Beverley, in the eastern part of the historic county of Yorkshire, was a thriving town by the 13th century. As such, it attracted the Dominicans, or Blackfriars, within a generation of their arrival in England. Their convent was established close to the Minster by 1240.

The house was of average size for a mendicant community, and flourished through the 14th century. Their is some evidence for decline and a fall in the number of friars in the 15th century, though the complex remained in their possession until its surrender to the crown in 1539.

This Dominican House was established on marginal land behind industrial tenements on Eastgate. Two successive timber halls lying to the north of the great cloister were occupied in the 13th century; their later occupation may have been secular. A 'little cloister' of two ranges was erected in this area in the early 14th century, and its development and occupation through the 14th century have been recorded. There was a functional division between private and communal accommodation in the larger of the two ranges, and environmental evidence suggests adherence to a diet in which poultry and fish were prominent. The lesser range was a narrow, perhaps subsidiary structure, and possibly overshot the cloister alley in the later stage of its development. The occupation of the little cloister closed with the stripping of the buildings in the early 16th century. They were very thoroughly robbed in the 17th or early 18th century.

The partial re-examination of the Priory church and great cloister has defined the final form and size of the church and the accretion to it of a chantry chapel, and has further indicated the adjacent projection of part of the east claustral range. The north claustral range was rebuilt in the later 14th century and accommodated a refectory; the modification of the west range is suggested, but remains undated. A latrine block and a cistern were associated with these ranges; the cistern may have later served as a wet fish store. An enhanced record of the precinct wall has also been achieved.

Finds included large quantities of building material (especially locally manufactured brick and tile), though the quality of these materials was often low. Window glass of 13th century grisaille pattern saw reuse in the little cloister. A miscellaneous collection of personal equipment indicates a cloistered status for this area, with the occasional presence of visitors, but not of female residents. The Dominicans appear to have been supplied with food and other materials from the same market sources as other sites in the town, though their diet was less varied and some of their domestic buildings of a modest vernacular standard.

Excavations which took place on this site between 1960 and 1983 form the subject of an earlier monograph. The present volume describes excavations between 1986 and 1989. In both works the site is called the Dominican Priory, although it is locally known as Beverley Friary (or, in the case of one surviving building, as the Old Friary).

Further Excavations at
the Dominican Priory, Beverley, 1986–89

by

Martin Foreman

with major contributions by

E.P. Allison, M.M. Archibald, David Atkinson, Roberta Gilchrist,
Alison Goodall, Ian Goodall, C. Pamela Graves, A.R. Hall,
Julian Henderson, H.H. Kenward, W.J.B. McKenna, C.M. Nicholson,
T.P. O'Connor, Stephen Potts and Gareth Watkins

principal illustrators

Mike Frankland and Linda Smith

Archaeology Unit
Estates and Property Management, Humberside County Council

SHEFFIELD EXCAVATION REPORTS 4
1996

Published by: Sheffield Academic Press Ltd.
               Mansion House
               19 Kingfield Road
               Sheffield S11 9AS
               England

Cover illustration shows a model depicting the Priory complex as it would have appeared in the first half of the fifteenth century. This model is on display at the Beverley Friary Youth Hostel.

The publishers wish to acknowledge with gratitude a grant from English Heritage in the production of this volume.

British Library Cataloguing in Publication Data
A catalogue record of this book is available from the British Library.

ISBN 1 85075 513 2

Copies of this volume and a catalogue of other archaeological publications can be obtained from:

     Sheffield Academic Press Ltd.
     Mansion House
     19 Kingfield Road
     Sheffield   S11 9AS
     Telephone: + 44 (0) 114 255 4433
     Fax: +44 (0) 114 255 4626

Printed in Great Britain

Contents

List of Figures

List of Tables

(Most of the tables are reproduced in the main text; however, the use of the abbreviation Mf. in brackets, denotes that it can be found in the microfiche.)

List of Plates

List of Contributors

E.P. Allison	Environmental Archaeology Unit, University of York
M.M Archibald	Department of Coins and Medals, British Museum
A.J. Clark	Consultant in archaeological prospecting and dating
Chris Clarke	Former illustrator, Humberside Archaeology Unit
Glyn Coppack	English Heritage
John Farrimond	Former finds researcher, Humberside Archaeology Unit
Martin Foreman	Assistant archaeologist, Humberside Archaeology Unit
Mike Frankland	Illustrator, Humberside Archaeology Unit
Roberta Gilchrist	Centre of East Anglian Studies, University of East Anglia
Alison R. Goodall	Consultant on non-ferrous metalwork
Ian H. Goodall	Royal Commission on the Historical Monuments of England
C. Pamela Graves	York Archaeological Trust
A.R. Hall	Environmental Archaeology Unit, University of York
Julian Henderson	Department of Archaeology and Prehistory, University of Sheffield
Jennifer Hillam	Department of Archaeology and Prehistory, University of Sheffield
H.K. Kenward	Environmental Archaeology Unit, University of York
Sarah King	Formerly Department of Geography and Earth Resources. University of Hull
Graeme Lawson	Cambridge Music/Archaeological Research Project
J.G.McDonnell	Department of Archaeological Sciences, University of Bradford
W.J.B. McKenna	Formerly Environmental Archaeology Unit, University of York
David Marchant	Former illustrator, Humberside Archaeology Unit
John Marshall	Illustrator, Humberside Archaeology Unit
D.T. Moore	Formerly Department of Mineralogy, British Museum (Natural History)
C.M. Nicholson	Environmental Archaeology Unit, University of York
T.P. O'Connor	Department of Archaeological Sciences, University of Bradford
Martyn Pedley	Department of Geography and Earth Resources, University of Hull
Stephen Potts	Former finds researcher, Humberside Archaeology Unit
Linda Smith	Former illustrator, Humberside Archaeology Unit
P.D. Spriggs	Scientific Services Laboratory, British Coal
Penelope Walton Rogers	Textile consultant
Gareth Watkins	Archaeologist (Finds), Humberside Archaeology Unit

Acknowledgements

The organisation of an archaeological response to redevelopment at the Beverley Dominican Priory was undertaken by Peter Armstrong, whose previous presentation of three decades of research at the Priory (Armstrong and Tomlinson 1987), and whose other extensive work in Beverley and Hull, have provided an indispensable context for the findings of this report. Dr. Bob Bewley and Andrew Davison acted in their capacities as successive English Heritage Inspectors of Ancient Monuments to initiate and subsequently extend the excavation of the site.

The team working for the Humberside County Council Archaeology Unit on the three seasons of fieldwork included Zena Ahmed, Caroline Atkins, Rob Baxter, Peter Didsbury, Ken Elders, John Farrimond, Mike Frankland, Tony German, Marcus Gledhill, Dave Marchant, Anne Saunders, John Tibbles and Jan Tully. Through the autumn and winter of 1986–87, in frequently atrocious conditions, they were assisted by a team recruited by Beverley Workbridge, funded by the Manpower Services Commission and administered by Vivian Metcalfe. The Workbridge team were Neville Barker, Andrew Cooper, Gary Coulbeck, Michael Footit, Tony Hatfield, Jeff Hobbs, Andy Hunter, Rob Ingram, Roy Lilley, Cheryl McDonald, Louise Muston, Jonathan Pool, Alan Rawe, and Martin Stothard, under the supervision of Dave Atkinson. The good humour and kindness of the entire workforce, who laboured with enthusiasm and vigour in difficult conditions, particularly in the rain and snow, is warmly acknowledged. Without their cheerful assistance little could have been added to our previous knowledge of the Priory. Voluntary help was kindly offered by Ruth Head and Norman Jackson. Throughout the programme of excavation David Bridgwood, warden for the Y.H.A. of the 'Old Friary' Youth Hostel, generously provided vital access to water supply and many welcome cups of tea.

The initial post-excavation analysis was carried out by Dave Atkinson, John Farrimond and Tony German, the latter joined by Steve Potts in work on finds. The willing and exemplary service offered by staff of the Humberside County Council Library Service, and most particularly Trevor Norman, was of incalculable benefit in the prosecution of post-excavation research.

The illustrations for the report were drawn and mounted by: Linda Smith, finds; Chris Clarke, pottery; Mike Frankland, phase plans and many sections; and Dave Marchant and John Marshall, the remaining sections, layer-plans and graphics work. Photographic plates were prepared by Bill Marsden, of B.M. Photographics. The contributors of specialist reports, named in the course of the text, are warmly thanked for their forbearance in the face of the author's impatient and meddlesome character. The typists of the Humberside County Council Property Services Department have suffered much with good humour during the writing and editing of the report. Valuable comment on the voluminous drafts of various reports, and much information not then available in print, was most kindly offered by Dr. James Bond, Dr. Paul Buckland, Dr. Glyn Coppack, Dr. Paul Drury, Dave Evans, Dr. Barbara Harbottle, Andrew Harris, Jenny Mann, Martin Stockwell, Bruce Watson and Dr. Andrew White. Staff of the Ancient Monuments Laboratory of English Heritage; Wendy Carruthers, Cath Mortimer and Sebastian Payne kindly commented on specialist reports. Andrew Davison must receive particular thanks for the patience and application he has brought to the onerous task of reading not one, but two versions of the draft report. Dr. Lawrence Butler, of York University, brought his wide knowledge of the medieval church to bear in the course of his service as an academic reader for this volume. The choice of the opinions cited and any erroneous conclusions reached in this report remain, however, the author's responsibility.

The excavations were funded by the Manpower Services Commission, English Heritage, Beverley Borough Council, and by the developers, T. Miller Homes. The day-to-day assistance of Mr. Bartholomew, site foreman for the developers was also important to the progress of the excavations. The post-excavation programme was funded by English Heritage, who have also made a grant towards the cost of publication. The material support of Humberside County Council's Property Services Department throughout all the stages of this process has been invaluable.

This volume was seen through the final stages of its production by D.H. Evans.

Abbreviations

Most of the bibliographical and historical abbreviations are in standard form: the exceptions are given below. Abbreviations which are used solely in individual finds reports are explained in the relevant sections (e.g. the pottery fabrics and forms can be found listed in section 3.16, 'The Pottery Type series').

ABQ	Animal Bone Quantification
A.M.L.	Ancient Monuments Laboratory
BL	British Library, London
Borthwick	Borthwick Institute of Historical Research, York
Cat.	Catalogue of small finds (see section 3)
C.B.A.	Council for British Archaeology
D.	diameter
E.A.U.	Environmental Archaeology Unit, York
H.B.M.C.	Historic Buildings and Monuments Commission for England
H.C.R.O.	Humberside County Record Office
L.	length
Max.	maximum
Mf.	microfiche
Min.	minimum
MNI	Minimum Number of Individuals
RF	recorded find
S.	section
Th.	thickness
W.	width
Y.A.J.	*Yorkshire Archaeological Journal*

Principal conventions used on sections and feature plans.

Clay	Limestone	Tiles on edge, to form hearth area
Burnt Clay	Chalk	Wood
Organic Loams	Chalk rubble, crushed chalk	Stakes, stake hole
Black Ash	Mortar	Cobbles
Ash laminate	Brick and Tile	Oyster shells

Conventions used on sections.

S1   section number

edge of baulk

7·50 m.   height above O.D. in metres

(453)   context number

Conventions used on plans.

►   ◄   end points of main section

site boundary

∟   ⌐   end points of feature section

+   grid intersection

edge of feature

hidden or proposed edge of feature

intrusion

xiv

1. Introduction

by Martin Foreman

The following report presents the results of research by the Humberside Archaeology Unit at the Beverley Dominican Priory carried out between 1986 and 1989. This was undertaken in advance of the proposed redevelopment of the area between Eastgate and Station Square, Beverley as residential housing by T. Miller Homes. These excavations could take place only because previous work (Armstrong and Tomlinson 1987) had defined the area of the Priory and enhanced its statutory protection as a Scheduled Ancient Monument. This status ensured that a record could be made of those parts of the Priory likely to be damaged or concealed by the accelerating rate of development within the town.

The Mendicant Orders — of which those of St. Francis and St. Dominic were the greatest — were a revolutionary force at the time of their inception, and their rapid spread through the towns of 13th–century Europe may in one way mark the maturing of medieval urban life. As their name suggests, the mendicant friars, or brothers, relied upon the donation of food and alms for both their day-to-day subsistence and for their building projects. They were thus intimately bound up with the life of the towns in which they chose to settle, and where they preached, taught and administered the sacraments. With the passage of time the rigorous constitutional limitations they set upon their personal comfort, and upon the ostentation of their buildings, were modified. The houses of the friars were to introduce, however, a distinctively urban ecclesiastical tradition. In architectural terms this may be traced in the later medieval provision and design of large parish churches with open preaching spaces, of which Hull's Holy Trinity is a good example. The spiritual contribution of the friars is less easily quantifiable. If one were to search for historical analogies for their work, one might consider the Nonconformist Missions, Chapels and Halls in the burgeoning towns and cities of the 19th century. The intellectual influence of the Mendicants, whether in the growth of the university towns, or in the diffusion of the ideas of Aquinas, was profoundly formative upon the later course of European thought.

The archaeological investigation of the Dominican Priory began with the excavation carried out between 1960 and 1964 by K.A. MacMahon and Mr. D.G. Lloyd at the west end of the Priory church and on the site of the west range of the great cloister. The partial surviving record of these works, limited excavations in and around the 'Old Friary' by R.W. Mackey in

1975; by the East Riding Archaeological Society in 1980–81, and by the Humberside Archaeology Unit in 1983 have been presented by P. Armstrong and D.G. Tomlinson (1987) (Figure 2). The results of watching briefs carried out on the eastern side of the precinct have also been published (Sanders and Armstrong 1983).

The significance of both the structures and the artefacts recovered by the recent excavations has been enhanced by the archaeological sampling of medieval Beverley which has been vigorously, if intermittently, prosecuted over the last decade. The result of this programme of excavation has been to allow the findings to be set in context within the fabric of the medieval town (cf. Armstrong *et al.* 1991; Evans and Tomlinson 1992). In this way, each successive contribution to the archaeological record of Beverley may be expected to bring perhaps fewer surprises, but, in compensation, a growing awareness of the organic functioning of the medieval town and an ever closer acquaintance with the townsfolk whose lives and work are recorded only in the soil.

The town of Beverley

The physical location of the town, and its early growth and development, have been described elsewhere (e.g. Armstrong *et al.* 1991, 243–6), and need not be reiterated here. Exploitations of parts of the surrounding landscape in the lower Hull valley is well attested from the Mesolithic period onwards (cf. Didsbury 1990). In the town itself, earlier prehistoric activity is attested by chance finds, whilst both Iron Age and Roman occupation have been demonstrated by recent excavations (e.g. Frere 1986; Armstrong and Didsbury 1992). Nevertheless, it is with the foundation of the monastery of St. John in the early years of the 8th century (Armstrong *et al.* 1991, 246–7) that we see the emergence of the first recognisable element of the medieval town — the future site of the Minster, which would become famous throughout the north of England as a goal for pilgrims to the shrine of St. John (canonised in 1037).

Although the earliest stages of its urban development remain uncertain, Beverley achieved borough status in the 12th century, under the lordship of the Archbishop of York. The industrial and commercial development of the town owed much to its position on the Beck, a canalised tributary of the River Hull which allowed shipping access into the southern part of the town. The exploitation of a ready water supply from the streams feeding the Beck also facilitated the growth of a textile industry, while pottery and tile manufacture grew up on its banks from the 12th century. The expansion and prosperity of the town are reflected in the two dependent churches — St. Mary's, established in the 12th century or before in the higher northern end of the town, and the 12th century church of St. Nicholas, serving the commercial and maritime community around the Beck to the east. There were 10 hospitals at Beverley — the term covers charitable institutions ranging from hostels to leper houses — whose numbers indicate that Beverley may have ranked among the ten most prosperous towns of the kingdom (Butler 1987, 169). The Poll Tax returns of 1377 showed Beverley was still at this date the eleventh most populous town in England, and twice as large as its rival, Kingston-upon-Hull, eight miles to the south at the river mouth. As the foremost town in the region it was natural enough that Beverley should attract the first of the mendicant friars within a short time of their arrival in England. The Dominicans, or Friars Preachers, who arrived in 1221, found a home close to the Minster before 1240. The Franciscans, who crossed the channel three years later, established themselves outside the town next to its western boundary before 1267. There is some evidence to suggest that the Carmelites too may have been present in the town, but this is less clear: certainly the site of their house is not known (Miller *et al.* 1982, 52).

Documentary evidence for the priory

The documentary evidence for the Beverley Blackfriars has been considered by Poulson (1829), Palmer (1882), and Goldthorp (1935), and has been selectively reviewed in the light of archaeological and topographical study by Miller *et al.* (1982) and by Armstrong and Tomlinson (1987). The later analyses have been assisted by the research of the Victoria County History committee which culminated in the publication of the volume on Beverley (Allison 1989). No major advance in the interpretation of the documentation has arisen from the recent excavations, so only certain aspects of this material are noted below. As all the documentary material considered here has been drawn from secondary sources, it is summarily presented in microfiche, in chronological order (Mf.1 A2–A8). Testamentary requests are noted only by date and number, save where they may have topographical relevance. They have been most fully enumerated by Goldthorp.

In an earlier report, Armstrong and Tomlinson (1987, 2–4, 49–51) discussed the disposition of areas within the precinct, the evidence for its evolution, and

its definition by a western wall and by the modern Friars Lane, Chantry Lane and Grovehill Road (Figure 1). They cited in that work the evidence for building work in 1263, 1449 and perhaps in 1524–5; however, archaeological research to date has failed to provide unequivocal evidence for any of these episodes of activity. These authors also drew attention to the expansion of the establishment from 33 friars in 1299 to 42 in 1310, and to its apparent contraction to 30 by 1335, and to 14 by the late 15th century. The only amendment necessary to their interpretation is to extend to the north the area of the buildings of the house, to which a suppression survey relates the position of closes and orchards in the north part of the precinct.

The documentary evidence illuminates aspects of the activity of the Dominicans in Beverley. In administrative terms the Beverley Priory fell under the 'Visitation' of York, one of four divisions of the English Dominican province, whose formation was advised *c.*1239–40 and firmly established by 1275. It was thus administered together with the Blackfriars' houses of Lincoln, Newcastle-upon-Tyne, Lancaster, Scarborough, Yarm, Carlisle, Bamburgh, Boston and Pontefract (Hinnebusch 1951, 209). The provincial chapters of the English Dominicans were held at Beverley in 1240, 1286, 1324 and 1342. An ordination at the church there is recorded in 1400. The General Chapter of the Dominicans was held in London in 1314, and among its acts was the deposing of several Priors, including the Prior of Beverley.

The friars' pastoral work brought them into occasional conflict with the collegiate Minster church at Beverley, the successful defence of whose privileges was recorded in 1269 and 1309. In 1301 the Dominican Provincial presented ten Beverley friars — out of an establishment of 36 recorded in the same year — to take confessions and grant absolution. The following year their activity led to conflict with the Archbishop of York over the shriving of intruders into the latter's park outside Beverley. The relationship between the Archbishop, as Lord of the town, and the friars appears to have been generally amicable; the Beverley Priory was on land held from the Archbishop, and the rents of tenements elsewhere in Beverley were accepted in commutation of the friars' obligations. The expansion of the Blackfriars precinct at the expense of further adjacent tenements was, however, quashed in 1309 by an *inquisition ad quod damnum*, in defence of the Lord's interests. The crusade of 1291 had seen the Archbishop deploy the Friars Preacher within his episcopate to preaching stations. Those of Beverley were allotted Preston in Holderness, or Hedon; Ravenser on the Humber; and Le Wyk (Hull). It is perhaps significant that these three stations, like Beverley itself, were ports.

```
━(■■■) TOWN DITCH KNOWN (UNCERTAIN)        1  EASTGATE EXCAVATION
●●(ooo) WALKERBECK KNOWN (UNCERTAIN)        2  CONSTITUTIONAL HALL EXCAVATION
□(□)  TOWN BAR KNOWN (UNCERTAIN)            3  WYLIES ROAD EXCAVATION
                                            4  DOMINICAN FRIARY EXCAVATION
                                            5  DYER LANE EXCAVATION
                                            6  HALL GARTH EXCAVATION
                                            7  LURK LANE EXCAVATION
                                            8  HIGHGATE EXCAVATION
                                            9  MINSTER MOORGATE EXCAVATION
                                           10  MINSTER
                                           11  ST.NICHOLAS' CHURCH
                                           12  ST.MARY'S CHURCH
                                           13  PRECEPTORY OF KNIGHTS HOSPITALLERS
                                           14  FRANCISCAN PRIORY
                                           15  ST.NICHOLAS' HOSPITAL
```

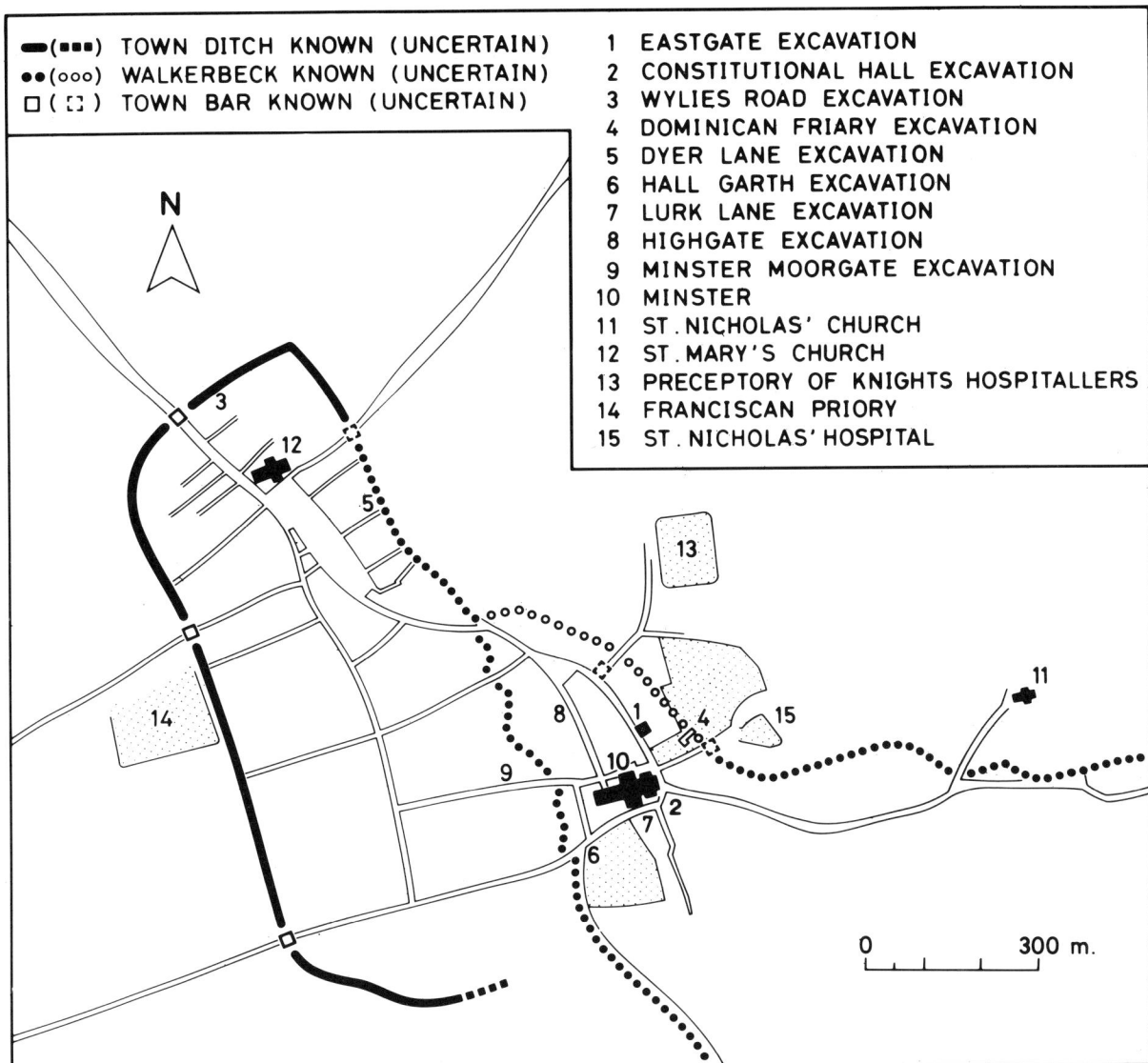

Figure 1   The location of the site within medieval Beverley.

The numerous gifts and testamentary requests to the friars must form only a sample of the donations which supported a mendicant house; a few may relate to the foundation or maintenance of chantries. They reach a marked peak in the years 1391–1410. The significance of the royal grants *pro rata* has been noted above, as this allows the numbers of residents at the house to be gauged. Gifts of corn in 1314, 1319 and 1320 may indicate the alleviation of particular distress in years of poor harvest, while an action for the recovery of debt in 1434, and the poverty of the friars cited in the royal grant of 10 marks in 1449 may indicate a further period of straitened circumstances. The description in Lord Darcy's grant of privileges of the house before 1524–5 as delapidated and non-functional is not entirely supported by other evidence: though no bequests in favour of the Blackfriars are known between 1505 and 1520, they figure regularly in wills before and after these dates. A grant of corn and malt

in 1493 may suggest the house had its own bakehouse and brewhouse at that time. A grant of six shillings for fish made to the Blackfriars in 1386 is held to have been in recompense for their guarding the town chest during disputes between the aldermen and keepers of the town, 1385–7, and betokens their status in the community. The same secondary source (Witty 1929), though of uncertain veracity, also alluded to the later connection between the *Porters and Creelers* (basket-men) of the town, who were by 1493 regular supporters of the Priory and held processions there on the first Sunday after the Assumption. This may indicate otherwise unrecorded institutional links between the Priory and the port community on Beckside. In 1414 the tailors of Beverley assembled in the garden of the Friars Preachers, a meeting at which 39 masters and 19 journeymen were present. A devotional Guild of St. Peter of Milan is also likely to have been linked with the Priory.

Site Location TA 0388 3936 (Figures 1–2)

The Dominican Priory is sited on a tract of boulder clay to the north-east of the Minster (Figure 1). Its topography and underlying geology are discussed in detail in section 6.1, below. Parts of a brick and stone patchwork wall, which is taken to be the precinct boundary, survive in Friars Lane and Eastgate. The position of the Eastgate section is wholly misleading today, since it was moved bodily in 1964 to its present location on the west of Eastgate from the opposite side of the road. Both lengths of wall are punctuated by gateways of brick with four-centred arches; the opening in Eastgate is topped by a triangular pediment, the one in Friars Lane formerly had a Dutch gable, now lost. The style of the gates and the reuse of masonry for patching suggests that the fabric as it survives today is mainly post-Dissolution work, but it conceivably maintains the precinct boundary position. Before the coming of the railway, Friars Lane was the western end of Chantry Lane whose winding route through to Grovehill Road on the north probably reflects the eastern boundary of the Priory, which is therefore effectively bisected by the Hull to Scarborough line.

A wall which marked the north-eastern limit of the precinct was demolished without record in May 1989; though this structure was indubitably post-medieval, it may have marked a pre-existing boundary alignment. The construction of a road which linked the station with Chantry Lane on the east side of the railway lines, was completed during the same programme of works; however, the carriageway design was modified to limit damage to the underlying deposits, principally those relating to the choir of the Priory church.

Two other religious houses can be seen to have been juxtaposed with the Dominicans; both appear to have preceded the construction of the Priory, and therefore they probably defined its grounds on two sides. The Preceptory of the Knights Hospitallers, established in 1201, occupied the Trinities, a moated enclosure now largely coincident with the Railway Station, and once within considerable grounds bounded by Trinity Lane on the west and Grovehill Road on the south. To the south-east of Chantry Lane lay Paradise Garth, another moated enclosure, believed to be the site of St. Nicholas' Hospital, and first documented *c.*1120 (Miller *et al.* 1982, 54).

The land on the western side of the railway line as far as the Eastgate frontage was occupied by factory buildings and local government offices until their demolition in 1983 (Evans and Tomlinson 1992, 1). At the present time, much of the Priory grounds has been absorbed by residential buildings. The area of the little cloister lies below these, but the great cloister survives substantially intact below the lawns fronting the new buildings.

The method of excavation (Figure 3)

The most recent work on the site began with a short programme of trial excavation consisting of three machine-cut trenches. Work began in May 1986, and continued for eleven months following the identification of structures in Trench 3 (Figure 3). Excavation continued throughout the winter of 1986–7, under the supervision of the Unit's staff, but were for the most part carried out by Beverley Workbridge, an agency deploying resources provided by the Manpower Services Commission.

Trench 1

Trench 1 examined an area north-west of the standing 'Old Friary' building. Although MacMahon had identified numerous structures immediately west of this building, which were of possibly medieval and definitely post-medieval date, excavation here was too shallow to locate any of these. The subsequent redevelopment of this area without further record has undoubtedly damaged, and for the present generation sealed, any surviving evidence.

Trench 2

Trench 2 investigated the course of the precinct wall, identified the extent of its survival, and attempted to establish its relationship to earlier features. Only the top of the wall was exposed, save for where later disturbance to the structure was examined, at its south end; and where the deposits to the west were partially recorded.

Trench 3

Trench 3 identified and investigated the north range of the great cloister, and the little cloister beyond it. From an early stage it was apparent that this area had seen occupation pre-dating the extension of the claustral plan. Effort was accordingly concentrated in this area. Attempts were made, by trenching in areas which for the most part had already been excavated in the 1960s, to correlate the most recent work with MacMahon's record. In the event this was not very precisely achieved, though valuable evidence amplifying his account was recorded. The northern part of Trench 3 was extended and rapidly examined before the close of site works in April 1987.

Trenches A–C

In 1988 and 1989 works in connection with a trunk road scheme on the east side of the precinct were carried out. These revealed the footings of the eastern part of the church, though neither more extensive nor more thorough excavation was permitted here. This area is now sealed by a new road whose carriageway

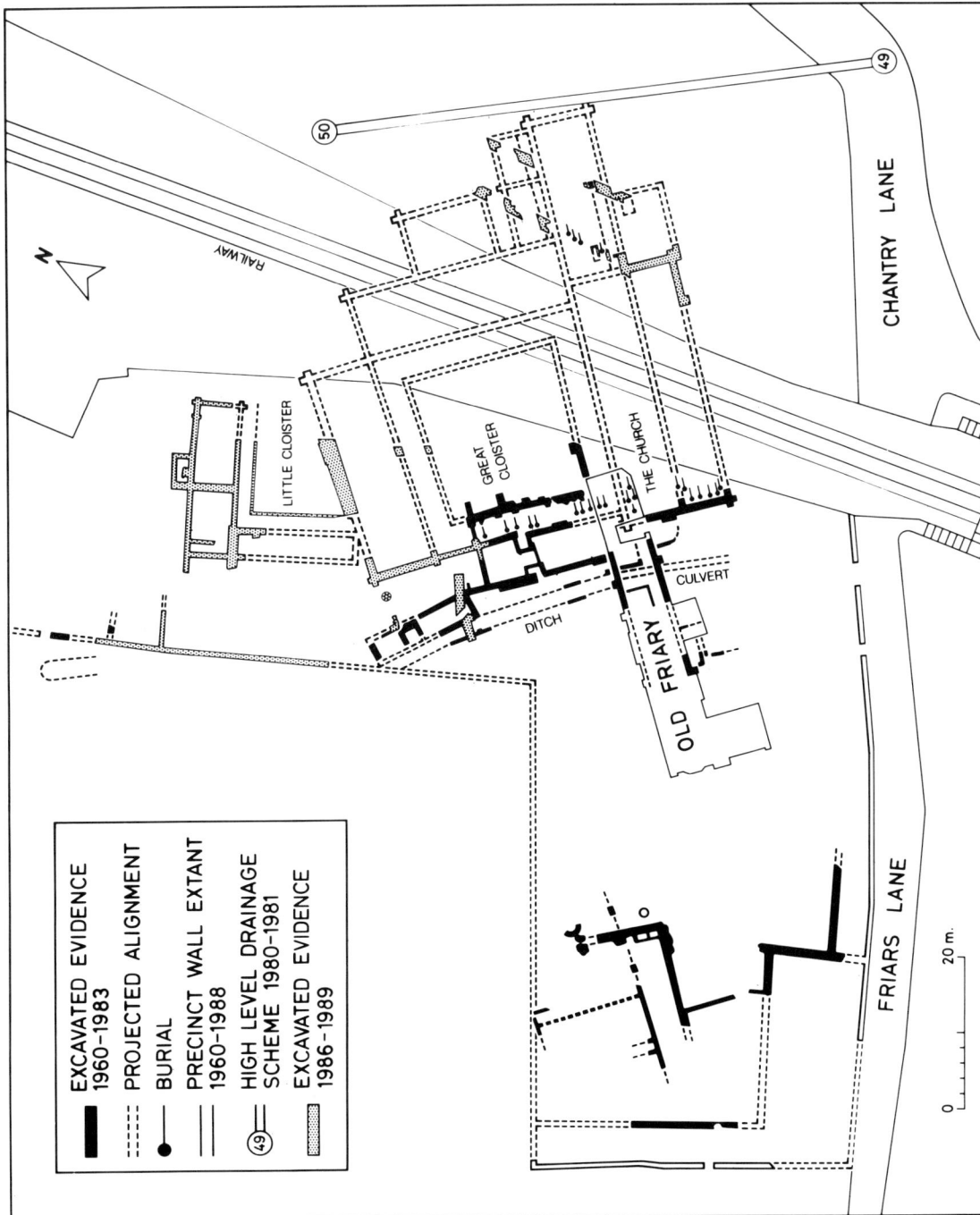

Figure 2 Excavations at the Dominican Priory 1960–89.

The following labels appear within the figure:

EXCAVATED EVIDENCE 1960–1983
PROJECTED ALIGNMENT
BURIAL
PRECINCT WALL EXTANT 1960–1988
HIGH LEVEL DRAINAGE SCHEME 1980–1981
EXCAVATED EVIDENCE 1986–1989

49
50

N

RAILWAY

LITTLE CLOISTER

GREAT CLOISTER

THE CHURCH

DITCH

CULVERT

OLD FRIARY

CHANTRY LANE

FRIARS LANE

20 m.

0

and drainage have been lifted above the level of the archaeological remains.

The Phasing of the Site

The Dominican Priory has been the subject of archaeological investigation since 1960, and the quality of record which survives from the several seasons of work is variable. The equation of phased activity in different areas is not possible in such circumstances. A detailed picture of the overall sequence of the physical development of the Priory has not, therefore, been achieved, though a broad sequence is becoming increasingly clear.

The excavations of 1986–7 examined the little cloister area in detail (Figure 2). This proved to include features related both to the great cloister and

to activity pre-dating both the little cloister and the Priory itself. Trenches were excavated into areas that had been previously exposed in the 1960s. The priority afforded to the protection of the monument dictated that these latter investigations should, in the main, be non-destructive. Similar non-destructive examination was carried out at the east end of the church in 1988–9. Very little dating evidence was recovered from areas examined in this way.

The phasing scheme adopted in the text is therefore one based on the examination of discrete areas. The approximate chronological relationships between the phase groups is illustrated in the table below.

The divisions between phases, particularly in Phases 5A to 5C, have usually been defined by events which show clearly in the archaeological record, such as the

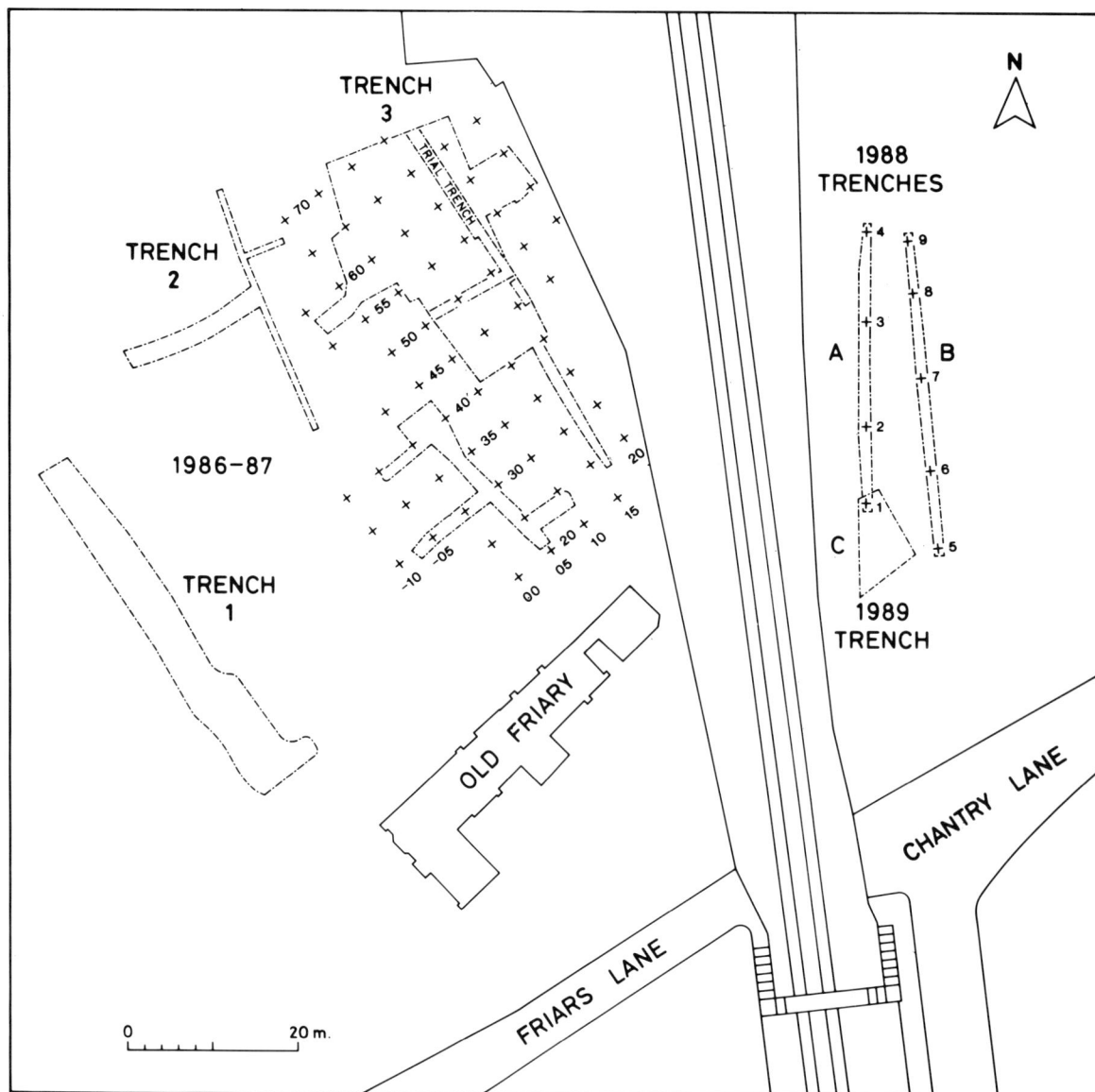

Figure 3 Excavations 1986–89 — trench layout.

Great Cloister

	Phase	
C13th	4A	First buildings of great cloister
?C13th	4B	Great cloister buildings extended/completed
C14th	4C	Further extension/modification in great cloister
Later C14th to C16th	6A	New *frater* built on north side of great cloister
	6B	Modifications to great cloister consequent on 6A
C16th	7	Partial demolition
C17th/18th	8	Later robbing and post–medieval activity

Little Cloister

Phase		
1	Early activity –?occupation — undated	
2	?Agricultural activity, preceding foundation of the Priory	C12th
3A	Timber building north of the great cloister	mid to late C13th
3B	A new timber building in the same general area	Later C13th
3C	Later modification and occupation of second timber building	Very late C13th/early C14th
3D	Demolition and abandonment of timber buildings	Very Late C13th/early C14th
5A	Little cloister constructed around previous site of timber buildings	First half of C14th
5B	Modification of little cloister buildings	Second half of C14th
5C	Modification of little cloister building	Later C14th to C16th
7		C16th
8		C17th/C18th

Suggested overall phasing scheme

renovation of floors or structural works. Although major interdependent episodes of activity have been identified, other changes are likely to have taken place as parts of a continuing process of development and maintenance. These may often have been carried out as the availability of funds or the convenience of the community permitted. It should be borne in mind that this organic process was probably under way throughout the occupation of the site. The imposition of phases upon it is a measure adopted to assist the understanding of the site, and should not be taken to indicate that the structural history of the Priory was divided into discrete bouts of activity punctuating a sedentary occupation.

The format and conventions of the reports

The principal drawing conventions which have been used on the plans and sections in this volume are illustrated on Figure 01; any deviation from these has been clearly indicated either on the relevant drawing, or in its caption. The principal features of each phase or sub-phase are shown on a series of plans of discrete areas (e.g. the choir, or the little cloister). Additional detailed plans have been provided, where necessary, to clarify complicated relationships, or to depict superimposed features; these can easily be tied into the main plans by cross-references to the grid shown on Figure 3. Individual feature sections have been grouped into figures, which have been placed as near as possible to the relevant piece of text: references to these are prefixed by an S (e.g. Figure 16, S22a).

The diagrammatic plan at the head of each section of the excavation text (Chapter 2) is intended to serve only as a guide to the general location of features within the precinct. It should not be taken as a representation of any particular phase of activity. Contexts marked with an asterisk are discussed in the environmental section of the report (4.2). The introduction of *c.* before measurements cited in the text indicates that these are taken from the drawn record rather than being measured on-site.

The finds reports have been grouped together into Chapter 3, the environmental reports into Chapter 4, and the analytical scientific reports into Chapter 5. Each principal report is treated as a numbered sub-section of the relevant chapter, in order to aid cross-referencing: hence, cross-references to the environmental evidence appear as 'see 4.2' ..... to the animal bone, as 'see 4.3', etc. The small finds or 'recorded finds' have been described in a cumulative catalogue order (nos 1–1142), and any cross-references to these in the text are by either that catalogue number (e.g. Cat. no. 452), or where appropriate, by a figure and catalogue number (e.g.

Figure 71, no. 60). Building materials have been given their own cumulative catalogue order, distinguished by the prefix 'B' (e.g. B229). For reasons of both space and economy, some of the more detailed specialist reports, catalogue listings, and many of the tables have been consigned to microfiche. An index to the fiche can be found at the end of the volume: any cross-references to this are preceded by the abbreviation Mf., followed by the relevant fiche number and frame number. Single context recording was used throughout the excavation; hence, some of the contexts listed in the finds catalogues are fills of pits, slots, post-holes or gullies, and may not otherwise be mentioned in the excavation text. Accordingly, the finds catalogues have been annotated, where appropriate, to make identification of features easier. In addition, the microfiche section contains a full list ascribing contexts to phase, in phase order (Mf. 1. A9–C4).

Chapter 6 presents a discussion of the archaeological evidence from Beverley and elsewhere. This summarises the evidence which is presented in detail in Chapters 2–5.

2. The Excavations 1986–1989

by Martin Foreman

Phase 1. Early features. 11th century and earlier (Figures 4–6)

The earliest activity on the site was examined only along the course of two trial trenches, aligned north–south and east–west (Figure 4). These trenches had identified features related to the occupation of the Priory at the start of the 1986 season of excavation. Their further excavation, down to the level of the natural subsoil, was undertaken in early 1987. The resultant keyhole view of the earliest features did not permit a coherent interpretation of activity carried on in the area. It did, however, indicate the proximity of early settlement (Figures 4–6).

Natural subsoil was not identified at a uniform level. Clays taken to be natural, with light coloured (1201) or sandy (1200) patches occurred in the northern end of the north–south trial trench at a level of c.6.30m OD (Figure 6, S5). To the south the natural was a stiff grey-brown clay, and was recorded as lying between c.6.07 and c.5.49m OD (Figure 5). The drainage of the site appeared to run from north to south.

The earliest features were identified as a group of shallow pits and layers; some of the latter may have represented pit-fills truncated by a later cut. At the west end of the east–west trial-trench the following sequence was noted in the section view of the north face (Figure 5, S1). Iron-stained clay (1159) formed the west side of a depression (1218), which was filled by layers of charcoal and daub-flecked clay (1157) and iron-stained clay (1156). These were sealed by silts flecked with burnt daub and charcoal (1155, 1122), and were cut by a shallow depression (1195) and by a Phase 2 feature (1158). A further flat-bottomed pit (1150) cut through the silts and was filled with clays and lenses of charcoal-flecked silt (1149*, 1151, 1152, 1153). Pit 1150 was recorded on both sides of the trench (Figure 5).

At the east end of the east–west trial trench lay an iron-stained clay (1185) and two shallow scoops: 1184* contained a fragment of slag, and 1160 small fragments of burnt daub. Further shallow deposits of clay were glimpsed along the north–south trial-trench; 1178, 1176, 1208, 1192 (Figure 6, S4). Features which probably post-dated these scoops and layers were identified in the northern part of the north–south trial trench. Their irregular contours may suggest they had been subject to re-cutting, though no evidence of this was recorded through the examination of their fills.

Shallow feature 1187 cut the north side of scoop 1184 (Figure 4). Its primary fill (1210*) was lightly flecked with daub. An iron-stained clay (1209*) on the steeper north side of the feature merged with its upper fill, 1186* (Figure 6, S3 and S5). Further north, a large feature (1197) was cut from a level of c.6.30m OD. It was filled with ash, charcoal and burnt daub (925*, 1193, 1214, 1215*, 1216*). The position of this feature was to lead later builders to employ very substantial footings in this area. Similar material (1198, 1212*) was deposited in a pair of smaller, later, pits dug in this area (1199, 1213).

There was little evidence for structures accompanying these cut features. A small depression (1203) in the clays at the north end of the north–south trial trench was only 0.06m deep. A possible feature (1205) aligned north–south in the same area was dismissed, because of the similarity of its fill (1204) to the slurry formed in the base of a narrow slot which had been cut to drain the trench.

Dating evidence

The Phase 1 deposits were aceramic; a fragment of slag was almost the only hand-collected find from this phase. Some of the features in the east–west trial trench were sealed by context 959, a layer which included Reduced Chalky ware which is unlikely to be earlier than the later 11th century. A large whetstone (Figure 85, no. 1001) was recovered from the base of a sondage in this area, and may have originated from the earliest levels.

Phase 2. Landfill. Early 12th – early 13th centuries (Figures 5–7, 13 and 36)

This phase was identified in the trial trenches, and in a sondage along the western excavation edge. It was recorded principally in the section drawings (Figures 5 and 6), together with the plan view of two cut features which were recorded in the east–west trial trench (Figure 7). An extensive range of soil samples, taken from the east–west trial trench, yielded a wealth of environmental and dating evidence.

These contexts were sealed by deposits associated with the construction of buildings which appear to relate to the Priory occupation. The archaeology of this phase therefore represents the usage and nature of the land which was made available to the Dominicans when they established their house at Beverley,

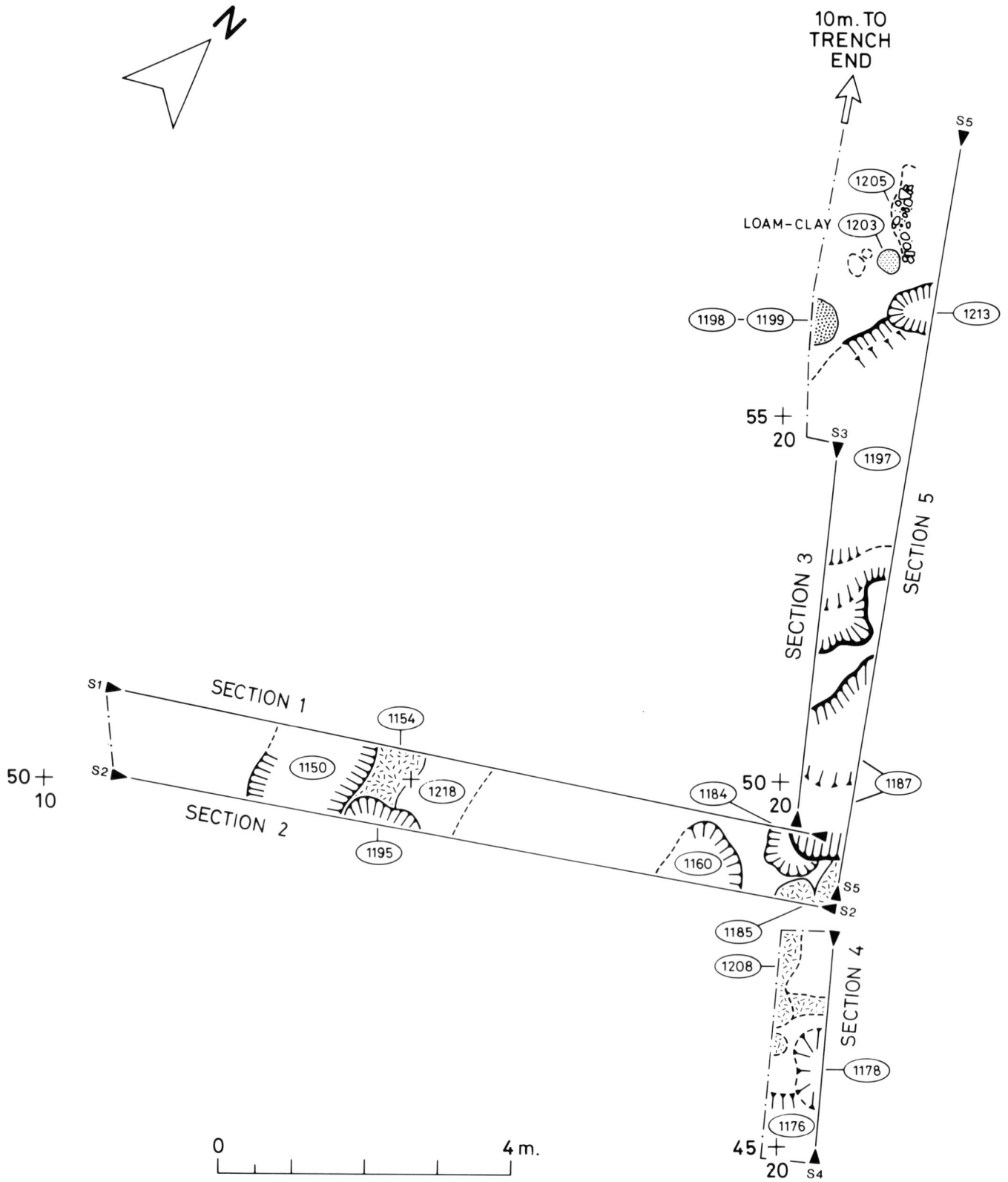

Figure 4　Phase 1, early features.

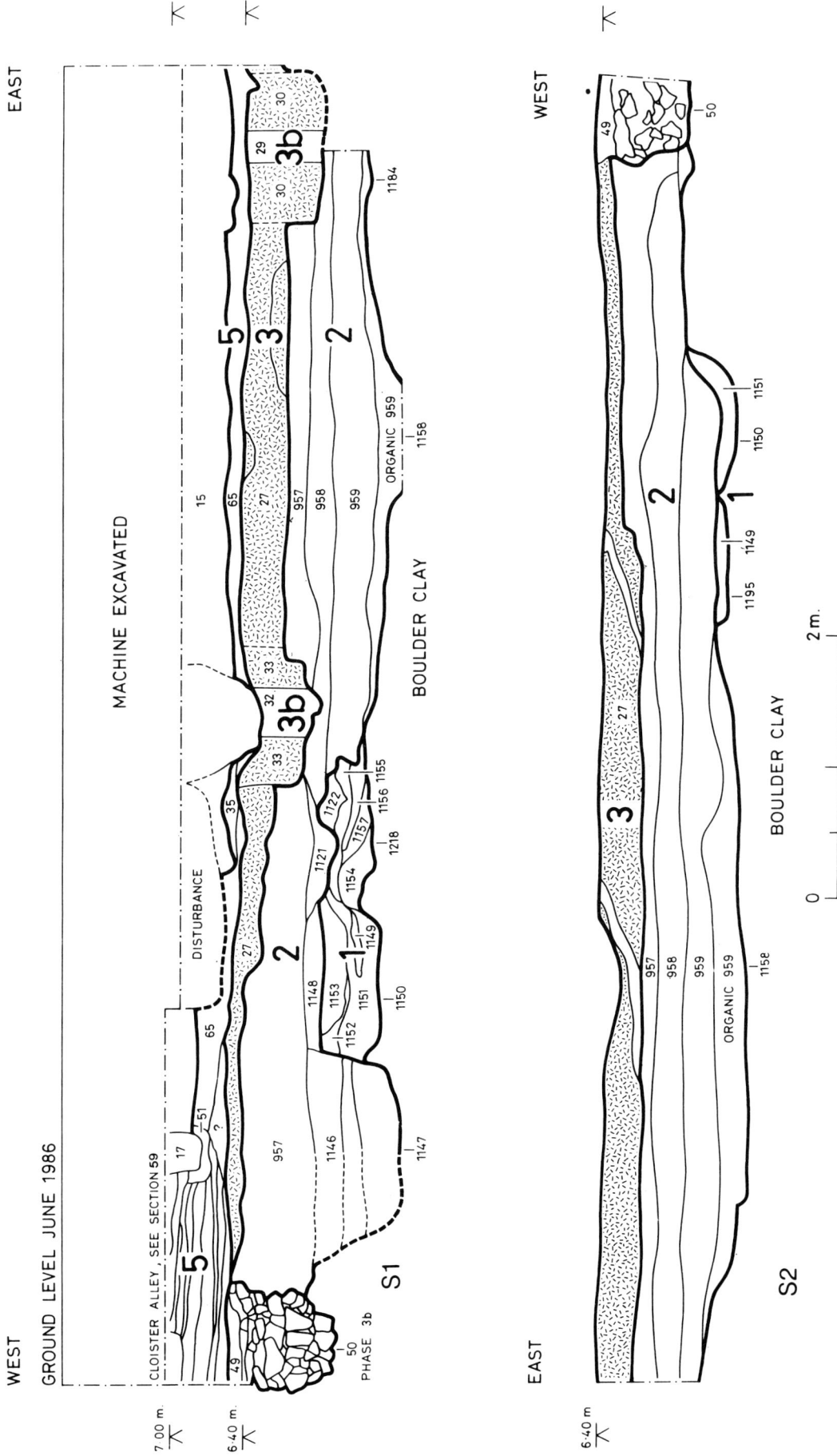

Figure 5 The east–west trial trench, Phases 1–3. S1–2.

*c.*1221–40. The Phase 2 deposits were at first assigned a single context number (28), which was only later divided into the series 957 to 959. This sequence was first distinguished in a sondage cut mid-way along the east–west trial trench. These deposits were excavated by hand, though the homogeneous character of the soils made it difficult at first to differentiate between them. The result has been the contamination of finds from 957* with those from 958*, and of finds from 958 with those from 959*.

The dark soils which made up the sequence 957 to 959 were also recorded along the north–south trial trench. They were not recorded as extending over the north part of the site where the subsoil rose. Here, the layers which pre-dated the construction activity were identified as 151 and 924* (Figure 6, S5; see also Figure 36, S43).

A sequence of layers which was seen in section along the west excavation edge (1188*, 1206*, 1211*), was also considered to form part of the Phase 2 activity (see below, Figure 13, S12). They were distinguished from 957, 958, 959 by the more prominent presence of organic fragments and by the absence of the iron staining which was a particular feature of 957. It is possible that the sequence 1188, 1206, 1211 may be associated with later pit-digging in this part of the site — unlike the other Phase 2 contexts it does not have a stratigraphic link with the Phase 3 clay platform — though such finds as were retrieved suggest an early date.

The earliest activity in Phase 2 was the formation of a large depression with gently sloping sides (1158). This was *c.*4.50m across (Figure 5), and was cut through the fills of the Phase 1 context 1218. It presumably resulted from the digging of clays for construction activity elsewhere. Its primary fill consisted of a firm dark grey silt (959), which was very dark at its lower levels. This layer also sealed the Phase 1 feature 1187, which was recorded in the north–south trial-trench.

This primary silt was sealed by a second layer of soft dark grey silt (958). It is possible that the northern extent of 958 was formed by 924, which rose with the subsoil towards the north end of the site. The upper surface of 958 was shown to undulate gently in the north–south trial-trench (Figure 6, S5). Two well-defined ridges lay *c.*2.35m apart: it is possible that these may indicate cultivation. A final layer of soft dark grey silt (957) covered 958. They were separated by greenish iron staining, which was also noted within layer 957. This latest element of the landfill horizon also sealed a daub-flecked layer (1148); a pit (1147) with its fill (1146), and a greenish clay, 1121, which perhaps represents the upcast from the digging of that pit (Figure 5, S1). In the north–south trial trench it is possible that layer 151 may represent a northern equivalent to 957.

The maximum overall depth of these three dark silt deposits was *c.*0.90m. Dr. McPhail, of the Institute of Archaeology, inspected the sequence of layers 957, 958, and 959, and considered that they could represent a 'dark earth' deposit formed by agricultural activity. This could account for both the homogeneous character of these soils and the breaking down of the organic content of the soils, which imparted a dark colour, but left little organic material. Daub-flecking and charcoal were noted in layer 1148, and also in parts of 958, and may have resulted from the disturbance of Phase I soils.

The finds

Roof tile: 0.023 m^2 of non-diagnostic tile.
Lead: melt (Cat. no. 707).
Iron: strip (no. 792); unidentified fragment (no. 818) and 1 nail.
Copper Alloy: needle (no. 912).
Worked Stone: hones (nos. 1001–2).
Pottery: 40 vessels.

Dating evidence

The pottery from this phase was mainly retrieved from sieved soil samples. The lowest silt in depression 1158 (959), contained a group of late 11th or early 12th century date, which was associated with two hone fragments (nos. 1001–2). The overlying layers (924 and 958) included sherds of Beverley ware types 1A and 2B, a little roof tile and a single ridge tile. The uppermost layer in the depression (957) incorporated much residual material and a single sherd of York White ware. The latest pottery in these layers would be consistent with a date in the early 13th century, albeit with a strong residual element. Lower context 924 included developed Stamford Ware (with a likely date-range of *c.*1150–1250) and seven Beverley ware vessels of types 1A and 2B. An early 13th century date would be appropriate for the material in this dark soil, which was on a similar horizon to that of 958. Context 151, above 924, bore pottery of similar date. This clearly pre-dated the Phase 5A construction activity in this area, but did not correlate with the other contexts in Phase 2. The soils in the northern part of the site may have remained open to disturbance until the 14th century.

In the western part of the site no glazed sherds were found in layer 1206, but Beverley ware type 1A and 2B sherds were present in a group from one of the upper layers (1188): a 13th century date could be appropriate for these. This sparse pottery evidence supports the notion that the sequence 1188, 1206, 1211 could belong to Phase 2.

The infill of the site began no earlier than the later 11th century, and Phase 2 seems to have been of 12th century date and later. Documentary evidence

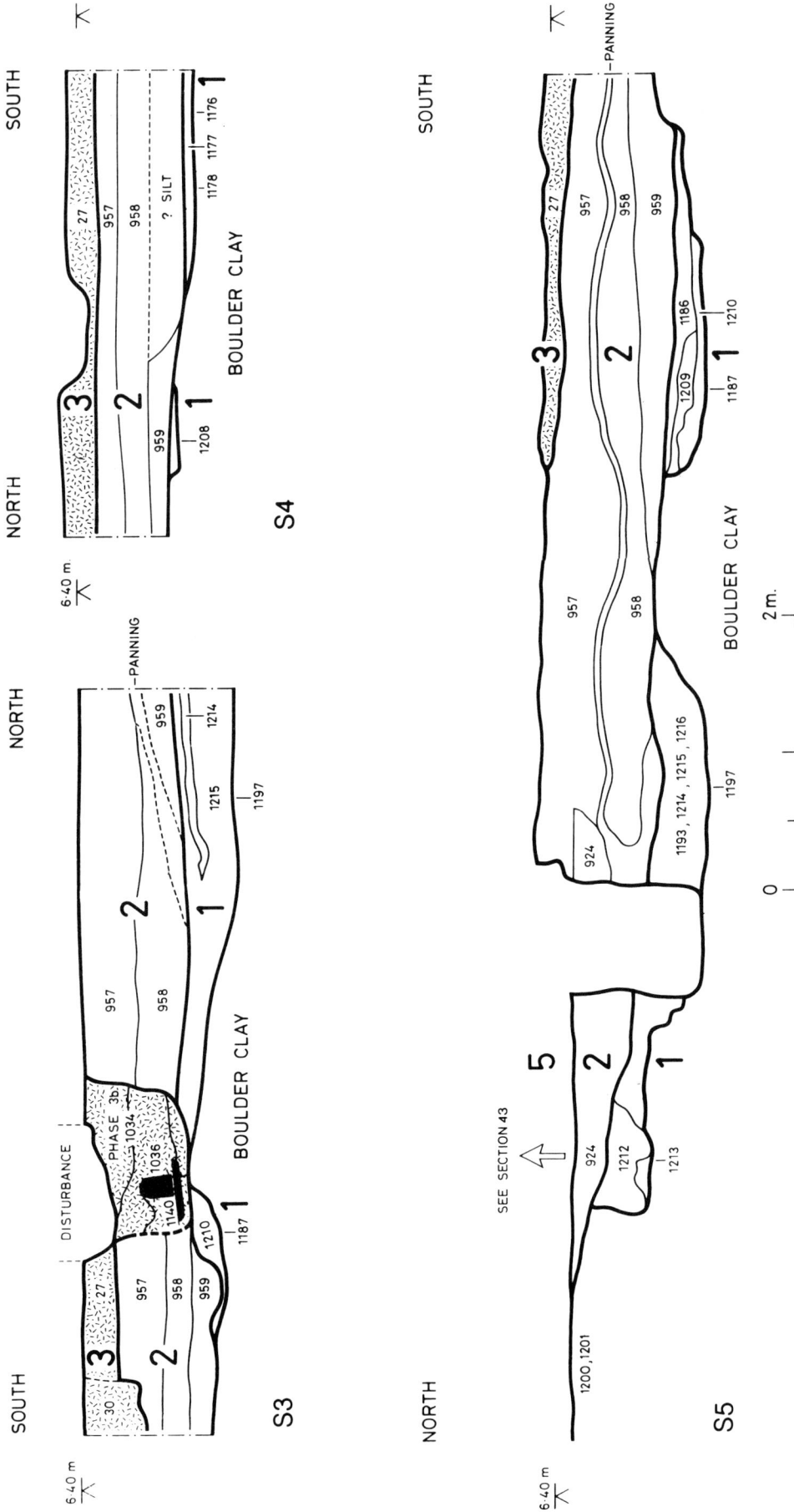

Figure 6 The north–south trial trench, Phases 1–3. S3–5.

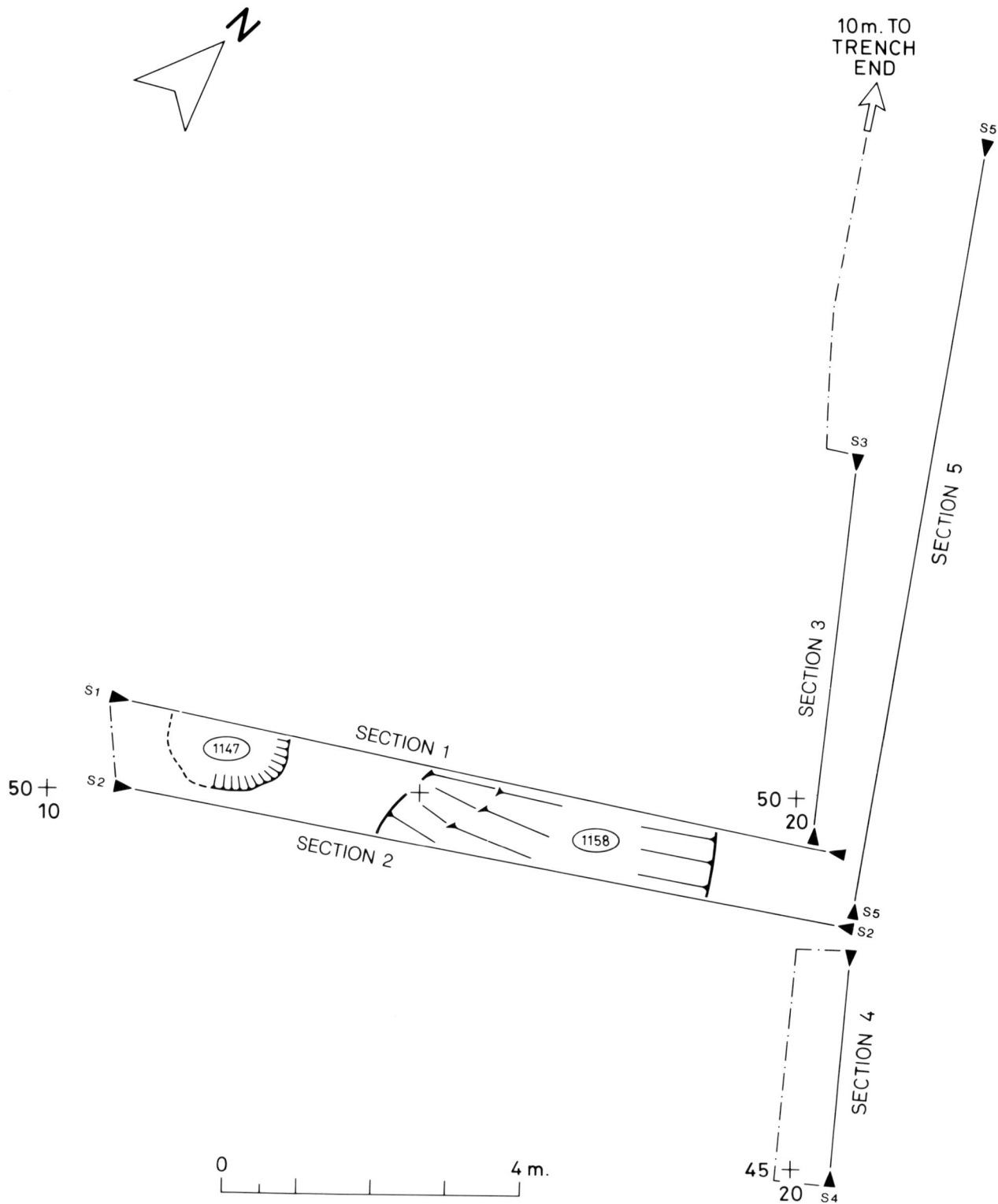

Figure 7   Phase 2 — cut features.

indicates that the Dominicans were established at Beverley between their arrival in England in 1221 and 1240, when a Provincial Chapter of the Order met in the town.

The western precinct boundary (Trench 2). ?11th century onwards (Figures 8–10)

Introduction

The excavation of Trench 2, westwards from the wall which defined the later medieval Priory precinct (see Figure 3), was undertaken in 1986. It was intended to determine whether the Priory was established within a truly urban context, or whether it was a suburban foundation from its inception. Previous research (Armstrong and Tomlinson 1987, 51–2) had suggested that the Walkerbeck may have taken a course which in part dictated the siting of the Priory, and may have formed an early eastern boundary to the town. It was hoped to identify this feature by deep trenching.

The depth and instability of the deposits, and constraints of time and funding, dictated a rapid investigation of this area. A preliminary excavation collapsed before any recording could be attempted. A second trench was excavated on a near-parallel alignment, and, once this had been extensively shored, it was possible to make a partial record of its sides (Figure 8). The two published sections distinguish between recorded evidence (depicted as solid lines) and the presumed continuation of deposits which were hidden by the shoring sheets (indicated by dotted lines). Small samples were recovered from the trench sides for environmental examination, but no stratified dating evidence was retrieved. A number of unstratified finds of wood (nos. 1071–1115) and leather (nos. 1116–42), were recovered during the machine excavation (see sections 3.17 and 3.18, below).

At the eastern end of the trench, a north–south boundary ditch (168/261) and a distinctive sequence of layers (199 and 197), were visible in both section faces, and represent early features. Along the south face, three major episodes of pit digging were recorded. This sequence closed with the raising of the land surface to the level from which the Priory precinct wall was subsequently built. The north face of the trench, in contrast, showed the deposit of deep layers of soil. Because of these marked differences, the north and south trench sections are discussed separately, though deposits common to both are indicated both on the illustrations and in the text.

The south section (Figure 8, S6)

The firm grey-brown boulder clay subsoil occurred at levels between 4.91 and 5.75m OD, an undulation ascribed to the cutting of features. The highest recorded level of the boulder clay was at the east end of the trench and is comparable to the range of subsoil levels recorded in Trench 3 (i.e. between 5.49 and 6.30m OD).

The earliest layer above the subsoil was identified at the east end of the trench, and was traced for *c.*6.40m westward. It may represent an ancient watercourse bed. It consisted of a mid-grey clay which was flecked with charcoal (165*), and had pebbles at its base. It rose slightly to the east, but mostly lay between *c.*5.04m OD and *c.*5.73m OD. A limited spread of material with the same distinctive pebble inclusions (275) was identified at the east end of the north section face (Figure 8, S7).

Layer 165 was cut from a level of *c.*5.31m OD. by a ditch with a U-shaped profile (168) which continued into the north section face as 261. It was *c.*1.80m — *c.*1.30m wide, steep-sided and flat-bottomed. A greasy grey clay (170) overlay a primary fill (187), and represents either slumping of the feature's side or its recutting. The more distinctive fills were black and greasy organic silts (169*, 164*); their counterpart in the north section was fill 262. An identical black material to layer 164 extended *c.*1.00m east of the cut, rising gently. An upper fill of soft greasy brown silt (167*) contained numerous twigs in a silty matrix: the survival of these twigs may indicate that layer 167 was sealed soon after its deposition.

A second, less regular, ditch or gully was dug *c.*1.00m east of 168/261. This was filled with a dark twiggy silt which lay up to *c.*5.60m O.D. It was not assigned a context number, though its continuation was noted on the north section as 166* (Figure 8, S7).

Activity further to the west began with the deposition of a greasy grey clayey silt, which was mistakenly identified with 165 in both section faces — this soil lacked the pebbles which were such a distinctive feature of layer 165. Over this accumulated a mixture of clay and organic material (199) and a firm silt with organic patches (197). All three layers were probably fills of a pit whose original limits are unknown because of later intrusions, but whose width was greater than 3.70m. They were cut from a level of *c.*5.32m OD by a flat-bottomed feature (207) which was subsequently filled with organic silts (208*, 209). The lower fill (209) was a greasy dark grey silt comparable with 169; the upper fill (208*) included patches of clay. Feature 207 was *c.*1.76m wide and *c.*0.82m deep.

Both the unnumbered pit and feature 207 were sealed by successive layers of silt (205, 204, 196, 211): the latest of these (211), included fragments of

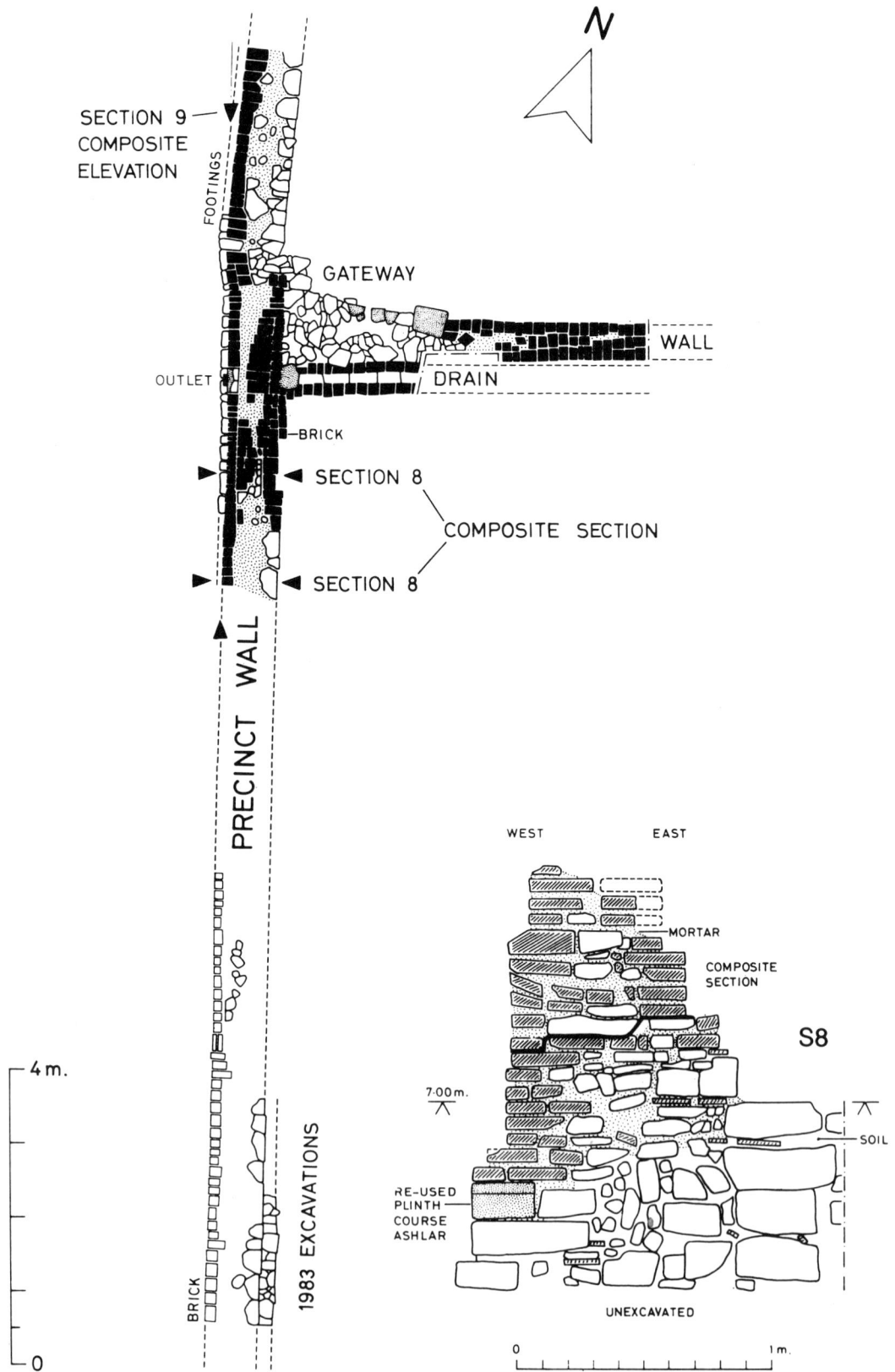

Figure 9   Trench 2 — the precinct wall, plan and composite section. S8.

tile. The general sequence of activity — cut features, recuts, and sealing deposits — mirrored that at the eastern end of the trench. Features and layers here were not, however, traced to the north section face.

At the east end of the section, a 4.60m wide depression with gently sloping sides was formed over the tops of the infilled ditches (168/261 and the unnumbered feature filled by 166). The lowest fill within this hollow consisted of a greasy grey-brown clayey silt (171). This was overlain by a clay matrix flecked with organic material (163*) which included chalk and tile. The basal layers within this depression (167, 171 and 163) all included a distinctive cobalt blue flecking, possibly vivianite; this material has been noted as possibly characteristic of ditch deposits elsewhere in Beverley (Armstrong *et al.* 1991, 131).

The deposit of chalk and tile in layer 163 may have been intended to seal the underlying ditches, and to serve as a bed for a new watercourse. In the north section a chalk spread (257) similarly sealed the earlier ditch, 261. The chalk and tile of layer 163 were sealed in turn by a thick layer of silt 162, into which had been driven a stake; this may have been part of a north–south alignment which was continued to the north by some driven timbers (253). Further unstratified timber, including stakes, was recovered from the east end of the trench. The presence of a possible timber revetment to the west side of this feature suggests that it was a pond or, more likely, a watercourse.

The deposits which accumulated within this hollow resulted in the raising of the ground level to between

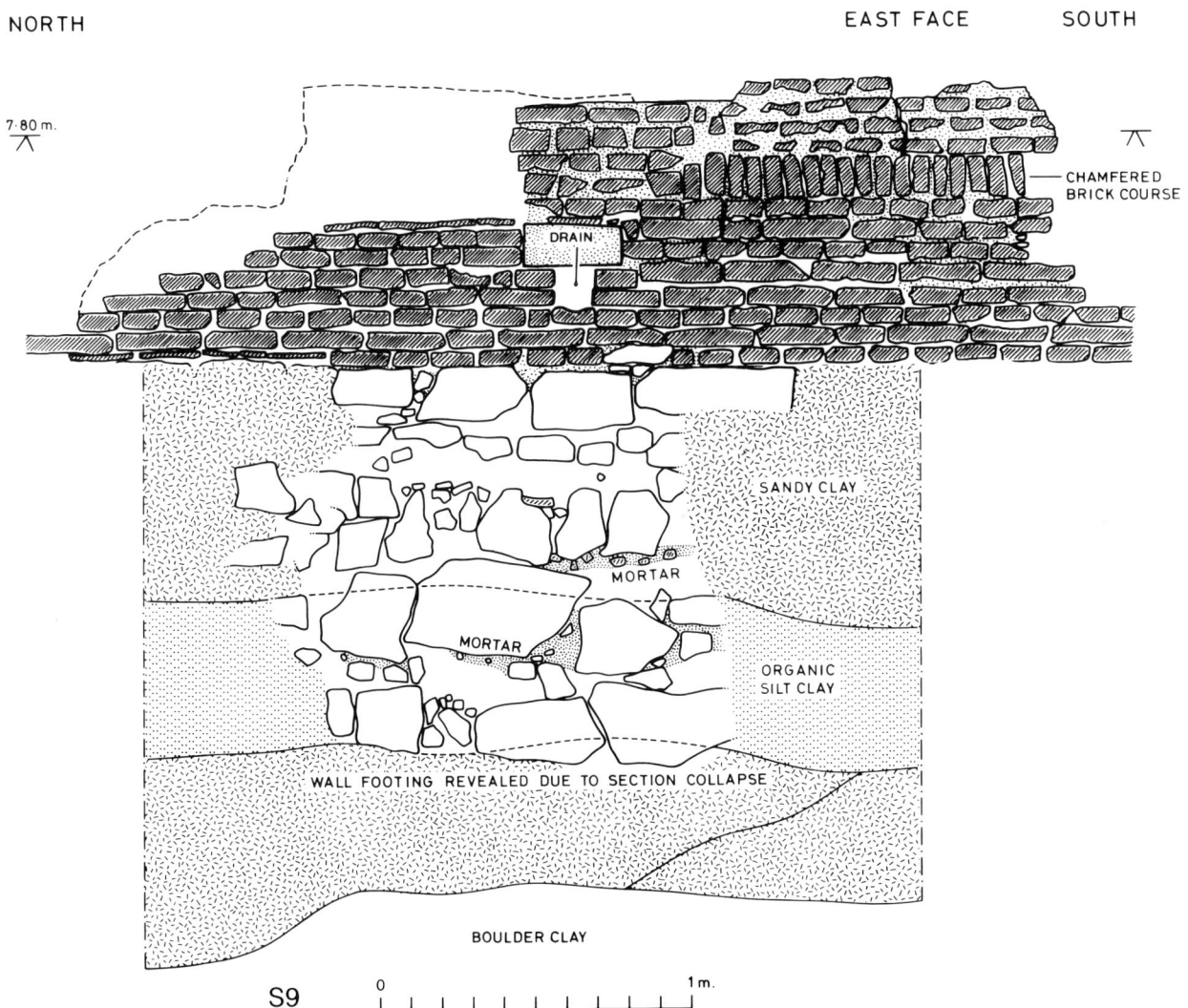

Figure 10 Trench 2 — the precinct wall, composite elevation. S9.

*c.*5.57 and *c.*6.19m OD. It seems reasonable to suggest that this was accompanied by the establishment of a boundary, which was represented by the timber alignment noted above. To the west of this boundary were a number of large flat-bottomed pits. The easternmost of these was *c.*0.90m deep and more than 2.90m across, with a gently sloping eastern edge. A greasy clay silt (183) accumulated within this feature. It was recut as a near-flat-bottomed pit (186), which was *c.*0.80m deep and *c.*3.24m across. Its east side may have been stepped, but the west was steeply sloped. A primary deposit of greasy clay and abundant charcoal (198) lay at the western end of the feature; this in turn was sealed by a soft dark brown organic silt (185*). The shape of these pits and the nature of their fills suggest that they served an industrial use of some sort: both were shallow and would, therefore, have been relatively accessible.

A third pit (216) was excavated *c.*3.00m to the west: it was more than 2.40m across and *c.*1.50m deep. This pit may have served a different function to the others, as its depth and steep sides would have rendered access difficult, and the deposits within it were of a different character. Its primary fill was a peaty soil (225*), which sloped markedly at its eastern end, over which had accumulated a thin organic spread (224). This was sealed with successive level spreads of silt (223*, 222, 221 and 215*), capped with a deposit of wet silt (220) and firm dark grey silty clay (219). The nature of these fills suggests that the pit was infilled over a period with rubbish which incorporated a heavy organic component. In contrast, the other two pits had been deliberately infilled once they had passed out of use.

These pits were sealed by layers which raised the height of the ground level to between *c.*5.34 and *c.*6.25m OD. The counterparts of these levelling layers in the north side of the trench may be fairly homogeneous spreads, such as clay-silt mix (238).

Pit 186 was sealed beneath silt 184, which in turn was covered by a mixture of clay, organic matter and silt (182), and an extensive spread of clay and tile (173): these layers also extended over the fills of the easternmost pit. To the west, pit 216 was covered by spreads of clayey silt (206, 214, 218), which appear to be broadly contemporary with 173. The tile and clay in the latter may indicate a deliberate intention to reclaim a boggy area. Some organic waste continued to be dumped in this area: a lens of fibrous organic peat (181) must have been rapidly sealed by a dump of greasy grey clay (180), to have preserved its characteristic vegetable inclusions.

The cumulative effect of this dumping was to raise the ground surface to *c.*6.25m OD. This was followed by the excavation of flat-bottomed pits which were shallower than their predecessors.

The easternmost of these pits was *c.*0.42m deep and *c.*2.75m across. Its grey primary fill was a soft dark grey silt (195); above this, the laminated fills consisted of successive lenses of silts (194, 193 and 191), capped with a layer of peat (189). A similar pit (230) was revealed at the west end of the trench. The primary fill was a soft organic silt (231*); above this lay layers of peat (229*), silt (228), and organic material (227, 226) which included twigs.

These shallow pits were sealed in their turn by further layers, some of which were very extensive and appeared on both sides of the trench. At the west end of the trench a layer of soft wet, grey silt (213*) contained charcoal and shell. This was overlain by loams 201, 202, and 203, which included clay, charcoal and chalk, and which formed a spread across much of this area: similar materials (237, 235) occurred in the north section (Figure 8, S7). These were capped by further loams (178, 177) which raised the ground level to *c.*6.70m OD. Incorporated within layer 177 were fragments of tile, brick and chalk: this marks the first appearance of brick on this site. It is possible that these fragments derived from the construction of the nearby precinct wall.

The layers described in the preceding paragraph did not extend as far as the precinct wall. Rather, they were cut through by a large depression over the site of the earlier hollow. This was infilled with a massive dump of greenish-brown clay loam (161). This was cut on its west side by a later pit which had a fill of firm clay (172). Further east, the depression was cut by a second pit or gully; this was *c.*3.00m wide, and was filled with a medium brown clay (160). The gently V-shaped profile of this feature, and its proximity to the later precinct wall could suggest this to represent an early boundary, pre-dating the construction of the precinct wall. Alternatively, it may have been associated with the supply of water to the Priory *reredorter*, *c.*21m to the south (see Phase 4 below), in which case it should be of later date.

The north section (Figure 8, S7)

The boulder clay subsoil lay between *c.*4.58 and *c.*5.33m OD along the north face of Trench 2. It had been subjected to less disturbance than was evident in the south section.

At the east end of the trench a stony clay (275) was the equivalent to 165 in the south face. Further west, an unnumbered clay-silt mix occurred at *c.*9.00m from the east end of the trench; it had a maximum depth of *c.*0.45m, and may represent an early soil or marsh horizon.

The earliest cut features recorded in the eastern part of the south section are considered to have continued here, to the north, as linear features following a north–south alignment.

The earliest feature was a steep-sided flat-bottomed gully (261), which was cut from between *c.*5.51 and *c.*5.31m OD; this has been interpreted as a continuation of ditch 168 (see above). Its fill (262) was capped by a soft organic silt (263) and a firm grey clay (259) — the probable equivalents of layer 167 in the southern section. At the extreme eastern end of the trench, the gully with fill 166* was similarly identified in both section faces.

At the opposite end of the trench a steep-sided pit (242) could be seen in section. Its primary fill was a greasy clayey-silt (241); this had been cut through by a gully filled with peat (240). The latter extended eastwards over a clay-silt mix (243), which may represent the upcast from the digging of 242.

A hollow or depression lay to the east of pit 242. At some stage, it had been deliberately infilled with a massive dump of firm grey silty clay (246) which contained flecks of charcoal and gritty organic fragments. At its eastern end, it was overlapped by the fill (262) of gully 261. Silt 258 accumulated over the latter, and was itself sealed by a chalk spread (257) which was *c.*0.20m thick.

In the area to the west of the former gully (261), the level of the prevailing ground surface was raised dramatically by a massive campaign of levelling. This is represented by an 0.60m thick layer of apparently homogeneous firm grey silty clays (239 and 250) which rose from 5.65m at the east to 6.10m OD at the west. These were separated from the deposits to the east by a line of closely driven stakes (253), some of which still survived in the section (Figure 8, S7); a solitary stake driven into layer 162 in the south section (Figure 8, S6) may suggest that these formed part of a north–south alignment on the edge of this feature. If this was indeed the case, then these stakes would have formed a revetment along the western side of a pond or watercourse; in which case, the upper surface of the firm silty clay to its west (250) would have formed a bank adjoining this feature.

Within the newly created pond or channel, dark silts (264, 256 and 255) accumulated over the earlier chalk spread (257): thus, the overall pattern of deposits revealed in the north section corresponds quite well with that seen in the south section.

The western side of this pond or channel was defined by firm silty clay 250: this achieved a maximum depth of 0.60m, and extended westwards for *c.*3.30m. It is interpreted as an embankment. It was capped with a thinner layer of silt and clay (249), and a clay silt (248). At some stage, the edge of the bank was made up with further dumps of clay (252) and silt (251). The top of the bank was thus raised to a level of *c.*6.50m OD, about 0.75m above the hard bedding of the water-filled feature. Further to the west, the composition of the embanking material became less clayey, and graduated into a thick deposit of firm silt

(239) whose surface lay between *c.*6.00 and 6.10m OD. All these layers were recorded without mention of the organic inclusions so common on the south side of the trench. They were presumably soils from which these had rotted out. The firm texture of 250 may have arisen from the ramming of this soil.

A further build-up of grey silty clay (238) which did include organic material, took place over the drier 239. This raised the ground level to *c.*6.50m OD, above the level from which the latest pits in the south section had been dug. This material was sealed beneath heavy deposits of loam (237, 235) which raised the ground surface by a further 0.50m. A solitary post-pit (244) was sunk into the level surface thus created.

Subsequently these loams were sealed by thick layers of clay (236, 234), the uppermost of which included chalk and limestone. A clayey-loam (247), which had been iron-stained by the percolation of water, was laid down over both the water-filled feature and the adjoining embankment. The deposit of this soil was followed by the insertion of various structural elements.

To the west an extensive layer of roof tiles set on edge possibly formed a path (233). About 1.70m to its east, a rectangular pit (245) was dug at the western edge of the former embankment. This pit had vertical sides and a stepped base lined with planks; it was subsequently infilled with chalk rubble. A further vertical-sided pit (271) lay to the east. This had chalk rubble (265) lining a central shaft. The latter — in which planking again occurred — was filled by even layers of loam (269), clay (268) and loams (267, 266, 270). It is uncertain what purpose this feature was intended to fulfil. Its extent is also uncertain, as later disturbance prevented any southward continuation of it being traced. It would appear to have been more complex than a simple footing, and the position of this feature over the infilled watercourse or pond suggests that its use may have been intimately associated with water.

The later features were sealed by a uniform deposit of loam (232) which closed the recorded sequence.

The finds (mostly unstratified)

Ridge Tile/Roof Furniture: unclassified glazed (1 fragment).
Lead: flashing (no. 674); ?line sinker (no. 766).
Worked Stone: ?weight (no. 1016).
Wood: stakes (nos. 1071–81); planks (nos. 1082–93); clinker (nos. 1094–1101); timbers (nos. 1102–3).
Leather: shoe uppers (nos. 1116–23); top band (no. 1124); rand (no. 1125); soles (nos. 1126–8, 1130–1, 1134); offcuts (nos. 1132, 1140); clump (no. 1133); fragment (no. 1142).

The precinct boundary. 14th century onwards (Figures 9–10)

Excavations in 1983 identified surviving elements of the precinct wall of the Priory (Figure 9: Armstrong and Tomlinson 1987, 19–24, figs. 13–14 and Pls. VII B and VII C). These formed its western boundary, dividing it from the tenements along Eastgate. Its identification has permitted the detailed discussion of the extent of the precinct (Armstrong and Tomlinson 1987, 49–52 and fig. 27). Excavation at the east end of Trench 2 in 1986 (Figure 3) allowed the recording of fuller elevation views of the precinct wall at the point, approximately midway along its surviving extent, where its broadly north–south alignment is kinked (Figures 9–10). These correspond to the position of an internal division within the precinct itself, for which limited evidence was recorded.

Since the completion of the non-destructive investigation of the precinct wall in 1986, the structure was seriously damaged by contractors in July 1987.

The precinct wall was set on a footing which was recorded to a depth of *c*.5.57m OD (Figure 10). Its lower reaches were filled with very substantial chalk rubble blocks, some over 0.50m long. These lower elements were randomly set, whilst the upper part of the footing was faced internally and externally with coursed chalk slabs; smaller chalk and a little tile provided a rubble core (Figure 9, S9). This suggests that the footing was built up as a free-standing structure from a height of *c*.6.30m OD. A fragment of ashlar plinth was recorded among the coursed slabs as a random inclusion — the chamfer ran back into the body of the wall. The slabs rose to a level of *c*.6.75m OD on the west (or external) side of the wall, and to *c*.7.00m OD on the east. The footing must have been almost immediately masked by soil, as no significant weathering damage to the chalk was recorded.

The superstructure of the wall was faced externally in brick, with a chamfer course set at a level of *c*.7.58m OD. The brick used for the precinct wall has been identified as Type 1, with the chamfer course made up of moulded variants. This course was in part decorative; chamfered bricks were also used to reduce the width of the wall as it rose in stepped sections. The coursed footings were *c*.1.40m wide, whilst the basal width of the wall was *c*.0.90m, diminishing to a thickness of *c*.0.70m where the chamfer was set, and to *c*.0.50m above it. The upper brickwork was coursed across the full thickness, but the wider base would have been built without incurring a significantly greater expenditure of shaped building materials. Brickwork survived in 1986 to a maximum height of *c*.1.30m.

The elevation of the wall showed a drain to have been built as an integral feature (Figure 10, S9): this ran through the structure *c*.0.35m below the external chamfer course. It was capped at this point with a limestone block, thus avoiding any undue stress which might have been occasioned by laying bricks over the outfall. It was fed by a channel which ran westwards from within the precinct. This channel was probably capped with bricks or slabs, though none of these had survived. Its very existence might argue for the continuing presence of a drainage ditch to the west of the precinct wall.

The drain ran along the south side of an east–west wall (Figure 9). It met the precinct wall at the point where the latter kinked slightly, though the lowest brickwork did not show any variation in its construction. This eccentricity may, therefore, have been a feature of the boundary which pre-dated the construction of the precinct wall. The internal wall was marked by a footing 0.50m wide, which was made up mostly of half bricks. At its west end an entrance surfaced with crushed chalk and mortar, 1.70m wide, gave access through this wall between the north and south parts of the precinct. A rectangular limestone block appears to have marked a gatepost. To the north the ground had been raised with a deposit of yellow-brown clay — either to cover the precinct wall footings, or as the floor of an otherwise unrecorded structure (a parallel wall was recorded *c*.9.00m to the north in 1983: Figure 2).

The brickwork of the early wall was laid in an irregular English bond, beginning with a course of header-laid bricks at its base. Rebuilding of the superstructure from the level of the splayed offset course was apparent in the elevation view: half bricks and header-laid work were prominent in this reconstruction work. No dating evidence was recovered during the excavation for either its original construction or for the later rebuilding. The survival of the precinct wall was recorded for an extent of *c*.30.60m: at both ends it had been destroyed by post-medieval disturbance of probably recent date.

The finds

Brick: Type 1 variant : B164 is illustrated.

Phase 3. Early timber buildings. 13th century

Introduction

Phase 3 consisted of two successive timber buildings of 13th century date which were established to the north of the great cloister. Although the first building may initially have served as temporary accommodation during the construction of the Priory, the rebuilding of this timber structure in the later 13th century indicates that it continued in use once the

Figure 11 Phase 3A — the clay platform and sill-beam hall.

cloister was established. Both of these buildings were set over a substantial clay raft or platform. The first belongs to Phase 3A, and was probably of sill-beam construction. This was replaced in Phase 3B by a post-built aisled structure on a different alignment. The new building, however, retained certain aspects of its predecessor, including drainage or soakaway features at the west end. These went out of use in Phase 3C.

In Phase 3D the aisled building was removed, and the area was disturbed, possibly by horticultural activity. This area was encroached upon by the construction of a subsidiary cloister in Phase 5, and by the extension of the north range of the great cloister in Phase 6.

All of the orientations described in the following excavation text apply to the ritual orientation of the Priory, unless otherwise stated.

The clay platform (Figures 11–14)

This structural phase was identified with the discovery of a thick yellow-brown puddled clay (27), which sealed the soils of Phase 2 (Figure 11). Variations in its character were noted on the southern part of the site (74). No clear boundary was identified between 27 and 74, and they are considered to have been part of the same series of dumps. Neither continued beyond the later Phase 6 footing to the south. The northern boundary of 27 was formed by a sill-beam alignment (1025), whilst its western limit was defined by a series of pits and scoops which were filled with clay and dark-stained soils. It did not appear in the western excavation edge, and was of a darker brown colour where overlapped by greasy dark soils.

Platform 27 was made up of successive dumps of material. The section view revealed three episodes of dumping, in a sequence which ran from west to east (Figure 5, S2). The yellow-brown clays were separated by greyer clay lenses. Other patches of greyish clay were identified towards the western limit of 27; these (961, 968) were interpreted as further lenses within the deposit. A charcoal-rich band of grey clay (1179) was also noted within 27 to the south-east. Clay 27 achieved its greatest depth, *c.*0.36m, over the Phase 2 depression. It became markedly shallower towards its northern and western limits. Nevertheless, its surface was level, lying between 6.44 and 6.37m OD. The close association between this deposit of clay and the overlying structural features indicates that it formed the floor or raft for a building.

The structural features above the platform were laid out on two different alignments (Figures 11 and 14). The cobble and chalk band (1025) was aligned NE–SW (ritual east–west) to match the orientation of the great cloister. It was the only structural element with such an orientation. Post-pits and other structural

features appear to have been laid out along broadly north–south and east–west axes, and both the occupation surfaces and the hearths appear to have been associated with this arrangement. Very little stratigraphic evidence was found to substantiate the interpretation of the Phase 3 buildings: it rests almost entirely upon the planned form and alignment of features.

Phase 3A. Sill-beam hall. Mid. to late 13th century (Figures 11–13)

The northern boundary of the clay platform (27) was formed by a sill, 1025 (Figure 11). This comprised an alignment of small chalk pieces and cobble, which were mixed with occasional lumps of burnt daub; it included several glazed potsherds. Roof tile, a common component of later deposits, was conspicuously absent from this material. Dark grey silt lay between the stones, contrasting with both the clay platform (27) to the south, and the sealing layer of clay (793). The cobbles which formed a distinctive feature of 1025 recurred to the north, but only as inclusions or small patches in later deposits. They were there considered to have been a product of later disturbance.

North of sill 1025 the soils were dark, in contrast to the yellowish clay of the platform (27). To the north-east, trial trenching had identified the northward continuation of the landfill soils of Phase 2. To the north-west an unnumbered dark grey soil with patches of orange clay was overlain by mottled clay (1144) with a maximum depth of 0.20m.

Possible post-settings were identified along the course of the northern sill (1025), only after an assiduous search for further structural elements. Most of these were filled with clays similar to the deposits north of 1025, and were considered as doubtful features at the time of excavation. Dubious bowl-shaped features (1161/1162, 1165/1166, 1169/1170, 1181/1182) mostly lay on the south side of the sill (Figure 12, S10–11). On the north lay the similarly ill-defined depression 1163/1164 (Figure 12, S11A). Three features on this alignment were more credible: 1171/1172 was a stake-hole; 1173/1174 was a small bowl-shaped depression at the west end of the sill, probably associated with later activity; and 1167/1168 had a distinctive gritty fill and was excavated to reveal a sub-rectangular pit with a lower part 0.22m square at one end (Figure 12, S11B–C). Though the latter could pass muster as a small post-pit, a later feature with fill of a similar character (789/790) occupied the same position. It is possible that the later feature had not been fully excavated.

Even if these dubious features are taken into consideration, Phase 3A presents only scanty evidence for substantial structural uprights. A more plausible interpretation is that the principal uprights were supported entirely on a sill-beam, laid on top of this alignment, with very little below-ground disturbance. It is probable that an alignment matching 1025 had been destroyed by the later insertion of a footing across the south side of the platform. No evidence was found for either a centre-line of posts, or for internal rows of aisle posts; however, the possibility that these could have been carried on padstones, which were later removed for reuse after the building had passed out of use, should be admitted.

Pits

A western boundary to the area of the clay platform (27) was marked by the irregular edge of a dark greasy clay-silt (937: Figure 11); its eastern edge ran at an approximate right-angle to footing 1025. The full extent of 937 was never revealed, as it extended beyond the excavated area; thus, though it directly overlay the western edge of the clay platform, it may have related to an unexcavated part of the building.

A series of cut features argued a distinct usage for the area which was sealed by 937. The fills of these features frequently included prominent iron staining. The similarity of 937 to some of these was noted at the time of excavation, and the layer may owe its

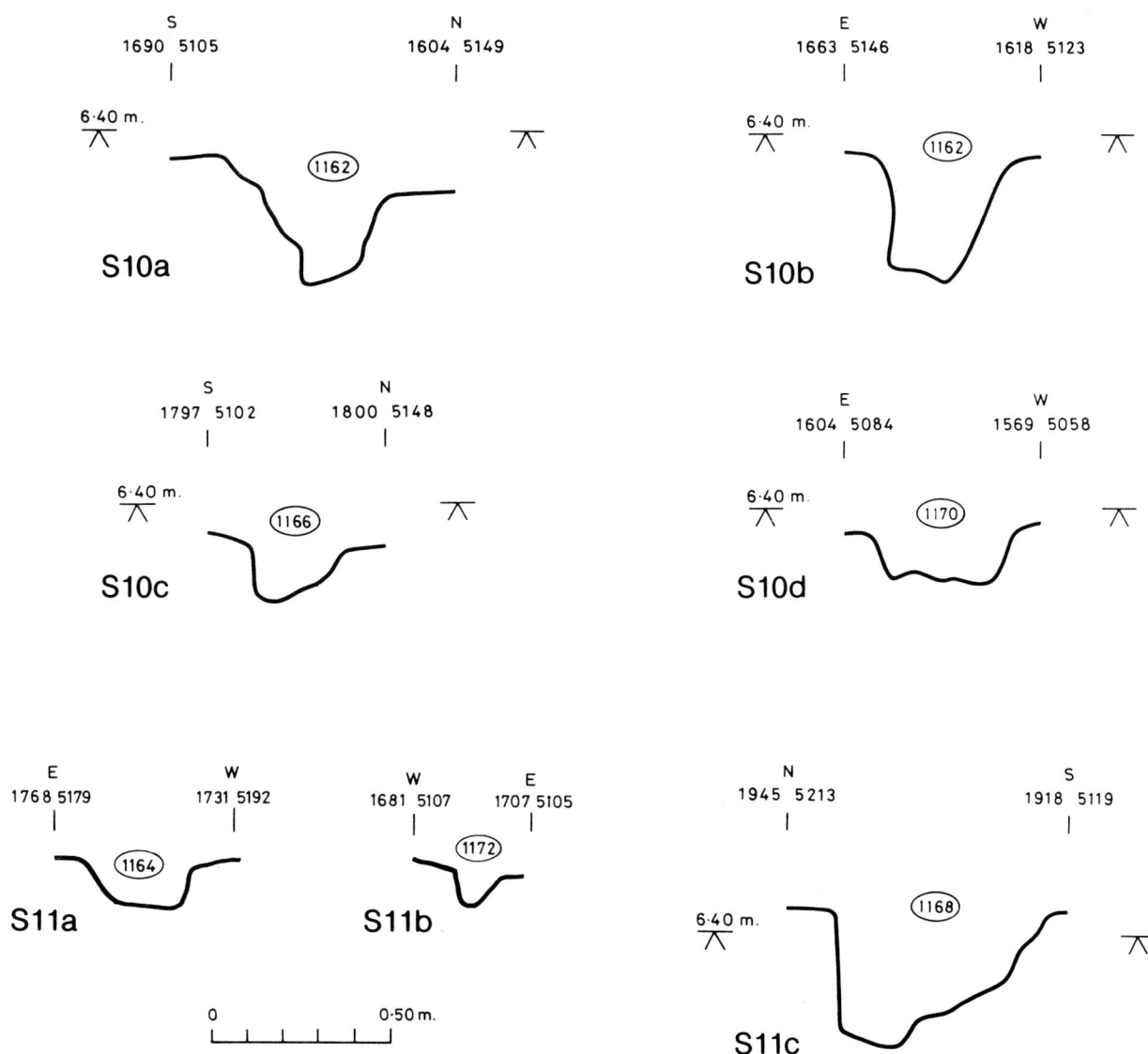

Figure 12 Phase 3A — features associated with sill-beam position. S10–11.

23

character to their proximity. Hollow 1061, which was a shallow feature over 5.00m long, was iron-stained on its base and sides. A crescentic depression (1062) ran alongside it. Both of these features respected the alignment of the east edge of 937. To the south lay a rectangular patch of bluish clay (1141) whose stratigraphic relationship to the other features was not determined. It was sealed by clay 1136. A shallow spread of clay (1056) separated features 1141 and 1061.

The lowest fill of hollow 1061 consisted of clay flecked with chalk and charcoal (1101: Figure 13, S12). This was overlain by iron-stained clay with charcoal (1074*) which was itself sealed by 1060; the latter was similar to 937, but included lumps of clay. It was sealed by iron-stained clay (1047*). Another hollow (1049), which was recorded as cutting 1061, but perhaps in reality represents its continuation, was filled with greasy clay-silt flecked with charcoal (1048*). The curving feature 1062 was filled by a soft greasy grey clay-silt (1055) which was very similar to 937, and was at first identified with it.

Some of these features may relate to the recutting of pits, though later intrusions have destroyed some of

the stratigraphic links between them. This activity closed with the sealing of the pits by the deposition of layer 937. Plastic clays (961*, 989, 962, 1053) were deposited at a similar level to the south of 937, and probably served to seal pits in that area.

The interpretation offered for this activity is that it indicates the use of the western part of the building as a service area, whose use was contemporary with that to the east. Although no structural evidence for a wall or partition separating this area from the eastern half of the building was recovered, the presence of two clearly defined surfaces, 937 to the west, and platform 27 to the east, may be taken as circumstantial evidence for such a division, or at least for a discrete use of these two areas.

Internal fittings

Most other features, on account of their alignment, are considered as belonging to the secondary use of the platform in Phase 3B. The exceptions to this are two successive early hearth contexts: a patch of reddened burning at the centre of the platform (963), and a small spread of brown clay (1017) on its east side, which apparently represents a repair of this fire

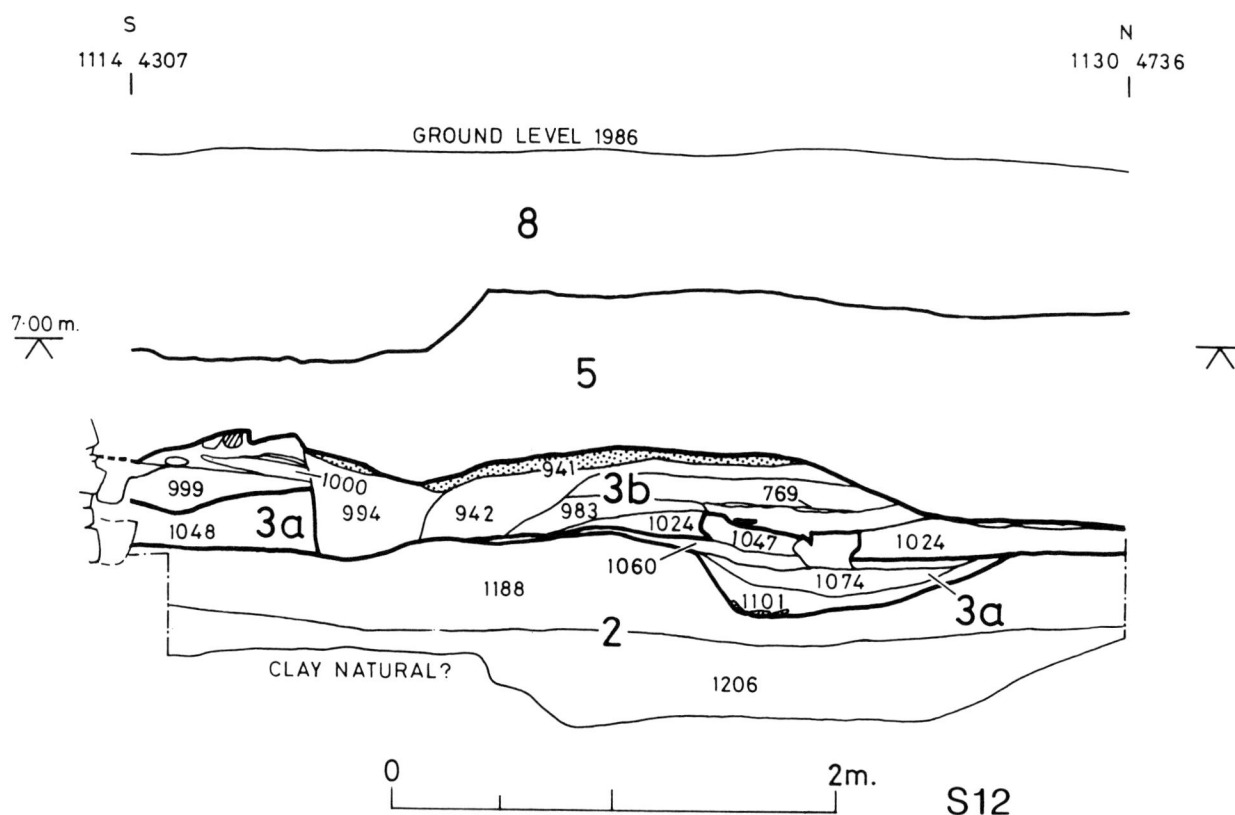

Figure 13 Phase 3 — pits in the Phase 3 hall. S12.

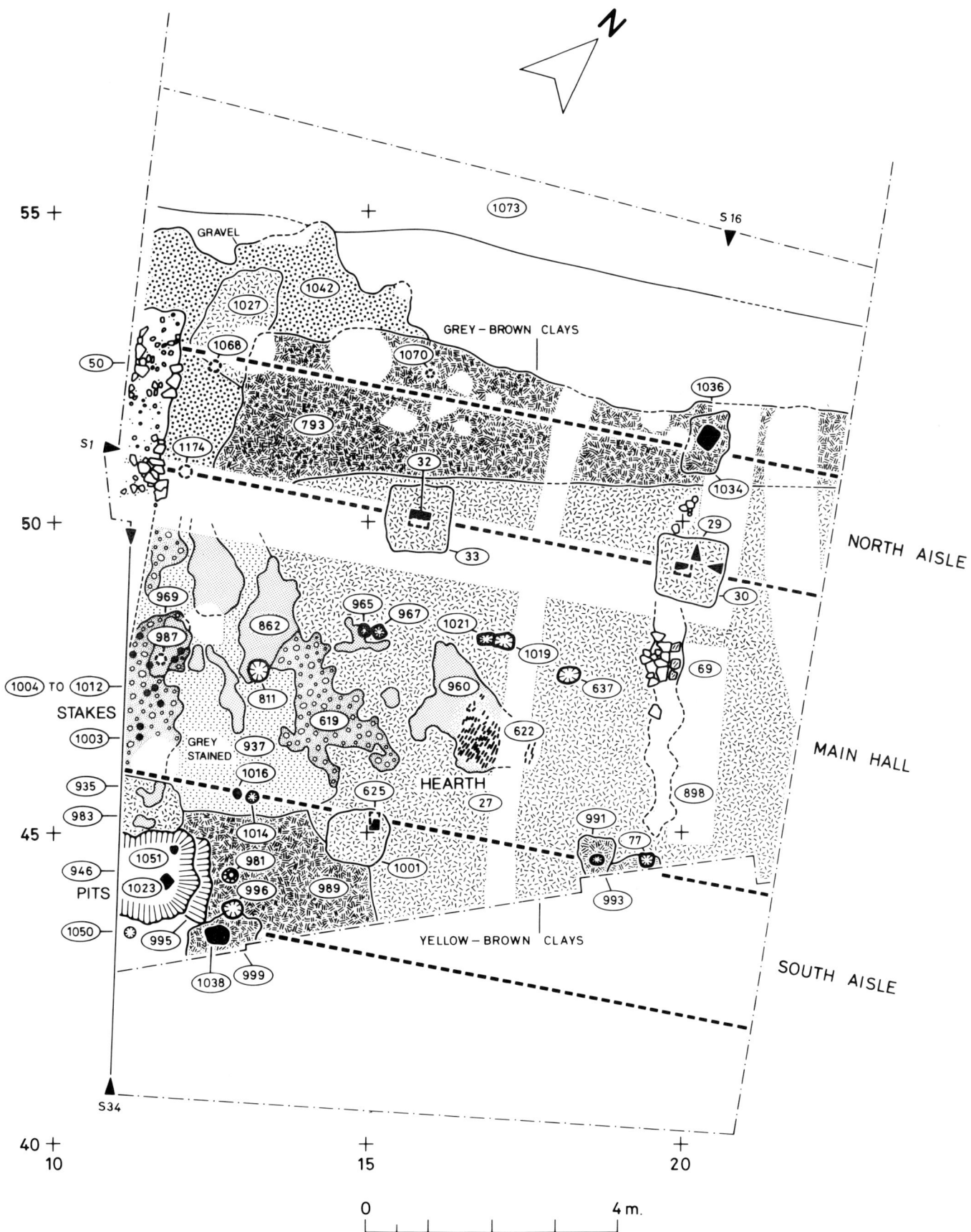

Figure 14 Phase 3B — the aisled hall.

position (Figure 11). Their central location indicates a hearth or brazier within an open hall structure during Phase 3A. Fragments of Type 6 roof tile were recorded from 963; these may, however, have been intrusive from a Phase 3B hearth structure in the vicinity.

The finds

Roof Tile: Type 1A (1 fragment); Type 2B (4); Type 6 (4), and 0.302 m² of non-diagnostic tile. All of these may be intrusive.
Lead: melt (no. 707A).
Iron: horse shoe nail (no. 811A), 1 nail and 7 nail fragments.
Copper Alloy: ?vessel fragments (no. 903).
Pottery: 16 vessels (nos. 1032–3 are illustrated).

Dating evidence

Pottery incorporated in the sill-footing (1025) included residual 12th century Beverley ware type 1A, and Coarse Sandy ware; the latter is more typical of 14th century contexts, but its appearance here may argue for an earlier origin. The pits in the south-west corner of the platform contained fragments of Coarse Sandy ware and Beverley ware type 2B (from contexts 1048 and 1074) which would normally be assigned to the later 13th or 14th century. Pottery from the surface of clay platform 27 was mostly of 14th century date, consisting predominantly of Humberwares, and should be regarded as intrusive from an overlying Phase 5 context (65); so too should examples of roof tile Types 1A and 2B.

Suggested date: mid. to late 13th century.

Phase 3b. Aisled hall. Later 13th century (Figures 14–16)

Introduction

The sill which marked the north wall of the Phase 3A hall (1025) was sealed by a mottled clay (793) which also overlapped gravel spreads to the north; this new clay surface formed an extension of the earlier clay platform (27). However, unlike the earlier building, its main axis was aligned NW–SE (Figure 14), rather than the approximate NE–SW orientation of its predecessor.

Clay 793 was laid down when the sill-beams of the early hall had been lifted, allowing their footings to be covered. It is less certain whether the platform was extended before the insertion of the structural elements which would support the Phase 3B building. The new clay overlay a limited spread of construction material (1142) at the north end of the building.

The structural account which follows is mainly concerned with the aisled structure which is orientated NW–SE, and is indicated by heavily dashed lines on Figure 14. A west wall is indicated by footing 50,

which is set at right angles to the main lines of aisle posts (32/33, 29/30 in the north aisle; 625/1001 and 991/993 in the south aisle). It is possible that there were two successive building phases represented. Support for this suggestion may be found in the fact that the northernmost post (1036) for the new building was not identified until after the removal of 793. The extension of the platform is therefore likely to have been a late episode in the reconstruction of the timber hall, post-dating the insertion of posts along its north side.

The structural features associated with the extended clay platform (27/793) consisted mainly of earth-fast wooden posts which were set in clay-packed pits, and a wall footing; a few minor elements were represented by posts, stakes, and hollows or depressions.

Four major post positions delineated a bay of a timber hall, and suggested a further bay on either side. It is likely that this was an aisled hall; a major post position at the outside of each aisle has been identified. The width of the central part of the hall was c.5.00m, the putative aisles were c.2.00m wide. The clay platform for the Phase 3A hall required extension 793 to serve the Phase 3B structure.

The structural elements — main hall

The north aisle was represented by at least two post-pits which were first identified in the base and north side of an east–west trial trench (29/30/31, 32/33/34: Figure 5, S1). These fell on a (ritual) east–west axis, with the posts set 4.25m apart, measured centre to centre. Their positions were indicated by post-pipes which were filled with soft plastic clay and the stubs of decayed wooden posts. The timbers measured c.0.18m by 0.17m (29) and c.0.35m by 0.20m (32). The pits had been cut through platform 27 and had been packed with clays (30, 33) which were initially indistinguishable from it. No further posts were identified on this east–west alignment; it is possible, however, that others may have existed beyond the excavated area. The eastern limit of the excavation lay only 2.50m to the east of post 29, whilst to the west, wall footing 50/1064 could mark either the end wall of the building or an internal partition.

The southern counterpart to post 32 lay c.5.00m to its south, and consisted of a post-pipe (625) which measured 0.40m by 0.30m. The timber had been set in a pit 1002 packed with clay 1001 (Figure 15, S13). The next post setting in this southern row lay c.4.50m to the east (77/978), and formed a pair with post 29 to the north. Setting 77/978 appeared as a rectangular hollow 0.17m by 0.20m, set in the north-east corner of a patch of clay that may have been all that remained of a clay-packed pit, which had been largely obliterated by a Phase 6A footing. Immediately adjacent, a square post-pipe (990/991) of 0.20m scantling was set in a

S13

S14

S15

S16

S17a

S17b

S18

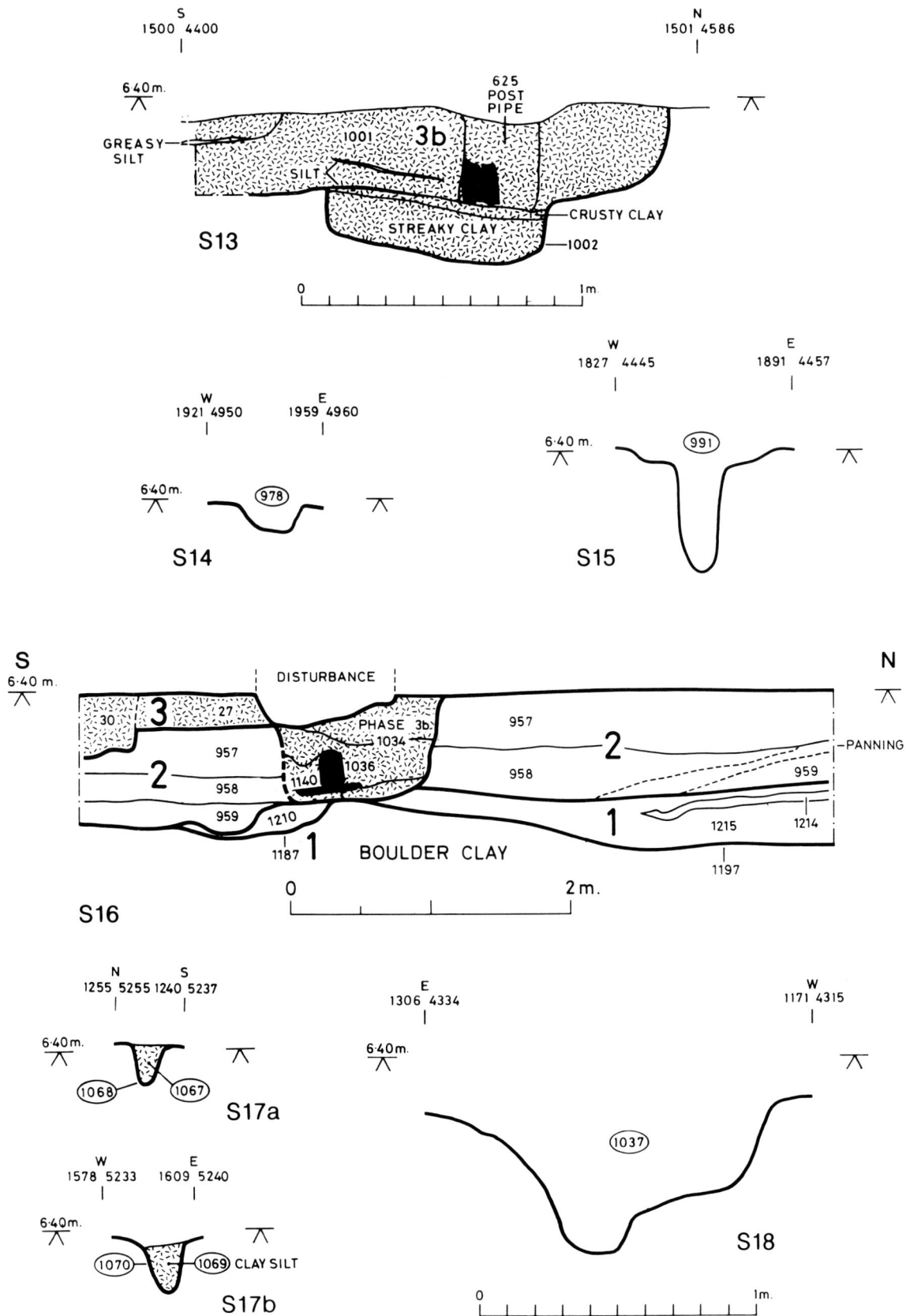

Figure 15 Phase 3B — post positions. S13–18.

sub-rectangular patch of mottled clay (992/993:Figure 15, S14–15), which may represent an additional or replacement post.

These four posts delineated a single bay of a timber hall on a broadly east–west alignment.

A solitary decayed timber (1036) which was 0.20m thick and which rested on a flat timber plank (1140), survived in the north wall. It was set in a

sub-rectangular post-pit (1035) and packed with clay (1034: Figure 15, S16). The post was set *c*.2.00m to the north of aisle post 29, in line with the bay division to its south. Further west along the north wall lay a pair of smaller post-holes, at *c*.4.50m and *c*.7.90m distance. The closer of these, (1069/1070) was rectangular and measured 0.13m by 0.11m; the further (1067/1068) was sub-rectangular and measured 0.12m

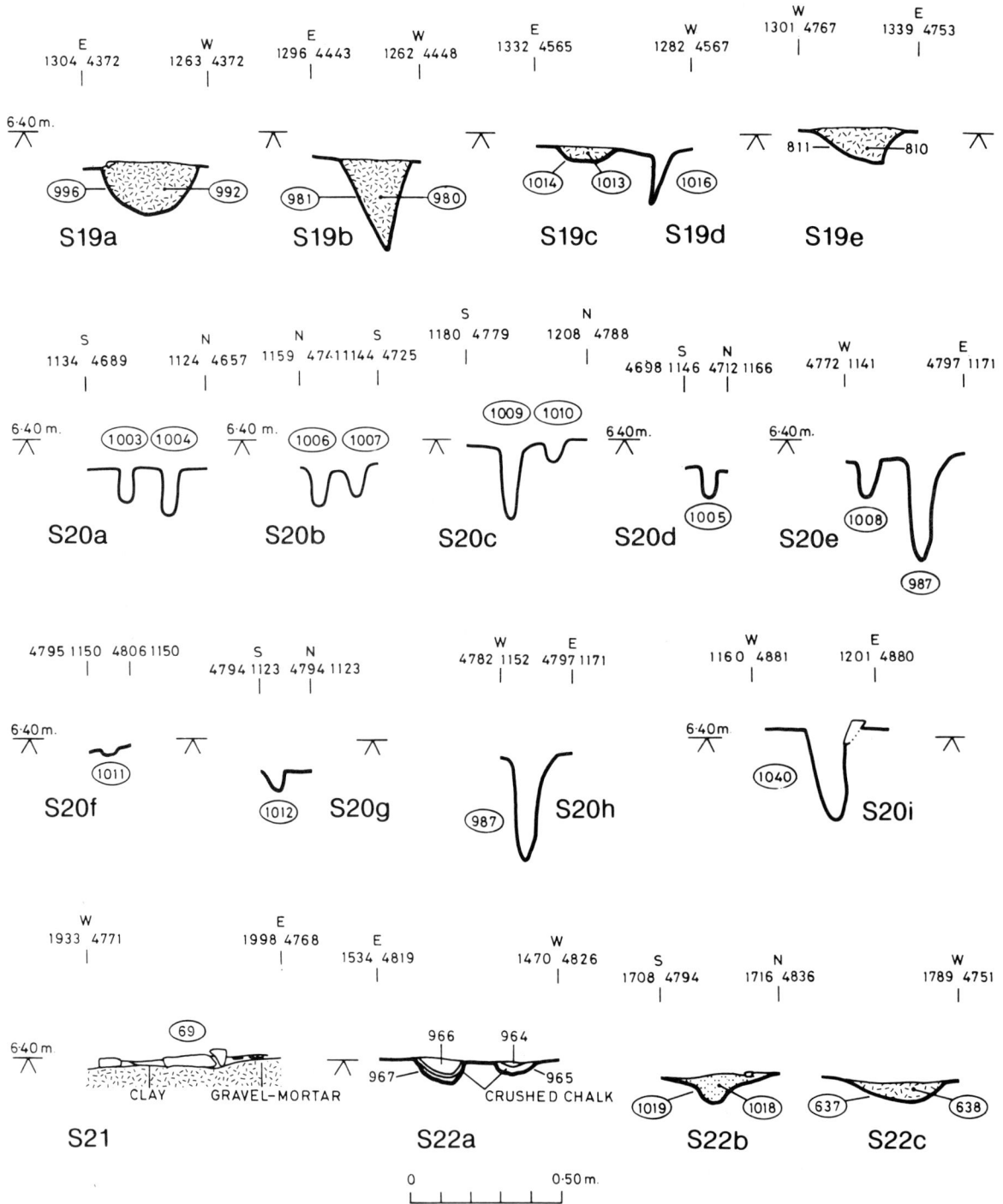

Figure 16 Phase 3B — partition elements. S19–22.

by 0.08m (Figure 15, S17A–B). The former lay *c.*2.30m north of aisle post 32, and was broadly in line with the bay division. Post 1067/1068 may have related to a partition within the timber building (see below). Neither 1069/1070 nor 1067/1068 contained any packing; nor were there any surviving traces of timber posts in these settings.

A solitary post survived on the line of the south wall of the building. Post 1038, with an approximate scantling of 0.24m by 0.18m lay in a sub-rectangular pit (1037) which was packed with clay (999: Figure 15, S18). This feature was identified only in the course of its excavation — its southern side having been obliterated by the insertion of a Phase 6A footing (Figure 14). The post lay *c.*2.00m to the south of the south aisle, and in line with a possible screen set across that aisle (see below).

West wall

The west end of the hall was defined by a north–south footing 50/1064 which was recorded along the edge of the excavation (Figure 14). It comprised a steep-sided trench 0.75m deep and in excess of 0.75m wide, which had been filled with pitched chalk rubble set in a mortary matrix (Figure 5, S1). This trench was cut through the Phase 3A platform (27) from its surface. Its position at the end of a bay of the new timber hall, and the absence of any post-pits adjacent to the wall, suggest it to have been integral to the plan of this building. The spread of occupation surfaces within the timber building post-dated the construction of this wall.

At the northern end of this footing a limited spread of crushed chalk (1142) marked its construction horizon. These were sealed by a limited spread of clay (1076), a more extensive spread of gravel, mortar, clay and cobble (1042), and by further spreads of clay (1027) and clayey-silt (1073). These were overlapped by the platform extension, 793 (Figure 14).

Compacted chalky layers (619, 969) are considered to have formed a common horizon running over the greasy clay-silt (937) and the earlier platform (27); it is possible that these may mark a similar construction spread to 1142. These chalky layers were overlain in turn by a dark gritty silty clay (979), and then by a patchy mortar spread (862) which was 0.04m thick (Figure 14). The various layers served as a floor surface for the west end of the building.

A dark clay (49/940) sealed the top of the chalk footing (50/1064), in the one section where it was cut by the east–west trial trench (Figure 5, S1). This may represent a break in the wall or, less likely, robbing. This material was thought to lie at a similar horizon to 935, an occupation silt within the aisled hall.

Screens and other internal partitions

Three north–south alignments and a single east–west partition were marked by features which related to the surfaces and occupation deposits which accumulated over platform 27 (Figure 14). These may indicate the position of internal features within the aisled hall.

The most prominent of these alignments was a group of five post-holes which ran across the south aisle from post 1038 (Figure 16, S19A–D). The most southerly of these was a bowl-shaped post-socket (996) which was 0.22m across and 0.18m deep. The next in the alignment (981) was of a similar diameter, though formed by the driving of a pointed timber 0.26m into the clay. Next was a bowl-shaped depression (1014) with a diameter of 0.18m; a 0.10m diameter driven stake at a raking angle (1016) was set next to it on the main south aisle alignment The line of this screen terminated with a bowl-shaped socket (811), with a diameter of 0.28m and a depth of 0.11m.

The partition began at the south wall and extended for *c.*4.50m — half the total width of the hall. All of the post-holes were filled with soft clays (992, 980, 1013, 1015, 810); those to the south were grey, whilst their northern counterparts were browner. The later occupation deposits within the hall did not respect this alignment: it is therefore probable that the partition was dismantled during the lifetime of the building.

A less well-defined north–south alignment extended across the west end of the building, between the two rows of aisle posts; it began *c.*1.50m to the west of the partition described above, starting close to its north end (Figure 14). The southern end of this alignment was marked by a cluster of stakeholes immediately to the north of the west end of the south aisle (1003–1012); these varied between 0.05 and 0.09m in diameter, and between 0.07 and 0.27m in depth (Figure 16, S20A–I). Some of these stakes may have been set in pairs, such as 1003/1004, 1006/1007, 1009/1010; others were apparently isolated; 1005, 1008, and two were unusually shallow; 1011, 1012. North of the centre of this grouping lay a circular post-hole (984/987) with a diameter of 0.12m and a depth of 0.35m. All of these features were revealed by the removal of a dark layer (979: see above), but it is possible that they in fact post-dated this layer and were simply not detected at a higher level: some support for this suggestion may be found in the fact that the one substantial post-hole (987) was first seen in the course of the removal of this 'sealing' layer. About 3.90m to the north, a bowl-shaped post-hole (1174), with a diameter of *c.*0.30m, lay on the same alignment as the north aisle posts, and should probably be related to this phase of activity (Figure 14).

A solitary post (1040) midway along this alignment was sealed below a construction layer (969), which was cut by the other features; it cannot therefore be considered contemporary with them.

The third north–south alignment lay between posts 29/30 and 77, towards the eastern end of the excavated area. It consisted of a shallow linear depression (69:Figure 16, S21), which was filled with small pieces of rubble, and was continued to the south by an irregular spread of similar material (898) for a total recorded distance of *c.*3.05m (Figure 14). There are problems in the interpretation of this feature, as much of its southern extent was disturbed and contaminated in the course of Phase 5, whilst its north end was destroyed by the east–west trial trench. It could have marked the position of a light sill for a screen; there is even the suggestion of a continuation of this feature across the north aisle, to the north of post 29.

A final series of shallow features appears to have followed an east–west alignment (965, 967, 1021, 1019, 637: Figure 14). Though similar in character to those at the west end of the building, these were shallower than the others (Figure 16, S22A–C), and their position within the building suggests that they formed part of a feature which was associated with the central hearth (see below). At the west end of this alignment, a pair of shallow oval depressions (965, 967) lay 0.10m apart. About 1.55m to the east a further pair (1019, 1021) were immediately adjacent to each other. They were filled with crushed chalk and silt laminates (964, 966, 1020, 1018), whose layering matched that of the surfaces within the building. The eastern end of this alignment was marked by a larger oval depression (637) which was filled with soft clay (638) — 0.75m to the east of 1019. These features probably marked a screen, but their partial filling with the material taken to form a construction spread or floor suggests that this was dismantled at some stage during Phase 3B.

The layer of greasy silty clay (937) which sealed the pits within the Phase 3A hall was itself sealed by the chalk and mortar construction spreads (619, 969) which spilled over the platform from the west. The earlier hall had seen a concentration of pits in its western half, which suggested that this part of the building had been used as a discrete service area (see above). Similarly, the only pits to be located within its Phase 3B successor were sited in its south-west corner. Here, a steep-sided sub-rectangular pit with a fairly flat bottom (994*/995) was set in the corner of the south aisle, up against the outside wall of the building (Figure 13, S12). Both its shape and its position are consistent with it having been used as a setting for a cask or other receptacle, which has been subsequently removed: the possible uses for such a vessel range from water butts to barrel cesspits. At some stage during the life of the Phase 3B hall, this pit was recut by a second rectangular pit (946). The new

cut was slightly smaller in extent, but once again had a fairly flat base. A neatly squared post (1023), measuring *c.*0.10 x 0.11m, was set into its base along the centre of its eastern side; whilst the remains of a second slightly smaller timber (1051) were found in the north-east corner of the pit. These two timber elements may have served to support the base of a cask, similar to that postulated for pit 994/995. Once this particular use of the pit had finished, the wooden vessel would have been removed, and the pit infilled with a succession of tips. The lowest fill consisted of ash (953*); this was covered by tips of greasy clay (942), ash and charcoal (941), and further greasy soils which were flecked with chalk grit (979, 1024). The position of these two pits in the far corner of the building, separated from the rest of the side aisle by a screen (the 996–811 alignment), could argue for the use of this area as a latrine or garderobe — in which case, the wooden container would have been a barrel cesspit which would have needed to be regularly emptied. Its siting against the exterior wall might suggest that provision was made for the removal of cess from the building at this point, thereby obviating the need to carry it out through the main hall. It is possible that post 1050, to the south of pit 946, may be part of this provision.

Hearths

The central hearth position which served the Phase 3A building continued in use when the Phase 3B aisled hall was erected (Figure 14). It was replaced, a little to the west of the original position, by a tile-on-edge hearth (622) set onto a sub-rectangular mortar base (960) which measured 1.60m by 1.36m. This hearth, though patched when the need arose, was to continue in use throughout the life of the building. The hearth was constructed out of reused tiles which included fragments of Type 6 roof tiles. Twelve samples were taken for archaeomagnetic assay of this hearth (see section 5.1: Mf.3. E5): three of these suggested a probable 13th century date for its last firing, but only a broad indication of the date could be obtained.

The finds

Masonry: ashlar (no. B77).
Roof Tile: Type 1A (1 fragment); Type 6 (31) and 1.812 m²
    of non diagnostic tile; no. B189 is illustrated.
Ridge/Roof Furniture: Type 1A (2 fragments); Type 1C (2);
    Type 1D (1); Type 2 (2); roof furniture (nos. B199,
    B206); finials (nos. B209–10); ventilator (no.
    B219).
Lead: offcut (no. 648).
Iron: 1 nail and 19 nail fragments.
Copper Alloy: needle (no. 913).
Worked Stone: fragment (no. 1019).
Wood: plank (no. 1105).
Pottery: 60 vessels; (nos. 1034 and 1036–7 are illustrated).

Dating evidence

Little datable material was removed from structural features of the Phase 3B hall. Fragments of Beverley ware type 2B came from post-pit 999, and from soil on top of footing 940. Some of the external spreads of material which post-dated the construction of wall 50/1064 were more productive. Context 1073 contained a range of later 13th or early 14th century material, including Humber 3 and Beverley ware type 2C. The clay (793) which extended the platform after the erection of the aisle posts included Beverley ware type 2B and Humber 3, together with residual sherds of Beverley ware type 1A. This is a combination which is unlikely to have occurred before the later 13th century. A fragment of tile Type 1A occurred in post-position 996.

The relative scarcity of Cowick-type Humberware from this phase (a solitary sherd from layer 1076) might argue that it did not continue far into the 14th century; however it should be stressed that the quantities of pottery present in these features are so small that their use for dating should be treated with caution.

An archaeomagnetic date for the tile-on-edge hearth within the hall suggested that its last use probably took place in the 13th century. The Type 6 tiles which were used in its construction were the first to be recorded at the Priory. The pits in the south-west corner of the hall produced small amounts of pottery: most of this was residual, but the occurrence of Beverley ware type 2C in their fills indicates that they remained in use until the later 13th or 14th century.

Suggested date: last quarter of 13th century or later.

Phase 3C. Aisled hall, later occupation. Very late 13th or early 14th century (Figure 17)

The final phase of occupation of the Phase 3B building is represented mainly by layers of silt which extended across the western part of the aisled hall (616/863:Figure 17). The deepest of these was silt 923 which accumulated at the western end of the hall, perhaps as a result of sweeping. None of these layers paid any respect to the Phase 3B partition positions, some of which were actually sealed by silts 616 and 923. As the maximum recorded depth of these silts was *c*.0.07m, their accumulation appears to have been strictly controlled.

In the centre of the hall a pad of hard clay (858) which measured *c*.3.00m by 1.60m, was laid down around the west side of hearth 622: the surface of this clay was distinctively pitted. This patching was overlapped by a further ashy silt (807*). On the north side of this hearth, two similar clay patches (621, 860)

were hard and fire-reddened. The first of these (621) was subsequently covered by a thin ashy spread 620. External ashy spreads 1043 and 1078 may represent sweepings from the hall, perhaps spread along a path.

A possible brazier position is indicated by an area of burning (863) to the west of the central hearth, at the lower 616 silt horizon. This should perhaps be regarded as a temporary fixture.

Isolated patches of ashy silt were identified during work on the north–south trial trench. In the north-east part of the hall 81, and at the south end of the trench lenses of sand, silt and ash 94, were the only occupation deposits noted east of the fireplace. These were both very insubstantial, are not illustrated, and cannot be ascribed to any particular sub-phase of the occupation.

The main alignment of the Phase 3B and 3C building was mirrored externally by an 0.90m wide band of ashy material which ran parallel to its long axis, just beyond the limits of any possibly drip line. Its regular form and position suggest that this was an external path along the north side of the hall. A similar feature (1078) was set approximately at right-angles to it in the north-west corner of the excavated area. The juxtaposition of these features, combined with the fact that there was a clearly defined hiatus at their postulated junction with the building, argue for the existence of an entrance into the north-west corner of the hall at this point.

The finds and dating evidence

Roof Tile: Type 6 (3 fragments) and 0.09 m² of
  non-diagnostic.
Lead: offcut (no. 648A).
Iron: 1 nail and 3 nail fragments.
Copper Alloy: ?patch (no. 906).
Pottery: 8 vessels. No new pottery types were present.
Suggested date: very late 13th or early 14th century.

Phase 3D. Garden features. Very late 13th or early 14th century (Figures 18–19)

A series of cut features post-dated the occupation of the timber hall (Figure 18), but were themselves sealed by context 65, which was a spread laid down after the construction of the little cloister in Phase 5. Though substantial, these could not be attributed to a structural phase. Some may well have been of natural origin. It is even possible that this activity may have occurred within the early garth of the little cloister in Phase 5 (Figure 18).

A discontinuous linear feature (629) with a total length of 8.55m, ran north–south, across the central hearth position within the timber building of Phases 3B and C, and thus clearly post-dated its disuse. It had a shallow dished profile, *c*.0.09m deep and

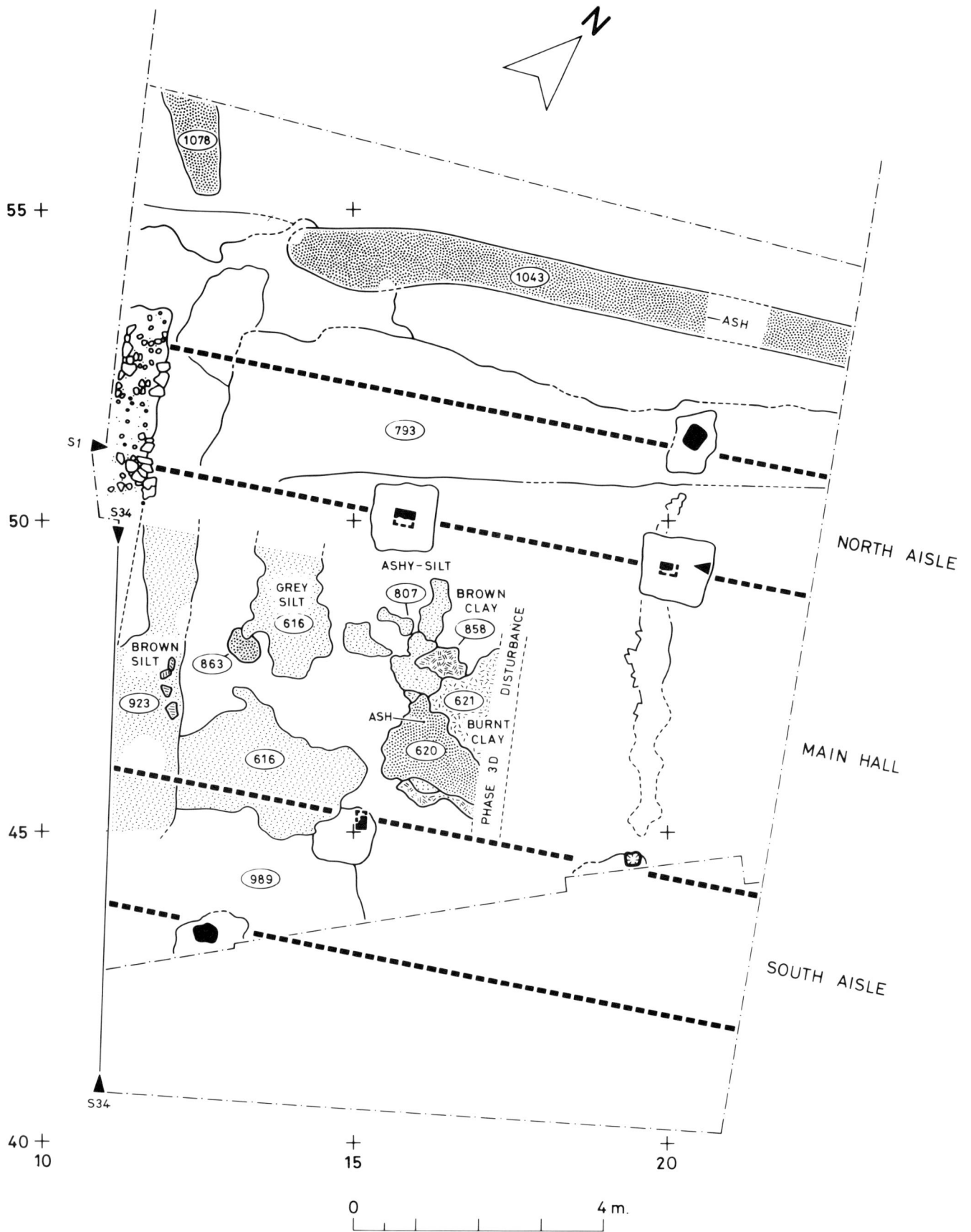

Figure 17 Phase 3C — later occupation of the aisled hall.

*c.*0.35–0.60m wide (Figure 19, S23A–B). It was filled with a gritty soil (633), which became a more patchy mixture of clays to the north — particularly beyond the break in gully 629 and to the north of platform 27.

A shallow and ill-defined gully (707/739) ran along the southern edge of 793, with its eastern end terminating close to gully 629 (Figure 18). It was filled with gritty soils (706/738) which was similar in their general character to the overlying layer, 65. This feature was only *c.*0.03m deep (Figure 19, S24 A–B).

A number of shallow irregular depressions (730, 733, 736, 764, 768, 775, 777, 790) cut through the former Phase 3B clay surface (793), close to the convergence of these two gullies (Figure 19, S25 A–D). (It is possible that 790 may have been an incompletely excavated post position, see Phase 3A above, though if so the timber had presumably been withdrawn.) Their fills (729, 732, 735, 763, 767, 774, 776, 789) were typically greasy clay soils, which were similar to the overlying 65. A further four patches of dark soil occurred at this horizon, and may have been comparable features; these were recorded in plan view (shown in dotted outline in Figure 18), but not assigned context numbers. Their irregular form led to their being considered as being of natural origin — perhaps the root action of small trees or shrubs. If this was indeed the process which led to their formation, it would suggest a hiatus in the occupation of this area, falling between the demise of the later timber hall and the construction of the little cloister.

The two gullies (707/739 and 629) could bear some structural interpretation. The latter could, for example, show the robbed out course of a sill, or of a narrow drain or waterpipe. No other features or layers which related to these alignments were identified. They were perhaps associated with some short-lived horticultural activity in this area.

A small group of other features should, by stratigraphic evidence, be included in Phase 3D. A stakehole (1029/1030) which was 0.23m deep (Figure 19, S25E) and a small circular pit (782/783) which had been filled with gritty grey soil both lay in the north part of the Phase 3B/C timber hall. A linear depression (903) wound south-westwards from the eastern excavation edge and passed underneath the straight line of 629 (Figure 19, S26 A–B); it was filled with clay 902. The irregularity of this feature suggested an interpretation as an animal burrow.

The finds and dating evidence

Roof Tile: Type 2B (3 fragments); Type 6 (7); Type 12B (2); and 0.675 m² of non-diagnostic tile.

Ridge/Roof Furniture: Type 1D (2); unglazed ridge (1): roof furniture (no. B207).

Lead: offcut (no. 649).

Iron: tenter hook (no. 776), hinge pivot (no. 785) and 9 nails and 2 nail fragments.

Copper Alloy: bell (no. 901).

Worked Bone: toggle (no. 953).

Worked Stone: strike-a-light (no. 1012).

Pottery: 52 vessels (no. 1038 is illustrated).

The pottery from Phase 3D was mostly of 13th century date. Context 633, the fill of the long shallow gully (629), included much residual material, but also one sherd of Beverley ware type 2C, placing this activity toward the end of the 13th or early 14th century. The first Pinky Buff ware also occurred here: this was first identified in late 13th century and early 14th century contexts at Eastgate, Beverley. Glazed roof tile was also found in this phase. The absence of Cowick-type Humberware from both Phases 3C and 3D might argue that they did not continue long into the 14th century; however, the strong residual element suggests that much of this pottery may be redeposited from other contexts.

Suggested date: late 13th/early 14th century.

Phase 4. The great cloister. 13th century onwards

Trenches were cut south of Trench 3 to enable the 1986–87 excavation to be correlated with the work carried out on the great cloister in the 1960s (Figures 2–3 and 23). MacMahon's record has enabled a summary description of the buildings in this area (Armstrong and Tomlinson 1987, 19–20, 54–5 and figs. 12 and 27). The re-excavation of parts of his trenches and the re-recording of structures has cast new light on this area, though few additional finds were recovered. A narrow trench, cut across the north range of the great cloister, produced further evidence of its development. The correlation of plans with MacMahon's record has proved problematical, as a disparity of *c.*1.60m along his north–south axis became apparent. Subsequent reference to his archive failed to trace the cause of this disparity, and so the plans were arbitrarily juxtaposed using salient features which had been recorded in both excavations as a guide.

Excavations in 1988–9 revealed elements of the east side of the great cloister and the choir of the Priory church. Investigation here was non-destructive, but has helped to clarify the form of the church and indicate the accretion to it of ancillary structures.

The great cloister is presumed to have been a quadrangular area, with the church to the south. The original form of the west and north ranges is, however, problematical, given the limitations of the record achieved. This layout is designated Phase 4A. Its construction was perhaps contemporary with the Phase 3 occupation to the north. Phase 4B involved the rebuilding of the great cloister, and it is possible that Phase 4C represents the continuation or

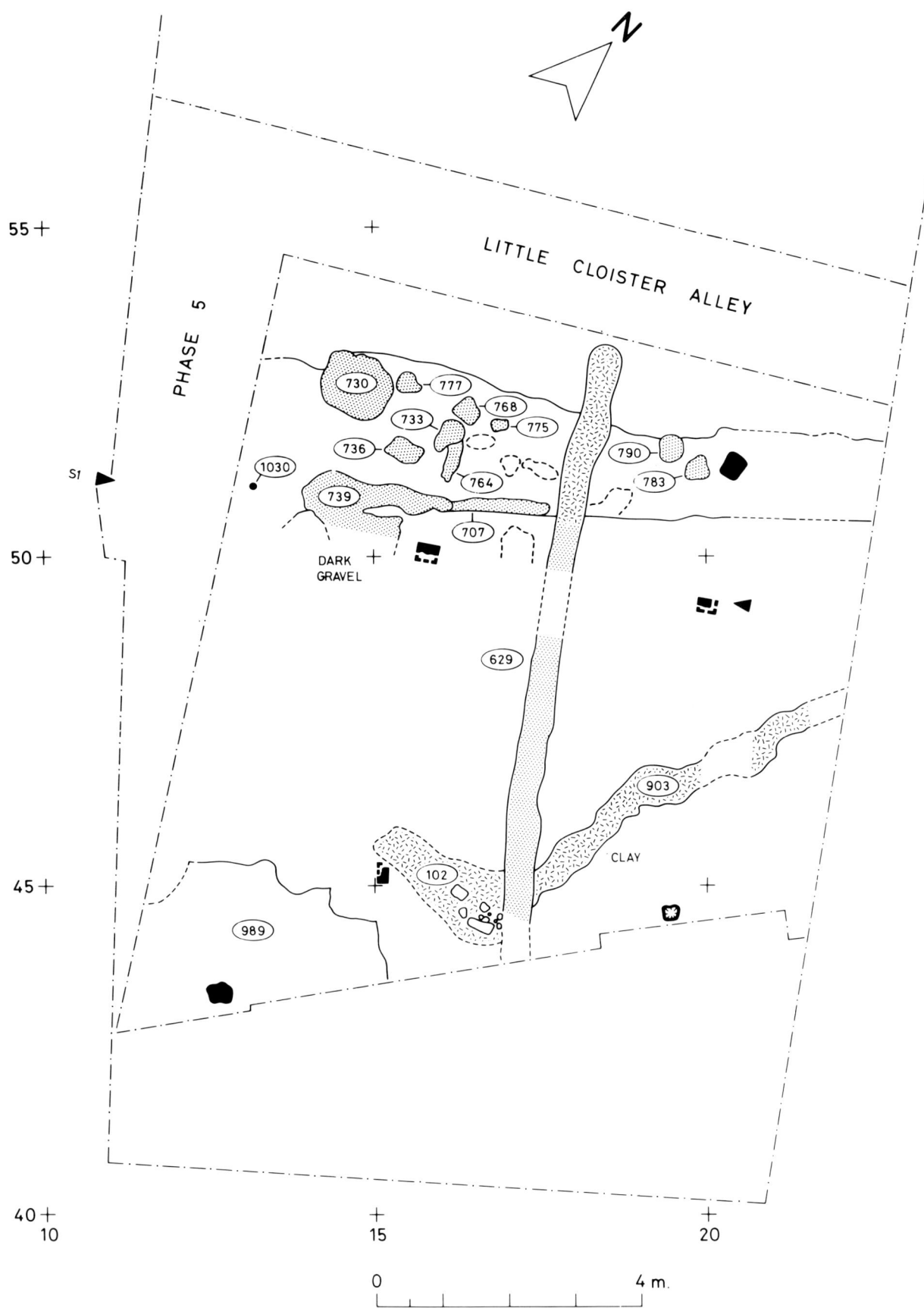

Figure 18 Phase 3D — end of the occupation of the aisled hall.

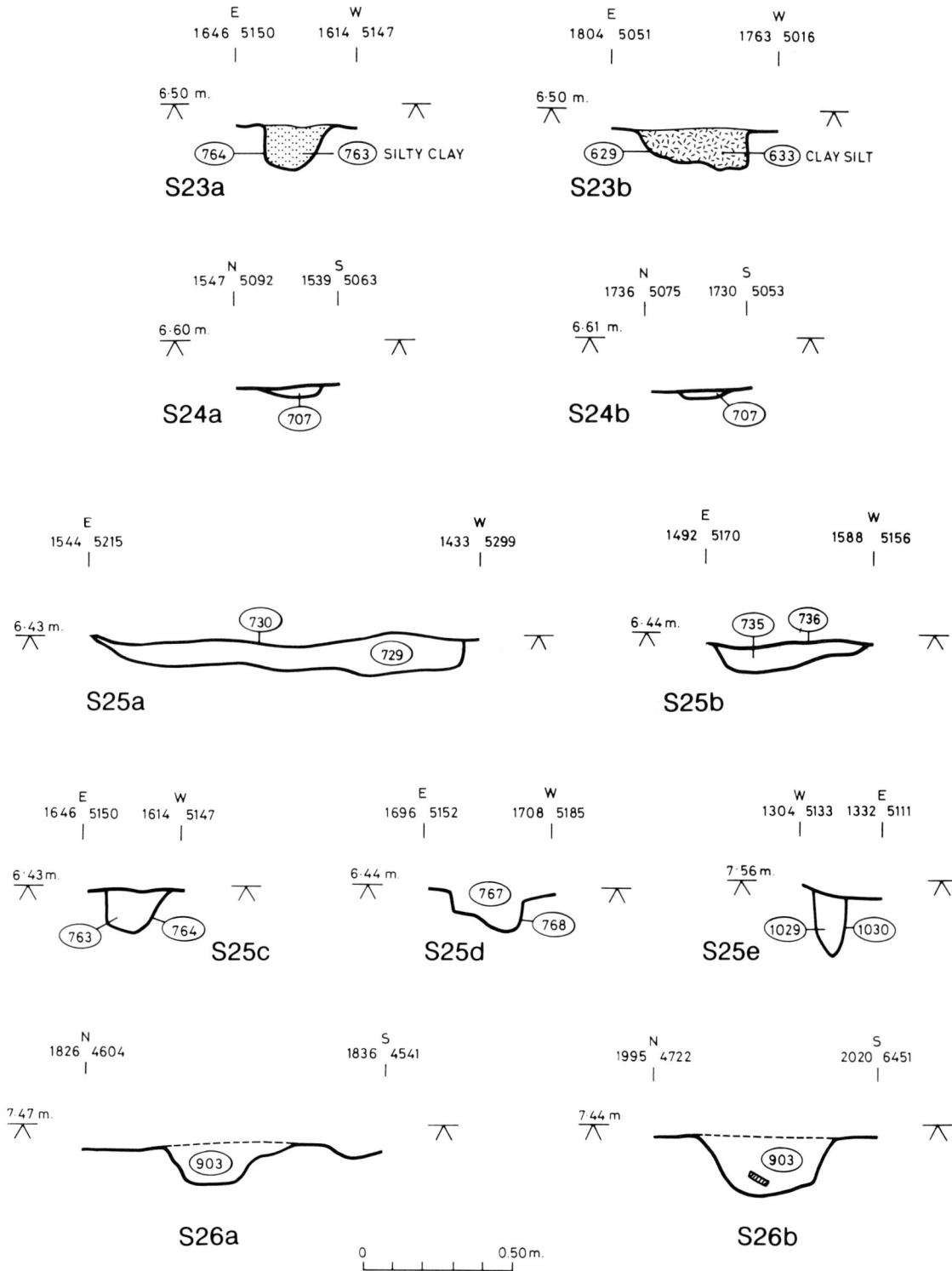

Figure 19 Phase 3D — features. S23–6.

completion of this work. Further reconstruction of the north range of the great cloister took place in Phase 6A.

Features which were associated with water management at the Priory are also described here, as their position was partly dictated by the layout of the great cloister.

The church (13th century onwards)

The church of the Dominican Priory was first located by MacMahon, who by 1964 had identified the full extent of its west end and a short stretch of its north wall (Armstrong and Tomlinson 1987, 7–9, figs. 3–5, and Pls. II–III). In 1983 a re-excavation of part of this area was carried out, and both sets of excavations were published as fully as possible (*ibid.*). The reader is referred to that account and particularly to its discussion (*ibid.*, 52–4). The main findings of the earlier excavations can be briefly summarised as follows: two major phases of construction were identified: an original nave; and the addition of a south aisle, western *galilee* porch and step. Fifteen burials were identified within the nave and the side aisle, together with a limited extent of floor tiles *in situ* within the nave.

The excavations in 1988–9 at the east end of the church are described with the context prefix 'C', to distinguish them from context numbers assigned during the excavations of 1986–7. They are discussed in an order which approaches the sequence of construction.

The choir (Figure 20)

The most substantial structural elements to be exposed during the excavations of 1988–9 (Trenches A–C: Figure 3) were two east–west alignments of chalk rubble, which formed the south (C1, C2) and north (C3, C4) wall footings of the choir of the Priory church (Figure 20). They consisted of rubble cores set in a mortar matrix and faced by slightly larger roughly worked slabs. The south side of footing C3 had suffered disturbance, while the north edge of C2 was obscured by later features which were butted against it. The width of footings C2 and C4 was *c.*1.60m; that of C1, *c.*1.64m. Tiles which were laid flat on the surface of C4 at a level of 6.75m OD are suggested to have been the basal levelling for the erection of stonework. The extent of mortar levelling on footing C1 indicated that it had supported walling *c.*0.92m thick.

The alignment of the south wall footings (C1 and C2) matched that to be expected from the projection of those at the west end of the church (Figure 2). The footings of the north wall of the choir (C3 and C4), however, lay *c.*1.00m to the north of their expected position. The implication may be that this footing related to an episode of reconstruction; alternatively, it

may represent an episode of building work that was executed when other works obstructed the establishment of a straight line along the north side of the church. The position of the walling which was set above the footing is not known, so it is not possible to determine whether any resulting error may have been partially corrected by offset construction. Almost all of the ashlar had been systematically removed, and the only surviving element of the superstructure was a chalk ashlar block which was set on the south side of the south wall (C1). This use of chalk in external walling was unusual, and may betray a later modification of the wall, as a result of the building of an ancillary structure against it (see below).

The western limit of the choir was indicated by the partial exposure of the east face of its end wall (C30). This was faced with chalk ashlar, and appeared to have a mortared core; it was more than 0.36m wide. The west end of the choir was marked externally by a buttress, which belonged to the original period of construction. At a later date, the east wall of the south aisle had been butted against this. It is not known whether the internal wall to the west end of the choir (C30) was a primary or secondary element of its construction, though a buttress which was set externally against that wall would clearly have fulfilled a structural function had wall C30 been early work. The presence, position, or nature of any 'walking space' to the west of the choir has not been determined by excavation. The evidence for this lies sealed beneath the Hull — Scarborough railway line. From the indications of footings glimpsed in the west face of a sewer trench in 1980 (Sanders and Armstrong 1983, 57), it would appear that the overall internal length of the choir was *c.*21.00m, and its width *c.*7.00m.

Features were identified within the choir, though the non-destructive method of investigation has prevented their being assigned a place within the sequence of development of the church (Figure 20).

Along the south side of the choir, 0.84m from the wall, ran a narrow internal wall of faced chalk ashlar C5. Only 0.20m thick, this is unlikely to have fulfilled a major structural role, and hence is interpreted as the foundation for a choir stall, 9.40m long. A small brick buttress or pillar (C7) was set against the main wall (C1) near the south-west corner of the choir. The east end of the stall was marked by another brick pillar (C8) and a block of chalk ashlar (C6). The space between this internal wall (C5/C6) and the south wall of the choir was covered with a mortary surface. The evidence for a corresponding stall set against the north wall is less convincing, consisting only of a mortary deposit (C9) and a small extent of chalk rubble footings which were glimpsed beneath it. Whatever had been set over C9 had limited the spread of an adjacent clay floor. The discovery of a slab of chalk

(C10) bearing two pivot-holes (one of which was stained with rust), at the east end of the southern stall, suggests an entrance to the stalls at this point. A small amount of reused tile and brick here may also have related to a step or entrance.

Flooring materials were not identified *in situ*, though several plain glazed floor tiles, which were coloured yellow or green, were found in the choir in demolition deposits (see below, section 3.6).

The sacristy (Figure 21)

On the north side of the choir a disturbed, and possibly robbed, footing alignment (C18) ran approximately parallel to the north wall (Figure 21). It was composed of small chalk gravel which was set over larger, rammed, elements of chalk rubble at a level of 6.71m OD. It lay *c*.2.00m north of the choir wall footing (C3/C4), and would thus have defined only a narrow chamber. The full extent of the latter is unknown, but it was probably between 1.44 and 2.00m wide. The floor surface within this chamber consisted of a clay pad which sealed a construction deposit of chalk. It is unknown whether this feature was a primary or secondary element of the complex.

To the east, the alignment of C18 was picked up by a wall or footing which was faced on its outer, or northern, side with brick (C19). From their recorded dimensions, these bricks are likely to have been of Type 1, which were in use at the Priory from the early 14th century (see below, section 3.3). The core and south face of the wall were built of chalk rubble. The room which was defined by footing C19 and the choir wall (C4) was floored with a mortar surface on which were laid flat fragments of roof tile — perhaps forming a light footing for an internal feature. External spreads of mortar and tile rubble (C21, C27), to the north of this building, may relate to an earlier structure in this area, which has yet to be located. (An interpretation as a robbed wall trench was considered for C21 at the time of its excavation.) The further alignment of these features is unknown.

Structures attached to the cloister side of the choir are frequently identified as the sacristy or vestry. It is uncertain whether the evidence from Beverley should be taken as representing the variable survival of a single structure, its extension, or a total rebuilding.

The south aisle (Figure 22)

The clearance of an area south of the choir in early 1989 revealed part of the south wall and east end of the south aisle (Figure 22). This had been previously confirmed as an addition to the preaching nave of the church (Armstrong and Tomlinson 1987, 8–9 and 53).

The footing of the south wall of the aisle (C31) consisted of coursed slabs of chalk, with an external offset capped with limestone slabs. The presence of an inner offset was not determined. The measured thickness of the footing was *c*.1.40m, 0.30m of which was the external offset. The internal face of the wall survived as an alignment of faced chalk ashlar blocks, which were finely tooled. This face retained a mortared rubble core *c*.0.50m thick; the outer cladding of limestone had been removed, though the irregular hollows left by this operation were clearly visible. The original width of the main wall above these footings was estimated to have been *c*.0.85–0.90m.

An external buttress was located at the west end of the excavated portion of footing C31. Here, the width of the surviving wall core increased to 0.90m, whilst a fragment of roof tile mortared into the top of the wider footing suggested that the ashlar superstructure at this point extended to an overall width of *c*.1.10m.

The footings for the east end of the aisle (C32) were of similar build to those of C31, to which they were butt-jointed. The east face of the footing had been robbed; this disturbance extended along the original choir wall east of the junction of the aisle and choir. The overall width of footing C32 was estimated to be *c*.1.26m; no evidence was found for offset footings. In the south-east corner of the aisle, an external clasping buttress position was indicated by limestone and a slightly offset chalk plinth which projected to the south and east; the combined width of the buttress and the wall footings was 1.63m. At the north-east corner of the aisle, chalk footings which were integral to the choir wall (C1) and which lay beneath the junction of aisle wall C32 and the choir indicated that a pre-existing buttress on the latter was used to support the thrust of the aisle roof.

The character, dimensions and alignment of the south aisle structures confirmed their identification with the equivalent work at the west end of the church. The aisle was *c*.31.50m long and *c*.5.10m wide internally. The only remnant of an internal surface consisted of a spread of tiles on the south side of the aisle, at its west end.

The chantry chapel (Figure 22)

A brick wall or footing (C22) was joined to the south side of the choir (Figure 22). The brickwork was 0.64m wide, and was set on a light footing of chalk and tile. The fabric of the earlier choir footing (C2) was disrupted at this junction, where the new structure had been bonded into it. The discovery of this feature was made in 1988, but its full extent was not identified; however, more extensive clearance in 1989 revealed the presence of a return wall to the west, which would have formed the south side of a room or chapel. A short length of this wall survived in brick, two courses high and *c*.0.54m thick; this was butted to the east side of the south-east corner buttress of the aisle. The walls C22 and C33 defined a space *c*.8.20m long and *c*.6.40m wide. The discovery of a brick-lined tomb (C17) close to the east end of the chamber has prompted its interpretation as a chantry chapel, whose construction post-dated both the choir and the south aisle. This area was floored with clay, which was overlain by a mortary demolition layer. Within these demolition deposits a copper alloy bell (no. 900) was found, hinting at a liturgical usage for the area.

The burials (Figures 20 and 22)

A number of possible grave cuts were identified within the east end of the church, but were not investigated, as they lay at a level which was not threatened by the development: in keeping with the non-destructive intention of the excavation, no attempt was made to either expose or lift the skeletons.

Within the choir four unlined grave cuts were identified (C12, C13, C14, C15), grouped towards the west end (Figure 20). No such cuts were identified to the east. In addition a solitary brick-lined grave (C16) was exposed in the south-west part of the choir; its width suggests that it was intended for a single individual. A further tomb (C17) was partially exposed in the area considered as a probable chantry chapel (see above, and Figure 22). The greater width of this second tomb, in excess of 0.80m, suggested that it was intended either for a particularly rich individual, or for the interment of more than one member of a family group. The fills of both the brick-lined graves were loose, mortary soils. No burials were identified within structures to the north of the choir, or outside the buildings, though in the latter area the examination of non-structural material was perfunctory.

The great cloister, east range (Figure 21)

The limited excavation which was carried out in 1988 aimed to determine the level of archaeological survival in the eastern precinct, and to indicate an appropriate response to the development proposals. Using the information which had been obtained by excavation in 1986–7, and through comparison with other Dominican sites, estimates were made regarding the nature of the features which were likely to occur within these trenches. Previous work around the great cloister had failed to identify a chapter house which projected back from a claustral range, as was a feature of Dominican east ranges at Bangor, Canterbury, Cardiff, Gloucester, Ipswich, Norwich, Oxford and Rhuddlan; yet a similar regular layout should have existed at Beverley. Accordingly, trenches were opened with the hope of locating the south-east corner of such a chapter house.

The excavation succeeded in revealing the footings of the corner of a building (C24), flanked on either side by an external clasping buttress (Figure 21). The footings of this building were composed of chalk slabs. The top of this foundation lay at a level of *c.*6.80m OD. Clasping buttresses have been identified

as a common feature of stone buildings at the Priory (cf. on the church, refectory and west range of the great cloister, and the north range of the little cloister).

A later brick-faced wall with a rubble core (C25) ran across these footings: the wall was 0.82m wide, and had been built on a flat bed of roof tile which had been reused to level the top of the earlier footing. The alignment of this wall bore no other discernible relationship to any of the structures associated with the Priory, apart from the fact that it was supported by the pre-existing footing. No continuation of the wall was noted in a trench *c.*4.80m further to the east, nor was a return identified. A brick-faced construction was, however, a technique employed for the building of later medieval structures at the Priory, as well as for internal features within buildings. It is therefore possible that the brick feature may represent an angle-buttress attached at a late date to the earlier building; it is even possible that it represents a comprehensive rebuilding of this structure in brick.

Phase 4a. The great cloister, north and west ranges. ?13th century (Figures 23–4. Plates 1–2)

West range

The earliest structural evidence along the west side of the great cloister was provided by two chalk rubble footings which were recorded in elevation (1118 and 1117); they lay at the base of the west range walls (Figure 23). Footing 1118 was formed of rubble capped with slabs, which had been cut by a later setting of larger slabs in Phase 4B (see below). This footing ran at a slightly different alignment to that of the walling above it, suggesting that the extant walling may have been rebuilt over older foundations.

Footing 1118 was separated from a northward continuation of larger foundations (1117) by a gap of *c.*0.60m (Figure 24, S27 B), which was occupied by a band of clay which included smaller fragments of chalk. Over this was set the finely worked limestone plinth-course of the east side of a buttress 1105 (*ibid.*). The west side of this buttress was incorporated into a later north–south wall (919) and butted by a later east–west wall (1103: Figure 24, S27 A–B). The south face of buttress 1105 bore a V-shaped groove which may suggest that a sluice had been sited immediately to the south of this structure, serving to control the flow along a channel which ran westwards to join the Phase 2 pond or watercourse (see below). At the north end of wall 919 lay a further buttress (916) which consisted of three courses of limestone, the lowest of which comprised another chamfered basal plinth course (Figure 23). This buttress also projected westwards. The common features of finely

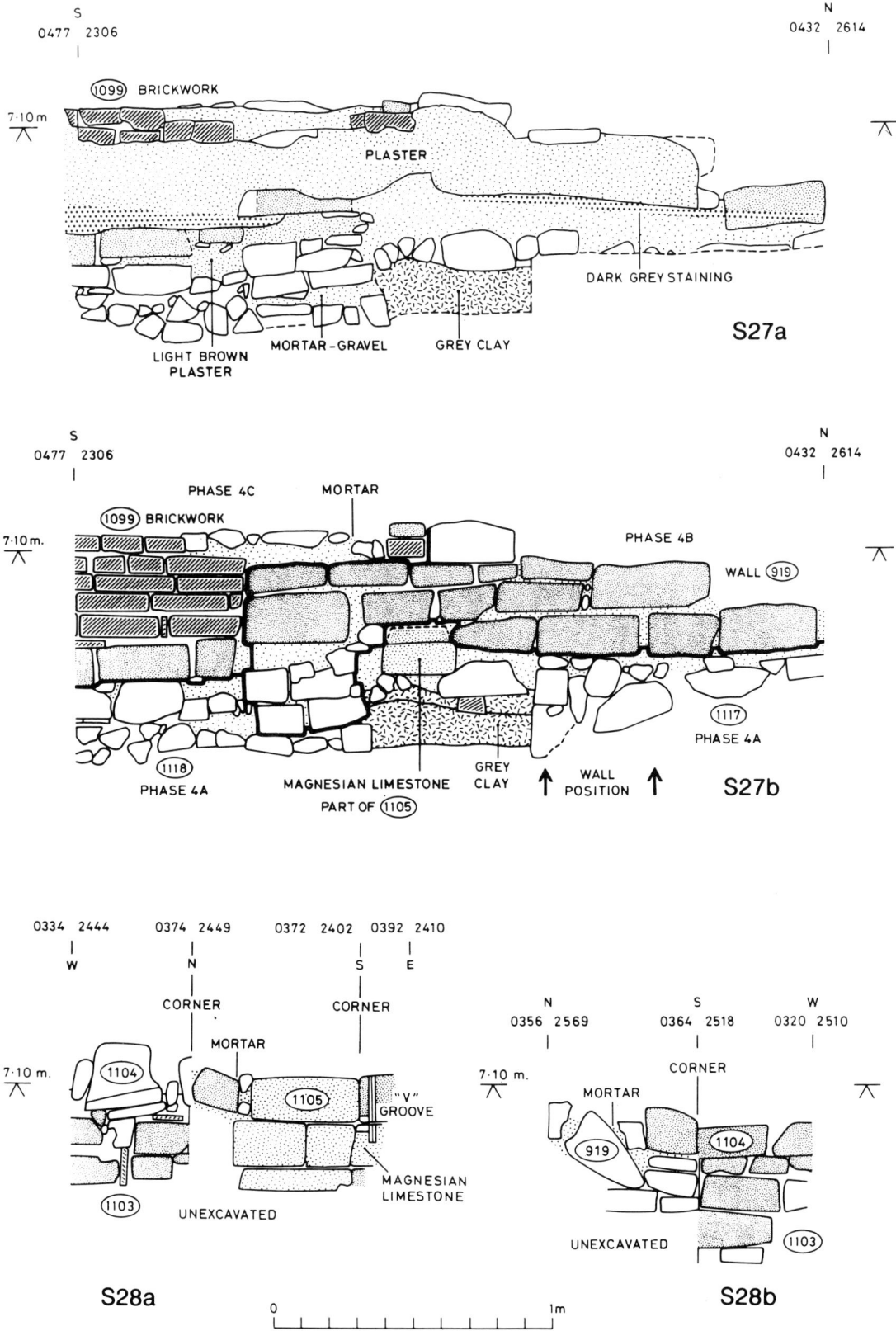

Figure 24 Phase 4A–C — west side of the great cloister. S27–8. S27b shows the same elevation as S27a, after the plaster had been removed.

worked limestone and chamfered plinths may suggest that these two elements belonged to the same campaign of building. The quality of their closely jointed ashlar masonry was in marked contrast to the later stonework of the building.

The northern part of the west range of the great cloister was represented by footing 1117; it was separated from footing 1118 to the south by an eastward return. The latter was partially exposed in the 1987 trench, but its full extent is shown on MacMahon's plans as a footing which was laid across the great cloister alley, and was wider at each end but narrowed in the middle (Armstrong and Tomlinson 1987, fig. 12). It has previously been considered as marking the position of responds flanking a step at a change in level in the alley (*ibid.*, 54); however, when considered together with the evidence for the setting of external buttresses along the west side of the walls of the range and the break in the foundation 1117/1118, this may indicate that the north-west corner of the great cloister was formerly defined by two free-standing buildings.

MacMahon recorded substantial footings which divided the great cloister alley from the cloister garth (*ibid.*, 54–5). The scale of these footings was illustrated by footing 1098, which was 1.00m wide with a further eastward projection of 0.63m. Such a foundation appeared rather massive to support a wall between the alley and the garth, but it would be eminently suited to a two-storied structure. However, as this alignment had been heavily robbed, the attribution of this foundation to any specific phase of construction was impossible. Its depth remains uncertain, as the full extent of its footings was never investigated.

The combined evidence of the footings and buttresses along the west range may suggest that the first phase of the north-west corner of the great cloister consisted of at least two separate ranges with an alley *c.*3.00m wide running through at ground floor level; there were presumably chambers or galleries at first floor level, No evidence for the early extent of the ranges west of the alley was recorded.

North range

A narrow trench was cut southwards from the main Trench 3 excavation (Figures 2–3); it was intended to locate evidence for any structures which accompanied the substantial Phase 6A chalk footing (24) which ran across the south side of that part of the site (see Figure 53). Stone-built structures were recorded in this trench, though as they lay outside the area threatened by development, they were not subjected to destructive investigation (Figure 23).

The earliest structure on the north side of the great cloister was a wall (566) which was aligned (compass) south-west – north-east: this alignment matched that of the Priory church. The north side of the wall was faced with a plinth-course of chamfered limestone ashlar; the south side was faced with chalk, and the wall-core composed of chalk rubble and a few tile fragments set in a pale buff mortar matrix. The total width of the wall was *c.*0.95m. Butted against its south face was a pair of chamfered limestone blocks with a core of mortared chalk rubble behind them (567); these formed a three-sided pier base or respond (Plate 1). The top of the chamfered plinth course lay at *c.*6.93m OD.

Possibly contemporary with wall 566 was a footing (727) on the south side of the later alley (Plate 2). It survived to a level of 6.45m O.D., and was in excess of 1m wide. It was sealed beneath footings which relate to the Phase 6 great cloister alley (649 and 716), but its width seems disproportionately large to relate to these later footings.

The use of limestone ashlar on the north side of wall 566 and chalk on its south suggests that the north face was on the exterior of a building, while the south face was sheltered from the elements. By extension, the use of an internal respond set against the south face indicates that a stone vault or arch rose above the ground floor, presumably supporting an upper storey. Footing 727 to the south of wall 566 may represent a parallel wall. The use of a chamfered plinth-course in the building can be paralleled in the Phase 4A buttressed structure at the north-west corner of the cloister (see above, and also Chapter 6, where Phase 4A on the west side of the great cloister is considered together with the development of the early north range).

The later modification of the north side of the great cloister is considered to have been associated with the construction of a refectory in Phase 6A (see below).

Phase 4B. Great cloister, north range. 13th or 14th century (Figures 23–4: Plates 3–4)

The major recorded element of Phase 4B was wall 919 on the west side of the great cloister alley (Figure 23). It defined part of the east side of the chambers which were excavated by MacMahon (Armstrong and Tomlinson 1987, fig. 12), and provided evidence of the second structural phase at the north-west corner of the great cloister (Figure 23).

Wall 919 was faced on its east side by roughly tooled limestone blocks (Figure 24, S27 B; Plate 4), which were laid rather haphazardly over the Phase 4A footing (1117) and buttress (1105). The extension of wall 919 over the Phase 4A footing (1118) and buttress (1105) clearly showed that the earlier 4A wall had been demolished to make way for it. The elevation view shows that this walling extended beyond that buttress and terminated on a large ashlar block which was set over a footing of rectangular chalk slabs. The west face of this wall was made up of roughly faced chalk slabs, whilst its core of chalk rubble was set in an orange mortar matrix. The overall width of the wall was 0.88m. It appeared to be of a single build with the north wall of the north range (917: Figure 23). The latter wall had a width of 0.95m, and was faced on its north side with limestone, and on its south side with chalk.

The south terminal of the Phase 4B wall (919), resting on its chalk slab footing, apparently marked a simple corner without a projecting buttress. This end of wall 919 was butted on its west side by an east–west wall (1103), which was 0.67m wide. The north face of this wall was formed by limestone slabs, and the south face by chalk. Excavation at this junction showed that chalk slabs formed an offset footing three courses down from the top of both 919 and 1103: this appeared to be continuous at a level of *c.*6.68–71m OD, and suggested that both these footings may have been built in a single episode.

At the south end of wall 919 a block of limestone was recorded standing on end. It is possible that this had marked the north side of a doorway (1119) through wall 919: if so, the doorway would have been *c.*0.80m wide. No other evidence was recorded for a doorway in this position, so the position of an entrance into the Phase 4B range remains uncertain.

Phase 4C. Great cloister, west range. ?14th century (Figures 23–4: Plates 3–4)

The onset of this phase was marked by a fresh campaign of building in the west range. The Phase 4B wall (919) was continued southwards by wall 1100 beyond the pre-existing buttress (1105:Figures 23–4, S27 B). The alignment of the new wall (1100) ran a little to the east of that of 919. The lowest course on its eastern side was built of rectangular limestone ashlar. This regular masonry permitted the coursing of stretcher-laid brickwork (1099) above it. The brick, which included examples of Type 4 size, was set in a pale buff chalk-flecked mortar. This brickwork was carried over the south end of the Phase 4B wall (919).

The west face of wall 1100 was made up of slabs of oolitic limestone at its junction with buttress 1105; further south it was faced with chalk. The wall-core consisted of rubble set in a buff mortar matrix. The overall width of the wall was *c.*0.60m. An east–west wall (1104) abutted its west face, and perhaps represents the reconstruction, repair, or completion of the Phase 4B wall in this position (1103). It was 0.66m wide and bonded with pale chalk-flecked mortar; it was faced with oolitic limestone on its

northern side, and chalk on the south (Figure 24, S27 B). A later tiled floor (1120) was recorded in the corner defined by these walls, at a level of *c.*6.72m OD.

The east faces of walls 1099/1100 and 919 had been heavily rendered with plaster above *c.*6.65m OD, thereby concealing the distinction between the brickwork of the Phase 4C wall and the stone slabs of its Phase 4B predecessor (Plates 3–4; Figure 24, S27 A–B). Fragments of roof tile were laid flush with the wall under the plaster, in an attempt to smooth the finished surface. Staining on the lower part of this plaster had been caused by the accumulation of silts in the alley between *c.*6.70 and 6.83m OD.

The MacMahon plan (Armstrong and Tomlinson 1987, fig. 12) shows walls forming the western limit of the range constructed in Phases 4B and 4C. Their alignment produced markedly asymmetrical rooms within this building. Neither MacMahon's excavations nor the more recent works have succeeded in locating a northern limit for a putative northern chamber.

A brick-built conduit (1082) was recorded in the south side of the trench cut across the west alley (Figure 27, S33). This feature was not recorded in plan by the recent excavations; however, its position suggests that it should be identified with a conduit on a north–south alignment which was excavated by MacMahon; this has been transposed onto Figure 23. The top of the conduit lay at a level of *c.*6.57m OD. It cannot be correlated with any particular phase of activity. Similarly, it was not possible to firmly establish the stratigraphic position of a burial, which would appear to have cut the line of this conduit (Figure 23).

The finds — Phase 4 overall

Masonry: ashlar (no. B78).
Roof Tile: Type 1A (4 fragments); Type 2B (1); Type 15A (?1).
Iron: knife (no. 780); strap (no. 791); 5 nails and 2 nail fragments.
Pottery: 13 vessels ranging in date possibly from the late 13th to the early 16th centuries.

The latrine block. 13th to 14th century (Figures 25–7: Plates 5–6)

The chutes and channel of a communal latrine or *reredorter* were identified by trenches cut to the south-west of the main 1986–7 excavation area (Figure 25). This investigation did not establish a structural history of the building; it did, however, enable the correlation of the findings with features identified by previous archaeological work in the 1960s, the 1970s, and in 1983 (Armstrong and Tomlinson 1987, 19, 54–5, and fig. 12).

The latrine block was built beside a ditch or culvert which ran north–south across the site, leading away

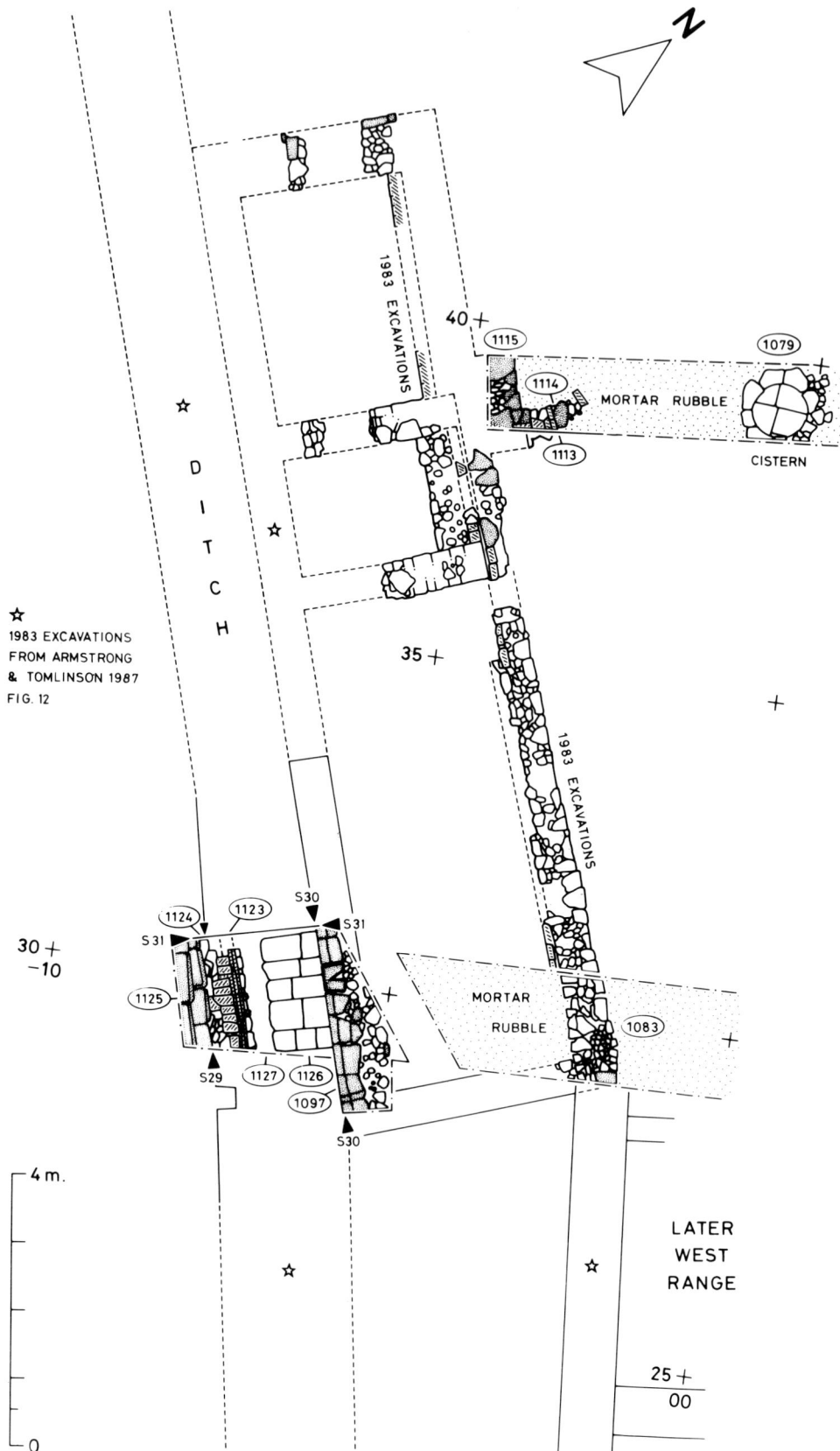

Figure 25 Phase 4 — latrine block and cistern.

under the standing 'Old Friary' building (Figure 2). The base of this culvert was formed by finely finished claw-tooled chalk slabs (1126) which rested on a base of close-set chalk rubble. A central channel (1127) which was 0.26m wide was faced on its east side by this slab floor; it was filled with a dark malodorous silt (1095*). The slabs ran under the structural elements which defined the east and west sides of the culvert, which was 1.06m wide at its base.

The west side of the culvert was faced with stepped brickwork (1123) which survived to a height of six courses: further brickwork had been removed by the insertion of a modern drainpipe (Figure 26, S29;Plate 5). Behind the brick, and originally revetted by it, lay a bank of small chalk rubble (1124). This appears to have served as the footing for a course of chalk slabs. These in their turn supported two courses of massive rectangular limestone blocks (1125). These latter do not appear to have formed part of the original structure: they bore no tool marks, and they were much larger (up to 0.80m by 0.25m scantling) than the medieval ashlar which was used elsewhere on the site. Both the brickwork and the limestone blocks were set in staggered courses which widened the culvert as the structure rose.

The east side of the culvert was formed by two bays of a *reredorter* (1097: Figure 26, S30;Plate 6). This was built of pale limestone ashlar, which rose from a chamfered plinth-course to a pair of angled chutes feeding into the culvert. Each chute was *c.*0.90m wide. The lower part of the structure was in an excellent state of preservation, the ashlar being finely finished and laid. The chutes, however, had been heavily pitted and weathered; both the chutes and the wall elevation below them were stained a dark grey-brown.

A chalk rubble footing immediately to the east of the chutes shows that they formed the lower part of the west wall of the latrine block (Figure 25). The east wall of the building (1083) lay *c.*2.60m distant, and was *c.*0.59m wide. The *reredorter* therefore appears to have been a narrow, possibly single-storied, building set parallel to the culvert. Previous excavations have shown that it extended northwards as a long two-chambered structure (Armstrong and Tomlinson 1987, fig. 12).

Further walling was identified *c.*8.00m to the north, and to the east of the northern chamber. This had been partially obscured by modern concrete footings. A north–south wall (1115) was formed by two courses of limestone rubble, which retained a core of chalk rubble set in an orange mortar matrix. An east–west footing of chalk and limestone (1114) abutted this wall, and supported a brick superstructure (1113); the last appears to have been a footing or an extended buttress, as it terminated *c.*0.72m east of 1115. The latter is assumed to have formed a northern

continuation of the east wall of the *reredorter*. The materials used in its construction (limestone slabs and brick), differ from those of the southern chambers (the ashlar of 1097 and the chalk blocks of 1083) and its alignment lies further to the east than does wall 1083, closely matching the position of walls recorded in 1983 (Armstrong and Tomlinson 1987, fig. 12). It would appear to have formed part of a rebuilding or extension northwards of the *reredorter* block. The use of brick in its construction suggests a possible association with works carried out on the great cloister during Phases 4C and 6B.

The cistern. 13th or 14th century (Figures 25 and 27: Plate 7)

A circular feature which had an internal diameter of 0.80m, and was built of blocks of finely claw-tooled chalk ashlar (1079), was discovered *c.*1.60m west of the north-west corner of the Phase 6 north range (Figure 25). Six courses of closely jointed masonry survived — the uppermost in fragments, but the rest in excellent condition (Figure 27, S32, Plate 7). The masonry rested on a flat base of chalk slabs which, when discovered, ruled out the initial interpretation of the feature as a well.

The relatively small size of this feature, together with the lack of heavy abrasions which would be caused by regular emptying, and the proximity of a latrine block nearby, all argued against an interpretation of this feature as a cesspit. An alternative identification as a cistern was suggested by a small rounded hole, measuring 50mm by 45mm, in one of the blocks on its south side (visible on the uppermost courses of undamaged masonry in Plate 7). This is taken to represent the position of a pipe leading into the tank; it was probably integrated into the lead-piped water supply system which was recorded in the 1960s along the west side of the great cloister (Armstrong and Tomlinson 1987, 19, 40–1, 54–5 and figs. 12 and 21).

It is alternatively possible that the tank may have been designed to hold water which had run off the roof of the Phase 6A north range, thus functioning as a water-butt and settling tank. It was, however, built with a degree of care which was not apparent in later work, but was more akin to the fine jointing of the *reredorter* structure.

Cistern — dating evidence

The uppermost fill of the tank consisted of loose rubble (1080) 0.38m deep. A further two layers of organic silt (1106*, 1107*) formed the secondary fill of the tank, while the lowest silt (1109) which was 0.10m deep, coincided with marked staining of the ashlar of the structure. This primary fill contained pottery of later 13th or early 14th century type,

S
−0723 2900

N
−0761 3070

GROUND LEVEL JUNE 1986

BACK FILL RUBBLE

LOAM–MORTAR
SILTY SOIL

6·60 m.

1125

LOAM–
MORTAR

1124

MORTAR

1123

S29

1095

N
−0616 3087

S
−0548 2825

GROUND LEVEL JUNE 1986

CONCRETE

BACK FILL
–RUBBLE

6·60 m.

LOAM–MORTAR

CHAMFER

1097

MORTAR

S30

CHAMFER

1126

| 1097 | LIMESTONE |
| STAINED |
| EROSION |

0   1 m.

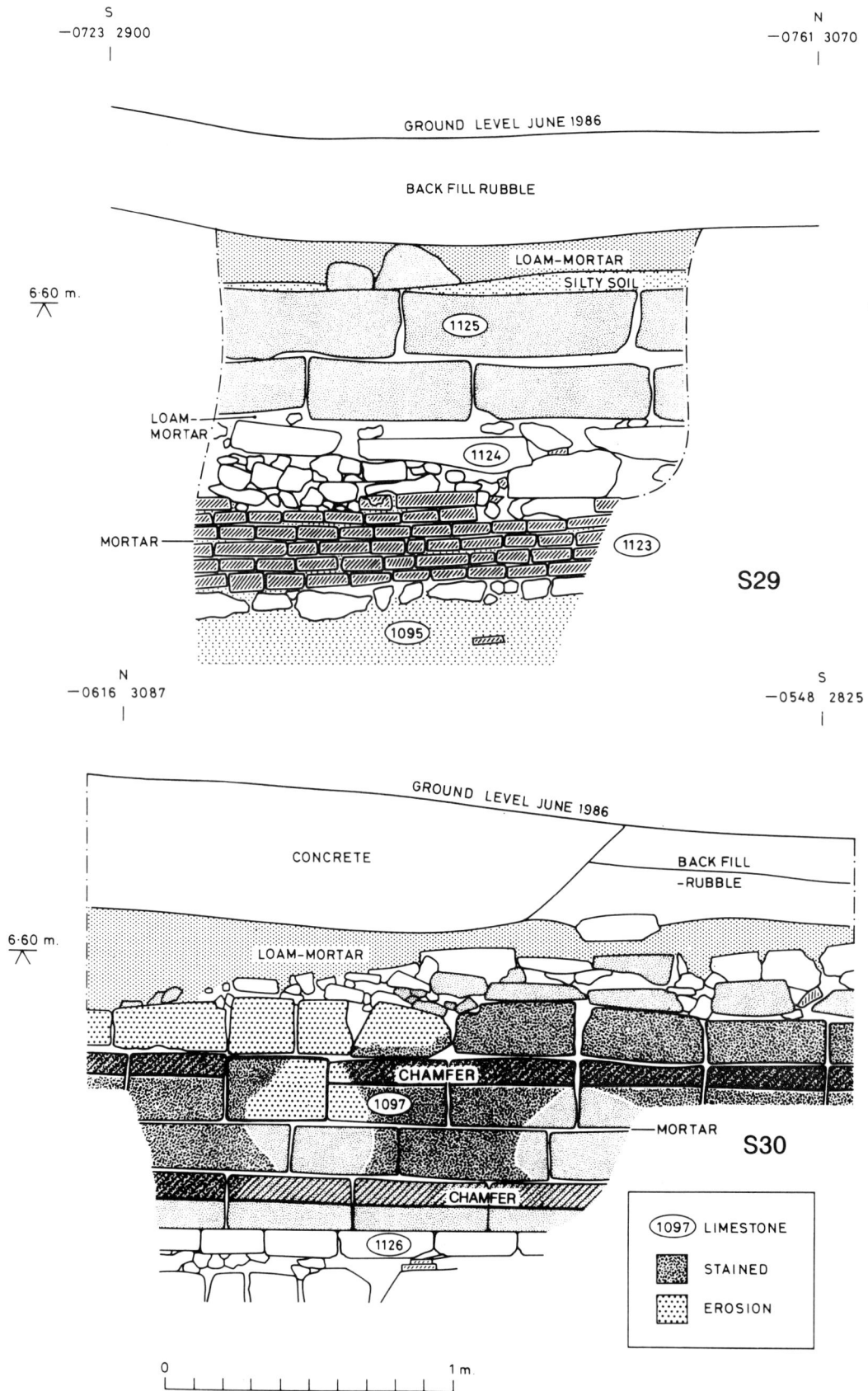

Figure 26 Phase 4 — latrine block. S29–30.

44

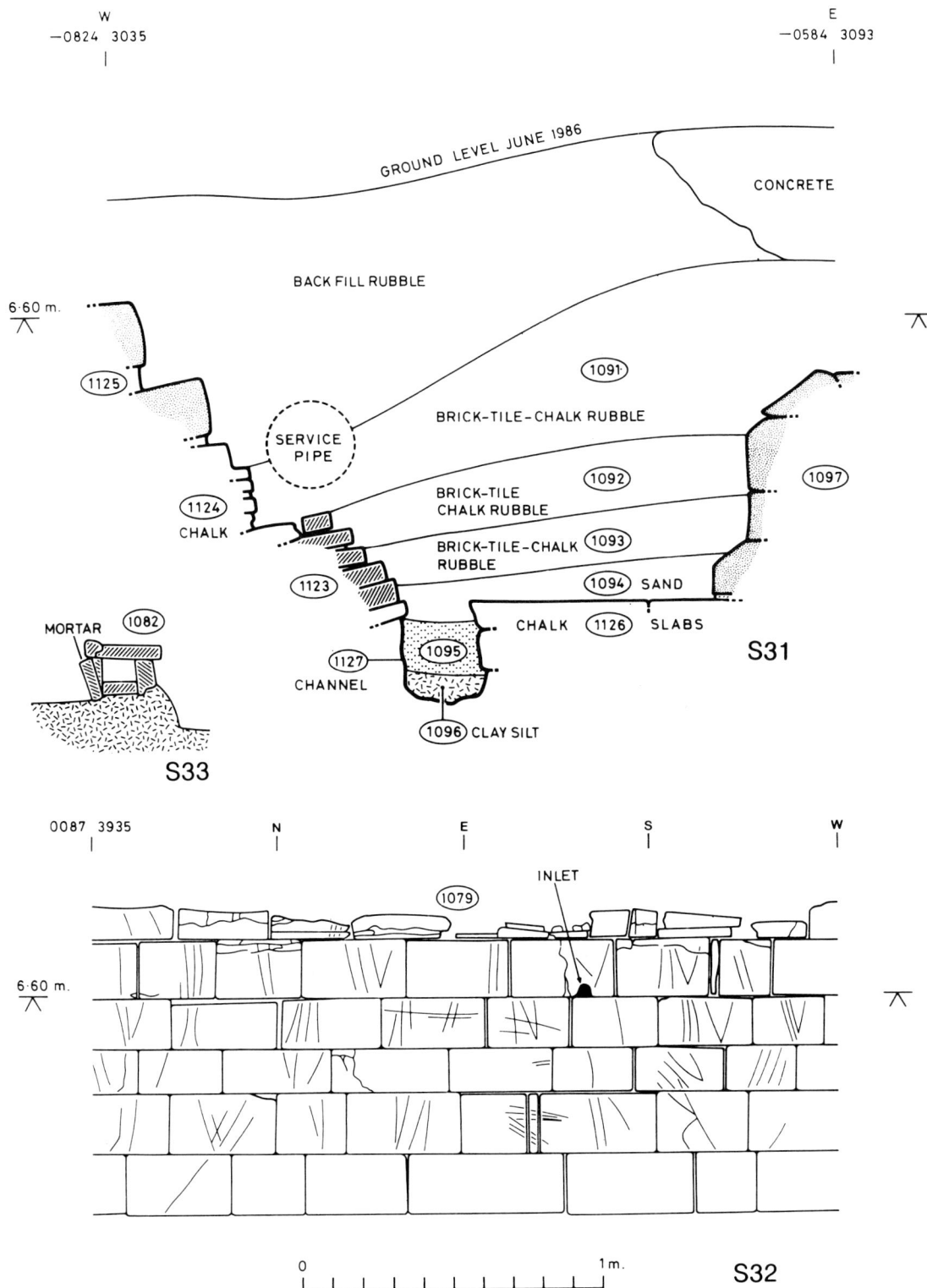

Figure 27 Phase 4 — latrine block and cistern. S31–3.

including a sherd of Saintonge polychrome, while the uppermost rubble included sherds of West Cowick Humberware. It is therefore likely that this feature was in use during the earlier part of the Priory occupation, and fell into disuse before its close. It may have originally served to supply water for use in the kitchen, or in a laver, and its proximity to the position chosen for the later Phase 6A refectory may be significant in this connection.

Phase 5. The little cloister. 14th — 16th centuries (Figures 28–52: Plates 8–11)

Phase 5 comprised the construction of the 'little cloister', its occupation, and its modification, up to the building of a refectory on the north side of the great cloister in Phase 6A. Phase 5C is considered as broadly contemporary with Phase 6A. The sequence of recorded events may be summarised as follows.

Footings for two ranges aligned on east–west and north–south axes were set into trenches. The upcast (possibly augmented with material derived from demolished structures) was used to raise the ground-level within and outside the new buildings. This raised ground formed an alley round the garth of the little cloister. The alley and garth were separated by a series of timber uprights which probably supported a pent-roof. It is likely that an eastern building was planned but not erected.

The cloister was conceived as a unitary whole from the beginning. The north range was the first to be constructed. It comprised two ground-floor chambers of approximately equal size, with the suggestion of a third room at its western end: this last room is imperfectly understood as its full extent was not recovered by excavation. For these reasons, the descriptions of the north range during Phases 5A — 5C refer throughout to the east (or eastern) chamber and the west (or western) chamber: although it is acknowledged that some sort of structure existed at the west end of the range, its plan, extent and function all remain undetermined. The western range was butted onto the north range, and was therefore technically secondary in construction, but still can be assigned to the same building campaign.

Substantial modifications to both chambers of the north range took place in the course of its occupation. These involved the relocation of doorways and other features. Some changes took place during episodes of construction activity over the little cloister area as a whole; others were part of a process of piecemeal adaptation and development. Major works may also have been carried out on the west range, though less evidence for this building was recorded. Occupation in the little cloister closed with the stripping of the

buildings at the onset of Phase 7.

Phase 5A. Little cloister. First half of 14th century (Figures 28–40)

The deposits laid down during the construction and occupation of the little cloister alley in this phase are shown schematically on Figure 30, whilst those for the north range are depicted on Figure 37.

The west alley (Figures 28–32)

The first operation to be carried out in the programme of works along the west side of the little cloister may have been the construction of a chalk structure, around which dumps of materials were laid down to raise the local ground level. Almost all of it was removed by robbing during Phase 5C, which was to leave a shallow trench on a north–south alignment (539: Figures 28 and 48). This possibly represents the remains of a robbed conduit — possibly a drain, or part of the piped water supply identified by previous excavations to the south (Armstrong and Tomlinson 1987, 19, 40–1, 54–5, and figs. 12 and 21).

Various features at the south end of this robber trench (539) may have been related to it (Figure 29, S34A). A clay-filled depression 770 (Figure 30A) was sealed by clay 757, which formed part of the construction horizon for the west range of the little cloister (see below). A second gully (745/746), joined trench 539 at right-angles, before exiting westwards over the top of depression 770; any pipe which had been set within this gully had been removed by later robbing, probably in the course of Phase 5B. A further linear feature (3012/3016/3027/3028) may also have been related to this water or drainage system, although it lay some distance away to the north and west of trench 539 (Figure 46). It led from the north to run alongside the Phase 5C alignment of the west wall of the west range; its southern extent is unknown. As it was infilled during Phase 5C, its construction can probably be assigned to either Phase 5A or 5B.

The west side of trench 539 was faced with chalk ashlar (554) which was aligned north–south and laid directly over the latest Phase 3 occupation. This lay at a level of *c.*6.45m OD. To the west deposits of mixed clay and gravel (769), chalk (909), tile (864) and clay (825) were laid down (Figure 30A). To the east the deposit of an extensive spread of soil (65) was to raise the level of the central garth of the new cloister (Figure 28; Figure 5, S1), though it is uncertain when this material was laid down.

The compacted soils may have been intended to seal structure 554. Over them was laid a soft greasy clay (938, 819) to a maximum recorded depth of 0.28m. The effect was to raise the ground-level to *c.*6.60m OD. This preparation pre-dated the construction of the

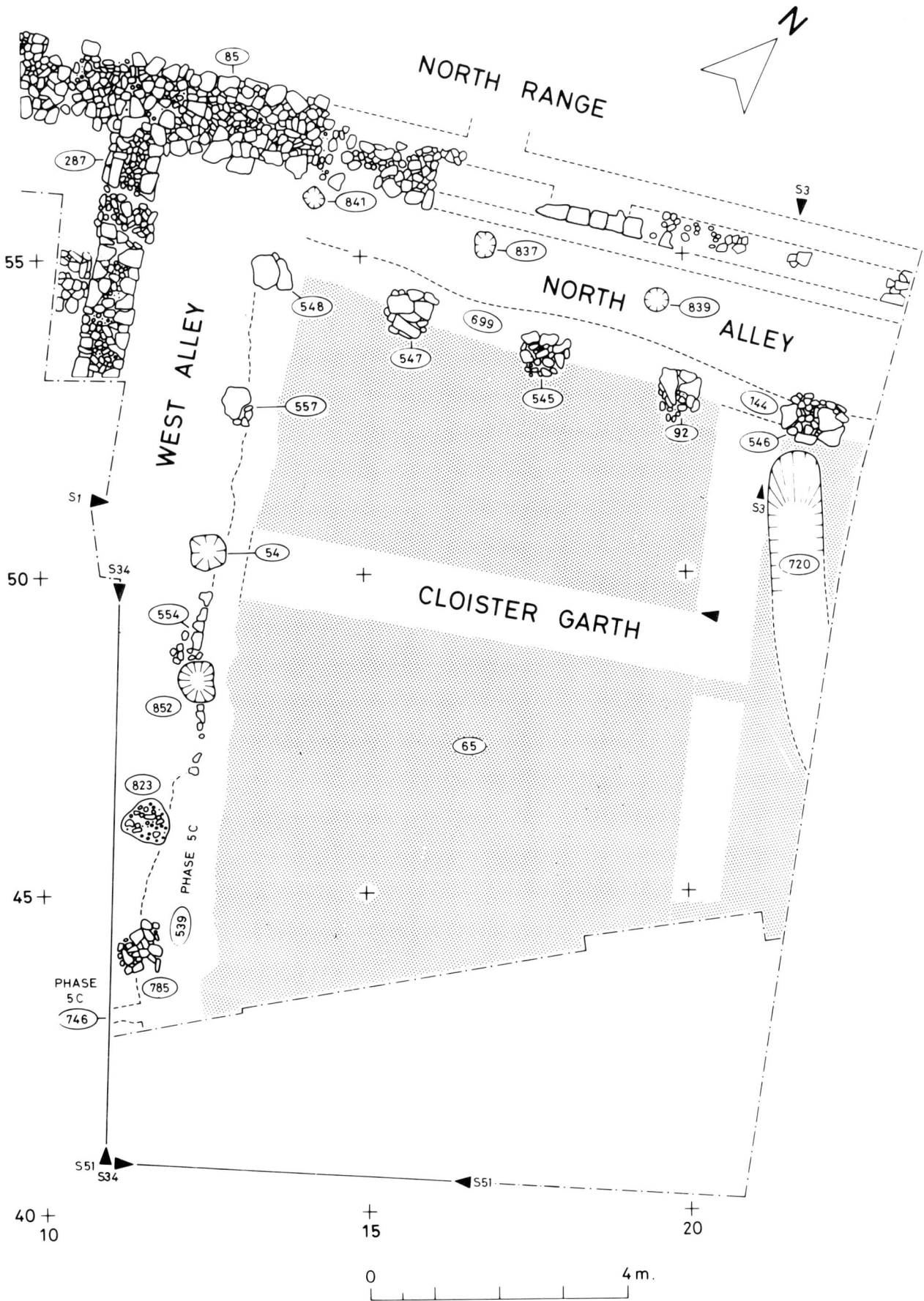

Figure 28 Phase 5A — little cloister alley and garth.

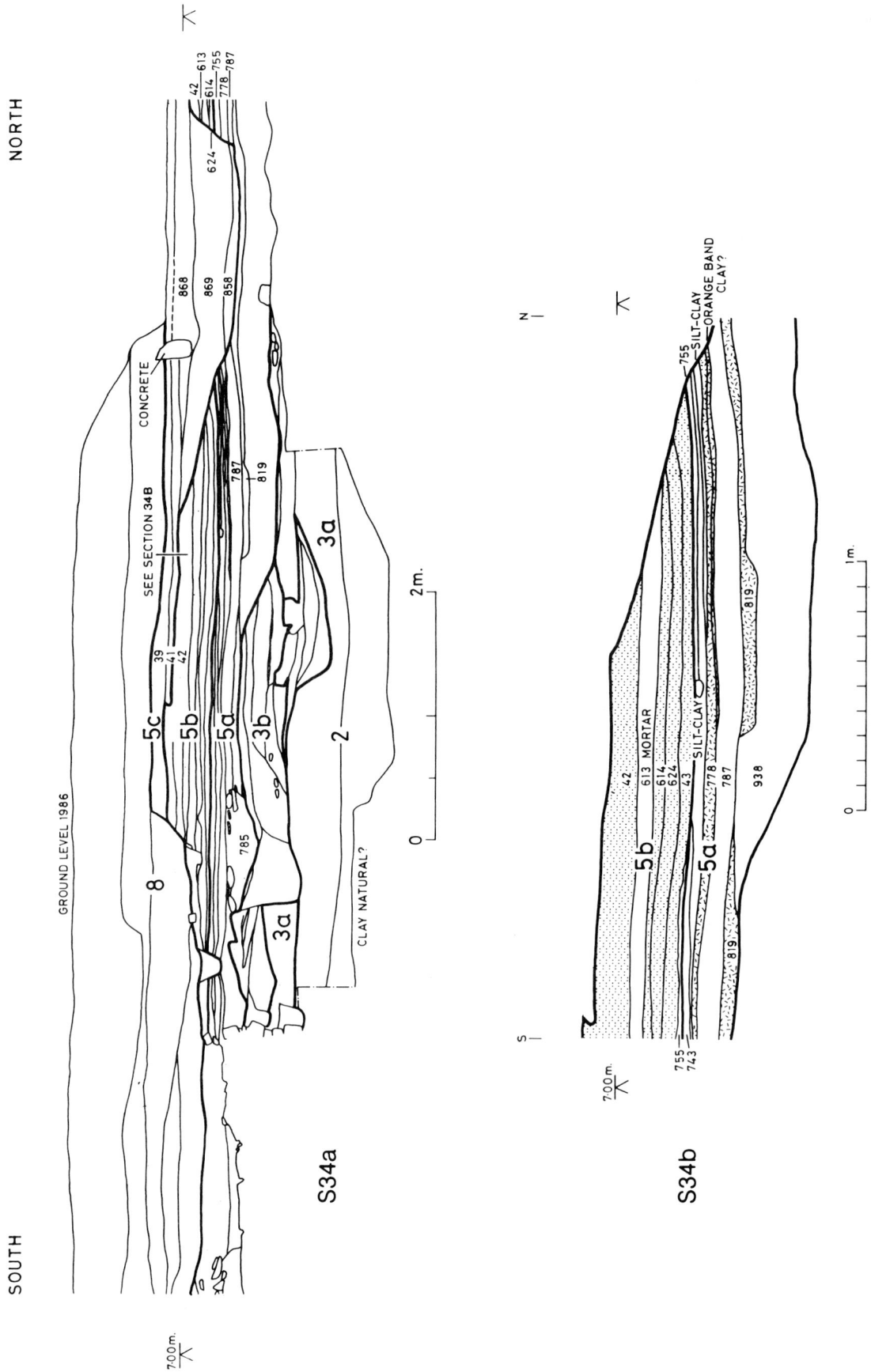

Figure 29 Phase 5A–C — little cloister alley. S34.

west range. The wall at the west end of the Phase 3B timber hall may have contributed material for this levelling; deposits here included more building debris than those laid down to the north.

The little cloister garth (Figure 28)

A fairly homogeneous layer (65) sealed the earlier buildings and was to form the surface of the garth of the little cloister (Figure 28). It lay up to 0.24m deep, as a gritty grey clay-silt which incorporated fragments of charcoal, roof tile (including a few glazed fragments), ironwork, and other finds. Patches of clay and ash also occurred in this thick layer, though only two lenses, of ash (35) and mortar (550), were individually recorded. Further north, a less gritty soil (120) was identified at this horizon during trial work. Pottery joins were noted between layer 65 and the occupation surfaces of Phases 5A, 5B and 5C. As layer 65 may have accumulated over a considerable period of time, it has been attributed simply to Phase 5. A section which was cut during trial work (Figure 54, S68) suggests that it may even have post-dated the construction of the Phase 6A structure, though this relationship was not confirmed by area excavation. (Evidence for phasing of this context is discussed below, with particular reference to the analysis of pottery; section 3.16).

A steep-sided U-shaped cut (720), on a north–south alignment, was revealed by the removal of layer 65; this gully was 0.80m wide and 0.45m deep (Figure 28; Figure 31, S35 A–B). Its north end sloped gently, but it continued as a deeper trench into the eastern excavation edge; hence its full extent was not determined. It had been capped with a layer of plastic clay *c.*0.12m deep, which overlay a gritty mixture of soil, chalk, tile, brick and mortar (719). This could represent demolition rubble deposited into a robbed wall-trench. The feature was cut through a thin layer (726) which was very similar to 65, and is thus considered to have been cut and filled during Phase 5.

The arcade footings (Figure 28)

Following the construction of footings for the north range and the raising of the ground level along the position to be occupied by the alley there (see below), the foundations for upright members were sunk in an alignment which divided the alley from the garth (Figure 28). These would carry the uprights which supported an arcade or pentice roof over the alley.

The footings of the north alley consisted of sub-rectangular pits which were filled with substantial chalk rubble blocks and packed with smaller chalk and gravel (92, 545, 546, 547, 548: Figure 35, S41 A–E). Three of these footings (92, 546, 548) were packed with coursed blocks; the others appear to have been more haphazardly filled. Their planned dimensions varied from 0.80m by 0.55m (no. 545,) to 0.92m by 0.75m (no. 547), and their depths from *c.*0.80m (nos. 546, 547, 548) to 0.94m (no. 92.) Two examples (nos. 92, 548) were capped with large flat slabs which could either have served as padstones, or as a levelling course. The upper surfaces of these slabs lay at 6.65m OD, at the east end of the alignment (92), and at 6.70m OD, at its west end (548). The footings lay *c.*2.20m apart, centre to centre, along the north alley.

The arcade footings along the edge of the west alley (Figure 28) were not as uniform as those of the north alley (Figure 35, S42 A–D), but both their common survival to a level of *c.*6.65m OD and their stratigraphic position demonstrated that they belonged to the same campaign of construction. At the north end of this alley, footing 557 had much in common with the northern group. It lay *c.*2.20m south of the latter's westernmost base (548), and consisted of coursed chalk blocks which supported a flat chalk slab. The dimensions of 557 distinguished it from the north alley footings: it was smaller, measuring 0.65m by 0.52m with a depth of 0.67m.

Approximately 2.50m to the south of 557 lay the gravel-filled base (53) of a circular feature (54) which was recorded in the base of the machine-cut east–west trial trench. Chalk rubble was glimpsed during the removal of this feature; however, the circumstances of its discovery were such as to preclude any further discussion. About 2.00m to the south of 54, however, lay a further pit (852) which was also filled with a buff gravel (851); its diameter was *c.*0.61m, but its depth no more than 0.30m.

Approximately 2.20m to the south of 851/852 lay a further circular pit (823), which was filled with gravel, chalk rubble and tile, (822). This feature lay a little to the west of the alignment of the other pits, and its stratigraphic position was later. It is not, therefore, considered to be a primary member of the group; however, the possibility exists that 823 was a replacement for an earlier post which lay further to the east, and which had later been removed by the Phase 5C robbing trench, 539.

The southernmost pit on the edge of the west alley (785) was of oval form, and filled with chalk rubble set in a matrix of crushed chalk and clay Its surface dimensions (0.83m long and over 0.72m wide) are comparable with those of the north alley footings, and its depth (0.65m), is similar to that of footing 557. These pits post-dated the alley make-up deposits. As with the north alley footings, they may have been intended to support timber uprights, though their smaller size indicates that they would have carried less weight. Their more erratic spacing would also render them less suitable to perform a major structural role. Footing 557 is closely comparable to those along the north alley, but the others appear to represent a distinct and less thorough episode of construction.

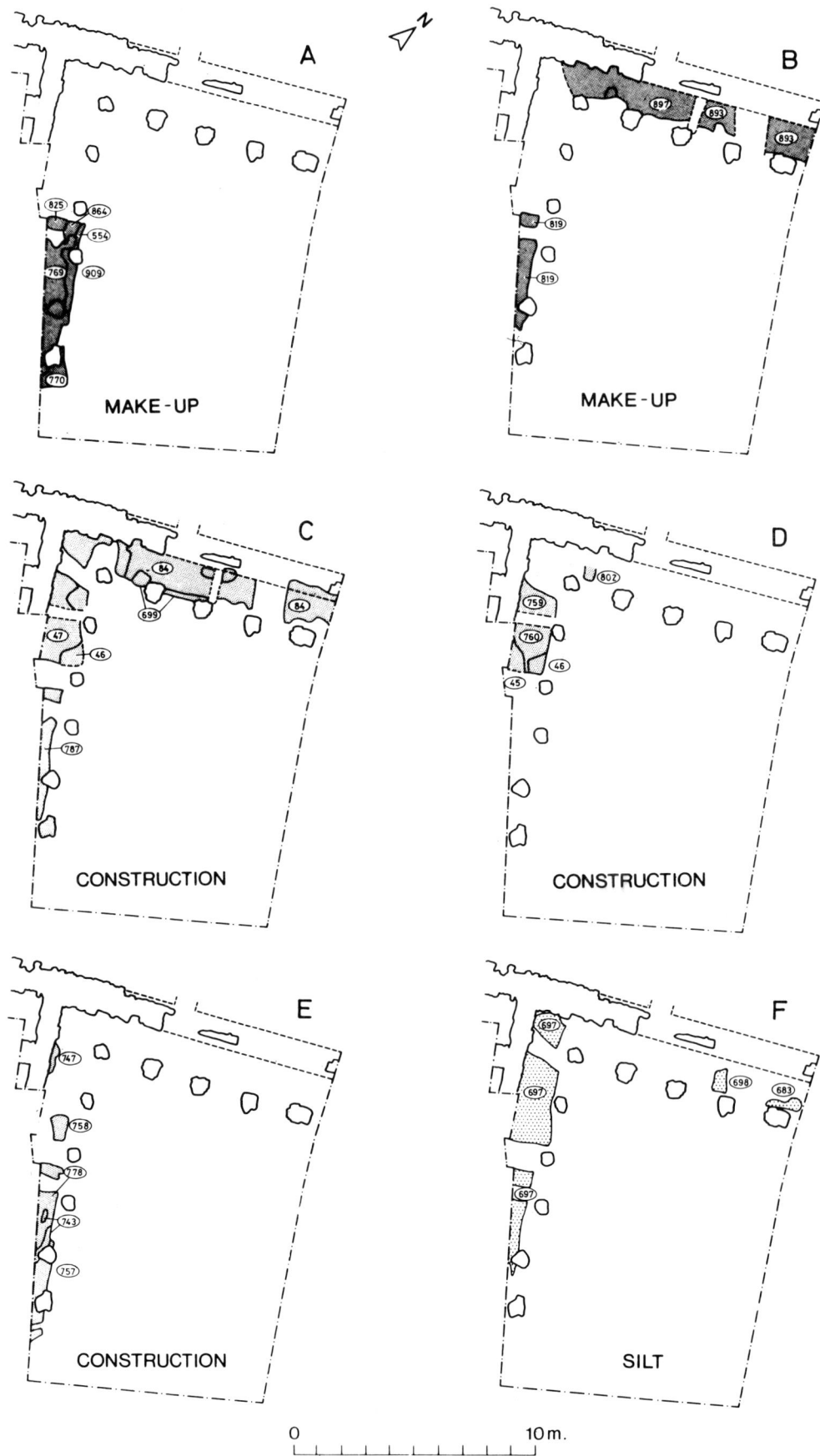

Figure 30 Phase 5A — little cloister alley - construction and occupation.

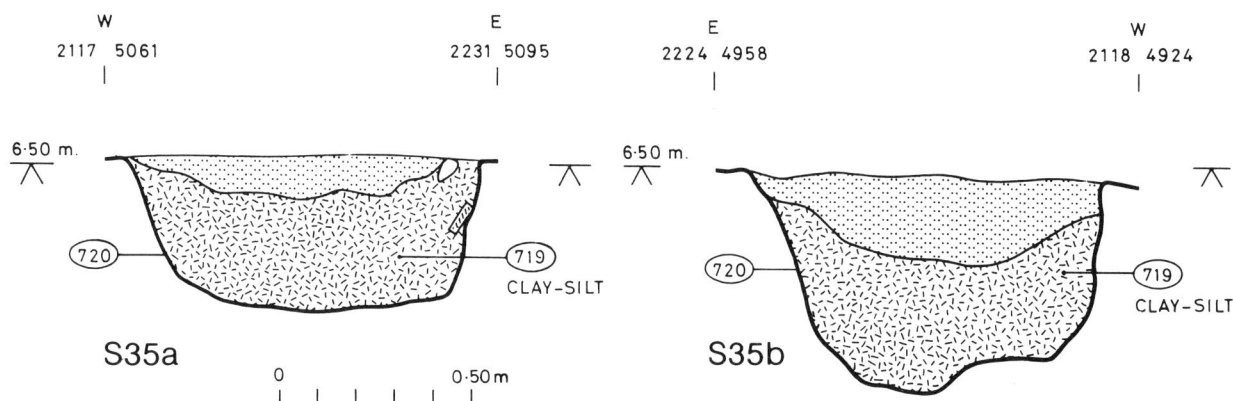

Figure 31 Phase 5A — little cloister garth, foundation trench. S35.

The north range footings (Figure 32)

A steep-sided trench (894) was dug to accommodate the foundations (85) of the south wall of the north range of the little cloister (Figures 28 and 32). This, the footing plan suggests, was originally intended to comprise two ground floor chambers of equal size; each was c.9.80m (c.32ft) long and c.4.80m (c.16ft) wide internally (Figure 32). This design was never to be fully executed: the west wall was of light construction and was subsequently rebuilt, whilst provision for buttresses was made at the east end and centre, but not to the west.

The footing for the south wall (85/3079) consisted of massive chalk rubble pitched into a trench (894) which was c.1.40m deep where fully bottomed (Figure 33, S36). The examination of this footing in section was carried out where an underlying Phase 1 pit (1197) dictated the use of deep foundations. The upper part of this footing was made up of smaller chalk rubble. Its total width was c.1.20m at the east end and c.1.30m to the west, and it appears to have been built in a single operation.

Along the course of the cloister alley the footing stood proud from its trench by c.0.30m. Its southern face was packed with clay 844 (Figure 32); this was perhaps intended to limit the flow of groundwater from the cloister alley into this foundation, thereby counteracting the tendency of such a structure to act as a land drain. The alley was then raised to the level of the top of the footing with the deposition of a series of dark loams (893*, 897 and 90, 91, 93, 104, 105, 133: Figure 30 B); the upper part of dump 893/133

included burnt clay and charcoal. These dark loams were noted in the fill of the Phase 1 pit (1197) which was cut by the footing. It therefore appears that the upcast from the foundation trenches was used to raise the level of the alley. A southern limit to these levelling deposits may have been formed by a narrow slot (900/901); this feature is not shown on the published plans, but it was traced for a length of 1.55m, between arcade footings 545 and 547 (see Figure 28).

The north wall of the west chamber of the range (Figure 32) was built on less substantial foundations, chalk rubble (146/3115/3193) which was set into a trench c.0.70m deep and c.1.15m wide (Figure 33, S37). The lesser depth of these footings compared to those of the south wall could be explained by the higher level of the subsoil here; however, it is possible that this might also reflect the choice of a different material for the building of the superstructure.

In the centre of the north wall, a projecting footing (564), which was c.0.80m deep and c.1.45m wide (Figure 33, S38), represented the foundation for a buttress. It was placed to take the thrust of the roof at the position of the internal cross-wall.

At a later stage, this buttress was extended to form the west side of a porch or tower structure. The eastern side of this structure may be represented by footing 874, which was encountered where the north–south trial trench intersected the north wall Figure 32). Pitched chalk under a course of flat tooled slabs lay in a trench c.0.55m deep and c.1.10m wide (Figure 36, S43). This footing lay slightly to the north of the new alignment of the north wall.

The history of this putative porch or tower is problematical. Its original north wall footing (141) was identified only in section, as a trench containing loose soil and rubble fragments (Figure 36, S43). This trench was *c*.0.65m or more deep and *c*.1.05m wide; the character of its fill may have resulted from either of the two following processes. A substantial footing may have been planned, and its trench excavated, but subsequently abandoned and backfilled after a change in plan. Alternatively, a structure on a substantial footing may have been built, but at a later date both the wall and its footing had been robbed. The latter interpretation may be preferred, as the reinstatement of a structure at this point is indicated by the provision of light footings (702) and a doorstep (145), in Phase 5B (see below, and Figure 42). The east side of this structure was not provided with substantial footings. An original threshold may have been supported by blocks of chalk and limestone (126), which were set in place at the same time as the north wall of the range (Figure 36, S43).

The east wall of the range was examined only in plan view, from which there was no evidence for the depth or full extent of footings.

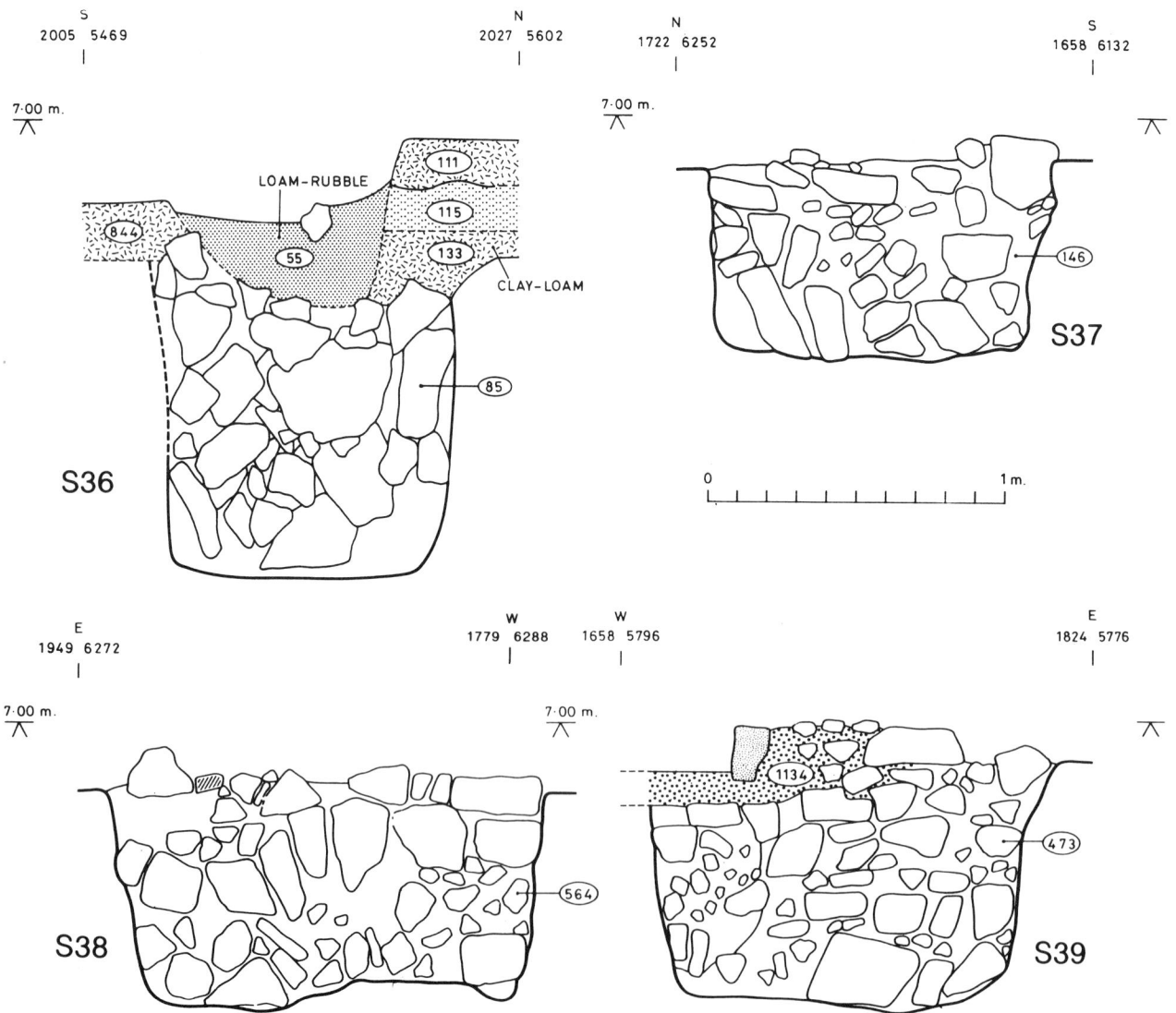

Figure 33 Phase 5A — little cloister, north range footings. S36-9.

The footing of the internal cross-wall (472, 473), which divided the range into two chambers, was formed of chalk rubble set in a trench *c.*0.85m deep and *c.*1.30m wide (Figure 33, S39). Set into the centre of this wall was a chimney above the fireplace in the western chamber; this functioned throughout the occupation of the north range.

The footing for the west wall of the range was of a lighter construction than had been used for the others (Figure 34, S40 A–B). Chalk rubble (3277) filled a trench (3278) which was *c.*0.50m deep and *c.*0.55m wide. The top of this footing lay at a depth of *c.*6.73m

OD. A construction horizon associated with this footing consisted of chalk and clay make-up (3160, 3159, 3163, 3158) and a layer of mortar (3156: Figure 34). The footings of the north (146/3115/3193) and south (85/3079) walls extended west of this light wall. The western limit of the west chamber was to be redefined in Phase 5B (see below).

At the extreme west end of the range the earliest features were the projecting footings of the north and south walls; no evidence survived for a superstructure (Figure 32). Midway between them, a rough limestone padstone (3279) was recorded at a level of *c.*7.01m

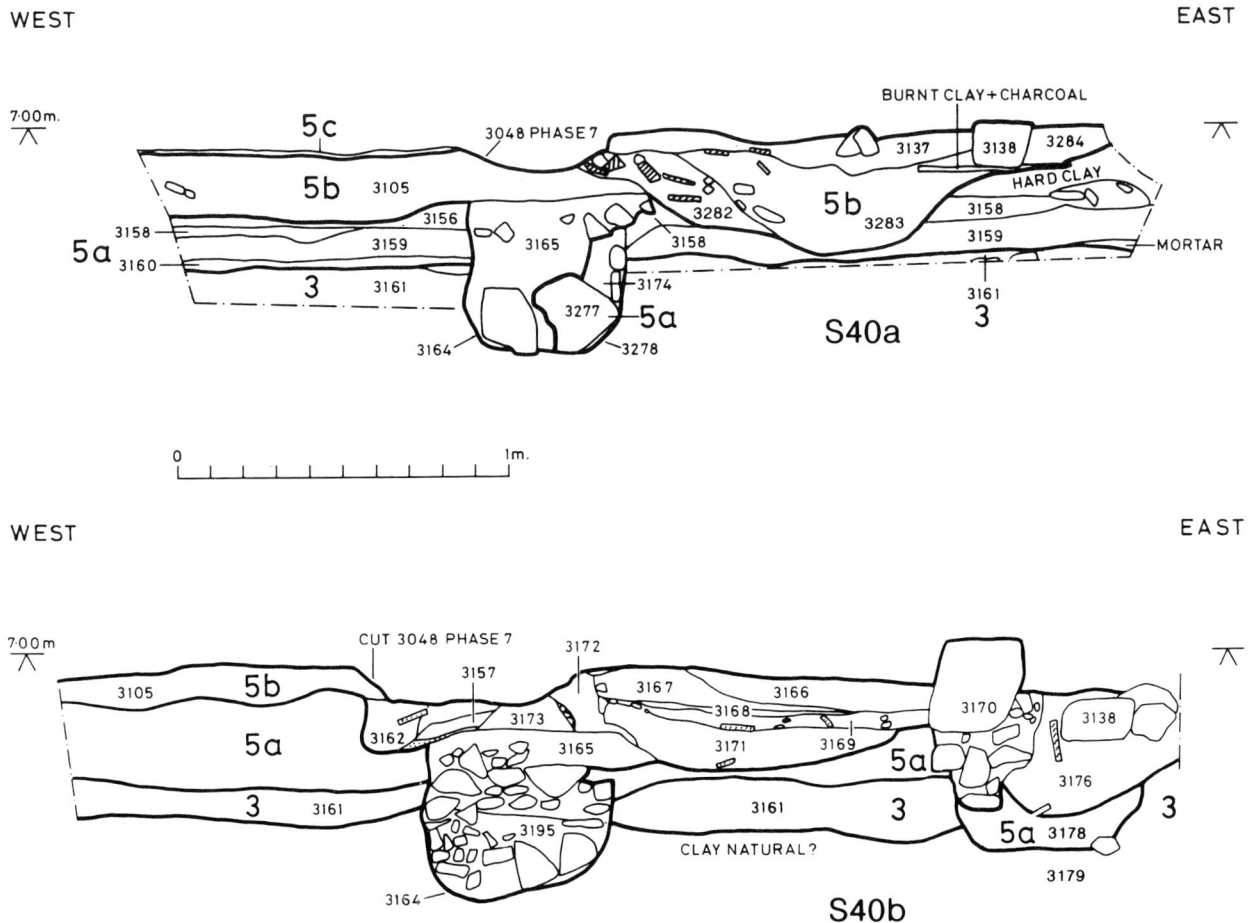

Figure 34 Phases 5A–B — north range footir ⁓est end S40.

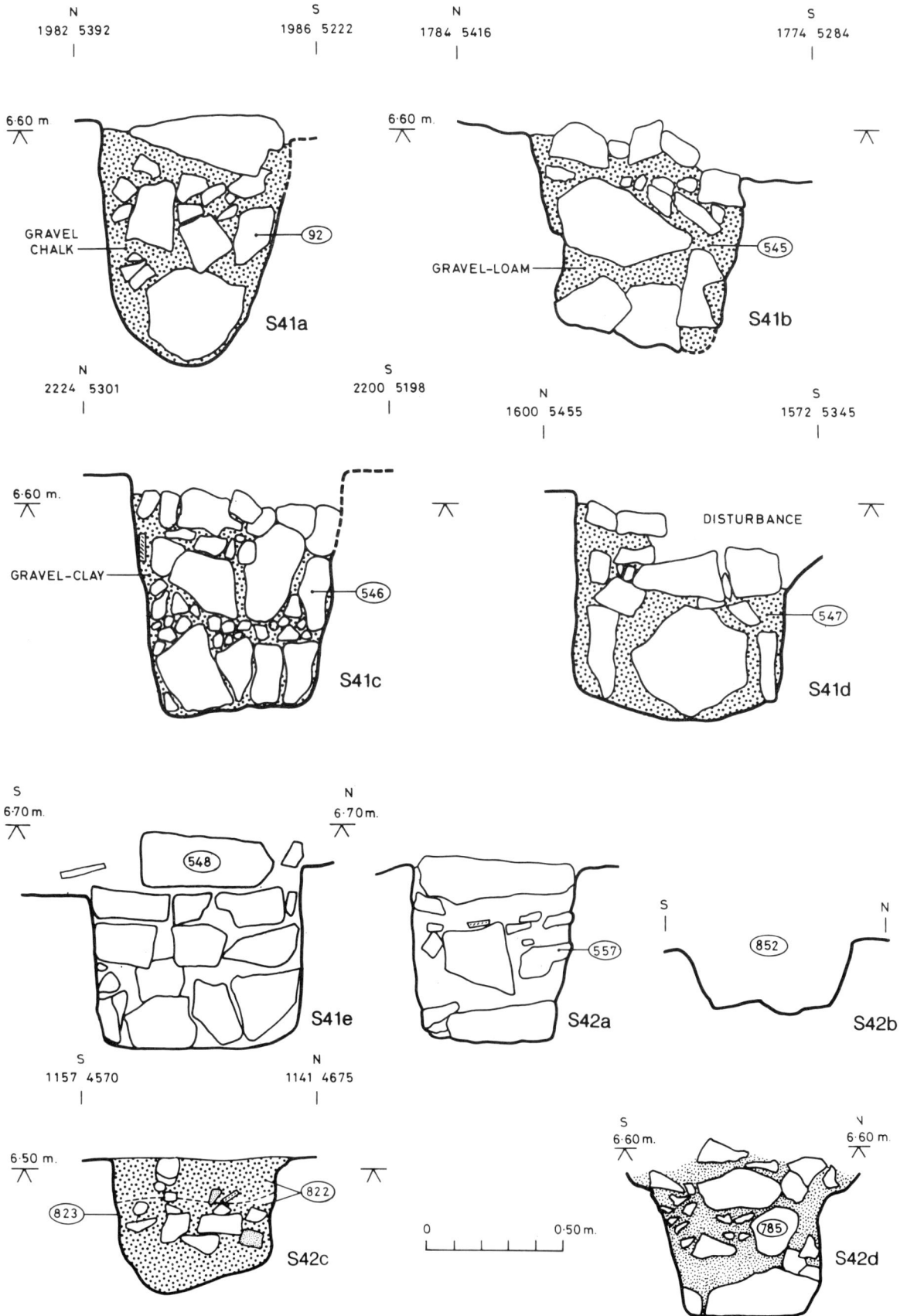

Figure 35 Phase 5A — little cloister, arcade footings. S41-2.

OD. This constituted the only structural evidence for a light building, presumably of timber, within which later occupation silts were to accumulate. The Phase 5A evidence for this end of the range is drawn from section views only; a full plan view of its early form was not achieved.

The north range walls (Figure 32)

The robbing of stone from the north range has left only fragmentary evidence for the original form of its superstructure (Figure 32). The ashlar blocks which formed the first course of the south wall survived for only *c.*1.70m as an undisturbed run, with a further extent rebuilt in Phase 5C (see below). The eastern part of the north wall survived as up to two courses of stone slabs over a length of *c.*5.20m.

The north wall of the east chamber (382) was the first to be built: it stood on a flat bed of chalk and limestone slabs, and was offset by *c.*0.08m over the threshold footing, 126 (Figure 36, S43). A construction spread (136) was sealed by a dark make-up layer (133) which was *c.*0.20m deep. Above this make-up deposit, which overlapped the south wall footing, lay a construction horizon (115) for the south wall (Figure 36, S43). Thus, levelling clearly continued as the building operations proceeded.

The outer face of the north wall was built of coursed limestone slabs, whilst the inner face was of tooled chalk, with a core of small chalk rubble. The total thickness of the wall was *c.*0.55m. Unless it had been heavily rendered (for which there was no evidence), the effect would have been less pleasing than that afforded by the ashlar of the south elevation of the building (Figure 36, S44–6).

Along the south footing (85) a level spread of mortar and roof tile was used to bed ashlar. The outer, or south, face of this wall (36, 37) was built of claw-tooled limestone (Figure 36, S46), whilst its interior was faced with tooled chalk blocks, retaining a core of small chalk rubble in sandy mortar. The total thickness was *c.*0.55m, matching that of the north wall. This scantling could suggest that a stone-faced ground floor wall rose either to a single storey, or carried an upper storey of timber-framed construction. Three possible scaffolding-post positions (837, 839, 841) were identified in an alignment which ran parallel to the south wall; these were sealed by a hard-standing (84) in the cloister alley.

The westward continuation of the south wall of this range was indicated by the survival of ashlar in two places — at threshold position 155, and at the junction with the west range wall (287). Beyond these, it was marked by the course of an 0.70m wide Phase 7 robber trench (3002/3001: Figure 57) which terminated at the west wall of the western chamber (3277: Figure 32). There was no evidence to indicate the nature of the superstructure of this wall save for

construction spreads of crushed chalk (3158, 3160), and mortar (3156), which ran up to its western edge. The insubstantial nature of wall 3277, coupled with the facts that both the east–west walls continued beyond it, and that a padstone (3279) was found further west on the centre-line of the building, all argue for this wall representing a screen or internal partition.

The east wall of the eastern chamber (2003) was faced with chalk slabs on both sides; its overall width of 0.68m may suggest either that it survived only to the level of an offset plinth, or alternatively that it served as a slightly more substantial gable end. Its junction with the north wall was marked by an external clasping buttress (2073). This formed one side of a doorway in the north-east corner of this chamber. The other side of this doorway was defined by a transverse line of chalk ashlar (2071) to the west (Figure 32). The entrance was *c.*1.34m wide.

A door in the north side of this chamber opened into the porch or tower structure set against the north wall. A light footing (865) which has been identified as a 1.00m wide stair-base ran through this entrance. Directly opposite this putative stair position were a pair of ashlar jambs which defined a south entrance *c.*0.90m wide. The eastern jamb (no. B12) was recorded *in situ*; the chamfered top of this block shows it to have been set at sill level. The infilling of a slot across the doorway (61) in Phase 5B, probably betrays the position of an original threshold which was removed at that time.

Further to the west the superstructure of the walls of the north range had suffered from later robbing. In the middle of the south wall (155) of the western chamber, limestone ashlar supported a tile threshold *c.*1.47m wide. This gave access from the north-west corner of the cloister alley to the west chamber. Opposite this doorway, a later conduit (426) which passed through the north wall, may have have been routed through an earlier entrance in this position (Figure 46).

Internal fittings — the north range, west chamber (Figure 32)

In the west chamber a fireplace was built against the cross-wall at the eastern end of the room. This fireplace was flanked by columns set on half-octagonal bases, nos. B14 and B15 (Figure 38, S47). The fireback was built of chalk ashlar, the whole being set on top of a light footing (1134) which had been inserted into the west side of wall 473 (Figure 33, S39). Parts of the superstructure of this wall (472) survived above this footing behind the fireplace (Figure 32). The latter was set slightly off-centre, perhaps to allow a doorway to communicate between the east and west chambers; however, no evidence for

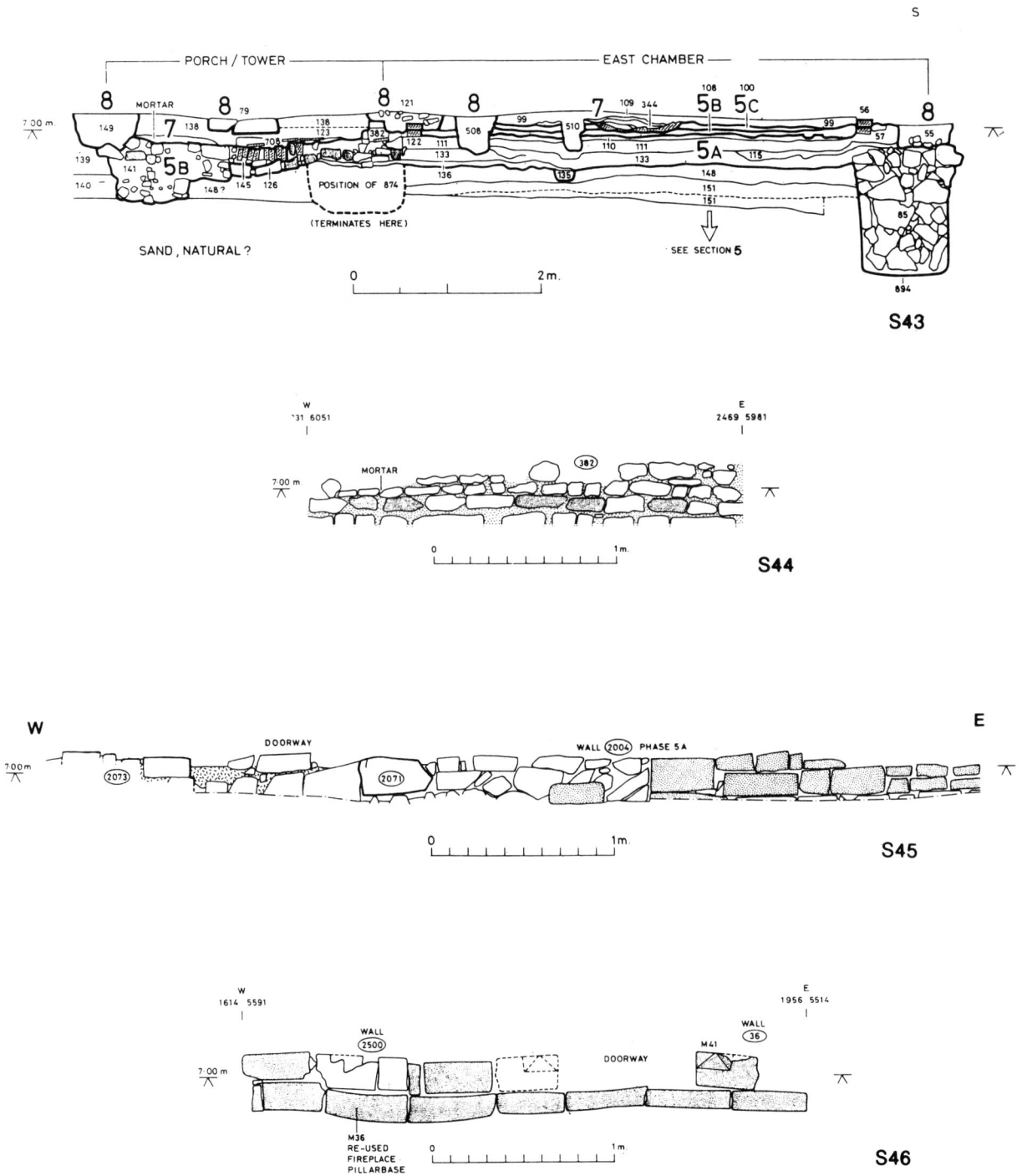

Figure 36 Phases 5A-C — little cloister, north range walls. S43-6.

a threshold in this position was recorded before Phase 5C. Alternative explanations for the off-centre position of this fireplace are that its chimney may have compensated for the lack of a buttress on the south side of the building, or that it may have been intended to bypass the ridge of the roof.

A spread of sandy clay (1132) ran across the south part of the room (Figure 37A). This was overlapped by a primary spread of ashy silt (1131) around the fireplace. This was sealed by a bright orange patch of burnt clay (1133) which marked the first recognisable hearth to accompany the fireplace. It had a sharply defined boundary which argues for the presence of a fender confining the hot ashes. The level of this burnt clay surface was *c.*6.75m OD. Archaeomagnetic assay of this surface produced a determination of AD 1140–90 at a 68% confidence level for its last firing (see section 5.1). This is clearly anomalous, as it is incompatible with other dating evidence for the little cloister, and indeed for the Dominican Priory itself.

No evidence was found for any floor platform or surfaces in the eastern half of this chamber. This could suggest that it had a surface of timber, tiles or flags during this phase. No evidence was found for any such surface surviving *in situ*, but later deposits included redeposited floor tile fragments. Moreover, numerous chalk slabs including reused flagstones, (nos. B27–8) were to be incorporated into a Phase 5C conduit here.

A mortar spread (1130) may have been associated with the construction of a tile-on-edge hearth (815) which overlay the previous fireplace (1133: Figure 32). This new hearth was built of reused roof tiles which were set into a plastic clay base. Its surface lay at a level of *c.*6.90m OD, and thus stood proud of the floor — again arguing for the former presence of a tiled or flagged floor. Archaeomagnetic assay of this hearth produced determinations of AD 1260–1300 or AD 1400–40 for its final firing; the later determination may be more acceptable (see section 5.1), but this would imply that it continued in use throughout Phase 5B. The archaeological evidence does indeed confirm its persistence into Phase 5B, though the dating achieved by other methods suggests that both of these determinations are questionable.

A solitary post-hole (3179) was found at the western end of this chamber, set to the south of the centre-line of the building (Figure 34, S40B). A chalk slab (3178) lay at the base of this post-pit. No other post-positions were identified in this area. It is possible that this one feature relates to a structure which was set against wall 3277 to the west.

Beyond the west wall (3277) a further deposit of clay 3157 overlay the construction horizon. On this surface was set a padstone (3279) along the centre-line of the building; it consisted of a rectangular block of limestone measuring 0.30 x

0.25m.

The north range, east chamber (Figures 32 and 37)

The internal fittings of the east chamber contrast with those in the west room. The floor was a platform of puddled clay (111) which overlapped the wall footings. The surface of this platform lay at *c.*6.88–6.92m OD. An extensive area of its northern surface was hardened and reddened by burning (843: Figure 37B). As this extended beneath other Phase 5A features, and was situated away from the hearth which served the chamber, it is taken to have represented activity which preceded the completion of construction work. Archaeomagnetic assay of this surface yielded a determination of AD 1360–90 at the 68% confidence level (see section 5.1): this does not appear compatible with other evidence for the construction of the range in the early part of the 14th century.

The formal fireplace which served this chamber was a rectangular structure built of re-used tiles set on edge into the clay platform (2072): the kerb which defined its edge was made from chamfered or rubbed brick. This hearth had been almost obliterated during Phase 5B by the insertion of a new fireplace of similar form (2011: see below). Only the eastern edge of the original structure survived; this was 1.36m long.

Along the north, east and south sides of the chamber low footings which were faced with brick (56, 122, 2005, 2006) ran round the inside of the walls (Figure 32). The brickwork was set directly onto the clay platform (111), and survived to a height of two or three courses (Figure 38, S48 A–B). Between the brick facing and the inside face of the walls was an infill of small chalk rubble (57, 2007, 2008). The total width of these footings was *c.*0.50m. They have been interpreted as the bases for wooden benches; comparable features occur elsewhere on the site. The dominant focus of the east chamber would therefore have been a hearth faced by benches along at least three of the walls.

Adjacent to the south doorway which gave access to and from the cloister alley, were a pair of small pits (928/929, 926/927): these may mark the course of a partition which extended into the chamber, and which would have screened the south door (Figure 32). This partition ended in a threshold paved with chalk rubble and slabs (818) which included reused fragments of grooved and chamfered mouldings (nos. B10, B11). The wear on these suggests that they continued to be smoothed by being walked on after the screen was dismantled.

In the area around the screen, and at the west end of the chamber, a series of thin interleaved deposits of silt and clay were laid down (Figure 37 C–F). These clay deposits were interpreted as either a localised

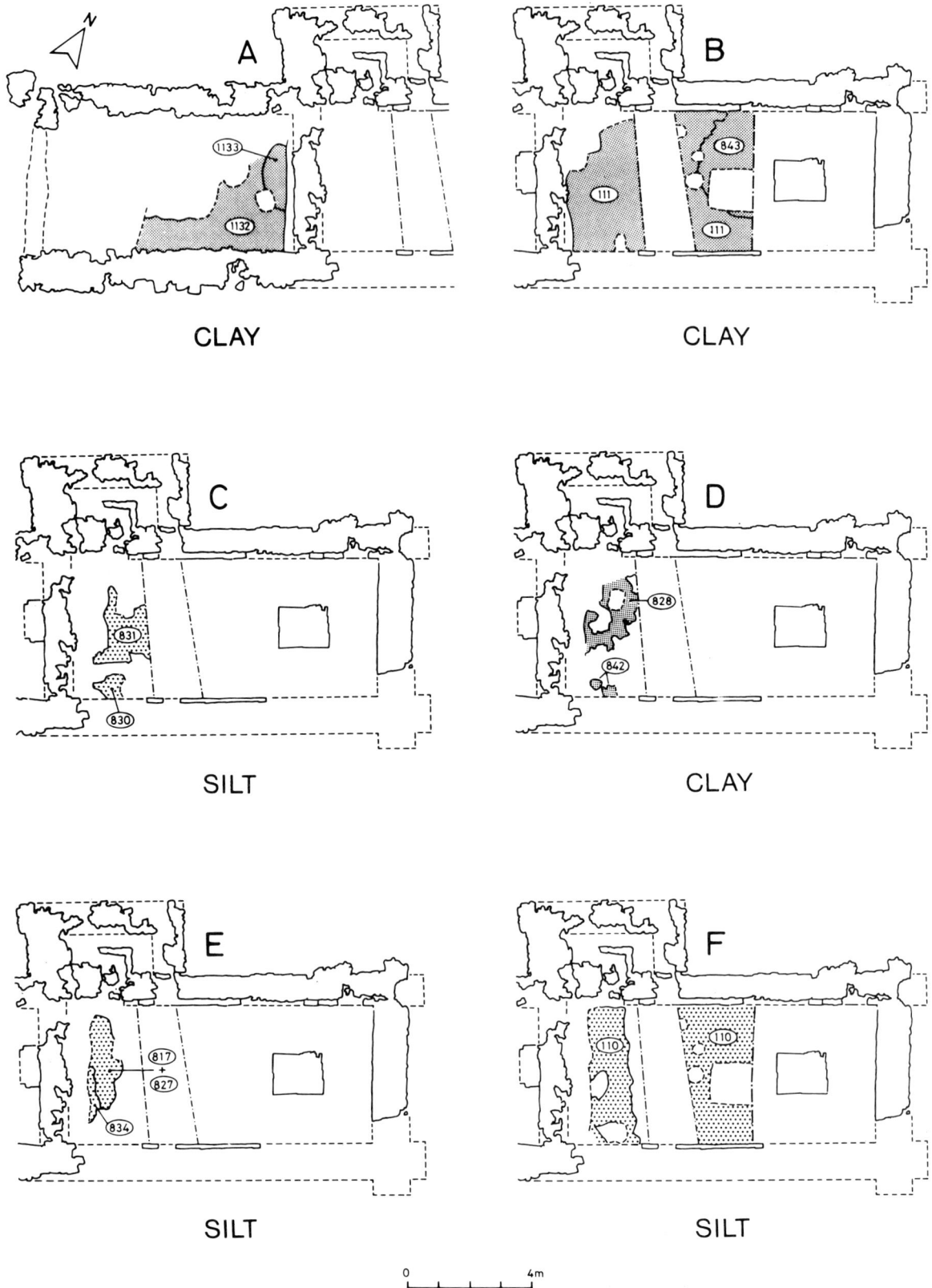

Figure 37 Phase 5A — little cloister, north range occupation.

patching of the floor or as material which had fallen from a partition. The sequence of silts (831, 830, 829, 827, 834, 826), clays (828, 842) and sand (817) was sealed by yet another silt layer (110*) which ran across the full width of the chamber.

In the area to the east of the building an external clay surface may have been associated with its use; however, no datable finds were recovered from this layer.

The west range (Figures 28 and 32)

The construction of the west range of the little cloister was clearly secondary to that of the north range, which its east wall (287) abutted (Figure 32). Nevertheless, the continuation of the cloister alley argues that both buildings formed part of a single scheme of construction (Figure 28).

A section across the east wall of the west range (287) identified chalk rubble footings (Figure 39, S50). Their depth was not revealed, but they were demonstrated to be at least 0.85m wide. Wall 287 was built from a level of *c*.6.65m OD. It comprised three courses of roughly worked chalk slabs (Figure 39, S50), and was 0.70m thick with a rubble core. The construction changed at the northern end: the slabs were replaced by a single course of blocks (892). These were set above an especially chalky patch in the construction horizon along the alley (795). This could suggest a doorway through the wall at this point (Figure 32): a later drain (426) was routed through here. A setting of chalk rubble (605), which may represent either an internal buttress or a partition footing, was recorded butting onto the west side of wall 287, though neither the further extent nor the date of this feature is known.

A wall to the west (3182) was examined more fully. It was positioned against the north range wall, directly opposite the north range internal wall (3277); however, if these footings were for an external buttress, it would appear to have extended further south from this wall than any of the other Phase 5A buttresses. Initially the ground level had been raised by a dense spread of rubble (3186), and a layer of clay (3184), both of which lay to the west of the projected wall alignment (Figure 39, S50); the comparable deposit to the east was a clay-silt mixture, 3189. A steep-sided trench, *c*.0.90m wide and *c*.0.65m deep, was then cut. Chalk rubble (3185) was laid in the trench in rough courses, and levelled up with crushed chalk on which further rubble was then set. The top of the footing lay at *c*.6.63m OD. On the east side of the footing, a layer of plastic grey clay (3187) was laid against the chalk rubble elements which stood proud. This recalls the treatment afforded to the footings of the north range.

Where the footing of the west wall was cut by the section, no superstructure was recorded above it. A band of grey clay (3181) was carried across these footings. No occupation material was recorded over the internal surfaces. (Further deposits of chalk 3037 and clay 3023 are considered to have been associated with later activity.) It is possible that although the footings had been laid, the programme of works was not completed; that construction in timber was resorted to, or that further walling was constructed beyond the limit of the excavation. Alternatively, this may have marked a doorway. A division may have been intended between a ground floor storage area and an alley which was integrated into the west range, though the evidence for a pent roof over the alley (see above) may indicate that such a scheme was not completed until Phase 5C.

The cloister alley layers

After the foundations of the alleys had been laid, and their ground levels raised (in the case of the north alley to *c*.6.60–6.76m OD, and of the west alley to *c*.6.60m OD), mixed deposits of gravel, crushed stone, sand and chalk were laid down (Figure 30 C–E). These are interpreted as forming a construction horizon for the superstructure of the north and west ranges. The spreads which comprised this horizon were more or less restricted to either the north or west alleys, and incorporated smaller patches within or between the major layers. All of these were sealed by the first extensive accumulation of occupation silts within the cloister alley.

A patch of crushed limestone and chalk (835) was sealed beneath an extensive spread of orange mortar, pea gravel, and chalk and limestone fragments (84) in the north cloister alley. The top of this spread lay at a level of *c*.6.73–6.89m OD. It overlapped an arcade post-footing (92: Figure 28) and the north range wall footing (85). Small patches of clay (737, 788) also formed part of this horizon. Along the west alley a spread of light brown gravel and mortar (47) was equated with 84 on the basis of its similar character (Figure 30C); it lay at a level of *c*.6.63–6.78m OD. A spread of crushed limestone *c*.0.05m deep was noted beneath 47 at its northern end, against the north range wall; a comparable deposit of crushed chalk (48) was recorded as its lower extent to the south (this is not shown on any of the published plans). These layers overlapped the wall footings along the west edge of the alley.

Above surface 47 small patches and layers were recorded along the northern part of the west alley (Figure 30, C–E). Some of these may have related to building activity (e.g. a spread of crushed limestone 46 and sand 797). Patches of clay or loam (760, 802, 45) may have been trampled about during the construction work; they were sealed by further spreads of crushed chalk and gravel (755, 747, 795, 758). A generally similar sequence was traced in the northern alley (Figure 29, S34). A chalk and gravel spread (787) was considered as an equivalent to contexts 46 and 47; this was sealed in turn by thin clays (778, 896, 757), sand (797), and finally by a second layer of sand (743).

The continuation of these cloister alley layers, in a similar series, was noted in the south-west excavation edge, to the south of an intrusive Phase 6A footing (Figure 40, S51). The lowest surface was a band of crushed stone fragments (888), c.0.11m deep. Above this was a soft clay flecked with grit and charcoal

(887) which was 0.05m thick; this was sealed by a further band of crushed chalk (886) c.0.06m deep, and a loose gravel (885) c.0.22m thick. These spreads accumulated between c.6.58m and c.6.87m OD. The comparable Phase 5A and 5B construction horizons at the south end of the alley lay between c.6.60m OD and c.6.79m OD. The implication is that the alley served not only the little cloister, but also provided a physical link with the north-west corner of the great cloister, which lay to the south.

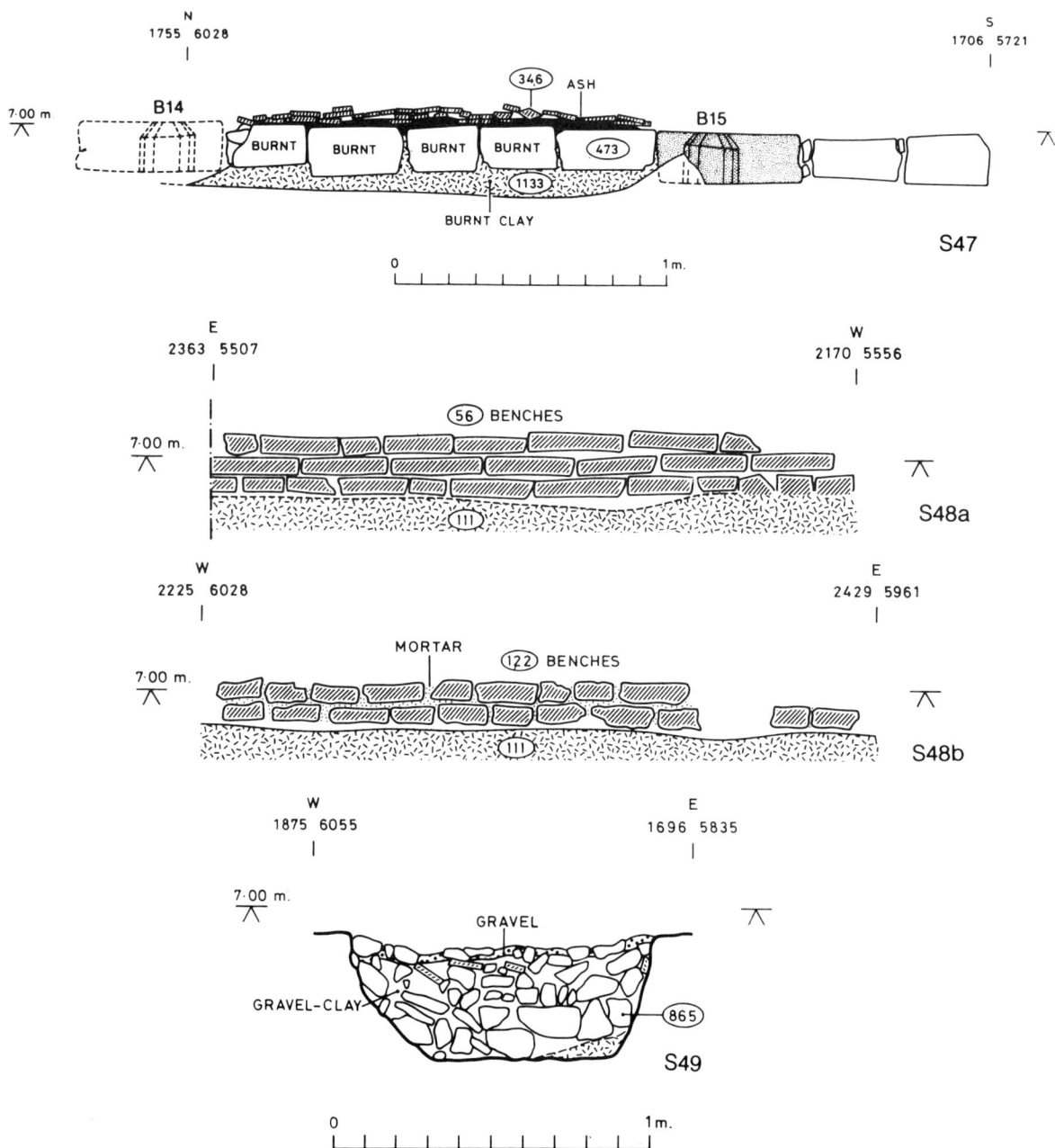

Figure 38 Phase 5A — little cloister, north range internal fittings. S47–9.

All the above deposits are considered to have related to the construction of the little cloister; they were all sealed by the first extensive occupation layer to be deposited in the alleys. The occupation silts were thin (Figure 30 F), which may indicate that the alleys were kept fairly clean. Silt 697 accumulated along the western alley, whilst in the north alley the accumulation of silts was restricted to its east end. Here, silt layer 698 was sealed by a chalky layer (679) on top of which accumulated further light silting (683).

The silting along these alleys was not continuous; a break occurred along the west end of the north alley, between the doorways in the south wall of the north range. This may betray a heavy traffic or regular sweeping which slowed the accumulation of silts; no evidence for any tiled or flagged floors was recovered from the early cloister alley layers.

These Phase 5A silts were sealed by extensive layers of crushed chalk (43, 44) which were associated with structural work in Phase 5B.

The finds — Phase 5A

Masonry: mouldings (B10–11); jamb (B12); base (B14); nook shaft (B24); floor slab (B26); ashlar (B51–8, B76, B79–89); slabs (B124–9).

Brick: Type 1 (20 fragments); Type 3A (1); Type 4 (34); Type 5 (2). Numbers B168–9 are illustrated.

Roof Tile: Type 1A (4 fragments); Type 2B (40); Type 2C (18); Type 6 (23); Type 7 (1); Type 12B (1); Type 15A (16); Type 15B (1) and 4.871 m² of non-diagnostic roof tile. Numbers B187, B192–3 and B196 are illustrated.

Ridge Tile/Roof Furniture: Type 1A (5 fragments); Type 1D (1); Type 2 (1); Type 3 (1); Type 5 (1); plain ridge tile (3); decorated unglazed ridge tile (2); unclassified glazed (2). Ridge tile/roof furniture (nos. B203–5, B214), ventilator (no. B217), and ridge tile (no. B222) are illustrated.

Window Glass: nos. 5–8.

Lead: sheet (no. 652); offcuts (nos. 653–4); melt (no. 710).

Iron: angle tie (no. 783); hinge (no. 787); strap (no. 788); nail (no. 796); disc (no. 802); washer (no. 804); horseshoe nail (no. 812); unidentified fragments (nos. 838–43); 29 nails and 63 nail fragments.

Copper Alloy: button (no. 884); key (no. 902); needle (no. 914).

Glass: bead (no. 998).

Worked Stone: mortar (no. 1009); millstone fragment (no. 1011); whorl (no. 1015).

Coins: An antoninianus of AD 270–273 (1021); Edward I farthing of 1272–1307 (1022).

Pottery: 125 vessels; numbers 1039, 1047 are illustrated.

The finds from the garth — Phase 5

Masonry: nook shaft (no. B21); ?floor slab (no. B32); ?splay (no. B33); ashlar (nos. B48–50).

Brick: Type 1 (15 fragments); Type 4 (13); Type 3A (1); Type 7 (20). Number B179 is illustrated.

Roof Tile: Type 1A (16 fragments); Type 1B (2); Type 2B (12); Type 6 (13); Type 15A (3); and 2.48 m² of non-diagnostic roof tile. Number B194 is illustrated.

Ridge Tile/Roof Furniture: Type 1A (3 fragments); Type 1C (3); Type 1D (2); Type 2 (2); Type 4 (3); plain ridge tile (9); decorated unglazed ridge tile (2); ridge tile or roof furniture (nos. B198, B200–2), roof furniture (no. B208), finials (nos. B211, B213) are illustrated.

Window Glass: (nos. 1–3).

Lead: flashing (no. 644); offcuts (nos. 650–1); melt (no. 708); eraser (no. 762); weight (no. 763).

Iron: wedge (no. 774); comb tooth (no. 775); looped staple (no. 781); straps (nos. 789–90); nail (no. 799); stud (no. 801); keys (nos. 806–7); horseshoe (no. 810); horseshoe nail (no. 815); strap slide (no. 817); unidentified fragments (nos. 820, 823–4, 831–6, 844) and 63 nails and 243 nail fragments.

Copper Alloy: brooch (no. 872); fitting (no. 892); strip (no. 894); vessel fragments (nos. 904–5); needle (no. 915); wire (no. 928); sheet fragment (no. 938); buckle (no. 949).

Worked Stone: hones (nos. 1004–6); 'pencil' (no. 1013).

Coin: Edward I–II farthing of *c.*1300–1310 (1020).

Pottery: 103 vessels; nos. 1040–6 are illustrated.

Phase 5A — dating evidence

The little cloister area provided the bulk of the finds from the 1986–9 excavations. It is therefore scarcely surprising that dating evidence for this area was relatively plentiful. In absolute terms the finds assemblage was not large — a common feature of monastic occupation areas.

The make-up layers along the west cloister alley included three fragments of Humber 1 (West Cowick type) in a layer of mixed clay and gravel (Context 769). This would suggest a date after *c.*1320.

The construction horizons which formed the first hard-standing along the cloister alley included fragments of thirty-three vessels with several joins between contexts. The group of contexts included ten vessels of Beverley ware type 2C, seven of Beverley ware type 2B, and a single example of Humber 1 — a combination which would be consistent with a date in the first half of the 14th century. A chalky construction spread (3158) at the west end of the north range included a slightly worn coin which was issued in 1280 (no. 1022) and deposited probably in the 1320s or 1330s, and certainly before 1351.

One of the pillar-bases which flanked the fireplace in the western chamber of the north range (no. B14), is of a form which is typical of 14th century work. Moreover, 14th century pottery was recovered from the fixtures and floor silts of the east chamber of the north range. A fragment of a Saintonge polychrome jug from context 830 is useful in dating the Phase 5A occupation of the east chamber: the main currency of this ware was during the late 13th and early 14th centuries.

No datable finds came from within the Phase 5A west chamber; however, a small purse hoard (no. 1026), which was found here in a Phase 5C context,

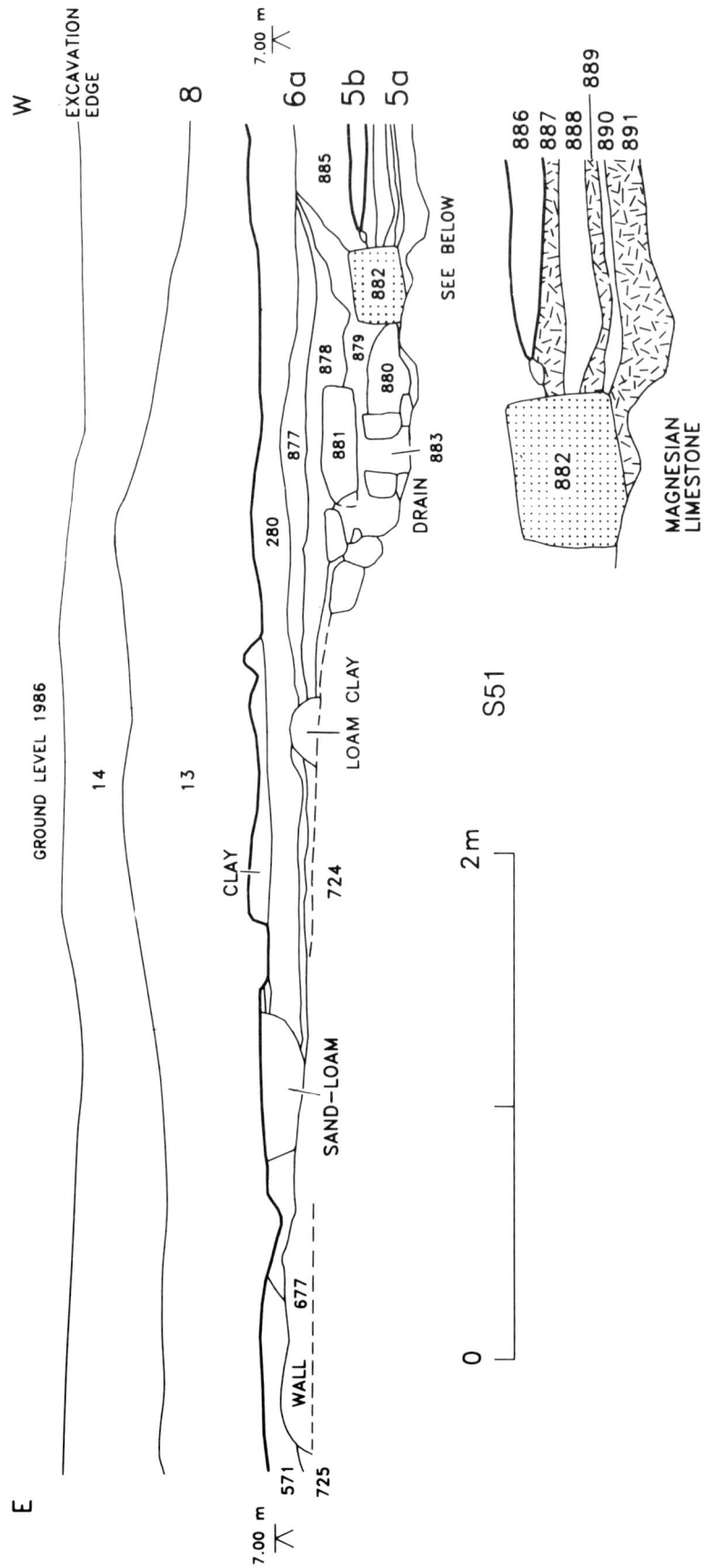

Figure 40 Phases 5A–6A — little cloister alley, south end. S51.

would seem more appropriate to the Phase 5A occupation of this chamber. The hoard included four Scottish coins issued between 1280 and 1296 and one English penny of 1280. It had certainly been deposited before 1351, possibly in the 1320s or 1330s. The loss of this group may have taken place during the construction or early occupation of the chamber. A similar residual find may be represented by a coin incorporated into the Phase 5B floor of the chamber (no. 1023) probably lost before *c*.1325.

The occupation silts which accumulated in the cloister alley included fragments of ten vessels, of Beverley ware types 1A, 2B and 2C, and a Coarse Sandy ware cooking pot. These are all consistent with a date in the first half of the 14th century.

Archaeomagnetic dates for Phase 5A were sought from the first and second hearths in the west chamber of the north range, and from an area of burning on the first clay floor of the east chamber (see section 5.1). None appears satisfactory, and all conflict with the ceramic and coin evidence. The construction of the little cloister would appear to date to the first half of the 14th century, and its earlier occupation to the third or fourth decade. The archaeomagnetic results for Phase 5 were uniformly at variance with other evidence, perhaps a result of localised subsidence.

Cloister garth context 65 has been attributed to Phase 5. (An attribution to Phase 5C on ceramic evidence is presented below; section 3.16). A feature (720) which was cut across the garth contained pottery of 14th century date and a coin (no. 1020) which was lost in the 1320s or 1330s. The garth soil (65) sealed this feature, which may have been related to construction activity in the area; sherds from ninety vessels were found in this soil. About 14% of this pottery group was residual; of the rest, Humber 1 made up 12%, Beverley ware type 2C 20%, and Beverley ware type 2B 23%. Sherd joins were noted with construction layers in the cloister alleys, perhaps arguing that layer 65 had begun to accumulate from the start of the Phase 5 activity in the area. There is no indication that the accumulation of material in the garth necessarily continued beyond *c*.1400: a single sherd of a Low Countries Redware pipkin could possibly be of 15th century date, but other common 15th century pottery types (e.g. Humberware cisterns or Rawmarsh wares) are absent.

Suggested date of construction: *c*.1325.

Suggested date of garth deposits: *c*.1325–*c*.1400.

Phase 5B. The little cloister. Second half of the 14th century

Introduction

Phase 5B saw the refurbishment of the little cloister.

In the alley this was shown by the laying of another hard standing deposit, and by alignments of scaffolding posts set parallel to the walls of the north and west ranges. The chambers were given new floors, and modifications to the access through the east chamber of the north range were carried out.

At the west end of the west chamber a new partition was inserted, to the east of its Phase 5A predecessor. This work was accompanied by the removal of the Phase 5A wall at this end of the building, and possibly by the extension of the range to include a larger third chamber. The major developments within the cloister alley are shown schematically on Figure 41, whilst those in the west and east chambers are similarly depicted in Figures 44 and 45, respectively.

The little cloister alley (Figures 41–3)

A thick layer of crushed chalk and mortar (44) was spread along the full extent of the west alley, forming the first evidence for a second phase of construction activity in the little cloister (Figure 41A). This layer reached its maximum depth of *c*.0.09m against the west range wall (287, 892: Figure 28). It was cut by a feature which was recorded only in the excavation edge (688): this had a diameter of *c*.0.40m, and was filled with mortary loam (687). A further cut through either 44 or the overlying layer (43: see below) was a U-shaped linear feature (746) which ran across the south end of the alley. It was 0.20m wide, 0.12m deep, and was filled with clay 745; it may have been related to the conduit feature which ran down the eastern edge of the west alley. This conduit (trench 539) has already been discussed under Phase 5A (see above; Phase 5A, the west alley).

Above layer 44 was a thick spread of gravel incorporating fragments of mortar, cobble and tile (43) which extended along both the north and west alleys (Figure 41B). This lay up to 0.07m deep, against the west range wall (287), and against the eastern part of the north range wall (36). The surface of this gravel spread lay between 6.93 and 6.79 OD, and sloped gently down from north to south.

Groups of post-holes were set parallel to the north and west range walls; these have been interpreted as scaffolding posts erected to permit work on the superstructure of the ranges (Figure 42). The more substantial of these features were round or oval (626, 653, 659, 661) with diameters of between 0.20 and 0.15m, and depths of 0.26 to 0.10m (Figure 43). A single square post position 665 was 0.18m across and 0.17m deep. The two least substantial features in this group were 0.04m deep depressions (655, 663) set into the surface of 43. All were filled with similar chalky or silty gravel (627, 654, 656, 660, 662, 664).

The post-positions parallel to the west range wall were set at intervals of *c*.1.20–1.50m, and at a distance of *c*.0.20–0.30m from the wall (Figure 42). The

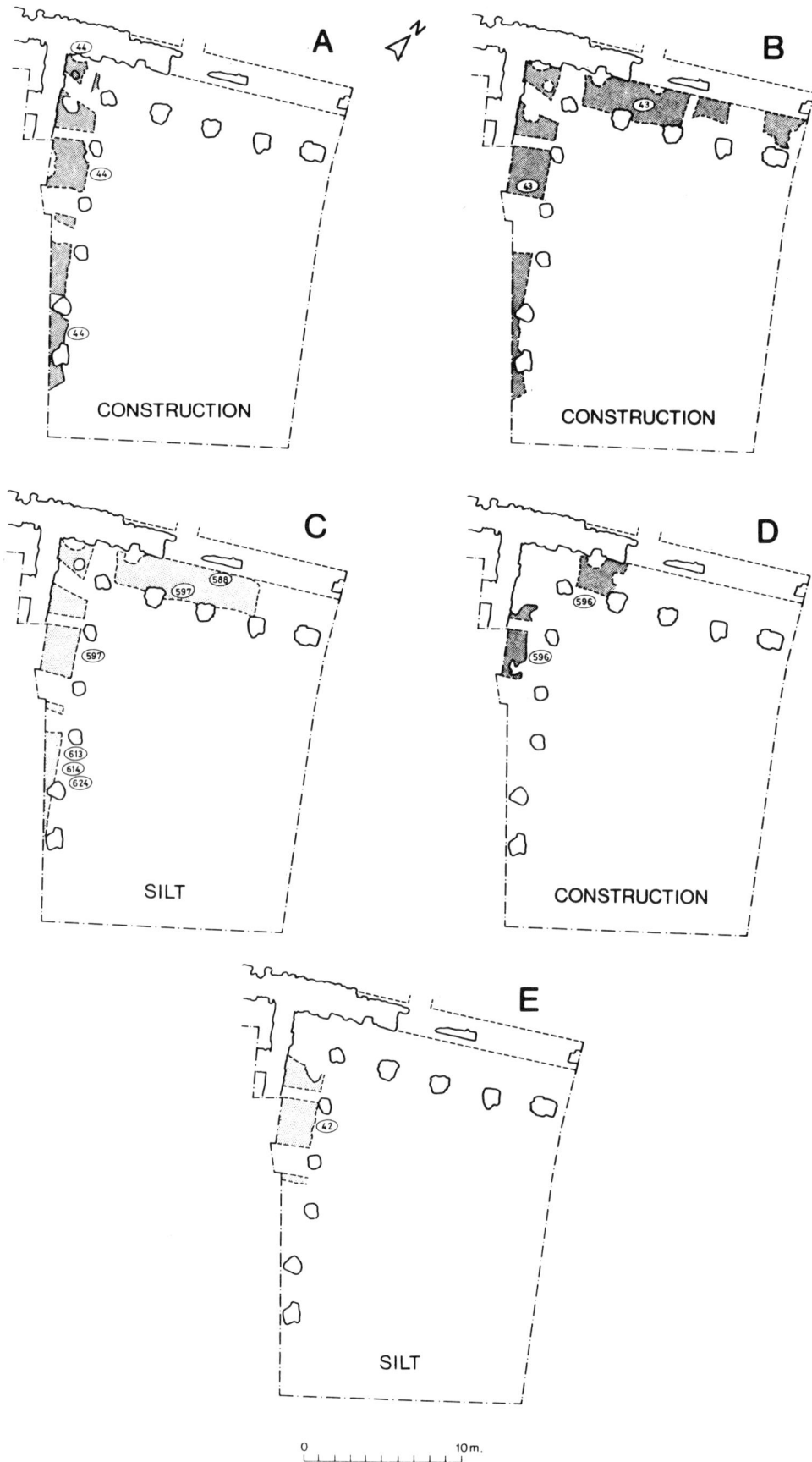

Figure 41 Phase 5B — little cloister alley, construction and occupation.

southernmost (655) was shallow; the others (653/654, 626/627) were of ovoid form and deeper. The post-positions in the north alley lay grouped together at the midpoint of the north range. Two deeper pits (659/660, 662/661) and a shallow feature (663/664) were set in a row alongside the wall, between 0.24 and 0.36m from its south face (Figure 43, S53 A–C). Further south, a square posthole (665/666) was set at right-angles to the wall, in line with post 661, close to the outer edge of the alley (Figure 43, S53 D). To the east, a larger cut (816) next to the position of footing 92 may also betray some work associated with the alley roof (Figure 43, S54).

At some stage, a shallow scoop (651) had been cut into one of the scaffolding-post positions (653), and was filled with gritty silt, 652 (Figure 43, S55). Subsequently, all of these features were sealed by silting from the continued use of the alley (Figure 41C). In the west alley these silts comprised layers 624, 614 and 613, whilst their northern counterparts were layers 645, 669 and 588. (The latter three contexts were all originally included within context 60). Silt 61 filled a depression across the south doorway of the east chamber, probably following the removal of a stone threshold. Layer 597 was a silt layer which was found in both alleys in the north-west corner of the cloister (Figure 41C). Subsequently, this was sealed by a thin chalky spread 596 (Figure 41D). Finally, a silt of uniform character (42) was laid down over the limited spreads in the west alley (Figure 41E). All of these layers were to be sealed by further mortar and crushed stone in Phase 5C.

The north range: west chamber (Figures 42 and 44)

The circumstantial evidence for a tiled, flagged or boarded floor in the western chamber during Phase 5A has been discussed above. The close of this first occupation phase left a jumble of deposits. Silt 855 was a loose, and possibly redeposited, patch of floor-silt. It was overlapped by a layer of soft brown clay (907) which lay across the south part of the chamber. Both these deposits were sealed by 867*, a mixture of clay, gravel, mortar and plaster; however, in some areas silt 855 was interleaved with this deposit (Figure 44A). Lumps of plaster also occurred in 859, a laminated deposit of clay and ash which overlapped a further layer of ash (780) on top of the Phase 5A tile hearth (815).

A pair of shallow gravel-filled pits (856/857, 853/854: Figures 42 and 43, S56) were cut into these churned deposits. These in their turn were sealed by a compacted mixture of clay and gravel (848) which formed the first floor platform within the west chamber (Figure 44B).

Patches of a very thin silt (805) accumulated over this platform; these were identified only where they had been sealed below a non-contiguous mortary spread, 803 (Figure 44C). The occupation which followed this was represented by a brown silt (754*: Figure 44D) which included a limited patch with much solidified copper alloy melt (796*), and a darker, ashier layer (772*), which overlapped the hearth. Silt 754 was not recorded as extending up to the south wall of the range; nor did it extend as far as the putative partition position at the west end of the chamber (see below). The surface level of this silt ranged from 6.84 to 6.91m OD; towards the western end of the chamber its level was *c*.6.87m OD.

A new rectangular tile-on-edge hearth (347) was constructed later in the course of Phase 5B; it was set on top of a pad of plastic clay (779) which sealed the Phase 5A hearth 815 (Figure 42). The new hearth was edged with a kerb which included a column fragment (no. B16), perhaps derived from the decorative Phase 5A fireplace. (The further reuse of an element of this fireplace was identified in Phase 5C). An ashy clay (750) was spread over the edge of this fireplace, towards the end of the Phase 5B occupation.

The north range: western end

During the course of Phase 5B, though not necessarily at its outset, further structural work was undertaken at the west end of the range (Figure 42). The attribution of this activity to this phase rests upon the identification of partition 3138/832 at the 754 occupation silt horizon. This alignment was not respected by the overlying Phase 5C silts (see below, Figure 47 C). Therefore, it represents a feature which was extant only in Phase 5B. The modifications involved the removal of the Phase 5A wall (3277: Figure 32) and its replacement by a screen further to the east (Figure 42). The latter passed over a post position (3179) which was considered to form an element of the original Phase 5A construction. This modification resulted in a smaller chamber in the western half of the building, than had existed during the previous phase.

The northern end of the Phase 5A west wall footing (3277: Figure 32) was partially robbed by trench 3164 (Figure 34, S40A); the latter was backfilled with chalk rubble and loam (3165). In contrast, at the south end of the wall only the superstructure was removed, and here the robber trench was backfilled with mixed clays (3162, 3157, 3173: Figure 34, S40B). A levelling deposit of clay (3105) was laid down after the robbing. Subsequently, a shallow pit (3281) was excavated on the east side of the wall, and infilled with clay and rubble (3283, 3282: Figure 34, S40A). This fill was sealed by a mortary lens (3284) which appears to have been contemporary with the construction of partition 3138/832.

The new partition was built after the removal (3177), of a Phase 5A post-setting (3179). The cut was filled by 3176, on top of which the partition was laid (Figure 34, S40B). The plan view suggests that the partition was itself of two phases (Figure 42).

The construction of this partition was followed by the deposition of further clays (3167/3137, 3166: Figure 34, S40B; Figure 44B). Of these, the earliest (3167) was flecked with mortar, chalk and tile. The others (3137, 3166) were cleaner clays which were more typical of platform deposits.

The north range: east chamber (Figures 42 and 45)

The modification of the east chamber of the north range cannot be directly correlated with work on the west chamber, though the uniform treatment of the cloister alley surface suggests that the area was still

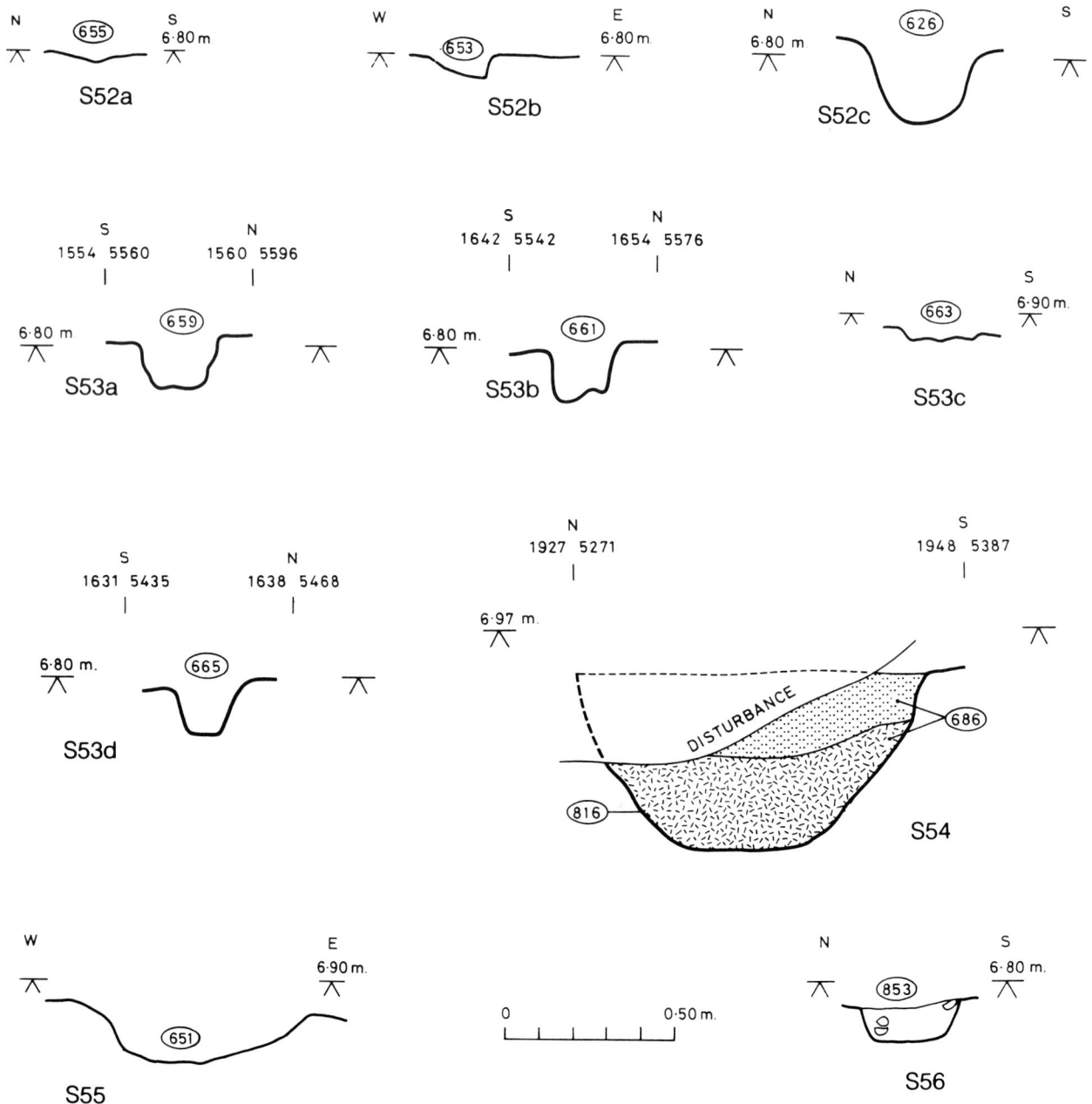

Figure 43 Phase 5B — little cloister alley, scaffolding positions. S52–6.

conceived as a single entity. It should be borne in mind that Phase 5B encompassed a variety of works which were secondary to the initial construction and occupation of the little cloister: this does not prove their contemporary execution.

The Phase 5A occupation surfaces in the eastern chamber were sealed by the laying of a new clay floor (108/2060) which was not recorded at the western end

of the room (Figure 45A). This floor seems to have largely coincided with the extent of the benches.

The Phase 5A hearth (2072: Figure 32) was replaced by a new rectangular brick-kerbed tile-on-edge hearth (2011). This is considered to have been done at this stage because the laying of the new floor would have presented a good opportunity for such renovation (Figure 42). (The relationship

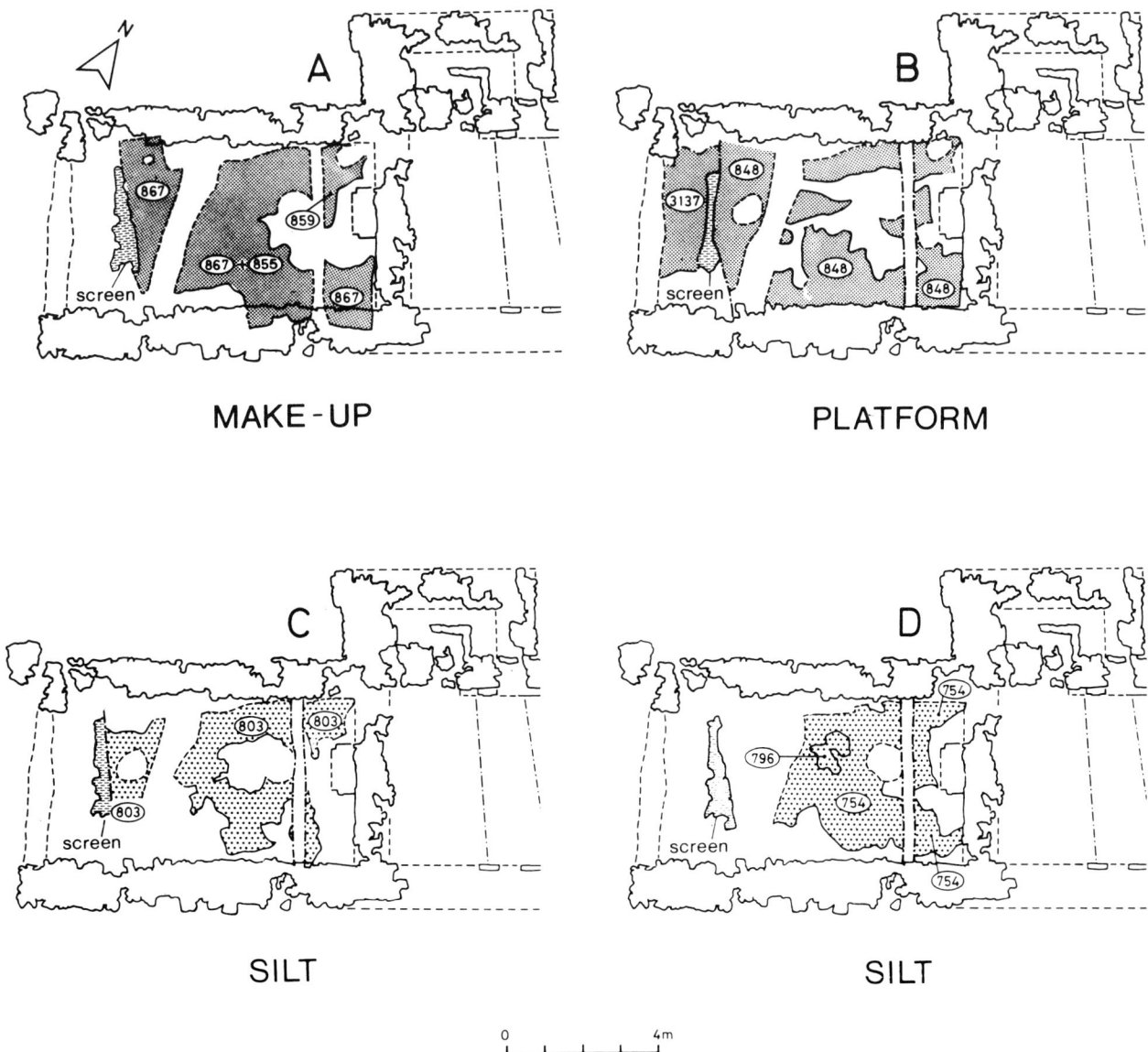

Figure 44 Phase 5B — little cloister, north range occupation — west chamber.

between the hearth structures is shown in plan, but the timing of the building of the first and second fireplaces is archaeologically unproven). Archaeomagnetic assay of this hearth yielded determinations of AD 1260–1310, of AD 1400–1450 at the 68% confidence level (see section 5.1, below).

The position of the fireplace relative to the north-east doorway into the chamber was clearly inconvenient, and the effect of a draught in a room where smoke would normally rise to a roof vent can be imagined. This was compensated for by the erection of a light screen, which was represented by an alignment of shallow stake-holes (2061) extending from the north-east corner of the fireplace to the doorway. This measure was not altogether satisfactory, and the doorway was subsequently blocked (2069): an additional element of brickwork (2074) was built in front of the old doorway linking the pre-existing benches along the north and east walls (Figure 42). Access to and from the north side of this chamber could now be gained only via the porch opening off its north-west corner (threshold 455).

The floor surfaces which accumulated over platform 108/2060 were composed of ashy silt (595) at the west end of the room and a more extensive dark ashy silt (2009*) over the greater part of the chamber (Figure 45B). Both incorporated mortary lenses or patches. Many small bones were recovered from a greasy patch (2019) within silt 2009 which lay next to the fireplace.

Evidence for continuing use of the hearth took the form of numerous interleaved lenses around it; these consisted of clay (2047, 2056, 2059, 2062) and silt (2046*, 2058: Figure 45C), capped with ash (2055, 2052: Figure 45D). On the west side of the hearth a patch of clay (2053*) included roof tile fragments, some of which were laid flat, and yet others were on edge (2054*); this may have represented a temporary extension of the hearth area.

A less typical deposit was laid down over floor surface 595 (Figure 45E). A mottled dark grey and brown mixture of clays (576) lay across the west end of the room; it did not appear east of the north–south trial trench, and was little more than 1.60m wide. The mixed clays of 576 included a well-defined brown patch of clay as it approached the south doorway. This deposit probably marked a well-used route from the alley, to the north door and stair.

The sequence of occupation during Phase 5B was terminated by the cutting of large features into the floor of the chamber, and by the sealing deposit of Phase 5C silts (100/381).

The porch (Figure 42)

The structure on the north side of the north range must have been of increased importance following the blocking of the north-east door. It now sheltered not only the stair, but also the sole exit from the chamber into the northern precinct. The limited spread of trampled clay (floor surface 576) at the western end of the room appears to indicate the use of this route. The attribution of these alterations to Phase 5B is based on circumstantial evidence: the blocking of the north-east door effectively removed the only other entrance into the chamber on the north side of the building; hence the entrance through this porch must clearly have continued in use.

The construction of a doorstep (455) marked the refurbishment of the north entrance (Figure 42). A less substantial threshold (145) was set on the east side of the porch: it consisted of roof tile mortared into a footing of bricks set on edge. This may represent an *ad hoc* replacement for an earlier feature: neither of these features (455 and 145) was stratigraphically tied to a particular phase, but they would clearly have been required from Phase 5B onwards.

The west wall of the porch was probably formed either by surviving elements from Phase 5A, or by a new structure set over a Phase 5A footing. The north wall was of lighter construction than its predecessor. The robbed foundation (703) was partially re-excavated, and was filled with a firmer mixture of rubble and clay (702) to a depth of *c*.0.70m. The fact that this porch had effectively been dismantled to foundation level and rebuilt on much the same alignment may signify little more than that the Phase 5A structure had become ruinous.

The finds

Masonry: nook shaft (no. B16); splays (nos. B34–6); ashlar (nos. B60–5).

Brick: Type 1 (12 fragments); Type 3A (1); Type 4 (4).

Roof Tile: Type 1A (2 fragments); Type 2B (12); Type 2C (1) Type 6 (2); Type 15A (2); and 1.555 m² of non-diagnostic roof tile. No. B181 is illustrated.

Ridge Tile/Roof Furniture: Type 3 (1 fragment); Type 5 (4); plain ridge tile (3); unclassified glazed tile (2); ventilator no. B220 is illustrated.

Window Glass: nos. 10–15.

Lead: came (nos. 541–5); sheet (nos. 655–6, 666); offcuts (nos. 658–60, 662, 675); melt (nos. 711, 713A–713D); dry point (no. 757); rod (no. 761); shot (no. 769).

Iron: spade iron (no. 777); nails (nos. 794–5); disc (no. 803); link (no. 805); horseshoe (no. 809); unidentified fragments (nos. 848–9); 14 nails and 52 nail fragments.

Copper Alloy: buckle (no. 874); lace end (no. 886); fitting (no. 891); stud (no. 896); chain (no. 898); repair clip (no. 902); tack (no. 910); pin (no. 920); sheet fragments (nos. 931, 937, 939, 940, 942, 952A); melt (948).

Gold: fragment (no. 897).

Glass: bead (no. 997); vessels (nos. 961, 981–2, 984).

Worked Bone: bead (no. 956).

Worked Stone: ?hone (no. 1007); mortar (no. 1010); flint (no. 1014).

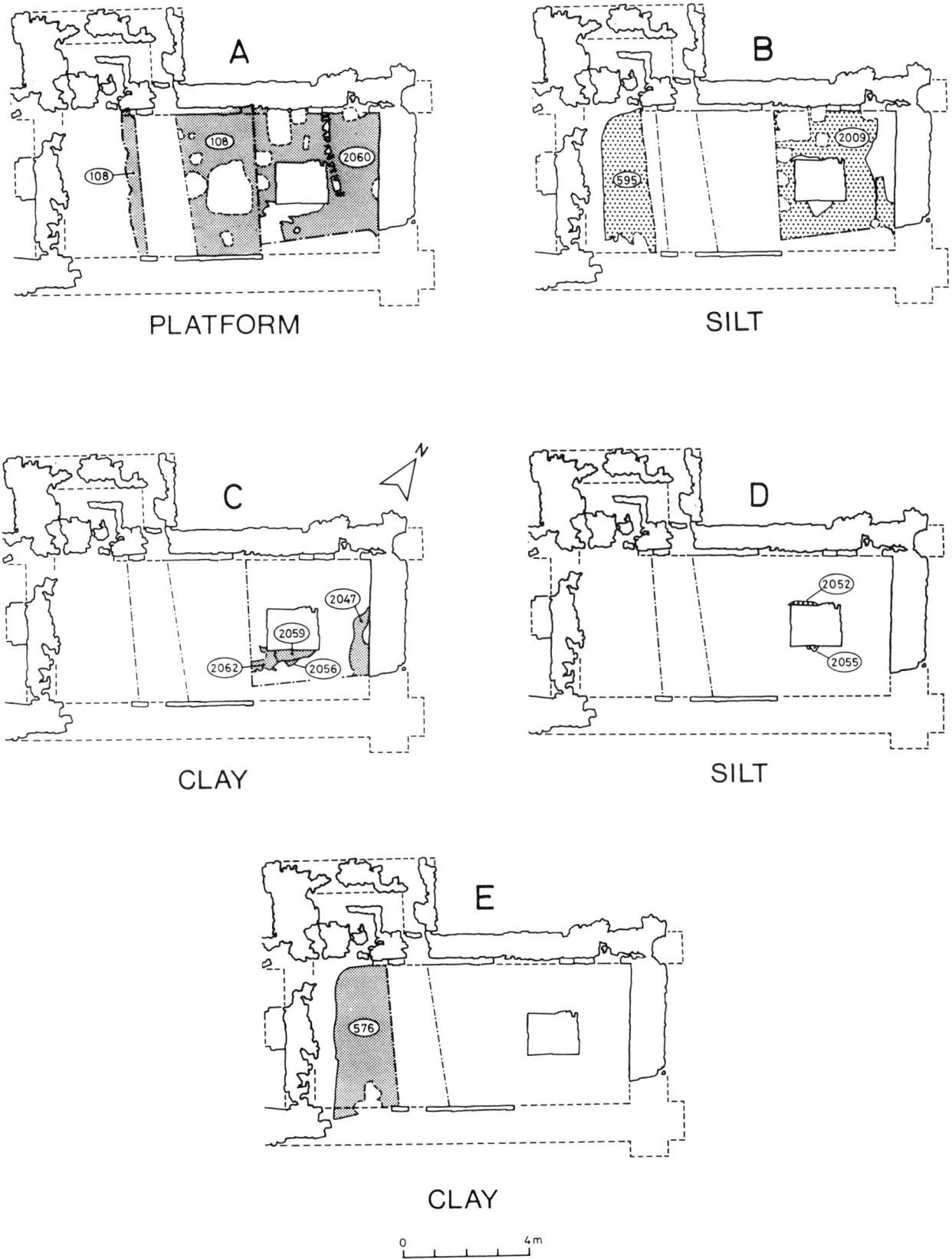

Figure 45 Phase 5B — little cloister, north range occupation — east chamber.

Coins: Edward I penny *c.*1280–1 (1023); Edward III
    halfpenny 1335–43 (1024); English jetton later 14th
    century (1025).
Pottery: 56 vessels, no. 1048 is illustrated.

Phase 5B — dating evidence

The renovation of the cloister alley surfaces saw the
deposition of pottery which was significantly distinct
from the Phase 5A material. Low Countries Redware
was present in context 44; in Hull this is rarely found
before *c.*1350, but thereafter is common in deposits
from the second half of the 14th until the mid. 17th
century. Beverley ware type 2C and Humberware
were also present in this phase, and there were
numerous sherds from a Scarborough 3 jug.

The deposits sealing the Phase 5A occupation in the
west chamber of the north range (855, 867, 848, 803)
included a fragment of a Low Countries Redware
frying pan (in layer 848). A coin which was lost by
1351 (no. 1023) was incorporated into mortary spread
803 over the platform. (It is possible that this may
have been residual from Phase 5A). The overall
character of pottery from the refurbishment of the
west chamber is similar to that of the cloister alley
group; both suggest a date after the mid. 14th century.

The hearth in the west chamber (815) was
constructed during Phase 5A, but continued in use for
some, or perhaps even most, of Phase 5B. One of the
possible archaeomagnetic determinations for its last
firing was AD 1400–1440 (see section 5.1); however,
this does not square happily with the other Phase 5B
material, especially as it was sealed by a new hearth
(347) late in Phase 5B. However, this is at least
internally consistent with one of the possible
determinations for the last firing of the Phase 5B
hearth (2011) in the eastern chamber, which was AD
1400–1450 at the 68% confidence level. This date is
more plausible because the latter was not sealed by a
new structure, and thus remained available for later
use.

Two coins were found in a floor silt (2009) in the
eastern chamber. The first of these (no. 1024) was an
Edward III halfpenny issued between 1335 and 1343.
The second (no. 1025) was an English jetton of the
later 14th century. The association of these coins
suggests that both were probably deposited in the later
14th century, and that this layer accumulated after
1351.

The pottery from the alley and the west chamber of
the north range appears to show that the Phase 5B
renovations took place about the middle of the 14th
century. The coins from the east chamber indicate that
deposits in that part of the range accumulated
thereafter. The archaeomagnetic dating of the eastern
hearth, if accepted, could be taken to show the later
use of that chamber.

Suggested date: second half of 14th century.

Phase 5C. The little cloister. Later 14th — 16th centuries

Introduction

Phase 5C marked a final attenuated series of
modifications in the little cloister. It began with work
on the south wall of the north range, followed by the
renovation of floors in its western chamber. Work
then extended to the rebuilding of the west walls of
both the north and west ranges, the latter perhaps
accompanied by rebuilding of the division between
the west alley and the garth. It is possible that this
permitted the integration of the west alley into a
timber-framed west range which overshot the alley.
This may have implemented a scheme which was
originally envisaged in Phase 5A, but whose previous
execution is uncertain.

Phase 5C is considered as being broadly
contemporary with part of the Phase 6A works to the
south. The Phase 6A refectory range had apparently
been constructed so as to permit the passage across it
of a Phase 5A conduit which was routed alongside the
west alley of the little cloister. This conduit was
removed immediately before the reconstruction of the
division between alley and garth, and also of a drain
which served the rebuilt west range. The drain had a
common stratigraphic relationship with the
reconstructed west walls of the north and west ranges,
in that it cut the new floor platforms and was
post-dated by occupation silting.

There are problems in correlating developments in
the little cloister area with those in other parts of the
precinct — a major handicap being the paucity of
dating evidence from the Phase 5C deposits.
Nevertheless, this phase encompassed a great deal of
structural activity; unfortunately, comparatively little
evidence survived for the occupation which followed.

The north range, south wall (Figures 46–8; Plate 8)

At the end of Phase 5B, works were undertaken which
are certain to have interrupted the use of the west
chamber, and may indicate some change in its
character (Figure 46).

The alterations began with the removal of the pillar
base on the north side of the fireplace (robber trench
749). The cavity was filled with brown plastic clay
(552). Fragments of pillars, which had possibly been
derived from the Phase 5A fireplace, had already been
used to form the kerb that bounded a tile-on-edge
hearth (347) in the later course of Phase 5B (see
above).

The pillar base which had been removed from this fireplace was incorporated into patching on the south wall of the range. The original fabric of this wall (36, 37) was composed of light limestone ashlar. The repaired section (2500) consisted of mixed chalk and limestone ashlar packed with smaller fragments (Figure 46). This was built to the same style and width as the original walling (Figure 50, S63B); its north face was abutted by a rebuilt T-shaped section of walling (516) — the join being packed with tiles on edge (Plate 8). This formed the eastern side of a new bench position in the western chamber, and was bonded into the cross-wall between the two chambers. It was 0.70m thick, and built of chalk ashlar and slabs which retained a narrow core of smaller rubble; this structure was cemented with a pale buff mortar. It extended northwards for a surviving extent of *c*.0.58m. It formed a rebuild over the Phase 5A spine wall footing (473), and was probably intended for the construction or reinstatement of a doorway connecting the east and west chambers. This interpretation is suggested by the extent of a contemporary platform deposit (523), which extended over footing 473.

The north range, west end

The separate excavation and recording of the west end of this range (Figure 3) has led to uncertainty in the correlation of the records of the main and subsidiary areas of excavation. Construction work on this range followed the laying of a platform of chalk-flecked clay (3042, 3030, 3031, 3137, 3105: Figure 47A), and a possible early phase of occupation which was indicated by silt 3006*. The construction horizon was marked by mortary spreads (3103, 3044, 3109, 3093: Figure 47B) at and beyond the west end of the building. The easternmost spread (3093) ran across the position of the Phase 5B screen 3138/832 (Figure 42), signifying its disuse.

A floor was laid down in the main part of the western chamber. This included some deposits which spread from the west (clays 3042, 3167, 3030, 3031: Figure 47A). Clay surface 485 lay at the same level in the north-eastern part of the room, sealing the top of the former hollow left by the removal of the fireplace pillar base; gravelly clays (483/523) formed the floor over much of the eastern half of the chamber. As noted above, a strip of hard brown plastic clay (523) overlapped the footing of the spine wall (473) at a putative doorway (Figure 47A). The surface level of the platform was *c*.6.90–7.04m OD.

Clays which were recorded as individual contexts, but were probably part of a single horizon, formed a floor for the area beyond the west end of the north range. These also extended behind the west range, suggesting an association with a separate structure, albeit one whose extent is unknown. A series of brown clays (3108, 3131, 3135) which incorporated

some chalky and orange flecking (Figure 47A), lay at *c*.6.89–6.96m OD — an equivalent level to the platform in the north range. These too were sealed by a mortary spread, which was probably associated with the reconstruction of the west walls of the north and west ranges.

The new west wall (3048: Figure 46) followed the approximate course of the Phase 5A footings (3277: Figures 32 and 34). This was apparently dictated by a broadly common alignment with the west wall of the west range (sill 3013: Figure 46, and see below). On the north side of this junction, a rectangular socket of brick (3112) was positioned on top of the original footing (85/3079) of the north range. A continuation northwards from here was marked by a shallow Phase 7 robber trench (3007/3048). This narrowed from a width of 0.97m to 0.41m as it continued northwards; its base was level at *c*.6.85m OD. The conjunction of a shallow footing with a socket suggests the use of an interrupted sill timber-framed construction.

Only a very thin, non-contiguous, silt (511) was identified as a primary deposit over the new floor platform in the west chamber (Figure 47C). It survived only where it was sealed by a skin of mortar. An extent of silt which was similarly sealed beneath this mortar was recorded in the south-east of the chamber, but was not distinguished from the later occupation deposit (349). To the west, various patchy silts (3006*, 3036 and 3092*) should probably be associated with this episode: silts 3006 and 3092 both included small fragments of melted lead. These deposits were cut by drain 435/556 (see below), and may indicate no more than a hiatus in the construction works in this area.

Surfaces west of the north range

Following the construction of the new west wall, a series of silts accumulated beyond the building (Figure 47C). The major concentration was an ashy silt (3111*), whereas the others (3035, 3032) formed non-contiguous spreads to the south. They were sealed by clays 3106, 3063, 3011, 3017, 3014, 3038, 3029, 3073 (Figure 47D). (Additional spreads of clay, 3100, and silt, 3099, may have extended this surfaced area up to 7.20m west of robber trench 3048; however as a modern concrete beam separated this area from the main excavation, this remains unproven.) The surface level of this platform ranged from *c*.7.00 to 7.08m OD. A series of burnt silts collected over it (3107, 3053*, 3052*, 3064*, 3010*, 3020*, 3070: Figure 47E); some of these were interleaved. Burning 3010 yielded an archaeomagnetic determination of AD 1330–1390 at the 68% confidence level (see section 5.1). The deposition of these silts was followed by further clay patching (3069, 3090, 3050: Figure 47F). The total duration of this intense activity is uncertain: it may have ended before the close of occupation within the rest of the little cloister area. The archaeological sequence was closed by the cutting of features which are thought to have been associated with robbing activity (see Phase 7, below).

The alley, conduit and drain (Figures 46, 48–9 and 52: Plates 9–11)

The Phase 5B occupation silts along the west side of the alley were sealed by a thin layer of mortar (41: Figure 52A). This is taken to be associated with construction work. The layer petered out to the north with a patch of crushed limestone (599: *ibid.*). Its northern counterpart was a mixture of soil and rubble (583), which extended for *c*.4.60m along the north alley. Deposits in the central part of this alley were not adequately distinguished, though layers of chalk and tile (668) and gravel (590) were identified at its eastern end.

The robbing of the Phase 5A conduit which ran down the east edge of the west alley took place in the course of Phase 5C (Figure 48). This left a shallow gully (539), which was deeper at its south end, but had a basal level of *c*.6.47m OD along most of its length (Figure 49, S57 A–B). It had been backfilled with loose loam and rubble (538); tilted tile fragments within this layer suggested that the infilling had been both deliberate and swift.

The conduit continued southwards into and beyond the refectory building (see below, Phase 6A). This is indicated by a modification which was made to the structure of the north wall footing of that building (24: Figure 53), at the point where the conduit entered. It then continued across the interior of that building as feature 881/884. If the conduit had been lined with brick or stone — there was no silting within it as might have been expected in an open channel — its level would have been close to that of 881/884 to the south.

It is not possible to state a direction for the fall of the conduit; however, the northern end of its robber trench was overlain by a later drain (426). The latter had a marked fall from south to north — from 6.70 to 6.48m OD — leading through the little cloister north range. The construction of the south end of drain 426 over trench 539 rules out a contemporary usage for drain and conduit.

The south end of this later drain (426) was contemporary with the construction of a brick wall (286/21) along the west side of the cloister (Figure 48). This replaced the alignment of uprights which formed the original division between the garth and the alley (Figure 49, S58). The contemporary building of the wall and the drain inlet was demonstrated by the fact that the former was overlapped by the capping slabs of the drain. These, in turn, were covered by further brickwork.

The drain (426) was set in a trench (435/556) which ran from the corner of the cloister alley into the west range (Figure 48). It then curved northwards to run across the west chamber of the north range and exit into the area behind the building (Figure 46; Plates 9–11). Its base was paved with Type 6 bricks, which occurred nowhere else at the Priory. The sides of the channel were also made of brick, and it was capped with slabs of chalk, and occasionally of limestone (Figure 46; Figure 49, S62). This structure was modified only where the drain passed across the footings of the north range walls: here, the base was formed of chalk ashlar. The drain cannot have served to take water standing in the cloister garth, unless this area was frequently and severely inundated — and deposits of a water-lain character were not recorded there. It was probably fed by a downpipe from guttering along the roof over the alley. A Phase 7 robbing pit at the inlet (64/317) may suggest that a lead pipe had fed into a silt trap (Figure 57).

The foundation trench for this drain (435/556) cut through the mortar and silt layers (511) inside the western chamber of the north range. This may suggest that a period of short-lived activity was interrupted by the construction of this drain and its associated works. The fill (436/555) of this foundation trench was sealed by silt 349, and its western equivalent (3051*: Figure 51). These formed the last occupation deposits to accumulate within this chamber. A large quantity of lead melt was recorded within layer 3051; this may relate to the Phase 5C occupation, or alternatively the stripping of fixtures from the range during Phase 7.

A tile-faced bench (38) was built along the inside face of the south wall of this chamber (Figure 46), but it is uncertain at what stage in the Phase 5C occupation this was constructed. It was butted against the internal angle of the junction of wall 2500 with 516. It was *c*.0.44m wide and 2.00m long, and was composed of four courses of flat-set roof tile fragments which retained a core of small chalk rubble. In character and location this footing was similar to the benches in the east chamber of the range.

The north range, east chamber (Figures 46, 50–1; Plate 12)

Works carried out in the east chamber of the north range appear, by Phase 5C, to have related principally to the continuing use of accommodation space at first-floor level. The access to an upper chamber was provided by the staircase in the eastern room, which had been in use throughout Phases 5A and 5B.

A large rectangular steep-sided and flat-bottomed pit (343) was excavated in the centre of the chamber. It was 1.40 by 1.45m in extent and 0.82m deep; it was filled with tightly packed heavy chalk rubble set in a loose sandy matrix (Figure 46; Figure 50, S64), which was sealed by the latest floor silt (100). The tightly

Figure 47 Phase 5C — little cloister, north range, west chamber, construction and occupation.

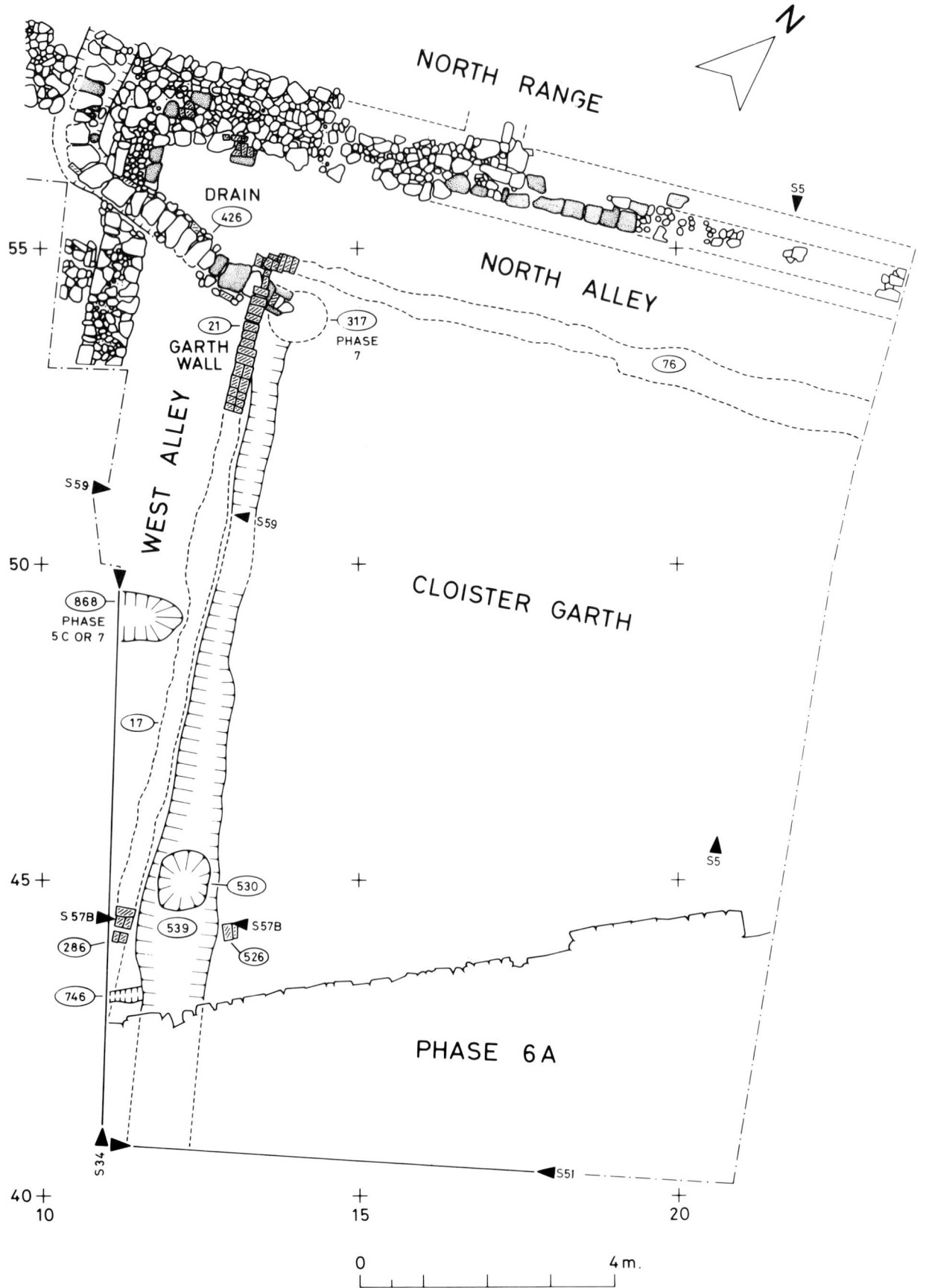

Figure 48 Phase 5C — little cloister alley, garth wall.

packed fill suggests that it was a footing for a timber or stone upright.

Pit 343 was cut through the fill of a smaller pit (2026). The latter was a shallow oval feature measuring *c.*0.40m by 0.47m and 0.17m deep. It was filled with a loose loam (2027) which incorporated brick and chalk fragments. This pit formed part of a line of features which ran north–south across this eastern half of this chamber with a single outlier to the east; they appeared to respect the central hearth setting in this room. Similar fills were recorded from all of the other pits (2021/2022, 2030/2031, 2042/2043, 2028/2029: Figure 50, S65 A–D). Most of these features were of sub-rectangular or oval form. Pit 2021 was *c.*0.48m across and 0.10m deep; 2030 was 0.60m by 0.45m and 0.14m deep; 2042 was a rectangular setting, 0.56m by 0.27m and 0.13m deep. Pit 2028 was a small round post-hole. The stratigraphic position of these pits was not recorded, but all respected the position of pre-existing features within the chamber, and may have related to works carried out at this time.

At the west end of the room a light tile footing (482) — perhaps a temporary bench position — was identified only as a robbed alignment (Plate 12). It has been ascribed to Phase 5C on the grounds of its similarity to structure 38 in the west chamber (see above). Immediately to its north lay a light brick structure (340, 341) set on top of the Phase 5B occupation horizon; this separated the north-west corner of the chamber from the rest of the room and may well have impinged on footing 482, if this continued northwards against the cross-wall. If this was indeed the case, then 340/341 would have been a later construction than footing 482. The brick was laid stretcher-fashion, without footings, so any superstructure which it supported must have been relatively insubstantial. The position of the brickwork appears to have been dictated by that of the stair and doorway giving access northwards and to the upper storey. It is thus interpreted as the base of a light screen which defined a stairwell. Its position also appears to relate to that of the doorstep in the porch (455: Figure 42); it may have been intended to screen the main part of the chamber from draughts from the north.

A new floor platform was not provided in the eastern chamber; silts accumulated directly over the earlier occupation deposits (Figure 51). The silt in the west part of the chamber (100) was very thin in places, but reached a depth of 0.07m to the north; it was not recorded at the east end of the building. A slightly different mortar-flecked silt (381) was probably confined by the brick stairwell (340, 341). No further occupation debris accumulated in the east chamber, and material which was spread about at the close of the occupation lay on the surface of the latest silts.

Later occupation (Figures 40, 48 and 52B)

Further silts accumulated in the cloister alley during Phase 5C. A uniform deposit (40) was identified along both the west alley and the west end of the north alley (Figure 52B). The central part of the latter was inadequately recorded, but at its east end a further fine silt (585) appeared to be an equivalent to layer 40. The surface levels of these deposits ranged from 6.98 to 6.93m OD, and were higher along the north alley.

To the south of the little cloister area, the Phase 5A and 5B banded chalk and gravel deposits which had been seen in section at the south-west excavation edge (Figure 40, S51) were capped by a thicker layer of soil and small rubble (885). The top of this deposit lay at 6.99m OD. This layer appeared to form a make-up deposit associated with Phase 6A.

The latest silts in the alley were sealed by a mortary rubble spread (39). This material was partially removed by machine excavation, but appears from section views to have risen to a level of at least *c.*7.12m OD. A large cut feature (593/868) in the western alley (Figure 48) was filled with loose grey-brown mortary loam (594, 869) in its upper reaches, and with brown plastic clay (850) in its base; it may have been sealed by layer 39, or possibly by the 41 construction horizon. This late-recognised feature may have introduced contamination into the finds assemblage in the west cloister alley. It was associated either with the Phase 5C works in this area, or with the Phase 7 stripping of the buildings.

The structural history of the west range has been considered above. The Phase 5A footing of the west wall of the west range had been sealed by clay 3181 (Figure 39, S50). The deposits recorded above this layer are considered to constitute a single episode of levelling following the construction work of Phase 5C.

A substantial deposit of clay (3015) was laid over 3181. Set into this clay was a heavy rubble footing for sill 3013, the west wall of the west range. It was set into a depression *c.*0.90m wide, with its base at *c.*7.00m OD. A short length of this sill was exposed, running southwards from the west end of the north range (Figure 46). Dumps of chalk gravel and cobble (3146), crushed chalk (3037), and clay (3023) were laid down against the clay bed of this sill (Figure 39, S50). These are interpreted as levelling deposits, which were perhaps capped by a floor platform. The top of the uppermost clay lay at a level of *c.*7.00–7.04m OD — comparable with the level of the Phase 5C platform deposits in the north range and to that of the deposits along the west cloister alley. Levelling apparently extended west of the wall, represented in section view by unnumbered deposits of clay and crushed chalk sealed by clay 3029 (Figure

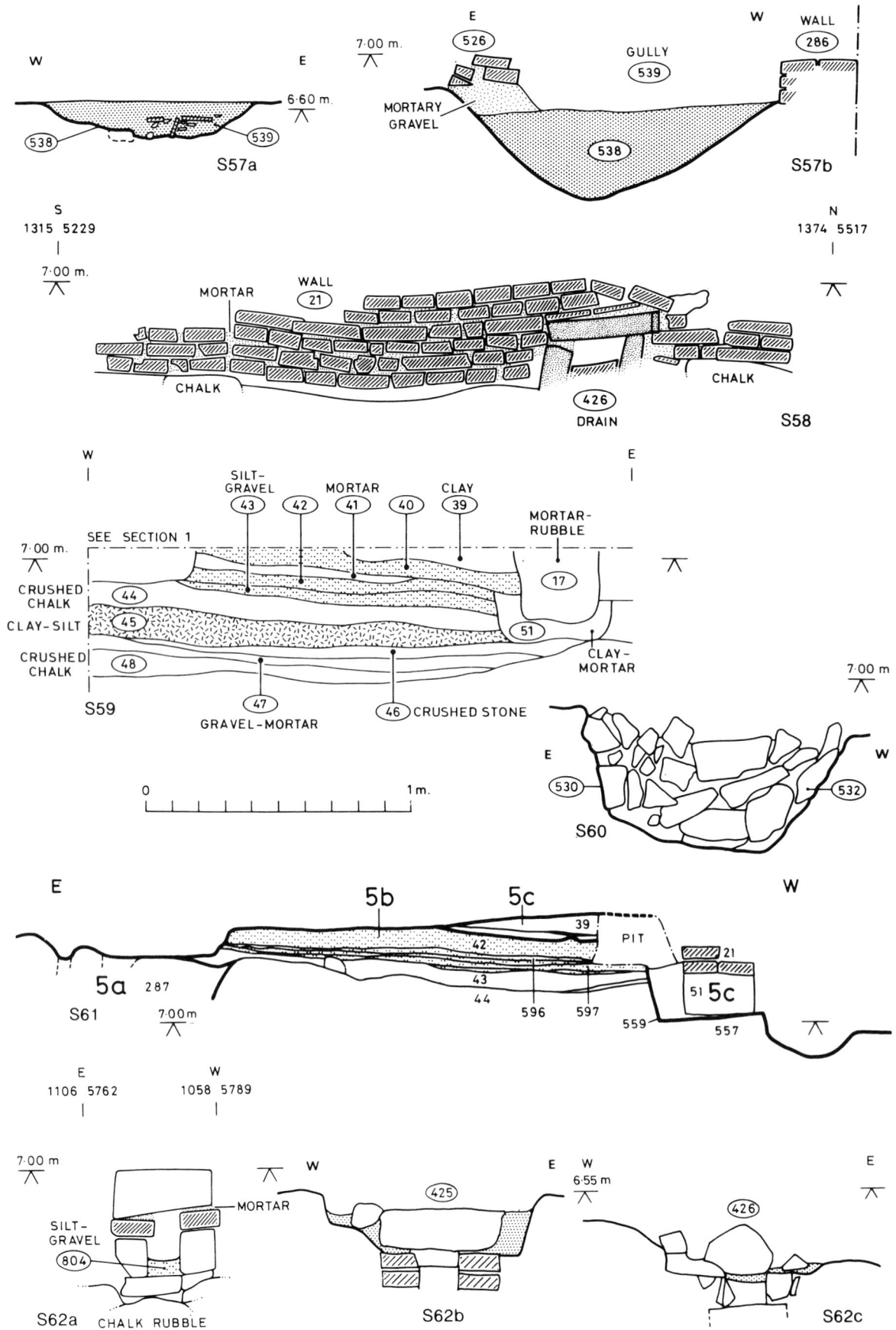

Figure 49 Phase 5C — little cloister alley; conduit, drain and wall. S57–62.

39, S50).

The internal make-up layers of the west range were cut by a large shallow feature (3003; not shown on published plans). Its function is not known, but it was recut before the end of occupation in this range. The latest occupation during Phase 5C was represented by a single thin silt layer (3280), lying at a level of *c.*7.07m OD. Further west, external activity may have been represented by the infilling (3012/3016) of cut 3027/3028 (Figure 46), which has been interpreted as a conduit alignment. This may indicate a modification to the system of water supply or drainage. The infilled feature was sealed by a layer of firm brown clay (3029).

The finds

Masonry: chimney (no. B2); base (no. B15); shaft (no. B22); floor slabs (nos. B27–8); splays (nos. B37–45); ashlar (nos. B47, B66–71, B90–112); slabs (nos. B130–57).

Brick: Type 1 (30 fragments); Type 2 (2); Type 3 (20); Type 3A (1); Type 4 (25); Type 7(1). Nos. B163,

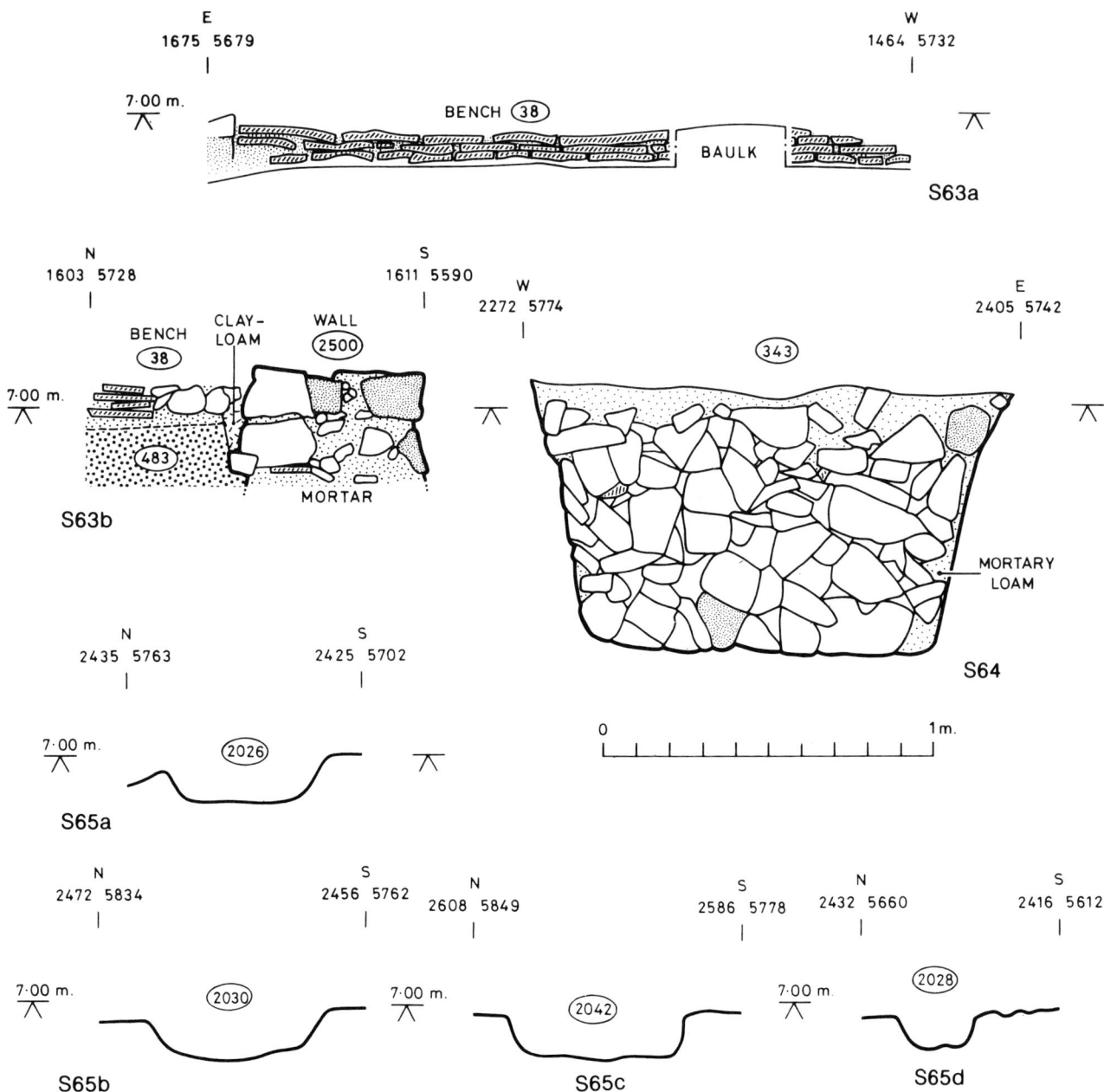

Figure 50 Phase 5C — little cloister, north range, internal features. S63–5.

B173, B177 are illustrated.

Roof Tile: Type 1A (19 fragments); Type 1B (3); Type 2B (46); Type 2C (4); Type 6 (7); Type 12B (1); Type 16 (1); and 5.916 m² of non-diagnostic roof tile. Nos. B185, B197 are illustrated.

Ridge Tile/Roof Furniture: Type 3 (1 fragment); Type 4 (5); Type 5 (1); plain ridge tile (10); decorated unglazed ridge tile (2); finial (no. B212) and hip tile (no. B227) are illustrated.

Floor Tile: Type 4 (1 fragment); Type 6 (1). No. B234 is illustrated.

Window Glass: (excludes Phase 5C/7 interface) Nos. 16–20, 23–8.

Lead: (excludes Phase 5C/7 interface) came (nos. 540, 550, 626A); sheet (no. 665); offcuts (nos. 663–4, 668, 672–4, 676, 680, 694); melt (nos. 716–17C); drypoint (no. 758).

Iron: staple (no. 782); horseshoe nail (no. 813); unidentified fragments (nos. 851, 853, 853A); 27 nails and 52 nail fragments.

Copper Alloy: ring (no. 873); buckle (no. 880); mount (no. 881); needle (no. 918); pins (nos. 926, 952); wire (no. 930).

Glass: vessel (nos. 962, 988–92); fuel/ash slag (no. 1000).

Worked Bone: tuning peg (no. 955); shell pendant (no. 960).

Coins: Hoard of five pennies struck between 1280 and 1296 (1026).

Leather: ?fragments (no. 1137).

Pottery: 77 vessels; nos. 1049–50 are illustrated.

Phase 5C — Dating evidence

The small quantity of pottery from Phase 5C included a marked residual component. Most was of 14th century date or earlier. Only in the east chamber of the north range did stratified 15th century material occur.

Mortary spreads (3093, 3103) at the west end of the north range contained fragments of residual pottery which was dated to the early-to-mid. 13th century. The platform deposits (3011, 3014, 3063) laid down at the west end of this range included fragments of three vessels, all of which could date to before 1350. Similar residual material came from platform deposits 3015 and 3037, and platform 483, 485 in the west chamber. Intense burning on the surface of silt 3010 produced an archaeomagnetic determination of AD 1330–90 at the 68% confidence level (see section 5.1, below). Demolition deposits sealing this western area contained no material later than 1400, perhaps arguing an early close to occupation in this area (see Phase 7, below).

The foundation trench for drain 426 contained two sherds of Humber 1 of 14th or 15th century type (fill 436/555). A sherd of Humberware from 555 joined to one from an overlying silt layer (349). The layer also produced a group of five coins which were corroded together (no. 1026), and was found adjacent to the course of the drain. These coins were probably

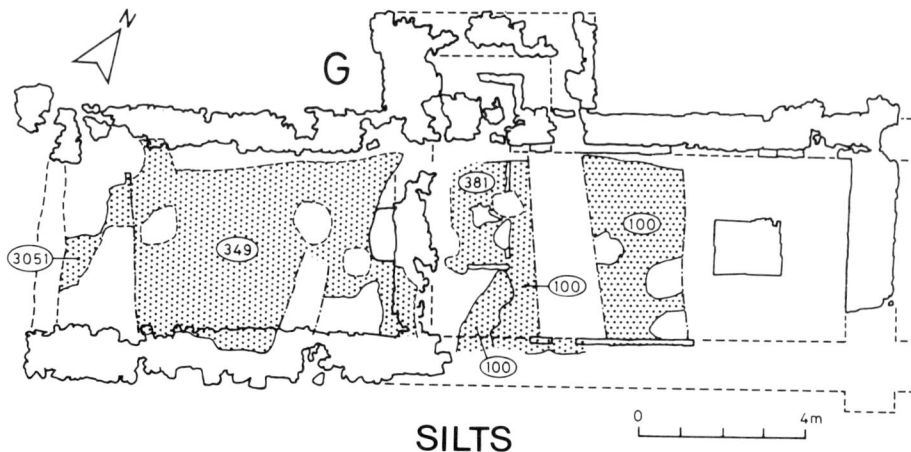

Figure 51 Phase 5C — little cloister, north range, later occupation.

deposited in the early 14th century and must have been disturbed during work on the construction of the drain. The later date of the latter was confirmed by its stratigraphic position: it post-dated the backfill (539) of a robbed conduit (538) which itself had produced 14th century pottery together with numerous roof tiles.

Later pottery was recovered from the floor of the east chamber of the north range. Low Countries Redware, a Humber 5 bowl fragment and a Cistercian ware cup (dated to after 1480) all came from this area. These wares may have been associated with the continuing use of this chamber in the later 15th and early 16th century. Archaeomagnetic assay of the hearths in this chamber produced a determination of AD 1400–1450 as a possible date for its last use (at a 68% confidence level: hearth 2011). A further jetton from the east chamber (no. 1027) was found in a Phase 7 context, and may have been residual from Phase 5C; it was probably deposited no later than 1450.

The archaeological record suggests that Phase 5C in the little cloister may have been near-contemporary with Phase 6A — the construction of a large north range alongside the great cloister. A joining sherd between a Phase 5C floor platform (485) and a putative Phase 6A construction trench fill (721) may tend to support this suggestion.

Suggested date: later 14th century with limited occupation activity continuing through the 15th century.

Phase 6. The great cloister. Later 14th century to 16th century

Phase 6A. The great cloister, north range. Later 14th century onward

Introduction (Figures 2, 23 and 53)

The rebuilding of the north range of the great cloister was contemporary with the Phase 5C works in the little cloister. It followed the construction (Phase 5A) and modification (Phase 5B), of the little cloister, and also some of the piecemeal works on the great cloister, such as Phase 4B. The original form of this building is

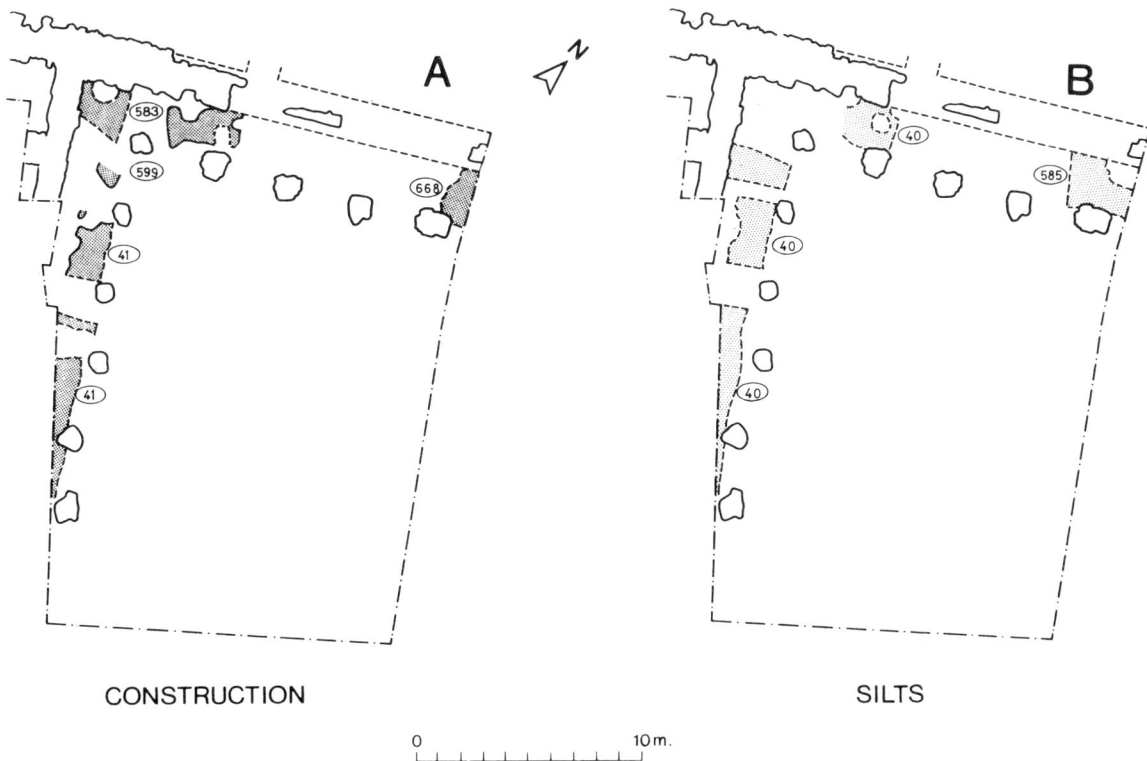

CONSTRUCTION

SILTS

0   10 m.

Figure 52 Phase 5C — little cloister alley, occupation.

considered above, as Phase 4A of the great cloister north range (see above, and Figure 23).

The new north range was built to the north of its Phase 4A predecessor, but reutilised the north wall of the earlier building (566) as the south wall of the new range (Figure 53; cf. also Figure 23). Once again, this range was sited across the alley between the great and the little cloisters, and abutted the Phase 4B west range of the great cloister. The new north range had an internal width of *c.*7.30m (Figure 53). Crushed chalk and gravel alley surfaces (886–90) were revealed in the excavation edge to the south of its north wall footing (24) at a maximum level of *c.*6.87m OD (Figure 40, S51). They were closely similar in character, level and position to the surfaces along the alley of the little cloister (see above). The superstructure of the new building was built from *c.*0.23m above the uppermost alley level.

The footings (Figures 53–6)

A chalk-packed foundation was constructed to carry the new building (Figure 53). A complete section was obtained across the north wall footing (24) within the main excavation area (Figure 54, S66), whilst part of the west footing (911) was exposed to a depth of *c.*0.75m close to its junction with the north wall (Figure 55, S69). These two sections suggested that slightly different construction techniques were adopted in the two wall footings.

The north wall footing (24) had an original depth of *c.*1.60m, though the upper part of it had been robbed to between 6.75 and 6.45m OD. The footing was *c.*2.15m wide, and was trench-built (Figure 54, S66), cutting through surfaces of Phases 3, 5A and 5B. No reliable cut for its construction trench was identified, though a series of discontinuous and ambiguous features (95/96, 106, 997/998, 1057/1058, 721/722) might have been part of such a trench (Figure 54, S67–68).

The lowest part of this footing consisted of irregular blocks of chalk of up to 0.40m scantling. A layer of smaller pieces was laid on top of these, and capped with rubble of intermediate size. The north side of the footing was then built up with roughly coursed slabs, some of which were sparsely tooled. Its centre section and south side were levelled up with additional rubble. At other points along the footing the larger blocks of chalk were laid flat-surface up.

At the west end of the excavated area particularly large blocks were used in this footing; a sub-rectangular hollow appeared to mark where the course of a conduit (539) had been carried across the line of the foundation (Figure 53). The robbed course of the north part of this conduit was identified in the little cloister (see Figure 48); the late insertion (884) of a trench-built conduit was also noted to the south of footing 24 (Figure 56, S72). This sides of this later conduit were set on clay, and it was part-filled with a fine silt (883). It could simply have functioned as a drainage channel for the removal of ground water. Alternatively, it may once have held water pipes which have been subsequently removed — in which case the silt would have accumulated after the removal of the pipes.

Towards the eastern limit of the excavation foundation 24 projected *c.*0.30m northward for a distance of *c.*2.75m (Figure 53). This offset was an integral feature of the upper part of the footing, and suggested an initial identification of the new north range as a refectory, equipped with a wall pulpit. (This interpretation is discussed below: Chapter 6.)

The upper part of the west wall footing (911) was *c.*1.80m wide at its lowest recorded point, narrowing to 1.56m where the wall rested on it (Figure 55, S69–70). The foundation here was faced with roughly coursed chalk slabs on both sides. This appeared to have been built as a free-standing structure, probably within a wide trench. Within the building the foundation was overlapped by successive dumps of clay (974, 971, 947, 956) and gravel (972–3). The lowest level reached by excavation here was a thick deposit of crushed chalk (975), which may mark a construction horizon: its top lay at *c.*6.36m OD. The external face of the footing was overlapped by dumps of clay (984, 933–4), and soils with a marked presence of building debris (931–2). Layers of dark mixed clay (306, 307, 309, 310, 762) had been recorded within the building in the east excavation edge, together with a mortary deposit (308), but later robbing had obscured their relationship to the north wall foundation (Figure 55, S71). Other deposits of clay (762, 891) should probably be taken as having fulfilled a similar purpose — i.e. raising the level within the building.

The walls (Figure 53)

The walls resting on these foundations survived for a single course at the west end of the building, as walls 911 and 910 (Figure 53). These walls were uniformly 1.13m wide, and were built from a level of *c.*6.97–7.02m OD. Both sides were lined with large roughly faced limestone blocks which retained wall-cores of small chalk rubble set in an orange mortar matrix. The limestone used for wall 911 was yellowish in colour, and was probably an oolitic limestone of indifferent quality. The junction of the walls was marked by an external clasping buttress (912). Its core was similar to that of the adjoining walls; however, the masonry was a lighter, more finely worked limestone which bore claw-tooling. It was possibly built with reused blocks of Magnesian Limestone.

The west wall (911) ran south to a butt-joint with the north-west corner of the great cloister (917/919).

N
1474 4351

S
1492 4108

6·50 m.

ROBBER TRENCH 95

24

S66

N
1750 4445

S
1754 4359

6·50 m.

CUT HORIZON
UNCERTAIN

95

FOUNDATION
24

S67

S

GROUND LEVEL 1986

N

22

CLAY–LOAM

20

15

95

CLAY–LOAM

6·50 m.

24

FOUNDATION

GARTH CLAY–SILT

65

106

SANDY SILT

S68

0   1 m.

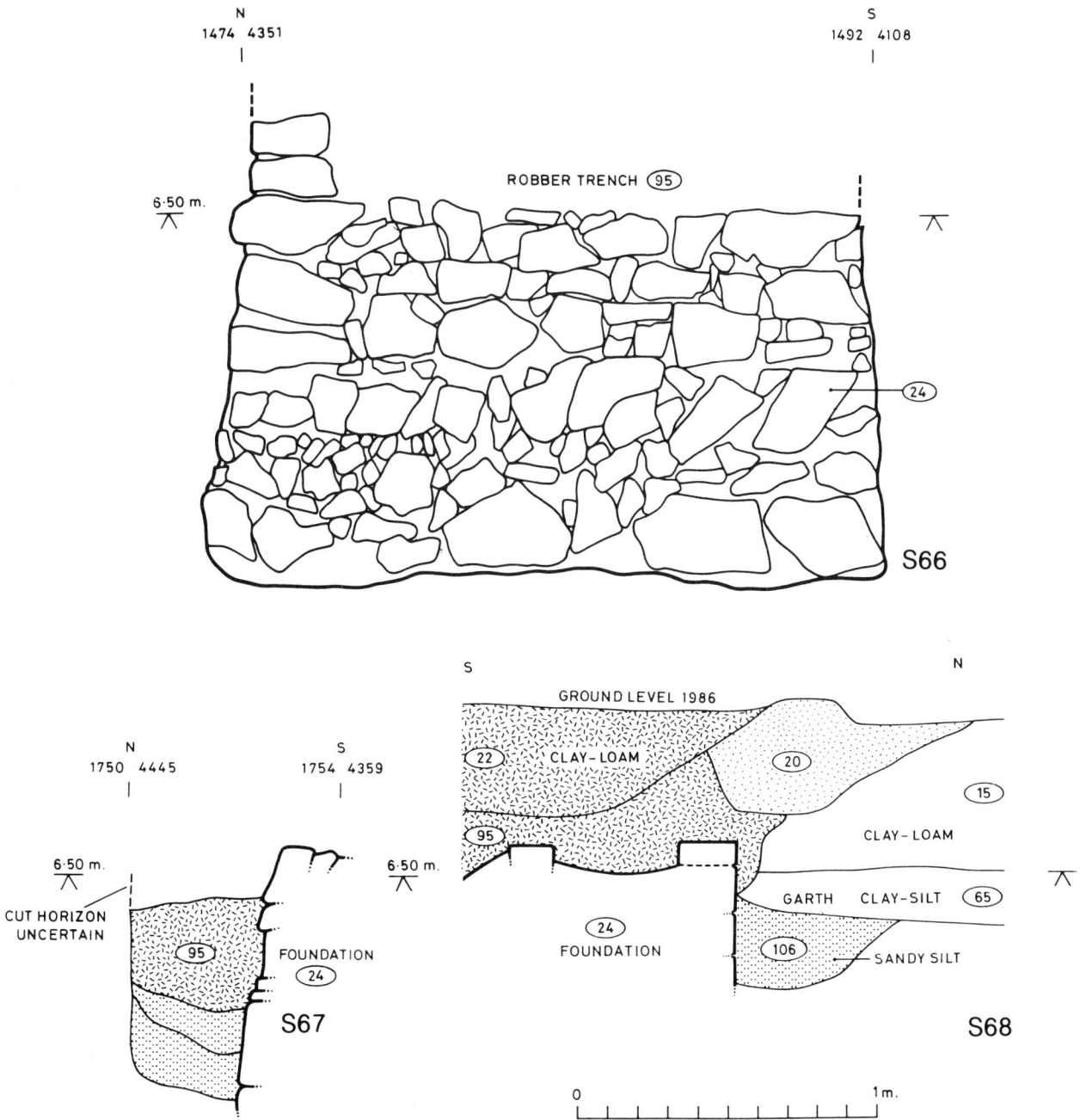

Figure 54 Phase 6A — the footings of the north wall. S66–8.

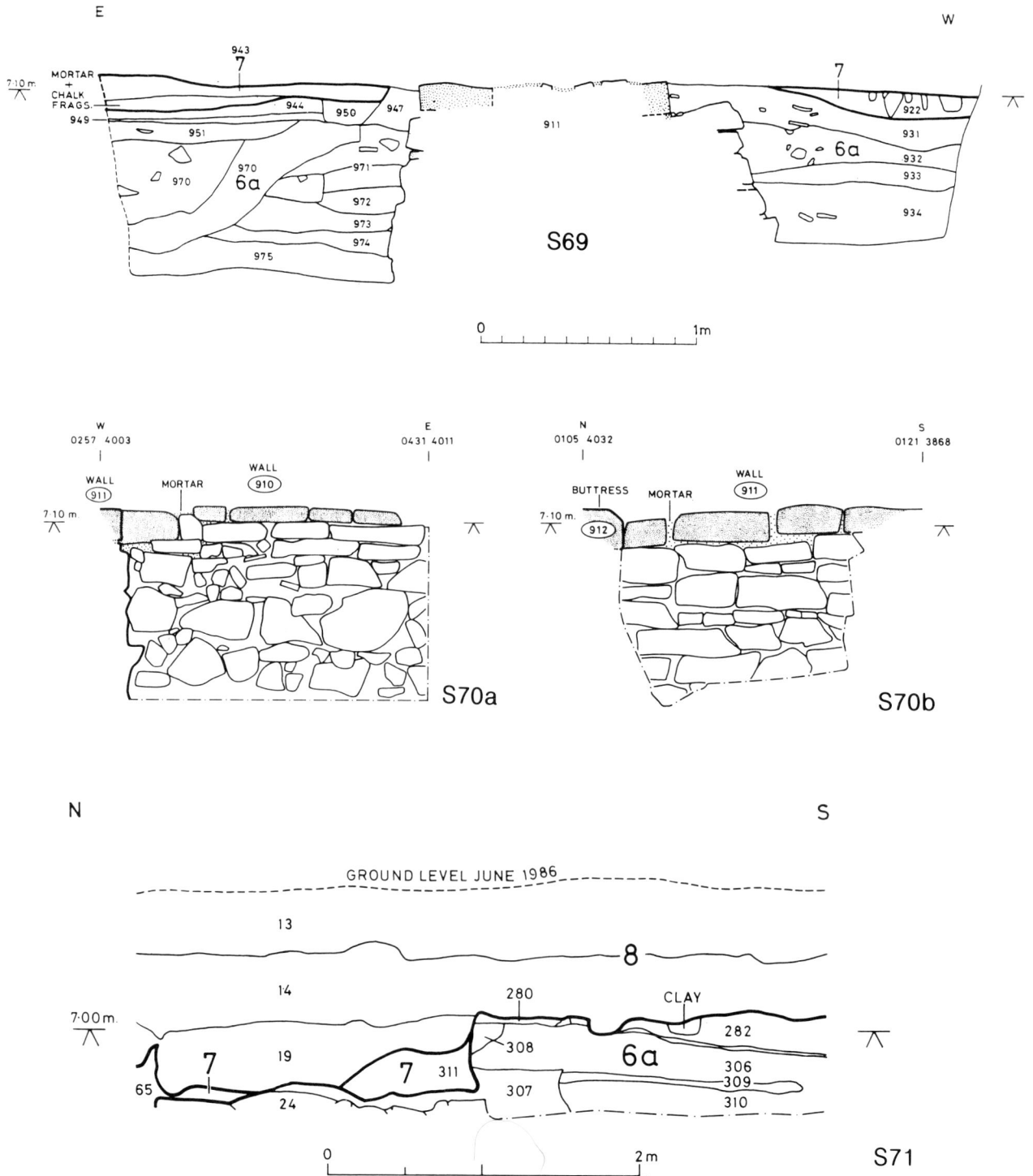

Figure 55 Phase 6A — the footings of the west wall. S69–71.

This junction was further marked by a setting of chalk blocks and rubble (915) which appeared to be the southern jamb of a doorway set into wall 911; the south face of 915 was set flush against wall 917. A surface of buff mortar (921) with tile fragments set flat into its top extended *c*.1.00m north of 915, indicating a possible paved threshold. A similar patch of light mortar with tile (913) occurred immediately to the north, at the midpoint of wall 911: here, the mortar spread was limited at its northern and southern ends by post-settings which were filled with post-medieval material; these defined a doorway or bay *c*.1.70m wide. Both of these putative thresholds had been disturbed by modern footings, so their identification must remain uncertain. Later disturbance has also removed any evidence for the relationship between these possible entrances.

Although no stone wall survived in the main excavation area, a spread of crushed yellow limestone (723) along the south edge of footing 24 may have marked its construction horizon (Figure 53). This occurred at a level of *c*.6.98m OD — about the same level from which the west wall was built. Similar crushed stone also appeared in gravel (682) immediately to the south of 723.

The internal features and occupation (Figures 53 and 55–6)

A light wall (677) was set on a mortar spread (282) on top of the construction horizon for the north wall of the building (clay 306: Figure 55, S71). This wall was faced on its south side by a single brick which remained *in situ*, and retained a core of small chalk rubble (Figure 53). This structure was set parallel to footing 24, *c*.0.30m to its south. If the dimensions of the actual north wall on top of this footing were similar to walls 910 and 911, this would have left a space of *c*.1.00m wide between wall 677 and the main wall of the building. This may have defined a passage, or, more likely, it indicates the position of a bench or other internal fitting, which did not continue up to the west end of the building. It was respected by the internal floor surface to the south (Figure 53).

Occupation within the building was represented by thin spreads of silt over clay floors (Figure 55, S69; 56, S73). Two occupation horizons were identified on the north side of the building (951, 725; 280, 949), but no clear continuation of the floor silts was recorded across the centre of the range (Figure 53). A single horizon of floor silt material (569) was identified on the south side of the building; the place of this material in the occupation is uncertain.

The first occupation horizon on the north side of the building was marked by floor silts (951) at the north-west corner (Figure 55, S69), and 725 against the south side of the internal wall 677 (Figure 56, S72). This occupation appears to have ended with the

insertion or repair of conduit 881, which ran from north to south through the west end of the building. The conduit construction trench (884) was backfilled with a layered clay and mortary rubble packing (878–80) and covered with mortar (877).

The second occupation phase began with the laying of a clay platform (280) along the northern side of the range (Figures 55–6, S71–2); this sealed the conduit (Figure 56, S72). The continuing significance of wall 677 is suggested by the straight edge of platform 280, which was apparently limited by the further eastward extent of the wall. Later layers did not, however, respect this alignment. A sub-rectangular mortar spread (279) formed a regular intrusion into the platform; a patch of later floor silt 278 also sealed its southern edge. These surfaces may, therefore, have post-dated its removal. In the north-west corner of the building a second clay floor (949) was covered by a silt which included much fishbone (944*: Figure 55, S69).

On the south side of the range, a soft floor-silt type material (569) overlapped the chamfer-course of the south wall (566). This material was cut by a gully which appeared to run parallel to wall 566 (Figure 53). The gully was 1.30m wide and 0.40m deep, and was filled with a loose mixture of sand, mortar and gravel (568: Figure 56, S73). This was sealed by a clay-loam mix (571) which, at the time of excavation, was taken to be at a similar horizon to early occupation silt 725 on the north side of the building (see above). However, the place of silt 569 and gully 761 in the occupation of the building remains in doubt: they may relate to an early occupation phase, to internal features, or even to an otherwise unrecorded structure.

The finds

Masonry: ?floor slab (no. B30); ashlar (nos. B72–3).
Brick: Type 1 (2 fragments).
Roof Tile: Type 1A (4 fragments); Type 2B (13); Type 6 (5); Type 12B (2); Type 15A (1); and 2.077 metres of non-diagnostic roof tile.
Ridge Tile/Roof Furniture: Type 4 (6 fragments); plain ridge tile (4); decorated unglazed ridge tile (2); unclassified glazed tile (4). Ridge tile B221 is illustrated.
Window Glass: nos. 29–30.
Lead: came (no. 552); offcuts (no. 702); melt (no. 718); patch (no. 767).
Iron: horseshoe (no. 811); unidentified fragment (no. 854); 6 nails and 31 nail fragments.
Copper Alloy: lace end (no. 887); chain (no. 889); rivet (no. 911); pin (no. 923); sheet fragments (nos. 941, 943).
Glass: vessel (no. 963); bead (no. 996).
Worked Bone: bead (no. 957); Romano-British toggle (no. 958).
Leather: heel (no. 1136).
Pottery: 63 vessels.

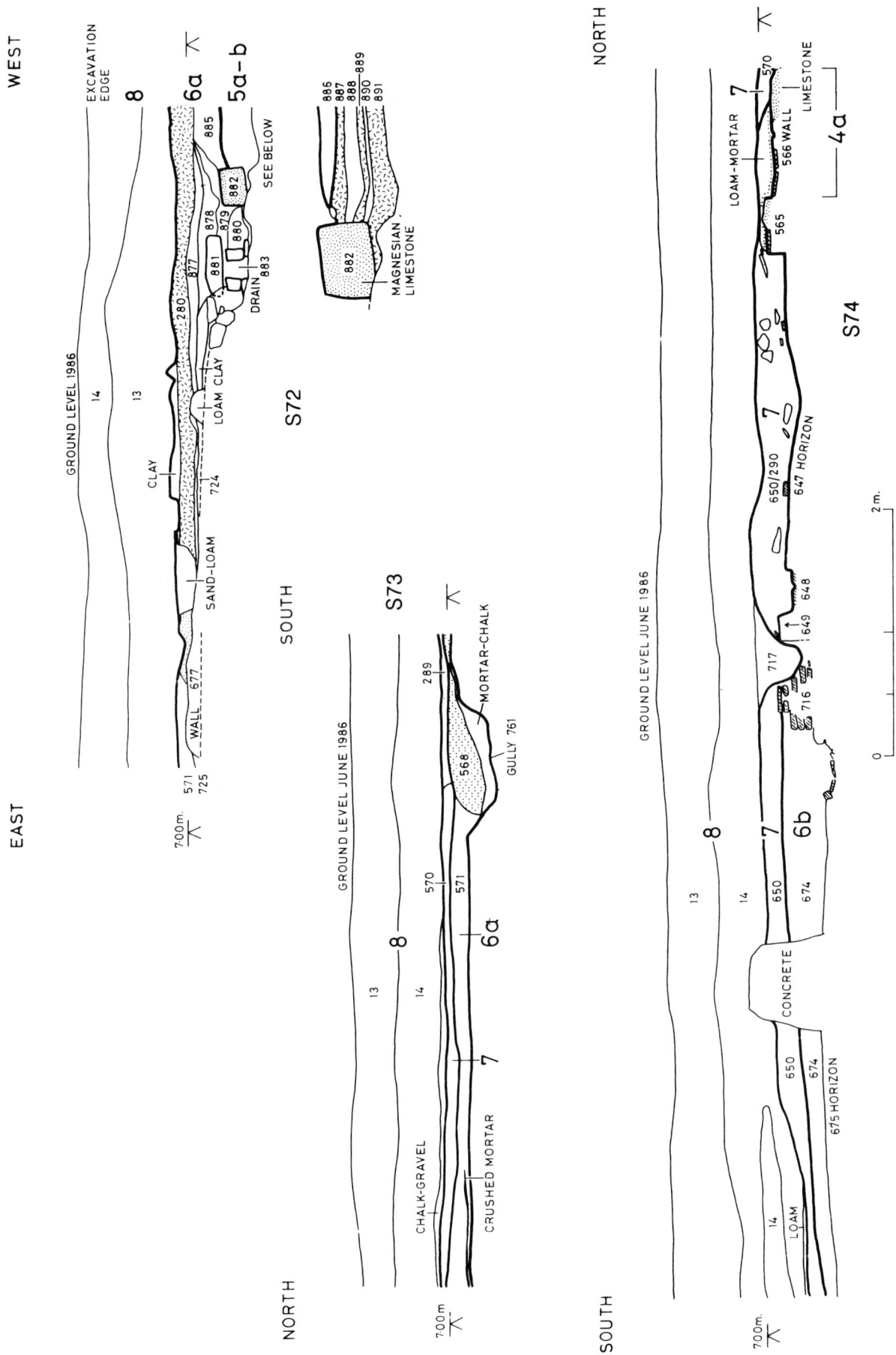

Figure 56 Phases 6A–7 — great cloister, north range and alley. S72–4.

Phase 6A — Dating evidence

Material associated with the construction of the Phase 6A structure included a large residual component, which probably resulted from the cutting of deep foundation trenches and the raising of the ground level by dumps of soil. Little, if any, of the material need be later than the 14th century.

The footing for the building contained a range of material, the latest of which was a sherd of a Humber 1 jug. Ambiguous features, some of which may relate to the construction of the footing, included Beverley wares, notably a pottery lamp (no. 1051) from Context 721; a bowl from the same context was linked by joining sherds to the little cloister Phase 5C floor platform (485). A levelling deposit within the Phase 6A building (956) included Beverley wares types 2B and 2C and Humberwares Types 1 and 3.

Of the layers lying against the outside of the footings, upper clay 934 included a sherd of Humber 5. Other, lower, dumps (931, 932) contained fragments of eleven vessels; five of these are Humberwares, and another four are vessels in Beverley ware type 2C. A similar combination of Beverley wares and Humberwares occurred in internal construction layer 282. Of all of these vessels, only the Humber 5 sherd is clearly later than 1400, whilst much of this material would be consistent with a date in the first half of the 14th century.

The first occupation of the west end of the building was represented by silt 951; the pottery from this layer consisted mostly of Beverley ware type 2C jugs, with no Humberwares. Such a group is likely to be earlier than 1350. It was sealed by a new clay floor platform (280), the material for which was clearly brought onto the site, as it incorporated residual material, including a Romano-British toggle (no. 958); a secondary silt layer (279) contained 14th century pottery.

The gully immediately to the north of the Phase 4A north range was sealed by layer 571, whose datable components could be regarded as of earlier 14th century date. It contained fragments of three Beverley ware types 2B and 2C jugs. The significance of this gully is, as indicated above, unknown.

Suggested date: second half of 14th century onwards.

Phase 6B. The great cloister. Later 14th century onward

North alley and garth (Figure 23)

The substantial footing (727) which suuported the south or median wall of the Phase 4A north range, later served as the foundation for a light wall 649 (see above, Figure 23;Plate 2). The south face of 649 was formed of limestone ashlar, whilst the north, or inner, face consisted of rough limestone slabs. This wall was less than 0.52m thick and did not have the rubble core which was associated with the more substantial structures on the site. Its construction is considered as the first event in Phase 6B. It maintained a division between the great cloister alley and the garth.

Set against the south side of this wall was a buttress (716: Figure 23) built of brick. The junction had been disrupted by later robbing, but both buttress and wall were set on a footing which rose *c.*0.15m above footing 727 (Figure 56, S74). This appears to indicate the re-building of a Phase 4A wall in a lighter form. Both the buttress and footing were overlapped by a fine loam which represented the later garth soil (674: Figure 56, S74). The spread of the latter also sealed a layer of compacted chalk and limestone (675), which was recorded only at the extreme south end of the trench (*ibid.*, and Figure 23), over a soft chalk-flecked brown clay 676. This may indicate that a surface or structure lay centrally within the garth; this has not been otherwise investigated

The surface dipped gently, within the alley defined by walls 566 and 649 (Figure 23). On either side of the alley, settings of flat-laid roof tile (565, 648) were built against the walls: these settings were possibly rendered on their outer (or visible) faces. On the north side of the alley the tile edging (565) terminated against a half-hexagonal respond (567); on the south side, edging 648 butted against projections from wall 649. Between these tile settings a floor silt (647) covered the alley surface.

The reconstruction of the south wall of the range in a lighter form may show the transition of a free-standing building over the great cloister alley into a pentice-roofed structure appended to the south side of the new north range.

The finds

Brick: Type 1 (2 fragments).
Roof Tile: Type 1A (4 fragments); Type 1B (1); Type 2B (3); Type 6 (1); and 0.24 m² of non-diagnostic roof tile.
Floor Tile: Type 1 (1 fragment). No. B228 is illustrated.
Window Glass: Nos. 31–2, 34–5.
Copper Alloy: Sheet (no. 936).
Glass: vessel (no. 964).
Pottery: 3 vessels.

Phase 6B — Dating evidence

The only context from Phase 6B of the north range to bear any datable finds was the fine loamy garth soil (674) from the great cloister. This overlaid the re-built wall which divided the alley from the garth, and incorporated a sparse mixture of residual pottery and glass. This phase of construction may have been contemporary with Phase 6A, but there are no direct stratigraphic or ceramic links to prove this.

Phase 7. Early 16th century

Introduction

The end of the Priory occupation was marked by a mortary demolition horizon in most parts of the site. Limited finds evidence and documentary history suggest that this be associated with either the Dissolution of the house, or perhaps with the state of dilapidation attested for the Beverley Dominican Priory before 1524–5 (see the Documentary Evidence in Chapter 1).

In the great cloister the demolition horizon covered the latest surfaces, and overlapped the structures of Phase 6B. In the little cloister area mortary demolition spreads covered some, but not all, of the surfaces within the excavated structures, suggesting that the character of the works at the close of occupation was variable. Three lead-burning hearths were identified, associated with spreads of broken glass and window-came. These, and other evidence, may show the stripping of fixtures from the buildings. A thick deposit of material within the cloister garth may have dated to the close of occupation, but was laid down before the robbing of building materials was completed.

The great cloister — demolition (Figures 27, 55 and 56)

Demolition deposits which were spread across both the Phase 6A north range and the great cloister, were identified in a trench to the south of the main area excavated in 1986–7 (Figure 53).

Within the refectory the deposit of a fine gritty clay (570) was shown (Figure 56, S73–4) to have post-dated the demolition of the south wall of the range (556). This layer of clay included a large number of very small tile fragments, but nothing larger: this could suggest that a floor of timber or some other obstruction prevented the deposition of heavier debris. Its identification as a demolition deposit rests upon its overlapping a mortar spread (289) which sealed the south wall of the refectory (566, 567). A lens of clay (288) appears to have formed part of this 570 horizon: it lay immediately to the north of the wall. (In this its position reflected that of the Phase 6A platform 280 — see above).

A more extensive spread of crushed chalk, mortar, gravel, and a little brick and tile (290, 650) extended across the great cloister alley and the great cloister garth (Figure 56, S74). The absence of this material over the interior of the Phase 6A refectory suggests either that the superstructure of the building was dismantled from the outside, or that robbed materials were cast southwards. This layer reached a maximum depth of *c.*0.35m in the great cloister alley. It followed the southward slope of the Phase 6B cloister garth towards the centre, and was capped by a thin spread of loam and charcoal.

The demolition horizon lay both inside (943) and outside (914, 922) the refectory at its west end (Figure 55, S69). Spreads of mortar (1084, 1116) were also identified within the chambers of the west claustral range, though these were subjected to minimal archaeological investigation as they lay outside the area threatened by development.

Although the latrine building to the north-west of the great cloister (Figure 25) was not fully excavated, the fills of its ditch or conduit were emptied along the trench which investigated this feature (Figure 27, S31: layers 1091–4). They were of a sandy or gravelly character which suggested that water had continued to pass through this conduit despite its partial infilling. This had left a remarkably clean series of gritty soils, with the finer particles washed out. A layer of coarse sand (1094*) was overlain by a mixture of sand and rubble (1093*), which in turn was sealed by a fine sand (1092*), capped by a layer of grit (1091). All of these layers appeared to post-date the use of the *reredorter*.

The little cloister: lead-burning (Figures 57–9; Plates 13–16)

The fuller excavation of the little cloister area provided correspondingly more complete evidence for the process of stripping of materials from the claustral buildings (Figure 57). The total demolition of the latter did not take place at this time: some walls were to be robbed after the Dissolution (see Phase 8, below).

Numerous pits which had been dug within the north range post-dated the final occupation of the buildings, but had been infilled before the deposition of layers associated with the abandonment of the building. The purpose of this activity is uncertain. The construction and use of three bowl-hearths (109, 753, 579) were contemporary with these pits: the former appear to have been related to the stripping and melting down of lead from the building — a process which left scatters of broken glass and smaller amounts of lead (both window-came and solidified molten fragments) (Figure 57; Figure 58, S75–7). These bowl-hearths were placed with regard to the existing ventilation of the rooms, and must, therefore, have been in use while the superstructure of the building still stood. They were sealed by demolition or disuse horizons (59, 99). The position and treatment of the hearths may also indicate that the building was stripped chamber by chamber.

A single hearth (109) was built in the east chamber (Figure 57; Plate 13). A circular pit, set near the middle of the room, was lined with Type 3 bricks:

these had been used on this site only for the Phase 5C works, mostly within this chamber. A further course of bricks formed the base of the hearth, and the structure was then used for lead-burning: some of this lead had seeped between the bricks, and solidified as a sheet (Figure 58, S75). A very dense scatter of glass and came fragments accumulated between the western screen walls (340/341: Figure 46) and the north and west walls of the chamber (Plate 16). This area has been interpreted above as a stairwell. The restricted area of the scatter (Figure 57) indicates that alignment 340/341 was still an effective barrier to its spread. If the interpretation of this as a stairwell is accepted, it could argue that the glass originated from a chamber or chambers on the first floor of the range. On the conclusion of works in the eastern chamber, the bowl-hearth was plugged with clay (344) which sealed a layer of ash and charcoal.

The western chamber was perhaps next to be dealt with. Here, a small bowl-hearth (753) only *c.*0.35m across was cut into the pre-existing fireplace at the eastern end of the room (347: Plate 14; Figure 58, S76). Glass from this chamber was recovered mainly from the demolition horizon which sealed the hearth, so it is uncertain whether this hearth was used for melting down window-lead or other fixtures. Its small size may indicate that it was used to melt window-came rather than larger pieces of pipe or sheet. At its disuse, the lead droplets, fine ash and charcoal (752) of the last firing were sealed with a clay plug (751), in a similar fashion to the hearth in the other chamber.

A second bowl-hearth (579) was set into the south-west doorway of the west chamber; this position clearly indicates that this entrance was no longer in use (Plate 15; Figure 58, S77), and it was inserted after the partial demolition of the adjacent wall (684/685). It was a more substantial hearth than the other two, being *c.*0.70m across. It saw heavy use, with its sides (534) being patched at least once; an operation which sealed a laminate of white ash between red-burnt clays. Perhaps significantly, at its disuse this hearth was left filled with ash (152), but (unlike the other hearths) it was not plugged. This may show that precautions against fire were now unnecessary. The hearth was close to a robbing pit (64/317) at the south end of drain 426 (Figure 57), and may have been used to deal with lead from its piping or guttering. Another possible role for this feature is indicated by glass fragments which were concentrated in a demolition layer (59) between this hearth and the stairwell in the next room (Figure 57).

A series of sub-rectangular pits was dug in both chambers of the north range (Figure 57; Figure 59, S79 A–D). In the eastern chamber the more substantial pits (500, 520, 2015, 2023, 2035) were cut into the bench footings. As this brickwork had not

otherwise been robbed, this activity may have related to the dismantling of timber fittings — perhaps to fuel the hearths. Pits 520 and 500 appeared to mark the west terminal of the south bench; they were backfilled with distinctively orange-stained loams which incorporated fragments of bricks of Types 3 and 4. Three pits were cut into the north bench footing towards its east end (Figure 57). One of these (2035) appeared to have marked the bench end, while two more *c.*2.00m to the west (2023, 2015) may show the removal of uprights. These later pits were backfilled with loam, and bricks of Type 7; the period of use of such bricks at the Priory has not been established, so a later date for these pits remains possible.

A further, shallow, cut (441) at the western end of the room included fragments of glass within its clay fill 443 (Figure 57; Figure 59, S79F). This scoop was only 0.07m deep, but it was positioned to interrupt the brick structure (340) which has been interpreted as the footing defining a stairwell. Here, too, a light timber member may have been removed. In addition to the robbing pits which have been described above, two further small cut features remain to be mentioned (Figure 57): 2044 was a small square feature in the south-eastern corner of the chamber, whilst 513 was a slightly larger cut to the north of hearth 109. The first may once have held a post, but it is not clear to what this would have related; the function of the second feature is equally unclear. Both were filled with small rubble and loam (512, 2045: Figure 59, S79G).

Other robbing (Figures 57 and 59)

In the western chamber a pair of pits (421, 469) was dug along its centre line: these lay *c.*1.44m and *c.*1.20m south of the north wall (Figure 57; Figure 59, S80 A–B). Pit 421 was 0.23m and 469 0.45m deep; both were filled with loam and rubble (427, 470). Another pair of shallow scoops (467, 464) lay close to the north-west corner of the chamber (Figure 57); these were filled with loose loams (468, 466: Figure 59, S80 C–D).

The spine wall which separated the east and west chambers was robbed, and the trench (453) filled with rubble. This robbing left a spread of mortar, rubble and tile (59) across the floor of the west chamber: this, in turn, may indicate that the debris from the spine wall was cast westwards. The eastward spreading of 59 was limited to the north-west corner of the east chamber, perhaps by the presence of the stairwell. The rest of this chamber was covered by dark loams (99, 2001) which contained mortar, brick and tile: finds from layer 2001 indicate a later date in Phase 8 for that context, at least. Further robbing of the structure at the east end of the room appeared to post-date the spreading of layer 99. The removal of the 59/99 deposits at the south door of the east chamber, perhaps by wear through pedestrian traffic, suggested that the shell of the east chamber survived this activity, and that the doorway continued in use.

At the west end of the building there was limited evidence for robbing of the south wall of the north range (Figure 57): here, a short trench (3001) was filled with mortary rubble (3002), whilst a loose grey loam covered the area. It is uncertain whether the sill of the west wall was robbed at this time, or at a later date. In general, the finds evidence from the backfill of the robber trenches suggested that the final demolition of the remaining parts of the little cloister took place in the 17th or early 18th century (see Phase 8, below).

Garth soils (Figures 5 and 28)

Within the garth of the little cloister a spread of clay, loam and rubble (15) was taken to mark the close of occupation; its extent was contiguous with that of an underlying layer (65: Figure 28). Layer 15 was truncated by machine excavation, but was recorded up to a level of 6.89m OD (Figure 5, S1). The nature of 15 was at first uncertain, as it appeared to have been cut by trenches robbing the garth walls (18, 76: Figure 48). The occurrence of window came, rubble, and late pottery in this deposit links context 15 to the Phase 7 activity. The similarity in character of finds from layer 15 to those from context 65 below may argue that it

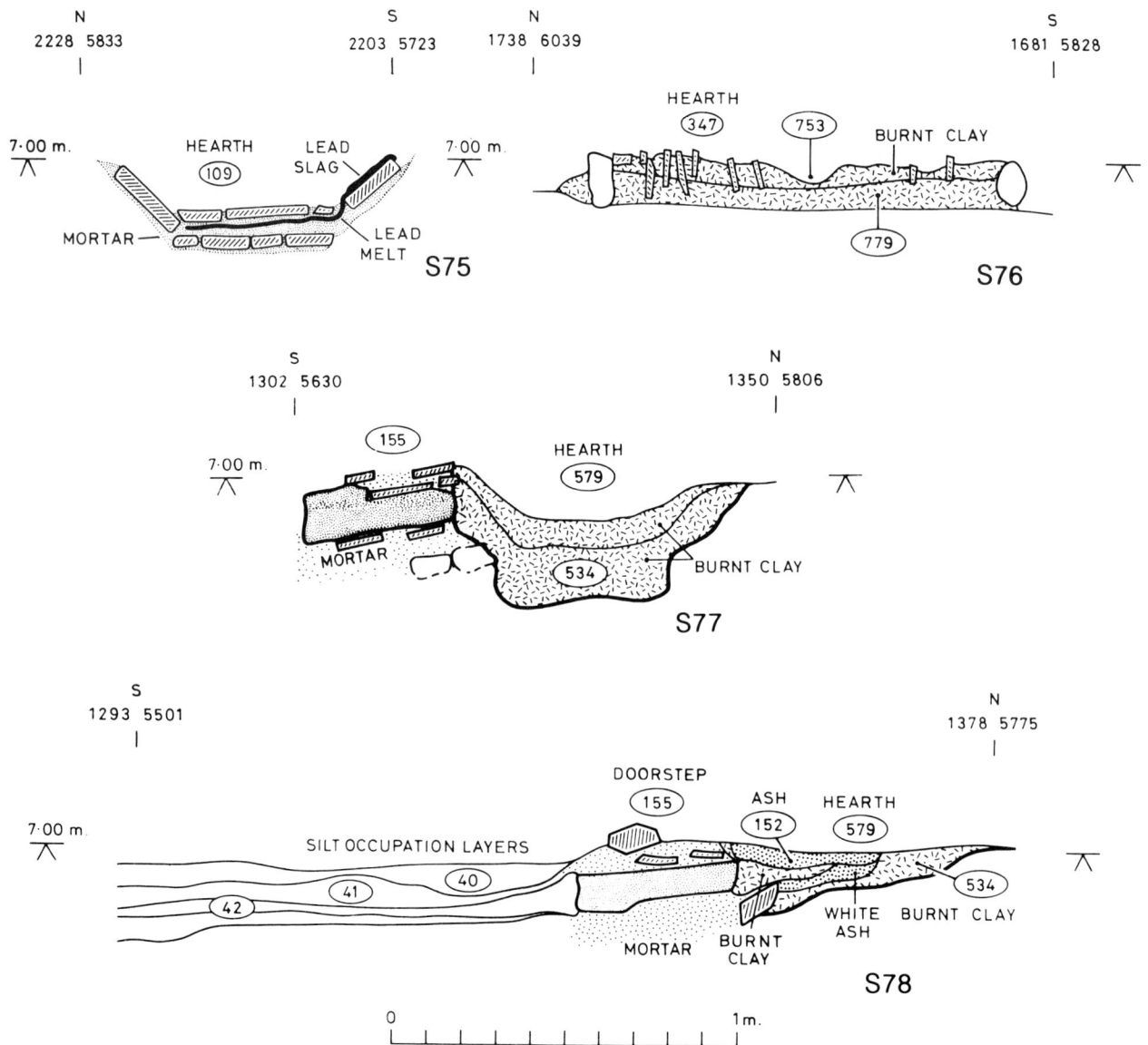

Figure 58 Phase 7 — little cloister — stripping. S75–8.

incorporates material derived from the Phase 5C occupation of the claustral ranges, cleared out at the close of occupation.

Some subdivision of layer 15 was attempted during its rapid excavation. Its upper levels included dense spreads of broken roof tile (62, 142) and a large shallow loam-filled pit, 304. The roof tile (142) was recorded at a level of *c.*6.90m OD. A lower element (16) was speculatively identified during the machine clearance of the site: this was held to have been a finer soil, but was not distinguished during subsequent excavation by hand.

The finds

Masonry: chimney (no. B3); tracery (nos. B4–5); ?plinth (no. B8); shafts (nos. B17, B23); floor slab (no. B29); ashlar (nos. B74–5, B113–18); slabs (nos. B158–62).

Brick: Type 1(59 fragments); Type 2 (8); Type 3 (131); Type 3A (4); Type 4 (54); Type 7 (6). Numbers B165–7, B171–2, B178 and B180 are illustrated.

Roof Tile: Type 1A (82 fragments); Type 1B (23); Type 2B (115); Type 2C (6); Type 3(1); Type 6 (13); Type 7 (8); Type 12B (1); Type 15A (17); Type 15B (2); and 19.518 m² of non-diagnostic roof tile. Numbers B183–4, B186, B188, B191, B195 are illustrated.

Ridge Tile/Roof Furniture: Type 2 (1 fragment); Type 3 (2); Type 4 (20); Type 5 (6); plain ridge tile (30); decorated unglazed ridge tile (8); unclassified glazed tile (2). Finial (no. B215), ventilator (no. B218), ridge tile (no. B225) and hip tile (no. B226) are illustrated.

Floor Tile: Type 1(1 fragment); Type 2 (2); Type 3 (1); Type 4 (1); Type 5A (1); Type 7 (1). Numbers B230–1 and B235 are illustrated.

Window Glass (includes 5C/7 interface): nos. 37–527.

Lead (includes 5C/7 interface): came (nos. 553–79, 582–625, 627–41); flashing: (nos. 645–6); sheet and offcuts (nos. 667, 680–700); melt (nos. 719–54); drypoint (no. 759); filter (no. 768); ?counter (no. 770).

Iron: file (no. 772); wedge (no. 773); knives (nos. 778–9); wall anchor (no. 784); hinge (no. 786); strip (no. 793); nails (nos. 797–8; stud 800); horseshoe nail (no. 814); bridle bit (no. 816); unidentified fragments (nos. 859–60, 863); 77 nails and 140 nail fragments.

Copper Alloy: buckles (nos. 878–9); button (no. 885); lace ends (nos. 888–9); book clasp (no. 893); skillet (no. 908); needles (nos. 916–17); pins (nos. 922, 924, 927); wire (no. 929); binding (no. 932); staple (no. 933); strip (no. 934); sheet fragments (nos. 944–6, 950).

Glass: vessels (nos. 965–6, 969, 972, 993) bottle seal (?intrusive) (no. 999).

Worked Bone: fragment (no. 959).

Worked Stone: hone (no. 1008); mould (no. 1018).

Coins: Charles VII *double-tournois*, 1422–1436 (no. 1027); two Nuremberg and one Tournai jettons, early 16th century (nos. 1028–1030).

Leather: upper (no. 1138); ?offcut (no. 1139); belt fragment (no. 1141).

Pottery: 162 vessels; nos. 1052–69 are illustrated.

Phase 7 — dating evidence

The great cloister

The deposits in the great cloister area provided a few diagnostic sherds to date the demolition activity in this area. Soil 570 within the area of the refectory contained a fragment of a Cistercian ware cup of probable 16th century date, and certainly later than 1480. The demolition material (650) which post-dated the abandonment of the alley and the demolition of the refectory also included a Raeren stoneware mug of late 15th or early 16th century type. Demolition spreads west of the refectory incorporated a Humber 1 jug, which could date from any time between the 14th and 16th centuries. A corroded Tournai jetton (no. 1030), of perhaps *c.*1500, was recovered from a demolition spread over the west claustral range (layer 1084).

Fill 1093 of the latrine conduit contained a group of 21 vessels which should be dated to the late 15th or early 16th century. This included two Cistercian ware cups, two Langerwehe stoneware jugs, a Low Countries Redware pipkin, a Humber 5 jar, fragments of seven Humber 1 jugs and a urinal, and a late York White/Hambledon-type ware salt: had such an assemblage been found on any of the Hull sites, then a date before *c.*1525 would have been suggested (see Watkins 1993). The overlying context (1092) contained a smaller group of similar material, together with a sherd from a Raeren stoneware drinking mug.

The little cloister

Little pottery was found in association with the Phase 7 stripping of the north range, and what little was present was mainly residual. The spread of mortary material in the west chamber (59) which was associated with the robbing of the internal spine wall included six vessels: Raeren stoneware, Cistercian ware, Humberware type 1, Humberware type 5, one residual and one unclassified vessel. The group was associated with an early 16th century Nuremberg jetton (no. 1029), and is consistent with this date. Jettons from the east chamber of the north range included a French *double tournois* of 1422–36 (no. 1027), possibly residual from the occupation during Phase 5C, and two Nuremberg jettons (nos. 1029, 1031) of mid. 15th and early 16th century type; their date of deposition is uncertain. The pottery from the east chamber (layer 99) was similar to that from context 59 in the western chamber (see above). Most of the pottery from the pits dug within the range was residual.

Context 15 in the little cloister garth provided the second largest group of pottery from the site: 59 vessels. It contained similar proportions of sherds per

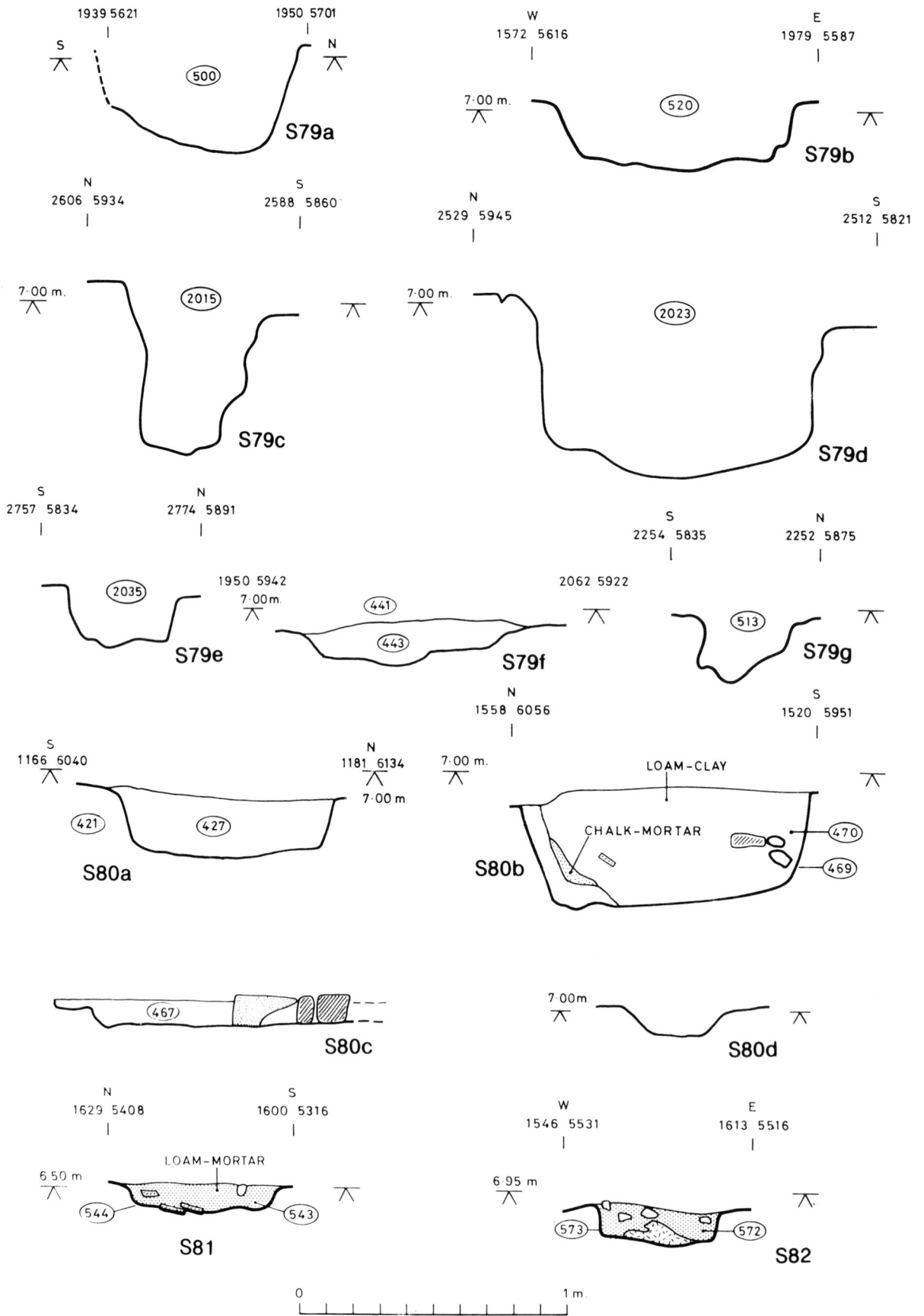

Figure 59 Phase 7 — pits. S79–82.

vessel and residual material as the underlying layer (65). A number of vessels were of 15th century type, but there was also a sherd of a Frechen/Cologne Bellarmine which might date to the second quarter of the 16th century, or later. Most of the rest gives the appearance of a group datable to the first quarter of the 16th century. The later spreads of material at the upper levels of layer 15 contained material of similar date: pit 303 contained fragments of six vessels, including Humber 1, Langerwehe stoneware, Cistercian ware and Low Countries Redware.

Suggested date: *c.*1500–39.

Phase 8. 17th or early 18th century

Introduction

Phase 8 embraced all the activity which took place on the site from the end of mendicant occupation, up to the time of the archaeological investigation in 1986–7. The evidence for the constraint of activity during Phase 7 by the partial survival of structures has been discussed above.

The final removal of the walls of the little cloister was carried out thoroughly and rapidly — most of the available stone being robbed. The depredations which were made upon the north wall of the great cloister refectory were unusually extensive, extending to the upper part of its chalk footing. This may suggest that even unworked chalk was required by the robbers, either for the footings of a new building, or perhaps to be burnt for lime.

The north-west area of the little cloister saw the continued erection and occupation of structures. It is not known whether these were sited with deliberate reference to any surviving elements of the medieval fabric. Even if the latter had been completely removed, it is still possible that the raising of the ground level throughout the occupation of the Priory had created a parcel of dry ground.

By the 19th century the greater part of the precinct was occupied by gardens or orchards (cf. Armstrong and Tomlinson 1987, fig. 29). The medieval outline of the Black Friars' holding became partly fossilised in the surrounding street plan and in the partial survival of its wall, while only the late medieval or early post-medieval 'Old Friary' building survived to mark the position of a small part of the formerly extensive complex of buildings. Some of the garden boundaries show an approximate, though not an exact, relationship to their medieval precursors within the precinct. Lines of drainage may have continued to follow some ancient routes, though these were to be supplemented by various culverts with little discernible relationship to early features. Neither the overall routing of these later features, nor their relationship to earlier schemes of water management

is understood.

Numerous pits may relate to the planting of trees or shrubs, though some, particularly at the west end of the area excavated in 1986–7, cannot be ascribed to any particular sub-phase of post-medieval activity. The dark tilled soils were themselves to be sealed by rubble rafts, and the stone, concrete, and brick footings associated with the industrial activity which spread over the site from the north; this culminated with the completion of the Armstrong Patents factory in the first half of the 1960s. This factory was itself cleared in the 1980s, causing considerable damage to the underlying deposits, particularly to the west of the Priory precinct.

Stone robbing (Figures 36 and 54–6)

A series of robber trenches dug along the alignments of the medieval footings resulted in the removal of nearly all the superstructure of the little cloister. The trenches (125, 131, 2067, 3116/3119) which robbed the north range were dug from a level of *c.*7.10m OD; little build-up of material had occurred between Phase 7 and this episode in Phase 8. The trenches were backfilled with mortary loams (55, 58, 121, 471, 2068, 3117, 3120): the loose consistency of the fills and the clear definition of the actual trenches show that the infilling followed rapidly upon the removal of the stone (Figure 36 and S43). A similar episode of robbing (293), followed by backfilling (292), took place along the east wall of the west range. The robbing of the spine wall within the north range has been considered to have been an earlier episode, during Phase 7, but dumps of clay (157), rubble (158) and loam (300) were also spread across this footing.

The robbing of the footings of the north range of the great cloister was not executed in the same thorough and consistent manner. This took place from an uncertain level of between *c.*7.20m and *c.*7.00m OD. along the north wall. A wide shallow trench (25, 277) extended southwards from the little cloister garth, and removed the upper part of the chalk footing. This trench was backfilled with small chalk fragments and loam (19, 22), and with mortar and tile (20: Figure 54, S68; Figure 55, S71). The west wall of the refectory, in contrast, was left with its first course and the footings completely untouched. The partial removal of the superstructure of this building southwards has been considered above as an aspect of the Phase 7 demolition work. There was, however, a further episode of limited disturbance of internal features along its north wall (284); these were backfilled rapidly (283). A trench (718) was also dug along the junction of the Phase 6B garth wall (649: see Figure 23) and the brick-built buttress which had supported it (716: Figure 56, S74). As this trench post-dated the spreads which were associated with the dismantling of the building, it cannot have been intended to jeopardise the latter's structural integrity, and must have had some other object. This robbing took place from a level of *c.*7.08m OD.

Post-medieval buildings (Figure 60)

The limited evidence for the continuation of occupation in the little cloister area was concentrated around the north-west part of the north range (Figure 60). The excavation here was rendered difficult by the contamination of soils with industrial solvents; in consequence, much of the later deposits which might otherwise have cast light on this activity were removed by machine without being recognised. Moreover, the recording of this area, in failing to recognise structural divisions, did not provide a clear and coherent picture of the later activity. The following description indicates such evidence as was recorded here.

The earliest activity to post-date the Priory occupation was represented by successive clay platform deposits (3142, 3140), whose uppermost surface lay at *c.*7.09m OD, a little higher than the last activity to be recorded at the west end of the north range. They were seen only in the west excavation edge (Figure 60, S83). On top of this platform accumulated a loose black silt (3058). This was sealed by a further platform (3141) which lay at *c.*7.19m OD. Close at hand, but with no stratigraphic link to it, was a spread of crushed chalk (3059) with further silting (3139: Figure 60, S83) over it to indicate that this, too, had served as a floor. Both platform 3141 and the chalk and silt sequence (3059, 3139) were sealed by another spread of reddish clay (3057), which related to two structural elements, both of which lay on a north–south axis (Figure 60). The easternmost of these structures was a narrow run of mortared chalk and limestone (3056), which possibly incorporated re-used materials. This was set above clay 3141. Lying *c.*2.40m to the west was a stretch of light brick walling (3060) which was also aligned north–south. To the east, but without any recorded stratigraphic link to either of the other structures, was a floor or path of brick-on-edge (3067) which was aligned north-east to south-west. This was furnished with a central gutter (3098) which drained from south to north. Silts 3110* and 3066* had accumulated over this surface. A pit (3054) filled with loose rusty material (3055*) was cut through the brick floor, perhaps suggesting some light-industrial activity. The overlapping of these structures with the west end of the north range — an area of distinct usage throughout the occupation of the little cloister — may hint at some continuing use of the area: it was the only such evidence to be encountered in the little cloister.

Post-medieval gardens (Figure 60)

Dark loams which are considered to have been cultivated garden soils covered most of the excavated area to depths of *c.*0.35 to 0.40m (2, 3, 12, 14, 2041, 137). The survival of medieval deposits beneath these soils may argue that this material had been imported at some stage to allow the agricultural or horticultural use of the area: however, as the tilling of these soils continued into the 19th century, it has not been possible to establish when this cultivation began. Some of the pits and other intrusions which were cut into the stratified deposits (particularly those which were filled with similar dark loams), should probably be associated with the planting of trees and shrubs. Pits (not illustrated) 128, 130, 150, 446, 480, 504–6, 508, 510, 521, 833, 2015, 3018, 3061, 3071, 3081, 3086 have been ascribed to such activity, though the position of contexts 3018–86 should be regarded as less certain. Their fills were respectively 127, 129, 149, 447, 503, 507, 509, 581, 2016, 3024, 3062, 3072, 3082 and 3086.

Two east–west brick walls in Trench 1 (4, 5: not illustrated) should probably be equated with property boundaries depicted on the 1854 Ordnance Survey map. So too should chalk footings (79, 80) which ran across Trench 3, just to the north of the robbed wall of the north range (Figure 60). Although these footings supported an unequivocally post-medieval brick wall, it is interesting to note the persistence of a boundary so close to the northern limit of the little cloister. This may betray the division between those areas of the precinct which were occupied by buildings and those areas which were recorded in the Dissolution survey as meadow, garden or garth (cf. Armstrong and Tomlinson 1987, fig. 27). A wall line running on the same east-west alignment, and recorded where it joined the precinct wall, had lain only a little to the north (see Trench 2: the western precinct boundary, above). It is therefore possible that later land use and division payed some slight respect to that which had obtained within the Priory during its occupation.

The finds

Masonry: moulding (no. B13).
Brick: Type 1 (14 fragments); Type 3 (8); Type 3A (1); Type 4 (6); Type 7 (2).
Roof Tile: Type 1A (9 fragments); Type 1B (8); Type 2B (13); Type 2C (1); Type 6 (1); and 1.895 m² of non-diagnostic roof tile.
Floor Tile: Type 2 (2 fragments); Type 3 (1); Type 5A (3); Type 5B (2). Numbers B229 and B232–3 are illustrated.
Window Glass: nos. 528–37, 538A.
Lead: came (nos. 580, 642–3); sheet (no. 701); offcuts (nos. 703–6); weights (nos. 764–5).
Iron: knife (no. 867); unidentified fragments (nos. 868–9); 5 nails and 3 nail fragments.
Copper Alloy: buckles (nos. 875, 877); harness boss (no. 890); strip (no. 895); spoon (no. 909); offcut (no. 919); ring (no. 935); sheet fragment (no. 947); ?stylus (no. 951).

N

3067

3056

BRICK

MACHINE
EXCAVATED

3054

65

3098 GUTTER

CHALK RUBBLE

80

79

3060

S83

60

3005

15

0   4 m.

55
10

S
0827 6411

7·30 m.

N
0877 6534

3060

3057

3141

3139

3059

3058

3142

3140

S83

0   1 m.

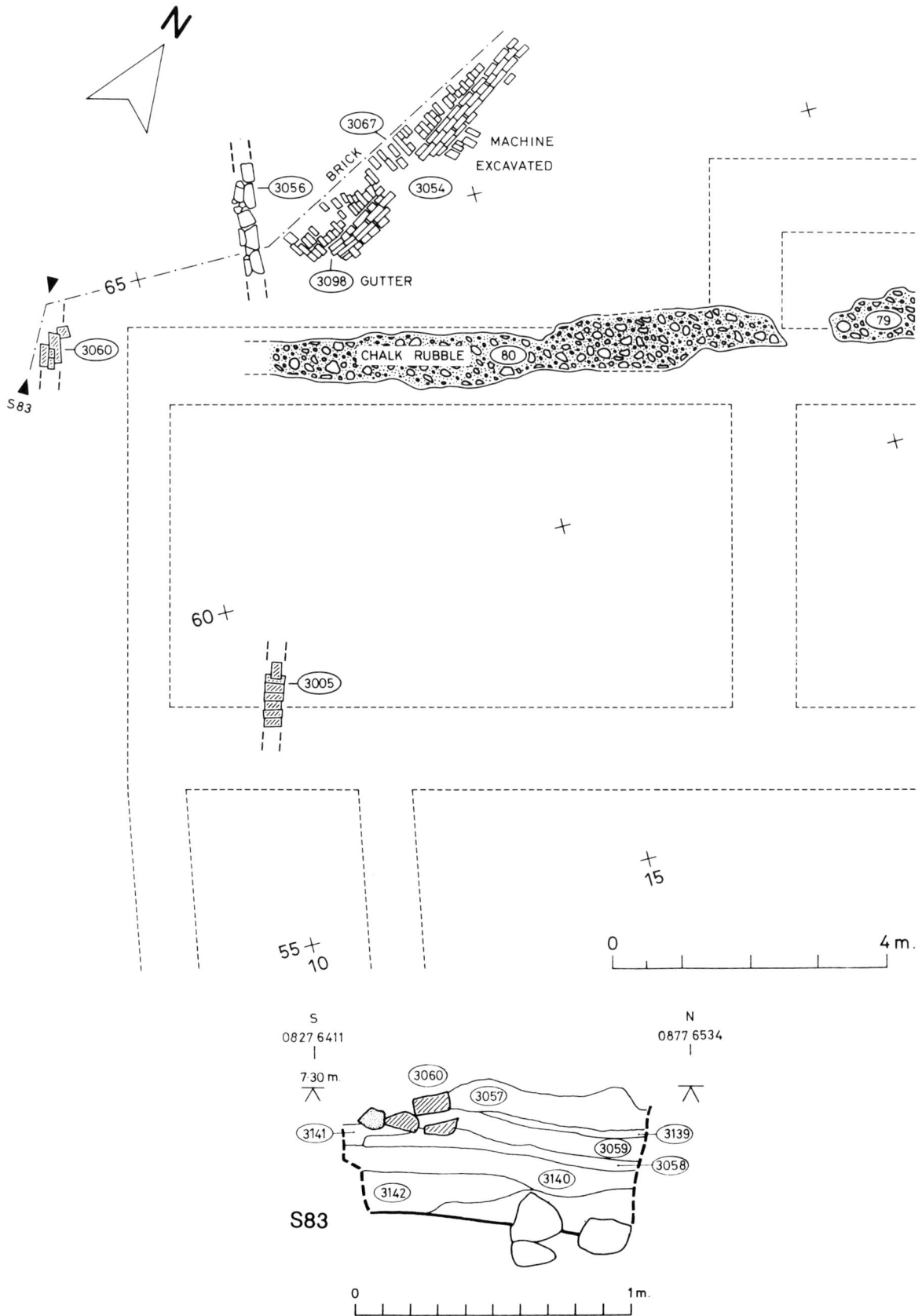

Figure 60 Phase 8 — post-medieval activity. S83.

Glass: vessels (nos. 967–8, 970–1, 973–9); fragments (nos. 994–5).

Coin: Nuremberg jetton mid. 15th century (no. 1031).

Pottery: 17 vessels; no. 1070 is illustrated.

Phase 8 — dating evidence

Pottery was found in the backfill of trenches in the little cloister area contexts (55, 471 and 2068). The material here was very mixed, ranging from 11th century wares to probably intrusive 19th century sherds. The latest material — disregarding the most modern — consisted of two Brown Glazed Coarseware pancheons from 55; these are likely to be 18th century in date. Similar pottery came from context 19, one of the fills of the robber trench over the refectory footings. Glass fragments from sack bottles (nos. 968–71) also suggest a 17th or early 18th century date for the final robbing.

No datable pottery was reported from the post-medieval features to the north of the little cloister. An assortment of residual pottery was present here, and also in the planting pits which intruded into the site. The garden soils which sealed the site included a little Romano-British material, though as these were imported soils they can have no relevance to the Priory area.

3. The Finds

3.1 Introduction

The finds from the 1986–9 excavations are presented in two major groupings. First are those materials whose primary use was as structural elements. The prefix 'B' for 'building materials' has been appended to the catalogues of the masonry, brick, and tile (sections 3.2 – 3.4).

The 'small finds' reports begin with the consideration of window glass and lead (sections 3.5 and 3.6) — materials whose principal importance was in furnishing the Priory buildings. The ironwork (3.7) follows, as it includes a variety of objects with uses in the fabric of the buildings. The other finds are considered to relate more closely to the occupation and use of these buildings. The coins and pottery, the major dating evidence for the site, fall towards the end of the report (sections 3.15 and 3.16). Waterlogged wood and leather, in the main from the deep Trench 2 excavation, are dealt with at the end of the report (sections 3.17 and 3.18): much of this material relates to the secular occupation on Eastgate, and very little of it was associated with activity within the Priory precinct.

Catalogues of building materials, other finds and pottery have been summarised, some in tabular form, for main text presentation. Fuller entries appear in the microfiche section of the report (Mf. sheets 1and 2); where detailed information about the provenance of objects is not given in the letterpress section, it occurs in fiche. A simple list of finds from each phase is also included in the relevant parts of the excavation report (see Chapter 2, above). Specialist technological analyses are presented in fiche (Mf.3), though the significance of the results is discussed in main text.

Discussion of the excavated finds includes consideration of the contexts from which they derive. Priority has been attached to the understanding of the objects in their setting, and to any evidence which the finds may offer for the interpretation of the site as a whole; however, a recurrent problem of any deeply stratified site is the residuality of early material in later contexts. Where high residuality or intrusion has been suspected, the reader's attention is drawn to the likelihood of objects being part of a mixed assemblage.

Summary of the excavation

The following brief description of the results of the 1986–9 excavations is presented to place the phasing of objects into proper context. The fuller discussion of the archaeology falls in the main excavation text, while the dating presented here is drawn principally from the evidence of excavated coins and pottery.

The Priory was founded between 1220 and 1240. Documentary evidence has indicated that building works were in progress in *c*.1263 and *c*.1449. The recorded number of friars appears, from the limited evidence of seven royal grants of food, to have peaked in *c*.1310, when 42 friars were present. The number had apparently fallen to 30 in 1335, and to 14 by the late 15th century; in national terms, the Priory was of average size. The house was surrendered to the Crown in 1539, when its precinct was surveyed.

Phase 1

The earliest activity on the site consisted of the digging and filling of pits: charcoal, grain and burnt clay were prominent in some of these features. These pits should be taken to indicate the proximity of settlement. This activity is undated, but is sealed by deposits of 12th-century date.

Phase 2

The Phase 1 activity was sealed by substantial deposits of silty loam. This activity represents landfill or some agricultural exploitation of the area. The suggested date for Phase 2 spans the 12th to early 13th centuries.

Phase 3

Phase 3 comprised evidence for timber buildings, considered to form early elements of the Priory.

Phase 3A was a structure aligned with the Priory church, but lying beyond the cloister on its north side. The building is considered to have been a hall of ground-sill construction. It is dated to the mid. 13th century.

Phase 3B marked the rebuilding of the ground-sill hall as an aisled building. It is dated to the last quarter of the 13th century.

Phase 3C comprised the latest occupation evidence within the aisled hall. A date in the late 13th century is suggested.

Phase 3D represented activity in the area of the aisled hall post-dating its occupation. An interpretation of this activity as gardening has been considered. Phase 3D is suggested to span the late 13th to early 14th centuries.

Phase 4

Phase 4 related to parts of the church and the great cloister, which were constructed after the 13th-century foundation of the house. Detached features (such as a latrine block and a cistern) and the east end of the church, are considered within Phase 4 because of their functional association with the great cloister layout. It should be noted that the earlier Phase 4 works were probably contemporary with Phase 3, and that later Phase 4 activity may have been contemporary with Phase 5. The designation of a separate phase is dictated by the topographical separation of the great cloister from the main area of archaeological investigation.

Phase 4A consisted of the evidence for earlier structures set about the quadrangular great cloister. These have been identified on the north and west sides of the cloister.

Phase 4B included evidence for the extension or rebuilding of the great cloister north range.

Phase 4C represented the continuation of works on the west range. This may have followed immediately upon Phase 4B. Little meaningful dating evidence can be presented for Phase 4, as its excavation was, in the main, non-destructive.

Phase 5

Phase 5 encompassed the construction and occupation of the little cloister, to the north of the great cloister and over or around the position of the Phase 3 timber halls. Phase 5 is divided into sub-phases, save for the important exception of context 65. This material lay in the little cloister garth, and appears to have included residual debris from the occupation of the timber halls. It may have remained open through Phases 5A, 5B and at least the start of Phase 5C. Over this period (the better part of the 14th century) small quantities of debris from the occupation of the surrounding ranges may have accumulated here. Alternatively, the evidence of the pottery may suggest its closer correlation with Phase 5C, or its deposition in a single episode.

Phase 5A included the construction of the two ranges and alley of the little cloister and their early occupation. The construction work probably began in the first quarter of the 14th century.

Phase 5B comprised structural modification of the cloister alley and north range: the latter included the shifting of doors and the movement of its west wall. Suggested date: mid. 14th century.

Phase 5C included the re-roofing of the cloister alley, the modification of drains and conduits, and further work on the ranges. Phase 5C is considered as broadly contemporary with Phase 6A, the construction of a refectory on the north side of the great cloister. The suggested date for the Phase 5C construction works is the later 14th century; limited activity continued into the 15th century.

Phase 6

Phase 6A was probably broadly contemporary with Phase 5C. It consisted of extensive soil movements to make up ground, and the construction of a range on the north side of the great cloister to replace the original north range. Two phases of occupation have been recorded in the ground floor of this building. Suggested date: later 14th century onwards.

Phase 6B consisted of the rebuilding of a wall between the great cloister alley and its garth. This may have followed directly on Phase 6A. No dating evidence was available for Phase 6B.

Phase 7

Phase 7 marked the close of occupation across the site, probably to be related to the 1539 Dissolution of the house. Intense activity within the north range of the little cloister involved the stripping and melting down of fixtures, and the partial robbing of structural elements. Dated to the early to mid 16th century.

Phase 8

Phase 8 included all the events between the end of the monastic occupation and the present day. Robbing of stonework was probably most extensive in the 17th or early 18th century. Limited post-medieval activity in the area was sealed by the deposition of garden soil, which was probably imported to the site; this in its turn was covered by a factory built in the 1960s.

Trench 2

The excavation of Trench 2 was not stratigraphically tied to the main excavation: its contexts probably span Phases 2 to 5. The finds from this area are more likely to relate to the occupation of Eastgate than to the Priory.

3.2 The masonry

by Martin Foreman

*with comments and architectural identifications by Dr. Glyn Coppack
and geological identifications by Dr. Martyn Pedley*

Introduction

Masonry was recorded from various contexts ranging from primary to secondary use, and finally in demolition debris. Some of the masonry had clearly been imported onto this site from other locations for reuse. This practice was noted during the investigation of the Priory church, where the source was almost certainly the Minster, following the rebuilding after *c.*1220 (cf. Armstrong and Tomlinson 1987, 54). Reuse of masonry was a prominent feature of structural activity at the Priory, as elsewhere in Beverley.

Materials

Inspection of samples of ashlar has shown that a variety of materials was used. The most common, and most readily available locally, was chalk. This saw use for interior walling, as slabs for walling or sill-walling, possibly also as floor slabs, and as rubble filling for foundation trenches and pits. The utility of chalk was limited by its fragility when exposed to weathering, and it appears to have been used externally only when partially sheltered, plastered or otherwise protected — or perhaps occasionally in response to the poverty of the house. The Dominican Church at Cambridge was, unusually, faced externally with clunch (Stubbings 1969, 101). The extensive use of chalk footings has been noted in contexts spanning the 13th to the 15th centuries in Beverley at Lurk Lane (Armstrong *et al.* 1991, 33–51) Eastgate (Evans and Tomlinson 1992), and at the Priory itself (Armstrong and Tomlinson 1987, 7–25).

Limestones from the site included oolitic stone, perhaps from the Cave beds which have been quarried at Brough, Brantingham and Newbald (Clifton Taylor 1972, 82), and Magnesian Limestone, as used in the fabric of the Minster (Miller *et al.* 1982, 9); a narrow strip of Magnesium limestone outcrops from Mansfield (Notts.), to the Durham coast at Hartlepool, and was extensively exploited during the Roman and Medieval periods. Hard slabs of fine oolitic limestone which were used for walling and thresholds were probably not Cave Stone. Limestone was typically employed for the external facing of buildings, and for buttresses, mouldings, windows and doors. A fireplace which formed an internal feature of the Phase 5A north range was flanked by pillars: the bases were of good Lower Magnesian Limestone, while the column fragments which possibly derived from this structure were of a more porous Lower Magnesian Limestone of indifferent quality. The limestone ashlar was of variable quality, sometimes mediocre or poor. The most extensive collection of masonry was recovered from feature 426, a Phase 5C drain, which incorporated both slabs and reused ashlar.

Architectural fragments (Figure 61)

No. B1 is a substantial rectangular padstone of fine-grained oolitic limestone, which was retrieved as an unstratified find during the clearance of the west end of the north range of the little cloister. The neatly executed chamfer suggests that the upper part of this stone was intended to be visible. It was eminently suitable for internal use, and would have supported a timber upright. Similar padstones at Lurk Lane were used in the interior of the Phase 7A aisled hall of 13th-century date: these had been set over rubble-packed pits similar to those which defined the Phase 5A cloister arcade at the Priory (Armstrong *et al.* 1991, 33–5 and fig. 20). If this example from the Priory had served in the later north range structure, it would probably have been as a reused element, drawn perhaps from the Phase 5C dismantling of the arcade, or from further afield.

Nos. B2 and B3 are substantial concavo-convex blocks of Lower Magnesian Limestone. Both were probably originally used in a chimney structure with an internal diameter of *c.*0.72m. No. B2 was reused in Phase 5C to cap a drain (426). A wall fireplace was an integral part of the west chamber of the little cloister north range, and there were probably others about the complex. The form of a later 14th-century chimney stack has been reconstructed from fragments found at the Royal Palace at Kings Langley, Hertfordshire (Neal 1973, 45, fig. 8:3).

Windows (Figure 61)

No. B4 is a fragment of finely claw-tooled window tracery of very high quality Lower Magnesian Limestone. It comes from the springing between the two pierced lights of a pointed window; double-ogee moulding survives around one side. Glazing would have been held in wooden frames with this piece. Dr G. Coppack comments that this is an example of

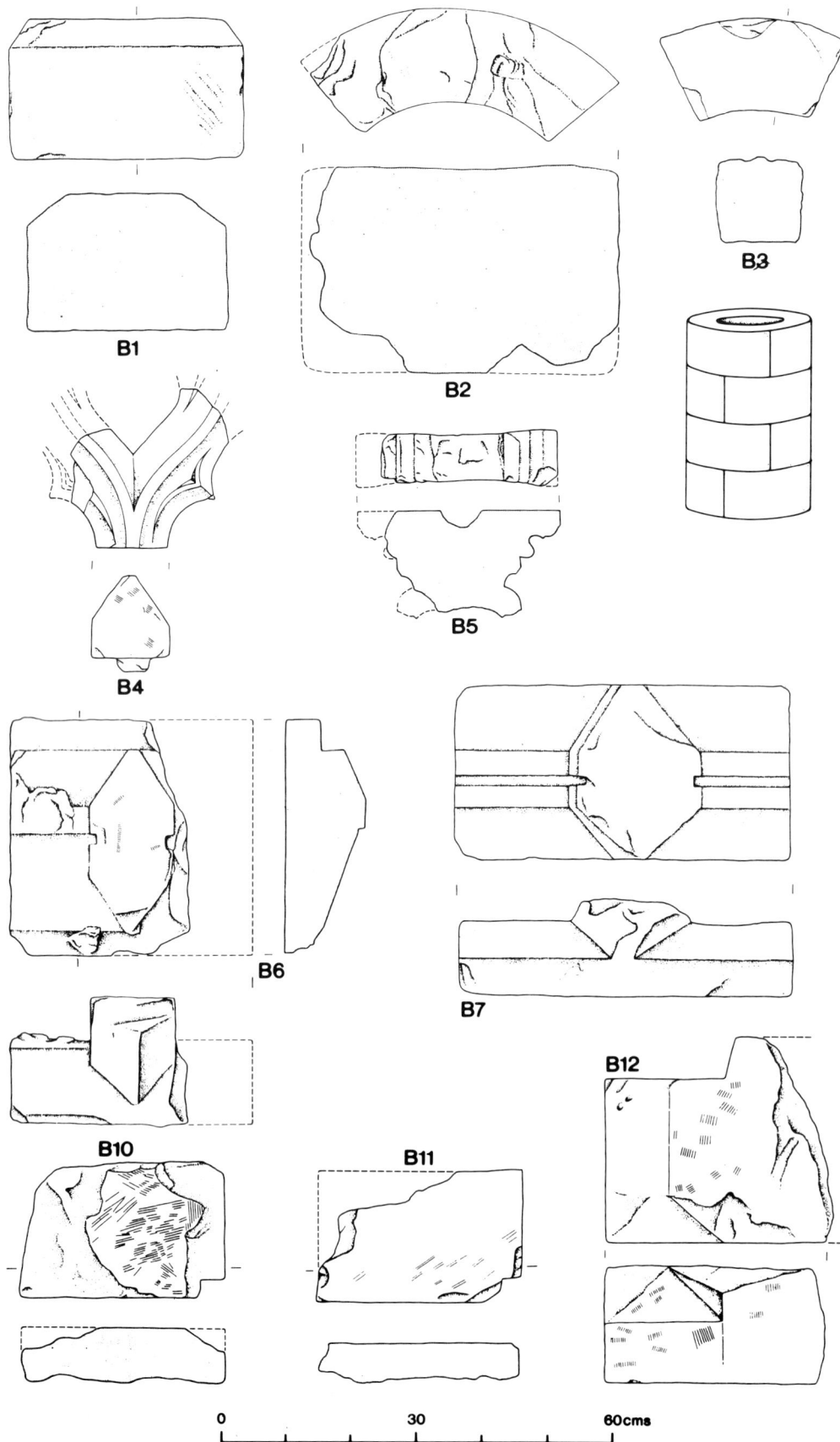

Figure 61 Masonry.

the later Decorated style, possibly reticulated, and suggests it to be stylistically dated to the mid.-to-late 14th century, though similar work is known to have continued in use after 1400 at Mount Grace Priory, North Yorkshire. This piece comes from demolition rubble over the refectory, which is thought to have been constructed in the later 14th century. A similar fragment, though without a double ogee moulding, was found at the west end of the church, and was considered to have been used in 14th-century works (Armstrong and Tomlinson 1987, 47, fig. 25:51). A comparable window from the Austin Friars, Leicester, was attributed to mid.-to-late 14th-century work on the refectory (Clay 1981, 46, fig. 11:19). A window head of 13th, or possibly 14th-century form, in Lower Magnesian Limestone (no. B5) came from a demolition deposit in the little cloister garth. The piece is two-sided, with flat fillets and repeated roll-mouldings — the roll which would have borne the glazing rebates is lost. This is again an example of Decorated work.

Unstratified window fragments (nos. B6 and B7) in fine Lower Magnesian Limestone, were recovered from 19th-century or later levels, and may have been disturbed by the construction of the Hull — Scarborough railway across the site. No. B6 was a six-sided, heavily chamfered mullion which bore rectangular rebates for glazing, a chamfered outer sill and an internal sill. No. B7 was the junction of a tracery bar, with a jamb. The mullion form is common in later medieval work, excavated from mendicant houses: it has been noted at Northampton Greyfriars (Wilson 1978, 119–20, figs. 14 and 15), the Austin Friars, Leicester (Clay 1981, 46, fig. 11:9) and elsewhere. Further examples of chamfered ashlar (nos. B8–9 and unillustrated) may be either from the capping of a plinth course or, in the case of B8 (which appears to bear cream-coloured paint on its lower surfaces) perhaps from a window sill, transom, mantlepiece or coping.

Simple mouldings (Figure 61)

Nos. B10 and B11 are internal window or door profile mouldings of chalk, both were reused in Phase 5A, and subsequently worn down. No. B12 is a limestone door jamb, which was set on one side of an entrance into the east chamber of the Phase 5A north range at sill level. It was intended to accompany a raised threshold or sill: this is indicated by the chamfer at the back, or internal side, of the jamb. The opposed jamb was noted *in situ*, but was subsequently removed without record. No. B13 is a chalk fragment (unillustrated) from an internal string-course moulding, of indeterminate 13th to 15th-century form, which was recovered from a post-medieval feature.

Shafts (Figure 62)

Nos. B14 and B15 are a matching pair of semi-octagonal wall-shaft bases of 14th-century form, fashioned in good Lower Magnesian Limestone. The use of a larger semi-octagonal base was recorded in the extension of the preaching nave of the Priory church in the early 14th century (Armstrong and Tomlinson 1987, 53; Watkins 1987b, 35). Octagonal bases have also been noted at the Dominican Priory at Chester (Ward 1990, 79, nos. 2–4) and at the Greyfriars, Hartlepool (Daniels 1986, 301). These pieces are of particular interest because B14 was recorded *in situ*, forming an element of a Phase 5A fireplace in the north range of the little cloister; while B15 was reused in Phase 5C to patch the south wall of the same chamber. No. B15 bears light burning on its display face, confirming its original use in a fireplace. A pillar or nook shaft fragment (B16) was incorporated into the kerb of this fireplace in Phase 5B, and may also have come from the original fireplace; this fragment bore indistinct traces of paint. A further shaft fragment (B17) bore clearer traces of blue and red paint, and had been coloured to resemble the shafts of Purbeck marble which form a distinctive feature of Early English and Decorated work at the Minster (Miller *et al.* 1982, 9–10). This attempt at ostentation may betray a certain relaxation of mendicant standards of austerity. Purbeck marble shafts have been recorded in mendicant churches at Sandwich Whitefriars (Rigold 1965, 18) and perhaps at Cambridge Blackfriars (Stubbings 1969, 97); and in the *frater* at Gloucester Blackfriars (W.H. Knowles 1932, 184). Other, unstratified, shaft fragments from the site include an example in a dark shelly limestone (B18) similar to Purbeck marble, and perhaps from the end of an arcade section; there are also two shafts of sub-circular section and inferior workmanship (nos. B19 and B20). Other pillar fragments were found in reuse or demolition contexts (nos. 21–3); Dr. G. Coppack comments that the beaked ovoid profile of no. 21 may show that it was intended to occupy a tight corner. All these shaft fragments were carved in a porous Lower Magnesian Limestone of indifferent quality. In style they appear likely to be of 13th-century date, if not earlier, and must therefore be considered as reused in their 14th-century or later contexts. No. B24 is a fragment of a mid.-12th-century nook-shaft base moulding which was reused in Phase 5A. A similar piece was incorporated into 14th-century work in the west end of the Priory church, and others occur in the relocated precinct wall on Eastgate (S.J. Armstrong 1987, 46–47, fig. 25:49).

B14

B15

B16

B17

B18

B19

B20

B21

B22

B24

B26

B27 & B28

B29

B33

B34

B30

B35

B36

0   30   60cms

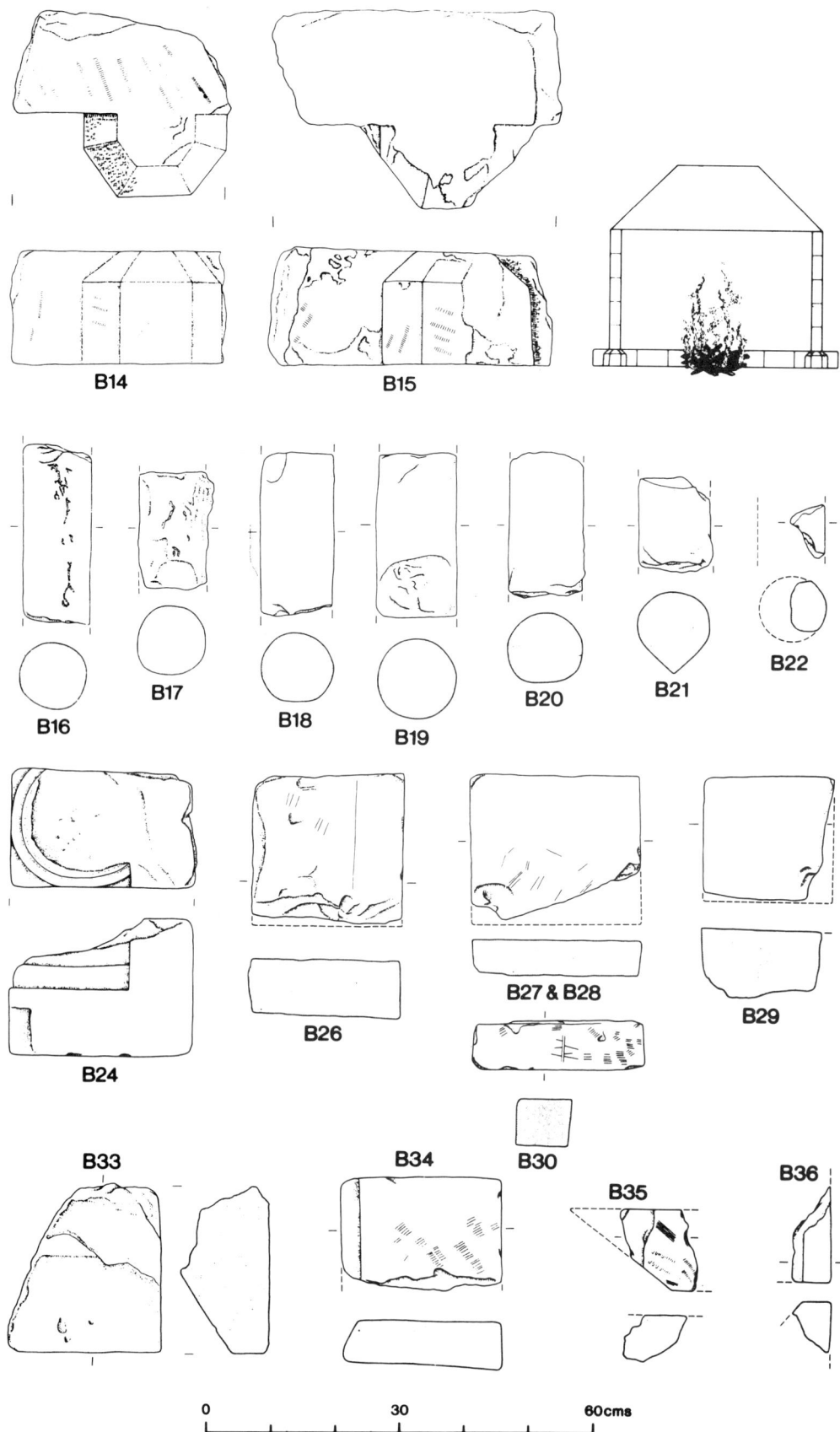

Figure 62 Masonry.

Floor slabs (Figure 62)

Nos. B26–8, and possibly B29–32, are floor slabs of chalk, which were reused in contexts of Phases 5, 5A, 5C, 6A, and 7; no examples were present in a primary context. Although the lack of occupation deposits from the west chamber of the little cloister north range might suggest that a floor covering was in place here during Phase 5A, no tiles or flags were actually found *in situ*. These slabs are finely worked for close setting, and bear smoothing from wear. A similar use of chalk slabs was recorded at the base of the water tank and *reredorter* of Phase 4, though for obvious reasons these were not worn by pedestrian traffic. Excavation in the great cloister west range and church showed only the use of plain tiled floors (Armstrong and Tomlinson 1987, figs. 11–12), so it must remain uncertain where, or indeed whether, any of these slabs saw their primary use within the Priory complex. The use of stone flags in a mendicant setting was uncommon, though by royal gift a floor of Purbeck marble was laid in the choir of the Newgate Greyfriars, London (Johnson 1974, 225), and the Linlithgow Whitefriars had floors of local sandstone (Lindsay 1989, 72).

Splays (Figure 62)

Nos. B33–7 are possible splay fragments, of Lower Magnesian and oolitic limestone, and thus were suited either for external use or in conjunction with the window mouldings discussed above. They are distinguished by finely claw-tooled faces which meet at a well-defined arris; where the upper and lower faces survive, these are flat. They were recorded in the little cloister garth, in secondary contexts and a floor platform in Phases 5 and 5B, and in the drain structure (426) in Phase 5C. Similar pieces of chalk ashlar (nos. B38–45) were for internal use; all but two of these were reused in drain 426. It may be significant that no splays were identified from demolition deposits associated with the little cloister, though chalk ashlar and slabs were incorporated into the superstructure of both the north and west ranges.

Ashlar and slabs (unillustrated)

The remaining masonry from the site consists of rectangular ashlar, fragments of ashlar whose original form is uncertain, and slabs. Of the ashlar, nos. B49–77 were mostly limestones, and were incorporated into structures and deposits of Phases 5, 5A, 5B, 5C, 6A and 7. The use of limestone ashlar in drain structure 426 was rare, suggesting that its value necessitated saving the durable stone for structural work. The stone typically bore claw-tooling, though broad diagonal tooling often occurred on faces which were intended to be mortared, and a few blocks showed overall broad or striated diagonal tooling of 12th-century character — occasionally retouched with a clawed tool. Nos. B78–119 were mostly chalk ashlar of rectangular or unidentifiable original form. These were excavated from Phases 3B, 4, 5A, 5C and 7, and were prominent among the reused elements of drain 426. The tooling characteristics were similar to those encountered on the limestone ashlar, save for the greater proportion of blocks which bore broad tooling, without any working or retouching by clawed tools. Nos. B120–4 were either crudely worked ashlar or slabs, and nos. B125–63 slabs. They included some threshold stones in a very fine-grained oolitic limestone which was probably not found locally; the others were mostly of chalk. Most bore little perceptible working, and had apparently been split along their natural bedding planes. The only exceptions were nos. B128–30, which served as the capping of a Phase 5A footing (126); they were heavily tooled to provide a flat bed for stone walling.

The full catalogue of masonry occurs in microfiche (Mf.1 C5–D9).

Catalogue of masonry

Architectural fragments (Figure 61)

B1. Oolitic Limestone, slightly finer than usual.
     Rectangular ashlar padstone with top chamfer on all four sides. Dimensions: 345mm by 300mm by 205mm.
     Weathered.
     From west end of north range, little cloister.
     M52, Unstratified.

B2. Lower Magnesian Limestone, very fine grained.
     Chimney-stack segment, part of 3 or 4 piece ring: concavo-convex. Dimensions: 425mm by 310mm; thickness: 140mm. Diagonal claw tooling on all visible mortared faces, slight tooling on external face. Two rebates, 25mm square, for cramps in one end. Reused, to form part of a drain.
     M127, Context 426, Phase 5C.

B3. Lower Magnesian Limestone.
     ?Chimney-stack segment or arch voussoir from an inner order: concavo-convex. Dimensions of concave face: 265mm by 130mm; thickness 125mm. Axe tooling on concave mortared surfaces, diagonal claw tooling on one end face. Roughly tooled on convex face. From a demolition spread over the frater.
     M58, Context 914, Phase 7.

B4. Lower Magnesian Limestone, of high quality.
     Window tracery of mid to late thirteenth century form or later, possibly reticulated. From a double-ended window with pointed light, a double ogee with window cusp in the middle. Glazing would be held in wooden frames. Dimensions: 240mm overall height, mullion: 155mm by 105mm. Fine striated tooling on external display faces, fine claw tooling on internal display faces and claw tooling on mortared face. From a demolition spread over the frater.
     M57, Context 914, Phase 7.

B5. Lower Magnesian Limestone.
Window head of thirteenth or possibly fourteenth century form, with flat fillets and repeated roll-mouldings; roll with glazing rebate is lost. Dimensions: 270mm by 165mm by 70mm. Fine claw tooling on display face, claw tooling on upper and lower faces. Three grooves for keying into mortar occur on upper face. From the little cloister garth.
M86, Context 15, Phase 7.

B6. Lower Magnesian Limestone, of high quality.
Mullioned window, with chamfered outer cill and stepped inner cill. Six sided mullion with rectangular rebates for glazing on either side. Claw tooled. Dimensions: 354mm by 270mm by 160mm. M176, Unstratified. (Recovered from demolition of nineteenth century shed on site of east end of church).

B7. Similar to B6 - now outside "Old Friary".

Simple mouldings (Figure 61)

B10. Chalk.
Internal window or door profile moulding, grooved at one corner. Dimensions: 305mm by 205mm by 85mm. Fine striated tooling on display faces and fine diagonal axe tooling on upper face. Wear may suggest reuse as a floor slab, or may arise from reuse as part of a partition footing.
M66, Context 818, Phase 5A.

B11. Chalk.
Internal window or door profile moulding. Grooved, with a chamfered corner. Dimensions: 300mm by 200mm by 50mm. Fine diagonal axe tooling on upper face and horizontal striations and axe tooling on display face. Wear and surface pitting may suggest reuse as floor slab, or may arise from reuse as part of a partition footing.
M61, Context 818, Phase 5A.

B12. Lower Magnesian Limestone.
Door jamb at cill level. Ashlar with 75mm rebate and chamfer at back indicating this was joined to cill.
Dimensions: 300mm by 160mm, thickness: 320mm. Fine claw tooling on all faces. Groove or scribe line along upper mortared face to position chamfer.
M41, Context 36, Phase 5A: formed doorway in north range, little cloister.

Pillars (Figure 62)

B14. Lower Magnesian Limestone, of high quality.
Semi-octagonal pillar base of fourteenth-century form.
Dimensions of display face: 300mm by 170mm, thickness: 240mm, diameter of pillar base *c*.125mm. Fine vertical and diagonal claw tooling on display faces, claw tooling on upper mortared face.
M46, Context 473, Phase 5A: formed part of a fireplace.

B15. Lower Magnesian Limestone, of high quality.
Semi-octagonal pillar base of fourteenth-century form.
Dimensions of display face: 380mm by 170mm, thickness: 300mm, diameter of pillar base:

c.125mm. Fine claw tooling on display face. Burning on display face which has been subsequently chipped and mortared. Reused to form part of mending of a wall.
M36, Context 2500, Phase 5C.

B16. Lower Magnesium Limestone, of mediocre quality; porous.
Pillar or nook shaft, of sub-circular section, in two joining fragments. Dimensions: diameter: 100mm, length: 265mm. Fine striated tooling on part of display face. Traces of paint survive on face. Burnt. Reused to form part of a hearth kerb.
M72, Context 347, Phase 5B.

B17. Lower Magnesium Limestone, of mediocre quality; porous.
Pillar or shaft fragment, of sub-circular section, of inferior quality, of thirteenth century form. Dimensions: diameter: 105mm, length: 180mm. Claw tooling on display face. Painted in red and blue to resemble Purbeck Marble. Slightly burnt.
M81, Context 466, Phase 7: from a pit.

B18. Purbeck Marble, though not of the classic series.
Pillar or shaft fragment, of thirteenth or fourteenth-century form, perhaps from end of an arcade.
Dimensions: diameter: 110mm. ?Claw tooling on end face, fine striated tooling on display face. Worn on one side.
M91C, Unstratified.

B19. Lower Magnesian Limestone, of mediocre quality; porous.
Pillar or shaft fragment, of sub-circular section, of inferior quality. Dimensions: diameter: 110mm. Vertical claw tooling on display face.
M91B, Unstratified.

B20. Probably joins with B19-identical material.
Pillar or shaft fragment of sub-circular section, of inferior quality. Dimensions: diameter: 110mm. Vertical claw tooling on display face.
M91A, Unstratified.

B21. Lower Magnesian Limestone, of mediocre quality; porous.
Nook shaft, for a tight corner: of beaked ovoid section.
Dimensions: diameter: 125mm-110mm, length: 130mm. Claw tooling touched up with a finer tool. Surface is burnt.
Reused to form part of a wall.
M47, Context 452, Phase 5.

B22. Limestone (not examined for geological identification).
Pillar or shaft fragment. Dimensions: *c*.100 mm original diameter, length: 40mm. Striated tooling on display face.
From a robber cut.
M77C, Context 552, Phase 5C.

B24. Oolitic Limestone, ?from Cave.
Fragment of round nook shaft base moulding, probably of mid-twelfth century form. Dimensions: 280mm by 170mm by 220mm. Diameter of shaft: *c*.160mm. Weathered diagonal striated tooling on display face and axe tooling on back.
Reused to form part of a wall.

M43, Context 37, Phase 5A.

Floor slabs (Figure 62)

B26. Chalk.
Floor slab. Dimensions: 220mm by 225mm by 90mm.
Axe tooling on all faces. Tooling on upper and lower faces. Reused to form part of a footing.
M83B, Context 126, Phase 5A.

B27. Chalk.
Floor slab fragment. Dimensions: 135mm by 105mm by 60mm.
Claw tooling on two faces, one face smoothed. Reused to form part of a drain. Joins with B28.
M139, Context 426, Phase 5C.

B28. Chalk.
Rectangular floor slab fragment. Dimensions: 190mm by 155mm by 55mm. Smoothed striated tooling on upper face, claw tooling on two side faces, axe tooling on one side face.
Reused to form part of a drain. Joins with B27.
M164, Context 426, Phase 5C.

B29. Chalk.
Floor slab. Dimensions: 190mm by 175mm by 100mm.
Diagonal axe tooling on side faces. Upper face smoothed, with two faint parallel scribed lines.
M63, Context 3080, Phase 7: from a robbed ?footing at the west end of the north range, little cloister.

B30. Chalk.
?Floor slab. Rectangular ashlar, cut to "brick shape". Dimensions: 250mm by 80mm by 75mm. Diagonal claw tooling on all faces, finer and smoothed on one long face.
M51, Context 956, Phase 6A: from a construction-phase pit.

Splays (Figure 62)

B33. Lower Magnesian Limestone.
Splay fragment or plinth. Dimensions: 240mm by 120mm by 250mm. Fine diagonal claw tooling on display face, flat mortared surface and on one end face.
M85, Context 65, Phase 5: from the little cloister garth.

B34. Oolitic Limestone, ?from Cave.
?Splay fragment, with chamfer. Dimensions: 243mm by 172mm by 73mm. Fine diagonal claw tooling on display faces. Claw tooling on one side face and mortared face. Subsequently smoothed overall. Reused to form part of a hearth kerb.
M71, Context 347, Phase 5B.

B35. Magnesian Limestone.
?Splay fragment, with chamfer. Dimensions: 120mm by 70mm by 120mm. Claw tooling on display face.
M79A, Context 848, Phase 5B: from a floor platform.

B36. Magnesian Limestone.
?Splay fragment, with chamfer. Dimensions: 140mm by 55mm by 80mm. Claw tooling on display face.
M79B, Context 848, Phase 5B: from a floor platform.

3.3 The brick

by Stephen Potts

Introduction

Brick occurs regularly on medieval sites in the region and there is a tradition of brick and tile manufacture in both Hull (Brooks 1939) and Beverley (Humberside County Council 1987; Youngs *et al.* 1987, 145–6 and fig. 4; Allison 1989, 41–2). Little systematic work has been carried out on the material excavated to date, and on surviving structures in the area. This report is mainly concerned with the brick recovered from the Priory; however, material from Lurk Lane and the Annie Reed Road tilery site has also been re-examined and placed in a typology. The study excludes brick from excavations in Hull, and in standing buildings. It has not had the benefit of petrographic analysis, and definition has been by visual and tactile means utilising lower power optics. The detailed typology appears in microfiche (Mf.1 D10–14). Brick was used extensively at the Priory, and the typology is based upon the classification of 822 complete and incomplete bricks, 100 of which are intact in all their dimensions.

A general account of the introduction of the use of brick for building in Eastern England has been given by Drury (1981, 126–30). Several notable examples of the early use of brick occur in Humberside. Brick was used extensively in the transepts and east end of Holy Trinity church, Hull, dating to *c.* 1300–20, whilst the complete circuit of the town walls which were built during the later 14th and early 15th centuries is estimated to have used *c.* 4.7 million bricks (Bartlett 1971, 21). Bricks were also used in the vault of the nave of Beverley Minster, *c.* 1320–40, and in the gatehouse of Thornton Abbey, South Humberside; the latter structure is of two builds, the earlier of which dates perhaps to the 1360s (Pevsner and Harris 1989, 757–8). The North Bar in Beverley was built of brick in 1409 (Bilson 1896). Several production sites are also known in the county. Two brickyards were in operation in Hull during the 14th and 15th centuries (Allison 1969, 57; Brooks 1939). A number of brick and tile production sites are documented in Beverley during the Middle Ages (Allison 1989, 41–2). Excavation at one such site in Annie Reed Road, Grovehill, Beverley, revealed evidence for manufacture of both brick and tile during the 13th century (Humberside County Council 1987, 17–18 and Pls 17–20). Some of the brick types from that site were identical to those used at Lurk Lane and this Priory (Mf.1 E13–F4).

Summary brick typology

Type 1 (137 examples)

Dimensions: L.245–260mm, W.122–137mm, Th.44–51mm.
Fabric: Fine alluvial clay, oxidised firing.
Manufacture: Moulded, pitted underside, straw/grass impressions common on underside.

Type 2 (10 incomplete examples)

Dimensions: L.?, W.135mm, Th.45–50mm.
Fabric: Fine alluvial clay, slightly micaceous, oxidised firing.
Manufacture: Moulded, sanded, straw/grass impressions on underside.

Type 3 (160 examples)

Dimensions: L.245–265mm, W.117–137mm, Th.40–48mm.
Fabric: Fine alluvial clay, variable firing.
Manufacture: Moulded, pitted underside, straw/grass impressions on underside.

Type 3A (10 examples)

Dimensions: L.220–240mm, W.103–120mm, Th.35–43mm.
Fabric: Fine alluvial clay, overfired Type 3.
Manufacture: As Type 3.

Type 4 (137 examples)

Dimensions: L.260–271mm, W.125–137mm, Th.55–62mm.
Fabric: Fine alluvial clay, oxidised firing.
Manufacture: Moulded, coarsely sanded, straw/grass impressions on underside.

Type 5 (1 incomplete example)

Dimensions: L.?. W.95–110mm, Th.37–45mm.
Fabric: Sandy alluvial clay, buff throughout, soft.
Manufacture: Moulded, pitted undersurface, straw/grass impressions on underside.

Type 6 (283 examples)

Dimensions: L.340–360mm, W.160–170mm. Th.50–57mm; also variants of thicknesses ranging from 45mm to 60mm.
Fabric: Coarse sandy clay with lithic inclusions — boulder clay, oxidised firing.
Manufacture: Moulded, pitted underside with angular chalk grit embedded.

Type 7 (31 incomplete examples)

Dimensions: L.?, W.120–125mm, Th.40–47mm.
Fabric: Sandy clay with lithic inclusions — ?boulder clay, oxidised firing.
Manufacture: Moulded with well-defined edges, sanded, white/buff slip on upper surface.

Raw materials

The region contains many sources of raw materials suitable for the manufacture of fired clay products. Much of the drift geology consists of superficial deposits ranging from the post-glacial alluvial clays of the Hull Valley and flanks of the Humber Estuary to an assortment of fluvioglacial clays, sands and gravels and glacial till (boulder clay), forming the region of Holderness to the east of the Hull Valley. As the available raw materials in the region are derived ultimately from the same sources — glacial deposits and alluvial deposits (largely derived from reworked glacial deposits) — the mineralogical compositions should not be expected to vary. A recent petrographic examination of tile from Hull (Dunham *et al.* 1987, 241–3) admitted an inability to make firm suggestions as to the origin of raw materials.

At the Priory the fine clay fabric of brick Types 1, 2, 3, 3A, and 4 is consistent with derivation from alluvial clays. Types 3 and 3A were present at the Annie Reed Road tilery site, and were probably manufactured there. Underlying that site is the alluvial clay of the Hull Valley (Humberside County Council 1987, 13–14). The fabric of Type 6 bricks, however, is a sandy clay with sub-angular and sub-rounded stones and rounded pebbles, of chalk, flint, sandstone, quartz and quartzite. These stones range from 2mm up to 40mm, and commonly exceed a 10mm long axis. The variety and size of stones, and the amount of sand in the clay groundmass, indicates that these bricks have been manufactured from glacial till (boulder clay). This probably applies also to Type 7 bricks. It is perhaps significant that the drift geology of the Priory consists of glacial till (British Geological Survey, Sheet 72, Drift).

It has been suggested that bricks in the 'Great Brick' tradition derive from southern Europe and were introduced into England by monastic establishments through their links with European houses (Harley 1974, 72). Gardner (1955, 31) regards it as likely that the manufacture of such bricks was carried out at the individual monasteries, citing Coggeshall Abbey as an example. At the Priory the boulder clay, from which the Type 6 bricks were made, is available on site. A feature of the rock fragments within Type 6 bricks is the presence of many chalk fragments in a few of the bricks, compared to its absence from most. Chalk is commonly present within the Devensian Tills of Holderness; at the Priory a thin covering of till overlies the chalk. Post-glacial weathering, however, would probably have removed limestones (chalk), shale, and calcareous sandstones from the top part of any soil profile developed on till (Madgett and Catt 1978, 78–9). Macroscopically, this is what the fabric of the Type 6 bricks presents. Those bricks containing no chalk fragments contain representatives of the more resistant types, such as quartz and quartzite pebbles. The implication is that the clay from which Type 6 bricks were made was obtained from near to the ground surface, which is consistent with the winning of this material from shallow pits or even from foundation trenches.

Manufacture

A number of methods can be employed to make and shape bricks (Harley 1974, 64–6). The most common medieval method was the impressing of a tempered clay plug into a sanded wooden mould, the 'form', with the surplus clay being struck off with a wooden bat, the 'strike.' The 'green' brick was then removed from the mould and transferred to a drying area. This basic method, with variations, was in use from the 13th to the 20th centuries. All bricks recovered from the Priory were manufactured in this way. The use of a rectangular open-bottomed mould is likely, since the general lipping of the upper arris is consistent with such a mould being removed vertically. The chamfered bricks (variants of Types 1, 3, 4 and 6) have also been moulded.

The presence of sanded surfaces on Types 1, 2 and 4 indicates the common use of sand to prevent the clay adhering to the sides of the mould. The absence of sanding on Types 3 and 6 from the Priory, and equivalent bricks examined from sites at Lurk Lane and the Annie Reed Road tilery site, suggests the use of a separator which was either too fine for the available magnification to distinguish, or which was of a combustible or impermanent nature. Alternatively, the water content of the clay used may have been sufficiently high not to require the use of applied separators. A limited number of the Type 3's which were examined did show examples of sags or runs that had been formed in the lipped upper surface edges, possibly indicative of the use of a softer clay. The weight of Type 6 bricks may have made a separator unnecessary.

Examples of brick Type 7 bear an applied white slip on the upper surface. There are no indications of brush marks, although the linear striations presumed to have resulted from 'striking off' are fainter than for other brick types.

Bricks were allowed to dry prior to firing. This sometimes took place in a drying shed, the 'hackstead', although at the Royal tilery in Hull documentary evidence suggests newly moulded bricks were covered with cloths or 'nattes' supported on spurs (Brooks 1939, 160). The Annie Reed Road tilery in Beverley was a probable source for Type 3 bricks, and there are indications that some drying took place in the open; bricks were recovered with raindrop pitted upper surfaces (Humberside County Council 1987, Pl. 20). Laying out probably took place on straw. Straw/grass impressions occur commonly on the bricks from the Priory, with the exception of Types 6 and 7. Sporadic straw/grass impressions would occur on any of the surfaces, though the tendency was for the undersurfaces to bear the most. Some variations on this have been noted. Three examples of Type 1 have a single end bearing prominent straw/grass impressions with associated impressions on the underside, consistent with end-stacking. Two showed prominent impressions on one of the side surfaces. Ten examples of bricks showed prominent straw/grass impressions on both upper and lower surfaces; the use of straw as a separator whilst stack drying could explain these imprints. Of the Type 4's; one example shows prominent straw/grass impressions on one end surface, again consistent with 'end' stacking.

The underside of Type 6 bricks always contains a large number of embedded angular chalk fragments (2–4mm). This is not a component of the fabric; although some Type 6's contain pieces of chalk, a similar effect is not displayed on any other surface. This may indicate moulding on a prepared flat piece of ground, 'the place', with the bricks being left to dry *in situ* (Harley 1974, 65), or on surfaces strewn with crushed chalk.

Accounts of brick-making methods (e.g. Harley 1974, 65) suggest that once a brick had been moulded, it was deposited on a pallet, and then transferred to the drying area or shed. A number of bricks from the Priory assemblage show finger-tip impressions, often quite numerous, which indicate post-formational handling. This was marked among bricks of Type 1 and 6, and infrequent on other types. A total of 66 bricks showed at least one finger-tip impression (8% of the total).

The author's experiments with local clay have shown that it will dry to a hardness sufficient for it not to take an impression after only a few days. Accordingly, it is likely that the impressions on the Priory bricks were sustained soon after moulding (when the clay would still have been plastic) in the process of transfer to the drying area, or during laying out for drying. (The most informative of these impressions are detailed in microfiche: Mf.1 E7–8). The best impressions were present on the Type 6's. This must relate to their size and weight, which would have necessitated lifting them with both hands. All the finger-tip impressions seem to have been incurred between the removal of the moulding frame and their arrangement for drying. Isolated groups of impressions on side or end surfaces may have resulted from attempts to free bricks stuck to the moulding surface, or in the process of laying them out for drying. Others suggest that bricks were carried by hand between the moulding and drying areas. If the brick was small, it was carried in one hand; larger bricks were carried in both hands.

Brick sizes

Two main categories of bricks are generally identified from medieval sites: 'Great Bricks', and smaller 'Flemish-type' bricks. The latter are generally regarded as superseding the former, whose manufacture is deemed to have ceased by the end of the 14th century.

Drury (1981, 129) distinguished two classes of 'Flemish' brick. A larger one (L.230–270mm, W.130–165mm, Th. 40–50mm) which is found mainly in the hinterlands of the East Coast towns, and a smaller one (L. 230mm, W. 115mm, Th. 50mm) of mainly southern distribution. The bricks from Beverley fall largely into the first class. The full dimensions of Types 2, 5 and 7 are unknown, though the known measurements are typically 'Flemish'. Type 6 bricks are larger. The dimensions of bricks recovered or recorded from sites in this region are shown below.

Ignoring the dimensions of bricks from the Annie Reed Road tilery site and the values for the Type 3A bricks — all thought to be Type 3 wasters — a 'Beverley brick size' of L.250–265mm,

Beverley Minster (Vault of Nave)	L.263mm, W.131mm, Th.50mm	(Bilson 1896, 47, 59)
Thornton Abbey (Gatehouse)	L.275mm, W.135mm, Th.50mm	
North Bar, Beverley	L.263mm, W.131mm, Th.50mm	
Annie Reed Road, Beverley	L.249mm, W.121mm, Th.44mm	(averages)
Lurk Lane (Type 1)	L.257mm, W.134mm, Th.49mm	Measured by the author (averages)
Lurk Lane (Type 3)	L.260mm, W.128mm, Th.44mm	
Lurk Lane (Type 3A)	L.245mm, W.115mm, Th.37mm	
Lurk Lane (Type 4)	L.266mm, W.136mm, Th.59mm	
Beverley Dominican Priory (Type 1)	L.253mm, W.130mm, Th.48mm	Mid-range values
Beverley Dominican Priory (Type 3)	L.255mm, W.127mm, Th.44mm	
Beverley Dominican Priory (Type 3A)	L.230mm, W.112mm, Th.39mm	
Beverley Dominican Priory (Type 4)	L.265mm, W.131mm, Th.59mm	

W.125–135mm, Th.45–60mm would appear to have been usual. No firm regulation of size is apparent.

The Priory Type 6 bricks are unusually large. All such bricks were known to medieval writers as 'Great Bricks', and dimensions given in Harley (1974, 71) of L.275–350mm, W.150–187mm, Th.33–50mm accommodate this type except with regard to thickness. The thickness range of Type 6's from the Priory is 50–57mm. Bricks of large size from Coggeshall Abbey (Essex) measured L.325mm, W.150mm, Th.50mm (Gardner 1955, 25), and from Pleshey Castle (Essex) Type A, L.305mm, W.130mm, Th.75mm (Drury 1977, 83).

The use of brick

The Priory underwent systematic demolition after the Dissolution, hence only ground level or sub-surface structures have survived (the surviving 'Old Friary' building has not been examined). Bricks had a wide variety of uses and forms in the medieval period, with specific shapes generally denoting a specialised function. At the Priory, bricks were used in the construction of walls (both internal and external), benches, steps, drains and hearths.

The Priory also provides examples of bricks with chamfered corners. Type 1 and 4 variants have a single chamfer; a Type 3 'special' is chamfered at both ends. Bricks with one chamfer are termed *plinth bricks*. They were commonly used in walls, header-laid to provide a reduction in thickness between plinth and main elevation, as with the Type 1 'specials' in the precinct wall (see above Figure 9). Type 4 variants were used randomly within the kerb of hearth 2072, along with reused roof tile, and in the outer facing of a bench position. Chamfered bricks occur commonly on medieval sites, and Coggeshall Abbey (Essex: Gardner 1955) provides a number of examples in doorway linings, arches, and the outside of single light windows. Bilson (1896, 39) records their use in the North Bar, Beverley. The standard Types 1, 3 and 4, were used extensively for walling, and also for internal fittings. The largest bricks found at the Priory, Type 6, were used in the base of a drain (426) whose sides were constructed from an assortment of brick types, with a capping of chalk slabs. The suggestion that they were made only for this purpose is contradicted by the presence of a chamfered example in the structure. Similar large bricks also formed part of a channel recorded to the west of the extant 'Old Friary' building (Armstrong and Tomlinson 1987, 23, fig. 2).

Types 1 and 3 frequently occurred together. This was feasible because of their similar dimensions. Since the Dominicans were a mendicant order this may reflect the *ad hoc* use of donations. It is likely that Types 1 and 3 were obtained from manufacturers who used slightly different moulding techniques. The North Bar at Beverley was built in 1409 with bricks from as many as 20 different sources (Bilson 1896, 44). The common occurrence at the Priory of overfired bricks and soft crumbly underfired bricks (especially Type 3), which in modern terms would be called 'rejects', is also consistent with their donation.

Phasing

This aspect of the brick assemblage is complicated by the possibility of reuse; however, no brick from the Priory was seen with two types of mortar adhering to it. As many appear to be 'rejects' (especially the Type 3's) the likelihood is that most bricks saw their first use on this site. The overall distribution of brick from Phases 5–5C is summarised in Table 1. More detailed descriptions of brick use and listings occur in microfiche (Mf.1 E1–6, E9–12). Appendices list and describe the bricks recovered from excavations at Lurk Lane and the Annie Reed Road site; these were

Table 1   Occurrence of brick types — by phase

Brick Type	Phases											
	3	3A	3B	3C	3D	5	5A	5B	5C	6A	6B	7
1						15	20	12	121	2	2	59
2									2			8
3							1		20			131
4						13	35	4	25			55
5							1					
6									286			
3A						1		1	2			4
7						20			1			

Figure 63   Brick types 1 (nos. B163–4), 3 (nos. B165–6), 4 (nos. B167–71) and 5 (no. B172).

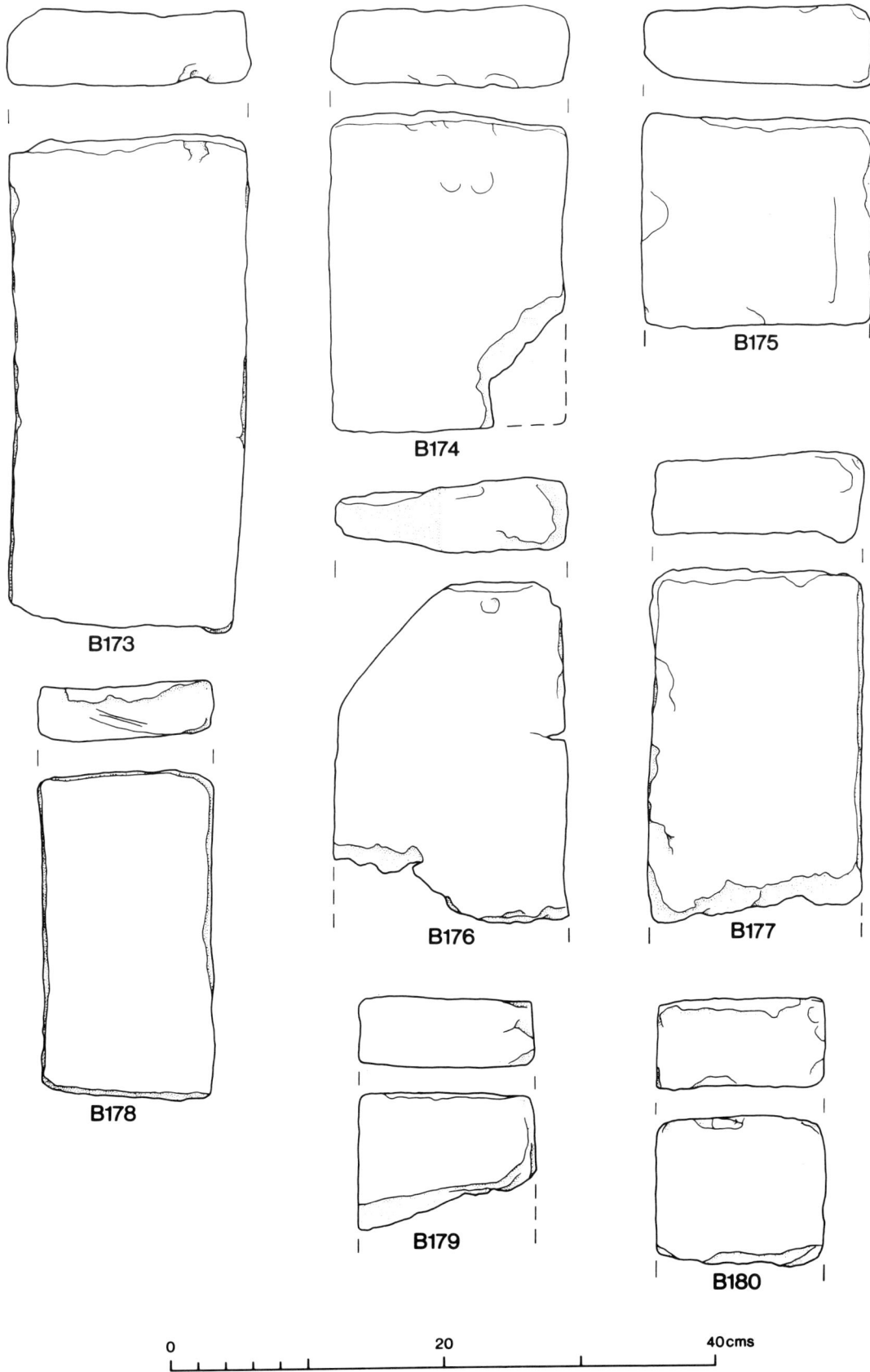

Figure 64 Brick types 3 (no. B178), 6 (nos. B173–7) and 7 (nos. B179–80).

examined to provide comparative material, and where possible have been placed within the typology (Mf.1. E13–F4).

The illustrated bricks (Figures 63–4)

B163: Brick Type 1. Context 21, Phase 5C.

B164: Brick Type 1 variant. From the precinct wall. Unphased.

B165: Brick Type 3. Context 109, Phase 7.

B166: Brick Type 3 variant. Context 109, Phase 7.

B167: Brick Type 4. Context 288, Phase 7.

B168: Fragment of brick Type 4 variant with bevelled side. Context 2072, Phase 5A.

B169: Brick Type 4 variant. Context 2072, Phase 5A.

B170: Brick Type 4 variant. Context 56, Phase 7.

B171: Fragment of brick Type 4 variant with chamfer. Context 56, Phase 7.

B172: Fragment of brick Type 5. Context 56, Phase 7.

B173: Brick Type 6. Context 426, Phase 5C.

B174: Brick Type 6. Context 426, Phase 5C.

B175: Brick Type 6. Context 426, Phase 5C.

B176: Fragment of brick Type 6 variant. Context 426, Phase 5C.

B177: Fragment of brick Type 6. Context 426, Phase 5C.

B178: Brick Type 3. Context 650, Phase 7.

B179: Fragment of brick Type 7. Context 719, Phase 5.

B180: Fragment of brick Type 7 variant. Context 2036, Phase 7.

3.4 The plain roof tile

by Stephen Potts

with a note on a fabric impression by Penelope Walton Rogers

Introduction

Only roof tile made of fired clay was present at the Priory; there was no evidence for the use of stone slates.

The site collection policy for roof tile was to retain all fragments: these were then sorted into diagnostic and non-diagnostic fragments. The former comprised 639 examples with evidence for suspension, and/or having one or other of the two principal dimensions intact. The non-diagnostic material was quantified by area, and then discarded. The quantification of classified fragments is presented in Table 2, with overall totals listed in microfiche (Mf.1 F5–G14, Mf.2. A2).

Roof tile from sites in Hull (Armstrong and Armstrong 1987, 234–6) served as the basis of a regional typology, which has been subsequently extended by work in Beverley (Armstrong *et al.* 1991, 207–7; S.J. Armstrong 1992). The present typology enlarges this range of plain tile types. The previous classification of roof tile benefitted from petrographical analysis which reinforced the distinctions between the (then) four types of tile. Additional material from the Priory has only been examined macroscopically, with the aid of a x20 achromatic hand lens. It should be noted that the brick and tile type series are independent; there is no correlation between, for example, brick Type 6 and tile Type 6, in fabric, manufacture or any other feature. The full regional tile typology appears in microfiche (Mf.1 F5–6).

Summary Tile Typology (types absent at the Priory omitted)

NB: Tiles are described as they would hang, not as manufactured, hence nib is on underside.

Type 1A (145 examples)

Dimensions: L.285mm, W.160–175mm, Th.13–15mm.
Fabric: Hard, no inclusions, usually oxidised throughout.
Suspension: Pulled semicircular nib, centrally placed.
Manufacture: Moulded, upper side pitted, lower side smoothed.

Type 1B (30 examples)

Dimensions: L.310mm, W.190–205mm, Th.15–18mm.

Type 2B (280 examples)

Dimensions: L.310mm, W.173–203mm, Th.13–17mm.

Fabric: Hard, calcareous inclusions, oxidised firing.
Suspension: Pulled central nib, often squared.
Manufacture: Moulded; upper side pitted.

Type 2C (32 examples)

Dimensions: L.275–295mm, W.185–195mm, Th.13–17mm.
Fabric: Similar to 2B, but more sand.
Suspension: Similar to 2B, but with round peg-hole usually to left of nib.

Type 3 (1 example)

Dimensions: L.320mm, W.205–210mm, Th.13–15mm.
Fabric: Sandy, with rough surface.
Suspension: Square tapering peg-hole.
Manufacture: Moulded; underside pitted and sanded.

Type 6 (108 examples)

Dimensions: L.270–280mm, W.180–205mm, Th.15mm.
Fabric: Sandy, usually oxidised margin and reduced core.
Suspension: D-shaped nib near left hand edge.
Manufacture: Moulded; underside pitted and sanded.

Type 7 (5 examples)

Dimensions: L.305–315mm, W.190–210mm, Th.15mm.
Fabric: Fine sandy, oxidised margin and reduced core.
Suspension: Tapering round peg-hole near centre of upper edge.

Type 12B (1 + 4 nibs of Type 12)

Dimensions: L?, W.190–192mm, Th.11–15mm.
Fabric: Dense with sand and chalk, oxidised.
Suspension: Triangular nib left of centre.
Manufacture: Moulded; underside finely pitted; smooth upper surface; exceptionally regular.

Type 15A (33 examples)

Dimensions: L.?, W.178–185mm, Th.13–17mm.
Fabric: Hard, with sand; oxidised throughout.
Suspension: Finger-moulded rectangular applied nib, towards left hand corner.
Manufacture: Moulded; underside slightly pitted.

Type 15B (3 examples)

Dimensions: L.?, W.180mm, Th.14–16mm.
Suspension: Same as Type 15A, with round peg-hole beside nib.

Type 16 (1 example)

Dimensions: L.?, W.?, Th.14–16mm.
Fabric: Hard, with calcareous inclusions.
Suspension: Nib close to right hand edge.
Manufacture: Moulded; underside pitted; upper side with slip.

Table 2   Number of diagnostic tile fragments recovered from the Priory.

Type	1A	1B	2B	2C	3	6	7	*12B	*15A	*15B	*16	Total
Nibs	63	18	235	31	1	105	5	1	33	3	1	496
Width of fragment	79	12	43	0	0	3	0	0	0	0	0	137
Length of fragment	3	0	2	1	0	0	0	0	0	0	0	6
Total	145	30	280	32	1	108	5	1	33	3	1	639

* New type

The tile types

Sixteen tile types, four of them subdivided, have so far been recognised from Hull and Beverley. The Priory assemblage contains nine types, five of which are new. One of these, a variant of Type 12, has forced the subdivision of this Type into a 12A and 12B. This is the only amendment of the pre-existing typology.

Three types predominate — Types 1A, 2B and 6. Of these 2B is the most common; Types 1B, 2C and 15A are moderately well represented, with Types 3, 7, 12B, and 16 being confined to few or even single examples. Hull Types 2A and 4 do not occur at the Priory, nor does Type 5, a poor quality product which was identified from Eastgate, Beverley. Of those identified at Lurk Lane, Types 6, 7 and a variant of 12 were present at the Priory. Overall this assemblage is dominated by tile types reported from other sites in Hull and Beverley. Of the new Types, only 2C and 15A can be regarded as being present in any quantity (Table 2).

A manufacturing source for Type 1A and 1B tiles has been located at the Annie Reed Road site, in the industrial suburb of Grovehill, Beverley (Humberside County Council 1987). Examples of Type 1A have also been found during fieldwalking at Castlethorpe, near Brigg, South Humberside, suggesting a wider regional distribution.

Manufacture

Visual analysis of the Priory's tile assemblage suggests manufacturing techniques similar to those described from other parts of the country. Fabrics are generally fine, lacking inclusions, with the exception of a sporadic speckling of chalk. This suggests the use of alluvial clays as a raw material, an observation consistent with the presence of Type 1A and 1B tiles at the excavated tilery at Annie Reed Road, Beverley.

The presence of lipped edges or mould extrusions suggests the tiles were moulded. Knife-trimming was practised on some tiles; this characteristic has also been noted on Type 4 and Type 10 tiles from Lurk Lane (Armstrong *et al.* 1991, 201–7). The nibs of some tiles were also trimmed (examples of Types 2B, 6, 12B, 15A and 15B show this) in order to improve the hanging edge of the tile. With Type 12 tiles, the triangular nib seems to have been achieved by the knife-trimming of a pre-existing, possibly semicircular, shape.

Linear striations on the upper surface (as moulded) suggest that the surplus clay was struck off lengthwise. Types 1A and 1B show finger ridging, indicating that for these types the fingers were used to achieve the same result. An applied white slip on the upper surface of these two tile types may have functioned as a lubricant, to prevent the fingers sticking to the plastic clay (it cannot be regarded as a

Table 3 Occurrence of tile types — by phase

Tile Type						Phases						
	3	3A	3B	3C	3D	5	5A	5B	5C	6A	6B	7
1A		1?	1			16	4	2	19	4	4	82
1B						1	1		3		1	23
2B	1	4?			3	12	40	12	46	13	3	115
2C							18	1	4			6
3												1
6		4	31	3	7	13	23	2	7	5	1	13
7							1					8
12B					2		1		1	2		7
15A						3	16	2		1		17
15B							1					2
16									1			

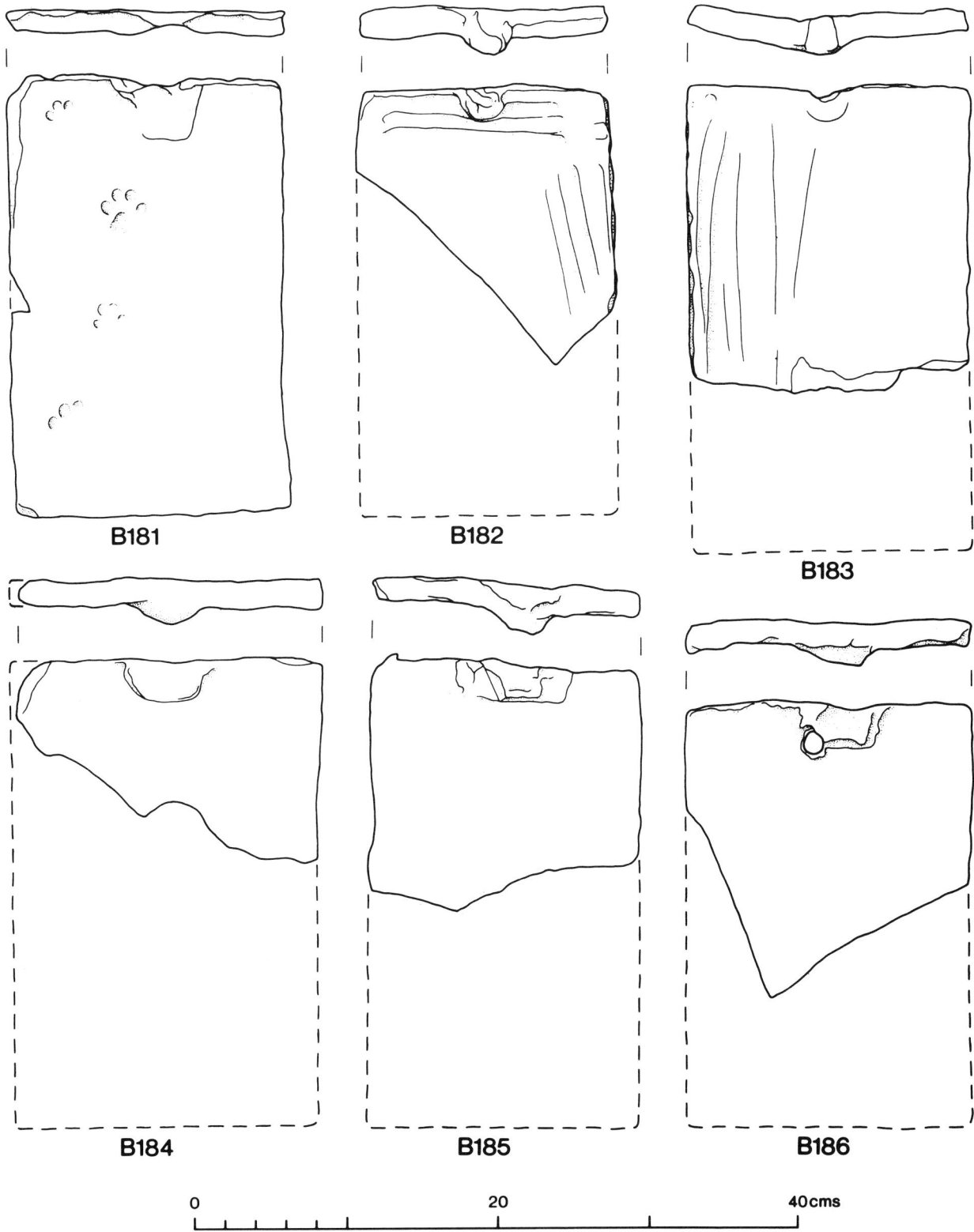

Figure 65 Roof tile types 1A (x2), 1B, 2B (x2) and 2C.

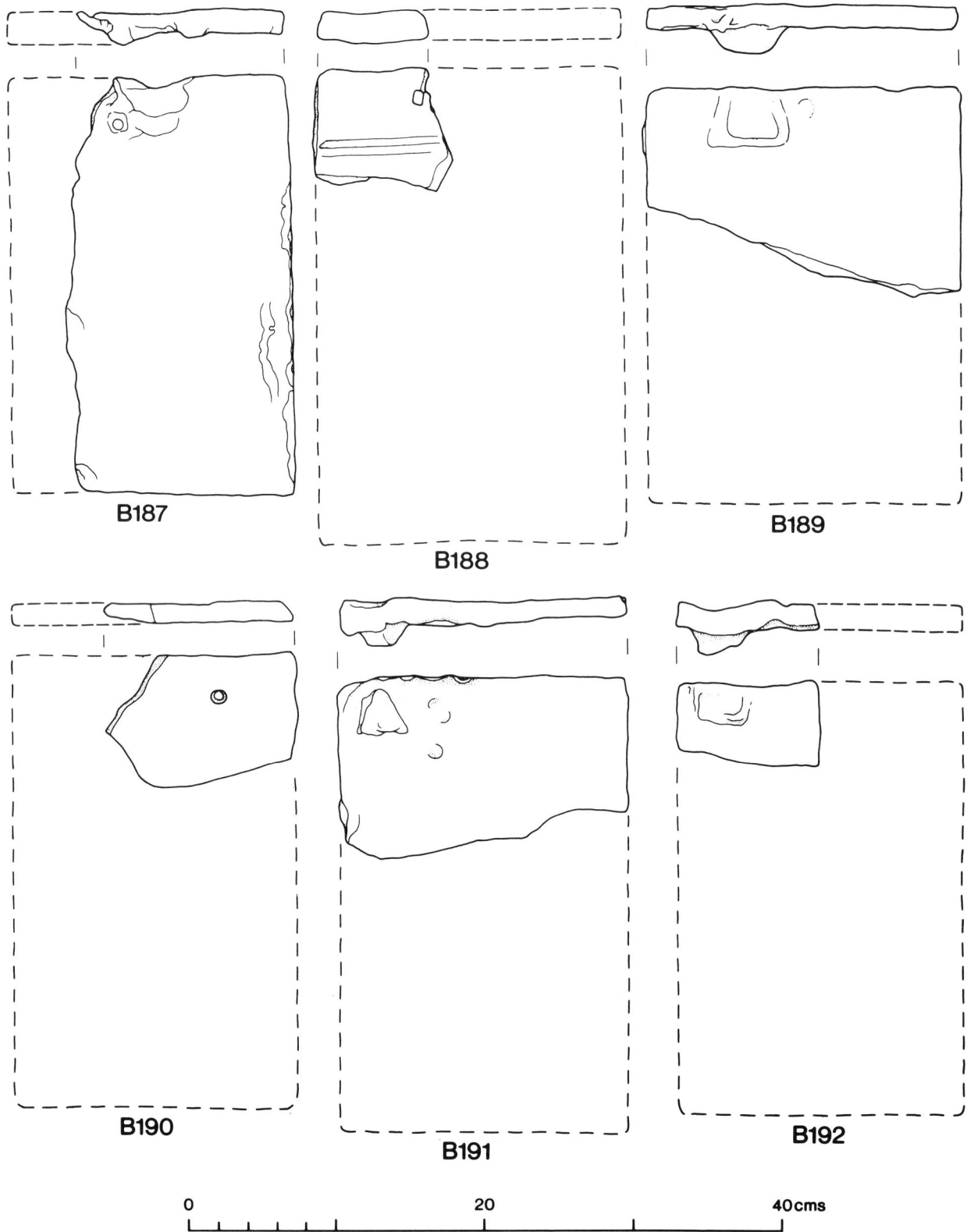

Figure 66 Roof tile types 2C, 3, 6, 7, 12B and 15A.

decorative effect since this surface would have been hung facing downwards). Striations on both upper and lower surfaces occur on a few examples of Type 15A. This may have resulted from the tile being slid across the moulding surface, possibly onto a pallet. Some means of supporting the tiles during their transfer to the drying area should be anticipated, since they would otherwise have been prone to buckling. Striations in more than one direction may indicate that some had brush-finished surfaces. Sand was sometimes used as a separator in the moulding process. Types 1A, 1B, 15A and 15B, however, do not appear to have been sanded — all have finely pitted undersides, which hint at the use of a separator that did not survive the firing process.

Straw or grass impressions on the surfaces of the tiles were rare; although, the latter were not examined for impressions as carefully as were the bricks, this may indicate a different drying practice. End or edge-stacking may have been used, though striated surfaces always seemed to be intact — this would not have occurred, had they been end or edge-stacked in a 'lean-to' fashion. Some of the tiles were laid flat for drying. This is indicated by no. B181, which shows paw prints on the striated upper surface.

Phasing and reuse

A common problem in considering the development of roof tile is the reuse of materials. At the Priory much of the tile and brick appears to have been of low quality. Underfired soft and crumbly tile, or overfired tile and tiles which were fired too quickly, producing sandwich fracturing (with layers of fabric separated by elongated voids), are common. In short, much of the building material at the Priory was probably only used there, perhaps after being obtained by donation.

Plain tile was reused in the construction of bench positions, door steps, and hearths. As with the brick, it was common for several tile types to be reused in the same structure. For example, a bench position (38) included flat-laid tile of Types 1A, 1B, 2B and 6, while hearth 815 was constructed from Types 1A, 2B, 2C, 12B and 15A. The prominence of tile Type 6 in the construction horizon for Phase 5A may have arisen from its prior use in structures of Phase 3B or 3C: it was common in deposits which had perhaps derived from the demolition of earlier buildings. Tile Types 1A, 1B and 2B were especially common in Phases 5C and 7, representing the later modification of the little cloister and the stripping of the Priory buildings at the close of occupation. This must reflect their importance as roofing materials in the Phase 5 little cloister.

The full listing of tile is summarised by Table 3. Tile Type 6 pre-dated the others, while Type 2B was unusually persistent in use. The occurrence of Type 6

with other types during Phase 5 can either be explained in terms of on-site recycling, or as a second input of the same type; the latter interpretation is perhaps more likely. Tile was not a dominant building material at the Priory before Phase 5 and its proven early use was confined to internal features in buildings of timber. It was most common in contexts of 14th-century date: the construction of the little cloister, and in contexts relating to its later history.

A coefficient of similarity (Brainerd 1951; Robinson 1951) was calculated for the diagnostic tile present in the various phases; these calculations are presented in Table 4 (Mf.1 G6). The most closely linked of the major groups were the demolition Phase 7, and the further progress of this activity in Phase 8; Phases 5B and 5C in the little cloister; and Phases 5C and 6A. This last result may support the interpretation of Phases 5C and 6A as being broadly contemporary.

Illustrated plain roof tile (Figures 65–7)

B181: Tile Type 1A, with cat paw prints. Context 1135, Phase 5B.
B182: Fragment of tile Type 1A. Context 79, Phase 8.
B183: Fragment of tile Type 1B. Context 303, Phase 7.
B184: Fragment of tile Type 2B. Context 15, Phase 7.
B185: Fragment of tile Type 2B. Context 3040, Phase 5C.
B186: Fragment of tile Type 2C. Context 1093, Phase 7.
B187: Fragment of tile Type 2C. Context 815, Phase 5A.
B188: Fragment of tile Type 3. Context 15, Phase 7.
B189: Fragment of tile Type 6. Context 625, Phase 3B.
B190: Fragment of tile Type 7. Trench 2, Unstratified.
B191: Fragment of tile Type 12B. Context 15, Phase 7.
B192: Fragment of tile Type 15A. Context 849, Phase 5A.
B193: Fragment of tile Type 15A. Context 770, Phase 5A.
B194: Fragment of tile Type 15A. Context 65, Phase 5.
B195: Fragment of tile Type 15B. Context 3123, Phase 7.
B196: Fragment of tile Type 15B. Context 37, Phase 5A.
B197: Fragment of tile Type 16. Context 3102, Phase 5C.

Appendix: A textile imprint on a medieval roofing tile

by Penelope Walton Rogers

The imprint of a medium-coarse textile is visible along one of the finished edges of roof-tile RF 3301 (from context 481, Phase 5); the area covered by the imprint is 100 x 30 mm. The middle part of the edge of the tile is pulled inwards, as if some fabric-covered object has been pushed against the side of the tile while the clay was still in a plastic state.

A plasticine impression of the imprint, viewed with a raking light, showed the textile to have been in tabby weave (syn.plain weave), with yarn spun in the Z-direction in both warp and weft. The thread-count (number of threads per cm in warp and weft) ranges from 8 x 10 to 10 x 12. The fibre is not identifiable from the imprint.

B193

B194

B195

B196

B197

0   20   40cms

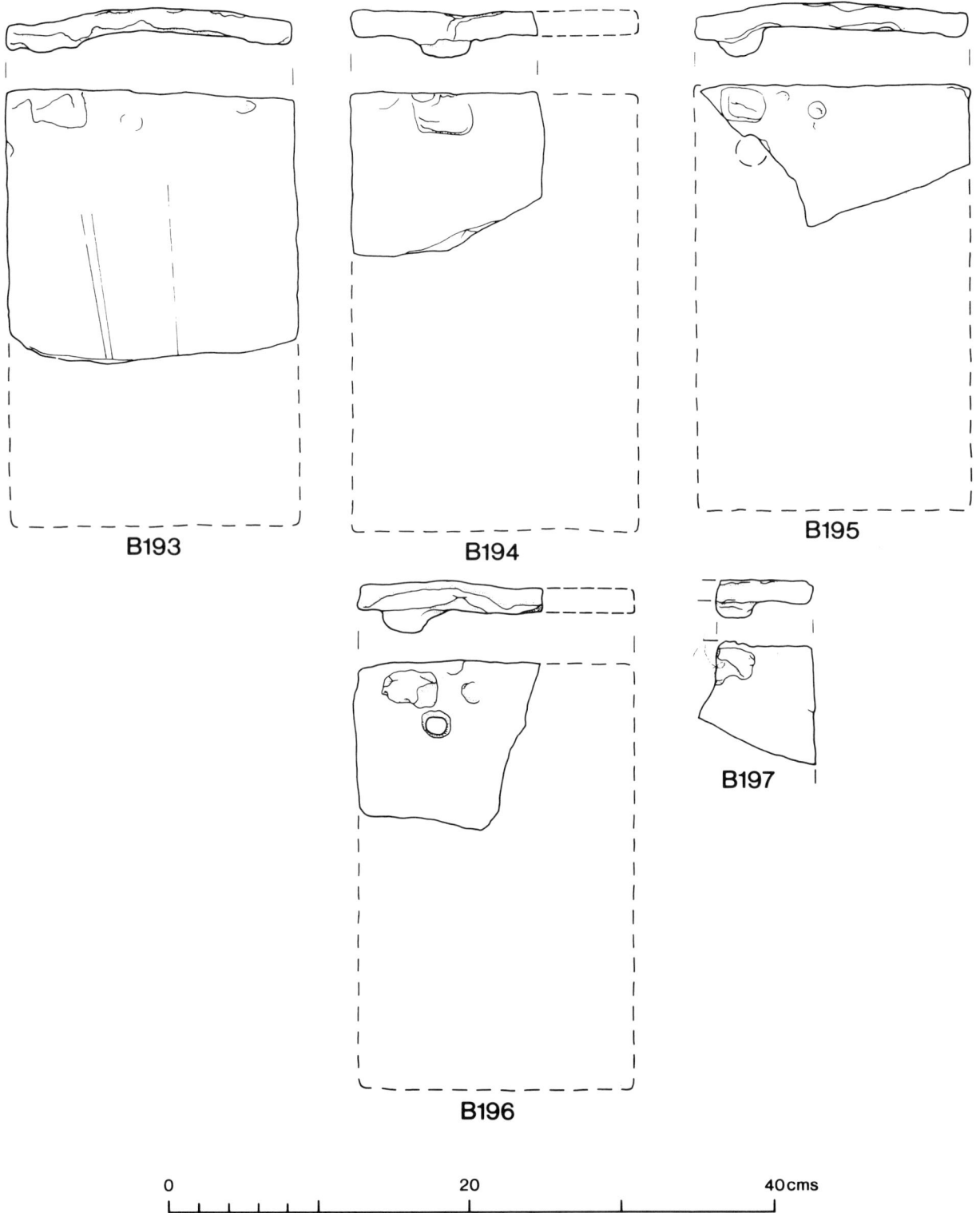

Figure 67   Roof tile types 15A (x2), 15B (x2) and 16.

116

The main types of fabric in use in the medieval period are now well-established (Walton 1989, 385–91). The weave of the Beverley imprint is one which was not common in wool until the 14th and 15th centuries, and even at that time was not usually produced with Z-spun yarn in warp and weft; when, rarely, Z-spun tabby weaves from medieval contexts do occur in wool, they are almost always much finer than the Beverley example.

The imprint in question is therefore more likely to be that of a linen textile. Medieval linens from Britain are almost without exception in tabby weave and worked from Z-spun yarn, in the manner of the Beverley example. The thread-counts of surviving linens range from 9 x 7, from a *c*.1300 AD burial at St. Bee's in Cumbria (J. Glover pers. comm.), to 24 x 24, from a 14th or 15th-century site in London (Pritchard 1982, 207). The Beverley example therefore falls towards the lower end of the range.

How a coarse linen textile came into contact with the roof-tile is a matter for conjecture. Researchers seem to be in agreement that textiles were not used during the manufacture of tiles. Freshly made tiles could well be carried on edge, in a row along the arm (pers. comm. Sarah Jennings): perhaps the imprint represents pressure from the tile-maker's overalls.

3.5 The roof furniture and ridge tiles

by Martin Foreman

Introduction

About 90 fragments of glazed tile were identified. Most were from ridge pieces, or from ceramic roof fittings. Unglazed ridge tiles, both plain and decorated, amounted to over 80 identified fragments. One group of half-glazed tiles was of uncertain original form, but was possibly comparable with the flat tile Type 4 identified from Hull (Armstrong and Armstrong 1987). This was perhaps of a different fabric, and certainly of an inferior quality. The low quality of some brick and tile from the Priory has been remarked upon, above (section 3.4).

The fabric groups have been defined purely on the basis of visual inspection; subdivisions have been made on the basis of differences in glaze finish, although it is acknowledged that these may sometimes have arisen fortuitously during manufacture. The summary typology which is presented here is not correlated with the typologies for plain brick and tile; nor does it include the undecorated forms of unglazed ridge tile. Detailed lists of the occurrence of fragments by context and phase can be found in microfiche (Mf.2 A3–10).

Summary typology of roof furniture and ridge tile

Fabric 1

This is reduced to a mid-grey colour through most of the fabric, orange oxidised surfaces appear typically only at the edges of the tile. The fabric is marked by occasional voids and sparse white quartz inclusions. The lower, unglazed, side is usually pitted. Finger smoothing occurs only where features have been added to the tile.

The upper surfaces are covered with lead glazes; their colours range from dark olive green (11 fragments), through mid-green (seven fragments) and mid green with brown speckles (76 fragments), to pale green (three fragments). Some of the glazes bear prominent grainy inclusions, but the majority are smooth. No convincing evidence was found for the use of an under-glaze slip.

Fabric 2

This is an almost completely oxidised sandy orange-to-buff fabric. None of the examples was glazed. This fabric was used only for finials. 6 fragments.

Fabric 3

This is a very fine, part-reduced fabric, lacking the inclusions typical of fabric Type 1. The tiles in this fabric were finished by finger-smoothing and knife cutting, and were glazed with a smooth mid-green finish. 6 fragments.

Fabric 4

This is a hard, red fabric with a charcoal-grey reduced core. All the tiles in this fabric are flat, finger-smoothed, and with the lower part of the tile glazed. Glazes are purple-brown, thick, and often bubbled, spilled or overfired. 29 fragments.

Fabric 5

This is a softer fabric than Type 4. It is pitted on the unglazed side, rather than being finger-smoothed. The tile fragments include curved examples, so are probably all from ridge tiles, which were fairly crudely fashioned. The glazes are yellowish-brown through to green. 14 fragments.

In addition, a few glazed fragments were considered as possible members of the groups listed above : these are not, however, included in the quantifications given above. The occurrence of the fabrics by phase groups is summarised in Table 5.

Manufacture

Ridge tiles were probably manufactured in bottomless moulds; it is uncertain whether sand or other media would have served as a separator. While the clay slab remained plastic, it would be shaped over a former to the desired angle. Any decoration or functional modification would be carried out at this stage; this could have involved the addition of wheel-thrown elements such as finials. Among the Priory tiles, it appears that this secondary working would usually be carried out by finger-shaping, though knife-cut slashing is a characteristic of some ventilator tiles. Glazing, either onto a pale slip or more usually directly onto the clay, would follow this shaping and precede the firing. The rough and uneven finish of some of the glazed surfaces may indicate that wind-blown sand or dust had adhered to the wet surface of the newly glazed tile.

Distribution

Table 5 shows that glazed roof tile first appeared in Phase 3B, in external surfaces associated with the aisled timber hall. The small fragments, lying mostly to the north of the building, could perhaps have derived from the earlier Phase 3A hall. Fabrics 1 and 2 were the only ones to occur in these 13th-century deposits. In context 65, the garth deposit of the little cloister, they were probably residual, and in the Phase 5A deposits they mostly derived from make-up layers laid down at the outset of construction activity. This would tend to confirm that their presence arose from the use of demolition debris from the Phase 3 structures in the levelling operations of Phase 5A. The later occurrence of fabrics 1B and 1D in Phase 6A, in the later 14th century, is again associated with a major episode of construction and the associated movement of soils. The virtual absence of these fabrics in later construction and demolition horizons is striking; it is unlikely that they were used on the 14th-century Phase 5 structures.

Fabrics 3, 4 and 5 are unlikely to have been used on the Phase 3 structures; only one ventilator tile fragment in a construction horizon of Phase 5A could possibly be residual from earlier activity. These fabrics were, however, present in contexts deposited during the Phase 5 occupation of the little cloister. It seems probable that they were used on the little cloister roofs from the outset. This is confirmed by their prominence in the Phase 7 demolition horizon. Fabric 4 was found in a limited area, in the north-west corner of the little cloister and — save for garth context 65 — only in Phase 5C. The plain ridge tile appears to have been in wide use in the little cloister from Phase 5A onwards. The decorated unglazed ridge tile fragments were not as common as the undecorated pieces — each broken tile produced more undiagnostic than decorated sherds.

Roof furniture (Figure 68)

Fragments in Fabric 1 with a dark olive glaze (nos. B198–205) include five whose curved hand-formed edges suggest them to be from 'horns': raised hollow projections. These could be decorative elements from a large finial (cf. Clarke and Carter 1977, fig. 136, no. 1) or may alternatively be fragments from vents on a ventilator tile or louvre. A further fragment in a pale green glaze could be from a similar object, as are two joining fragments (nos. B207–8) in a medium green glaze. Several of the Fabric 1 sherds may derive from a louvre such as that reconstructed from fragments at the Austin Friars, Leicester (Allin 1981, fig. 18, nos. 20–1). Similar 'horns' have been identified at the neighbouring Eastgate site (S.J. Armstrong 1992).

'Spinning top' finials are a form best represented at the Priory by Fabric 2, an unglazed ware. These include three body sherds from wheel-thrown finials (nos. B209–11), three hand-pulled spurs (nos. B214–16), and a wheel-thrown flat top which is probably from a finial (no. B213). A fragment (no. B212) of a hand-made 'spinning top' finial was made in glazed Fabric 3. Similar finials were present at Eastgate (S.J. Armstrong 1992, nos. 820, 830–2), and at a nearby grange of Meaux Abbey (Eames 1961, 166, fig. 45, h–i); they are also common elsewhere (cf. Clarke and Carter 1977, 301).

Ventilator tiles (Figure 69)

A straight-edged cut in no. B217 indicates that it is a fragment of a ventilator: this example may have been a simple ridge tile with slots cut into its sides. A second ridge tile with a crest (no. B220) has a similar cut aperture. A more complex form occurs with no. B218. Here, a ridge tile with a decorated crest was cut, and the clay pulled upwards and outwards, flaring around the oval vent: the flared surface would have sheltered this vent, helping to keep rain from entering.

As noted above, the hollow 'horns' of some roof furniture may also have served as ventilating features. The adaptation of a ridge tile to form a ventilator has been identified at Hull (Armstrong and Armstrong 1987, 238–40, fig. 145). Neither the Hull ventilator tiles nor those from the Priory are sooted, and the function of a ventilator should not be equated with that of a chimney or smoke louvre.

Ridge tiles (Figure 69)

Ridge tiles from this site include glazed, unglazed, plain and decorated products. The form of decoration at the Priory was usually a simple finger-formed banding, either pinched or applied, which ran either along (nos. B218 and B220–21) or across (nos. B222–5) the crest of the tile. The latter form would have helped to seal the joints between overlapping tiles. The simplest pinched decoration occurred on the unglazed tiles; whereas glazed pieces could have more carefully formed features, including a motif executed by the finger-pressing of squares in series along a tile (no. B223). These forms of decoration were established by the time of the little cloister construction in the early 14th century. A similar ridge tile with bands of thumb-applied clay across its top was present in a kiln at Boston, Lincolnshire, dated to the early 14th century (Mayes 1965, 99). Moorhouse (1983, 315) holds the shallow finger-formed crest to be peculiar to the north, and of wide distribution in Yorkshire. Simple fingered decoration has been noted on ridge tile previously excavated at the Priory (Armstrong and Tomlinson 1987, 47) and at Eastgate (S.J. Armstrong 1992, 224–5 and fig. 104, no. 822).

Half-glazed tiles (not illustrated)

The purpose of the tiles in Fabric 4 is uncertain; they included no curved elements to suggest a function as ridge pieces. The half glazing of the tiles — on the

B199 & B203

B206

B207 & B208

B209

B210

B211

B212

B213

B214

B215

B216

0   5   10   15 cms

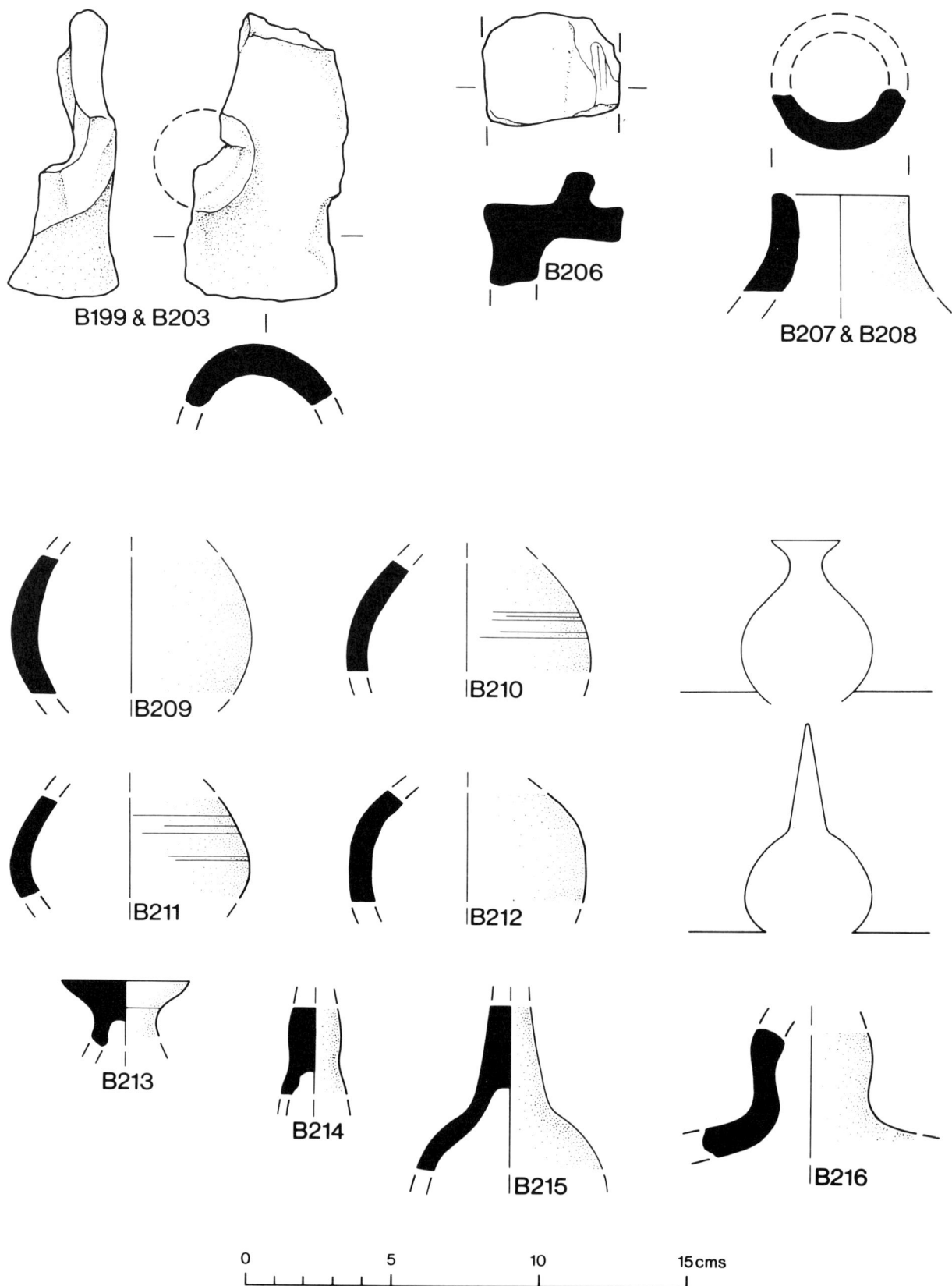

Figure 68 Roof furniture.

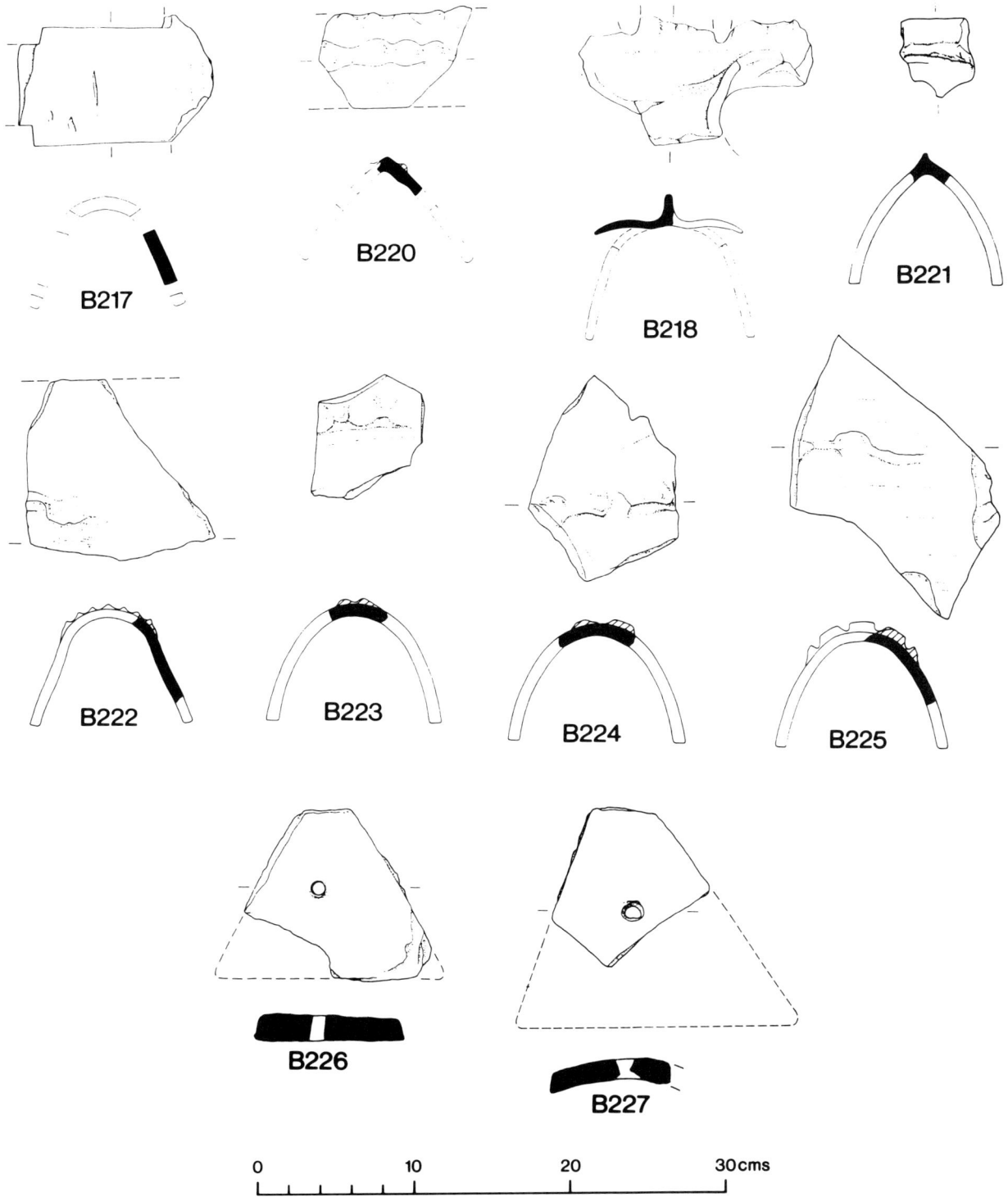

Figure 69 Ventilator, ridge and hip tile.

lower surface — is also inappropriate to ridge tiles, as it suggests that the upper part of the tile would be overlapped. These tiles were particularly common at the north-west corner of the Little Cloister. It is possible that they were deposited from the roof during the demolition and rebuilding of walls at the west end of the north range in Phases 5B and 5C. An alternative use, as in a hearth or stove, is also possible.

Hip tiles (Figure 69)

Two hip tiles (nos. B226–7), one of which was curved to form a bonnet hip, were identified; a few other fragments might have been from either hip or ridge tiles. These come from Phase 7 and Phase 5C. Hip tiles may have seen use in the reconstruction of the Phase 5C little cloister ranges, which are considered to have shared common timber-framed elements at ground level, and perhaps also above.

Catalogue of illustrated material (Figures 68–9)

B199. Roof furniture fragment.
Broken on all sides. Joins to B203, forming part of an object with an open 'horn' or vent. ?Joins to B200, B202, B204 and RF 3363 also.
RF 3358, Context 1073, Phase 3B.

B203. Roof furniture fragment.
Broken on all sides. Joins to B199, forming part of an object with an open 'horn' or vent. ?Joins to B200, B202, B204 and RF 3363 also. Fabric 1, Glaze type: A
RF 3361, Context 787, Phase 5A.

B206. Roof furniture or ridge tile fragment. Broken on all sides. A raised rib runs along ?crest. Fabric 1, Glaze type: C.
RF 3357, Context 1073, Phase 3B.

B207. Roof furniture, 'horn' fragment. Joins with RF 3356.
Fabric 1, Glaze type: D
RF 3355, Context 729, Phase 3D.

B208. Roof furniture 'horn' fragments. Joins with RF 3355.
Fabric 1, Glaze type: D
RF 3356, Context 65, Phase 5.

B209. 'Spinning top' finial fragment. Wheel-thrown body sherd.
Fabric 2
RF 3329, Context 1073, Phase 3B.

B210. 'Spinning top' finial fragment. Wheel-thrown body sherd.
Fabric 2
RF 3353, Context 1027, Phase 3B.

B211. 'Spinning Top' finial fragment. Wheel-thrown body sherd.

Fabric 2
RF 3330, Context 65, Phase 5.

B212. 'Spinning top' finial fragment. Hand-fashioned body sherd. Fabric 3
RF 3354, Context 40, Phase 5C.

B213. ?Finial top, flat. Wheel-thrown flat-topped object. Fabric 2
RF 3299, Context 65, Phase 5.

B214. ?Finial top spur. Hand drawn fired clay point. Fabric 2
RF3303, Context 893, Phase 5A.

B215. ?Finial top spur. Hand drawn fired clay point, rising from a rounded body. Fabric 2
RF 3328, Context 15, Phase 7.

B216. ?Finial top spur. Hand drawn fired clay point. Fabric 1, Glaze A ?Joins to B205.
RF 3407, Context 18, Phase 7.

B217. Ventilator fragment. Flat tile fragment with straight knife-cut edges marking two straight horizontal vents.
Fabric 3
RF 3302, Context 702, Phase 5A.

B218. Ventilator ridge-tile fragment. Ridge tile with low crest, with cut or impressed hollows. Side of tile flares out around a round or oval vent. Fabric 3
RF 3300, Context 303, Phase 7.

B220. Ventilator fragments. Decoration formed as two applied finger-formed strips running along the crest. A straight horizontal knife-cut vent runs along the tile below the crest. Fabric 3
Context 624, Phase 5B.

B221. Ridge-tile fragment. Decoration formed as a simple finger-pulled strip, running along the crest.
Fabric 1, Glaze type: B
Context 997, Phase 6A.

B222. Ridge-tile fragment. Decoration formed as an applied strip, ?running along the crest.
Context 815, Phase 5A.

B223. Ridge-tile fragment. Decoration formed as an applied finger-formed strip running across the crest. Unglazed fabric.
Context 65, Phase 5.

B224. Ridge-tile fragment. Decoration formed as an applied finger-formed strip running across the crest.
Context 65, Phase 5.

B225. Ridge-tile fragment. Decoration formed as an applied finger-formed strip running across the crest. Fabric uncertain.
Context 303, Phase 7.

B226. Hip tile. A flat hip tile, with hole for suspension.
Context 15, Phase 7.

B227. Bonnet hip tile. Curved hip tile, with hole for suspension.
Context 583, Phase 5C.

3.6 The floor tile

by Stephen Potts

Manufacture

Twenty-two undecorated lead glazed floor tiles were recovered from the Priory; of these only one was a near-complete example (no. B234). The fabrics are of better quality than those of the brick or roof tile, generally being a hard fine clay with a little sand. The absence of pebbles or lithic fragments and the presence of only small infrequent voids suggest the use of a well-puddled clay. The degree of firing is also more even. All the tiles show an even orange colouration on their fracture surfaces, and none of the cores is reduced. These characteristics are indicative of a uniform oxidised firing. The detailed descriptions of these tiles are presented in microfiche (Mf.2 A11–13).

The tiles were made in sanded moulds; all the examples have a sanded undersurface. A white/cream slip was painted on the struck surface of some tiles and brush-marks are visible on most examples. Lead glazes were used either applied to a white slip resulting in a yellow/buff colour on firing, or, with added copper, producing a dark green.

Distribution

No floor tiles were excavated from *in situ* positions, though a late, plain, and apparently unglazed tile floor was noted within the west range of the great cloister. Most came from demolition horizons in Phase 7, or from the post-medieval contexts of Phase 8. As only one complete tile was recovered, it seems almost certain that they were removed when the buildings were stripped. The three examples which were recovered from contexts representing the occupation of the Priory lay on the north side of the great cloister, and close to the junction of the north and west ranges of the little cloister. Three others probably derived from the choir of the Priory church. This small collection of green or yellow tiles (except for no. B235 which lacks a glaze over its slip) is of similar character to the nine tiles previously recovered at the Priory (S.J. Armstrong 1987, 48). The earlier excavations at the Priory (1960–83) revealed the presence of late-medieval plain tile floors, both in the church and in the Old Friary building, though no examples of these tile floors were lifted (*ibid.*, 48). 'Tessellated pavements' have also been recorded in the area of the Beverley Franciscan Priory (Miller *et al.* 1982, 51–2).

The uniformity of the tiles from the Priory should probably be taken to indicate that a decorative scheme for their use would have consisted, at its most elaborate, of a chequered setting of yellow and green tiles. A triangular tile, such as no. B234, would have had its place at the edge of this arrangement of tiles. Such a scheme has been noted at Greyfriars, Hartlepool, in the church (Young 1983, 51), and a comparable pattern in black and yellow has been suggested for the cloisters of the Carmelite House at Newcastle-on-Tyne (Harbottle 1968, 192), and at Newcastle Blackfriars (B. Harbottle, pers. comm.). Tiled floors in the Dominican churches at Guildford (Poulton and Woods 1984, 23–5) and Ipswich (Loader 1986) were lifted and reset frequently, as burials intruded into them. The negative evidence for tiled, flagged or suspended floors — a lack of occupation deposits — has been noted at Beverley in the west range of the little cloister, perhaps also in the Phase 5A occupation of the west chamber of the north range; and in the Phase 6 occupation of the great cloister north range. Green and yellow tiles excavated at Lurk Lane were considered to have been of local manufacture, and of 15th-century date (P. Armstrong 1991, 199).

Catalogue of illustrated floor tile (Figure 70)

B228: Floor tile, dark green glaze. Context 674, Phase 6B.
B229: Floor tile, dark yellow glaze. Context 2068, Phase 8.
B230: Floor tile, dark yellow glaze. Context 15, Phase 7.
B231: Floor tile, dark yellow glaze. Context 17, Phase 7.
B232: Floor tile, dark green glaze. Context 303, Phase 8.
B233: Floor tile, dark green glaze. Context 303, Phase 8.
B234: Floor tile, dark green glaze. Context 3015, Phase 5C.
B235: Floor tile. white slip, no glaze. Context 142, Phase 7.

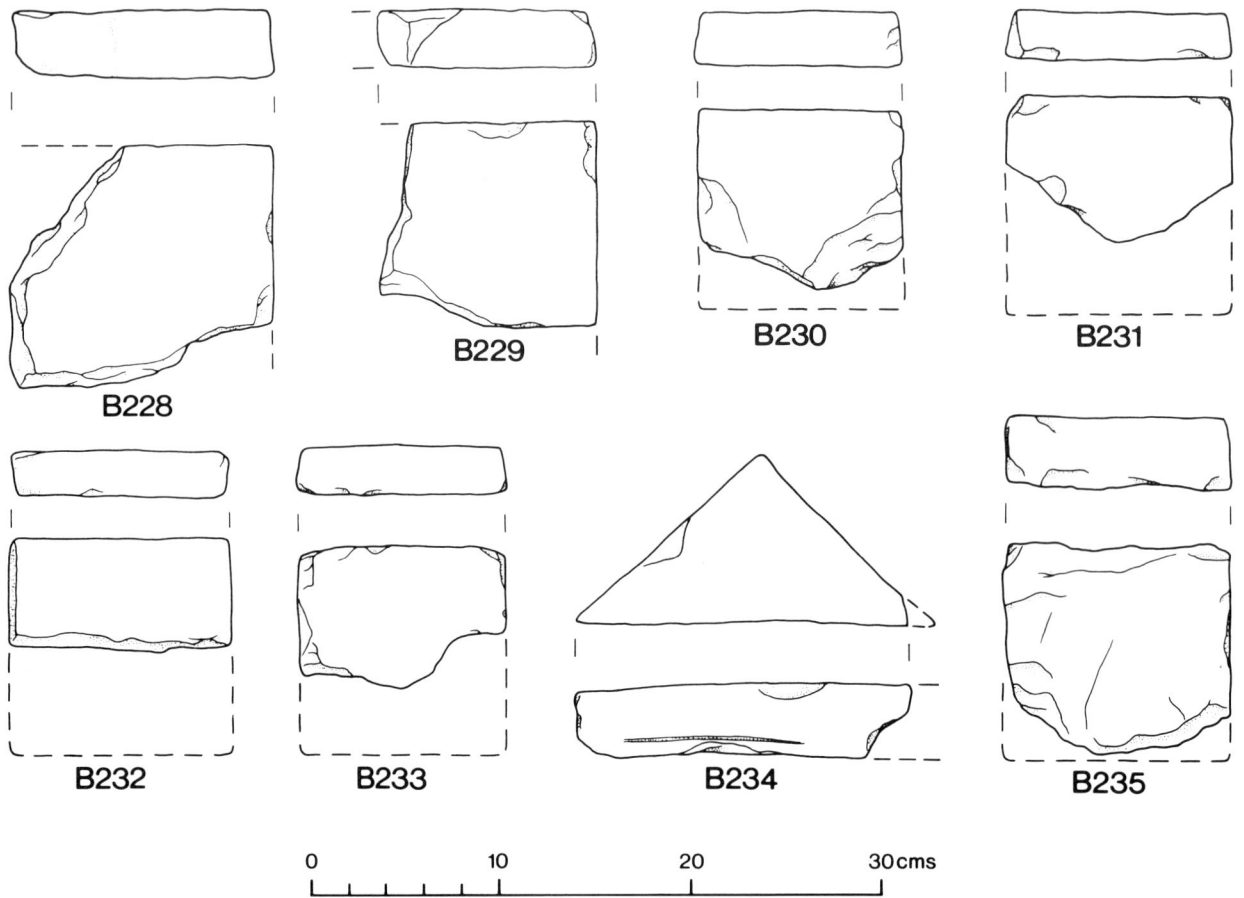

Figure 70 Floor tile.

3.7 The daub

by Martin Foreman

A small amount of burnt daub with reed or lath impressions was identified from the site. Most of the smaller pieces appear to originate from Phase 1, occurring within the fills of features. In his examination of some small fragments of slag-like material from these features, Dr. Gerry McDonnell commented that the ashy slags found in them could have originated in the burning of wattle-and-daub structures (Section 5.2: Mf.3 E6–8). The daub from Phase 1 may further illustrate the clearing of debris after a fire.

Lumps of daub were deliberately used among chalk and cobbles to form the footing for the Phase 3A timber hall. At no point after this did daub make a significant appearance among the finds. There is no evidence for its later use in any of the Priory structures.

Daub from the excavation is listed here — none is illustrated.

Context	Phase	Quantity
925	1	1 small bag — from soil-sieving.
1209	1	1 small bag — from soil-sieving.
1212	1	2 small bags — from soil-sieving.
1214	1	1 small bag — from soil-sieving.
959	2	Small fragment.
1121	2	Very small fragment.
1025	3A	Large pieces of (selected) daub.
90	5A	A little (?residual) daub.
223	7	Very small quantity.

3.8 The window glass

by C. Pamela Graves

with a note on the chemical analysis by Julian Henderson

Introduction

This report is prefaced by notes to the catalogue and a brief summary of the distribution of the glass. The art-historical affinities of the painted glass are examined, followed by a summary consideration of the context of Dominican glazing elsewhere in England. The report concludes with an integrated discussion of the archaeological patterning on this site.

Catalogue Notes

The catalogue of window glass is presented in microfiche (Mf.2 A14–C4). It omits individual reference to fragments deemed to have been adequately presented by their illustration.

This glass has been illustrated in context groups; all of the glass bearing painted decoration or grozed edges has been illustrated, whereas glass without either of these features has not usually been illustrated unless its quantity appeared to be significant. The quantification of glass in the contexts, by area, is presented in Table 6.

The fragments are briefly described in the catalogue; the term 'white glass' has been used for originally colourless translucent metal, regardless of its tint. Dr. Julian Henderson examined a small sample of the excavated window glass, some of which proved to be pot metal blue; he has also noted the thickness and condition of those fragments which he examined, and this information has been incorporated into the catalogue. The character of the window glass from the site was superficially consistent, probably justifying the limitation of detailed analysis to sample pieces.

Distribution of window glass (Table 6)

Window glass was recovered from occupation Phases 5, 5A, 5B, 5C, 6A and 6B, and from demolition Phases 7 and 8. Undecorated 'white' glass was found within the east chamber of the little cloister north range in Phase 5B, and in the west chamber and the lean-to or ancillary area at its west end in Phase 5C. Fragments were also recovered from the little cloister alley and garth, including cat. nos. 3 and 4 which are recorded from construction-phase trench 719

The bulk of the window glass, and almost all the painted fragments, came from either the Phase 5C/7 interface, or from demolition Phases 7 and 8. Most was concentrated in the east chamber of the little cloister north range; unpainted 'white' glass was more prominent in the west chamber. It had been deposited here during the retrieval of lead cames, and extensive evidence for the gathering and melting down of this material has been recorded (see Chapter 2, Phase 7, and section 3.9, below). Glass may also have been retrieved at this time. A concentration of painted glass was confined by a stairwell in the eastern chamber (see Figure 57). A little glass, both unpainted (nos. 516–17 and 521–2) and painted (no. 526), came from a demolition spread which was probably associated with the buildings on the west side of the great cloister. A fragment of window glass, perhaps of 14th-century date, was also excavated in the 'Old Friary', where it may have derived from either the nearby church or from other buildings in the south part of the precinct (S.J. Armstrong 1987, 45, no. 37).

The Painted Glass (Figures 71–7)

Almost all the glass is of the type known as grisaille, with designs of stylised foliage on either plain or cross-hatched grounds. Grisaille on a cross-hatched ground was less common than grisaille without cross-hatching (c.238.48 square cms., or 9.5% overall, glass with cross-hatching; c.1360.43 square cms., or 54.4% overall, glass without cross-hatching). There was a proportionately large amount of unpainted plain glazing (664.6 square cms or 26.6%). Most of the remaining glass was painted with a wavy border design (237.28 square cms or 9.5%).

The first type of grisaille employs trefoils on curling stems, sometimes with a short tapered line or spur within the stem where it joins with the trefoil head (e.g. no. 502). These designs are consistent with patterns which appear in panels of the Five Sisters window (nXVI) in the north transept of York Minster, completed by c.1250 (O'Connor and Haselock 1977). The grisaille on plain ground employs similar trefoils, on curling and crossing stems (e.g. no. 122), often in association with a group of three or more berries (e.g. nos. 75, 116–17, 122, 225, 250 and 255). The stems are generally emphasised with fine, attenuated lines drawn from the spurs at the head. This type of grisaille is found in the second half of the 13th century (generally the later part), and into the early 14th century, e.g. Westwell, Kent (Winston 1867, Pl. 1); Chartham, Kent (Westlake 1891–4, I, Pl. LXXXIX; II, Pl. LXCIId; Winston *op.cit.*, Pl. 10). It should be noted that the designs are not mutually exclusive and, for example, both cross-hatching and portions of plain

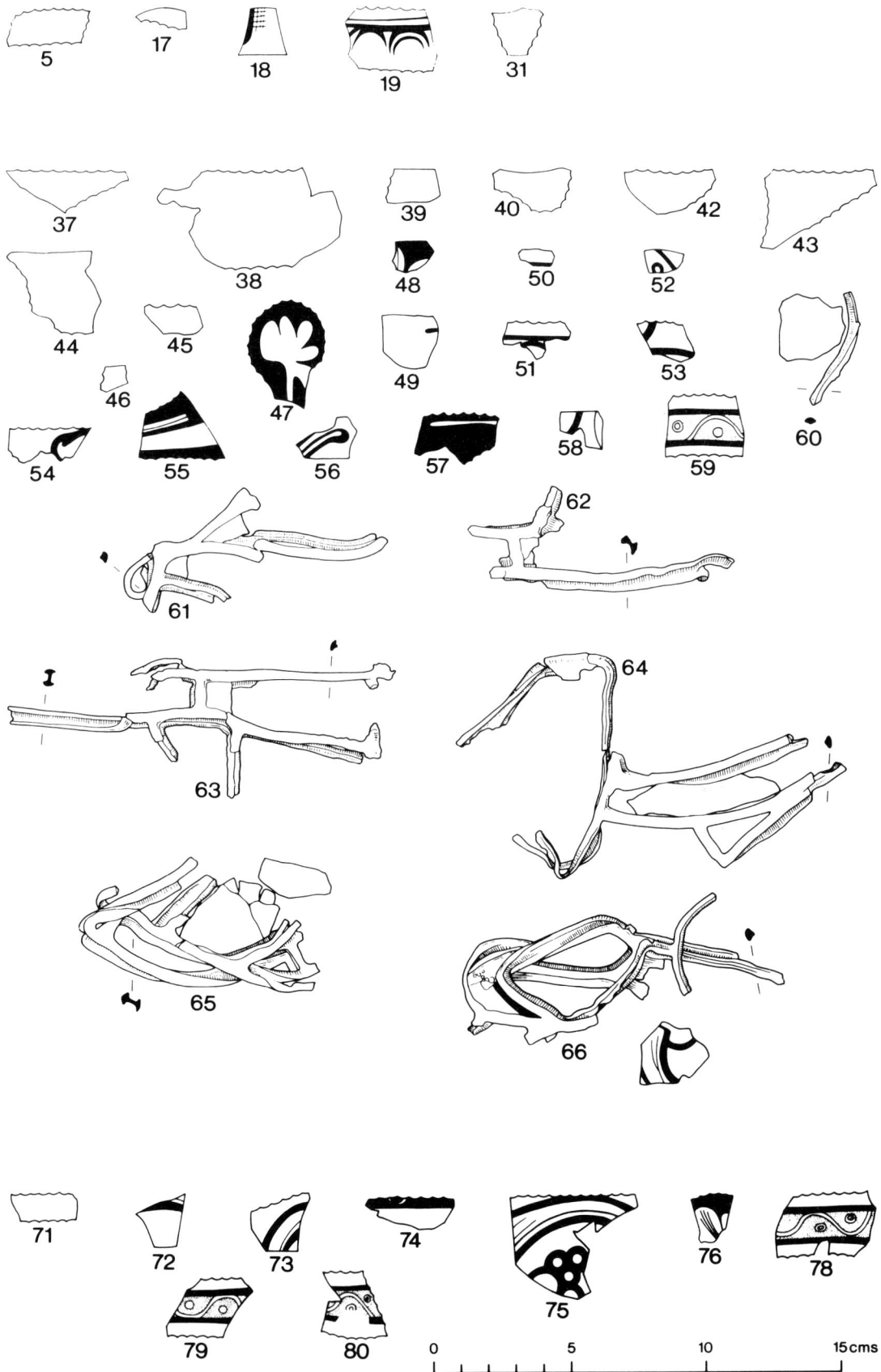

Figure 71 Window glass and came. Nos. 5-66, glass and came from RF439, context 381. Nos. 71–80, other glass from context 381.

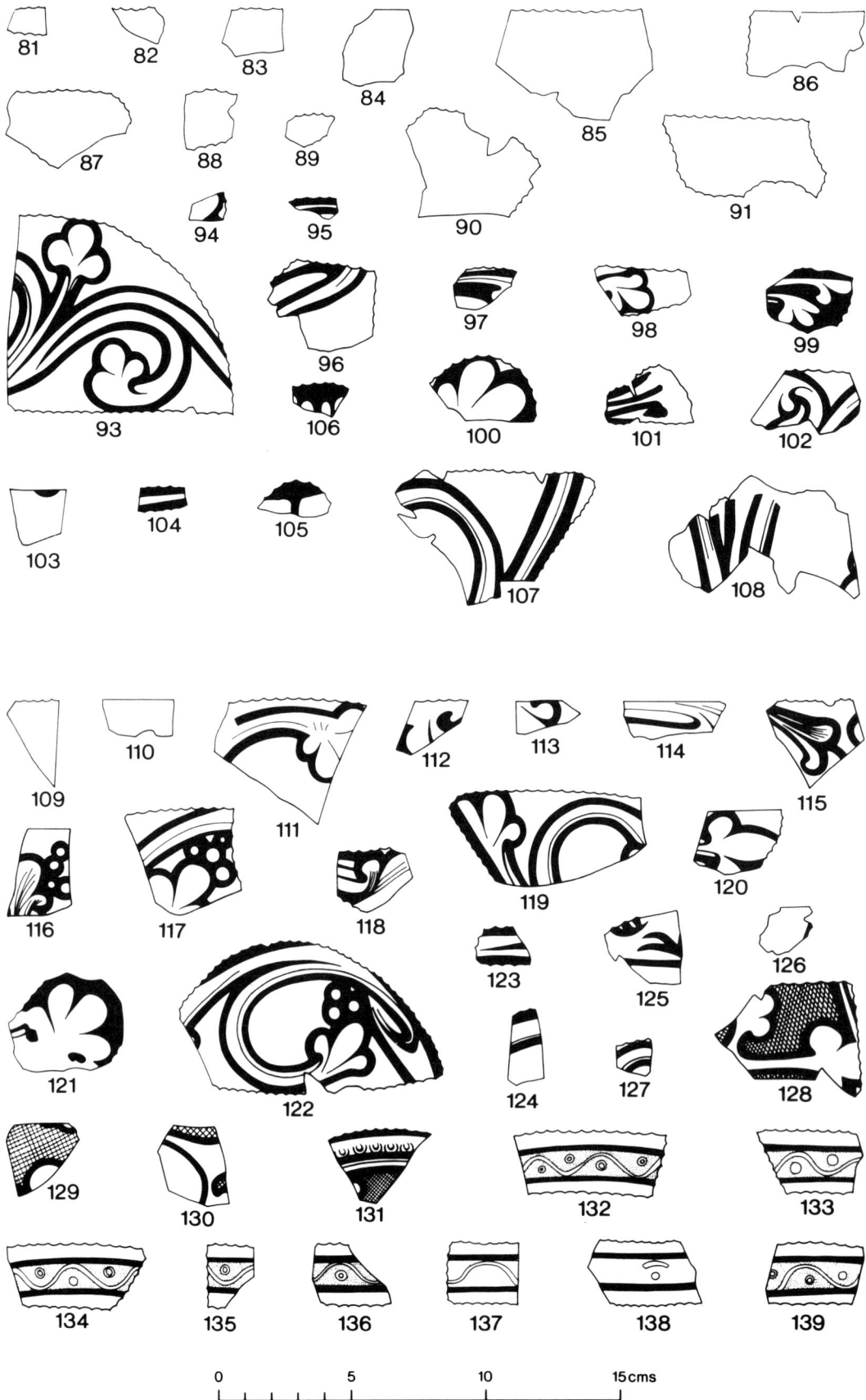

Figure 72 Window glass. Nos. 81–108, glass from RF440a, context 381. Nos. 109–39, glass from RF440, context 381.

ground appear on no. 383. This combination is also found on examples of similar grisaille excavated from the Gilbertine Priory of St Andrew, Fishergate, York (Graves in prep.). Combinations of these two forms of grisaille can be found together at Selling, Kent; Stanton St John and Stanton Harcourt, Oxfordshire (Kerr 1983, 61). It is also clear that some of the foliage of the second category is articulated with fine lines like radiating veins (e.g. nos. 116, 221 and 222).

Amongst the first group, the arrangement of the trefoils on no. 128 resembles a fragment from Battle Abbey (Kerr 1985a, 129, fig. 40, 6), which was described as a radiating frontal trefoil; like the Battle example, the trefoils on no. 128 have not been drawn with spurs within the stems. One of the largest fragments (no. 466) has a central upright trefoil flanked by two curling trefoils on one side. This may be a variant on a design found at Lincoln (Morgan 1983). As the edge has been painted with a curved line, it may have been part of a circular design resembling one specific Lincoln arrangement (*ibid.*, fig. C, 12). A parallel motif with short central trefoil and curling subsidiary foliage, but without the curved edge, has been excavated from the Gilbertine Priory in York (Graves in prep.); it also occurs amongst excavated material from Rievaulx Abbey, North Yorkshire. Beverley fragment no. 305 is also paralleled in the York Gilbertine assemblage, and compares with a grisaille fragment from the Gilbertine Priory at Ellerton, outside York, releaded into a window in the north nave aisle of Selby Abbey.

The crossing of the stems (e.g. no. 122) is common to grisaille both on plain and cross-hatched grounds, and can be seen amongst excavated material from the Premonstratensian Abbey at Bayham, Sussex (Kerr 1983, 60 Group A; fig. 16, 13); the Gilbertine Priory at Fishergate, York (Graves in prep.); and in the Five Sisters at York (J.A. Knowles 1936, Pl. XXXVI).

The design of the multilobate foliage on no. 358 appears to have a multiple stem, and the leaves, like the individual trefoils of nos. 116, 118, 221 and 222, have fine radiating veins. Fragment no. 358 has been grozed to a curved edge around the design, and is similar to no. 236 which is semicircular, no. 239 which has a multiple stem, and nos. 238 and 240. This may be a variation on a palmette design. Grisaille borders and quarries with palmettes were recovered from Bayham Abbey, but these had strap-work edges, cross-hatched grounds, and leaves which were less densely veined (Kerr 1983, 63, figs. 17, 35 and 38; 61, Group D).

There is a repeated pattern of partial beading or arcs of paint appearing at the edge of grisaille fragments 131 and 536, and on a larger scale on nos. 19, 373, 377–8. The border design can be compared with designs in the glazing of Canterbury Cathedral (Caviness 1981, figs. 127, 169), in the grisaille of

Stanton Harcourt, Oxfordshire (Westlake 1891–4, I, Pl. 1vib), and at Snodland, Kent. Comparisons may be found in the excavated material of the Benedictine Battle Abbey, Sussex (Kerr 1985a, 131; 129 fig. 40, 16). This design could have framed the geometric shapes into which the trefoil designs were leaded, as no. 536 suggests.

The pattern employing an undulating line interspersed with small circles is an example of a stickwork border (the pattern being picked or scratched out of a matt wash with a stick). This pattern can be found, defining a geometric shape in grisaille on cross-hatched grounds, together with a border of partial beading comparable to the above, at Stanton Harcourt, Oxfordshire (illustrated by the vesica panel in Winston 1867, II, Pl. 5). Fragments of a similar border were found amongst excavated Dissolution debris from Rievaulx Abbey, North Yorkshire. The background wash of the Beverley fragments, however, appears as a white or cream colour. This may be due to the effects of corrosion on a very dilute wash of paint and can be seen in other examples of excavated glass. On medieval glazing still *in situ* thin washes of paint which have been used on the exterior as back painting, to emphasise details or as shading, have often developed a white corrosion product similar to the Beverley phenomena.

There appear to be no examples of figural scenes except perhaps no. 468, which may be a piece of architectural detailing, implying a narrative scene.

A few fragments retain painted lines at the edges of the pieces, where the basic shapes were traced through from the cut-line of a cartoon, and then grozed to shape (e.g. nos. 119, 122, 131, 228, 389 and 536). These lines would have been covered over by the leads of the panel when mounted in a window.

No. 464 appears to be an example of late 13th/early 14th-century grisaille, using a more naturalistic leaf form, in contrast to the earlier material of stiff-leaf trefoils. It is paralleled by a number of fragments from excavations at Jedburgh Abbey, Borders Region, Scotland (Graves forthcoming). Although the transition to naturalistic leaf forms can be seen in the Five Sisters window at York, the windows of the chapter house display a variety of foliage set in patterned grisaille, dating to the 1270s (O'Connor and Haselock 1977). No. 467 is probably from a 14th-century painted quarry, with a central stylised rose or eglantine. Variations on this theme were common in England and France.

The context of Northern glass-painting

Although there are stylistic parallels in glass of the 14th century between York workshops and sites throughout the North of England, including Beverley (see French and O'Connor 1987), no systematic study

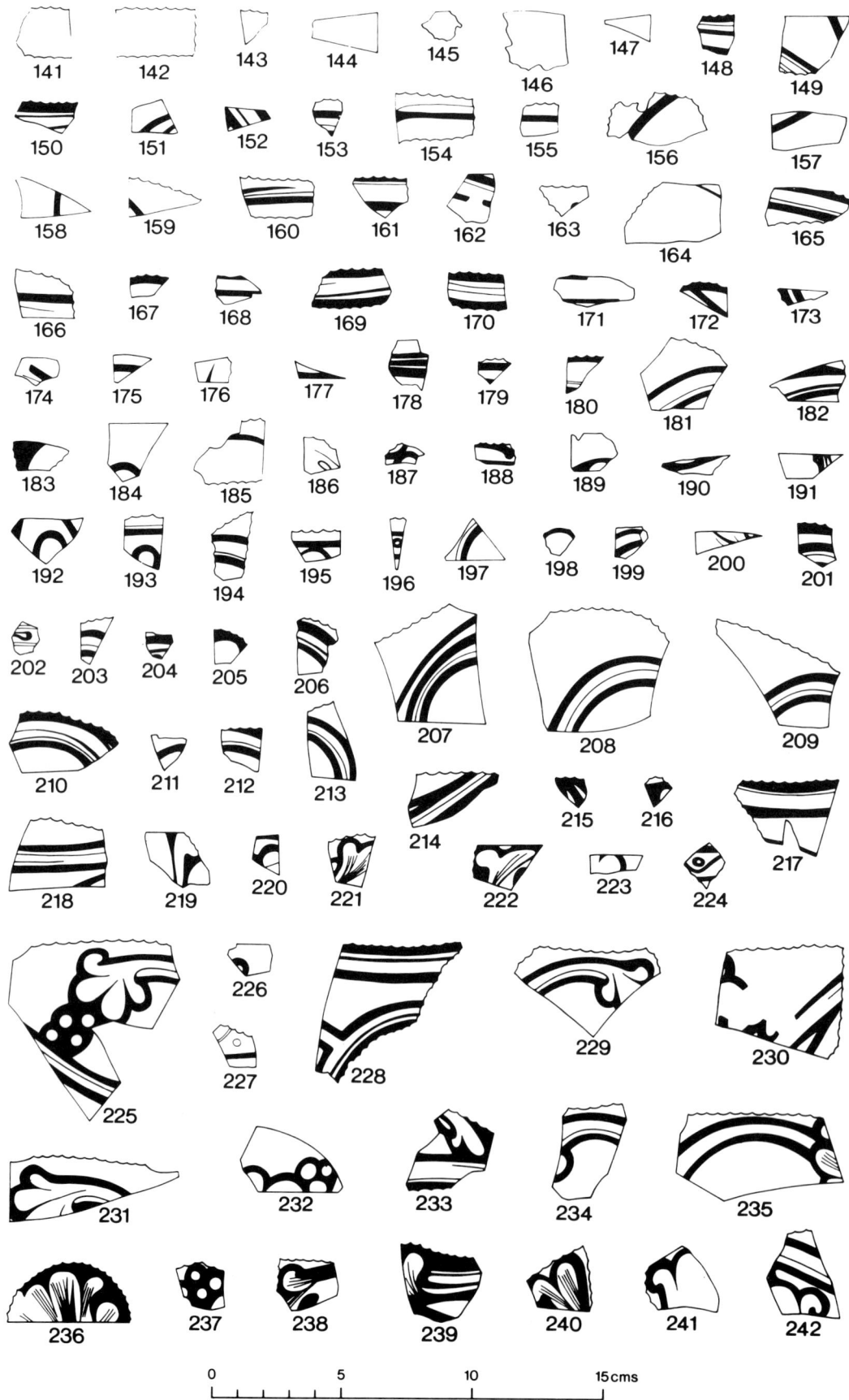

Figure 73 Window glass. Glass from RF440, Context 99 (Phase 7).

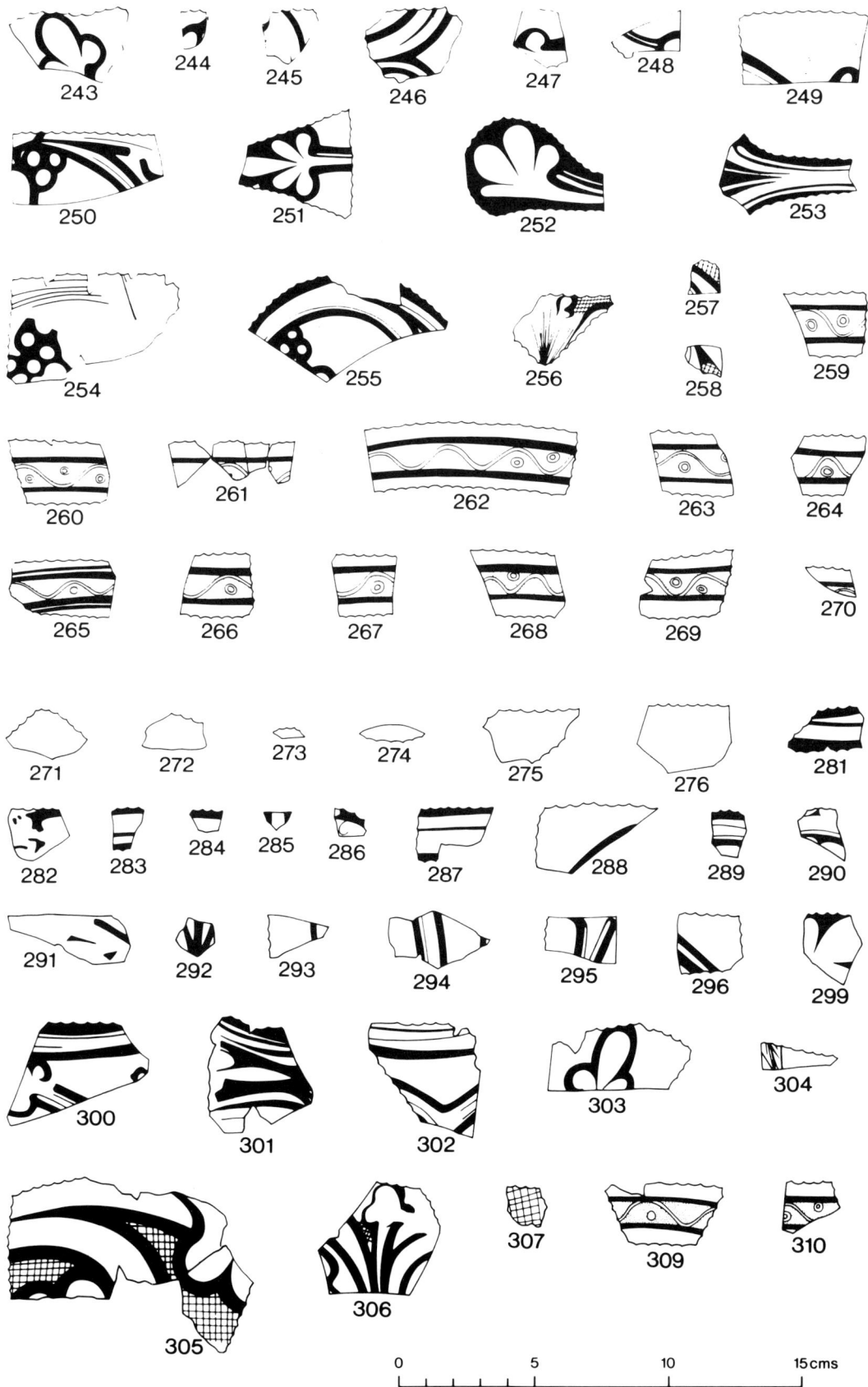

Figure 74 Window glass. Nos. 243–270, glass from RF440, context 99; nos. 271–310, glass from surface of context 100.

131

has yet appeared of 13th-century grisaille in the North. The comparanda cited above show the extent to which shared motifs occur in excavated assemblages from various Northern monasteries, including Rievaulx and some lesser York houses. There is no grisaille from the mid. to late 13th century in Beverley Minster with which to compare this glass: the background foliage and stiff-leaf border patterns which do survive have been dated to the second quarter of the 13th century (O'Connor 1989, 66–8). The forms of border types 1 and 3, as identified by O'Connor, are suggestive of the stiff-leaf arrangement of no. 466, and it may be that the tradition of grisaille in Yorkshire developed out of earlier foliage forms, such as these (*ibid.*, Pl. XIV E (window I 1b); Pl. XIV G (I 2c)). The other major *locus* of grisaille which may have been influential is Lincoln, and it has been noted elsewhere that the affinities between Lincoln and York grisailles are strong (O'Connor and Haselock 1977, 326 no. 75). Given the limited sample of the Beverley glass, there is little further that can be said concerning the origins of the glass-painters who may have worked on the Dominican Priory glass, although York would seem the obvious centre. The raw material, the glass itself, could have come from Europe: coloured glass came from areas around the Rhine, the Moselle, the Maas and the Meuse, and was river-borne to ports such as Rotterdam; thence to York via the Hanse depot at Hull (J.A. Knowles 1936, 115; 196). It is known that some white glass was made in England, in forested areas like the Sussex Weald which supplied St Stephen's Chapel, Windsor, in 1352, whilst a 1333 subsidy roll mentions possible glass-makers in Staffordshire (*ibid.*, 202; 199).

The context of Dominican window glass

Most window glass excavated from Dominican institutions in England has come from post-Dissolution or post-medieval contexts. The painted glass from the Oxford house was mainly grisaille of the cross-hatched variety, dated to after *c.*1240–50 and thought to be the original glazing (Kerr 1985b, 170–2, fig. 17). There were about 180 fragments, of which around 50 were painted. A limited repertoire of trefoil designs was recovered from this house, together with the same border pattern of arcs or open beading as was found at Beverley. This border accompanies grisaille glass in existing windows at Stanton Harcourt, Oxfordshire (Winston 1867, II, Pl. 5). There is limited evidence for reglazing in the 14th and 15th centuries. The distribution of the glass suggested that only the church and chapter house had painted windows (Kerr 1985b, 170).

The Dominican house at Chester also produced grisaille of the mid. to late 13th century, possibly going into the 14th century, the bulk again coincided

with construction dates for the Priory (Axworthy Rutter 1990, 115–18). One rectangular grozed quarry has a design with central upright trefoil and side-curling foliage which resembles Beverley fragment no. 466 (*ibid.*, 117, fig. 81, 7). Only two out of 510 fragments (a surface area of approximately two-thirds of a square metre) were proven to be coloured. The distribution of the glass was largely in and around the church building (*ibid.*).

Chelmsford, Essex, produced a small collection of stained and painted glass from demolition debris, which was mainly white, although there was some flashed ruby (Drury 1974, 59). A comparison with Beverley would be biased in this case, however, as only the *reredorter* was excavated at Chelmsford — and this was unlikely to yield much glazing evidence. Great Yarmouth produced 20 fragments of burnt window glass which was identified as 15th-century (Rye 1973, 502). At Guildford, Surrey, saltire lead cames with plain glass, probably from latticed quarry glazing, were found (Poulton and Woods 1984, fig. 48, 32). Painted glass which may have come from the Dominican Priory was releaded into windows at the Abbot's Hospital in that town (Hinnebusch 1951, 146). A fragment from the centre-piece of a spun sheet of glass, as well as window debris, was recovered from demolition deposits at Ipswich, Suffolk (Blatchly and Wade 1977, 30). Excavations in 1988 at Dunstable Friary, Bedfordshire, located large quantities of window glass and tracery (Clark and Maull 1989). The glass includes both geometric and *rinleau diaper* patterns on thick glass, and of the first half to mid. 14th century, a running border design of quatrefoils. There is also some much finer glass, with three-dimensional representations of buttress offsets, gothic script (probably from a scroll) and some quarry work — all of the late 14th and 15th centuries. A well, lined with 15th-century moulded stones and window tracery, from the Blackfriars Priory, London, produced associated fragments of 'fine, decorated 15th-century Venetian stained glass' (Heathcote 1990, 161).

Two documentary references have been found: for the Blackfriars of Canterbury, to whom King Henry III gave 100s. on September 25, 1256, to make the glass windows of their church; and the Rhuddlan friars, to whom Edward I gave 50s. for windows to be installed next to their altar of The Blessed Mother (*ibid.*).

The Dominican house at Newcastle provides a closer geographical comparison for the Beverley material. Amongst a quantity of excavated window glass from this house is mid. to late 13th century grisaille, 14th-century figured glass, diaper backgrounds and architectural detail, and evidence of 15th-century quarry glazing (unpublished, but see

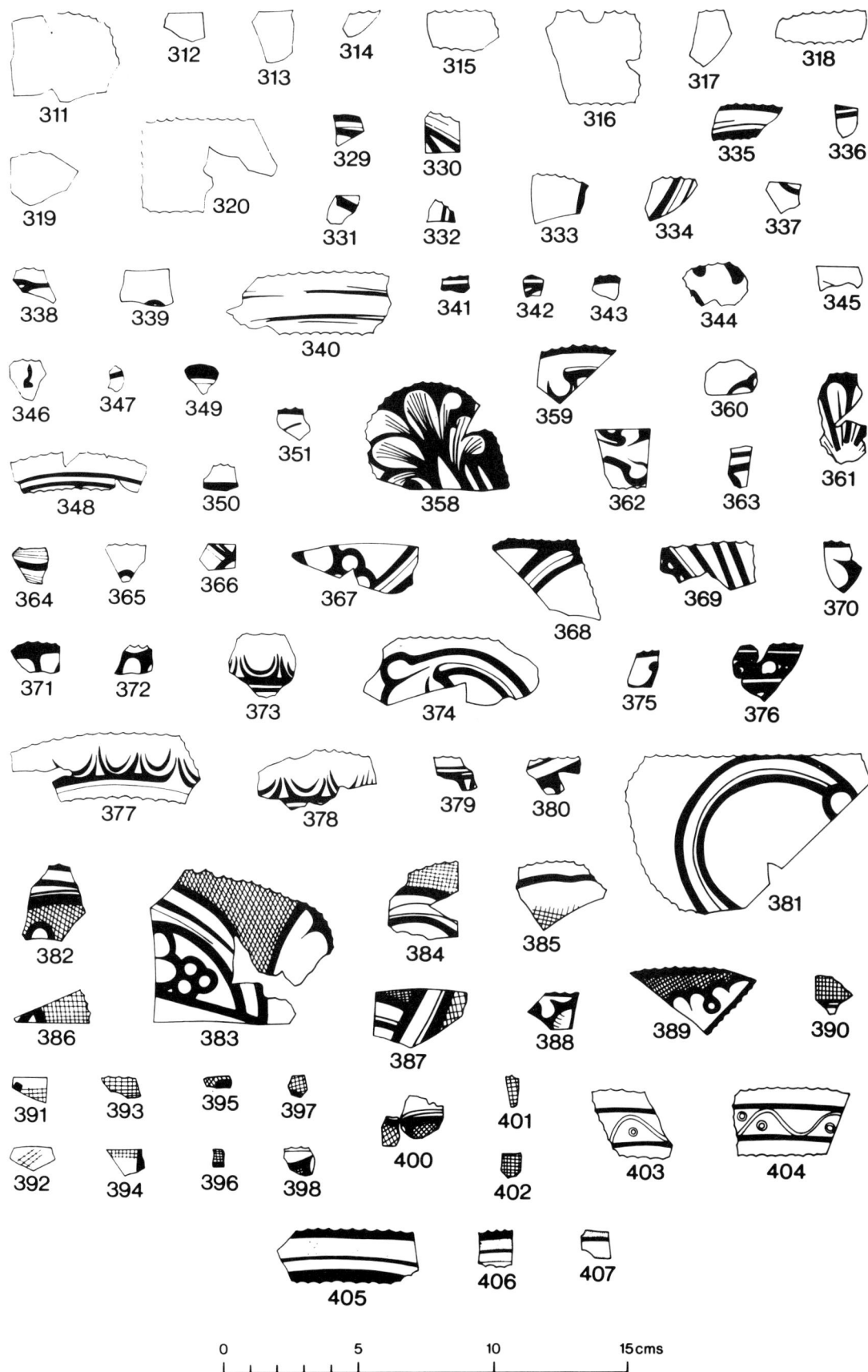

Figure 75 Window glass. Glass from context 99 (Phase 7).

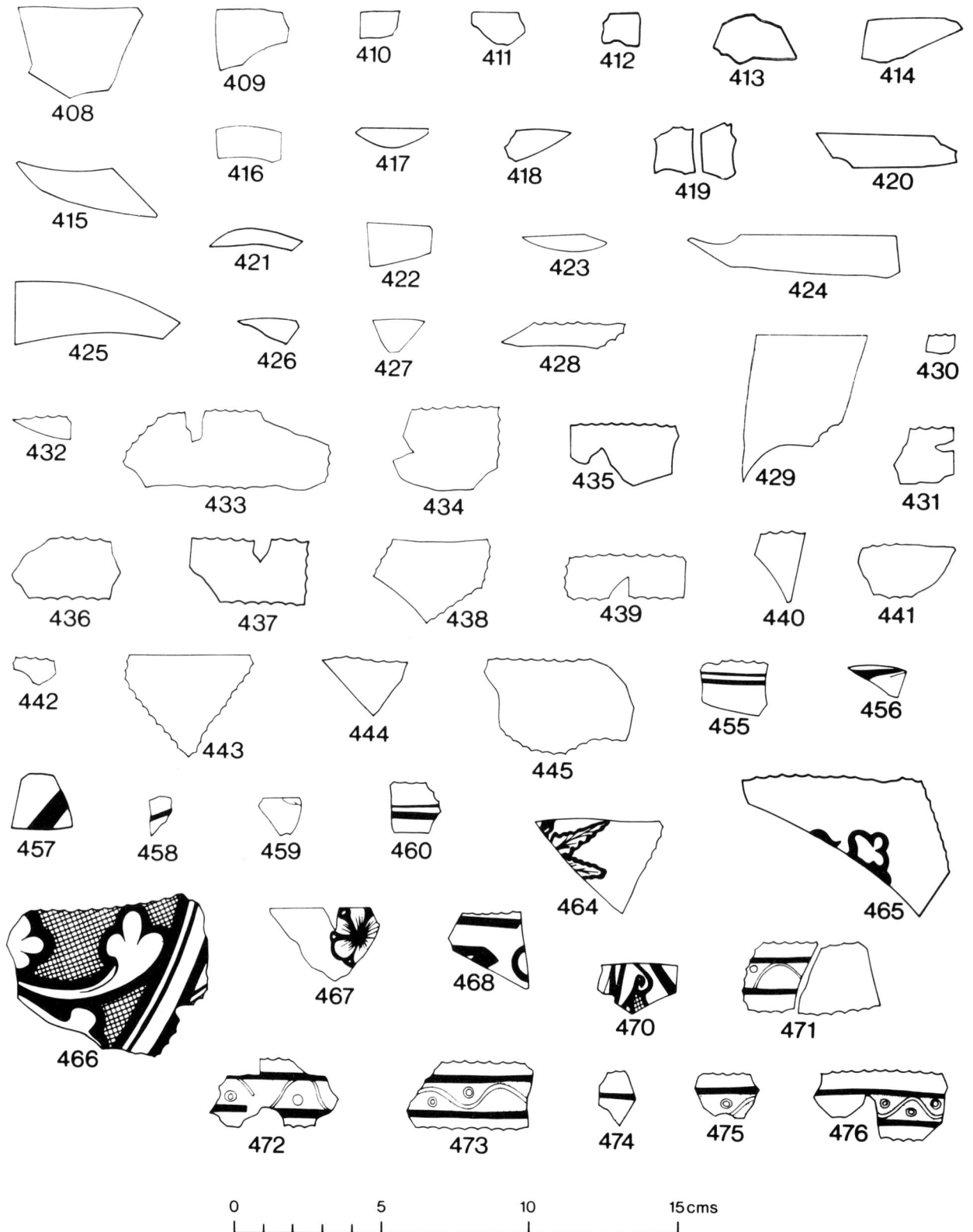

Figure 76 Window glass. Glass from context 59 (Phase 7).

Harbottle and Fraser 1987, 102–5 for post-Dissolution retrieval contexts).

In contrast to the foregoing, the Dominican Priory at King's Langley, in close proximity to the Royal Palace, and a recipient of documented royal patronage, has yielded fragments of architectural detail, figures, diaper background and heraldry suggesting painted windows of a very different nature (Gamlen 1973, 73–7). Over 3,000 fragments of glass were found on the south side of the Lady Chapel and the south aisle of the chancel. The assemblage is dominated by fragments with yellow stain and pot metal yellow; ruby and blue were reckoned to be present in a proportion of 1:3 (*ibid.*, 75). Most of the detail was dated to the late 14th century, suggesting canopies with architectural detail of buttresses, window tracery, crockets and finials. A number of pieces of background diaper were found, mainly on blue; there was also some lettering which may have identified saints, figures from scripture or donors. Figures were indicated by a crown, two portions of hair, and a hand holding a staff. It was suggested that the glass may have been attributable to an Oxford workshop, but no more detailed study seems to have been undertaken (*ibid.*).

For the purposes of comparison with the Beverley material, one is obviously looking at the contrast in patronage and wealth between these two houses which was made manifest in the glazing. Although it might be argued that there is no way of assessing how representative each sample is of the glazing of their respective houses, it should be noted that Gamlen thought the King's Langley assemblage comprised mostly peripheral rather than central features. Even if the *caveat* is accepted that the Beverley material may only be residual background glazing upon which figured panels could have been placed, there is still a striking contrast in the nature of the painted material and the amount of colour.

Synthesis

Based on the sample recovered, the majority of the glass was grisaille on a plain background; this was twice the amount of plain glass, and five times as much as the older grisaille on cross-hatched backgrounds. With no conclusive evidence for figural glazing, and very little colour, it might be argued that the Beverley Priory had windows made up of largely foliate designs set in geometric shapes, with very little coloured glass, and devoid of figures. On the other hand, small figured or heraldic panels may have been set on these geometric grounds, as seen at Selling, Kent. Although a proportion of the smaller plain fragments may have come from these windows, larger quarries might be expected to have come from plain windows in less important, perhaps more utilitarian

buildings of the complex: the grozed fragment (no. 517) amongst those from the demolition deposits on the west side of the great cloister is of this kind, and the majority of larger fragments of lead came defined rectangular or sub-rectangular quarries, which are characteristic of plain glazing (see section 3.9, below). If the position of the reredorter suggests that the dormitory range was over the western range of the great cloister, it might be expected that the windows here were plain; and indeed, about half the sample of window glass from this area is unpainted. Based on analogy with other Dominican precincts, however, the prior's lodgings might have been on this side, in which case painted glass might have been expected, to reflect his status; the few painted pieces from this part of the site are mostly on cross-hatched grounds. It is possible that glass from several sources on this side of the cloister was mixed in the demolition debris.

The statutes of the first Dominican general chapters emphasised poverty and austerity in the architecture of their houses, and plain glass alone was permitted in the windows (Hinnebusch 1951, 127). By the second half of the 13th century, however, the order had begun to erect churches described as *opera sumptuosa* (King 1955, 329). From *c*.1240, other religious orders and institutions became less willing to let the Dominicans use their churches for preaching, which forced the Order to develop the capacity and aesthetics of their own churches towards a lay audience. Their apostolic work as friars preacher led them to advocate the use of images in the instruction of the laity — visual stimuli to their sermon *exempla* (cf. *ibid.*, 295–312). At the same time, individual Dominicans would argue fine points of theological distinction in the reverence due to images (e.g. Robert Holcot d.1349, author of a widely-used commentary on the Book of Wisdom, and the sermon in MS. Harl. 2398 quoted in Aston 1988, 118–19). The distribution pattern at Beverley cannot tell us if there was a distinction, for example, between a figured glazing scheme in the nave of the church, and a plainer scheme in the friars' choir. On the whole, the friars' churches were lit by many windows, often of large proportions (Hinnebusch 1951; Aston 1988, 145–6). Relatively plain glazing at Beverley might have been simply a matter of economic exigency — white glass being less expensive than fully coloured schemes (Morgan 1983, 39; Salzman 1952, 175–6).

As the archaeological evidence suggests that the ranges around the little cloister were built in the early 14th century, the preponderance of grisaille of the second half of the 13th century here may imply two alternative interpretations. The first would be that, in this instance, a very conservative type of glass design was employed in the early 14th century. Given, however, that formalistic foliage such as this had been replaced by more natural forms in the chapter house

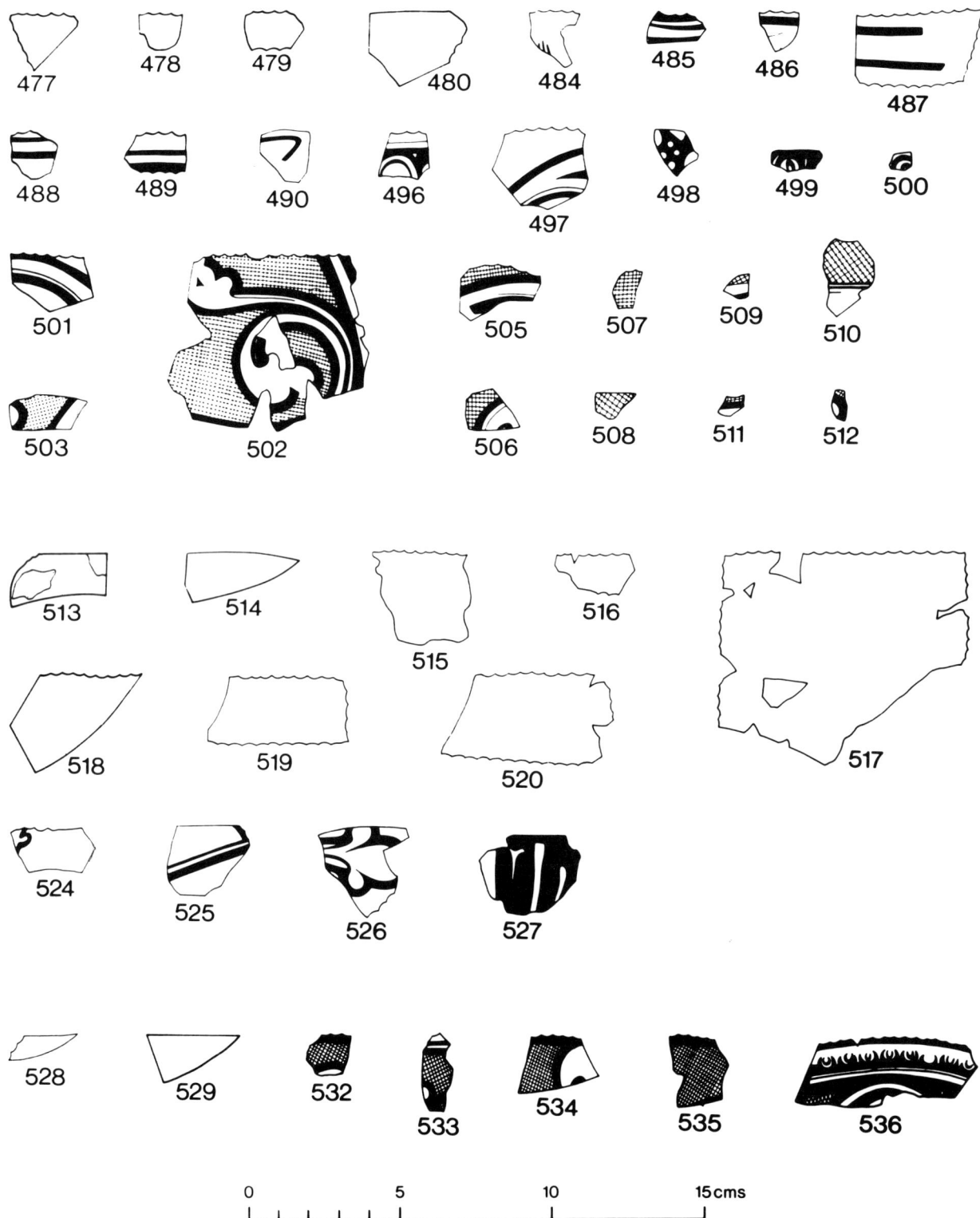

Figure 77 Window glass. Nos. 477–512, glass from demolition contexts (Phase 7); nos. 513–36, Phases 7–8.

and vestibule of York Minster as early as 1285 (O'Connor and Haselock 1977, 334–41), this would seem unlikely. The second interpretation might be that glass from some earlier buildings was reused in the little cloister range. If the glass were to be used as a background for figural panels in geometric shapes, the friars may not have been so concerned to have up-to-the-minute designs. The glass may have come from buildings which were invested with a greater ritual and social significance than those in the little cloister complex, during a period of refenestration. This may have been connected with extensive 14th-century building works on the priory church, including the demolition of the south wall and the addition of an aisle (see Chapter 2). In this case it might have mattered little that the glass was old. This might lend further support to an interpretation which suggested differential investment in the furnishing and maintenance of different areas of the monastic complex, the little cloister receiving less attention. Comparison with Bristol Priory suggests that buildings like the infirmary and calefactory were situated round the lesser cloister (Hinnebusch 1951, 179, fig. 18). The explanation rehearsed above might be compatible with a calefactory or an infirmary. At least two fragments were associated with construction phases in this area, suggesting primary glazing (nos. 3 and 4).

The above interpretation largely depends, however, on whether or not the glass debris might be thought to have originally come from the little cloister buildings. The distribution of Dissolution debris in the northern building is consistent with the stripping of lead window came, and the bowl hearths and melted lead certainly confirm lead gathering. The fact that the west room has predominantly plain (i.e. unpainted) glass, whereas the east chamber has mainly grisaille on plain grounds, does indeed suggest some cursory sorting process. There is not enough differential evidence, however, to further imply whether this glass was gathered from windows throughout the Priory complex, or simply from the immediate vicinity. The concentration in the putative stairwell (see Figure 57) is the strongest evidence that some of the glass, at least, did originate in the upper chamber of the north range itself — suggesting that it had been thrown downstairs, where the burning of the lead was carried out.

Conclusion

As stated above, the glazing schemes from several parts of the complex may have had similar grisaille backgrounds, leaving similar residual patterns. Compared with the amount of glass there would have been when the Priory was fully glazed, the excavated sample must be a very small amount. Analogy with

Dissolution activity at other Yorkshire sites might suggest that the best glass was certainly taken off site, or sold to private residences or other churches. Ripon Minster bought glass from Fountains Abbey in 1540 (J.A. Knowles 1936, 46). At Rievaulx the glass was *'sortyd into iij partes, the fayrest to be sortyd, the second sort to be sold, the iij sort to be taken out of the lede and the lede molten'* (*Cartulary of Rievaulx*, quoted in Knowles, op. cit.). This would lead us to conclude that our sample is from the poorest quality of glazing at Beverley. Rievaulx was one of the wealthiest houses in England, and it is perhaps appropriate to draw again on the aforementioned comparisons with other Dominican houses, especially the contrast with King's Langley. I would conclude that the glass in the northern range of the little cloister has probably been gathered from several buildings, although all may have been in the little cloister itself. The glass had probably been removed from an earlier building, in which (possibly) devotional glazing was more appropriate, and then releaded in the little cloister ranges without much further renewal in the later Middle Ages. The spread at the base of the stairwell suggests an upper floor room with glazing. As more painted glass was found in the eastern room, which contained this stairwell, it might be tentatively inferred that the upper chamber was of relatively high status compared with the west room. Although only representative of a fraction of the former glazing, the surviving glass suggests a modest glazing scheme of moderate quality.

Chemical analysis of window glass
by Julian Henderson

Seven window fragments (nos. 524, 514, 276, 465, 460, 459, 425) formed a compositional group that was characterised by potassium-rich glasses, with very low sodium oxide contents and high phosphorus pentoxide and magnesium oxide levels; these fragments were found in 16th-century contexts, but were dated on stylistic grounds to the mid. 13th century. A further unusual and very interesting compositional feature of these glasses is the occurrence of a minimum level of between 0.4% and 0.8% barium oxide. These relatively high levels of barium oxide in the glasses apparently occur with high levels of manganese oxide, although the few data suggest that these are not related. The presence of barium oxide at these levels will probably prove to be a useful way of chemically characterising window glass of this period. The fact that the very similar glass compositions in this group were used for window fragments found in contexts dating to the 16th century suggests either that the fragments found in 16th-century contexts were residual, or that the same glass production technology continued from the 13th to the 16th centuries; at the Priory site the former interpretation appears more likely.

The analysis of a 14th-century window glass fragment (no. 529) differs from the above group by having significantly higher silica, lower alumina and lower manganese oxide levels. The durability of the glass is, however, apparently very similar. This compositional difference may simply reflect a slight change in the use of raw materials in the 13th or 14th century (i.e. being the results of using a different glass melt). Another compositional difference between no. 529 and the group discussed above is its relatively low level of barium oxide. The green colour in the window samples would be due to iron oxide (ferric and ferrous) ions in the presence of manganese oxide.

Two window panes which were analysed (from among nos. 37–66) were blue rather than green. These can be distinguished compositionally from the first group by having very low sodium oxide levels, lower silica, significantly higher potassium oxide and the highest barium oxide levels which were detected. The colourant is principally cobalt oxide, modified by copper, zinc and manganese oxides. The trace of arsenic in analysis no. 14 is not considered to be significant, with respect to the type of cobalt mineral used. The primary (mineral) source is therefore likely to have been manganiferous, though it is also possible that manganese may well have been introduced 'accidentally' (Newton 1978), if beech ashes had been used as a source of alkali (potassium). The two analyses of blue window fragments are sufficiently close for them to have originally formed part of the same window pane. Soda-lime-silica cobalt blue window glasses have recently been reported from York Minster (Cox and Gillies 1986), and are of an entirely different chemical composition.

The last window pane composition to be considered (no. 538A) is definitely of a later date. It is characteristically thinner than medieval window glass, and is more durable; its mixed-alkali composition is more typical of a post-17th-century date, which is consistent with its Phase 8 context.

Analysis of the window glass has provided some new evidence for the existence of three compositional types of medieval glass, which can be distinguished by levels of potassium oxide and the oxides of phosphorus and magnesium. Both of the latter tend to be linked with the alkali raw material which was used (species of vegetable ash or mineral). Another very unusual compositional characteristic of the 13th or 14th-century window glass is the relatively high barium oxide content (maximum 0.9%). Further quantitative analyses of medieval glass will place this compositional feature in context.

(Dr Henderson considers the chemical composition of vessel glass from the site in section 3.13; the quantitative analysis of glass is tabulated in microfiche, Mf.3. E9).

Catalogue of window glass

Note: Given the presentation of glass by a comprehensive series of illustrations, those catalogue entries which denote glass whose characteristics and provenance are adequately presented there, are omitted from this listing. The term 'white glass' is used for originally translucent metal, regardless of its tint. The colour of glass has, however, been considered by Dr. Julian Henderson in his examination of a small sample of the window glass. When excavated the metal was typically black in colour, partially devitrified, with red painted decoration. The '(now) white painted' decorative fields are considered to be as a probable corrosion product formed over a thin wash of paint applied to the exterior as back painting.

Glass from occupation Phases 5 to 6b (Figure 71)

5.   Quarry: Blue coloration. Four grozed edges.
        RF3209, Context 849, Phase 5A.
17.   Fragment: White glass. One grozed edge.
        RF462:2, Context 348, Phase 5C.
18.   Fragment: Painted grisaille decoration comprises one red line and fine cross-hatching.
        RF462:3, Context 348, Phase 5C.
19.   Fragment: Painted grisaille decoration comprises fine red lines and double open crescents. A (now) white painted or stained line occurs on one edge. Two grozed edges.
        RF462:4, Context 348, Phase 5C.
31.   Fragment: White glass. Two grozed edges.
        RF710, Context 674, Phase 6B.

Glass and came from RF439, Context 381 - Phase 5c or 7 (Figure 71)

Dr. Henderson writes of a sample of glass fragments from RFs 439/440, Context 381: 'Four fragments cobalt blue with 'black' and iridescent weathering. Max. thickness: 2.9mm. Analysis nos. 14 and 15.' He continues: 'twelve fragments similar, but with stripes of red fired on paint. Max thickness: 3.6mm.'
Catalogue nos. 37-40 are omitted from list. See Figure 71
42.   Quarry Fragment: ?Triangular, white glass. Two grozed edges.
        RF439:20, Context 381, Phase 5C/?7.
43.   Quarry: Triangular, white glass. Three grozed edges.
        RF439:21, Context 381, Phase 5C/?7.
Catalogue nos. 44-6 are omitted from list. See Figure 71
47.   Quarry Fragment: Oval, with painted red ground framing an uncoloured floriated design. One curved grozed edge.
        RF439:6, Context 381, Phase 5C/?7.
Catalogue nos. 48-58 are omitted from list. See Figure 71
59.   Border fragment: Painted grisaille decoration comprises two red lines enclosing a (now) white painted central field, an uncoloured wavy line and

open ring and filled dot pattern along central field. Two grozed edges.
RF439:18, Context 381, Phase 5C/?7.

60. Fragment: White glass with associated came of T-section.
RF439:24, Context 381, Phase 5C/?7.

61. Fragments: White glass still attached to came of H-section. This defined parts of four quarries, two include glass fragments.
RF439:25, Context 381, Phase 5C/?7.

62. Fragments: Still attached to came of H-section. These defined parts of three quarries, one includes glass fragments.
RF439:26, Context 381, Phase 5C/?7.

63. Fragment: Still attached to came of H-section. These defined parts of five quarries, one includes a glass fragment.
RF439:27, Context 381, Phase 5C/?7.

64. Fragments: Still attached to came of H-section. These defined parts of at least five quarries, three include glass fragments.
RF439:29, Context 381, Phase 5C/?7.

65. Fragments: Still attached to came of H-section. These defined parts of at least four quarries, one of which includes glass fragments.
RF439:30, Context 381, Phase 5C/?7.

66. Fragments: Painted grisaille decoration comprises curved red lines. Still attached to came of H-section. These defined parts of at least five quarries, one of which includes glass. A further fragment of painted glass is associated with this came.
RF439:31, Context 381, Phase 5C/?7.

Other glass from Context 381 - Phase 5c or 7 (Figures 71–2)

Catalogue nos. 71–6 are omitted from list. See Figure 71

78. Border fragment: Painted grisaille decoration comprises two red lines enclosing a white-painted central field, an uncoloured wavy line and ring pattern run along central field. Two grozed edges.
RF400:6, Context 381, Phase 5C/?7.

79. Border fragment: Painted grisaille decoration comprises two red lines enclosing a (now) white painted central field. An uncoloured wavy line and dot pattern runs along central field. Two grozed edges.
RF400:7, Context 381, Phase 5C/?7.

80. Border fragment: Painted grisaille decoration comprises two red lines enclosing a (now) white painted central field, an uncoloured wavy line, and ring pattern along the central field. Two grozed edges.
RF400:8, Context 381, Phase 5C/?7.

Glass from RF440a, Context 381 - Phase 5c or 7 (Figure 72)

('A' denotes lower layer of a dense spread.)
Catalogue nos. 81–90 are omitted from list. See Figure 72

91. Quarry: White glass. All edges grozed, two straight, the others curving.
RF440A:27, Context 381, Phase 5C/?7.

93. Quarry fragment: Painted grisaille decoration

comprises red lines forming floriated tendrils. One curved and one straight grozed edge.
RF440A:2, Context 381, Phase 5C/?7.

Catalogue nos. 94–9 are omitted from list. See Figure 72

100. Quarry fragment: ?Oval, painted grisaille decoration comprises a looping red line forming a floriated design. One curved grozed edge.
RF440A:10, Context 381, Phase 5C/?7.

Catalogue nos. 101–8 are omitted from list. See Figure 72

Glass from RF440, Context 381 - Phase 5c or 7 (Figure 72)

(Middle layer of a spread of glass)
Catalogue nos. 109-121 are omitted from list. See Figure 72

122. Quarry fragment: ?Semicircular; painted grisaille decoration comprises red lines, circles and floriated tendrils. Two grozed edges, one curving markedly.
RF440:26, Context 381, Phase 5C/?7.

Catalogue nos. 123–30 are omitted from list. See Figure 71

131. ?Border fragment: Painted grisaille decoration comprises red lines, crescents and fine cross-hatching. One grozed edge.
RF440:17, Context 381, Phase 5C/?7.

132. Border fragment: Painted grisaille decoration comprises two red lines enclosing a (now) white painted central field. An uncoloured wavy line and ring pattern runs along central field. Three grozed edges.
RF440:5, Context 381, Phase 5C/?7.

133. Border fragment: Painted grisaille decoration comprises two red lines enclosing a (now) white painted central field. An uncoloured wavy line and dot pattern runs along central field. Three grozed edges.
RF440:6, Context 381, Phase 5C/?7.

134. Border fragment: Painted grisaille decoration comprises two red lines enclosing a (now) white painted central field. An uncoloured wavy line and ring and dot pattern runs along central field. Three grozed edges.
RF440:7, Context 381, Phase 5C/?7.

135. Border fragment: Painted grisaille decoration comprises two red lines enclosing a (now) white painted central field. An uncoloured wavy line and ring pattern runs along central field. Three grozed edges.
RF440:8, Context 381, Phase 5C/?7.

136. Border fragment: Painted grisaille decoration comprises two red lines enclosing a (now) white painted central field. An uncoloured wavy line and ring pattern runs along central field. Two grozed edges.
RF440:9, Context 381, Phase 5C/?7.

137. Border fragment: Painted grisaille decoration comprises two red lines enclosing an uncoloured wavy line running along the central field. Three grozed edges.
RF440:10, Context 387, Phase 5C/?7.

138. ?Border fragment: Painted grisaille decoration comprises two red lines enclosing a central field. An uncoloured wavy line and dot pattern runs along the central field. Two grozed edges.
RF440:11, Context 381, Phase 5C/?7.

139. Border fragment: Painted grisaille decoration comprises two red lines enclosing a (now) white painted central field. An uncoloured wavy line and ring pattern runs along the central field. Two grozed edges.
RF440:12, Context 381, Phase 5C/?7.

Glass from RF440, Context 99 - Phase 7 (figures 73–4)

(Upper layer of a spread of glass)
Catalogues nos. 141–227 are omitted. See Figure 73

228. Quarry fragment: Painted grisaille decoration comprises six curving red lines. Three curved grozed edges.
RF440:115, Context 99, Phase 7.

Catalogue nos. 229–235 are omitted from list. See Figure 73

236. Quarry fragment: ?Semicircular; painted grisaille decoration comprises a red ground and lines forming a floriated design. One semi-circular grozed edge.
RF440:127, Context 99, Phase 7.

237. Fragment: Painted grisaille decoration comprises four or five red rings. One curved grozed edge.
RF440:129, Context 99, Phase 7.

Catalogue nos. 238–51 are omitted from list. See Figures 73–74

252. Quarry fragment of elongated oval form; painted grisaille decoration comprises red ground forming open floriated design.
RF440:159, Context 99, Phase 7.

253. Fragment: Painted grisaille decoration comprises seven red lines. Possible (now) white paint survives between them. Two curved grozed edges.
RF440:160, Context 99, Phase 7.

254. Fragment: Painted grisaille decoration comprises thin red lines and rings. Three grozed edges.
RF440:161, Context 99, Phase 7.

255. Quarry fragment: ?Semicircular; painted grisaille decoration comprises red lines and rings. One curved grozed edge.
RF440:162, Context 99, Phase 7.

Catalogue nos. 256–8 are omitted from list. See Figure 74

259. Border fragment: Painted grisaille decoration comprises two red lines enclosing a (now) white painted central field. An uncoloured wavy line and ring pattern runs along the central field. Three grozed edges. Dr. Henderson writes of an unspecified but typical one of the RF440, Context 99, fragments: 'Complex decoration, comprises two red strips with enclosed wavy line and open circle. Dark brown weathering; thickness 3.6mm.'
RF440:38, Context 99, Phase 7.

260. Border fragment: Painted grisaille decoration comprises two red lines enclosing a (now) white painted central field. An uncoloured wavy line and ring pattern runs along the central field. Three grozed edges.
RF440:40, Context 99, Phase 7.

261. Border fragments: Painted grisaille decoration comprises a red line and a (now) white painted field. An uncoloured wavy line and dot pattern runs along the field. One grozed edge.
RF440:41, Context 99, Phase 7.

262. Border fragment: Painted grisaille decoration comprises two red lines enclosing a central field. An uncoloured wavy line and ring pattern runs along the central field. Three grozed edges.
RF440:42, Context 99, Phase 7.

263. Border fragment: Painted grisaille decoration comprises two red lines enclosing a (now) white painted central field. An uncoloured wavy line and ring pattern runs along the central field. Two grozed edges.
RF440:43, Context 99, Phase 7.

264. Border fragment: Painted grisaille decoration comprises two red lines enclosing a (now) white painted field. An uncoloured wavy line and ring pattern runs along the central field. Two grozed edges.
RF440:44, Context 99, Phase 7.

265. Border fragment: Painted grisaille decoration comprises four red lines enclosing (now) a white painted central field. An uncoloured wavy line and dot pattern runs along the central field. Two grozed edges.
RF440:45, Context 99, Phase 7.

266. Border fragment: Painted grisaille decoration comprises two red lines enclosing a (now) white painted central field. An uncoloured wavy line and ring pattern runs along the central field. Three grozed edges.
RF440:46, Context 99, Phase 7.

267. Border fragment: Painted grisaille decoration comprises two red lines enclosing a (now) white painted central field. An uncoloured wavy line and ring pattern runs along the central field. Two grozed edges.
RF440:47, Context 99, Phase 7.

268. Border fragment: Painted grisaille decoration comprises two red lines enclosing a (now) white painted central field. An uncoloured wavy line and ring pattern runs along the central field. Two grozed edges.
RF440:48, Context 99, Phase 7.

269. Border fragment: Painted grisaille decoration comprises two red lines enclosing a (now) white painted central field. An uncoloured wavy line and ring pattern runs along the central field.
RF440:49, Context 99, Phase 7.

270. Border fragment: Painted grisaille decoration comprises one red line and a (now) white painted field. An uncoloured wavy line runs across the field. One grozed edge.
RF440:110, Context 99, Phase 7.

Glass from surface of Context 100 — Phase 5c or 7 (Figure 74)

271. Fragment: White glass. Two grozed edges.
RF319:1, Context 100, Phase 5C/?7.

*272. Fragment: White glass. One grozed edge. Dr. Henderson writes of RF321: 'fragments totally weathered with strips of opaque fired on red decoration. Thickness 3.2mm.' These are marked *.
RF321:1, Context 100, Phase 5C/?7.

Catalogue nos. 273–4 are omitted from list. See Figure 74

275. Fragment: Two grozed edges. Dr. Henderson writes:

'Undecorated translucent blue. Thickness 2.7mm.'
RF361, Context 100, Phase 5C/?7.

276.   Fragment: One grozed edge. Dr. Henderson writes: 'Undecorated pale green. Thickness 2.2mm.' Analysis No. 14.
RF494, Context 100, Phase 5C/?7.

*281.   Fragment: Painted grisaille decoration comprises three slightly curving red lines. Three grozed edges.
RF321:3, Context 100, Phase 5C/?7.

*282.   Fragment: Painted, indistinct red patches survive. One grozed edge.
RF321:4, Context 100, Phase 5C/?7.

*283.   Fragment: Painted grisaille decoration comprises three red lines. Two grozed edges.
RF321:5, Context 100, Phase 5C/?7.

*284.   Fragment: Painted grisaille decoration comprises one red line. One grozed edge.
RF321:6, Context 100, Phase 5C/?7.

*285.   Fragment: Painted grisaille decoration comprises two red lines.
RF321:7, Context 100, Phase 5C/?7.

*286.   Fragment: Painted grisaille decoration comprises one red line. One grozed edge.
RF321:8, Context 100, Phase 5C/?7.

Catalogue nos. 287–96 are omitted from list. See Figure 74

299.   Fragment: Painted grisaille decoration comprises a red ground forming an open floriated design. One grozed edge.
RF319:3, Context 100, Phase 5C/?7.

Catalogue nos. 300–3 are omitted from list. See Figure 74

304.   Fragment: Painted grisaille decoration comprises ?naturalistic foliage. One grozed edge.
RF338:3, Context 100, Phase 5C/?7.

Catalogue nos. 305–7 are omitted from list. See Figure 74

309.   Border quarry: Painted grisaille decoration comprises two red lines enclosing a (now) white painted central field. An uncoloured wavy line and dot pattern runs along central field. Four grozed edges.
RF335, Context 100, Phase 5C/?7.

310.   Border fragment: Painted grisaille decoration comprises two red lines enclosing a (now) white painted central field. An uncoloured wavy line and ring pattern runs along the central field. Two grozed edges.
RF337:1, Context 100, Phase 5C/?7.

Glass from Context 99 — Phase 7 (Figure 75)

311.   Fragment: White glass. One curved grozed edge. Dr. Henderson writes: 'Dark brown weathering, no visible glass; fragment with a curving ?grozed edge. Thickness: 3.1mm.'
RF326, Context 99, Phase 7.

Catalogue nos. 312–19 are omitted from list. See Figure 75

320.   Quarry fragment: ?Rectangular; White glass. Three grozed edges.
RF424:2, Context 99, Phase 7.

Catalogue nos. 329–30 are omitted from list. See Figure 75

331.   Fragment: Painted grisaille decoration comprises red line. Dr. Henderson writes of RF399: 'Thirteen fragments, red painted, decoration in stripes and branching at right angles, no visible glass, brown weathering. Thickness: 3.2mm.'

RF399:7, Context 99, Phase 7.

332.   Fragment: Painted grisaille decoration comprises two red lines. One grozed edge.
RF399:9, Context 99, Phase 7.

333.   Fragment: Painted grisaille decoration comprises a red line. One curved grozed edge.
RF399:12, Context 99, Phase 7.

Catalogue nos. 334–51 are omitted from list. See Figure 75

358.   Quarry fragment: ?Elongated oval; painted grisaille decoration comprises red lines and ground forming a floriated design. One curved grozed edge.
RF328, Context 99, Phase 7.

Catalogue nos. 359–68 are omitted from list. See Figure 75

369.   Fragment: Painted grisaille decoration comprises three thick and one thin red lines. Also a red ground with open semi-circular pattern. Two grozed edges.
RF406:3, Context 99, Phase 7.

Catalogue nos. 370–2 are omitted from list. See Figure 75

373.   ?Border fragment: Painted grisaille decoration comprises two red lines and crescents. Two grozed edges.
RF410:4, Context 99, Phase 7.

Catalogue nos. 374–6 are omitted from list. See Figure 75

377.   Border fragment: Painted grisaille decoration comprises two red lines and crescents, with (now) white paint at edges. Three grozed edges.
RF415:2, Context 99, Phase 7.

378.   ?Border fragment: Painted grisaille decoration comprises two red lines and crescents. One grozed edge.
RF419:3, Context 99, Phase 7.

379.   Fragment: Painted grisaille decoration comprises two red lines and ?crescents. One grozed edge.
RF419:4, Context 99, Phase 7.

Catalogue nos. 380–98 and 400–2 are omitted from list. See Figure 75.

403.   Border fragment: Painted grisaille decoration comprises two red lines enclosing an uncoloured wavy line and ring pattern. Two grozed edges.
RF404:3, Context 99, Phase 7.

404.   Border fragment: Painted grisaille decoration comprises two red lines enclosing an uncoloured wavy line and ring pattern. Three grozed edges.
RF411:1, Context 99, Phase 7.

405.   Border fragment: Painted grisaille decoration comprises two thick red lines enclosing one thin one. Some (now) white paint survives in central field. Two grozed edges.
RF410:5, Context 99, Phase 7.

406.   Fragment: Painted grisaille decoration comprises two red lines enclosing a (now) white painted central field. Two grozed edges.
RF420:1, Context 99, Phase 7.

407.   Fragment: Painted grisaille decoration comprises red line and (now) white painted field.
RF420:2, Context 99, Phase 7.

Glass from Context 59 — Phase 7 (Figure 76)

Dr. Henderson examined a group of glass fragments from Context 59. Their usual thickness was *c.* 2.3-2.7mm.

408.   Fragment: White glass. Dr. Henderson writes of one of the RF285 fragments: 'Brown weathering, but

retains a pale green translucency. Muff Glass.'
RF285:1, Context 59, Phase 7.

409. Fragment: White glass.
RF285:2, Context 59, Phase 7.

410. Fragment: White glass. Dr. Henderson writes: 'Brown weathering but retains a pale green translucency. Muff Glass.'
RF357, Context 59, Phase 7.

Catalogue nos. 411–13 are omitted from list. See Figure 76

414. Fragment: White glass. Dr. Henderson writes: 'Brown weathering, but retains a pale green translucency. Muff Glass.'
RF364, Context 59, Phase 7.

415. Fragment: White glass. Dr. Henderson writes: 'Brown weather, but retains a pale green translucency. Muff Glass.'
RF365, Context 59, Phase 7.

Catalogue nos. 416–17 are omitted from list. See Figure 76

418. Fragment: White glass. Dr. Henderson writes: 'Brown weathering, but retains a pale green translucency. Muff Glass.'
RF375, Context 59, Phase 7.

Catalogue nos. 419–23 are omitted from list. See Figure 76

424. Fragment: White glass. Dr. Henderson writes of one of the RF387 fragments: 'Brown weathering, but retains a pale green translucency. Muff Glass. Thickness: tapers from 5.2mm (max.) to the edge to 2.3mm at the thinnest part. From a window edge.'
RF387:2, Context 59, Phase 7.

425. Fragment: White glass. Dr. Henderson writes: 'Brown weathering, but retains a pale green translucency. Muff Glass.' Analysis no. 19.
RF388, Context 59, Phase 7.

426. Fragment: White glass. Dr. Henderson writes: 'Brown weathering, but retains a pale green translucency. Muff Glass.'
RF392, Context 59, Phase 7.

427. Fragment: White glass. Dr. Henderson writes: 'Brown weathering, but retains a pale green translucency. Muff Glass.'
RF396, Context 59, Phase 7.

428. Fragment: White glass. Two grozed edges. Dr. Henderson writes: 'Brown weathering, but retains a pale green translucency. Muff Glass.'
RF351, Context 59, Phase 7.

429. Fragment: White glass. One grozed edge. Dr. Henderson writes: 'This fragment is from a window edge. It has brown weathering, but retains a pale green translucency. Its thickness tapers from 5.2mm (max.) at the edge to 2.3mm at the thinnest part. Muff Glass.'
RF352, Context 59, Phase 7.

Catalogue nos. 430–2 are omitted from list. See Figure 76

433. Quarry fragment: White glass. Four grozed edges.
RF367, Context 59, Phase 7.

434. Fragment: White glass. Two grozed edges. Dr. Henderson writes of one of the RF369 fragments: 'Brown weathering, but retains a pale green translucency. Muff Glass.'
RF369:1, Context 59, Phase 7.

Catalogue nos. 435–8 are omitted from list. See Figure 76

439. Quarry fragment: White glass. Three grozed edges. Dr. Henderson writes of one of the RF378

fragments: 'Brown weathering, but retains a pale green translucency. Muff Glass.'
RF378:1, Context 59, Phase 7.

440. Fragment: White glass. One grozed edge. Dr. Henderson writes: 'Brown weathering, but retains a pre green translucency. Muff Glass.'
RF380, Context 59, Phase 7.

Catalogue nos. 441–3 are omitted from list. See Figure 76

444. Fragment: White glass. One grozed edge. Dr. Henderson writes: 'Brown weathering, but retains a pale green translucency. Muff Glass.'
RF391, Context 59, Phase 7.

445. Fragment: White glass. Two grozed edges.
RF395, Context 59, Phase 7.

455. Fragment: Painted grisaille decoration comprises two red lines, one thin. One grozed edge.
RF350, Context 59, Phase 7.

456. Fragment: Painted grisaille decoration comprises one red line and a thin line. Dr. Henderson writes: 'Brown weathering, but retains a pale green translucency. Muff Glass.'
RF358, Context 59, Phase 7.

457. Fragment: Painted grisaille decoration comprises a thick red line. Dr. Henderson writes: 'Brown surface weathering, crystalline turquoise centre, presumably originally a green colour, with the addition of fired-on reddish paint. The stripe is wide: 5.6mm.'
RF371:4, Context 59, Phase 7.

458. Fragment: Painted grisaille decoration comprises one red line.
RF373:1, Context 59, Phase 7.

459. Fragment: Painted decoration comprises two thin curved red lines. Dr. Henderson writes: 'Brown weathering, but retains a pale green translucency. Muff Glass.' Analysis no. 18.
RF374, Context 59, Phase 7.

460. Fragment: Painted grisaille decoration comprises one thick and one thin red line. Two grozed edges. Dr. Henderson writes of one fragment of RF386: 'Brown surface weathering, crystalline turquoise centre, presumably originally a green colour, with the addition of fired on reddish paint - stripes, including an unusually thin one, only 1.2mm thick. Glass unusually thick: 3.4mm.' Analysis 17: of one fragment RF386.
RF386:1, Context 59, Phase 7.

464. Fragment: Painted grisaille decoration comprises naturalistic foliage. One grozed edge. Dr. Henderson writes: 'Brown weathering, but retains a pale green translucency. Muff Glass.'
RF355, Context 59, Phase 7.

465. Fragment: Painted grisaille decoration comprises red lines forming a floriated design. Two grozed edges. Dr. Henderson writes: 'Brown weathering, but retains a pale green translucency. Muff Glass.' Analysis no. 16.
RF368, Context 59, Phase 7.

466. Fragment: Painted grisaille decoration comprises two thick and one thin curved red lines. Floriated tendrils and ground of fine cross-hatching. Two grozed edges.
RF372, Context 59, Phase 7.

467. Fragment: Painted grisaille decoration comprises red

lines forming a floriated design. Dr. Henderson writes: 'Brown weathering, but retains a pale green translucency. Muff Glass.'
RF377:1, Context 59, Phase 7.

468. Fragment: Painted grisaille decoration comprises three red lines. One grozed edge. Dr. Henderson writes of one fragment of RF387: 'Brown surface weathering, crystalline turquoise centre, presumably originally a green colour, with the addition of fired-on reddish paint.'
RF387:1, Context 59, Phase 7.

470. Fragment: Painted grisaille decoration comprises red lines and ground of fine cross-hatching.
RF379, Context 59, Phase 7.

471. ?Border fragment: Painted grisaille decoration comprises two red lines enclosing a wavy line and dot pattern. Three grozed edges. Dr. Henderson writes: 'Brown surface weathering, crystalline turquoise centre, presumably originally a green colour.'
RF378:2, Context 59, Phase 7.

472. Border fragment: Painted grisaille decoration comprises two red lines enclosing a wavy line and ring and dot pattern. Two grozed edges.
RF383, Context 59, Phase 7.

473. Border fragment: Painted grisaille decoration comprises two red lines enclosing a (now) white painted central field. An uncoloured wavy line and ring pattern runs along the central field. Three grozed edges.
RF353:1, Context 59, Phase 7.

474. ?Border fragment: Painted grisaille decoration comprises one red line and a (now) white painted area. One grozed edge.
RF373:2, Context 59, Phase 7.

475. ?Border fragment: Painted grisaille decoration comprises one red line and a (now) white painted area. An uncoloured wavy line and ring pattern runs along white area. One grozed edge.
RF373:3, Context 59, Phase 7.

476. Border fragment: Painted grisaille decoration comprises two red lines enclosing a (now) white painted central field. An uncoloured wavy line and ring pattern run along central field. Two grozed edges.
RF373:4, Context 59, Phase 7.

Glass from other demolition contexts — Phase 7 (Figure 77)

477. Fragment: White glass. Two grozed edges.
RF478:2, Context 345, Phase 7.

478. Fragment: White glass. One grozed edge.
RF478:3, Context 345, Phase 7.

479. Fragment: White glass. Two grozed edges.
RF478:4, Context 345, Phase 7.

480. Fragment: White glass. One grozed edge.
RF478:5, Context 345, Phase 7.

484. Fragment: Painted grisaille decoration comprises three thin red lines; (now) ?white paint on one edge. One grozed edge.
RF450:1, Context 443, Phase 7.

485. Fragment: Painted grisaille decoration comprises three red lines. One grozed edge.

RF451:1, Context 443, Phase 7.

486. Fragment: Painted grisaille decoration comprises one thicker red line and two thin lines. One grozed edge.
RF451:3, Context 443, Phase 7.

487. Fragment: Painted grisaille decoration comprises two red lines: ?eroded - terminating. Three grozed edges.
RF734:1, Context 443, Phase 7.

488. Fragment: Painted grisaille decoration comprises two red lines. One grozed edge.
RF478:6, Context 345, Phase 7.

489. Fragment: Painted grisaille decoration comprises two red lines. Two grozed edges.
RF478:7, Context 345, Phase 7.

490. Fragment: Painted grisaille decoration comprises one curved red line.
RF490:2, Context 345, Phase 7.

496. Fragment: Painted grisaille decoration comprises red lines forming loops and one thin straight line. One grozed edge.
RF402:1, Context 345, Phase 7.

497. Fragment: Painted grisaille decoration comprises three thick and one thin curving red lines. One grozed edge.
RF402:2, Context 345, Phase 7.

498. Fragment: Painted grisaille decoration comprises red ground with uncoloured dots.
RF403, Context 345, Phase 7.

499. Fragment: Painted grisaille decoration comprised red ground with uncoloured features.
RF528:3, Context 75, Phase 7.

500. Fragment: Painted grisaille decoration comprises two curved red lines.
RF528:5, Context 75, Phase 7.

501. Fragment: Painted grisaille decoration comprises three curved red lines, one thin. One grozed edge.
RF734:2, Context 443, Phase 7.

502. Fragment: Painted grisaille decoration comprises red lines forming two floriated tendrils and ground of fine cross-hatching. One grozed edge.
RF528:1, Context 75, Phase 7.

503. Fragment: Painted grisaille decoration comprises two red lines and ground of fine cross-hatching.
RF528:2, Context 75, Phase 7.

505. Fragment: Painted grisaille decoration comprises two red lines and ground of fine cross-hatching. One grozed edge.
RF476:1, Context 345, Phase 7.

506. Fragment: Painted grisaille decoration comprises red lines and ground of fine cross-hatching.
RF476:2, Context 345, Phase 7.

507. Fragment: Painted grisaille decoration comprises fine cross-hatching. One grozed edge.
RF478:1, Context 345, Phase 7.

508. Fragment: Painted grisaille decoration comprises fine cross-hatching.
RF478:8, Context 345, Phase 7.

509. Fragment: Painted grisaille decoration comprises a red line and fine cross-hatching.
RF478:9, Context 345, Phase 7.

510. Fragment: Painted grisaille decoration comprises two red lines and fine cross-hatching.

RF490:1, Context 345, Phase 7.

511. Fragment: Painted grisaille decoration comprises one red line and fine cross-hatching.
RF528:4, Context 75, Phase 7.

512. Fragment: Painted grisaille decoration comprises one red line and ground of fine cross-hatching.
RF528:6, Context 75, Phase 7.

Glass from other areas or demolition - Phases 7 and 8 (Figure 77)

513. Fragment: White glass.
RF434:1, Context 428, Phase 7.

514. Fragment: Dr. Henderson describes this as follows: Translucent green with patchy brown weathering: Thickness: 2.2mm. Analysis no. 11.
RF475, Context 470, Phase 7.

515. Fragment: White glass. One grozed edge.
RF610, Context 303, Phase 7.

516. Fragment: Two grozed edges. Dr. Henderson describes this as follows: 'Brown surface weathering, crystalline turquoise centre, presumably originally a green colour. Thickness: 2.9mm.'
RF1089:2, Context 1084, Phase 7.

517. Quarry fragment: ?Rectangular: White glass. Three grozed edges.
RF1110, Context 1084, Phase 7.

518. Fragment: White glass. One grozed edge. Dr. Henderson writes: 'Fragment, badly weathered. Thickness: 1.0mm.'
RF3213, Context 3047, Phase 7.

519. Fragment: White glass. Three grozed edges. Dr. Henderson writes: 'Fragment, badly weathered, pale green translucent. Thickness: 3.4mm.'
RF3214, Context 3047, Phase 7.

520. Fragment: Blue coloration. Three grozed edges.
RF3211, Context 3047, Phase 7.

524. Fragment: Painted grisaille decoration comprises one red line. One grozed edge. Dr. Henderson writes: 'Fragment translucent green with dark brown

weathering. Thickness 1.9mm.' Analysis no. 10.
RF515, Context 499, Phase 7.

525. Fragment: Painted grisaille decoration comprises two red lines. One grozed edge.
RF2034, Context 2013, Phase 7.

526. Fragment: Painted grisaille decoration comprises red lines forming a floriated design. One grozed edge.
RF3210, Context 1084, Phase 7.

527. Fragment: Painted grisaille decoration comprises red ground and uncoloured lines.
RF3211, Context 3047, Phase 7.

528. Fragment: One grozed edge.
RF3205:2, Context 471, Phase 8.

529. Fragment: Dr. Henderson writes of 528 and 529: 'Two fragments, thin, colourless, with iridescent and brown weathering. Thickness: 1.2mm.' Analysis no. 12.
RF3205:1, Context 471, Phase 8.

532. Fragment: Painted grisaille decoration comprises red lines and ground of fine cross-hatching. One grozed edge.
RF448:5, Context 121, Phase 8.

533. Fragment: Painted grisaille decoration comprises red lines and ground of fine cross-hatching. One grozed edge.
RF448:4, Context 121, Phase 8.

534. Fragment: Painted grisaille decoration comprises red lines and ground of fine cross-hatching. One grozed edge.
RF448:3, Context 121, Phase 8.

535. Fragment: Painted grisaille decoration comprises red lines and ground of fine cross-hatching. One grozed edge.
RF448:2, Context 121, Phase 8.

536. ?Border fragment: Painted grisaille decoration comprises curved red lines and ground of fine cross-hatching. A crescent shaped pattern runs along one edge. One grozed edge.
RF448:1, Context 121, Phase 8.

3.9 Objects of lead

by Martin Foreman

Introduction

Lead was used at the Priory as window came mounting glass panes, as flashing for roofing or guttering, and for the piping of water to various parts of the complex (Armstrong and Tomlinson 1987, figs. 12 and 21). A small number of other lead artefacts were also found on the site. Lead was a valuable and reusable material, and at the close of the occupation of the little cloister it was systematically stripped from the buildings and melted down or 'burnt' in three bowl hearths. This activity left solidified lead melt to form a significant proportion of the lead recovered from Phase 7.

Structural interpretation

Table 7 shows the phase by phase occurrence of window came, lead sheet and lead melt as numbers of catalogued items. Despite this imprecise tabulation, certain tendencies are apparent. First, there is no indication that glazed windows were used within the Phase 3 timber halls. The very slight occurrence of sheet lead in Phase 3 — only two fragments — also argues against any widespread use of the material for the roofing or damp-proofing of these buildings. The use of glazed windows and other structural leadwork appears, however, to have been a feature of the Phase 5 little cloister from the outset. The accumulation of lead came, sheet and melt in Phases 5B and 5C argues that window settings, and gutters or roof flashings, were modified or renovated at these times. Work on windows is confirmed by the presence of small amounts of white glass incorporated in occupation deposits. This is not surprising in the light of other site evidence for considerable programmes of modification and renovation carried out in the little cloister area. The relative scarcity of material derived from the great cloister (Phases 4 and 6) is a result of the non-destructive investigation applied to these parts of the site. The preponderance of window came recorded from the Phase 5/7 interface may indicate that the stripping of the window came was an early step in the gutting of the little cloister ranges, whilst the sheet lead fittings were attacked immediately afterwards (Phase 7).

Window came (Figures 71 and 78)

The window came was recovered either with its original H-section (e.g. most of nos. 539–80) or with a T-Section resulting from the rough dismantling of glazed panels (nos. 591–626), or as pieces without a discernible form to their surviving sections (nos. 627–42). This last group may incorporate some fragments of composite openwork ventilator panels, or fragments of lead ribbon for the attachment of panels to glazing bars. No assembled ventilators have, however, been identified from the site. All the came appears to have been cast.

The larger fragments of came define a variable number of quarries, often of rectangular or subrectangular form. Some still retained devitrified glass (see Figure 71). Soldering to join the came sections is apparent on some examples. Most of the glass stylistically pre-dated the building in which it was found; the decoration of the glass is typical of the mid. 13th century, while the little cloister ranges were built in the early 14th century. It is uncertain whether the came was recast when the building was erected, or whether windows were installed after their bodily removal from another structure. The life expectancy of cast lead exposed to weathering is 100 — 200 years (Clifton-Taylor 1972, 376), which suggests that the cames would have required recasting at some time.

The distribution of the window came shows a clear concentration in the north range of the little cloister. At the time of the stripping of the building in Phase 7, the greatest accumulations of window glass and came were limited by a sill or footing taken to define a stairwell. The distribution of glass and lead within the range is illustrated by Figure 57, and discussed above (section 3.8). The scatter of window debris in the west part of the range is less informative: most of this material was incorporated into mortary demolition-type spreads and may, therefore, have been disturbed after its initial deposition.

Sheet lead (Figure 78)

Lead was used in England for the roofing or cladding of important buildings from the later Saxon period, and evidence for the large scale casting of lead for major building projects in Beverley has shown that its local use was already firmly established by the 11th century (Armstrong *et al.* 1991, 17–20). At the Dominican Priory the use of lead was less extensive, though offcuts of sheet from the little cloister area show that some fittings were of lead. The site evidence for conduit systems and their later robbing suggests that gutters took rainwater from the roof, and down to a drain leading out of the north range — a system installed during Phase 5C, in the later 14th or early 15th century (see above, Chapter 2).

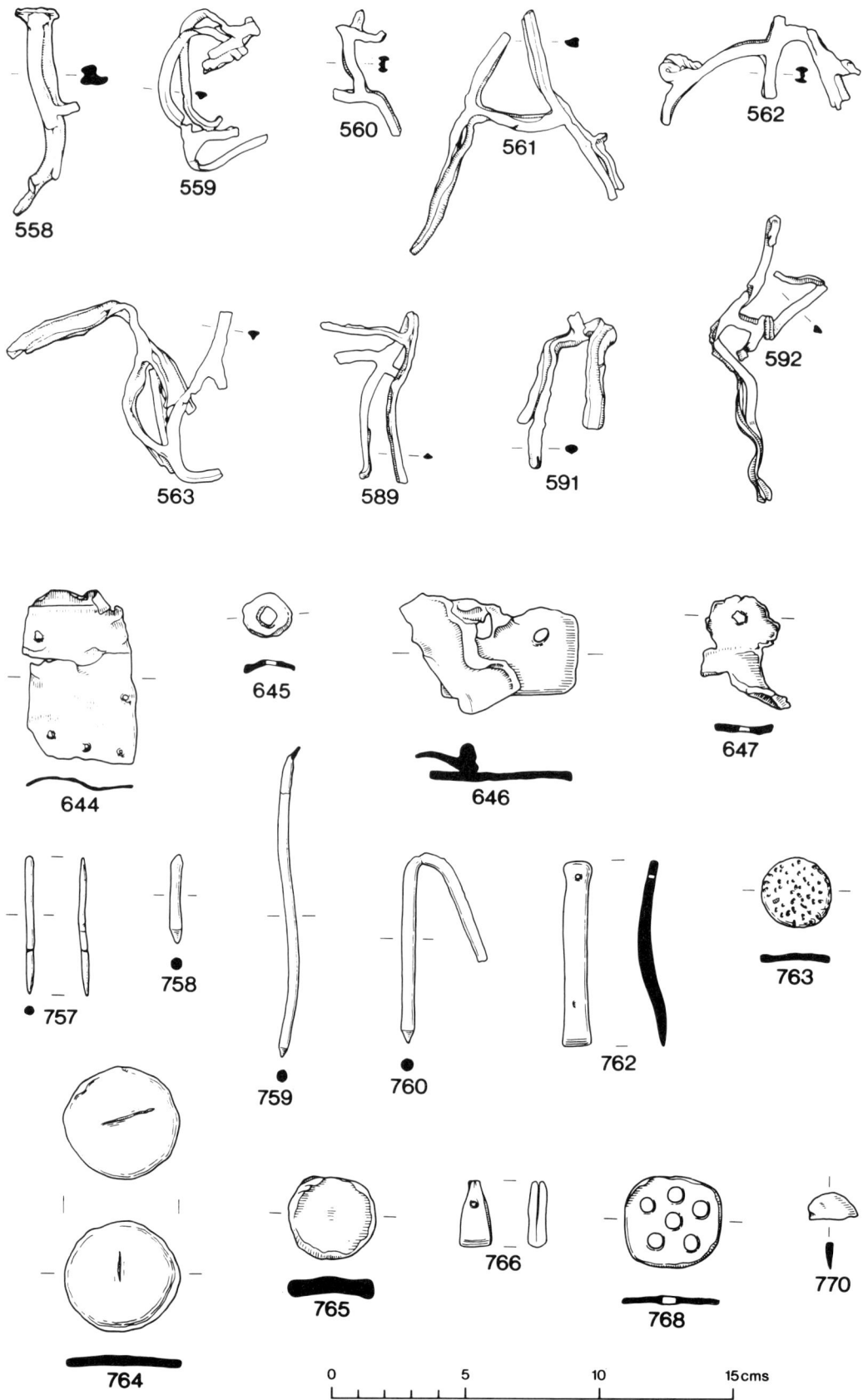

Figure 78 Objects of lead.

Utilised fragments of lead bearing a variable number of nail holes (nos. 644–7), were found in contexts of Phase 5A, and from the close of occupation (Phase 7); they were also present in an area of pits or gullies immediately outside the precinct. These are suggested to be fragments of flashing. The circular form of no. 645, with its central square perforation, appears to show how this fragment was trapped beneath the head of the nail which held it in place. The overfolding of no. 646 may show where a flap of lead was laid over the nail which secured it, to retard the corrosion of the nail. This practice has been noted at Kirkstall Abbey (Moorhouse and Wrathmell 1987, fig. 73 nos. 306 and 307:1) and at Lurk Lane, Beverley (Foreman 1991a, no.744). The thickness of lead offcuts and sheet ranges from 1mm to 8mm, indicating that a range of purposes could be served by lead sheet. As well as flashing roofs, it may also have been used to seal joins in water pipes or gutters made of other materials — a usage recorded at the neighbouring industrial site at Eastgate (Foreman 1992c). A perforated object (no. 768) which may have been a filter for such a system, is discussed below.

Lead melt (Figure 57)

The 'burning' or melting down of lead during the occupation, either for reuse or for removal, was an activity which is represented only by small fragments of solidified spillage weighing a little over 370g. These would appear to indicate works on the fabric of the little cloister ranges. The solidified spillage was found in the cloister garth; in floors of the east and west ranges in Phases 5B and (more prominently) 5C, and in a pit in the area of the Phase 6A refectory. Only three fragments of lead melt occurred among the numerous glass and came fragments from the Phase 5C/7 interface, suggesting that the material began to accumulate here before the burning got under way. The upper part of the lead and glass concentration RF 440 did, however, include numerous melted fragments. The most significant quantity of melt (nos. 721–54, weighing over 8623g) came from the close of occupation, Phase 7. Most was concentrated within the north range of the little cloister; the single largest piece weighed 5939g. This was formed by lead which had seeped between the bricks of bowl hearth structure 109. Lead was also present in the other bowl hearths, though in smaller quantities. The other melt included recognisable fragments of window came and lead sheet.

The site evidence for this activity may suggest that wooden fixtures were dismantled at this time, perhaps to fuel the hearths (see Chapter 2, Phase 7). The scatters of glass and lead do not appear at their densest around the hearth positions, but rather where the materials were gathered together (Figure 57). Similar activities are recorded in documentary accounts of the Dissolution from Northampton Greyfriars, where the choir of the church was the site of a furnace used to melt lead fixtures, perhaps because the stalls provided a supply of fuel. Archaeological evidence for this pattern of activity has been recorded from Northampton (Williams 1978, 106, Pl. 3) Chelmsford (Harris forthcoming) and elsewhere. Although a Dissolution date for this activity would be in accord with the archaeological evidence, the documentary account of the poor state of the house before 1524–25 may impose some caution on firmly attributing such activity to the suppression — it may have been an aspect of a slightly earlier contraction of the house.

Writing gear (Figure 78)

As well as serving in the furnishing and water management of the Priory, lead was also employed for other, minor, tasks. Nos. 757–9 came from the little cloister area, and no. 760 from a robber trench just to the south. These are cast rods with a point at one end; most are broken, but no. 757 retains a slightly flattened blunt end. Lead rods are sometimes considered to have served to secure panels of glass, but they did not occur in association with the large collection of window came from the site. Similar rods were found together with sturdier lead drypoints at nearby Lurk Lane, a medieval site attached to Beverley Minster (Foreman 1991a, nos. 711–21). The drypoints may have served to rule lines on parchment (MacGregor 1985, 125), being used together with pricking wheels, frames or bone-handled iron points (Jones 1946, 389): two of the latter have been found at the Beverley Priory. Similar rods have been excavated at other monastic and secular sites, and at mendicant houses including the Austin Friars, Leicester (Clay 1981, 49, fig. 13:49) the Oxford Blackfriars (Lambrick and Woods 1976, fig. 12:30), and Guildford Dominican Priory (Poulton and Woods 1984, fig. 46:44).

A strip of offcut lead sheet (no.762) is a small improvised tool with a perforation at one end, and a flattened wedge-shape at the other. The perforation of a drypoint for suspension and the improvisation of drypoints from offcut lead has been noted at Lurk Lane and elsewhere (Foreman 1991a, 156–7). This object would be unsuitable for drawing or ruling, as it lacks a point, but is comparable to one from Seacourt, Berkshire, which is considered to have perhaps served as an eraser for use with wax tablets (Biddle 1961–2, 198, fig. 32:14). The Beverley example was found in the garth of the little cloister, and relates to the Phase 5 occupation.

Weights (Figure 78)

Three cast discoid weights have been excavated from

the site. No. 763 was from the little cloister garth, and probably derives form the occupation of the surrounding ranges. The object is marked by numerous tiny indentations on both sides. It weighs 14g, just short of one half imperial ounce. Nos. 764–5 are both from post-medieval contexts; weighing 32g and 48g respectively, these may also represent one ounce, and perhaps a one and a half ounce weight. No. 763 bears crudely incised lines on one surface. These are similar to heavier examples from Trig Lane and Swan Lane, London, dated mostly to the later medieval period (D.U.A. 1984a, 1) and to others from High Street, Hull (Watkin 1987, 207, fig. 119: 286–7). No. 766 is a weight formed by the overfolding of a small fragment of sheet lead; it is furnished with a perforation at the top and weighs 14g. It is similar in form to medieval line-sinkers from the Thames estuary (Steane and Foreman 1988, fig. 26:4), and in function may be compared with larger suspended weights from Hull (S. Jackson, pers. comm.) and from the medieval borough of Yarm, Cleveland (Evans and Heslop 1985, 75). Though unstratified, this weight was excavated from an area considered at the time of excavation to be a channel or water-course; the same trench also yielded a small semi-perforated stone weight. An alternative use as an improvised 'bob', for a builders plumb-line, might also be considered for this object.

Vessel patch (unillustrated)

A flattened, waisted casting is considered to be a repair piece for a perforated vessel (no. 767). This object was found close to the Phase 6A great cloister north range. Other evidence for the repair of vessels was recovered from Phases 3C and 5B in the form of copper alloy patches or repair clips (nos. 906–7).

Water filter (Figure 78)

No. 768 is a small cast piece with six perforations integral to its original form. The holes are too large for this to have served as a strainer, but it may have been associated with water management — as a filter to prevent leaves or other debris from clogging a gutter or pipe. The object is a little small to fit into the bore of the lead water pipe previously recovered at the Priory (Armstrong and Tomlinson 1987, 40, fig. 21), so the evidence for guttering around the little cloister ranges may be significant for its interpretation (see Chapter 2). The object was found in demolition deposits of Phase 7, in the little cloister garth. A fragment of a similar object from Kirkstall Abbey has been considered as part of a drain cover, strainer or filter (Duncan and Moorhouse 1987, 138, fig. 71:251). A stone filter was incorporated into one end of an improvised cistern or settling tank at Chelmsford Dominican Priory (Drury 1974, 51–3, fig. 6).

Miscellaneous (Figure 78)

A lead shot (no. 769, not illustrated) with one flattened face, suggesting that it has been fired, was recorded in a 14th-century occupation horizon in the north range of the little cloister. This is considered to have been intrusive from the continuing use of the chamber as a route to other parts of the complex, or perhaps from its stripping or demolition. No. 770 is a small fragment of lead from Phase 7, the close of the Priory occupation. It may be a small offcut, however, small blank lead discs or tokens have also been recorded from ecclesiastical contexts at Lurk Lane, Beverley (Archibald 1991, 173), and this may be comparable.

Catalogue of lead

Window Came - H-Section (Figure 78)

558. Window came; fragment defining parts of two or three quarries, of H-section. Weight: 17g
RF439:75, Context 381, Phase 5C/?7.

559. Window came; fragment defining a rectangular quarry, H-section, split. Weight: 14g
RF298:2, Context 15, Phase 7.

560. Window came; fragment defining parts of at least two quarries, of H-section with double groove on one side. Weight: 9g
RF320:2, Context 99, Phase 7.

561. Window came; fragment defining parts of two rectangular quarries and two other quarries, of H-section. Weight: 23g
RF330, Context 99, Phase 7.

562. Window came; fragment defining parts of five quarries, of H-section. Weight: 25g
RF440:163, Context 99, Phase 7.

563. Window came; fragment defining parts of at least two quarries, of H-section, twisted. Weight: 31g
RF440:164, Context 99, Phase 7.

Window came - T-Section (Figure 78)

589. Window came; fragment defining four quarries, of T-section. Weight: 12g
RF439:71, Context 381, Phase 5C/?7.

591. Window came; fragment defining part of a rectangular quarry. Weight: 15g
RF296, Context 15, Phase 7.

592. Window came; fragment defining parts of two rectangular quarries, split to T-section. Weight: 18g
RF320:1, Context 99, Phase 7.

Flashing, sheet and offcuts (Figure 78)

644. Flashing; sheet, with five nail holes. Thickness: 1mm. Weight: 18g
RF600, Context 65, Phase 5.

645. Flashing; fragment of sheet with central nail-hole and cut edges. Weight: 4g
RF558, Context 534, Phase 7.

646. Flashing; sheet, with two nail-holes, folded. Weight: 68g
RF398, Context 345, Phase 7.

647. Flashing; fragment with 4mm nail-hole at one end. Thickness: 7mm. Weight: 26g
RF3280, Trench 2, Unstratified.

Other objects of lead (Figure 78)

757. Cast rod or drypoint, of rounded section. Pointed at one end, slightly flattened at the other.
RF1129, Context 867, Phase 5B.

758. Cast rod or drypoint, of round section. Pointed at one end, broken at the other.
RF3126, Context 3093, Phase 5C.

759. Cast rod or drypoint, of round section. Pointed at one end and a flattened point at the other.
RF689, Context 303, Phase 7.

760. Cast rod or drypoint, of round section. Pointed at one end, broken at the other. Bent double.
RF692, Context 19, Phase 8.

762. ?Eraser: strip of sheet flattened at one end and perforated - ?for suspension - at the other.
RF70, Context 65, Phase 5.

763. Weight: cast disc bearing numerous small impressions on both sides. Weight: 14g
RF549, Context 65, Phase 5.

764. Weight: cast disc, incised lines on both sides. Weight: 32g
RF459, Context 137, Phase 8.

765. Weight: cast disc with slightly raised edges on both sides and a circular cast impression on one side. Weight: 48g
RF3118, Context 3072, Phase 8.

766. Line sinker; sheet folded to sub-triangular form, perforated at top. Weight: 14g
RF3281, Trench 2, Unstratified.

768. Filter: sub-rectangular plate, edges rounded, with six round cast perforations, each with a slightly upstanding lip on both sides.
RF608, Context 303, Phase 7.

770. Semi-circular fragment, probably part of a circular object. The edge is slightly rounded. Weight: 2g
RF458, Context 99, Phase 7.

3.10 Objects of iron

by Ian H. Goodall

Introduction

The ironwork from the Priory is small in quantity though comparatively wide in its range. It contrasts with ironwork from other Beverley sites such as Lurk Lane (I.H. Goodall 1991) and Eastgate (I.H. Goodall, 1992) in the relative scarcity of craft gear and horse furniture.

Most iron objects have been X-rayed; the detailed interpretation and illustrations of those discussed below are based on the X-radiographs.

Tools and knives (Figure 79)

No. 771 is an auger bit with a damaged blade tip. The tapering tang, which was inserted into a wooden handle, is of a type known in the medieval period, although it has never been common. No. 772 is a file with a short tang and circular-sectioned, slightly tapering blade with teeth around its full length. Nos. 773 and 774 are wedges with damaged, burred heads — no. 773 with a broad and slender blade, no.774 with a substantial blade. Nos. 771–3 come from the close of occupation in the little cloister area (Phase 7); no. 774 is from garth context 65, which may have remained an 'open' context during the Phase 5 use of the little cloister.

No. 775, a tooth from a flax or wool comb, has an expanded head and broken stem. No. 776 is a tenter hook. Tenter hooks had several uses, being used to secure cloth during its stretching and drying on tenters after fulling, and also to support wall hangings. This single example could have had either use, or might even have held a tile in place: roof tiles of Type 7 include examples with iron pegs or nails in the perforations, furnished to assist their suspension. Artefacts associated with textile crafts have been common finds on sites excavated in Beverley, but are rare at the Dominican Priory. No. 775 comes from the Phase 5 context 65, while no. 776 is from a shallow feature which post-dates the Phase 3 timber buildings, and is perhaps residual from their occupation.

No. 777 is the nailed terminal from a spade iron, completely lacking the grooved blade mouth, but retaining traces of the wooden blade. It comes from a construction layer in the alley of the little cloister attributed to Phase 5B, and may have been discarded during the deposit of this material.

No. 778 is a whittle-tang knife, with the blade tip lost. No. 779 is a whittle-tang knife with its blade and tang broken. The tang retains substantial areas of coating, identified as tin; such coating is rare on whittle tangs, and it may have served to secure an otherwise loose handle. No. 780 is a fragment of a scale tang from a knife with a hollow copper-alloy rivet and a shaped copper-alloy end-plate impaled on a projecting nib. The whittle-tang knives come from the close of occupation in Phase 7, while the scale tang fragment may have been incorporated in the 13th-century footings of structures set about the great cloister, though it could be an intrusive find deposited during robbing of this structure.

Building ironwork (Figure 79)

Nos. 781 and 782 are staples — no. 781 looped, no. 782 rectangular with a shaped back and broken arms; the shaping on the latter is decorative and perhaps suggests use on furniture. No. 783 is an angle tie, and no. 784 a wall anchor with an incomplete head, probably broken across a hole. No. 785 is a hinge pivot with a broken shank. No. 786 is a hinge with a looped eye, and a broken strap with incised decorative grooves next to the outer edges. No. 787 is a shaped and perforated hinge terminal, while nos. 788–91 (not illustrated) are strap fragments, all with parallel sides, but only 791 has a nail-hole. Nos. 792–3 are strip fragments, 792 broadening to a shaped but incomplete terminal; no. 792 came from the deposits pre-dating the Priory. Nos. 783, 785, 787 and 788 were all found in construction horizons of Phase 5A, and may therefore have been residual from the timber buildings of Phase 3. No. 781 from context 65 could similarly derive from the earlier structures. Nos. 789 and 790 were found in occupation deposits of Phase 5A, and 782 from the later little cloister, Phase 5C. Only nos. 784, 786 and 793 were attributed to Phase 7, which may hint at the systematic removal of building fittings at the close of occupation. No. 791 came from the great cloister. Given the eventful structural history implied by the archaeological record, the building ironwork is a small collection.

Nails (Figure 80)

by Martin Foreman

Many timber nails were excavated, but heavy corrosion has obscured the shape of most of the surviving heads. Nos. 794–9, however, indicate the range of recognised head types in use at the Priory. Table 8 (compiled by Stephen Potts and Tony German) illustrates the numbers of complete and incomplete nails attributed to the various phases of occupation. The results are biased by the mainly

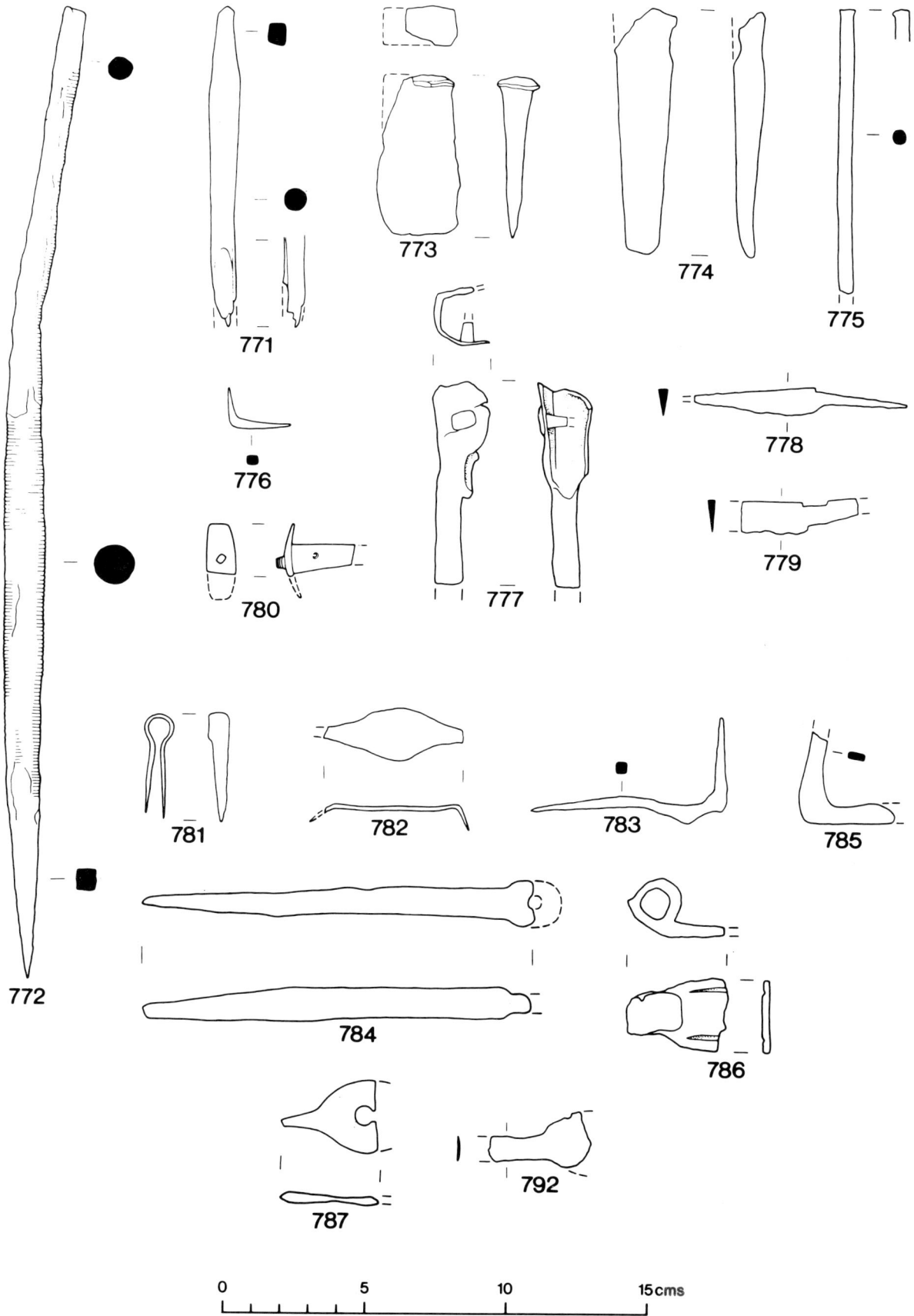

Figure 79 Objects of iron.

151

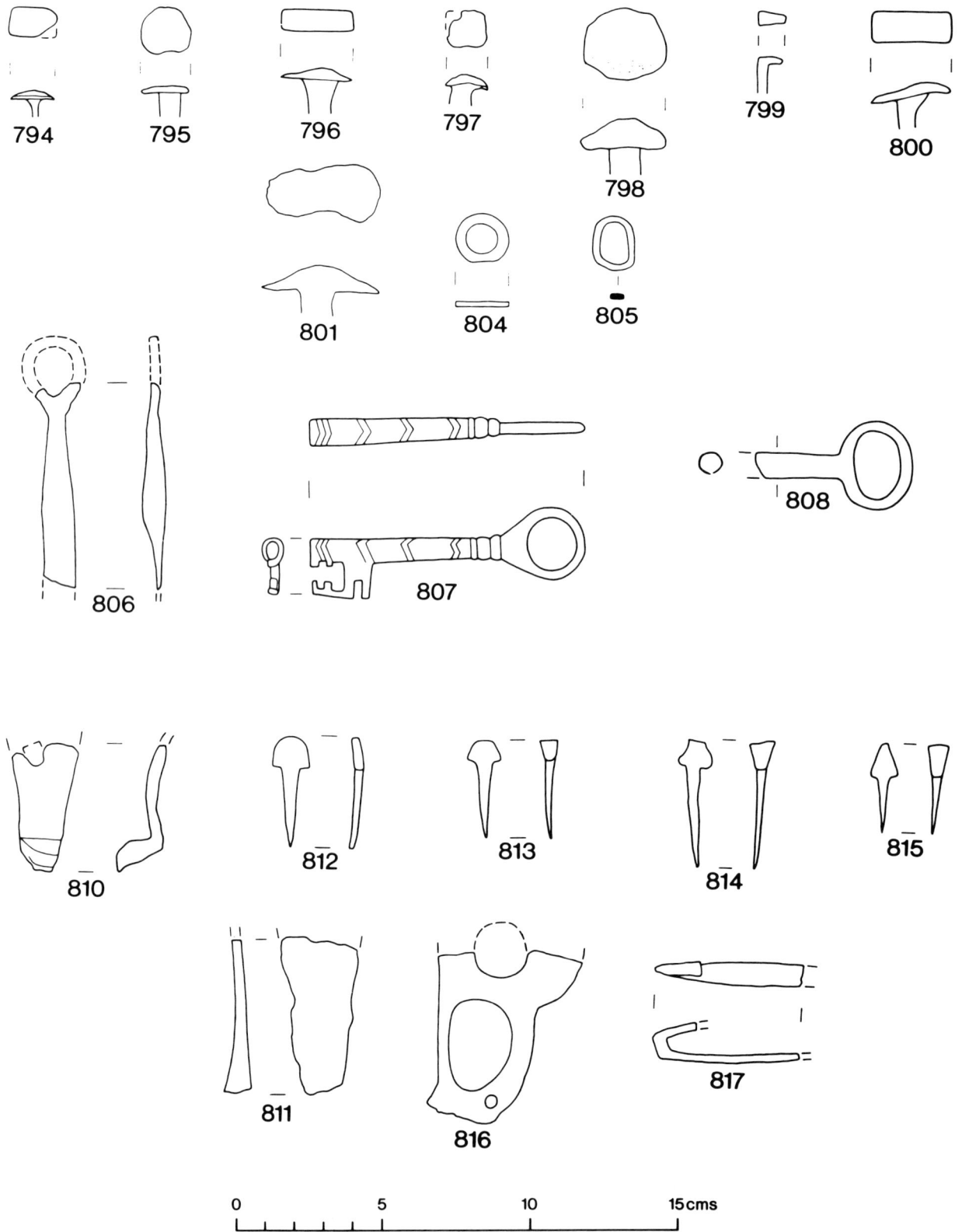

Figure 80 Objects of iron.

non-destructive investigation carried out in the great cloister of Phases 4 and 6, but nevertheless illustrate a general trend in which fragments out-number complete examples, particularly in Phase 5. This may indicate a reluctance to discard any nails which were capable of reuse; this would be in accord with the mendicant status of the house. The largest single group of nails comes from context 65, the 'open' context within the little cloister garth, in which both residual finds from Phase 3 and material which probably derived from the Phase 5 ranges accumulated. Here 236 incomplete nails and 53 complete examples were recovered. The Phase 7 deposits when the close of occupation timber fixtures may have been stripped out, included 77 complete nails and 140 fragments. Nails had evidently been significant in the structures around the little cloister, but had perhaps been less common in the sill-beam structure of Phase 3A. Nails were not present in any significant quantity in layers which pre-dated the Priory; this may argue against the proximity of earlier medieval structures.

Nos. 800–1 are studs, both with broken shanks, and both from the little cloister. Nos. 802–3 are circular discs, which are raised in side view, while no. 804 is a flat circular washer: all come from the 14th-century construction and occupation of the little cloister (Phases 5A and 5B). A D-shaped link, no. 805, comes from a 14th-century construction horizon in the same area.

Keys (Figure 80)

No. 806 is a padlock key with a broken ring bow and swollen stem. No. 807 is a key with its ring bow and hollow stem rolled in one with the bit — the stem with a moulded head and clusters of decorative grooves. The whole key retains abundant traces of a tin coating. No. 808 is a key with an oval bow and a broken, hollow stem. Nos. 806–7 both come from the little cloister garth context 65 — no. 808 from the close of occupation in the north range.

Horse furniture (Figure 80)

Nos. 809–11 are horseshoe tips, nos. 809–10 with calkins, no. 811 with a thickened tip. No. 810 is broken across a rectangular nail-hole. Nos. 812–15 are horseshoe nails, all medieval. No. 812 is a fiddle-key nail, its head no thicker than the shank; it is of a type which was in use until the mid. to late 13th century. Nos. 813–15 are succeeding types, with thickened and sometimes eared heads. No. 816 is a cheek-piece from a bridle bit with coating identified as tin. The cheek-piece is incomplete, and probably comes from a curb bit; it may have resembled, when complete, a cheek-piece from Somerby, Lincolnshire (Mynard 1969, 81, fig. 11: 1.W 28). No. 817 is an incomplete

strap slide. The horseshoe fragments come from a 14th-century Phase 5B floor silt, in the north range of the little cloister (no. 809), and from the open cloister garth (no. 810); no. 811 was residual within the footings of the refectory lying north of the great cloister (Phase 6A). The fiddle-key nail (no. 812) was incorporated into construction levels of Phase 5A, and is probably residual from the 13th-century Phase 3. Nails 813–15 are from the later occupation and stripping of the little cloister — their contexts confirming the typological development of horseshoe nail forms through the 14th and early 15th century. The bridle bit and strap slide (nos. 816–17) are both from the early 16th-century stripping of the little cloister. The infrequent appearance of horsegear among the finds suggests that these fragmentary artefacts represent a residual component of the assemblage.

Unidentified objects (unillustrated)

Nos. 818–71 include numerous small fragments of sheet or strip, and many small rod (?or nail) fragments. Much of this material derives from the little cloister garth context 65; there is a smaller amount from the stripping of the buildings in Phase 7. Little iron came from the post-medieval Phase 8. These objects are described in microfiche (Mf.2. D6–11).

Catalogue of iron objects (Figures 79–80)

771. Auger bit with tapering tang, for insertion into a wooden handle. Blade tip is damaged.
RF3230, Context 3046, Phase 7.
772. File with short tang; of circular section with teeth around the full length.
RF297, Context 15, Phase 7.
773. Wedge with a broad and slender blade. Head is damaged and burred.
RF3262, Context 99, Phase 7.
774. Wedge with a substantial blade. Head is damaged and burred.
RF609, Context 65, Phase 5.
775. Comb tooth from flax or wool comb, with an expanded head. Stem is broken.
RF67, Context 65, Phase 5.
776. Tenter hook.
RF1175, Context 1090, Phase 3D.
777. Nailed terminal from a spade iron. This retains traces of the wooden blade, but the grooved blade mouth is absent.
RF681, Context 43, Phase 5B.
778. Whittle-tang knife. Blade tip is absent.
RF315, Context 15, Phase 7.
779. Whittle-tang knife. The tang retains substantial areas of tin coating. Blade and tang broken.
RF3261, Context 59, Phase 7.
780. Fragment of scale tang from a knife with hollow copper-alloy rivet and shaped copper-alloy end plate impaled on a projecting rib.

RF728, Context 727, Phase 4A.

781. Looped staple.
RF3253, Context 65, Phase 5.

782. Rectangular staple with decorative shaped back.
RF3091, Context 3051, Phase 5C.

783. Angle tie.
RF1028, Context 893, Phase 5A.

784. Wall anchor with incomplete head. Probably broken across a hole.
RF305, Context 15, Phase 7.

785. Hinge pivot with broken shank.
RF920, Context 902, Phase 3D.

786. Hinge with looped eye and broken strap with incised decorative grooves next to the outer edges.
RF3308, Context 59, Phase 7.

787. Shaped and perforated hinge terminal.
RF3271, Context 759, Phase 5A.

792. Strip fragment broadening to a shaped but incomplete terminal.
RF3226, Context 1188, Phase 2.

794. Timber nail with flat rectangular head.
RF644, Context 645, Phase 5B.

795. Timber nail with flat sub-rectangular head.
RF628, Context 597, Phase 5B.

796. Timber nail with long rectangular head of slightly domed profile.
RF3274, Context 755, Phase 5A.

797. Timber nail with sub-rectangular head, slightly domed in profile with four angled facets.
RF3294, Context 15, Phase 7.

798. Timber nail with round domed head.
RF498, Context 499, Phase 7.

799. Timber nail with integral flat rectangular head at right angle to shank.
RF3248, Context 65, Phase 5.

800. Stud with flat rectangular head. Shank is broken.
RF3237, Context 499, Phase 7.

801. Stud with slightly domed sub-rectangular head. Shank is broken.
RF640, Context 65, Phase 5.

804. Flat circular washer.
RF895, Context 897, Phase 5A.

805. D-shaped link.
RF618, Context 596, Phase 5B.

806. Padlock key with ring bow and swollen stem. Broken at ring.
RF73, Context 65, Phase 5.

807. Key with ring bow and hollow stem rolled in one with the bit. The stem has a moulded head and clusters of decorative grooves. The whole key retains abundant traces of tin coating.
RF553, Context 65, Phase 5.

808. Key with oval bow and hollow stem. Stem broken.
RF3263, Context 99, Phase 7.

810. Horse-shoe tip with calkins. Broken across a rectangular nail-hole.
RF3245, Context 65, Phase 5.

811. Fragment of horse-shoe with a thickened tip.
RF3309, Context 24, Phase 6A.

812. Fiddle-key nail from a horse-shoe; head of equal thickness to shank in profile.
RF3255, Context 45, Phase 5A.

813. Horse-shoe nail with thickened eared head.
RF3229, Context 3103, Phase 5C.

814. Horse-shoe nail with thickened eared head.
RF3232, Context 303, Phase 7.

815. Horse-shoe nail with thickened angular head.
RF3241, Context 65, Phase 5.

816. Cheek-piece from bridle bit. Tin coating. Cheek-piece is incomplete, probably from a curb bit.
RF1137, Context 1084, Phase 7.

817. Strap slide, incomplete.
RF3250, Context 2036, Phase 7.

3.11 Objects of copper alloy and gold

by Alison R. Goodall

Finds of copper alloy were most common in the occupation deposits of the little cloister, or in the garth deposits whose composition shows that they include material tidied or dumped from occupied areas. Objects of copper alloy were rare within the timber building of Phase 3. They were also infrequent in the early occupation of the little cloister (Phase 5A), but became more common in Phases 5B and 5C. The accumulation of material appears to have been strictly controlled, perhaps by regular cleaning; the best groups came from the garth. The use of copper alloy at the Priory appears to have been for decorative mounts or fittings, needles and pins, clothing fasteners, and for other purposes including vessels. The simple yet decorative buckles which were common at Lurk Lane, Beverley (A.R. Goodall 1991a) are extremely rare on this site.

Personal equipment and fittings (Figure 81; Plate 17)

No. 872 is a tiny brooch of plated copper alloy. It has a constriction where the missing pin would have been, and a projecting ornament in the form of clasped hands. A crude four-petalled rosette has been stamped on the ring opposite the projecting hands, and in the position where the point of the pin would have rested. A similar, but slightly larger, brooch was found at Lyveden, Northants (Cherry 1975, 111–12). In other examples of this kind of brooch the hands have been made to clasp a jewel (Evans 1970, 58–9, Pl. 14c, fig. 42:39). The type should probably be dated to the 13th century. This example was incorporated in a lower garth soil (899) in the little cloister, where building work began in the early 14th century (Phase 5) over earlier occupation (Phase 3). This find may, therefore, be residual from 13th-century activity.

No. 873 is a finger ring with simple decoration. It came from the Phase 5C occupation of the west chamber of the north range, from the later 14th century onwards. No. 874 is part of the frame of a large buckle; it may have been single or double-looped. It lay in floor silts of 14th-century Phase 5B. No. 875 is probably part of a rectangular shoe buckle; it has cast decoration and white metal plating on the surface and was found in a post-medieval context. So too were 876–7, double-looped buckles. No. 877 has lost the separate bar which would have been held in the holes in the top and bottom of the frame: it seems to have had a black coating on its surface. No. 878 is a buckle pin. No. 879 is an incomplete buckle plate made from thin sheet. It has five rivet-holes and traced border decoration, and was found in layers spread across the little cloister garth at the close of the monastic occupation. No. 880 is a strip, possibly originally a buckle plate or strap end: the position of the rivet-holes at one end suggests that the object has been damaged and reused. The plate is inscribed 'MARCIALL' in Lombardic letters on an all-over traced background (Pl. 17). It was found in the fill of a cut attributed to Phase 5C, the later 14th or early 15th century. The reuse of book fittings to make belt ends has been suggested at Dominican Guildford (Poulton and Woods 1984, 79) to have indicated the poverty of the friars.

Nos. 881–2 are rosette mounts stamped from sheet metal. No. 881 is made from thicker metal; it has two rivet-holes, one still containing the rivet. No. 882 has a central rivet-hole. Similar mounts to these were used to decorate belts, as on an example from Newgate, London (London Museum 1954, 198, fig. 63:7). Rosettes from the Dominican Priory, Guildford have been alternatively identified as book mounts (Poulton and Woods 1984, 77, fig. 45:30–1). No. 881 came from a Phase 5C floor platform of the later 14th or early 15th century, while 882 was unstratified. No. 883 is a repoussé decorated mount with a plated surface: it has two rivet-holes. It was originally round, with a raised ring within a beaded border. It was found in floor silts within the Phase 5B little cloister north range.

Nos. 884–5 are buttons. No. 884 has a plain, flat top with a soldered loop at the back. Found in the structure of a Phase 5A bench footing, this could be intrusive from its robbing. No. 885 is the metal back from a button, the front of which would have been made from a different material. It was found in a demolition spread of Phase 7.

Nos. 886–9 are lace ends. No. 886 is very large and contains remains of an organic material which may be leather. Nos. 887–9 are made from rolled sheet metal; 888–9 are pinned, and both appear to contain leather. The large lace end (886) was incorporated into the make-up layers for the Phase 5B reflooring, and may derive from previous occupation. No. 887 came from a later floor silt (944) within the ground floor of the Phase 6A refectory, associated with possible food debris. Nos. 888–9 came from demolition rubble and a robber trench respectively.

No. 890 is a harness boss of sheet metal, with scalloped edge and a raised cabled band. There are no rivet-holes on the surviving part. It was found in a

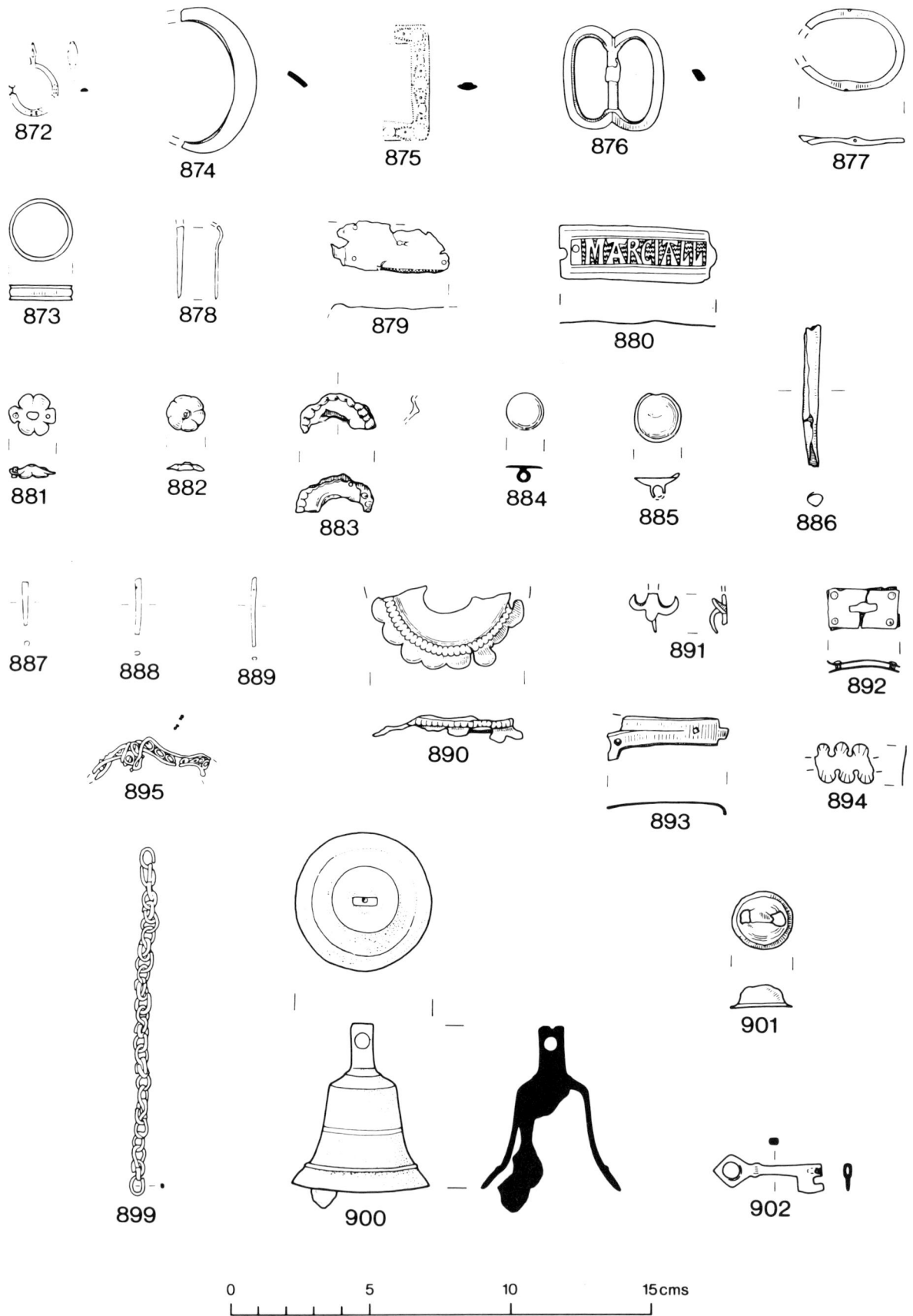

Figure 81 Objects of copper alloy.

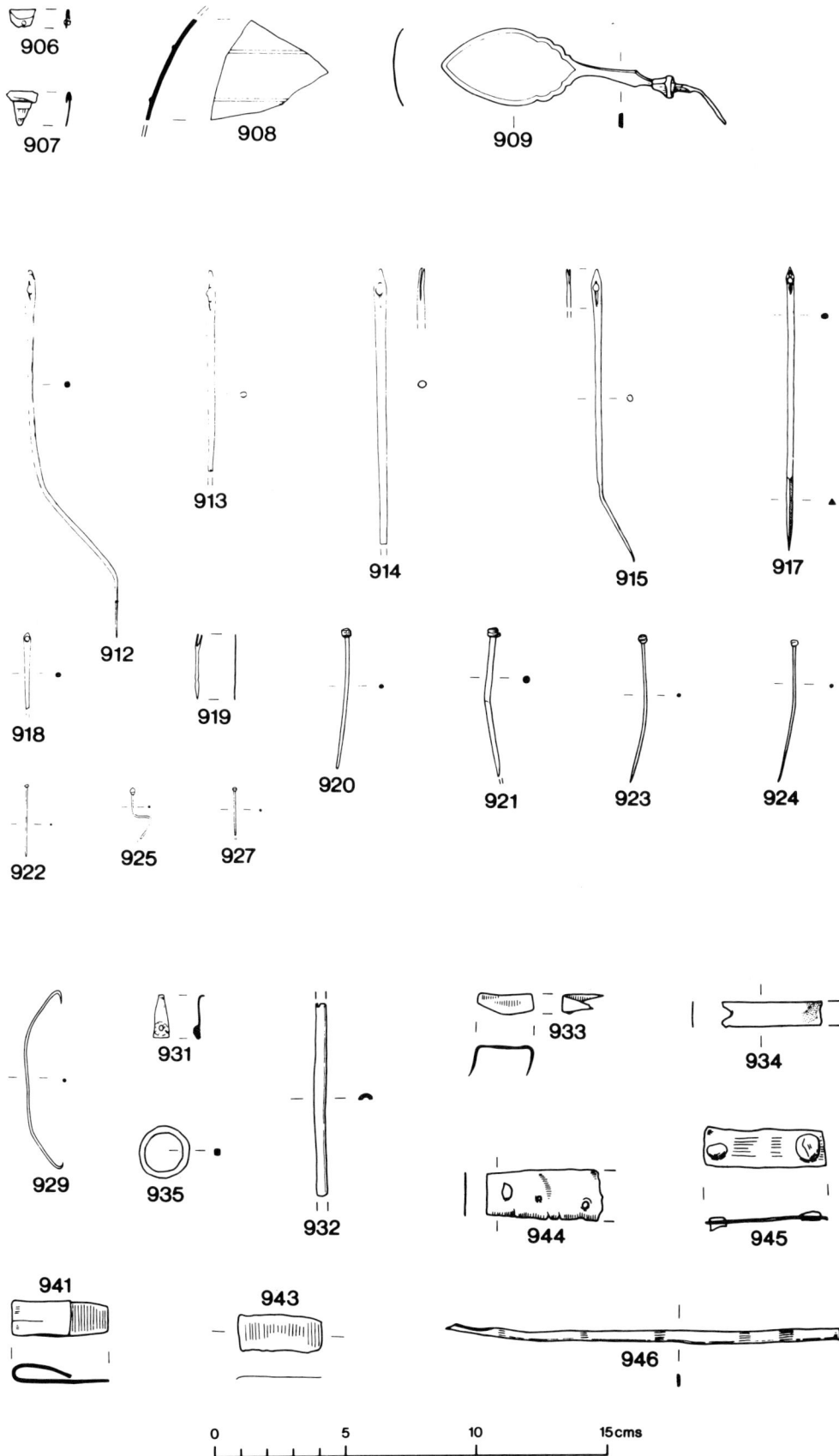

Figure 82 Objects of copper alloy.

post-medieval context.

No. 891 is a fragment of a decorative fitting, probably representing the lower part of a fleur-de-lis. It has a long, hooked shank at the back. It was found in Phase 5B occupation silts within the little cloister alley. The stratification of this motif within the monastic occupation is of interest because the fleur-de-lis is a symbol appropriate to Our Lady, and was specifically associated with St. Dominic (Farmer 1982, 109). No. 892 is a pair of plates joined at the corners by four rivets and having a central slot. It would have been attached to leather, and might have been a book or strap fitting. It came from cloister garth context 65. No. 893 is a book clasp of common 16th-century form with simple decoration of a single groove. It was found amongst the accumulation of material, context 15, in the little cloister garth at the close of the monastic occupation. Nos. 894–5 are decorative strips. No. 894 has scalloped and incised edges. No. 895 is an openwork strip made from two wires with small rings soldered or brazed between them. The former came from the Phase 5 cloister garth, the latter from a post-medieval context. Fragments of a gilded stud head, 896, were found in the floor silt (754) within the west chamber of the little cloister north range, Phase 5B; while 897 is a minute fragment of gold from floor silt 2009, a broadly contemporary deposit in the east chamber.

Nos. 898–9 are two lengths of chain, each made from S-shaped links, joined so that alternate links are attached to the further loop of the previous link. No. 898 has much corrosion; 899 consists of 18 links, each approximately 11 mm in length. Chains like these could have had a variety of uses; a similar example of S-shaped links came from the Austin Friars, Leicester (Clay 1981, 137, fig. 49: 58). Of the chains at Beverley, 898 came from floor silt 754 (Phase 5B), along with the gilt stud; and 899 from a robbed internal feature in the Phase 6A refectory.

No. 900 is a cast, open-mouthed bell with a pierced lug for suspension: it retains a corroded iron clapper. The find-spot of the bell, in demolition rubble within a chantry chapel, suggests that it might have had a liturgical use; however, typologically it strongly resembles post-medieval and recent harness bells which were sometimes suspended within terrets on similar long, pierced lugs (Keegan 1973, 170–2). No. 901 is the lower half of a sheet metal bell. It was found in Phase 3D, post-dating the 13th-century timber buildings. No. 902 is a key with a pierced lozenge-shaped head; the lower part of the stem has been hollowed out. Small keys such as this would have operated the locks of caskets. It was found in a Phase 5 pit in the north range of the little cloister.

Vessels (Figure 82)

Nos. 903–5 (not illustrated) are fragments from sheet metal vessels. No. 903 is a piece of thick sheet, and may be from the body of a vessel. It probably derives from the Phase 3 occupation of timber buildings in the 13th century. Nos. 904 and 905 are rim fragments, probably from plates: they do not join, but could come from the same object. They were found in the little cloister garth. No. 906 is a small, folded sheet with a rivet through it — possibly a patch. Under the rivet head is what appears to be the remains of gilding. No. 907 is a clip made from folded sheet, such as is used to attach a patch to a sheet metal vessel, or to repair a small hole. No. 906 came from the later 13th century occupation of the aisled timber building in Phase 3C; while 907 was found in a little cloister alley floor silt of Phase 5B. No. 908 is a body fragment from a cast skillet with two horizontal cordons (London Museum 1954, 205–7, Pl. 55), which was incorporated into the backfill of a robber pit at the close of occupation. The pottery from the little cloister garth, where material collected from the occupation of the ranges during Phase 5, included few cooking pots and vessels. A spoon (909) is of recent date.

A small tack (910; not illustrated) has a rectangular head and is 8 mm long. No. 911 (not illustrated) is a rivet passing through a washer. The tack came from a silt (597) in the Phase 5B cloister alley along with patching clip 907; while the rivet and washer was found in the later occupation of the ground floor of the Phase 6 refectory.

Needles and pins (Figure 82)

Nos. 912–18 are needles. No. 912 is a long needle with a flattened and pointed head and an almost lozenge-shaped eye set in grooves: it is solid in section. Nos. 913–16 are similar in form (although no. 916 has lost its head), but all have been made by rolling sheet metal, giving a hollow section. A smaller needle from Wharram Percy was also made by rolling sheet metal, but in that example it did not give a hollow section (A.R. Goodall 1979, 112, fig. 57:8). In contrast, the large group of needles from the neighbouring Eastgate excavations in Beverley all appear to have solid sections and to have been made from drawn metal (A.R. Goodall 1992, 138–42, fig. 76, nos. 138–50). A similar solid character is apparent among needles from a further industrial site at Dyer lane, Beverley (in prep.). There may be a distinction between the needles used in domestic and industrial settings in medieval Beverley. No. 917 has a triangular-sectioned tip, and was probably used for stitching fine leather. The possible association between lace ends and leather thongs, which were perhaps used as garment fasteners as at Coventry and Leicester (Clay 1981, 137), has been noted above.

Needle no. 918 is incomplete and, unlike the other examples, does not have the eye set in grooves or gutters. The needle of solid section, 912, which more closely resembles Beverley's 'industrial' needles, indeed came from deposits which which pre-date the priory occupation. Three of the others were found in a Phase 3B post-pipe (probably an intrusive position: no. 913), in the early garth soils of Phase 5 (no. 914), and in the garth context 65 (no. 915); the rest were found in the deposits laid down in the garth at the close of occupation. All of these probably derive from the little cloister occupation. A further fragment (919) has a split end; it is possibly a damaged needle but is more likely to be an offcut. It came from post-medieval deposits.

Nos. 920–7 are pins. No. 920 is a large pin with a drum-shaped head, broken away on one side to show the top of the shank inserted through it. Nos. 921–2 have heads of coiled wire. The head of 927 is also coiled, but has been stamped to a globular form, while 923–5 are similar but less well formed. The head of 926 is missing. Only 926–7 have evidence of white metal plating. Drum-headed pin 920 came from 14th-century occupation silts in Phase 5B; wire-headed pins 921–2 were found in post-medieval deposits and in the demolition horizon respectively. Pins with stamped globular heads were found in the Phase 6A frater footing (no. 923, perhaps an intrusive find), in demolition deposits (no. 924), and in the later occupation of the refectory (no. 925). The plated pins are also of later date, from Phase 5C occupation in the little cloister (no. 926), and from a demolition phase pit (no. 927).

Miscellaneous (Figure 82)

Nos. 928–30 are fragments of wire. No. 928 (not illustrated) is a coil of fine wires, partly embedded in ferrous corrosion. No. 929 has been hooked and pointed at both ends, and no. 930 (not illustrated) is a fragment, possibly from a pin shank. No. 928 came from a trench in the little cloister garth, which was backfilled during Phase 5 *c*.1325. This object is possibly intrusive from the excavation edge. The hooked wire (no. 929) was found in a demolition spread over the north range of the little cloister; while 930 came from the Phase 5C occupation of the range.

No. 931 is a triangular fragment, hooked at its narrow end, and with an oval hole at the wider end made by a daisy-shaped punch. It was found in floor silts of Phase 5B. No. 932 is a length of U-sectioned binding strip, without pin-holes. It was found in the demolition spread across the little cloister garth. So too was 933, a staple-like object, cut from sheet metal: it could perhaps have served as a crude belt loop. No. 934 is a strip with a V-shaped notch cut out at one end; at the other end there appear to be traces of solder

on both faces. It lay in a demolition spread. A ring, 935, is approximately rectangular in section, and was found in post-medieval deposits.

Nos. 936–47 are fragments of sheet metal. No. 940 (not illustrated) comprises three or four layers, and may be from the terminal of a strap end. No. 942 (not illustrated) has gilding on one surface, and 945 has two large rivets in it. Fragment 938 came from the garth which was open during Phase 5; 937, 939 and 940 (not illustrated) came from the Phase 5B occupation of the west chamber, north range, close to the fireplace; 942 (not illustrated) was found in the Phase 5B occupation of the east chamber; 936, 941, and 943 came from the alteration, construction and occupation of the Phase 6 refectory. Nos. 944–6 are from demolition horizons, and 947 from a post-medieval context. A small fragment of fused bronze, 948, was also found in Phase 5B occupation silts in the cloister alley. Catalogue nos. 949–52 were stolen from the site, or were unavailable for examination at the time of writing.

Catalogue of copper alloy and gold objects

Personal equipment and fittings (Figure 81)

872. Tiny brooch of plated copper alloy. It has a constriction where the missing pin would have been and a projecting ornament in the form of clasped hands. A crude four-petalled rosette has been stamped on the ring opposite the projecting hands and in the position where the point of the pin would have rested.
RF954, Context 899, Phase 5.

873. Finger ring with simple decoration.
RF460, Context 349, Phase 5C.

874. Fragment of a large buckle frame, either single or double-looped.
RF2057, Context 2009, Phase 5B.

875. Fragment of a rectangular ?shoe buckle with cast decoration and white metal plating on the surface.
RF86, Context 55, Phase 8.

876. Double looped buckle.
RF691, TR1A, Unstratified.

877. Double looped buckle. The separate bar which was held in holes in top and bottom of frame is lost. Black coating on surface.
RF6, Context 2, Phase 8.

878. Buckle pin.
RF527, Context 15, Phase 7.

879. Fragment of buckle plate made from thin sheet. It has five rivet holes and traced border decoration.
RF68, Context 15, Phase 7.

880. Strip, possibly originally a buckle plate or strap end. The position of the rivet holes at one end suggests that the object has been damaged and reused. The plate is inscribed 'MARCIALL' in Lombardic letters on an all-over traced background.
RF2032, Context 2031, Phase 5C.

881. Rosette mount stamped from sheet metal. Two rivet holes, one still containing the rivet.

RF3019, Context 3009, Phase 5C.

882. Rosette mount stamped from sheet metal, with a central rivet hole.
RF781, Trench 3, Unstratified.

883. Repoussé decorated mount with plated surface. Two rivet holes. Originally round, with a raised ring within a beaded border.
RF2049, Context 2046, Phase 5B.

884. Plain flat-topped button with a soldered loop at the back.
RF3194, Context 2005, ?Phase 5A.

885. Metal back from a button the front of which would have been made from a different material.
RF3195, Context 914, Phase 7.

886. Very large lace end containing remains of organic material.
RF1128, Context 867, Phase 5B.

887. Lace end made from rolled sheet metal.
RF3370, Context 944, Phase 6A.

888. Lace end made from rolled sheet metal, pinned. Appears to contain leather.
RF1088, Context 1084, Phase 7.

889. Lace end made from rolled sheet metal, pinned. Appears to contain leather.
RF696, Context 123, Phase 7.

890. Fragment of a harness boss of sheet metal, with scalloped edge and a raised cabled band.
RF497, Context 509, Phase 8.

891. Fragment of a decorative fitting, probably representing the lower part of a *fleur-de-lys*. It has a long hooked shank at the back.
RF592, Context 42, Phase 5B.

892. Fitting: pair of plates joined at the corners by four rivets and having a central slot. For attachment to leather.
RF657, Context 65, Phase 5.

893. Book clasp with simple decoration of a single groove.
RF432, Context 15, Phase 7.

894. Decorative strip with scalloped and incised edges.
RF454, Context 65, Phase 5.

895. Decorative openwork strip made from two wires with small rings soldered or brazed between them.
RF89, Context 80, Phase 8.

899. Length of chain made from 18 S-shaped links, each approximately 11mm in length, joined so that alternate links are attached to the further loop of the previous link.
RF680, Context 682, Phase 6A.

900. Cast, open-mouthed bell with a pierced lug for suspension: it retains an iron clapper. Unstratified, from chantry chapel, east end of Priory church.

901. Lower half of a sheet metal bell.
RF765, Context 776, Phase 3D.

902. Key with pierced, lozenge-shaped head: the lower part of the stem has been hollowed out.
RF936, Context 101, Phase 5A.

Vessels (Figure 82)

906. ?Patch; small folded sheet with a rivet through it. Under the rivet is what appears to be the remains of gilding.
RF615, Context 616, Phase 3C.

907. Clip made from folded sheet, such as is used to attach a patch to a sheet metal vessel or to repair a small hole.
RF630, Context 597, Phase 5B.

908. Body fragment from a cast skillet, with two horizontal cordons.
RF66, Context 62, Phase 7.

909. Spoon with an ornamental leaf-shaped bowl and a tang to insert into a handle of organic material. Stamped E.P. N.S. on back of stem. Of recent date.
RF8, Context 3, Phase 8.

Needles and pins (Figure 82)

912. Long needle with a flattened and pointed head and an almost lozenge-shaped eye set in grooves. Solid in section.
RF1112, Context 957, Phase 2.

913. Long needle with flattened and pointed head an an almost lozenge-shaped eye set in grooves. Hollow in section, made by rolling sheet metal.
RF988, Context 990/1, Phase 3B, ?intrusive from Phase 5.

914. Long needle with a flattened and pointed head and an almost lozenge-shaped eye set in grooves. End lost. Hollow in section, made by rolling sheet metal.
RF985, Context 899, Phase 5A.

915. Long needle with a flattened and pointed head and an almost lozenge-shaped eye set in grooves. Hollow in section, made by rolling sheet metal.
RF71, Context 65, Phase 5.

917. Needle with a triangular sectioned tip, probably used for stitching fine leather.
RF524, Context 15, Phase 7.

918. Fragment of needle with simple eye.
RF561, Context 63, Phase 5C.

919. Fragment with a split end. Possibly a damaged needle but more likely an offcut.
RF78, Context 14, Phase 8.

920. Large pin with a drum-shaped head. Top of shank is inserted through head: this is revealed by breakage.
RF2037, Context 2009, Phase 5B.

921. Pin with head of coiled wire.
RF87, Context 80, Phase 8.

922. Pin with head of coiled wire.
RF1086, Context 1084, Phase 7.

923. Pin with poorly formed coiled head stamped to globular form.
RF291, Context 24, Phase 6A.

924. Pin with poorly formed coiled head stamped to globular form.
RF119, Context 123, Phase 7.

925. Pin with poorly formed coiled head stamped to globular form.
RF3368, Context 944, Phase 6A.

927. Pin with white metal plating.
RF463, Context 468, Phase 7.

Miscellaneous (Figure 82)

929. Wire pointed and hooked at both ends.
RF418, Context 59, Phase 7.

931. Triangular fragment, hooked at its narrow end, with an oval hole made by a daisy shaped punch at the wider end.

RF3326, Context 2009, Phase 5B.

932. Length of U-sectioned binding strip, without pin holes.

RF316, Context 15, Phase 7.

933. ?Staple/?Belt loop, cut from sheet metal.

RF301, Context 15, Phase 7.

934. Strip with a V-shaped notch cut out at one end: at the other end there appear to be traces of solder on both faces.

RF359, Context 59, Phase 7.

935. Ring, approximately rectangular in section.

RF461, Context 137, Phase 8.

941. Fragment of sheet metal.

RF281, Context 24, Phase 6A.

943. Fragment of sheet metal.

RF945, Context 944, Phase 6A.

944. Fragment of sheet metal.

RF356, Context 59, Phase 7.

945. Fragment of sheet metal with two large rivets in it.

RF690, Context 15, Phase 7.

946. Fragment of sheet metal.

RF1138, Context 1094, Phase 7.

3.12 Objects of worked bone and shell

by Martin Foreman

with a contribution by Dr. Graeme Lawson

Objects of worked bone form only a small proportion of the finds from the excavations of 1986–7. Categories of objects associated with crafts, especially weaving, which are common on other Beverley sites are absent from the Priory. This may reflect the residential and cloistered status of the excavated areas, and the later-medieval date of the occupation.

Toggles and Pins (Figure 83)

A pig metapodial drilled at the mid-shaft, no. 953, is the sole representative of a class of objects which are ubiquitous on early medieval sites, and are considered to have probably functioned as toggles for the fastening of garments. In Beverley these have been excavated from 9th to 12th-century levels at Lurk Lane (Foreman 1991c, nos. 1109–13), and from 12th-century and later deposits at Eastgate (Foreman 1992b, nos. 505–9). The latter group included an example with a knotted leather thong threaded through the hole. A toggle from High Street, Hull, was found in a late 13th-century context (Armstrong and Ayers 1987, 217, fig. 127:393). A similar date obtains for the Priory toggle, which came from a feature post-dating the 13th-century occupation of the Phase 3 timber buildings. (For an alternative interpretation of these objects as primitive musical instruments, see Lawson forthcoming.)

An abraded object (no. 953A) was recovered by from the infill layers of Phase 2. This is the head of a bone pin worked into the form of a coiled worm or serpent, and bearing two opposed transverse perforations. Though the shaft is missing, the object is considered, on account of its early context, to be a further example of the class of veil or hair-fastening hipped pins which are known from Castle Acre Castle, Norfolk (Margeson 1982, 248–9, fig. 47), and Lurk Lane (Foreman 1991c, no. 1108) and Eastgate (Foreman 1992b, no. 500) in Beverley. Such pins have a currency up to the later 12th century. The serpentine motif and double perforation are unusual features, though pins of this class from Beverley and Lincoln (J. Mann, pers. comm.) show an idiosyncratic variety compatible with their local manufacture.

Writing Instruments (Figure 83)

A parchment pricker, no. 954, was an unstratified find recovered during the cutting of the east–west trial trench across the little cloister garth and earlier buildings. Its iron point is held in a lathe-turned ball-headed handle. Such objects have a general urban currency, rather than a specifically ecclesiastical provenance. A fragmentary pricker, also unstratified, has already been published from the Priory (Armstrong and Tomlinson 1987, 42, fig. 22:22). Stratified examples in this region come from Lurk Lane dated to the 13th century and after (Foreman 1991c, nos. 1175–6), from 14th-century Eastgate (Foreman 1992b, no. 496), from late 13th/early 14th-century levels in Chapel Lane Staith, Hull (Jackson 1979, fig. 22, no. 4) and Sewer Lane, Hull (Armstrong 1977, fig. 29, no. 137); and from High Street, Hull from the first half of the 14th century (Armstrong and Ayers 1987, 217, fig. 127, no. 394). MacGregor (1985, 124–5) has discussed the use of prickers with drypoints of lead; rods which may have served this function are discussed above (see section 3.9, nos. 757–60).

The tuning peg (Figure 83)

by Dr. Graeme Lawson

A tuning peg, no. 955, was found in occupation levels of Phase 5C, within the east chamber of the north range of the little cloister.

The find is incomplete, but its shape, size and method of working confirm its inclusion among the category of stringed instrument tuning pegs, as recovered from other medieval and early post-medieval sites in Britain, including Lurk Lane, Beverley (Lawson 1980, 219–28; Lawson 1991, no. 1172). Slight irregularities in the shaping of the shaft represent inferior workmanship, but would not have seriously affected function. The absence of clear signs of wear — knifed facets are still distinct — suggests that breakage occurred before much use, and possibly even during manufacture. The surviving length of the object is 46mm, the total length when complete would probably have been in excess of 58mm. The form corresponds to Type A, which has been reported from sites such as St. Aldates, Oxford (Durham 1977, 163–6, fig. 39), Lower Brook Street, Winchester (Lawson 1990) and Battle Abbey, Sussex (Lawson 1985, 154, fig. 47). This type is consistent with the late medieval date of context 100. Whilst it is most probably associated with small harps, other possibilities include bowed instruments of fiddle type which possess simple peg-boards, but are distinct from those with more complex peg-boxes such as viols.

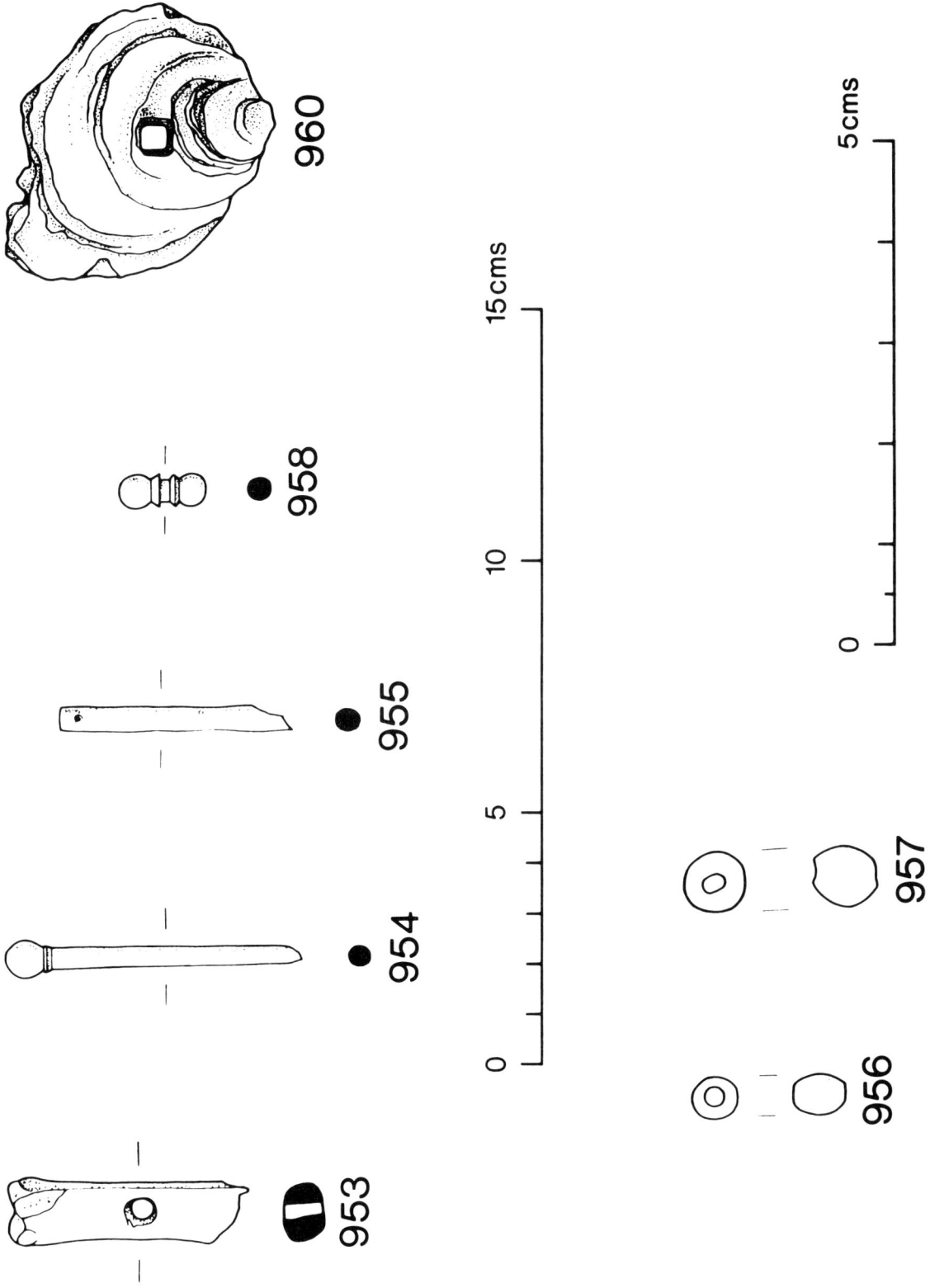

Figure 83 Objects of bone and shell.

163

Miscellaneous Objects (Figure 83)

Two ovoid bone beads (nos. 956–7), were excavated from the mid. 14th century occupation of the little cloister north range (Phase 5B), and from the occupation of the ground floor of the Phase 6A refectory. The Dominicans are traditionally associated with the devotion of the Rosary, though the popular attribution of its invention to St. Dominic is unauthenticated (Farmer 1982, 109). A bone bead was recorded at Pontefract Cluniac Priory, in Dissolution layers (Bellamy 1965, 125) and a bronze paternoster bead at Dominican Guildford (Poulton and Woods 1984, 79, fig. 44:24). Other, glass, beads have also been recovered from the Beverley Priory, nos. 996–8 (see section 3.13).

A further turned piece (no. 958) is a Romano-British object, kindly identified by John Dent as a dumbbell button — a form of toggle or fastener. The distribution of these objects in Scotland is listed by Morna MacGregor (1976, 137, fig. 8: 13–16). Closer to Beverley, examples have been excavated in Yorkshire at Rudston (Stead 1980, 105, fig. 69: 13–19), North Elmswell (Congreve 1938, 33, fig. 8:13) and Wetwang (Dent forthcoming, nos. 127 and 135). The incorporation of this find into a clay platform of Phase 6A indicates that it may have originated from a location used to supply building materials for the Priory. In this, it is similar to a Roman coin (no. 1021) which was found in a chalk footing of Phase 5A.

Perforated Shell (Figure 83)

An oyster shell with a neatly cut rectangular hole (no. 960) was incorporated into the gravel and clay patching of a floor platform in the little cloister north range of Phase 5C. A similar perforated oyster shell, perhaps intended for suspension or attachment to a hat or garment, has been excavated at Eastgate, Beverley (Foreman 1992b, 168). Shells other than oyster saw some use as amulets or fertility charms among the Anglo-Saxons (Meaney 1981, 123–30), and scallop shells were the Pilgrim sign *par excellence* in the later Middle Ages because of their association with the shrine of St. James at Compostella (Spencer 1968, 143).

Catalogue of bone and shell objects (Figure 83)

953. Toggle. Metapodial bored dorso-ventrally at mid-shaft. One end lost.
RF918, Context 901, Phase 3D.

953A. ?Pin. Fragment of ?hipped pin. Head carved with intertwined segmented body of serpent or worm. Two opposed transverse perforations drilled through lower part of pin-head. One side of head and shaft of pin broken, heavily abraded throughout.
Context 1188, Phase 2.

954. Parchment pricker. Lathe-turned; ball-headed and collared handle, holding corroded stump of an iron pin at the other end.
RF26, TR3 unstratified.

955. Knife-cut tuning peg, Lawson type A. Broken at one end.
Length: 46mm
RF112, Context 100, Phase 5C.

956. Lathe-turned ovoid bead.
RF3344, Context 2009, Phase 5B.

957. Lathe-turned ovoid bead.
RF3369, Context 944, Phase 6A.

958. Dumb-bell button. Two spheres of unequal size, separated by a sharply defined double collar. Lathe-turned on a single piece of bone. The smaller sphere bears a partial perforation, the larger a flat surface where the button has been cut from its parent material.
RF430, Context 280, Phase 6A.

960. ?Pendant. Oyster shell, with near-central rectangular perforation cut from one side.
RF905, Context 583, Phase 5C.

3.13 The vessel glass

by Julian Henderson

Introduction

Most of the glass vessel fragments from the Priory are undiagnostic, mainly because they are too small. A single translucent yellow fragment (no. 963) can, however, be identified as deriving from a fragment of goblet, chalice or beaker with a decorative trail of the same glass colour. Vessel glass of this type with applied trails has been found on other sites in the area, such as Sewer Lane, Hull (Armstrong 1977, 61, no. 53) and Lurk Lane, Beverley (Henderson 1991). Other examples of fine, often colourless, decorated, 14th-century and later, vessel glass have been found, for example in Southampton (Charleston 1975) and Swan Lane, London (unpublished; excavated by the Department of Urban Archaeology).

Chemical analysis of representative glass vessel fragments

(Table 36: Mf.2. E4–6)

Glass fragments were chosen for analysis so as to represent the full spread of dates from the site, and, where possible, so that the glass chemical composition could be linked to the vessel type. Since one could construct a vessel form from very few of the vessel fragments, samples were chosen according to the context dates supplied. For details of analytical conditions and a description of the equipment used for electron-probe micro-analysis, see Henderson 1988.

One vessel fragment, which is definitely in its correct 14th or 15th-century context, is the fine yellow trail-decorated piece (no. 963). Analysis no. 1 shows its major chemical composition to be a flint glass (lead oxide-silica) with low levels of potassium oxide (1.2%), negligible calcium oxide (0.2%) and 0.3% iron oxide (probably a mixture of ferric and ferrous ions), accompanied by 0.1% copper oxide and 0.2% sulphur trioxide. These last two oxides probably contribute to the final colour; sulphur trioxide might be present as part of an iron-sulphur chromophore, though a technique such as electron paramagnetic resonance would be required to prove this. This early example of a 'flint' glass is unexpected, since one would normally expect to find such glass from around the 17th century onwards, when it was introduced into England by George Ravenscroft. The fragment derives from a vessel which was probably imported from Italy, where at this time soda (low lead) glass was in use. Recently, 14th-century lead-rich glass has been found in the City of London (pers. comm. J. Clark,

Museum of London), so the introduction of this glass composition evidently pre-dates the 17th century. Further analytical research may reveal other examples of lead-rich 14th-century glass, although, as yet, we are unable to state with certainty where or when such European medieval glass was introduced.

Analysis no. 2, of a fragment of undiagnostic colourless glass from the site (no. 964), shows it to be of a soda-lime-silica composition. This may mean that it was imported in the 14th century, or more likely, that the context is contaminated by later material.

The analysis of a green vessel fragment (no. 962: analysis no. 3) from a late 14th or early 15th-century context, shows an unusual low alkali (4.1%), high lime (26.6%) composition. This is interesting, because in medieval glass one would expect a high lime content to be accompanied by a high potassium oxide content. Since there are very limited comparative data, this composition will have to stand alone, till further analytical research is carried out on vessel glass of this age.

Analysis no. 4, of another green vessel glass fragment (no. 965), shows it to be of a mixed-alkali content with a reasonably high calcium oxide content, comparable to the glasses being manufactured at Bagot's Park, Staffordshire in the late 16th century (Thorpe and Sykes 1967), a possible date for the context in which the fragment was found.

Analyses 5 and 6 were of fragments of thin green vessel glass (nos. 972, 961), both of which probably date to the 16th century, though a 14th-century date cannot be ruled out; the fragments derive from contexts respectively dated to the mid. 14th century (context 596), and the early 16th century (context 15). These fragments are thin-walled, but are otherwise undiagnostic. They do, however, display a brownish weathering. The glass is a lead oxide-silica composition, and, despite deriving from two separate archaeological contexts, they both were probably originally part of the same vessel. The colour of the glass is probably due to *c*.1% copper (cupric) oxide. Irrespective of whether these vessel fragments are of 14th- or of early 16th-century date, the occurrence of green lead oxide-silica ('flint') glass is very interesting in either period.

The analysis of the translucent green beaker base (no. 973; analysis no. 7) again reveals compositional characteristics (mixed-alkalis and medium calcium oxide level) of glass which may have been made in northern England and other centres from the late 16th century onwards. The beaker base derives from a

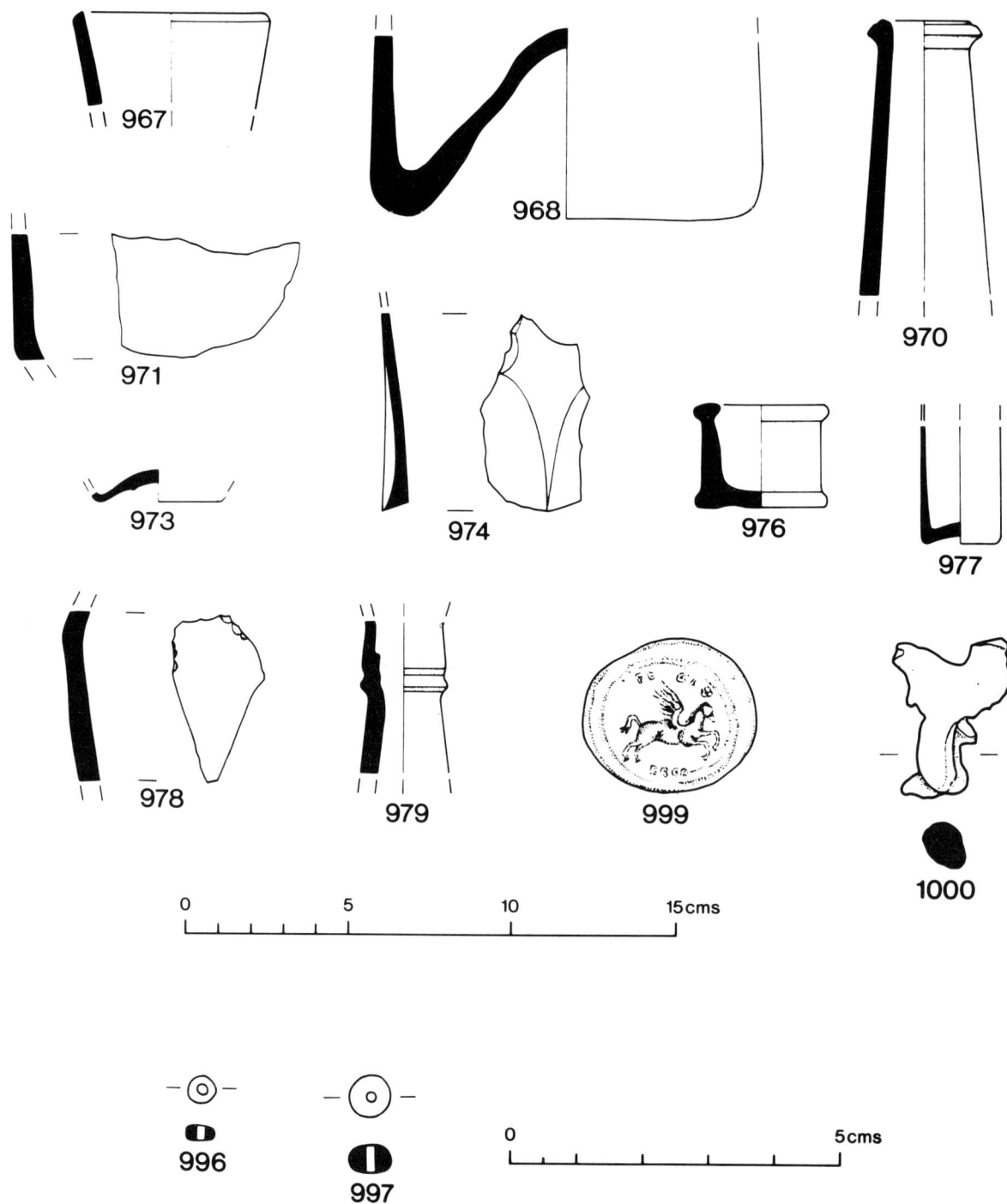

Figure 84 Vessel glass.

context dating to the 17th or 18th century.

Analysis of an unweathered sample taken from the base of a sack-bottle (no. 968; analysis no. 8) shows high calcium oxide (22.6%) and relatively low total alkali content (5.1%). The green colour is due to the iron oxide in the glass, which was probably present as mixed ferric and ferrous ions. This composition provides a parallel for no. 962 (analysis no. 3), possibly implying that the latter in fact dates to a later period of use.

A pale green handle with negligible signs of weathering is of a soda-lime-silica composition (no. 975; analysis no. 9); its form, together with its composition, strongly suggest a 19th or 20th-century date. It was found in a Phase 8 context.

Overall, these analyses have provided some very useful data for medieval vessel glass, showing that lead oxide-silica glass was in use in the area in the 14th century, and was used for the manufacture of fine thin vessels.

The vessel glass — a note on its distribution

by Martin Foreman

The medieval vessel glass was represented for the most part by tiny non-diagnostic fragments, some of which were recovered by hand (nos. 961–79, 981, 988, 993, 996–7, 999, 1000), and others during the sieving of soil samples (nos. 980, 982–7, 989–92, 994–5, 998). Of the latter group nos. 982–3 and 985–7 were post-medieval intrusions into Phase 5B, and nos. 990 and 992 intrusions into Phase 5C. In all these cases, the movement of these fragments by worm action is the probable cause of their inappropriate position, as the contexts concerned lay almost immediately below the post-medieval deposits of garden soil which sealed the archaeological features.

A glass bead (988) came from occupation silting within a refectory area of the little cloister in Phase 5A; a further bead (997) and vessels 961, 982, 984 came from the same chamber in Phase 5B. A fragment of imported glass (963) lay within the Phase 6A refectory; this was either a residual find, or one which had slipped through a floor covering. A bead (996) was probably residual in this phase. Most of the rest of the vessel glass was incorporated in demolition horizons of 17th-century date or later, or in the post-medieval topsoil sealing the site. The illustrated vessel glass derives in the main from Phase 8.

Catalogue of illustrated vessels (Figure 84)

967. Two weathered rim fragments, colours not determinable, weathered brown; thickness: 4.1mm.
RF 3206, Context 471, Phase 8.

968. Base of wine (sack) bottle with pointed kick and punty. Iridescent weathered surface. Maximum measurable thickness: 10.06mm. Probably 17th century.
RF 3322, Context 55, Phase 8.
Analysis No. 8.

970. Part of neck and top of rim of wine (sack) bottle in olive green glass: thickness (maximum): 5.7mm.
RF 3316, Context 3, Phase 8.

971. Fragment of wine (sack) bottle in olive green glass; thickness: 5.7mm.
RF 3315, Context 3, Phase 8.

973. Base of small pale green vase with pushed-in domed base and punty; iridescent weathering; thickness (base of wall): 1.5mm.
RF 3314, Context 3, Phase 8.
Analysis No. 7.

974. Fragment of moulded colourless vessel; iridescent weathering: thickness: 9mm.
RF 3318, Context 3, Phase 8.

976. Base and walls of glass cylinder with expanded ends; thickness: 6.7mm.
RF 3320, Context 3, Phase 8.

977. Fragment of flat base and walls of colourless glass specimen tube, with brown weathering; thickness: 2.7mm.
RF 3317, Context 3, Phase 8.

978. Fragment of green bottle glass; thickness: 6.4mm.
RF 3321, Context 14, Phase 8.

979. Top of pale green bottle with part of neck attached; thickness: 6mm.
RF 3319, Context 3, Phase 8.

996. Translucent, annular, pale yellow bead; diameter: 4.2mm.
RF 3366, Context 944, Phase 6A.

997. Translucent, orangey-yellow, partly devitrified bead; diameter: 6.5mm, depth: 4.4mm.
RF 3352, Context 2009, Phase 5B.

999. Glass seal. Badly devitrified, yellowy-green colour. Moulded design of winged horse. Letters above horse are P E G A with a small detailed flower to the right-hand side. Letters below horse possibly read E B O R, though these last four letters are unclear. Length: 50.9mm, width: 46mm, Depth: 9.7mm.
RF 3345, Context 15, Phase 7 (?intrusive from Phase 8).

1000. Lump of glassy slag. Dark green, vitreous, slaggy lump; probably a fuel-ash slag deriving from a high temperature process at or near the site. It has fused to a fragment of pale calcareous-looking stone.
RF 3325, Context 583, Phase 5C.

3.14 The objects of worked stone

by Martin Foreman

Introduction

The objects of worked stone from the site have been examined by Dr. Martyn Pedley of Hull University, who has also carried out a thin-section investigation of the mortars. The hones were examined in thin-section by Mr. D.T. Moore, formerly of the British Museum (Natural History).

The hones (Figure 85)

Nos. 1001–2 were found in deposits pre-dating the foundation of the Priory; the others (nos. 1003–9) are associated with its establishment or occupation. Those hones deriving from the Dominican occupation appear to be mostly smaller 'personal' hones, which would be easily portable, either hung from a belt or carried in a wallet. This may reflect the essentially residential character of the area excavated in 1986–7 (though the possibility of residuality should be considered, see below). Other hones from mendicant houses tend to share this characteristic: examples may be cited from Guildford Blackfriars (Poulton and Woods 1984, fig. 47:48), the Austin Friars, Leicester (Clay 1981, 144, fig. 54: 101–4), and from previous excavation at this Beverley Priory (S.J. Armstrong 1987, 44, fig. 24:34).

A large hone fragment (no. 1001) in a fine light grey sandstone (sub-arkose), perhaps Millstone Grit, was lightly worn, and broken at both ends; it was found in a Phase 2 pre-Priory context (959), which represents an episode of landfill and possible cultivation. The pottery from this context suggests an 11th or 12th-century date for this activity. The weight of the fragment rules out an interpretation as a readily portable hone; it may have been used in a workshop, or in an agricultural context. A further fragment from the same context (no. 1002) is perhaps from a smaller hone of fine-grained quartz phyllite or slate: it appears to have been sawn on both sides. At the nearby industrial site on Eastgate the large or craft hones of local (i.e. northern British) origin predominated until the later 13th century (Foreman 1992a).

No. 1003 is a hog-backed hone. The material is identified as sandstone (orthoquartzite) with chert, clay and rare alkali-feldspar, and accessory tourmaline. It was incorporated into a cobble footing for a 13th-century building in Phase 3A. The form is comparatively rare; it has been noted from a Saxon context at Yeavering, Northumberland (Hope-Taylor 1979, 196, fig. 92:1), and at Lurk Lane, Beverley in 10th or 11th-century contexts (Foreman 1991b, nos. 16–18). The shape is well adapted to hold in the hand,

for the sharpening of long-bladed tools such as scythes. Two longitudinal grooves along one side of the hone show that it was also used to sharpen smaller, pointed, tools.

Nos. 1004–8 are all fragments of personal hones. No. 1004 is a weathered fine grained quartz phyllite/slate. No. 1005, a quartz and chlorite-bearing phyllite/slate is perforated for suspension; no. 1006 has been used to sharpen points. Nos. 1004–6 came from the garth of the little cloister, and may derive from either the Phase 3 or the Phase 5 occupation of the area. No. 1006 is a purple phyllite, of a type usually associated with Viking-age sites and may, therefore, be a residual find. No. 1007 was incorporated into a platform deposit laid down during Phase 5B in the north range of the little cloister, and no. 1008 came from demolition deposits. No. 1008 is a Norwegian Ragstone (a quartz-muscovite -calcite-schist). Excavations at Lurk Lane and Eastgate have demonstrated that the dominance of this imported stone over the local market for small, or personal, hones was established by the early 13th century. The other personal hones are either phyllites or slate, types which tend to occur more often in early medieval horizons, though their local persistence into the 12th century has been noted at Lurk Lane (Foreman 1991b, 106), and into the 13th at Eastgate (Foreman 1992a, 122).

The mortars (Figure 86)

The two mortars from the Priory were both excavated from secondary contexts. No. 1009 was incorporated into a Phase 5A arcade footing — perhaps a secondary reuse, as the stone had already been carefully reworked; no. 1010 was built into a Phase 5B footing. No. 1009 is a rim and wall fragment, with one partially surviving lug and part of a pouring spout; it is made from a light pelloidal oolitic limestone. It is internally and externally smoothed. The stone may be Cave Oolite, and quarried relatively locally. A Cave Oolite mortar of simple form, but without lugs, is known from High Street, Hull, where it was also a residual find (Armstrong and Ayers 1987, 190, fig. 169: no. 17). The Priory mortar had found its way to a secondary reuse by the early 14th century. No. 1010 is a more substantial fragment. Its most striking characteristic is the pronounced concave swelling of the wall between vertical fillets; one of these fillets survives, widening towards a rectangular footring. A square footring is a characteristic of Caen-stone mortars of Dunning's types 1, 6 and 7 (Dunning 1977,

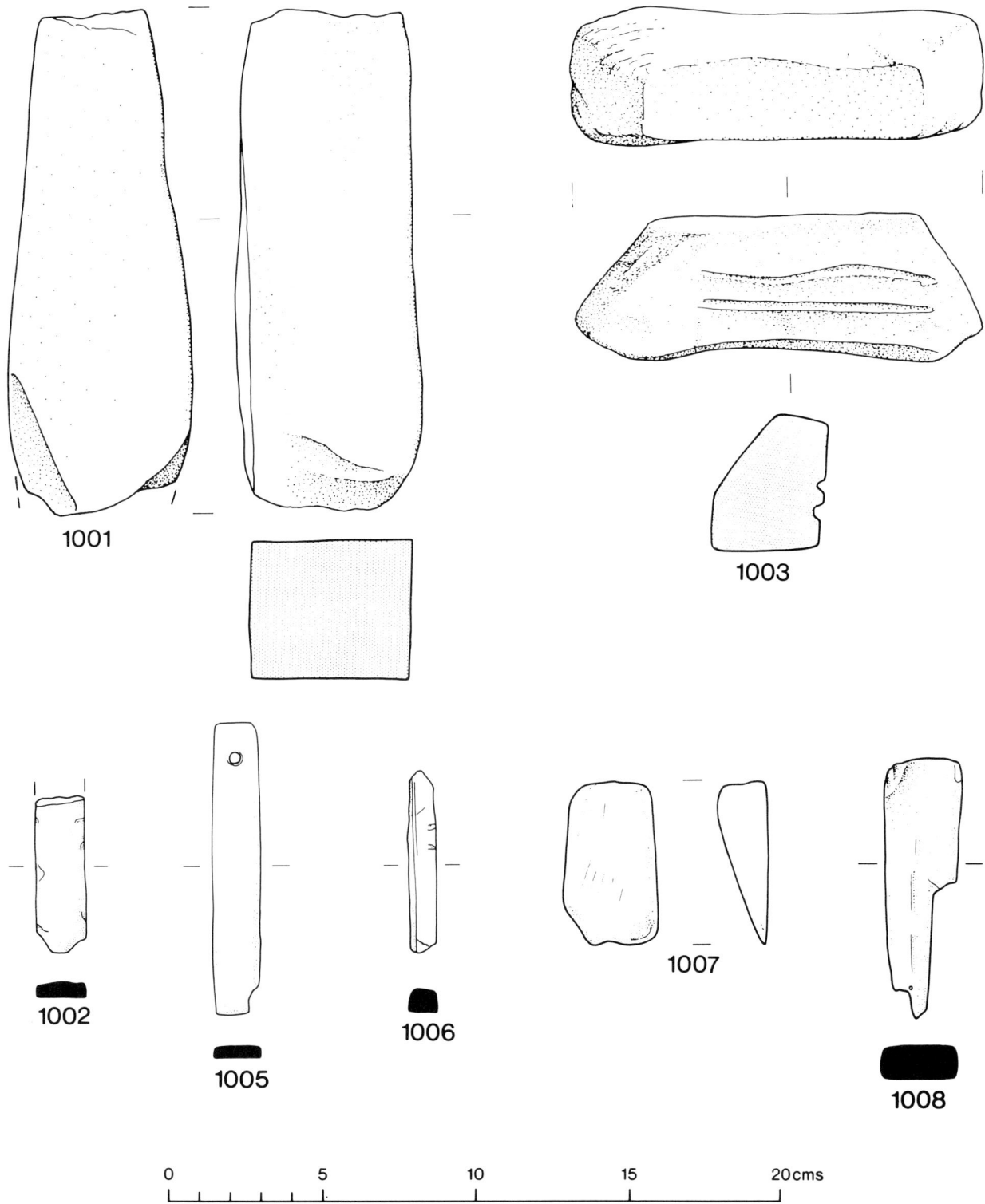

Figure 85 Objects of stone — hones.

169

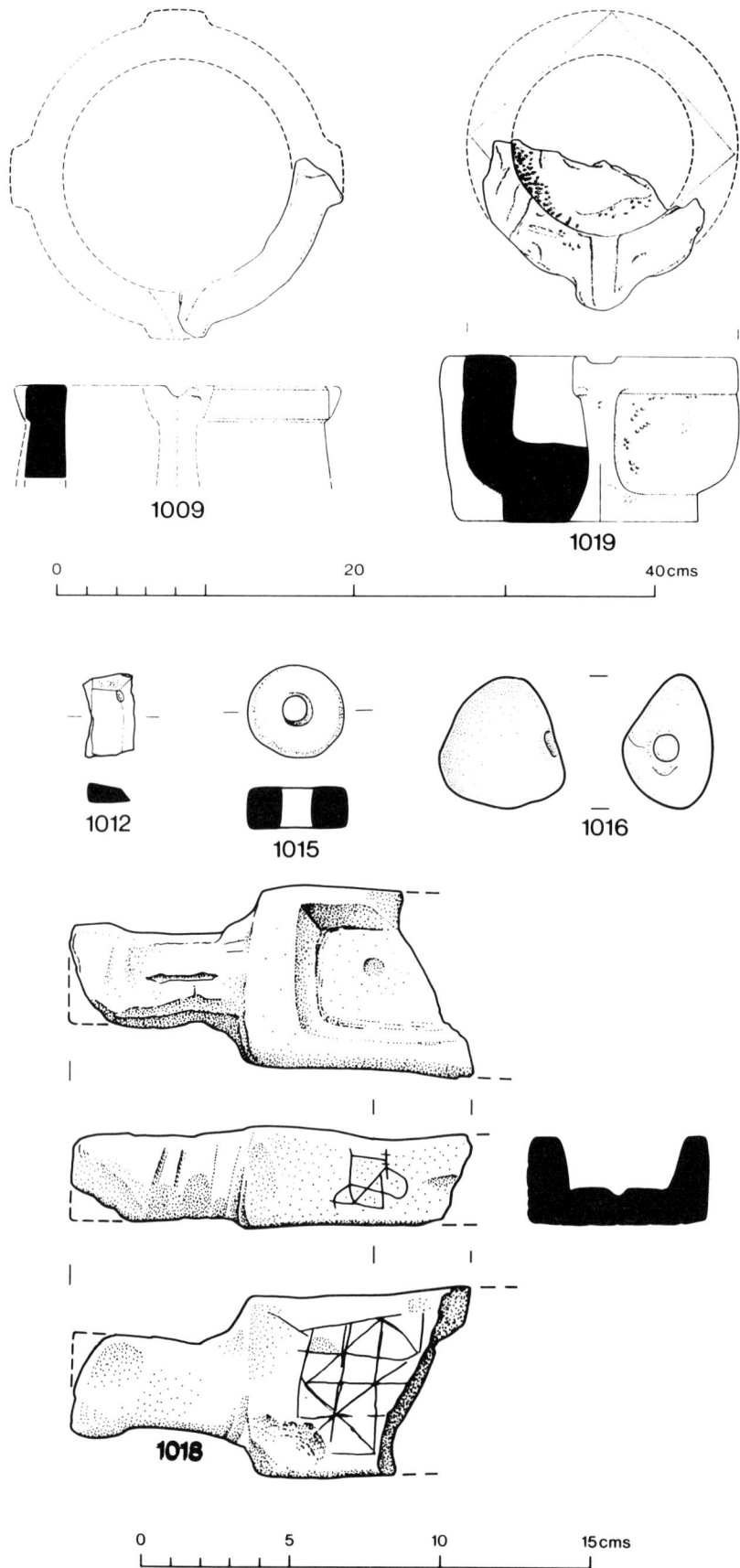

Figure 86 Objects of stone — mortars and miscellaneous.

331–46), and is also an occasional feature of Purbeck marble mortars. The thin-section of this mortar indicates that the stone is an even-grained medium quartz sandstone, with burrowing and detrital glauconite grains suggesting its marine deposition. It is possibly Jurassic, and not dissimilar to material occurring north of Scarborough. It would therefore appear to be an imitation of an imported form, executed in stone which was available locally.

Miscellaneous (Figure 86)

No. 1011 is a small millstone or quern fragment from a Phase 5A levelling spread, and is presumably a residual find. No. 1012 is also likely to be residual, perhaps from the Phase 3 occupation of timber buildings in the 13th century. It is a tabular worked flint with four flakes removed, and is suggested to be a flint striker for use with a 'fire steel'. This would usually be used with a pouch or tinder-box filled with inflammable material. A comprehensive collection of firelighting paraphernalia has been illustrated and discussed by Christy (1926). No. 1013 is a small stone rod — perhaps of shale — which has been ground to taper towards an even-faceted point. This is comparable to a faceted slate pencil found at Eastgate in later medieval deposits (Foreman 1992a, no. 83). No. 1015 is a discoid spindle whorl of chalk; this form of whorl was common at Eastgate, where it was current between the 11th and later 13th centuries (*ibid.*, nos. 57–60). The Priory whorl was incorporated as a residual find into a Phase 5A construction spread, and is the only spindle whorl to be recorded from this site.

No. 1016 is a small sandstone weight with a perforation part-drilled from both sides, but not carried through. This may be an unfinished weight, or may alternatively have been pegged when in use — a fastening method suggested for larger stone plugs and sinkers for use with fishtraps (Mynard 1979). The provenance of this object, as an unstratified find from an area of deep pits and channels, may conceivably support its association with fishing. A small lead weight (no. 766) was also excavated from this area. No. 1017 is a rough disc of tile, possibly to be compared with a collection from Hull, of 13th-century date (Armstrong and Ayers 1987, fig. 108, nos. 11A–D); another example came from a 14th-century horizon at Lurk Lane (Foreman 1991b, no. 80), and there were also two from Baile Hill, York (Addyman and Priestley 1977, 143).

No. 1018 is a chalk object, apparently carved as an oblong handled box; one end has been lost. This piece is of interest both for its location in the demolition or clearance material lying in the little cloister garth, and also for the graffito scratched on its base. The regular form of the cavity in the box, with a dimple in its base, may suggest that it was intended to serve as a small ingot-mould. The long handle would have permitted the mould to be moved before it had fully cooled. A large ingot mould of limestone has been excavated from the Franciscan church at Hartlepool (Daniels and Gill 1986, 291, fig. 15 no. 59). Graffiti on the side of the Beverley object, both straight and curvilinear, is not readily interpreted. The crudely incised vertical, horizontal and diagonal lines on the base, however, form a small playing board. The game may be *Alquerque*, a variant of Nine Mens Morris held to have been introduced into Europe via Spain. Twelve pieces on each side would take each other by leaping over, as in draughts (Murray 1952, 65). Slightly simpler boards of similar character are considered to be for Three Men's Morris: a group of these are inscribed on a 13th-century coffin lid from Holy Trinity church, Little Woolstone, Buckinghamshire (Croft 1987). A simple Three Men's Morris board, cut into a board or paddle of 13th century date, was excavated at Eastgate, Beverley (Morris and Evans 1992, 191, fig. 95, no. 652). As is usual with medieval playing boards, these were ephemeral objects which enjoyed only a brief lifespan.

No. 1019 is a chunk of dark igneous stone, which was found in a Phase 3B context. Its smooth, and regular shape suggests that it is a small fragment from a large vessel or object. No other pieces of this material were recovered during the excavations. Use or reuse of the object as a smoother is possible, as has been suggested for an object of basalt from Wharram Percy, North Yorkshire (Andrews 1979, 124–5, fig. 67:2).

Catalogue of stone objects

(* Indicates thin-sectioned for identification)

Hones (Figure 85)

1001. *Sandstone (Sub-arkose), with chert and clay. Perhaps Millstone Grit.
        Large slightly tapered hone of rectangular section. All four faces smoothed, and three lightly dished. Both ends broken.
        RF952, Context 959, Phase 2.

1002. *Fine-grained quartz Phyllite/Slate.
        ?Hone. Rectangular object sawn on both sides. Upper and lower surfaces lost due to splitting along bedding planes, both ends lost.
        RF3198, Context 959, Phase 2.

1003. *Sandstone (Orthoquartzite) with chert, clay and rare alkali-feldspar, and accessory tourmaline.
        Large hone of hog-backed form. Upper and lower surfaces smoothed, lower surface dished by longitudinal wear. Two point-sharpening grooves occur on one side.
        RF1194, Context 1025, Phase 3A.

1005. *Quartz and chlorite-bearing Phyllite/Slate.
        Small, rectangular, personal hone, with suspension hole drilled at one end. Worn thin by use, split along

bedding plane.
RF72, Context 65, Phase 5.

1006. *'Blue' or 'Purple Phyllite' (a well-known Viking Age material for hones). The rock is a slate or fine-grained quartz, mica and ore-bearing phyllite.
Small personal hone of sub-rectangular section, smoothed by wear on all faces. Possible small point-sharpening grooves occur on one face. Both ends lost.
RF643, Context 65, Phase 5.

1007. Fragment of tapered ?hone of rectangular section, smoothed on upper and lower faces, and at one end. One end lost.
RF731, Context 108, Phase 5B.

1008. *'Norwegian Ragstone' quartz-muscovite-calcite schist (a well-known material used from medieval to recent times for hones).
Fragment of a hone of rectangular section, smoothed by wear.
RF299, Context 15, Phase 7.

Mortars (Figure 86)

1009. Oolitic Limestone, ?from Cave.
Mortar fragments; three rim and upper body sherds, joining. Rim is squared in section with one lug and a spout partially surviving, body slightly concave. Smoothed on internal and external faces. Re-worked with claw tool forming flat surfaces along side and lower breaks.
RF847, Context 822, Phase 5A.

1010. *Even grained medium quartz Sandstone; some burrowing and detrital glauconite grains suggest this is a marine deposit. Could be Jurassic, possibly middle Jurassic deltaic series or equivalent; not dissimilar to material occurring north of Scarborough (e.g. Cloughton Wyke).

Mortar fragment; squared rim, with shallow pouring spout. A vertical fillet runs beneath spout to widen as it joins a square foot-ring. The wall is markedly convex. External surface is perhaps diagonally tooled, bowl vertically tooled, both now heavily weathered; internal surface is pecked, and worn towards base of wall.
RF939, Context 702, Phase 5B.

Miscellaneous (Figure 86)

1012. Flint.
?Strike-a-light. Tabular worked flint with four flakes removed, one end and one side lost.
RF1059, Context 1046, Phase 3D.

1015. Chalk.
Spindle Whorl. Knife-cut and smoothed discoid whorl. Round central perforation. Tapers inward from one side.
Weight: 18g
RF930, Context 795, Phase 5A.

1016. Pebble. ?Fishing weight.
?Unfinished sinker. A sub-rectangular pebble with perforation part-drilled from two sides. The perforations have not been completed.
RF3311, Trench 2, Unstratified.

1018. Chalk.
?Ingot mould. Sub-rectangular carved handled box with a neatly defined cavity of trapezoidal section. A round dimple occurs on internal base of cavity. A crudely incised pattern of squares intersected by diagonals occurs on the outside of the base, apparently forming a small game board. A further crudely incised design of rectangle, diagonal and curving lines occurs on one outer side. Other end lost.
RF147, Context 15, Phase 7.

3.15 The coins and jettons

by M.M. Archibald

Many of the coins, and especially the jettons, are corroded and chipped. The weights and diameters are those of the pieces in their present condition. References to standard works (e.g. North 1960; Stewart 1967; Lafaurie 1951; Mitchiner 1988) are given where possible, but the corroded state of some of the pieces can sometimes make it impossible to quote a precise number.

Coins of standard type are not described, except where variants occur.

Dr. Mitchiner's recently-published catalogue (1988) lists and illustrates a very much larger number of jettons than was included in Barnard (1916), but such is the variety of detail on these pieces that it is still rarely possible to find a piece which is identical in all respects. 'Cf.' in what follows denotes that the Beverley coin differs in detail from all the Mitchiner pieces, but the number quoted is the closest. The difference is usually just one of minor additional decoration, but if all Mitchiner's examples seem to differ appreciably, then just his general type rubrics are quoted, especially if the piece is so corroded that few of the details are visible at all.

The deposition dates suggested are based on the average condition of coins from that issue surviving to those dates. The possibility of earlier or later deposition dates must be allowed for, to take account of coins in abnormally good or bad condition.

1020. Edward I–II, farthing, class X, *c.*1300–10.
Obv. EDWARDVS REX A.
Wt. 0.13g.
Ref. North II, 1058.
From a cut feature in the little cloister garth.
RF 806, Context 719, Phase 5.
This coin shows slight wear, but is unclipped. It was certainly lost before 1351, but was probably lost rather earlier — in the 1320s or 1330s.

1021. Roman, Tetricus I, 270–273, radiate (so-called '*antoninianus*').
Rev. Spes.
Wt. 1.83g.
From a wall footing, north range.
RF 3078, Context 3079, Phase 5A.
The details of the legends are illegible, so a precise reference cannot be quoted. This is an official coin, not a barbarous imitation.

1022. Edward I, 1272–1307, farthing, class II, 1280, London.
Rev. LONDONIENSIS (reverse-barred N).
Wt. 0.28g.
Ref. North II, 1052.
From a construction level, north range, west end.
RF 3148, Context 3158, Phase 5A.

This coin shows a little wear, but is not clipped. Deposition dates as 1020 above (before 1351, probably in 1320s or 1330s).

1023. Edward I, 1272–1307, penny, class IIId, *c.*1280–1, London.
Wt. 0.66g.
Ref. North II, 1019.
From occupation, north range, west chamber.
RF 814, Context 803, Phase 5B.
This coin is only a little worn, and is unclipped. It was certainly lost before 1351, and probably before *c.*1325.

1024. Edward III, 1327–77, halfpenny, 2nd Coinage, 1335–43, London.
Star after obv. and rev. legends, usual rough style.
Wt. 0.33g (mended fragments).
Ref. North II, 1102.
From occupation, north range, east chamber.
RF 2050, Context 2009, Phase 5B.
This coin is badly corroded, especially on the obverse, and it is therefore more difficult to assess its condition at deposition. The areas of the reverse which are visible look quite sharp, and it was probably unclipped. It was possibly lost by 1351, but a later survival would be acceptable. This coin can be associated with the later 14th century jetton no. 1025; this would suggest that the halfpenny is a post–1351 deposit.

1025. English jetton, later 14th century.
Obv. irregular symbols in place of legend. King standing under canopy.
Rev. irregular symbols in place of legend. Cross fleury.
Wt. 1.38g, Diameter 22mm.
Ref. Mitchiner cf. No. 278 (but rev. cross on Beverley coin is fleury).
From occupation, north range, east chamber. See no. 1024.
RF 2051, Context 2009, Phase 5B.

1026. Group of five pennies:
(a) *Three coins found stuck together*
All are pennies of Scotland, Alexander III, 1249–86, 2nd Coinage, 1280–88 (some are posthumous):
(i) Rev. Four mullets of six points.
Wt. 1.09g.
Ref. Stewart class G.
(ii) Rev. Four mullets of five points; two extra pellets in second and fourth numismatic quarters.
Wt. 0.96g.
Ref. Stewart class E, but cross potent.
(iii) Rev. Two mullets of six points and two stars of seven points.
Wt. 1.08g.
Ref. Stewart class G, but cross potent.
(b) *Two separate coins*
(i) Edward I penny, class IIa, *c.*1280, London.

Wt. 0.99g.

Ref. North II, 1014.

(ii)   Scotland, John Baliol, 1292–6, 1st Coinage.

Rev. Four mullets of six points.

Wt. 1.08g.

Ref. (Stewart does not differentiate classes in this coinage).

From occupation, north range, west chamber.

All part of RF 484, Context 349, Phase 5C.

The English coin is of no use in establishing the date of deposition of this group, as pennies of this type survived for a long period in circulation. As the coins of John Baliol's second issue and of Robert Bruce are rare, the absence of these later Scottish issues from such a small group is not necessarily significant. The coins show a little wear, but are not clipped, so they were certainly deposited before the reduction in standard weight in 1351, and could have been deposited earlier, even in the 1320s or 1330s.

Scottish coins of this period were of comparable weight and fineness to the English pennies, and the issues of each country were allowed to circulate freely in the other. Hoards suggest, however, that Scottish coins normally represented not more than about 5% of the English currency at this time. The abnormal composition of this find does suggest that the coins had originated in a group which had come south from Scotland. How long before, or at how many removes, it is not possible to say.

1027.   France, Charles VII, 1422–61, 1st part of Reign, 1422–36, *double tournois*.

Obv. almost all of legend corroded away. Details of type uncertain.

Rev. almost all of legend corroded away. Cross pattée, nothing in angles.

Wt. 0.40g.

Ref. Lafaurie cf. 484ff.

From close of occupation north range, east chamber.

RF 2048, Context 2012, Phase 7.

Very little of the original surface of this coin remains, and the edges are badly chipped. Foreign issues, such as this base billon French coin, were not allowed to circulate in England, and, in consequence, are generally found at coastal sites or at places, like Beverley, where foreign travellers may have been given hospitality. It is unlikely that this coin survived for very long in circulation, giving a *terminus* for its deposit of *c*.1450.

1028.   Nuremberg jetton, early sixteenth century.

Obv. illiterate legend. Lion of St. Mark of Venice, lion with halo, plain field.

Rev. illiterate legend. *Reichsapfel* in cartouche, no initial mark above orb.

Wt. 5.26g, Diameter 26mm.

Ref. Mitchiner 21b(3), cf. No. 1102ff.

From a pit, close of occupation.

RF 514, Context 512, Phase 7.

This is a thick, heavy, jetton of good style, and while not one of the first of this obverse design, it falls quite early in the type.

1029.   Nuremberg jetton, early 16th century.

Obv. illiterate legend. Crowned shield of France modern.

Rev. illiterate legend. *Reichsapfel* in cartouche.

Wt. 2.32g, Diameter 26mm.

Ref. Mitchiner Group 21a(2), cf. No. 1080.

From close of occupation, north range, west chamber.

RF 276, Context 59/121, Phase 7.

This piece has been pierced towards the edge with a knife blade, which suggests that someone may have tried to pass it off as a groat, and that it had been pierced in the manner prescribed for false coins.

1030.   Tournai jetton, *c*.1500(?).

Obv. illiterate legend. Four fleur-de-lis in a lozenge, other details illegible.

Rev. Cross fleury in a quatrefoil, other details illegible.

Wt. 2.16g, Diameter 22mm.

Ref. Mitchiner cf. No. 648 for the type.

From close of occupation, great cloister.

RF 1087, Context 1084, Phase 7.

So little is visible on this very corroded jetton, that it is not possible to assess its place in the chronology of the type. It appears to be pierced at the edge, but its condition makes it difficult to be sure whether this is deliberate or not.

1031.   Nuremberg jetton, mid. 15th-century.

Obv. +AVE MARIA GRACR (sic), double annulet stops. Moor's head to right.

Rev. +A / VE / MA / RIA. Voided cross fleury with a fleur-de-lis in centre and a saltire in each angle.

Wt. 1.00g, Diameter 20mm.

Ref. Mitchiner 11b(3), cf. No. 373 (Beverley coin has shorter obv. legend).

From north range, east chamber.

RF 2002, Context 2001, Phase 8.

This is a very long-lived type, and it is difficult to date the issue of the various groups precisely.

General remarks

Most of the coins from this site at Beverley seem to have been deposited in the first half of the 14th century — many of them possibly in the middle of that half century rather than at the end of it. There are no jettons from this early period; they are generally not uncommon, although scarcer than the late medieval pieces. There is only one coin whose deposition might be dated into the second half of the 14th century, and then not too far into it (no. 1029). One jetton is of the later 14th century (no. 1025), and might have been around at the same time. One base

French coin (no. 1027) is datable to the second quarter of the 15th century; a jetton apparently only a little later (no. 1031) was found in the later demolition levels. The demolition levels contain several jettons, but no coins. This might indicate a different use of the building after the early part of the 14th century.

Of the jettons from Beverley, nos. 1028–30 all seem to be of a plausible date to have come from the levels associated with a demolition period of 1524–5 or of 1537. Jetton no. 1031, which also comes from a level of this same period, appears to be rather earlier in date. This piece could be residual, but the occasional earlier jetton might have survived in use. (Bags of jettons regularly appear in inventories of deceased persons' property, so they were clearly handed down.) It is not possible at present to decide which of these possibilities is the more likely.

Very little is known about how long the various issues of jettons remained is use, as there are few hoards or securely associated site groups. The metal from which they were made was much harder than the silver of the coinage, and so they may be expected to be slower in showing wear. In any case, many jettons from excavations, as at Beverley, are so corroded that it is impossible to form any view on the duration of use from relative condition. As it is difficult to date the various sub-groups of many of the long-lived basic types, it is impossible to suggest narrow limits for their likely date of deposition, or to be very sure about whether jettons of apparently different issue dates were in use at the same time.

3.16 The pottery

by Gareth Watkins

Introduction

The Priory has been investigated on a number of occasions. An account of the excavations which took place between 1960 and 1983 has already been published (Armstrong and Tomlinson 1987), and includes an assessment of the pottery recovered throughout that period (*ibid.*, 30–6). This present report summarises the results of the study of the pottery recovered during an eleven month period of investigation in 1986–7, when an area to the north of the extant 'Old Friary' building was examined. Although more ceramic material was recovered than in the previous investigations, the amount was nonetheless small in view of the extent and duration of the excavation. All the material from contexts before *c.*1550 was analysed and quantified; a total of 853 different vessels (on a minimum vessel count; Watkins 1987a, 55) was identified.

In common with most other urban monastic sites — with the notable exception of the Leicester Austin Friary (Woodland 1981, 81–130) — the Priory excavation produced very little in the way of large groups of contemporary pottery; the majority of the material being obtained from contexts containing less then ten sherds. The only notable exceptions were the garth area of the little cloister, contexts 65 (Phases 5A–C) and 15 (Phase 7), which contained fragments of 88 and 56 vessels respectively, and the group from the Phase 7 fill of the latrine conduit, contexts 1091–4, which contained fragments from 32 different vessels. Because of the soil disturbance caused by successive rebuilding operations, residuality was a major factor from Phase 3 onwards; the quantity of intrusive material was also somewhat disturbing. Given these limitations, where other more reliable types of evidence are available they should be given precedence.

The method of study employed was the same as that used for the material from the 1983 Priory excavation, and for the Beverley Lurk Lane and Eastgate sites (Watkins 1987b, 30–6; Watkins 1991, 61; Didsbury and Watkins 1992, 81), and is based on the reduction of the raw material (i.e. the individual sherds) to the number of different pottery vessels found in each context. Details of each vessel (fabric, glaze, decoration, condition, joins and number of sherds) were entered into a database using Dbase III+. The same type series has been used throughout these Beverley studies, and so it is superfluous to repeat it here. The analysis of the pottery from the Priory

benefited greatly from the earlier work carried out on much larger assemblages from Lurk Lane and Eastgate, for these two nearby sites established a number of fixed points in the development of local pottery types, and provided a chronological framework into which the Priory material could be integrated. It is noteworthy that, despite the difference in social status presumed between the medieval inhabitants of the three sites, the pottery used by each group, in terms of both vessel type and place of manufacture, was almost identical. The proportion of 13th to 15th century imported pottery at each site, for example, is around 3% — in contrast to the 20–25% level of imports which obtains for medieval sites in Hull. The obvious conclusion is that the medieval inhabitants of the two towns obtained the vast majority of their everyday ceramics at their respective local markets. Vessels from the Low Countries or the Saintonge were freely available at their point of importation in Hull, but no retail mechanism seems to have existed to carry any quantity of such wares seven miles up the River Hull to Beverley. The much higher proportion of imported wares found at the site of the Dominican Priory in Boston (Moorhouse 1972, 30–2) should not therefore be taken as a measure of the wealth of the house relative to that of Beverley, but rather as a consequence of that town's position as a port engaged in foreign trade.

Phase 1

The earliest evidence of occupation consisted of a number of shallow pits dug into the natural. No pottery or other datable finds were associated with these features, and so the period of their use is unknown. It is worth noting that, in common with most other medieval Beverley sites, a small quantity of Romano-British material was found residually in upper layers; two Roman sherds were found in the garden soil which overlay the site, perhaps an imported soil, and a fragment of an Iron Age vessel was found in context 902, Phase 3D.

Phase 2 (early 12th to early 13th century)

Documentary evidence indicates that the Priory was founded between 1221 and 1240. Pottery and other evidence from the 1986–7 excavations accords with the conclusion reached in the previous report; that the Dominicans were granted land which, despite its proximity to the Collegiate Church of St John, the present Minster, was undeveloped and used perhaps for agricultural purposes. The small quantity of

Table 9 Number of vessels of each pottery type present, by phase

Phase	2	3A	3B	3C	3D	3	4	5A	5B	5C	5	6A	6B	7	8
Beverley 1A	10	5	15	–	9	–	–	13	3	8	11	3	2	7	–
Beverley 2B	5	3	16	4	17	4	2	42	9	15	24	12	–	9	–
Beverley 2C	–	–	8	–	5	–	–	20	7	17	24	19	–	21	3
Brown Glz.	–	–	–	–	–	–	–	–	–	–	–	–	–	18	7
Cistercian	–	3	–	–	–	–	–	–	–	–	–	–	–	–	1
Coarse Sandy	–	–	1	–	2	–	2	2	4	3	4	–	–	6	–
Fr/Cologne	–	–	–	–	–	–	–	–	–	–	–	–	–	1	–
Humber 1	–	–	1	–	–	–	2	5	7	9	13	9	–	1	2
Humber 3	–	–	3	–	–	–	–	4	5	3	4	1	–	40	–
Humber 4	–	–	–	–	1	–	1	–	–	–	–	–	–	5	–
Humber 5	–	–	–	–	–	–	–	2	1	1	–	1	1	11	1
Iron Age	–	–	–	–	1	–	–	–	–	–	–	–	–	–	–
Langerwehe	–	–	–	–	–	–	1	–	–	–	–	–	–	7	–
L.C. Red	–	–	–	–	–	–	1	–	2	1	1	–	–	9	–
N. Yorks 1	–	–	–	–	–	–	–	–	2	–	1	1	–	1	–
Pimply	–	–	2	–	–	–	–	–	–	–	–	2	–	–	–
Pinky Buff	–	–	–	–	2	–	–	–	–	–	–	1	–	–	–
Raeren	–	–	–	–	–	–	–	–	1	–	3	–	–	3	–
Red. Chalky	6	1	3	–	–	–	–	–	–	–	–	–	–	6	–
Saintonge 1	–	–	–	–	–	–	1	–	–	–	–	–	–	–	–
Saintonge 2	–	–	–	–	–	–	1	1	–	–	–	–	–	–	–
Saintonge 4	–	–	–	–	–	–	–	–	–	1	–	–	–	–	–
Scarboro 2	–	–	–	–	–	–	–	1	–	–	–	–	–	–	–
Scarboro 3	–	–	–	–	–	–	–	–	2	–	–	–	–	–	–
Shell Temp	2	1	1	–	1	–	–	–	–	–	–	1	–	–	–
Staffs 1	–	–	–	–	–	–	–	–	–	–	–	–	–	–	1
Staffs 2	–	–	–	–	–	–	–	–	–	–	–	–	–	–	1
Stamford	1	–	1	–	–	–	–	–	1	1	1	–	–	–	–
Staxton/PB	1	–	4	–	3	1	1	4	1	2	2	1	–	2	–
S. Yorks GR	–	–	–	–	–	–	–	–	–	–	1	–	–	3	–
Torksey–type	3	–	–	–	1	–	–	1	–	–	–	–	–	–	–
Unclassified	9	3	3	3	6	2	2	18	9	8	6	7	–	10	–
Unc. Splashed	2	–	–	–	1	–	–	3	2	2	2	–	–	–	–
York White	1	–	2	1	3	–	–	9	–	2	6	5	–	5	1
Total	40	16	60	8	52	7	13	125	56	73	103	63	3	162	17

Note: Vessels which are obviously intrusive have been omitted, i.e. Context 27 (Phase 3A) — all vessels, Context 100 (Phase 5C) — all vessels, Context 282 (Phase 6A) — 1 sherd Eng. s'ware 1, Context 303 (Phase 7) — 1 sherd Misc. White, Context 55 (Phase 8) — 1 sherd Misc. White.

Table 10   Selected groups, showing percentages of pottery types present. Table 9 shows the total number of vessels of each pottery type which were identified from each phase of the site. The figures were not presented as percentages, since the quantities involved are in many cases rather small. The following table attempts to rectify the situation by taking vessels from the larger groups only, or by combining the vessels from a number of related groups, and expressing these figures in terms of percentages; a general picture of the overall trends is thus produced.

	Group				
	1	2	3	4	5
Beverley 1A	22.1%	6.1%	10.2%	6.2%	5.4%
Beverley 2B	29.4%	16.3%	22.7%	3.1%	8.9%
Beverley 2C	11.8%	14.3%	20.4%	6.2%	16.1%
Cistercian	–	–	–	6.2%	1.8%
Coarse Sandy	1.5%	6.1%	4.5%	3.1%	1.8%
Fr/Cologne	–	–	–	–	1.8%
Humber 1	1.5%	16.3%	12.5%	43.8%	14.3%
Humber 3	4.4%	4.1%	4.5%	3.1%	5.4%
Humber 5	–	4.1%	–	3.1%	12.5%
Langerwehe	–	–	–	6.2%	5.4%
L.C. Red	–	–	1.1%	6.2%	7.1%
N. Yorks 1	–	4.1%	1.1%	–	–
Pimply	2.9%	–	–	–	–
Pinky Buff	–	2.0%	3.4%	–	1.8%
Raeren	–	–	—	3.1%	3.6%
Red. Chalky	4.4%	–	1.1%	–	–
Saintonge 2	–	2.0%	–	–	–
Shell Temp	1.5%	–	–	–	–
Stamford	1.5%	4.1%	1.1%	–	–
Staxton/PB	5.9%	4.1%	2.3%	–	1.8%
S. Yorks GR	–	–	–	–	5.4%
Unclassified	8.8%	12.2%	6.8%	6.2%	3.6%
Unc.Splashed	–	–	1.1%	–	–
York White	4.4%	4.1%	6.8%	3.1%	3.6%
Total Vessels	68	49	88	32	56

Key to Groups:

1   all pottery Phases 3B and 3C (late 13th century)
2   Phases 5A, 5B and 5C, occupation surfaces only (14th century)
3   Phase 5, context 65 (14th century)
4   Phase 7, fill of reredorter conduit (early 16th century)
5   Phase 7, context 15 (early 16th century)

pottery associated with features of Phase 2 (40 vessels in total) bears close comparison with that from the immediate pre-foundation layers of the 1983 excavation (Watkins 1987b, 33–4); comprising sherds of Torksey-type, Reduced Chalky, Shell Tempered and splash glazed local wares of the type referred to as 'Oxidised Chalky' in the previous report, but now redefined as 'Beverley 1A' (Didsbury and Watkins 1992, 108–11). In addition to these types, which point to a horizon of activity of 12th or possibly late 11th-century date, the pre-Priory levels contained fragments of five vessels in the developed local ware defined as Beverley 2B (*ibid.*, 114–17) — providing useful evidence that this major technological and stylistic transition in the local industry had probably taken place before 1240.

Phase 3A (mid. to late 13th century: Figure 87)

Features allocated to this phase represent the earliest

occupation activity which can be correlated with the establishment of the Priory, namely the construction of a hall in the area in which the little cloister was later established. Unfortunately, the largest pottery assemblage from this phase — a group recovered from the surface of the clay platform which was laid down immediately prior to the erection of the building (context 27) — proved on analysis to be heavily contaminated with wares of 14th-century date, although some of its contents (such as a jug in Beverley 2B; no. 1032) were probably deposited at the time of construction.

In addition to those from platform layer 27, fragments of 16 other pottery vessels were recovered from contexts allocated to Phase 3A, including a further jug rim with applied bosses in Beverley 2B (no. 1033) from pit fill 1074. The phase also saw the first occurrence on site of Coarse Sandy Ware, a type in which most of the cooking pots used in the 14th century were manufactured, but which, as the Priory

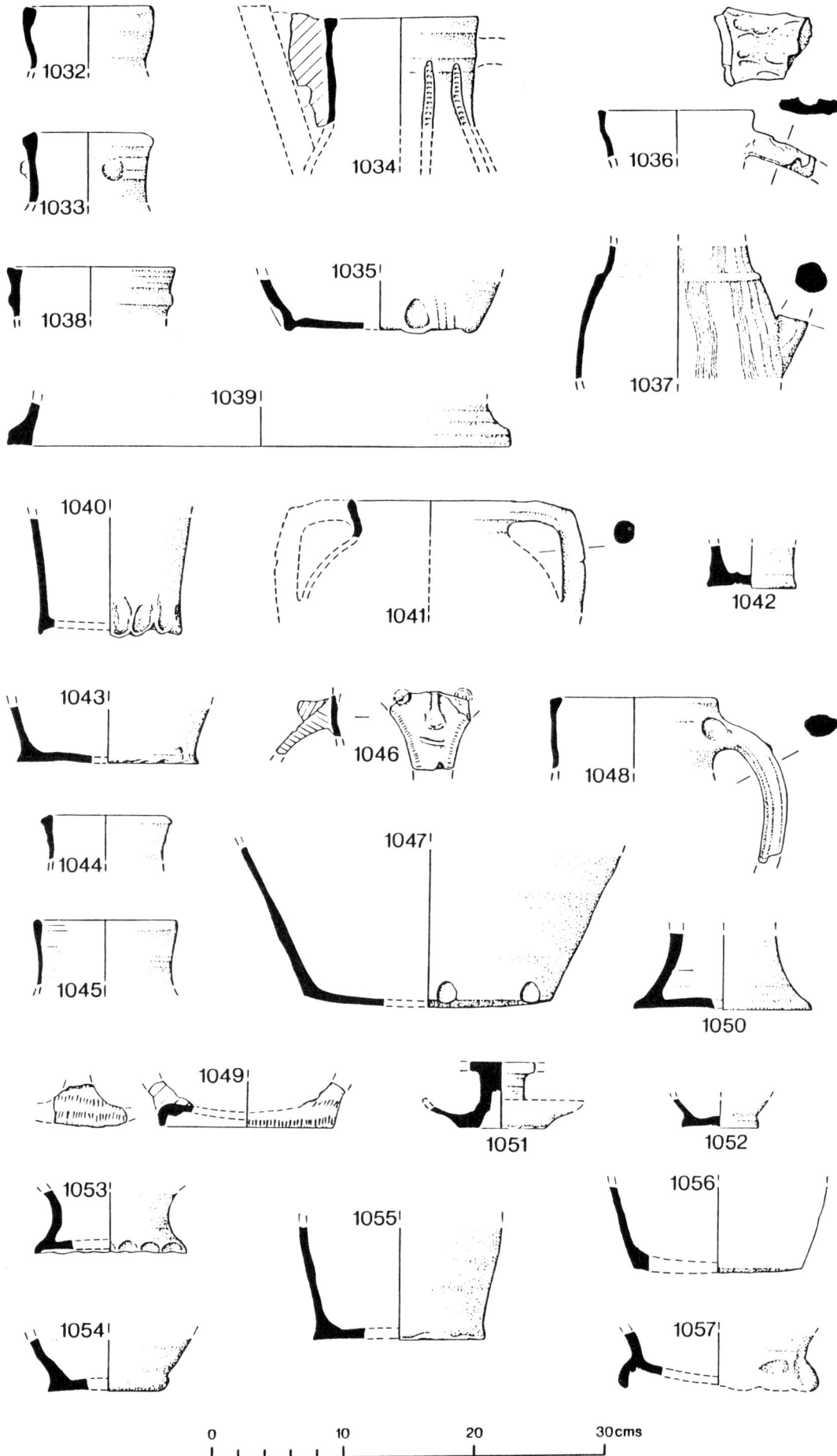

Figure 87 Pottery.

site demonstrates, may have originated before the middle of the 13th century. This phase also saw the first occurrence on site of a pottery curfew; this vessel, in Beverley 2B ware, was also found in 1074.

Phase 3B (later 13th century: Figure 87)

The Phase 3A hall was dismantled and replaced by an aisled hall in Phase 3B; fragments of 60 pottery vessels from 11 different contexts were found in association with the construction and occupation of the new building, and so the relative proportions of the types of pottery present may be of some significance: Beverley 2B was the most common type, forming some 27% of the total; 25% were in the earlier Beverley 1A fabric, and thus residual in this phase; 13% were of Beverley type 2C, and 7% in Staxton/Potter Brompton ware. Various other types all formed 5% or less of the total. The first occurrence here of Beverley 2C has significant implications for the dating of this period of activity, for this type (classed as 'Orangeware' in reports dealing with pottery from excavations in Hull) can be shown, on evidence from excavations in Eastgate, Beverley (Didsbury and Watkins 1992, 117), to have originated in the late 13th century. In addition, the Phase 3B layers produced sherds from three vessels in a type defined as Humber 3 — a type whose fabric is similar to the products of the later Humberware kilns at West Cowick, but which is more finely potted, and contains copper as a colorant in its glazes. It seems unlikely that the type was in production before *c*.1275. One vessel from this phase has been identified as of type Humber 1, i.e. a product of West Cowick. It is considered that this vessel, represented by a single sherd from layer 1076, is intrusive in this context, since no further examples of the type were found until Phase 5. Phase 3B saw the first appearance on site of the pipkin — two vessels in Beverley 2C being present.

Four vessels from the Phase 3B context 1073, a layer of mixed clay and silt outside and to the north of the building, are illustrated: no. 1034 is part of a jug in York White ware, with applied laddered strips and part of a strut which linked a tubular spout to the body; no. 1035, the base of a Beverley 2B jug; no. 1036, the rim and handle from a residual Beverley 1A jug, showing a handle which was thumbed on the edges, and which was typical of the pottery from the waster pits at the Albion House site in Beverley; and no. 1037, a Beverley 2C jug, which was unusually decorated with the type of wavy combing that was current at the time of the 1188 fire in Beverley (Watkins 1991, 66).

Phase 3C (very late 13th/early 14th century)

Minor modifications were made to the Phase 3B aisled hall in this period, but only eight pottery vessel fragments were recovered from the layers associated with this occupation. None was of types which had not already been identified in earlier layers, and so no conclusions for the chronology of the site can be drawn.

Phase 3D (very late 13th/early 14th century: Figure 87)

Following the latest occupation of the aisled hall, this area of the site appears to have lain vacant until the construction of a little cloister (see Phase 5A, below); it may temporarily have been used as a garden. The pottery assemblage of this period is little different from that of Phase 3B. Fragments of 52 different vessels were found in the contexts allocated to the phase; Beverley 2B was still the most common single type, forming 33% of the total, with 17% in residual Beverley 1A, and 10% in Beverley 2C. One vessel of Humber 3 was recovered, but none in Humber 1. One new fabric, however, had its first occurrence in Phase 3D, this being Pinky Buff ware, a minor type of unknown origin which was first isolated during the study of the Eastgate site (Didsbury and Watkins 1992, 117) where it appeared in contexts of the late 13th and early 14th centuries. No new vessel types appeared during the course of this phase; none of the pottery from 3D contexts needs to be any later than 1300 in date. Beverley 2B jug rim, no. 1038, was found in the Phase 3D context 1044.

Phase 4 (13th to 16th centuries)

In the area of the little cloister, Phase 3D was succeeded stratigraphically by Phase 5A (below). Features described as 'Phase 4' are those which were excavated in an area to the south of the main excavation, in the great cloister. Major structural remains were encountered, but since non-destructive excavation techniques were employed in this area, in an attempt to link the features discovered in the 1986–7 season with those located by earlier work, the recovery of finds was low. Fragments of 13 different pottery vessels were recovered; they range in date from late 13th or early 14th-century Saintonge Polychrome ware (Saintonge type 2) to late 15th or early 16th-century Purple-Glazed Humberware (Humber type 4). The Polychrome fragment, which consisted of a modelled face mask from the rim of a jug, was found in the fill of a cistern, context 1109, where it was associated with two jug fragments in West Cowick-type Humberware.

Phase 5A (first half of the 14th century: Figure 87)

After a hiatus in occupation (Phase 3D), the land where the aisled hall had formerly stood became the site of the Priory's little cloister, with ranges to the north and west. The total assemblage from contexts allocated to Phase 5A, the period of construction and early occupation, consists of fragments of 125 different vessels. Inevitably, given the soil movement caused by the digging of foundations, the assemblage contains a high proportion of residual material; it is surprising therefore that no pottery joins were found between any of the 5A vessels and those from Phase 3 (Table 13).

The relative percentages of the types of pottery from 5A contexts are shown in Table 9, where it can be seen that the proportions of types found is not dissimilar to those from Phase 3D and indeed 3B; however, three fabrics which did not occur in the Phase 3 groups (or four if the sherd of Humber 1 from Phase 3B is counted as originating from Phase 5) were now present, and it is these which can be used to assess the chronology of the site's development. Phase II Scarborough ware was found in context 822, a footing pit in the Cloister's western alley; the type is considered to have been in production between *c.*1225 and *c.*1366 (Farmer and Farmer 1982), and so does not help to refine the dating in this area. More significant is the sherd of Saintonge Polychrome ware (Saintonge 2) which was found in a floor surface in the eastern chamber of the north range (context 830): this could be taken to demonstrate that the floor was in use and open to deposition in the late 13th or early 14th century. Sherds of Humber 5 (Late Humberware) made their first appearance in Phase 5A, examples being found in contexts 110 and 760, but these are clearly intrusive. The only other distinguishing factor between the pottery assemblages of Phases 3 and 5A is the occurrence in the latter of fragments from five vessels in Humber 1, West Cowick-type. Two sherds from a jug were found in context 802, a cloister alley construction layer, and a single sherd from a jug was found in context 2008, a bench footing in the eastern chamber of the north range. The only Phase 5A group in which Humber 1 outnumbered Beverley wares was that from context 769, a make-up layer in the western alley. In the study of pottery from sites in Hull, the relative proportions of Humberwares and Orange (i.e. Beverley) wares was found to be a useful chronological indicator (Watkins 1987a, 55–6). Although it is by no means certain that the same rise in the use of Humberware at the expense of Beverley ware took place in the two towns, the comparative rarity of Humber 1 ware in the contexts of Phase 5A argues for a date around the beginning of the 14th century for the construction and early occupation of

the little cloister. Two vessels from contexts of this period are illustrated; the rim of a Beverley 2B curfew from pit fill 836 (no. 1039), and the base of a large jug in Beverley 2C (no. 1047), which was found in alley construction layer 760.

Phase 5B (second half of 14th century: Figure 87)

Phase 5B consists of modifications made in the area of the little cloister; reflooring was undertaken throughout, but there was also evidence for structural alterations. The pottery assemblage consisted of 56 vessels, and contrasts significantly with that from Phase 5A. Humber 1, which formed only 4% of the total in Phase 5A contributed 12.5% to the total in 5B. This rise in the use of the type is even more pronounced, if one omits the various disturbed or redeposited contexts of this period, and examines the pottery from floor surfaces only (this should give a more accurate picture of the types in contemporary use, although the quantities involved are admittedly small); of the 16 different vessels from these selected layers, seven were in Humber 1 and four in Beverley 2B and 2C. It may therefore be argued, on the basis of evidence from Hull, that Phase 5B of the Priory dates to the middle years of the 14th century, for that was the period when Humberwares achieved numerical dominance over Orange/Beverley wares; however, the coin evidence clearly takes this phase into the second half of the 14th century. Three new fabrics appeared amongst the Phase 5B material, these being Low Countries Redware, Scarborough variety 3 and North Yorks. variety 1; all are acceptable in a phase of mid. 14th-century date. Low Countries Redware is represented by single sherds from two different frying pans; such vessels are invariably soot-blackened on their undersides, and seem to have been used exclusively for the preparation of food. Neither of the Priory examples, however, was recovered from occupation surfaces, being from construction layer 44 and platform 848, respectively; no inferences for site usage can be drawn from their find-spots. A Humber 1 jug rim-and-handle sherd from context 867 is illustrated, no. 1048.

Phase 5C (later 14th–16th centuries: Figure 87)

This represents a final modification of the buildings of the little cloister; fragments of 77 different pottery vessels were associated with these activities. As can be seen from Table 9, the overall composition of the pottery assemblage is generally similar to that from the preceding phase, with Humber 1 again contributing 12% to the total (though note the omission of Context 100 from this tabulation, considered below). The three major types of Beverley pottery (1A, 2B and 2C) had, however, all substantially increased in proportion, demonstrating that residuality must have been a major factor in the Phase 5C deposits, since the production of Beverley Ware 2 was by now in decline, if not at an end, and the production of Beverley Ware 1 had ceased at least a century before. Very little pottery was found in occupation layers, and the disturbance to the underlying stratigraphy caused by structural alteration to the buildings was substantial. It is therefore difficult to estimate a date for the Phase 5C activity on pottery grounds alone. The only new pottery type to occur in the phase is the variety of Saintonge ware known as 'All-over Green Glaze' (Saintonge 4); joining sherds from a single jug in this fabric were found in a number of contexts, of which the earliest on stratigraphical grounds was northern alley layer 583. The type, though akin to the better-known Polychrome ware of late 13th or early 14th-century date, may still have been in production in the middle years of the 14th century.

The pottery evidence can be taken to suggest, however, that the reconstruction activities of Phase 5C did not extend into the 15th century. The argument is a negative one, based on the non-occurrence amongst the sherds recovered of types of wares which are characteristic of local deposits of the 15th century;

however, the lack of such ubiquitous types as Langerwehe stoneware, Humber 1 bung-holed cisterns, and South Yorkshire Gritty (Rawmarsh) wares, may well be of significance.

One context allocated to this phase contained pottery that was out of character with the remainder, which, has been argued above, are all acceptable in groups of the mid. to late 14th century. Context 100, a floor layer in the east range of the north chamber, which lay immediately under strata of Phase 7, produced four sherds: one each of Low Countries Redware, Unclassified, Late Humberware (Humber 5), and Cistercian ware; it must therefore date to the very end of the 15th, or to the early part of the 16th century. Two explanations are possible; either the layer is contaminated with Phase 7 material, or the use of the area throughout the 15th century left no trace in the pottery record. The latter interpretation would be consistent with the introduction of planked floors or other removable floor surfaces within the buildings: pottery would thus be present inside the building in the construction layers only, whilst the alleys would have been kept fairly clean — fresh material being introduced only in patching the surfaces of the cloister walk.

Two vessels from this phase are illustrated in Figure 87. No. 1049 appears to be a fragment of a lid. It was

Table 11   Number of vessels of each vessel type present, by phase

	Phase														
	2	3A	3B	3C	3D	3	4	5A	5B	5C	5	6A	6B	7	8
Bellarmine	–	–	–	–	–	–	–	–	–	–	–	–	–	1	–
Bowl	–	–	–	–	–	–	–	–	–	2	1	–	–	2	1
Chafing dish	–	–	–	–	–	–	–	–	–	–	–	–	–	1	–
Cistern	–	–	–	–	–	–	–	–	–	–	–	–	–	1	–
Condiment	–	–	–	–	–	–	–	–	–	1	–	–	–	–	–
Cooking pot	9	6	13	1	5	1	3	12	6	9	6	4	–	9	–
Cup	–	–	–	–	–	–	–	–	–	–	–	–	–	6	1
Curfew	–	1	–	–	–	–	–	2	–	–	1	–	–	–	–
Drinking jug	–	–	–	–	–	–	–	–	–	–	2	1	–	–	–
Dripping pan	–	–	–	–	–	–	–	–	–	–	3	1	–	–	–
Frying pan	–	–	–	–	–	–	–	–	2	–	–	–	–	3	–
Jar	1	–	–	–	1	–	–	1	2	–	1	1	–	6	2
Jug	13	7	37	5	32	4	9	90	39	53	72	51	3	94	5
Lamp	–	–	–	–	–	–	–	–	–	–	–	1	–	–	–
Lid	–	–	–	–	–	–	–	1	–	1	–	1	–	–	–
Mug	–	–	–	–	–	–	–	–	–	–	–	–	–	7	–
Not known	16	2	8	2	13	2	1	13	5	7	10	1	–	22	3
Pancheon	1	–	–	–	–	–	–	–	–	–	1	1	–	1	3
Pipkin	–	–	2	–	1	–	–	6	2	–	6	1	–	7	–
Posset pot	–	–	–	–	–	–	–	–	–	–	–	–	–	–	2
Salt	–	–	–	–	–	–	–	–	–	–	–	–	–	1	–
Urinal	–	–	–	–	–	–	–	–	–	–	–	–	–	1	–
Total	40	16	60	8	52	7	13	125	56	73	103	63	3	162	17

Note: Vessels which are obviously intrusive have been omitted, i.e. Context 27 (Phase 3A) — all vessels, Context 100 (Phase 5C) — all vessels, Context 282 (Phase 6A) — 1 bowl, Context 303 (Phase 7) — 1 bowl, Context 55 (Phase 8) — 1 teapot.

found in drain fill context 538, and is in Beverley 2B ware, and so is probably residual in this context; however, it is the only example of this form which has been identified locally. No. 1050 is the base of a jug in Beverley 2C, which came from context 3015; such baluster-shaped bases are rare in this local fabric.

Phase 5 — The garth

The largest single group of pottery from the entire excavation came from context 65, an extensive spread of soil which accumulated within the garth of the little cloister. Fragments of 90 different vessels were identified. Humber 1 was well represented (11 vessels, 12% of the group), including the first stratified example of a drinking mug of Skipton-upon-Swale type from the excavation. Of the locally-produced wares, Beverley 2C accounted for some 20% of the assemblage (18 vessels), with jugs, pipkins, a jar and a dripping pan being identified; whilst Beverley 2B accounted for 23% of the total (jugs, dripping pans, a pipkin, a bowl, a pancheon and a curfew being present). Eleven of the vessels of the group were in fabrics which had gone out of production before 1300, and a further two vessels consisted of sherds which joined to earlier contexts 633 and 902, giving a residual element of some 14% of the total.

Seven of the vessels from the group are illustrated: no. 1040, the base of jug in North Yorks. 1 (Brandsby-type) ware; no. 1041, the rim from a *grape* or pipkin in Low Countries Redware; no. 1042, the base of a Humber 1 drinking jug; no. 1043, the base of a Humber 1 jug; nos. 1044 and 1045, jug rims in Beverley 2C ware, and no. 1046, a long-bearded face mask from a jug in Beverley 2C.

As was the case with the wares from Phase 5C (above; with the exception of context 100), there is no indication from the types of pottery present that the deposition of layer 65 continued after 1400. A pottery join was noted between a vessel in 5C layer 538 and the garth soil 65. The pottery was therefore examined to see if any corroborative evidence could be found. A coefficient of similarity (Robinson 1951; Brainerd 1951; Watkins 1983, 245) was calculated between the group from context 65 and various other groups of material, in order to determine which group or groups matched each other most closely in composition. The groups chosen for comparison with 65 were (a) all the pottery from Phase 5A, (b) all the pottery from Phase 5B, (c) all the pottery from Phase 5C; (d) all the pottery from Phases 5A, B and C contexts combined; (e) the pottery from Phase 5 occupation layers only; and (f), as a control, the pottery from all Phase 5 layers apart from occupation contexts. If, as evidence from the bone deposited in the later garth suggested (see section 4.3, below), the material in the garth soil was derived preponderantly from the occupation

activities in the surrounding buildings, then the closest match to the group in context 65 should be group (e). The results of this exercise are set out in Table 12, where it can be seen that this is not the case; in fact that material from context 65 matches more closely to the control group (f), which consists of the material in platforms, construction trenches and other non-occupation contexts. The next group with which 65 was found to match was (c), the combined occupation and non-occupation material from the heavily residual Phase 5C.

Phase 6A (later 14th century onwards: Figure 87)

A substantial new refectory was constructed on the northern side of the great cloister in Phase 6A. It is thought probable on stratigraphic grounds that this work was contemporary with the later refurbishment works (Phase 5C) in the area of the little cloister. The pottery recovered from contexts allocated to Phase 6A tends to support this view, for there is the similar lack of pottery groups which are clearly of 15th-century date, although the picture is again distorted by large quantities of residual material. One instance of a pottery join was found between contexts in the two areas: sherds of a bowl in Beverley 2C were found in Phase 6A trench 721 and in Phase 5C platform 485. The same trench also produced an example of a lamp in Beverley 2C (no. 1051); such items are rare finds on Beverley sites; it probably represents an attempt by a local potter to copy a prototype of Low Countries origin.

A total of 63 vessels from Phase 6A contexts was identified. As with Phase 5C, the single most common fabric was Beverley 2C (30% of the total), with Beverley 2B contributing 19% and Humber 1 14%. Small quantities of other 14th-century fabrics, such as North Yorks. 1 (Brandsby-type) and Scarborough variety 3 were also present, but the area produced no examples of imports such as Saintonge or Low Countries wares which, as noted above, were in use in the area of the little cloister. The quantities of pottery involved, however, are too small to allow any speculation about differences in status implied by the lack of imports in the refectory area. Given the nature and use of the building, it is probably worth noting that only four of the 63 vessels of this phase were cooking pots; moreover, three of these were certainly residual (being in Pimply and Beverley 1A wares). The phase produced only one example of the other common type of medieval cooking vessel, the pipkin, from context 956. One of the four Beverley 2B dripping pans found on this site came from Phase 6A layer 279, but once again this is likely to be residual, and no frying pans were found. Pottery evidence strongly suggests that the kitchen which supplied the refectory was not located in the immediate vicinity.

Phase 6B

This includes works which were carried out in the great cloister alley and garth area. Only residual pottery was obtained from the contexts of this period, and thus its date cannot be established.

Phase 7 (early 16th century: Figure 88)

This phase marks the demolition of major buildings of the Priory, or, in some cases, the stripping of structures of any salvageable material — the buildings being left to stand as uninhabitable shells. Although most of this activity might have been expected to have taken place immediately after the Dissolution, in certain areas of the site there are indications of at least partial demolition work which could have pre-dated the suppression of the house; these works may be related to the documented refurbishment in the 1520s.

The largest single pottery group of this period was that from context 15, a layer of soil in the garth area of the little cloister, which immediately overlay context 65 (above). Context 15 produced fragments of 59 vessels, of which three were found to be parts of vessels from stratigraphically earlier contexts. Of the remainder, the most common fabrics present were Beverley 2C (16%), Humber 1 (14%) and Humber 5 ('Late Humberware'; 12.5%). A number of vessels from this layer are illustrated; no. 1052, a Cistercian ware cup; no. 1053, which is probably the base of a chafing dish in South Yorkshire Gritty ware, and nos.

1054–6, all bases from Humber 1 jugs. Other noteworthy vessels include three Langerwehe jugs, two Raeren mugs, a Humber 1 cistern, and four vessels in Low Countries Redware (two frying pans, a pipkin, and a bowl). The latest vessel in the group is a Frechen/Cologne bellarmine, represented by a single sherd; this is out of character with the remainder of the group, and, given the layer's proximity to the surface of the site, is highly likely to be intrusive. If this sherd is discounted, the group has the appearance of a deposit of the first quarter of the 16th century with an admixture of material from the 14th and 15th centuries.

A comparison between the assemblage from context 15 and that from the underlying layer 65 yields some interesting similarities. In terms of the quantity of residual material present, the lack of joins to other layers, and of the number of sherds per vessel (which is a measure of the degree of homogeneity of each group), the two groups are alike; these factors could be taken to indicate that the circumstances of deposition of both these groups were the same. Did both groups result from a process of gradual accumulation, or were they both laid down in a single operation — 65 as a levelling deposit at the time of the construction of the little cloister and its garth, and 15 as a clearance or levelling operation following the stripping of the building? It has already been demonstrated that the material in context 65 does not have a close relationship with the pottery in the surrounding occupation areas; the evidence may thus favour an interpretation as a single levelling deposit.

Table 12 Phase 5: comparison between selected pottery 'groups' (% of pottery types present — in order of occurrence)

	5A	5B	5C	total Ph 5	Ph 5 occ	Ph 5 excl occ	ctxt 65
Beverley 2B	34	16	20	26	16	28	23
Beverley 2C	16	12	23	17	14	18	20
Beverley 1A	10	5	11	9	6	10	10
York White	7	4	3	5	4	5	7
Humber 1	4	12	12	8	16	6	12
Humber 3	3	9	4	5	4	5	4
Staxton/PB	3	2	3	3	4	2	2
Unc. Splashed	2	–	–	1	–	1	1
Coarse Sandy	2	7	4	3	6	3	4
Humber 5	2	2	1	2	4	1	–
Saintonge 2	1	–	–	0	2	–	–
Scarboro 2	1	–	–	0	–	0	–
Torksey–type	1	–	1	1	–	1	–
Scarboro 3	–	4	–	1	–	1	–
N. Yorks 1	–	4	1	1	4	0	1
L.C. Red	–	4	–	1	–	1	1
Pinky Buff	–	2	1	1	2	0	3
Stamford	–	2	1	1	4	–	1
Saintonge 4	–	–	1	0	–	0	–
Red. Chalky	–	–	–	–	–	–	1
Unclassified	14	16	11	14	121	14	7
Total vessels	125	56	73	254	49	205	88

Context 15 may thus also have been deposited in a single operation, with the two events being separated by a period of over a century.

Perhaps the single most instructive group of material from the 1986–7 excavation at the Priory is that which was recovered from the conduit which led under the reredorter block, standing to the north-west of the great cloister. Context 1093, a layer of sand and rubble within the backfill of this conduit, contained an excellent group of twenty-one vessels, a few of which are undoubtedly residual — two Beverley 1A vessels, one Beverley 2B pipkin (no. 1064) and probably also

the one jug in Beverley 2C; however, the remainder comprised a classic group of early 16th-century date, including a Low Countries Redware pipkin (no. 1061), two Cistercian ware cups (nos. 1062 and 1065), two Langerwehe stoneware jugs, a small modelled fragment from the inside of a salt in Late York White/Hambledon ware (Brooks 1987, 159–60), a jar with thumb-impressed applied decoration around the rim in 'Late Humberware' (Humber 5; no. 1065), the only example from the site of a urinal (appropriately enough, in such a context), which was in Humber 1 ware (no. 1066), and fragments of at

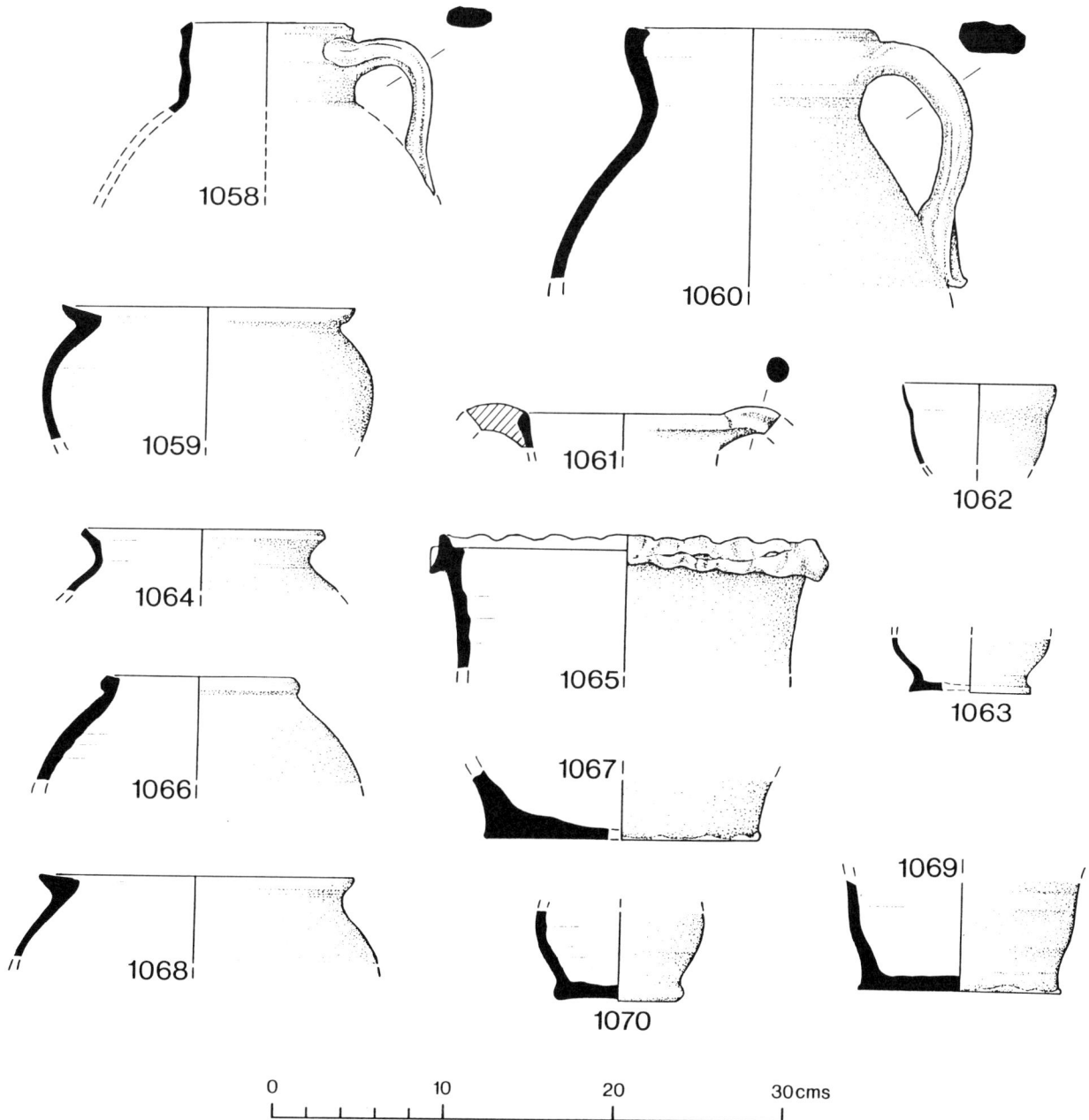

Figure 88 Pottery.

185

Table 12b Coefficients of similarity with context 65

(a)	Phase 5A	50
(b)	Phase 5B	56
(c)	Phase 5C	24
(d)	all pottery, Phase 5	30
(e)	Phase 5, occupation contexts only	49
(f)	Phase 5, excluding occupation contexts	33

(Note: vessels from context 100, Phase 5C, have been omitted throughout.)

least seven Humber 1 jugs, including no. 1067. Context 1094 (the lowest fill) contained fragments of three vessels, all of type Humber 1 and consisting of two jugs and a vessel of cooking pot-shape (though not necessarily of this function; no. 1068). Context 1093 was overlain by 1092, a fine rusty-brown sand which contained a smaller group of similar material, but with the additional presence of a sherd of Raeren stoneware. No pottery was found in context 1091, the uppermost fill. It seems probable that the conduit was back-filled with material abandoned on site at the time of the Dissolution. However, all of the types of pottery found within the fill were current in the early years of the 16th century, and it is therefore possible that the group pre-dates the Dissolution by some twenty to thirty years (cf. Hayfield 1985, 117–18, figs. 115–16). Such a combination of vessel types from a site in Hull would be taken to date before *c*.1525 due to the lack of types of the second quarter of the century such as Saintonge chafing dishes and Beauvais plates, but the comparative scarcity of imported pottery on all but the very wealthiest sites in Beverley (Watkins and Williams 1983, 80) means that the same argument need not necessarily apply in this town.

Very little pottery was recovered from the layers which are considered to represent the horizon of demolition in the area of the great cloister, its northern range and refectory, but the combination of types found — two Humber 1 jugs, a Cistercian ware cup and a Raeren ware mug — is indicative of activity in the early part of the 16th century. Rather more ceramic material was recovered from the area of the buildings of the little cloister, where the overall picture is one of the removal from the site of salvageable material, such as window lead and roof tile, followed by the abandonment of the structures. The various robbing or destruction layers in this area contained a selection of material of later 15th and/or early 16th-century date such as Langerwehe, Raeren, Low Countries, Cistercian, Humber 5 and Humber 1 wares. They included Langerwehe (no. 1057) and Humber 1 jugs (no. 1058: both from pit fill context 62), a Humber 1 cooking pot (no. 1059, from robber trench fill context 123), a Humber 1 jug (no. 1060,

from pit fill 303), and a Humber 1 jug base (no. 1069, from pit fill context 2023).

A total of 163 vessels were identified from the whole of Phase 7; for the first time on site the proportion of Humber 1 present exceeded the proportion of Beverley 2, with the former contributing 25% to the total, and the latter 24% (13% Beverley 2B and 11% Beverley 2C). The next most common type was Humber 5, at 7%.

Phase 8 (post-Dissolution to present day: Figure 88)

The pottery from the post-Dissolution layers on the Priory site was treated in a different way to the pre-Dissolution material, since the primary objective of the study of the site's pottery finds was to aid in the establishment of a chronology for the development of the site during the period of monastic occupation. The only pot-bearing contexts of Phase 8 which were recorded in detail and are noted below are those few which contained pre-industrial wares only.

As was stated above, it seems probable that some of the walls of the former little cloister were left standing after the suppression of the house. The fills of the robber trenches may provide some clues as to the length of time for which the walls survived, for they contained fragments of two wide pancheons in Brown Glazed Coarseware. This type of ware was in common use in eastern Yorkshire by 1600, but the production of the pancheon may have been a later introduction to the repertoire of the Brown Glaze potters, and a date of after 1700 for the filling of these trenches seems more likely. Robber trench 19, however, in the area of the great cloister, contained a Brown Glazed jar which could well be of 17th-century date (Watkins 1987a, 115–17). The only other pottery-bearing context which can be placed in the period before *c*.1750 is demolition layer 3046; in addition to a pancheon fragment in Brown Glazed Coarseware, this contained a fragment of a Staffordshire-type Slipware posset pot of early 18th-century date. Part of a Cistercian ware cup came from the same context (no. 1070).

Table 13 Pottery joins

Primary context and vessel no.	Phase	Joins from (number of sherds)	Phase
1027.1	3B	1073.1 (4)	3B
		1044.1 (7)	3D
1073.12	3B	729.1 (1)	3D
		1044.2 (1)	3D
		1090.1 (1)	3D
633.5	3D	65.1 (2)	5
902.6	3D	15.13 (1)	7
		65.90 (5)	7
65.2	5	522.1 (1)	5C
		528.3 (1)	5C
65.3	5	15.14 (2)	7
757.1	5A	743.1 (10)	5A
760.1	5A	759.1 (1)	5A
		282.6 (1)	6A
760.5	5A	822.2 (1)	5A
769.9	5A	824.1 (1)	5A
787.7	5A	757.6 (1)	5A
		770.2 (1)	5A
797.1	5A	759.6 (1)	5A
		760.2 (68)	5A
662.1	5B	583.3 (2)	5C
		596.1 (30)	5B
		597.1 (3)	5B
867.1	5B	1135.1 (6)	5B
485.2	5C	721.1 (2)	6A
555.4	5C	349.1 (2)	5C
583.1	5C	15.1 (1)	7
		40.1 (1)	7
		76.1 (1)	7
		534.1 (1)	7

Catalogue of illustrated pottery

Figure 87:

1032.   Jug rim, Beverley 2B. Phase 3a, context 27, vessel no. 11.

1033.   Jug rim, Beverley 2B. Phase 3a, context 1074, vessel no. 6.

1034.   Jug rim and strut, York White. Phase 3b, context 1073, vessel no. 12.

1035.   Jug base, Beverley 2B. Phase 3b, context 1073, vessel no. 13.

1036.   Jug rim and handle, Beverley 1A. Phase 3b, context 1073, vessel no. 14.

1037.   Jug shoulder, Beverley 2C. Phase 3b, context 1073, vessel no. 15.

1038.   Jug rim, Beverley 2B. Phase 3d, context 1044, vessel no. 16.

1039.   Curfew rim, Beverley 2B. Phase 5a, context 836, vessel no. 1.

1040.   Jug base, North Yorks 1. Phase 5, context 65, vessel no. 6.

1041.   Pipkin rim, Low Countries Redware. Phase 5, context 65, vessel no. 24.

1042.   Drinking jug base, Humber 1. Phase 5, context 65, vessel no. 52.

1043.   Jug base, Humber 1. Phase 5, context 65, vessel no. 53.

1044.   Jug rim, Beverley 2C. Phase 5, context 65, vessel no. 69.

1045.   Jug rim, Beverley 2C. Phase 5, context 65, vessel no. 76.

1046.   Face mask from jug, Beverley 2C. Phase 5, context 65, vessel no. 89.

1047.   Jug base, Beverley 2C. Phase 5a, context 760. vessel no. 3.

1048.   Jug rim and handle, Humber 1. Phase 5b, context 867, vessel no. 1.

1049.   ?Lid, Beverley 2B. Phase 5c, context 538, vessel no. 1.

1050.   Jug base, Beverley 2C. Phase 5c, context 3015, vessel no. 1.

1051.   Lamp, Beverley 2C. Phase 6a, context 721, vessel no. 4.

Figure 88:

1052.   Cup base, Cistercian. Phase 7, context 15, vessel no. 2.

1053.   Chafing dish base, South Yorks Gritty. Phase 7, context 15, vessel no. 15.

1054. Jug base, Humber 1. Phase 7, context 15, vessel no. 54.
1055. Jug base, Humber 1. Phase 7, context 15, vessel no. 56.
1056. Jug base, Humber 1. Phase 7, context 15, vessel no. 53.
1057. Jug base, Langerwehe. Phase 7, context 62, vessel no. 1.
1058. Jug rim and handle, Humber 1. Phase 7, context 62, vessel no. 4.
1059. Cooking pot rim, Humber 1. Phase 7, context 123, vessel no. 1.
1060. Jug rim and handle, Humber 1. Phase 7, context 303, vessel no. 1.
1061. Pipkin rim and handle, Low Countries Redware. Phase 7, context 1093, vessel no. 1.
1062. Cup rim, Cistercian. Phase 7, context 1093, vessel no. 2.

1063. Cup base, Cistercian. Phase 7, context 1093, vessel no. 3.
1064. Pipkin rim, Beverley 2B. Phase 7, context 1093, vessel no. 10.
1065. Jar rim, Humber 5. Phase 7, context 1093, vessel no. 11.
1066. Urinal rim, Humber 1. Phase 7, context 1093, vessel no. 14.
1067. Jug base, Humber 1. Phase 7, context 1093, vessel no. 20.
1068. Cooking pot rim, Humber 1. Phase 7, context 1094, vessel no. 3.
1069. Jug base, Humber 1. Phase 7, context 2023, vessel no. 1.
1070. Cup base, Cistercian. Phase 8, context 3046, vessel no. 1.

3.17 The worked wood

by John Farrimond and Martin Foreman

Introduction

Most of the wood recovered from the Priory excavations came from two trenches cut to the west of the precinct wall. The first cutting collapsed before any recording could be undertaken, the second was designated as Trench 2. *In situ* timbers were recorded in both the north and south sections of Trench 2 (Figure 8), and some of the unstratified timbers may relate to these. Most of the timbers were stakes or planking; some of the latter was reused ship's timber.

Only two fragments of wood were recovered from the main excavation area, Trench 3: these were a rotted post, and a board used to support it. Other structural timbers were recovered during contractor's work to the west of the Priory site; the cutting of a sewer trench immediately to the south of the site of the 1984 Eastgate excavations. Although unstratified, these provide further evidence for the occupation of the medieval tenements along Eastgate, the Priory's nearest neighbours. They are briefly presented here, as minor addenda to the report presented by Evans and Tomlinson (1992).

Stakes (Figure 89)

Nos. 1071–80 were stakes, for the most part crudely worked. No. 1071 was an offcut trimmed from a larger log, sharpened at one end. Nos. 1072–80 were slender tree-trunks or boughs, crudely pointed. Little working was visible on these stakes, which sometimes retained their bark, and were sharpened with between one and four angled cuts. None was complete; it is uncertain whether this arose from the rotting of the upper ends, or from their excavation by machine. No. 1080 featured a blind peg-hole; otherwise the stakes were all very simple. The species used to make the stakes included oak and alder. No. 1081 was either a small stake of rectangular section, or a lath. The rough working of these timbers is consistent with their use in a light revetment or fence, and similar timbers were recorded fulfilling such a role in Trench 2.

Planks (Figure 89)

Nos. 1082–93 were fragments of planking; nos. 1082–6 were considered to have been sawn. The planks were between 12mm and 25mm thick; only no. 1093 bore any other features, being slightly bevelled at one end. They have all been identified as oak.

Ship's timber (Figure 89)

Some elements of planking were distinguished by either traces of nailing or the survival *in situ* of clench bolts. These have been identified as fragments of ship's timber (cf. Olsen and Crumlin Pedersen 1967; McGrail 1982). No. 1094 may be included in this group, as it bears a broad nail shank *in situ*. No. 1095 is either a fragment of ship's timber, or perhaps a shingle. It was an unstratified find, but was considered likely to have originated from a deep pit at the west end of Trench 2. So too were clench-nailed clinker fragments, 1096–8. Other clinker planking, nos. 1099–1101, came from elsewhere along Trench 2. The clinker planking included fragments from the upper and lower edges of strakes. One fragment (no. 1099) is of a form which indicates that it came from the port bow of a vessel. The thickness of the planks, between 15 and 21mm, indicates that they probably came from a sizeable ship. As no other elements of ship timbering were present (with the possible exception of no. 1102 which could represent a rotted fragment of keel), it is unlikely that an actual ship was present. Given the presence of stakes, it is likely that some of the clinker planking was reused in a revetment. Light timber stake and plank revetments have been identified in a 9th-century context at Lurk Lane, Beverley; these served to support the side of a ditch or culvert (Armstrong *et al.* 1991, 10–12). More substantial sections of reused ship's timber have been recorded from medieval waterfronts at London (Milne and Milne 1974), Hull (Ayers 1979), and Grimsby (pers. comm. D. Evans).

Structural timbers (Figure 89)

Evidence for the structural use of larger timbers is scarce in the artefactual record: where timbers were identified, their position was marked usually by a hollow, or post-pipe left by the decay of the wood. A sawn offcut found in Trench 2 (no. 1103) bore cut-marks suggesting that it had been used as a saw-rest for the cutting of wood. The rotted stub of a post (no. 1104) from the putative north aisle of the Phase 3B timber hall was recovered, together with a thick board (no. 1105) on which it had been set. This method of setting a post has also been recorded at Eastgate, Beverley, in structures of 13th-century date (Evans and Tomlinson 1992).

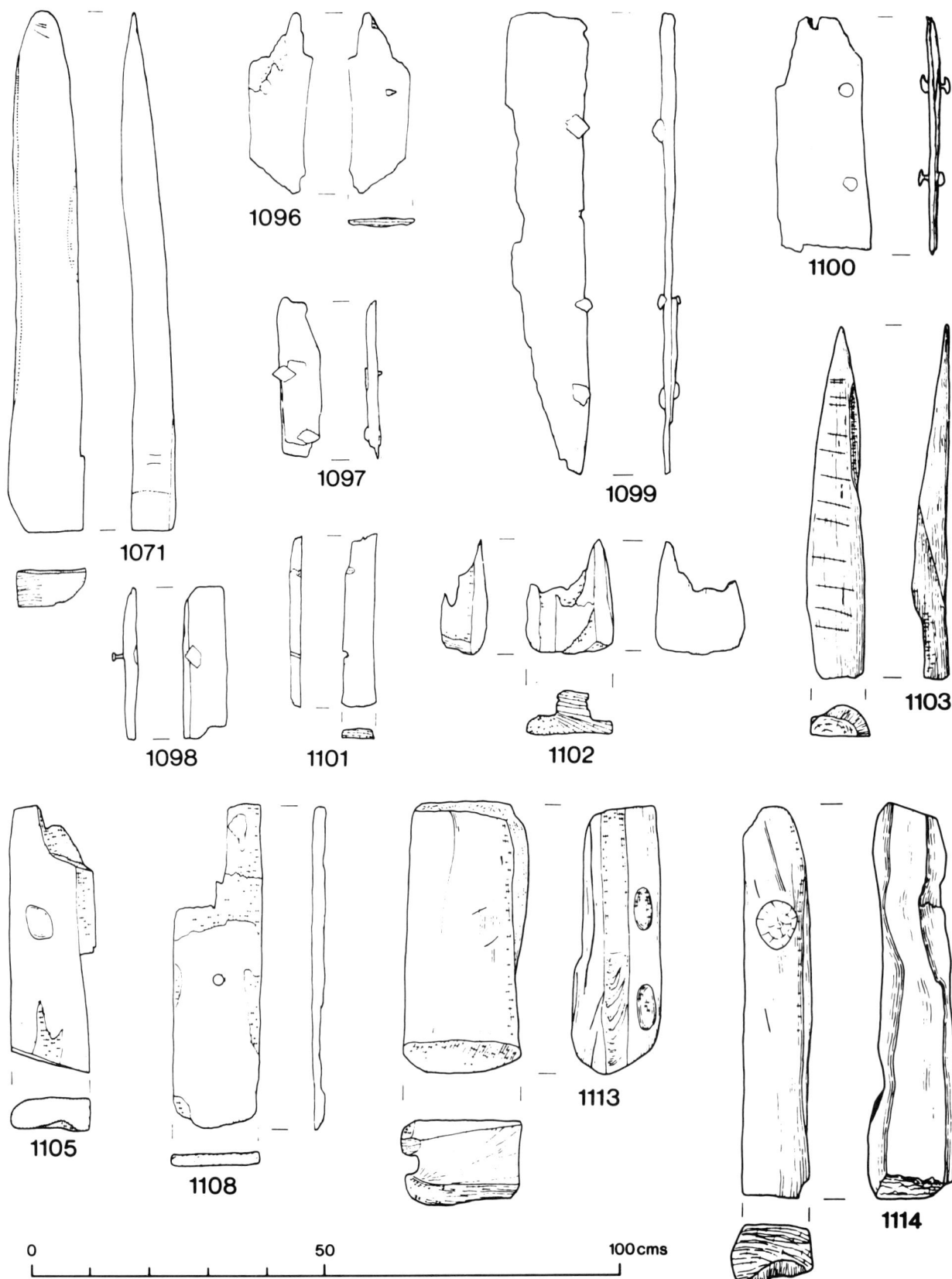

Figure 89　Wood.

Timbers from Eastgate (Figure 89)

Excavation by machine of a deep trench, which ran from a main sewer routed under Eastgate into the area west of the Priory, uncovered substantial structural timbers. The trench was considered to lie immediately to the south of the area excavated in 1984. A few timbers were recovered, though no more precise record of their provenance was achieved.

No. 1106 was a branch, perhaps pointed at both ends. Nos. 1107–9 were plank fragments. No. 1108 bore a single transverse peg-hole, and no. 1109 had been cut from the edge of a larger log. So too had no. 1110, an offcut, which was subsequently re-used as a sawing rest.

No. 1111 was a fragment of a post base, chamfered at the bottom and perhaps along its sides. It came from a deep trial pit on the course of Trench 1. No. 1112 was a similar piece, but was of a more massive squared section, chamfered along one side as well as at the base. Two fragments of a lighter timber sill were also recovered: no. 1113 bore a longitudinal rebate flanked by two oval hollows to one side, while no. 1114 bore only a round hollow or socket. The variety of structural forms which these finds represent is fully discussed by Morris and Evans (1992); the dendrochronological dates indicated for the felling of these more recently excavated timbers fall after the mid. 11th century AD (Mf.2 G3–6).

Catalogue of wooden objects (figure 89)

1071. *Quercus*
Stake cut from the side of a larger log, sharpened by two cuts at one end. Length: 894mm x 127mm x 83mm
Timber 6, Trench 2, Unstratified.

1096. Fragment of clinker plank, with one clench nail *in situ*. Possibly from the lower edge of a strake. Length: 360mm x 115mm x 15mm
Timber 21A, Pit at west end of Trench 2, Unstratified.

1097. Fragments. Consisting of two planks secured by two clench nails set 110mm apart but not in the same horizontal plane relative to the edge of the plank. This may represent a repair. Length: 270mm x 75mm x 20mm
Timber 21B, Pit at west end of Trench 2, Unstratified.

1098. Fragment; the top edge of a clinker plank with one clinker nail *in situ*. Length: 260mm x 75mm x 20mm.
Timber 21C, Pit at west end of Trench 2, Unstratified.

1099. Clinker planking. One plank and a fragment of another with luting surviving in the joint. The main plank probably represents the end of a strake, the orientation shows that this was from the port bow of the ship. Length: 790mm x 135mm x 21mm
Timber 16, Trench 2, Unstratified.

1100. Fragment of clinker plank. Possibly the lower edge is represented. Length: 405mm x 150mm x 15mm
Timber 17, Trench 2, Unstratified.

1101. *Quercus*
Fragment of plank with two rust stained holes 150mm apart.
Length: 300mm x 61mm x 20mm
Timber 18A, Trench 2, Unstratified.

1102. Fragment, possibly of a house structural timber or from a ship's keel. Too rotted and damaged for positive identification. Length: 198mm x 150mm x 75mm
Timber 36, Trench 2, Unstratified.

1103. *Quercus*
Probably an offcut from sawing logs into planks. Subsequently, the series of diagonal saw marks suggest that it was used as a saw-rest. Length: 608mm x 96mm x 55mm
Timber 3B, Trench 2, Unstratified.

1105. *Quercus*
Fragment of a thick plank, both ends cut. Used as a support under 1036 post. Length: 460mm x 145mm x 50mm
Timber 10, Context 1036, Phase 3B.

1108. *Quercus*
Fragment of plank, with one peg-hole. Length: 550mm x 150mm x 25mm. Diameter of peg-hole: 17mm.
Timber 13A, from a contractor's sewer trench at Eastgate street front.

1113. Sill beam, one end sawn the other chamfered. With longitudinal rebate and two oval depressions on upper surface. Length: 455mm x 205mm x 200mm. Rebate: 40mm wide and 25mm deep. Depressions: 70mm x 30mm.
Timber 12, from a contractor's sewer trench at Eastgate street front.

1114. Sill beam?; both ends sawn, a single depression on ?upper surface. Length: 665mm x 140mm x 100mm. Depression: 70mm x 70mm, 50mm deep.
Timber 14, from a contractor's sewer trench at Eastgate street front.

3.18 The leather

by David Atkinson and Martin Foreman

Introduction

A small quantity of leather was retrieved, mostly as recognisable but unstratified finds (the exception to this was a small group from context 225) from the Trench 2 excavation. This examined an area immediately to the west of the Priory precinct, which is considered to have been the site of pits and of a conduit. The latter was filled or narrowed in the course of the medieval period. It may perhaps have been continued by a deep feature to the south of the existing 'Old Friary' building which produced a box padlock of pre-Conquest form (I.H. Goodall 1987, 37–8, fig. 18) and a small collection of shoe fragments (Armstrong and Tomlinson 1987, 42–4, fig. 23).

The dumping of waste in this area should probably be associated with activity carried out in tenements along Eastgate, as the channel would have formed the eastern boundary of these plots — later redefined by the building of a precinct wall. Substantial quantities of leather have been examined from excavations on Eastgate. This evidence has suggested that shoe-making, cobbling and translation were significant activities there throughout the 12th and 13th centuries. The detail of shoe styles, fastenings and repairs at Eastgate suggested that craft practices or fashions probably conformed to a norm for sites of low social status. In view of the likely association between the Eastgate tenements and the bulk of the material reported here, it is briefly described with reference to the more comprehensive discussion of leather finds from that site (Atkinson and Foreman 1992).

The terminology used to describe the shoe fragments broadly follows that set out by the Museum of London (D.U.A. 1984b). All are of turnshoe construction (Thornton 1973, 7–9). Certain amendments have been suggested by Miss June Swann (formerly of the Northampton Museum Service) who has kindly commented on this and previous papers on excavated leather from Beverley. The leather was drawn and measured before conservation.

The shoes — Uppers (Figure 90)

No. 1116 is a quarter of an ankle boot, formerly fitted with a triangular heel stiffener shown by V-shaped stitching, and with a vertical thong under which two horizontal laces were threaded. Another thong, knotted at one end, is also threaded through the quarter. At Eastgate this method of fastening had

appeared by the later 12th or early 13th century, and it has been dated to the late 12th century in London (Grew and De Neergaard 1988, 14–15, fig. 16). No. 1117, a boot quarter, came from Trench 1, closer to the Eastgate street frontage. It bears two slots, apparently to accommodate simple horizontal lacing, a form of fastening which was possibly superseded in Beverley by laces attached to vertical thongs. Another quarter, no. 1118, with a single slot for a horizontal lace, is probably from a shoe made in separate quarters: this is a form which occurs among shoes from Eastgate only in a child's boot of early 12th-century date (probably a translated piece). In London the manufacture of new shoes with separate quarters is considered as a development of the mid.-to-late-14th century (Grew and de Neergaard 1988, 49–51).

Nos. 1119–22 are fragments, probably from one-piece uppers, the most usual shoe form from Eastgate and from early medieval sites generally. Nos. 1119–21 are vamps; no. 1121 has an edge-flesh side seam, edge-flesh seams around the throat, and three thong or lace-holes. No. 1124 is a fragment of a top band, which as a fitting on shoes from York has been considered to reflect Scandinavian practice (MacGregor 1982, 146); however, the presence of a top band is usually necessary to stop the stretching of unlined shoes (J. Swann, pers. comm.). Top bands from London are usually attributed to the later 13th century or after, but there are occasional examples of earlier date (Grew and de Neergaard 1988, 11, figs. 89, 90, 94). No. 1125 is a rand fragment — a small part of the shoe inserted between the upper and the sole, which is often lost when shoes have disintegrated (J. Swann, pers. comm.).

Soles (Figure 90)

Nos. 1126–7 are nearly straight-sided, a form characteristic of shoes from mid.-to-late 12th-century deposits at Eastgate. No. 1127 came from Trench 1. A fragmentary sole of similar form was recovered from a deep trench immediately to the south of the standing 'Old Friary' (Armstrong and Tomlinson 1987, 43, fig. 23, no. 25). At Hungate, York, straight-sided soles have been associated with Anglo-Scandinavian material (Richardson 1959, 87, fig. 21); however, this form continued in use as late as the 14th century at Aberdeen, perhaps for work-boots (Stones 1982, fig. 112, nos. 131–2, 134, 136). Nos. 1128–31 are progressively waisted with a slight inswing. This form occurred at Eastgate from the later 12th century

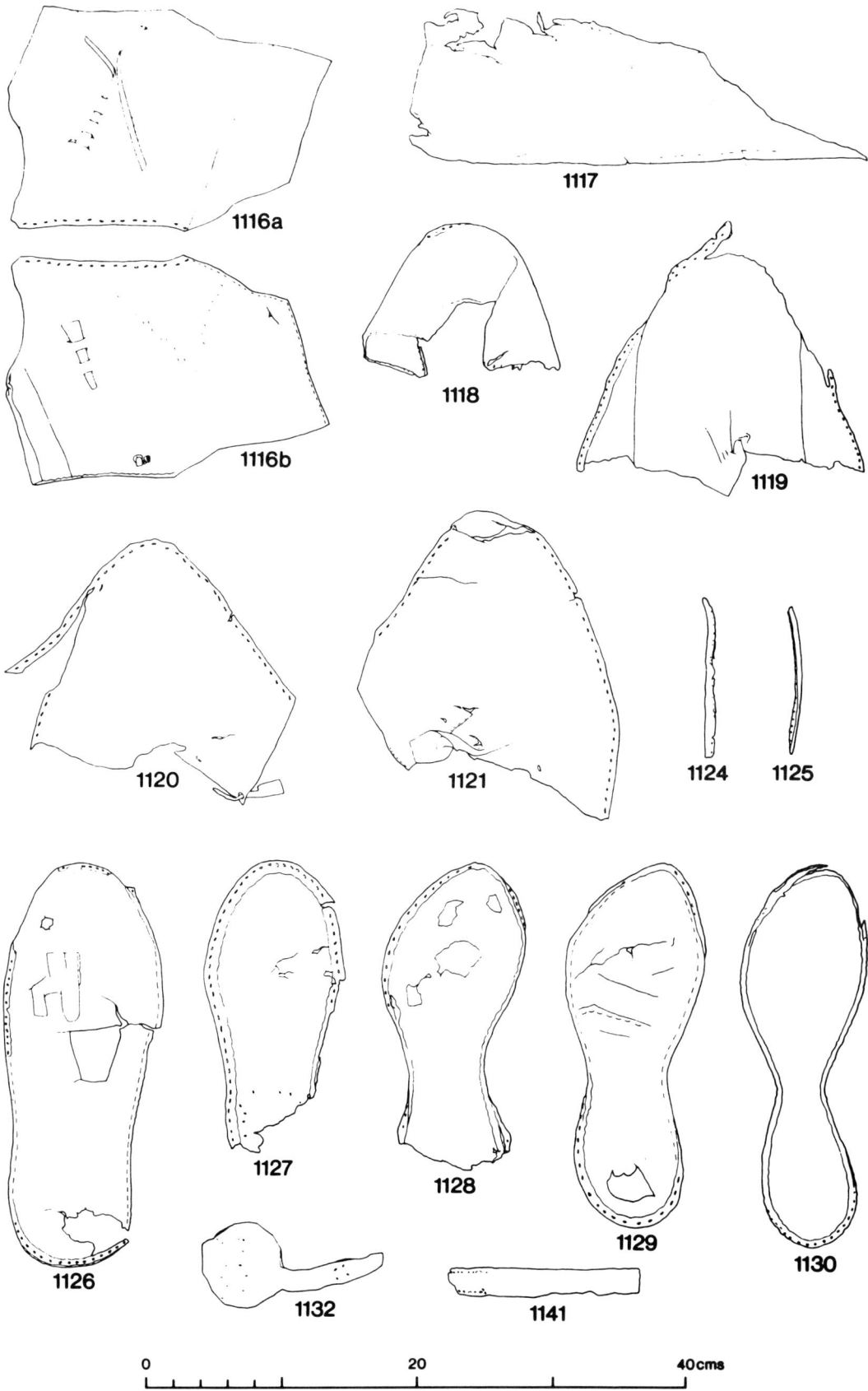

Figure 90 Leather.

onwards. No. 1129 came from a late intrusive feature. Similar soles have been excavated south of the 'Old Friary' (Armstrong and Tomlinson 1987, 43, fig. 23, nos. 27–8). The form is common at Kings Lynn through the period 1250–1350 (Clarke and Carter 1977, 358–9). In London the rounded or oval toe accompanies a waisted form as a development from the later 12th century onwards (Grew and de Neergaard 1988, 13). These shoe-types could be contemporary with the earlier Priory occupation, and, with this in mind, it is interesting to note that the Dominicans were nicknamed '*Shodfriars*' to distinguish them from the Franciscans who went barefoot (Hinnebusch 1951, 245–6; 259).

Cobbling (Figure 90)

There is limited evidence from the excavation finds for re-use or mending of shoes. As suggested above, it is possible that no. 1118 may be a fragment of a translated shoe. An unusual H-shaped repair piece has been inserted from the flesh side into sole no. 1126 and another rectangular piece cut out, while nos. 1127 and 1129 also bear stitching which indicates the former presence of repair pieces. No. 1132 is a piece of sole cut down for reuse, while no. 1133 is a tunnel-stitched clump for repair of a sole.

No. 1136, a possibly nailed heel with repair stitching, was incorporated within an internal structure of Phase 6A, while a stitched fragment and an offcut, nos. 1138–9, were identified within deposits laid down at the close of the Priory occupation (Phase 7). Phase 7 also produced a needle, no. 917, which was probably used for stitching fine leather. It is thus possible to identify very limited evidence for leatherworking in the later stages of the occupation of the Priory.

Catalogue of leather (Figure 90)

1116. Quarter of ankle boot.
   Stitching on flesh side indicates former presence of a heel stiffener. A vertical thong for lacing is woven through. Impressions of two horizontal laces appear on the grain side. One lace is present knotted on the flesh side. Edge/flesh seams. Stitch length: 5mm.
   RF3397, Trench 2, Unstratified.
1117. Fragment of a boot quarter.
   It has two slots for thongs/laces. Edge/flesh stitching along the bottom edge.
   RF3378, Trench 1, Unstratified.
1118. Quarter from a composite upper.
   Length: 250mm, width: 90mm. Thong hole in one corner. Edge/flesh seams all round. Stitch length: 4mm.
   RF3382, Trench 2, Unstratified.
1119. Vamp.
   Probably part of a one-piece upper. Length: 180mm, width: 210mm. Stitch length: 5mm.
   RF3395, Trench 2, Unstratified.

1120. Vamp.
   Probably part of a one-piece upper with a side seam. Length: 185mm, width: 210mm. Edge/flesh seams run up one side and along part of the throat. A fragment of a thong remains in a slot at the corner of the side seam and throat. Stitch length: 5mm.
   RF3396, Trench 2, Unstratified.
1121. Vamp.
   Possibly part of a one-piece upper with edge/flesh side seam. Stitch length: 4mm. Edge/flesh around the throat and three thong/lace holes.
   RF3384, Trench 2, Unstratified.
1124. Fragment of top band.
   Length: 120mm, width: 7mm. Stitch length: 5mm.
   RF3394, Context 225, Trench 2.
1125. Fragment of rand.
   Length: 112mm. Stitch length: 5mm.
   RF3390, Context 225, Trench 2.
1126. Sole.
   Adult's shoe, right foot. Length: 290mm, width at tread: 118mm, width at heel seat: 90mm. Unusual repair piece ('H' shaped) inserted from flesh side in tread. Also piece cut out indicating re-use. Worn through at heel seat. Edge/flesh seam all round. Stitch length: 5mm.
   RF3389, Context 225, Trench 2.
1127. Sole.
   Adult's Shoe, right foot. Length: 210mm, width at tread: *c.* 95mm, at waist *c.* 70 mm, Part of heel seat missing. Probably of turnshoe manufacture worn through at tread and heel seat. Stitching at heel seat indicating repair.
   RF3377, Trench 2, Unstratified.
1128. Part of sole, left foot.
   Length: 226mm, width at tread: 95mm, width at waist: 55mm. Heel seat missing. Worn through at tread. Edge/flesh seam all round.
   RF3388, Trench 2, Unstratified.
1129. Sole.
   Adult's shoe, left foot. Length: 257mm, width at tread: *c.*90mm, at waist: 50mm, at heel seat: *c.*65mm. Worn through at tread and heel seat. Stitching at tread indicating repair.
   RF3376, Context 503, Phase 8.
1130. Sole.
   Adult's shoe, left foot. Length: 272mm, width at tread: 92mm, width at waist: 35mm, width at heel seat: 68mm. Marked narrowing at waist. Worn at toe with remains of edge/flesh seam all round. Stitch length: 5mm.
   RF3387, Trench 2, Unstratified.
1132. Offcut.
   Part of sole cut down for re-use; stitching indicates former presence of repair pieces.
   RF3392, Context 185, Trench 2.
1141. Fragment.
   Strap or belt end. Length: 135mm, width: 20mm. Stitch at one end may suggest repair. Stitch length: 3mm.
   RF3386, Context 289, Phase 7.

4. The Environmental Reports

The environmental evidence from the Priory illuminates both the character of activity which preceded the Dominican occupation, and aspects of that occupation. It also supplements the results of the previous excavation of the Eastgate tenements, which were the western neighbours of the Priory.

The analysis of macrofossil remains has shed some light on the character of the soils which were deposited before the mendicant occupation began. Pollen cores taken from these deposits are reported in microfiche (section 4.1: Mf.2 G10–14). Those plant macrofossils from beyond the precinct have revealed a close relationship between the activities in the front and rear areas of the Eastgate tenements.

Both plant and invertebrate macrofossils attest the prevailing conditions within the Priory ranges and details of their occupation. The bone from within and around the buildings provides a valuable corpus of material, suggesting the distinction between those areas devoted to the preparation and those connected with the consumption of food, and also allowing comparison with evidence for the diet observed elsewhere in the medieval town. This latter category of evidence may be especially valuable for the calculation of the relative prosperity or status of areas and periods of occupation.

4.1 The pollen

by Sarah King

Summary

Two pollen cores were extracted from the surface of clay platform 27. Eighteen samples from these cores were analysed for pollen, and the counts and the diagram compiled from them are presented in Tables 14–16 (Mf.2 G10–14).

The pollen evidence suggest that the pre-Priory deposits indicate the existence of ponds or small streams in wet grassland within an area of partly deforested landscape. No clear changes are apparent in the sequence, which may argue for the homogeneity of the deposits examined. Evidence for the reworking of deposits drawn from raised bog environment — as with the incorporation of peat fuel drawn from further afield (see below, 4.2) — must qualify the interpretation of the pollen evidence, and detract from its value in the assessment of the early landscape.

(The full text of this report can be found on Mf.2, frames G10–14.)

4.2 Environmental evidence

by E.P. Allison, A.R. Hall, H.K. Kenward, W.J.B. McKenna, C.M. Nicholson and T.P. O'Connor

Introduction

This report discusses the results of analyses of invertebrate animal and plant remains from deposits excavated from the site. Limitations of time and technical assistance have precluded as detailed a survey as might have been desirable, but much useful information about the nature and formation of the deposits has been obtained.

Methods

Samples of raw sediment were taken by the excavator (a full list is given in Table 17: Mf.3 A2–8). The majority of these have been processed by bulk-sieving (Kenward *et al.* 1980), the samples (of between 5 and 70kg) being sieved by B. McKenna to 1mm, either at the Humberside Archaeological Unit, or in the Environmental Archaeology Unit after the sediment had been described. This resulted in a series of residues (retained on the mesh) and washovers (of lighter, mainly organic material, which 'floated' from the samples during sieving). Initially, residues from a modest proportion of these samples were sorted for the larger animal and plant remains and for artefacts. Selected residues and washovers were later 'rough' sorted more thoroughly — primarily for plant remains, though other components were recorded; these are listed in Table 19 (Mf.3 A14–C4). The residues from bulk-sieving consisted largely of stone and building debris, but also contained charcoal, seeds, mineralised root moulds, wood, nutshells, fragments of mammal, bird and fish bone, shellfish, snails, avian eggshell, earthworm egg capsules, and a few insect fragments. Some samples contained coke or clinker, coal, slag, glass and metal fragments. Washovers contained mainly charcoal, seeds, wood fragments, organic concretions, snail shells and coke or clinker. Bone from the residues is reported below (section 4.3).

Sub-samples of raw sediment from selected samples were examined in the laboratory for parasite eggs, insect and plant remains. A proportion of these was judged to have only a small organic content at the time at which the samples were inspected; their sedimentary characteristics were recorded, and no further action was taken (Table 17, column NFA).

Sub-samples from fifteen samples were examined for the presence of eggs of intestinal parasites. Sub-samples of 6g were taken from the raw sediment and processed following a procedure outlined by the Ministry of Agriculture, Fisheries and Food (1977, 3) for examining modern faecal samples. Accurate identification of ova is only possible when samples are prepared using reagents which do not alter egg size (Hall *et al.* 1983); the method used in the present study is believed to be appropriate in this respect. All parasite ova recovered were counted and measured using an eyepiece graticule calibrated to a stage micrometer. Ova of *Trichuris* and *Ascaris* were recorded. Measurement of those of *Trichuris* were compared with data given by Beer (1976), leaving little doubt that they were from the human whipworm *T. trichiura*. The ova of *A. lumbricoides* and *A. suum*, the large roundworm or maw-worm of man and pigs respectively, are of identical size, and cannot be distinguished by measurement. A number of cysts of testate amoebae were also noted in the parasite samples; these are common soil organisms of no further significance.

A 'general biological analysis' was carried out on the twelve more 'promising' samples. 'Test' sub-samples of 1kg were taken and processed by paraffin flotation (Kenward *et al.* 1980) to extract insect remains. Six of these produced sizeable assemblages of beetles (Coleoptera) and bugs (Hemiptera) and numbers of individuals (N in Table 21, Mf.3 C11–D12) and numbers of taxa (S in Table

21) from each sample were recorded. Taxa were divided into broad ecological groups for analysis, following the methods of Kenward *et al.* (1986), using a PASCAL computer program. Diversity of the assemblages was estimated by calculating the value of *alpha* of Fisher *et al.* (1943). Other insect and invertebrate taxa present in the flots were also recorded, but were not included in the statistics.

Plant remains in the 'test' sub-samples were recorded from both the flots from paraffin flotation and from the residues; the latter were mostly examined wet. Components other than plant macrofossils were also recorded (Table 19, Mf.3 A14–C4), as for the bulk-sieved sub-samples. For all the lists in Table 3 the remains have been scored using a three-point (bulk-sieved) or four-point (test samples) scale of abundance. For the three-point scale this was: 1 — rare to occasional; 2 — frequent to common; 3 — abundant. For the four-point scale, the scores were 1 — rare; 2 — occasional; 3 — frequent to common; 4 — abundant. For discrete items such as whole seeds or fruits the numbers can be translated as 1 — 1–4 per kg; 2 — 5–*c.*49 per kg; 3 — *c.*50–*c.*200 per kg, 4 — more than *c.*200 per kg. The lists of identifiable plant remains have been subjected to computer analysis in which each taxon is assigned to one or more ecological and use groups (Table 20, Mf.3 C5–9). For each of the test samples, the numbers and percentage of taxa scoring in each group are presented, together with a statistic — the abundance-indicator value (AIV) — which reflects both the abundance of the taxa scored for that group in the sample and how indicative the taxa are for the group. Thus a taxon which has an abundance score of 3 and is a good indicator of, say, cornfields, will have an AIV of 9 (the product of these), and this AIV contributes to the total AIV for group SECA (cornfield weeds) for the sample. (A more detailed explanation of this method is described by Hall and Kenward 1990).

All data pertaining to these biological analyses are stored on the mainframe computer at the University of York and as paper copy within the EAU.

The samples and results of the analyses

The analyses carried out on each sample, and the remains recovered, are described below, together with a laboratory description of the sediment where available. Samples yielding no significant evidence are omitted from this section of the report, though they are listed in Table 17. Those of only scant interest, or offering repetitive results, are described in microfiche (Mf.3 A9–13). The order follows the phasing supplied by the excavator; within contexts, samples are presented in numerical order. A brief archaeological description and/or interpretation of the context is given in parenthesis. Animal and fish bone recovered by sieving is considered below (section 4.3).

Phase 1

Phase 1 includes evidence for the earliest activity on the site. This activity is undated, though it preceded landfill of ?12th century date. Sampling was intended to clarify the nature of early activity.

Context 1149 (pit fill):

Sample 48 [Mf.3 A9] Sample yielded remains of a few charred cereals and weeds of no interpretative significance.

Context 1184 (clay–filled scoop):

Sample 91184 [Mf.3 A9] Traces of *Fumaria* sp(p). (fumitory) and *Avena* sp(p). (oats) were recorded.

Context 1210 (primary fill of feature 1187):

Sample 50 Black, soft, peaty, ashy organic sediment with patches of soft greenish-grey clay.

An 18kg sample of sediment was bulk-sieved, but only the residue was examined in detail. It yielded a modest assemblage of plant remains including charred cereals, some of which were identifiable as barley and bread/club wheat. There were also fragments of the rachis (stalk) from the ears of either or both of these crops. All the other remains were weeds of waste places and cultivated soils, though there was a trace of hemp (*Cannabis*), perhaps another crop plant. The residue also contained small amounts of daub-like material and charcoal.

Sample 91210 Black, wet, smeary silt with abundant charcoal and patches of olive, dark grey and mid grey material. It was considered to be mainly charcoal.

An 8kg sub-sample was bulk-sieved, and a 1kg 'test' sub-sample was processed by paraffin flotation. The washover from the bulk-sieved sub-sample contained a modest number of charred cereal grains of barley, with traces of cultivated oats (*Avena sativa*), though much of the grain was too badly damaged (?during charring) to be identified beyond Cerealia indet. There was also a component of charred chaff fragments; this may have been threshing waste, or simply debris from the disintegration of whole cereal spikelets between charring and deposition, or during disaggregation in the laboratory. The remainder of the assemblage comprised mainly weed seeds, many of them charred; these were probably crop contaminants. Hempseed was again present.

No insect or other invertebrates were recovered from the flot from the 'test' sub-sample, and no parasite ova were present in the 6g sub-sample. The flot and residue contained a substantial quantity of plant material; however, most of it consisted of charred cereal, grain and chaff.

It seems most likely that charred cereal waste was discarded in this feature; the absence of more than traces of other rubbish suggests that perhaps this was fairly pure, rather than a mixture of domestic waste.

Context 1186 (upper fill of 1187):

Sample 87 Soft, sticky orange and grey clays mixed with charcoal.

A 20kg sub-sample was bulk-sieved. The residue contained abundant, mainly waterworn, stones. Charcoal was also abundant. A small quantity of slag, brick or tile fragments, several carbonised cereal grains (?barley and oats), and a few fragments of mammal and fish bone were also recorded. The washover contained abundant charcoal. It appears likely that this deposit was a dump rather than a primary ditch fill; the laboratory description of the material as a sticky clay is at variance with the excavator's description of it as 'silt'.

Context 1209 (iron-stained clay merging with 1186):

Sample 97 Dark grey and brown silty sands with abundant charcoal inclusions.

A sample of 21kg was bulk-sieved. Stone, daub and half-fired clay or brick/tile were abundant in the residue, as was charcoal. A few, mostly burnt, fragments of large and small mammal and fish bone were present. The washover from the bulk-sieving consisted mainly of charcoal, but carbonised grain was also present, together with a few weed seeds, hazelnut shell fragments and hempseed.

Context 1214:

Sample 51 (fill of cut 1197) Grey and yellow silt.

A sample of 11kg of sediment was bulk-sieved. The residue was mainly daub and stones, some of which were chalk. There was also some slag and a few fragments of mammal bone. The washover consisted of charcoal with traces of waterlogged plant remains, including shoot fragments of the bog moss, *Sphagnum imbricatum*, discussed in more detail below.

Context 1215 (fill of cut 1197):

Sample 126 Bulk-sieving was carried out, though no weight was recorded. Brick or tile, stone, daub and charcoal were abundant in the residue. Charred grain, mortar or plaster, coal, slag and mammal and fish bone were present in small quantities. The very small washover consisted almost entirely of charcoal with small numbers of charred barley, wheat and unidentified cereal grains.

Context 1216 (fill of cut 1197):

Sample 83 [Mf.3 A9] The very small residue consisted mainly of stone, charcoal and root moulds, with some slag.

Context 925 (cut fill — upper fill of 1197):

Sample 39 Dark grey silt, burnt clay and ash.

A 6kg sub-sample of sediment was bulk-sieved. The residue consisted chiefly of daub with abundant stones and charcoal. Burnt fragments of both large and small mammal bone were also present. There was no washover from the bulk-sieving and the residue was not re-examined.

Context 1212 (pit fill):

Sample 76 [Mf.3 A9] This included some fragments of burnt oolitic limestone, otherwise it was similar to Sample 99 (below).

Sample 99 Soft, very dark grey-black clay silt with abundant charcoal.

A 10kg sample was bulk-sieved. Brick or tile, daub and charcoal were abundant in the residue. Some mortar or plaster, slag, charred grain, and a few fragments of large and small mammal and fish bone were also present. The washover consisted mainly of charcoal with a little charred (barley) grain and charred weed seeds.

Phase 2 (?12th century)

Phase 2 comprised evidence for excavation of a shallow hollow and subsequent landfill. Sampling aimed to determine the date of this activity — probably 12th century — and the character of land use at this time.

Context 959 (primary fill of depression 1158):

Samples 3, 8, 4, 9–11, 65–74, 107–8, 114 [Mf.3 A9] See list (Table 19, Mf.3 A14–C4); the small assemblages from samples 3 and 8, including several weeds, charred bread/club wheat grains, hempseed and blackberry, cannot be used interpretatively.

A total of 460kg was bulk-sieved for finds retrieval; no further examination of these samples was made.

Context 958 (?levelling to fill depression 1158):

Sample 60 Moist slightly clayey grey silt.

Bulk-sieving was carried out on 27.5kg of sediment. The plant macrofossils recovered from the washover were mostly from plants that are weeds of cultivated soils and waste places, but with traces of hempseed and hazelnut shell, wheat and blackberry. The presence of bogbean (*Menyanthes trifoliata*) and sedge (*Carex* sp(p).) may point to damp habitats nearby, or the inclusion in the deposit of, say, reworked fen peat, though this is hardly conclusive.

Sample 103 [Mf.3 A9] Small fragments of mammal and fish bone, slag, mortar or plaster, and brick or tile fragments were prominent. The assemblage of plant remains was essentially similar to that from Sample 60.

Samples 2, 29, 30–33, 59, 61–4, 115 Dark grey silts.

A total of 295.5kg was bulk-sieved for finds retrieval but none of the residues was examined.

Context 957 (silt filling depression 1158):

Sample 36 [Mf.3 A10] Similar to 958, with the addition of slag and lead. Plant macrofossils were a depauperate collection of the same taxa as those from 958 and 959 and have little interpretative significance.

Context 924 (layer pre-dating Phase 5A construction activity, ?early 14th century):

Samples 26, 1, 24–5, 27–8, 57–8 [Mf.3 A10] A total of 204kg was bulk-sieved, but the residue from Sample 26, the only one examined, yielded scant environmental evidence.

Context 1188 (?fill or dump):

Sample 5 Wet dark grey silt.

A sample of 32kg of sediment was bulk-sieved, and plant macrofossils were recorded from the washover. They included a modest range of weed taxa, together with some plants suggestive of damper soils (*Thalictrum flavum, Menyanthes, Scirpus lacustris* and *Eleocharis palustris*). The trace amounts of amorphous peat in this fraction may point to the presence either of reworked peat incorporated into the sediment (along with small amounts of occupation debris), or the growth of a marsh/fen kind of vegetation at or very near this part of the site.

Sample 16 Moist dark grey silt.

A sample of 15kg of sediment was bulk-sieved. The washover yielded trace amounts of weed taxa, with evidence, again, for plants of waterlogged soils or marginal-aquatic environments — *Scirpus* cf. *lacustris, Eleocharis palustris*, together with saw-sedge, *Cladium mariscus*.

Sample 75 Wet, dark grey silt with chalk gravel inclusions.

A 28kg sample of sediment was bulk-sieved, and the residue gave a very small list of plant taxa, most of which might merely have been weeds. The presence of fish bone and scale, and mammal bone with chalk, charcoal and mortar suggests the incorporation of occupation debris into the deposit.

Sample 92 [Mf.3 A10] Similar to Sample 75, with the addition of hazelnut shell, oyster shell and avian eggshell.

Sample 105 [Mf.3 A10] Charcoal was prominent in this sample.

Samples 110, 12–15, 17, 144 [Mf.3 A10] Traces of unidentified charred cereal grains and wheat caryopses were present in Sample 110.

A further total of 171kg was bulk-sieved for finds retrieval.

Sample 91188 More of the raw sediment was examined in the laboratory. A 1kg 'test' sub-sample was processed by paraffin flotation. The very small insect assemblage obtained (4 fragments) was uninterpretable. A single *Trichuris* ovum was recorded from a 6g sub-sample; this is at the level of contamination or 'background'.

Plant remains from the flot and residue from this sub-sample formed a modest assemblage. The only taxa scoring more than 1 (trace amounts) were stinging nettle (*Urtica dioica*), fat hen (*Chenopodium album*), deadnettles (*Lamium* Section *Lamiopsis*) (all scoring 2) and mud rush (*Juncus gerardi*) (scoring 3). The last of these is usually found today in the upper reaches of salt marshes, and would be unexpected as far inland from, for example, the Humber estuary, as Beverley; however, there is evidence that it may have been formerly more widespread in the less saline parts of coastal meadows and perhaps therefore more widely distributed in inland habitats. Another explanation that has been put forward for the regular records of seeds of this plant (together with other, more definitely halophyte, taxa) from Roman York, is that it arrived in the town in the guts of cattle grazed a day or two previously on salt marsh downstream (Kenward *et al*. 1986; Hall and Kenward 1990). The same group of probable marsh/fen or waterside taxa recorded from other samples from this context were also present here (giving a rather high AIV for group PHRA, cf. Table 20, Mf.3 C5–C9).

Context 1206 (?infill):

Sample 49 [Mf.3 A10] The plant taxa were essentially weeds or indicators of human occupation and offer little useful interpretative information.

Context 1211 (?pit fill):

Sample 46 Moist grey clay with patches of harder yellow clay.

A 25kg sample of sediment was bulk-sieved. Stone, mostly in the form of rounded pebbles, was very abundant in the residue. Slag, and a few fragments of mammal bone, fish bone, and shell were also present. The washover contained a small quantity of charred grain, though this was not available for examination. The washover, when rechecked, was found to have traces of two weed taxa, together with charcoal, fish and mammal bone, shellfish, shell fragments and slag.

Context 1146 (pit fill):

Sample 91146 Mid. grey/grey-brown to reddish grey-brown, moist, plastic silty clay, with charcoal, bone and possibly redeposited natural inclusions.

A sample of 39kg was bulk-sieved, from which the washover yielded a small range of weed seeds, together with leaves and shoot fragments of the bog moss *Sphagnum imbricatum*; this last is a typical component of Flandrian (post-glacial) raised bog peats, and is perhaps an indication of the exploitation an area of raised bog, or of imported peat cut from such a location. Unfortunately, in the absence of peat fragments, it is not possible to say which is the more likely explanation. A sample of the raw sediment was examined in the laboratory, but no further action was taken.

Trench 2 (?12th — 14th century)

This trench examined the area immediately to the west of the Dominican precinct. Gullies, pits and levelling were considered to relate to activity in tenements along Eastgate. Evidence for the development of the boundary between the Priory and these tenements was also recovered. Most of the activity recorded by Trench 2 pre-dated the construction in the ?14th century of a precinct wall around the Priory, and probably dated from the early 12th century onwards.

Early horizon:

Sample 165 [Mf.3 A10]

Context 164 (black, greasy fill of U-shaped feature):

Sample 164 Mid grey, moist, plastic/crumbly, slightly sandy, silty clay, with abundant humified organic remains including wood, yellow patches, chalk gravel, a flint pebble, and a few tile fragments.

A 1kg 'test' sub-sample was processed to extract insect remains, and a reasonably sized assemblage of beetles and bugs was recovered (131 individuals of 71 taxa). The assemblage was fairly diverse (alpha = 63, SE = 10), and outdoor forms were numerous (%S OB = 30; %N OB = 19). Aquatics made up 5% of the individuals (28% of the outdoor component); there were three *Ochthebius minimus* and two *Helophorus* sp., both common denizens of small water bodies. Decomposers were rather well represented, making up 62% of the individuals (%N RT); taxa coded 'RD' contributed 17% of the assemblage, those coded 'RF' only 3%. Much the most abundant taxon was a *Corticaria* sp., with 17 individuals. There were eight each of an aleocharine and a *Cryptophagus* species, and seven of a second species of *Corticaria*. It appears very likely that there was fairly dry decaying organic matter at or near to the point of deposition, but there is no evidence that this was very persistent. The fauna is very typical of that from many urban sites examined, and includes some species which are largely, but not exclusively recorded from buildings. Conceivably some aquatics lived in the cut. The record of ephippia (resting eggs) of a water flea *Daphnia* sp. from this

sample supports this, but much of the fauna could be of background origin.

Other invertebrates recovered in the flot were: mites, a spider, an earthworm egg capsule, insect larvae, an earwig, parasitic wasps, fly puparia, heteropteran nymphs, a sheep ked (*Melophagus ovinus*), and a body segment of a flea.

Two fertilized *Ascaris* ova were recorded from the 6g parasite sample; given the presence of cereal 'bran' and other foodplants (below), this probably indicates the presence of some (?human) faeces in the deposit.

Plant remains from the flot and residue from this sub-sample of 164 were abundant and diverse. The best represented ecological and use groups were weeds of waste places and cultivated land — some (e.g. docks and stinging nettles) more indicative of neglected land with a perennial weed flora; others were annual weeds of regularly tilled soils. The single nutlet of cat-nip, *Nepeta cataria*, in this sub-sample may have originated in a plant in this category, though this is a species with medicinal uses and, like *Marrubium vulgare* (see below, sample 136) may have been grown deliberately in the area at this period, or earlier. Foodplants scored highly (Table 20) and the small fruit seeds of elder, blackberry and strawberry, together with wheat/rye 'bran', may be evidence of the presence of faeces, perhaps human. Other food remains included charred cereals, notably barley which showed signs of having started to sprout prior to charring; this may have been spoilt grain or perhaps waste from brewing, but the quantities of grain were not large.

Two dyeplants were recorded from this sample: weld (*Reseda luteola*) (which might easily also be a weed of waste places, especially on the kind of calcareous soil likely to have been prevalent in and around Beverley), and madder (*Rubia tinctorum*). The latter was recorded in some quantity from deposits excavated in 1984 in Eastgate, adjacent to the present site (McKenna 1992; see also below, context 167).

As is usual in medieval urban archaeological deposits, there was a component of wetland taxa, including marsh lousewort (*Pedicularis palustris*), saw-sedge and several mosses of marsh/fen habitats. They may have grown locally if there was a ditch or wet meadow in the vicinity, though there is no evidence for a ditch carrying nutrient-rich water.

Context 169 (black, greasy fill of U-shaped feature):

Sample 127 (no description).

A 14kg sample of sediment was bulk-sieved. The residue consisted of wood fragments, mainly twigs, charcoal and stone. The washover was made up of wood fragments (small twigs) and plant debris; the plant macrofossils included several woody taxa which perhaps indicate the presence of scrub or a hedge, though this has not been confirmed by more detailed analysis. Charred cereals were quite well represented, including barley, bread/club wheat and cultivated oats. Mosses of marsh/wet grassland habitats were again present.

Context 167 (upper fill of U-shaped feature):

Sample 167 Mid/dark, varicoloured (grey with brown and olive mottling), moist, plastic/crumbly, humic, silty clay, with small patches of pure sand and organic detritus and twig fragments.

A 1kg 'test' sub-sample was processed to extract insect remains, and a large assemblage of 219 individuals of 96 beetle and bug taxa was obtained. Like the assemblage from the sub-sample of 164, it was of rather high diversity (alpha = 65; SE = 7) and included a substantial 'outdoor' component (%N OB = 18). There was a substantial proportion of decomposers (%N RT = 62), and RD taxa were quite important (%N RD = 22, N RD as %N RT = 35). 'Foul' decomposers were not especially important (%N RF = 5). A good number of taxa (22) were represented by three or more individuals. The more abundant were: *Lathridius minutus* group (17); a *Corticaria* sp. (16); *Anobium punctatum* (woodworm beetle; 10); *Cercyon analis*, a *Cryptophagus* sp. and an *Atomaria* sp. (all with 6). It appears that decomposer habitats for species favoured by fairly dry to somewhat damp material were available nearby or in the cut, or that rubbish containing insects was thrown in, while a few taxa indicated the presence of fouler material. Woodworm is indicative of timber on a structural scale, when found in large numbers; the longhorn *Gracilia minuta* attacks smaller wood, basket-work, and the like. The list obtained (Table 22) is subjectively very similar to that from 164/T.

Also present in the flot were: mites, spiders, an earthworm egg capsule, an abdomen of a louse (Ischnocera: Trichodectidae), parasitic wasps, adult flies (including a bibionid), fly puparia, a flea body segment, a caddis wing, heteropteran nymphs and an aphid.

Plant remains were abundant in the flot and residue from the 'test' sub-sample. The two kinds of macrofossil scoring 3 on a four-point scale of abundance were willow (*Salix* sp(p).) buds and epidermis of Cyperaceae (perhaps sedges, *Carex* sp(p).) which, together with a range of other taxa, may indicate the presence of wetland nearby, or the disposal of materials (perhaps cut vegetation for roofing or flooring) exploited from it.

In addition to more madder root (scoring 2), a further dyeplant was recorded from this sub-sample — pod fragments of woad (*Isatis tinctoria*). Seeds of weld and leaf fragments of bog myrtle might also be present as waste from dyeing — both plants yield good yellow dyes, complementing the red of madder and blue from woad. The last-named was also recorded from Eastgate (McKenna 1992). The presence of both flax seeds and capsule fragments perhaps gives evidence of textile working, too — though both might be present in waste from processing of seed for use as a food or as a source of linseed oil.

A further component of these deposits was evidently human faeces. Although the 6g sub-sample examined for parasites yielded only a single ovum of *Ascaris*, disaggregation of a fragment of material in the residue thought to be a faecal concretion showed that both *Ascaris* and *Trichuris* were present. Wheat/rye 'bran' (and concomitant milled corncockle (*Agrostemma githago*) seed fragments) also support this interpretation. Faecal concretions made up a considerable proportion of the residue (scoring 3 on a four-point scale), though few fruit remains were present — merely apple endocarp ('core') and elderberry seeds.

Context 166 (cut fill):

Sample 136 (not described after sampling; field description as 'dark mottled and twiggy silt').

A sample of 20kg was bulk-sieved; both washover and residue were available for examination in detail. Somewhat similar plant remains were recovered from this as from contexts 164 and 167. Of note were the common nutlets of white horehound (*Marrubium vulgare*), a plant with medicinal uses, but equally likely to have grown in waste places or near hedges. Taxa that could be interpreted as coming from hedges or scrub are also rather well represented, though they may be debris from clearing such vegetation, as much as evidence for its growth in the vicinity. Supporting evidence from insect remains would have been highly desirable.

Context 185 (pit fill):

Sample 185 Dark grey, moist, crumbly, humic, sandy silt, with some wood and bone fragments, and patches of light grey clay and peaty organic matter.

A 1kg 'test' sub-sample was processed by paraffin flotation to extract insect remains. An assemblage of 152 individuals of 65 beetle and bug taxa was obtained. It was of moderate diversity (alpha = 43; SE = 6) and had a clear but modest 'outdoor' component (%S OB = 25; %N OB = 14). This component in turn was of fairly low diversity (alpha OB =32, although SE = 16), depressed by taxa such as *Platystethus nitens*, *Cercyon ustulatus* and *Carpelimus* ?*corticinus*, all of which might have exploited damp organic rich mud within the pit. Several other 'damp ground' and aquatic taxa may have been attracted to suitable, if transient, habitats in the pit. Such taxa made up three-quarters of the outdoor component. There was in addition a single ephippium of the water flea *Ceriodaphnia* sp.

Decomposers were numerically well represented, and made up just over half the fauna (%N RT = 53). Dry decomposers were not very numerous (%N RD = 7), and foul decomposers just sufficiently abundant to suggest they found attractive habitats nearby (%N RF = 7). The decomposer component was of low diversity (alpha RT = 19; SE = 3). It is probable that some or all of the more abundant taxa invaded different aspects of the pit fills, ranging from somewhat to fairly foul matter.

Also recovered from the flot were: several species of adult flies (including several individuals of a bibionid) and fly puparia, two sheep keds *Melophagus ovinus* (evidence of sheep, sheepskins or wool), a thrip, two lice (including a species of Anoplura), parasitic wasps, a flea body segment, nymphs of two species of bug, mites, spiders and an earthworm egg capsule. There was modern fly contamination.

A single *Trichuris trichiura* ovum was present in the sample examined for parasites. Cysts of testate amoebae were also noted.

Plant macrofossil remains were recorded in some quantity in the flot and washover; the most notable amongst these were fruits and receptacular bracts of teasel. Indeed, one fragment comprising a group of associated bracts indicated that whole or partly fragmented teasel heads had been thrown into the pit. On initial inspection, it was thought that the material was of the wild teasel, *Dipsacus fullonum*, but closer examination of both fruits and bracts suggested fullers' teasel (*D. sativus*) was the plant concerned (and it is interesting in this context to speculate, with regard to wool processing, about the possible significance of the sheep keds — see above — from the same deposit). In the light of this determination, other fossil material of teasel heads from Eastgate (McKenna 1992) and from Anglo-Scandinavian Coppergate, York (Hall, unpublished) have been examined, and, where identifiable to species, all the material is *D. sativus* (Hall 1992).

Possible evidence for textile dyeing resides in the abundant weld seeds and presence of leaf fragments and fruits of bog myrtle. The rest of the assemblage is accounted for by weeds (perennials being rather well represented: cf. sample 163/T), wetland taxa and perhaps also some grassland plants, though this last component is not sufficiently large to suggest the presence of, for example, cut vegetation like hay (cf. samples 134/B and 229/T).

Context 225 (pit fill):

Sample 134 Mid/dark, grey-brown, amorphous organic deposit, with some herbaceous detritus, twig fragments and lumps of light grey silty clay.

A 13kg sub-sample of sediment was bulk-sieved, and the residue and washover gave a very large assemblage of plant macrofossil remains (91 taxa), representing the highest number of groups (46) for any sample from the site (though most taxa were present in small numbers). This high diversity perhaps reflects a mixed origin for the remains, for, although the majority are weeds, there are several plants suggestive of grassland, wetland and perhaps even heathland habitats. The record for trace amounts of dyer's greenweed (*Genista tinctoria*) stem fragments is of interest; this was an important dyeplant in the Anglo-Scandinavian period at York (to judge from evidence from three sites) and was probably used throughout the Middle Ages. It is also a plant of lowland pastures, however, and might have arrived in the town by other routes than deliberate collection for dyeing. Evidence for other possible dyeplants from 134/B is restricted to *Myrica* leaf fragments and fruits, though there are other uses to which this plant might have been put (including medicinal applications and brewing).

The records for culm-nodes ('knees') of cereals (and perhaps also grasses) argues for the presence of straw (and perhaps hay: though the data are not presented here, this sub-sample gave the second highest AIV for the grassland group MOAR for the site as a whole). Amorphous peat fragments were present at a score of 2 on a three-point scale and these may account for the records of wetland taxa like *Potentilla palustris*, *Hydrocotyle vulgaris* and *Menyanthes trifoliata*.

A 1kg 'test' sub-sample was processed to extract insect remains. Apart from beetles and bugs, other taxa present in the flot were *Ceriodaphnia* and *Daphnia* sp. ephippia, spiders, mites, insect larvae, a scale insect, fly puparia, larval spiracular processes of a Syrphidae sp., a bibionid fly, an earwig, parasitic wasps, and a head and abdomen (containing male genitalia) of *Pulex irritans*, the human flea.

An estimated 102 individuals of 71 beetle and bug taxa were recorded. The estimate of Fisher *et al.* 1943's alpha was high (103), with a SE of 21. This, combined with the presence of a substantial 'outdoor' component (%S OB = 30; %N OB = 23), suggests exposure to the open air. (The presence of an *Olophrum* sp. offers a very small hint of an alternative source — in gathered moss, of which there was rather a diverse range, see below). The water flea ephippia suggest that the pit held fairly clean water at some stage, unless the ephippia came from elsewhere. Water beetles

were rare (only two individuals — *Helophorus* sp., and *Chaetarthria seminum*; these may well have originated in waterside moss with *Olophrum* sp.).

Decomposers were fairly well represented (%N RT = 59), with the RD component modest for an urban assemblage (%N RD = 13) and the foul component quite substantial (%N RF = 10). The decomposer component was rather diverse (alpha RT = 41, although SE = 10). The species list gives some evidence that a few decomposers bred in or by the pit — there were eight *Lathridius minutus* group, six *Cercyon analis* and four *Platystethus arenarius*. There is no evidence of a long-lived foul decomposer community, although the syrphid fly, a 'rat-tailed maggot', probably did live there. It is possible that much of this fauna was introduced from elsewhere, in moss or water, in sweepings (in which the flea may have originated), and as background fauna. If so, the pit may have been short-lived or covered.

A single *Trichuris trichiura* ovum was recorded from the sample examined for parasites; the only other evidence for faeces is of ?faecal concretions from the bulk-sieved sub-sample, but their identity could not be confirmed.

Plant remains from the 'test' sub-sample were, again, abundant, well preserved and diverse in their origins. Together with *Juncus gerardi* (see above, sample 91188/T), there was a more strictly halophile plant, sea arrow-grass (*Triglochin maritima*), whose presence in the deposit is not easily explained unless brought to the town in the guts of livestock grazed on salt-marsh (the nearest would perhaps have been about 12–13km away on the Humber foreshore). It is of interest, therefore, that this sample gave the third highest score (20) for the grassland group, MOAR, for the site, and the presence of grassland taxa in hay or herbivore dung is a possibility. Straw may also have been dumped in the pit (there were culm-nodes, as in the bulk-sieved sub-sample). The range of mosses is quite wide, with taxa of bark and shaded rocks predominating; some are taxa typically associated with medieval latrine pits (where they were certainly used as toilet paper), though all were present in small quantities and might have arrived accidentally on timber or as packing for goods in transit, for example. Stem fragments of dyer's greenweed were again present.

Context 223 (spread in pit):

Sample 139 (not described after sampling).

A sample of 18kg of sediment was bulk-sieved. Twigs and fragments of bark, many of them charred, were abundant in the residue, as were stone, charcoal, plant stems (again mostly charred), and organic concretions (?peat). Carbonised and uncarbonised seeds were also fairly abundant. Mortar/plaster, daub, hazelnut shell, moss, bone (mostly burnt), insect and fly puparia fragments, snails, shell and avian eggshell were also recorded. The washover was mainly of plant stems, charred grain and seeds. Wood, charcoal, moss, organic concretions (?un-disaggregated humic sediment), and snails were present.

Although only a few snails were recorded from this sample, most were *Oxyloma pfeifferi* and *Zonitoides nitidus*, implying an input of vegetation from base-poor marsh. This perhaps correlates with the presence of a component of marsh/fen/waterside plant taxa from the residue and washover, especially in the case of mosses (the same five taxa contributing to both groups MARS and FENS resulted in an AIV of 10, the largest in each case for the samples from this site as a whole). There were certainly other components in the sample, however. The stalk and pinnule fragments of bracken (*Pteridium aquilinum*) perhaps indicate disposal of bedding, as might the culm-nodes of cereals and/or grasses. Charred grains of wheat, oats and barley were all moderately well represented, and all showed signs in some specimens of having begun to sprout prior to charring; it may be that this was spoilt grain that was deliberately burnt. Other food remains included charred field bean (*Vicia faba*) and ?pea (cf. *Pisum sativum*), and waterlogged remains of celery seed (*Apium graveolens*), apple (*Malus sylvestris*) and blackberry. The range of foodplants present is reflected in the high AIV for group FOOS, though it appears to have been non-faecal waste.

Context 215 (spread in pit):

Sample 137 (not described after sampling).

A 14kg sample was bulk-sieved but only the washover was examined. This gave a small assemblage of plant remains including weeds and charred cereals in small to moderate quantities. The only unusual taxon was *Berula erecta*, an umbellifer of waterside habitats.

Context 231 (pit fill — primary):

Sample 124 (no description after sampling; excavator described this as a 'soft dark brown organic silt').

A 9kg sample was bulk-sieved. The residue was mainly charcoal, ?ash, wood and twig fragments with some chalk and charred grain (including wheat, barley and oats, some grains showing signs of germination, as in previous samples). Amongst the weed seeds (a good proportion of which were charred and are likely to have been crop contaminants), there were various other foodplants — field bean, hazelnut, 'cherry' (*Prunus* Section *Cerasus*), blackberry and linseed.

Context 229 (pit fill — over 231):

Sample 229 Dark grey-brown, moist, crumbly, layered, ?silty, amorphous organic sediment, with traces of herbaceous detritus within laminae.

A 1kg 'test' sub-sample was processed to extract insect remains. A beetle and bug assemblage of 106 individuals of 59 taxa was recovered. Other taxa recorded were: *Daphnia* sp. ephippia, mites, a spider, bug nymphs (all but one being heteropteran), a parasitic wasp, fly adults and puparia, a flea body segment, and insect larvae.

The beetle and bug assemblage was of moderate diversity (alpha = 55, SE = 9), but had a rather small 'outdoor' component (%N OB = 9). Two of the most abundant taxa were, however, borderline in this respect but not coded 'OB' — *Carpelimus* ?*bilineatus* and *C. fuliginosus*. Decomposers made up 58% of the assemblage, and considerably more if some uncoded (U) probable decomposers are included. The more abundant taxa perhaps included invading decomposers. *Carpelimus* ?*bilineatus* and *C. fuliginosus*, *Cercyon analis*, *C. atricapillus*, *Oxytelus sculptus* and *Sphaeridium bipustulatum* seem likely to have exploited foul organic matter in the pit, and others such as *Atomaria* sp., *Lathridius minutus* group, *Ptenidium* sp. and *Xylodromus concinnus* may have lived in the drier parts of the fill. It seems likely that there was some breeding — diversity of the RT component was fairly low (alpha RT = 21; SE = 5). There was probably some 'background' fauna,

although this may have originated in sweepings, together with a suite of 'domestic', 'pest' and dry decomposer taxa. The specimens of the bean weevil *Bruchus* ?*rufimanus* may have been passed through human intestines, if this was a cess pit.

Since only single ova of *Ascaris* and *Trichuris trichiura* were recorded from a 6g sub-sample examined for parasite ova interpretation, this seems unlikely, until the list of remains from the botanical analyses are consulted; here, faecal concretions scored 2, and *Ascaris* and *Trichuris* ova were recorded from a fragment of concretion disaggregated in dilute hydrochloric acid and scanned quickly under the transmission microscope. The presence of modest number of fig (*Ficus carica*) seeds agrees well with this interpretation, though there are few other foods of this type in what is otherwise a very long species list.

The plant macrofossil assemblage is, in fact, the largest for the site, with 94 taxa (though it did not give the largest number of ecological and use groups). One of the chief components is charred cereal remains, both caryopses (of wheat barley, and oats — including cultivated oats), and chaff and culm-nodes, suggesting straw and threshing waste were also partly burnt prior to disposal. Hay and/or herbivore dung may also be present, for this assemblage has by far the highest AIVs (38 and 15 respectively) for grassland plants (groups MOAR and FEBR, to which many taxa are common) for the site.

Conduit — context 163 (layer of chalk and tile in clay):

Sample 163 Mid/dark, grey-brown, moist, plastic/crumbly, humic, silty clay, with large chalk fragments and some wood fragments.

A 1kg 'test' sub-sample was processed by paraffin flotation, and it yielded a rather small assemblage of beetles and bugs (60 individuals of 42 taxa). This assemblage was of quite high diversity (alpha = 62; SE = 16) and included a very substantial proportion of 'outdoor' forms (%S OB = 40; %N OB = 30). A death assemblage of this kind seems very likely to have formed in the open. Aquatics were rather abundant, accounting for 10% of the whole assemblage and 33% of the outdoor component. Decomposers were rare — by comparison with most assemblages from occupation sites — making up only 38% of the fauna. Within this component, 'dry' (RD) decomposers were relatively poorly represented (7%), and 'foul' ones (RF) relatively numerous (8%). This is also characteristic of deposition in the open. Decomposers may have been attracted to the site of deposition, but the evidence is weak. The only numerous taxa were a *Corticaria* sp. (5 individuals), two aleocharine staphylinids (with 4 and 3 individuals), and *Platystethus arenarius* (3). Although uncoded, the aleocharines were quite possibly also decomposers. *Corticaria* species are mainly associated with rather dry decaying matter, and *P. arenarius* with foul matter, so it is more likely that these, and the rest of the assemblage, were of 'background' origin — deposited *in situ*, imported in 'clay', or of mixed origins.

Other invertebrate remains recovered in the flot were an earthworm egg capsule, an ostracod, mites, insect larvae, fly puparia, several individuals of at least two species of parasitic wasp, a caddis fly wing, and a heteropteran nymph.

A single *Trichuris trichiura* ovum was recorded from the sample examined for parasites, but no other evidence for faecal material was found amongst the plant remains. A more modest assemblage than those from 164 and 167 was present in this sub-sample, and it was marked by the presence of a high proportion of perennial weeds (group ARTE, Table 20), perhaps suggesting the presence of neglected land in the area. Wetland taxa are again moderately well represented, notably the celery-leaved crowfoot (*Ranunculus sceleratus*). This is usually taken to be an indicator of mud at the margins of ponds or ditches where there is disturbance and high nutrient status — for example, where cattle drink, or where organic waste is being deposited. Together with five other taxa assigned to the group — especially *Chenopodium* Section *Pseudoblitum* (also scoring 3) — this gives rise to the highest AIV for BIDE in this series of samples, and suggests the presence of drying mud, or a ditch in the vicinity. The extremely common achenes of stinging nettle (*Urtica dioica*) also suggest nutrient-rich soils, though this plant is also typical of fens.

Phase 3A (13th century)

Samples from Phase 3A were drawn from an area of pits, at one end of a timber hall, with the intention of clarifying their function.

Context 1074 (pit or hollow fill in 1061):

Sample 42 Moist grey clay with very hard buff clay patches.

Bulk-sieving was carried out on 27.5kg of sediment, but only the washover was examined. It gave a modest list of taxa, the only one of which was present in more than small amounts being deadnettle (*Lamium* Section *Lamiopsis*). Most of the other taxa were also weeds, though there was a distinct component of wetland plants, notably cf. *Oenanthe aquatica*, *Menyanthes trifoliata*, *Scirpus lacustris*, *Eleocharis palustris*, *Cladium mariscus*, and probably most if not all of the *Carex* sp(p). The assemblage is too small for confident interpretation, however; the taxa are all regularly recorded from urban archaeological deposits of the medieval period.

Sample 118 Wet, sticky greenish-grey silty clay.

A 23kg sample of sediment was bulk-sieved, but no further action was taken. A 6g sample was examined for the presence of parasite ova, but none was recorded.

Context 1047 (pit or hollow fill, sealing/?plugging 1061):

Sample 123 (no description made after sampling; excavators' description is 'grey-green panned clay with charcoal flecking').

A 14kg sample was bulk-sieved, the residue 'rough-sorted' and the washover examined further in detail. There was a small assemblage of weeds, together with blackberry and charred bread/club wheat; the residue contained modest amounts of chalk and of concreted root moulds (?associated with panning). There is thus little evidence for the origin of the deposit, though deliberately dumped clay soil with a 'background' content of seeds is a reasonable interpretation.

Context 1048 (pit fill in 1049):

Sample 41 [Mf.3 A10–11] A few fragments of mammal and fish bone were recorded, with charcoal, seeds (mainly of weeds) and a charred bread/club wheat grain.

Context 961 (stained layer):

Sample 104 [Mf.3 A11] Similar to 1048, with small quantities of building debris and slag. A few seeds of elderberry were also recovered.

Phase 3B (later 13th century)

Samples from Phase 3B were drawn from pits at the end of a second timber hall, and as with Phase 3A were intended to clarify their function.

Context 994 (trench/pit fill):

Sample 121 [Mf.3 A11] No action was taken after bulk-sieving and paraffin flotation of a sample. Building debris was abundant, and traces of charcoal, bone and mussel shell were present. A sub-sample was examined for parasite ova, but none was noted.

Context 953 (ashy pit fill):

Sample 113 Waterlogged, soft, sticky, gritty clay silt.

A 15kg sample of sediment was bulk-sieved. Stone (mainly chalk), charcoal and root moulds were abundant in the residue, with some mortar or plaster, a few fragments of calcined mammal and fish bone, snails, oyster shell and avian eggshell. The washover contained abundant charcoal and very small root channels, with trace amounts of charred bread/club wheat grain, elderberry seed and snails. The assemblage of snails from this sample was too small to be of interpretative value.

Two *Trichuris* ova were recorded from the 6g sub-sample examined; this is barely evidence for the presence of faeces, unless this kind of material was present in very small amounts through low input, or because only very little had survived decay processes.

Phase 3C (later 13th century)

Floor silt deposits associated with the second timber hall are considered to be associated with its later occupation. They were sampled to elucidate the character of this occupation.

Context 807 (floor silt — in timber hall):

Sample 122 [Mf.3 A11]

Context 1043 (floor silt (sweepings) — outside timber hall):

Sample 40 [Mf.3 A11]

Context 1078 (floor silt (sweepings) — outside timber hall):

Sample 135 [Mf.3 A11]

All three samples included small building debris — brick or tile, mortar, or plaster — and charcoal. Mammal and fish bone, and fragments of snail and oyster shell and avian eggshell were present in the sample from within the hall, while external deposits also included hazelnut shells and amphibian bone.

Phase 4 (?14th century onwards)

Samples from Phase 4 were taken from contexts relating to waste and water management at the Priory (the latrine or *reredorter*, and a cistern).

Context 1095 (latrine/conduit fill — ?16th century):

Sample 129 (no description made after sampling).

A 12kg sample was bulk-sieved. The residue from this consisted mainly of stone (mostly chalk), mortar or plaster and charcoal. Brick or tile, fragments of twigs, coal, hazelnut shell fragments, a sloe (*Prunus spinosa*) fruitstone, and fragments of mammal and fish bone, oyster shell and avian eggshell were also present. The very small washover was mainly charcoal. There was thus only very limited evidence for the nature of the fill.

Context 1109 (cistern/water tank fill — 14th century)):

Sample 45 Wet, gritty, grey silt, with chalk rubble and peaty lumps, ?similar to samples from 1106 in appearance.

Bulk-sieving was carried out on 31.5kg of sediment. Oyster shell was abundant in the residue (this was extracted before sorting for plant remains and is not recorded in large amounts in the list in Table 19), as was charcoal, with modest amounts of amorphous peat, earthworm egg capsules, eggshell fragments and fish bone. The assemblage of seeds was dominated by weed taxa, but with wetland plants (probably from the peat), and traces of hempseed and fig. Domestic refuse clearly formed a considerable proportion of the deposit, and this may have included the peat (which may have been imported for fuel), though the exact nature of its use remains uncertain.

Context 1106 (cistern/water tank fill — 14th century)):

Sample 6 Moist, crumbly, black silt.

A 23kg sample was bulk-sieved and both residue and washover sorted for plant remains. The bulk of the residue comprised amorphous peat fragments with a small range of plant taxa including bogbean and marsh pennywort (see below).

Sample 120 Dark brown, moist, crumbly, with ?lumps of peat in grey-brown humic silt matrix, ?wood fragments present. Contaminated by modern algae.

Bulk-sieving was carried out on about 12kg of sediment. The main component in the residue was amorphous peat. Chalk gravel and oyster shell were also abundant. Small amounts of brick or tile, mortar or plaster, charcoal, worm egg capsules, and mammal and fish bone were recorded. Seeds were abundant in the washover, and most of these were of bogbean (*Menyanthes trifoliata*) and marsh pennywort (*Hydrocotyle vulgaris*), together with other taxa of fen/marsh habitats likely to have derived from the fen peat that formed such a large component of the fill. Why this should be so is difficult to explain unless the cistern was simply being used for the disposal of waste. There is some similarity here with a context from the Gilbertine Priory at Fishergate, York (Kemp forthcoming): there, amorphous peat formed a large proportion of layer 4188 (interpreted as a dump from robbing the lining of a drain or pit and dated to the mid. to late 14th century).

A 1kg sub-sample diagaggregated gave essentially the same range of taxa, though it was possible to look at each fraction only very cursorily. Peat fragments again formed a major component of the residue.

Sample 140 Wet, dark-brown organic silt with abundant oyster shells.

The residue from a bulk-sieved sample of 35kg contained rather large numbers of bogbean and marsh pennywort seeds and sedge nutlets, with some other aquatic or wetland taxa and large amounts of peat, as in the previous samples from this context.

Context 1107 (water tank/cistern fill — 14th century):

Sample 132 (not described prior to processing).

A total of 30kg of sediment was bulk-sieved. Oyster shell, chalk stones, peat fragments, faecal concretions and brick/tile fragments were abundant in the residue. Charcoal, seeds (including substantial quantities of *Menyanthes trifoliata* and sedges), moss, plant debris, mammal and fish bones, and avian eggshell were present. The washover contained abundant plant debris, and smaller quantities of wood, charcoal, seeds, moss, and insects. It may be significant that this uppermost part of the organic fill of the cistern contained faecal concretions; what had previously perhaps been a water tank, had evidently become a repository for waste.

Phase 5A (early 14th century)

Phase 5A little cloister deposits sampled included occupation horizons and material laid down as make-up in the course of construction work. The most useful information thus retrieved is considered below (section 4.3) with the animal and fish bone of the site.

Context 110 (floor silt — east chamber of little cloister north range):

Sample 37 Moist, very gritty, brown, silty sand.

A 19kg sample was bulk-sieved. The residue contained abundant mortar or plaster, chalk and other stones, and clinker. Fish bones, brick or tile fragments, and coal were fairly abundant, with smaller quantities of mammal and bird bone, snails and avian eggshell. The washover was of charcoal and clinker, with a small amount of wood and fairly abundant snails. Neither fraction was investigated in detail for plant remains.

The presence of small numbers of freshwater and semi-aquatic snail taxa suggests some input of waterside vegetation, which would have provided a good habitat for colonisers such as *Trichia* spp., *Cochlicopa lubrica* and *Discus rotundatus*.

Context 893 (dump/levelling in alley, little cloister):

Samples 106, 111 [Mf.3 A11] Traces of charred wheat and charcoal were considered likely to have been from ash incorporated into the make-up. This material was comparable with that from Phase 1 pits (see above) which are considered to have been cut by the excavation of construction trenches in Phase 5A, the spoil being used as make-up along the cloister alley (see Chapter 2, the north range footings).

Phase 5B (mid. 14th century)

Phase 5B construction and occupation deposits were sampled. As with Phase 5A, significant assemblages of animal bone and fish bone were recovered, discussed below (section 4.3).

Context 867 (construction level — west chamber of little cloister north range):

Sample 38 Moist, brown silty clay, with plaster and red mortar.

Bulk-sieving was carried out on 31.5kg of sediment. Chalk pebbles and mortar were abundant in the residue. Brick/tile, slag, mammal, fish and bird bone, snails, shell and avian eggshell were also present. The washover was mainly charcoal fragments, but also contained some snails. The small snail assemblage consisted of typical urban taxa. No plant remains other than charcoal were recovered during 'rough-sorting'.

Sample 867 (no description made prior to disaggregation).

A sample of 18kg of sediment was bulk-sieved. The residue contained brick or tile, stone, slag, wood, charcoal, charred grain, bone and shell.

Context 754 (floor silt — accumulation associated with hearth — west chamber of the little cloister north range):

Sample 754 Mid-brown, moist, plastic-crumbly, sandy, silty, clay, with chalk pebbles and bone fragments as common inclusions. ?Mortar and ash also present.

Bulk-sieving was carried out on 57.5kg of sediment. The residue contained brick or tile, stone, coal, iron slag, charcoal, bones, shell and avian eggshell. Many of the bones were stained green (?from copper alloy melt in context 796).

A 5kg 'test' sub-sample was processed by paraffin flotation in the laboratory. The small flot contained a thrip (Thysanoptera) and an aphid, both of which were modern contaminants, a mallard femur fragment, several earthworm egg capsules, a rotted mite, an unidentifiable beetle fragment and a small snail assemblage (21 individuals). The following species of snail were recorded: *Caecilioides acicula* (15 individuals), two *Carychium* species (probably one each of *C. tridentatum* and *C. minimum*), and single individuals of *Cochlicopa lubrica*, *Discus rotundatus*, *Trichia* cf. *hispida* and *Oxychilus alliarius*. *C. acicula* is a burrowing species and must be assumed to be intrusive. The other species are typical of the urban 'background' fauna, although the *Carychium* species suggest a wet pasture or swamp habitat.

The only plant remains, other than charcoal, were trace amounts of corn gromwell, *Buglossoides arvensis*, a weed of arable land.

Context 796 (floor silt — west chamber of little cloister north range):

Sample 796 [Mf.3 A12] As noted above, copper alloy melt may have contributed to staining of bone in this area.

Context 772 (floor silt — west chamber of little cloister north range):

Sample 772 [Mf.3 A12] A similar residue to that from Context 754, with the addition of ?slag, nutshells and a ?coprolite. No plant remains other than nutshell were available for examination.

Context 2009 (floor silt — east chamber of little cloister north range):

Samples 52, 79, 89, 100 [Mf.3 A12] These samples included brick or tile, coke or clinker, mortar or plaster, as well as mammal, bird and fish bone, shellfish and avian eggshell. It is noted of Sample 100 that it is rather surprising that so much burnt material was present in the sample without identifiable charred plant remains also being recorded. Snails were abundant throughout, and are discussed below.

Sample 101 [Mf.3 A12] Similar to those described above, though with more chalk pieces. Oyster and mussel were identified among the shellfish.

Sample 92009 Mid. grey-brown, moist, plastic-crumbly, slightly sandy, silty clay, with some bone and mortar fragments.

An estimated 30kg of sediment was bulk-sieved but not examined further. A 1kg 'test' sub-sample was processed by paraffin flotation. A worm capsule and an unidentifiable beetle fragment were present in the flot. There was also modern fly contamination. Plant remains were restricted to two weed taxa, though there was a range of evidence for occupation debris in the residue. A 6g sub-sample was examined for parasite ova, but none was found.

The snails from context 2009:

The five snail assemblages from this context were very similar, and gave an intriguing mixture of taxa. A synanthropic element such as might have lived in and around a stone building included *Trichia* spp., *Discus rotundatus*, and *Oxychilus alliarius*. In addition, there was also an obvious freshwater component (*Theodoxus fluviatilis*, *Valvata piscinalis*, *Bithynia tentaculata*, *Aplexa hypnorum*, *Lymnaea* spp., *Anisus leucostoma*, *Planorbarius corneus*, *Oxyloma pfeifferi*), comprising taxa which are typical of a range of conditions from flowing water to muddy pond margins. There was also a grassland association (*Vallonia* spp., *Pupilla muscorum*, *Vertigo pygmaea*), the presence of *Vallonia costata* suggesting dryish, turfy grassland. If this deposit truly accumulated during the use of the north range, and was not merely a dump of mixed origins, then it seems likely that the mollusca came into the deposit with vegetation brought in for fuel or floor covering. If so, then two main sources are indicated: a swampy marsh such as might have been cut for reeds, and a drier, tussocky grassland, perhaps used as a source of hay.

Context 2046 (floor silt — east chamber of little cloister north range):

Sample 81 [Mf.3 A12] Similar components to those recorded in Context 2009.

Context 2053 (patching — floor in east chamber of little cloister north range)

Similar components to those recorded in Context 2009, with the addition of burnt clay. The snail assemblage was very much like those from Context 2009.

Sample 88 Moist, dark grey, brown and orange heterogeneous silty clays (?burnt). Similar material to that from Context 2009, with a little coal and prominent charcoal. The snail assemblage was very much like those from Context 2009.

Context 2054 (floor silt ash — east chamber of little cloister north range):

Similar to Context 2053.

Sample 96 Moist, gritty, brown silt with orange-red (?burnt) clay inclusions. Again, the snail assemblage was very much like those from Context 2009.

Phase 5C (later 14th century)

As with the preceding phases of little cloister occupation, the mammal and fish bone recovered by sieving proved a useful component of samples drawn from occupation deposits.

Context 3092 (floor silt — west chamber of little cloister north range):

Sample 80 Moist, light grey-brown silty sand with abundant chalk grit inclusions.

A 30kg sample was bulk-sieved. Mortar or plaster, chalk and other stone, coal, and coke or clinker were abundant in the residue, with smaller quantities of brick or tile, charcoal, mammal, bird and fish bone, snails, oyster and mussel shell fragments, and avian eggshell. The washover was mainly clinker and charcoal. Snails were plentiful, and a few fragments of mammal and fish bone were present.

The snail assemblage from this sample was dominated by *Trichia* spp., with taxa such as *Lauria cylindracea* and *Oxychilus cellarius* suggesting a habitat analogous to a damp stone wall. A dump of material containing brick, stone and clinker in a damp, probably abandoned, stone building might well have accumulated such a death assemblage.

Context 3051 (floor silt — west chamber of little cloister north range):

Sample 53 Dry, brown silt-like very fine sand, loose, only very slightly damp.

A sample of 15kg of sediment was bulk-sieved. Mortar or plaster and stone (mainly chalk) were the major components in the residue. There were smaller amounts of brick or tile, coal, coke or clinker, slag, charcoal, mammal and fish bone, snails, shellfish and avian eggshell. The washover was mainly charcoal and contained snails.

Sample 95 Similar to Sample 53, with the addition of brick or tile.

The snails from Context 3051:

Samples 53 and 95 gave samples dominated by *Trichia* cf. *plebeia*, with small numbers of *Discus rotundatus*. This would indicate a short-lived, rather damp habitat, liable to disturbance.

Context 3006 (floor silt — west chamber of little cloister north range):

Sample 85 Moist, light grey-brown silt with abundant chalk grit inclusions.

A 12kg sample was bulk-sieved. The residue consisted chiefly of brick or tile, mortar or plaster, stone, and charcoal. Fish bone was also plentiful. Smaller quantities of slag, mammal bone, and snails were present. The washover from the bulk-sieving was mainly charcoal with fairly abundant snails, some shellfish fragments, and avian eggshell. The snail assemblage was small, and dominated by *Trichia* cf. *plebeia*.

Context 3111 (floor silt — from structure at west end of little cloister north range):

Sample 84 Moist reddish-brown silt with chalk gravel inclusions.

A sample of 6kg of sediment was bulk-sieved; the washover yielded trace amounts of blackberry (*Rubus fruticosus* agg.) seeds and modest amounts of charcoal and snails, with some coal and fish bone.

Context 3052 (floor silt — from structure at west end of little cloister north range):

Sample 130 Similar to Context 3006 above.

Context 3010 (floor silt — from structure at west end of little cloister north range):

Sample 94 Moist, brown and grey-brown very heterogeneous silts, with abundant chalk gravel inclusions.

Bulk-sieving was carried out on 21kg of sediment. The residue was mainly chalk and mortar or plaster. Some brick or tile, coal, clinker, charcoal, mammal, fish and bird bone, snails, shellfish and avian eggshell were also present. The washover was mostly clinker and charcoal, but snails were also present. The snail assemblage was of typical urban taxa.

Context 3020 (floor silt — from structure at west end of little cloister north range):

Sample 93 Moist, light brown silt with abundant chalk grit inclusions.

An 11kg sample was bulk-sieved. Stone (mainly chalk), brick or tile, mortar or plaster, clinker or coke were more abundant in the residue, and fish bone was also well represented. There were smaller quantities of mammal bone, coal, snails, shellfish, avian eggshell, and a fossil. The washover was mainly coke or clinker. The snail assemblage was too small for comment.

Context 3053 (floor silt — structure at west end little cloister north range):

Sample 98 Wet, heterogeneous, brownish-red and light brown silts with abundant chalk grit inclusions.

A sample of 35kg of sediment was bulk-sieved. The washover yielded traces of several weed species, charred barley, and blackberry. There were more snails.

Phase 6A

Floor silts within the Phase 6A building were sampled in order to determine its function; the most useful component of these deposits was again the mammal, fish and bird bone.

Context 944 (floor silt — great cloister ?refectory):

Sample 35 Wet, gritty, brown silt.

Bulk-sieving was carried out on 26.5kg of sediment. Brick or tile, mortar or plaster, stone (mainly chalk), clinker, and mammal bone were abundant in the residue, with smaller quantities of coal, fish and bird bone, snails, shellfish and avian eggshell. Clinker and charcoal were the principal components of the washover, and snails were fairly abundant.

Discus rotundatus and *Trichia* cf. *plebeia* were much the most abundant of the snails, with other taxa similarly indicative of damp conditions.

Phase 7

Samples from Phase 7 were drawn from the material

filling the latrine or *reredorter* conduit. This was considered at the time of excavation to be unassociated with its use.

Context 1092 (conduit fill):

Sample 117 Wet, mid-dark reddish- brown silty chalk grit.

A sample of 23kg was bulk-sieved. The washover yielded traces of hemlock (*Conium maculatum*) fruits and seed fragments of *Sambucus*, probably elderberry. They offer no evidence about the nature of the deposit.

Context 1093 (conduit fill):

Sample 133 (not described prior to disaggregation; excavators' description is 'sand and rubble'. A further sample (44) was described as 'wet, brown sand with abundant chalk and tile'.)

A 37kg sample was bulk-sieved and the washover yielded quite a large list of taxa, including traces of hempseed and moderate numbers of fig and elderberry seeds, and a range of taxa including weeds, plants of scrub/hedgerow (including buds and/or scales of several trees and leaf epidermis fragments of holly, *Ilex aquifolium*), and moderate numbers of leaves of bog moss, *Sphagnum imbricatum* — a species typical of raised-bog peats (see above). Remains of woody plants are often an indication of deposition in a ditch under or near a hedge or area of scrub, though it is possible that the material in this context is secondarily derived from, for example imported brushwood.

Conduit 1094 (conduit fill):

Sample 138 (not described prior to disaggregation; excavators' description: 'loose sand').

A sample of 22kg of sediment was bulk-sieved. The residue was mainly chalk and brick or tile, with smaller quantities of mortar or plaster, coal, slag, mammal bone, mussel and oyster shell, and avian eggshell. Wood, charcoal, hazelnut shells, fruit stones of *Prunus spinosa*, fish bone, leather, and snails were all represented by a few fragments. Plant remains examined from the washover and the 'rough-sorted' residue included woody taxa (as in sample 133), fig and several weeds. The presence of pondweed, *Potamogeton* sp(p). in isolation, is probably not good evidence for standing or slow-moving water in the conduit; the fig seeds might be domestic waste (?faecal), though there is no supporting evidence for this.

Phase 8

Phase 8 comprised the fragmentary record of activity post-dating the close of Dominican occupation on the site.

Context 3110 (floor silt — post-medieval structure in area of little cloister):

Sample 55 Moist grey silt.

Bulk-sieving was carried out on 15.5kg of sediment. Chalk and other stones, brick or tile, coke or clinker, and mortar or plaster made up the bulk of the residue. A few fragments of coal, burnt daub, mammal and fish bone, snails, shell, avian eggshell, and mica were also present. The washover from the bulk-sieving consisted mainly of coke or clinker, but some snails were present.

Sample 102 Compact, mid-dark brown silty clay, with chalk grit, charcoal and brick or tile inclusions.

A sample of 19kg of sediment was bulk-sieved. Chalk and other stone, brick or tile, and coke or clinker were abundant in the residue. Mortar or plaster was also plentiful. Fragments of coal, slag, bone, snails, shell and a 'fossil' were present. The washover was mainly coke or clinker, and snails were fairly abundant.

The snail assemblages from Context 3110:

Samples 55 and 102 gave snail assemblages of low diversity, with *Oxychilus alliarius* particularly common. This facultative carnivore is often abundant in 'midden' deposits into which quantities of bone and shell have been incorporated.

Context 3055 (pit fill — little cloister area):

Sample 54 Moist, reddish brown silt with tile fragments.

A sample of 7kg of sediment was bulk-sieved; the small washover contained only scraps of charred organic material (not charcoal) and snails.

Summary

Activity attributed to Phase 1 related in part to the use or processing of crops, particularly cereals (oats, barley and wheat), though hemp may also have been cultivated. Where occupation material occurred, it was in association with debris perhaps cleared from a timber structure destroyed by fire (cf. section 5.2, Mf.3 E6–8). These deposits were subjected to only limited investigation, and produced no datable finds; an origin for them in an area peripheral to agricultural activity may be suggested.

Phase 2 included more material derived from occupation activity, including a heavily residual assemblage of pottery. This may argue that extensive movement of soils had taken place. It is debatable whether marsh and wetland species should be regarded as originating in this area, or whether they derived from the incorporation of peat into dumps of soil. The limited return of plant macrofossils from large sieved samples may indicate that these soils had been aerated by reworking prior to their deposition on this site.

The Phase 3 samples included a variety of wetland and weed species, with a proportion of occupation and structural debris compatible with the location of these contexts in a building. Neither in Phase 3A nor 3B did significant evidence for the use of pits as latrines occur, so the function of these features must remain obscure. The detection of concreted root moulds did, however, bear out the excavator's identification of panning within these features. The most prominent components of sieved residues from the pits comprised 'background' material derived from occupation. This material was similar in character to that from Phase 3C floor silts and sweepings, though a significant variation in the profile of skeletal material was noted between Phases 3B and 3C, and is discussed below (section 4.3).

Samples from both the base (Phase 4) and the infilling (Phase 7) of the latrine conduit or *reredorter* did not relate to its primary use; nor, for that matter, did samples examined from a nearby cistern. The secondary use of the cistern as an area for the disposal of peaty fuel debris, food preparation waste (see section 4.3 below), and faecal material must betoken its disuse, or a marked change in its function. It is uncertain, though likely, that the oyster shells common in its fill formed part of this deposit. These could alternatively have been associated with an earlier function as a live store for fish or shellfish.

Make-up deposits of Phase 5A incorporated material comparable with that identified in some of the Phase 1 pits, confirming that these soils derived from the cutting of footing trenches through early horizons. The subsequent occupation of the little cloister north range through sub-phases 5A to 5C was examined by extensive sampling of floor silts. The animal, fish and bird bone is considered below (section 4.3). The recovery of snails indicated an input of waterside vegetation — perhaps rushes spread on the floor — during Phase 5A; and the use of both rushes and hay for this purpose in Phase 5B. Both Phases 5B and 5C yielded snails typical of a habitat within a stone-walled building. Those from Phase 5C were considered to have accumulated in a damp, probably abandoned, stone building. This complements other evidence suggesting a diminished intensity of ground floor activity at this time. These damp conditions also obtained in the west end of the north range, where a short-lived occupation is suspected (see Chapter 2). Similar conditions were recorded in the ground floor of the Phase 6 great cloister north range, though in samples deriving from an area perhaps detached from the main chamber of that range.

No significant information was recorded relating to the post-medieval use of the area, save for the identification of 'midden' type deposits associated with floor silts in the vicinity of the former little cloister.

The area immediately west of the Dominican precinct, designated Trench 2, was the most productive area examined in 1986–7 for both plant and insect macrofossils. A sequence of gullies and pits here produced assemblages comparable with those examined from the Eastgate tenements, to which they may relate (McKenna 1992). The samples derived from contexts pre-dating the construction of the ?14th-century precinct wall, all lying on the south side of Trench 2.

The earliest features furnished evidence for water-filled features, with decaying organic and human faecal waste deposited nearby. Weld, woad and madder (all dyeplants prominent at Eastgate: McKenna 1992) were also present, as was flax. Invertebrate species suggested the proximity of buildings, or of waste including vegetation from their roofing or flooring. The proximity of scrub or hedges was also suggested.

A conduit bed, which post-dated these early features, yielded evidence for a ditch that was subject to both disturbance and fertilisation, as might have arisen with the grazing of livestock. The land through which this passed was apparently somewhat neglected and overgrown with perennial weeds; as such, it attracted an 'outdoor' assemblage of insects.

The formation of the conduit was followed by the digging of pits whose varying characteristics are held by the excavator to have denoted different functions. The fills of the shallower of the pits examined included sheep keds, heads from fullers' teasel, and abundant weld seeds and bog myrtle fragments, all suggesting an association with the processing of wool or cloth. A deeper pit included trace amounts of dyeplants, including dyer's greenweed, but there were also larger quantities of straw, bracken, peat, and spoilt grain (perhaps domestic or byre sweepings) which probably accumulated rapidly. Later shallow pits were likewise used for the disposal of domestic or grain preparation waste, perhaps betokening a change in the character of the occupation to which this area related. The precinct wall was erected after the sealing of these pits.

Table 18   Complete list of plant and invertebrate taxa from excavations at the Priory, in taxonomic order. Plant names follow Smith (1978) and Tutin *et al.* (1964–80), insects follow Kloet and Hincks (1964–77) and non-marine molluscs follow Kerney (1976). Note that 'indet.' indicates records which may include taxa already listed.

ALGAE
Chara sp(p).
MUSCI
Sphagnum sp(p).
S. imbricatum Hornsch. ex Russ.
Bryum capillare Hedw.
Plagiomnium cf. *affine* (Funck.) Kop.
Plagiomnium sp(p).
Antitrichia curtipendula (Hedw.) Brid.
Neckera complanata (Hedw.) Hüb.
Thuidium tamariscinum (Hedw.) Br. Eur.
Cratoneuron filicinum (Hedw.) Spruce
Cratoneuron commutatum (Hedw.) Roth
Campylium stellatum (Hedw.) Lange & Jens.
cf. *C. elodes* (Lindb.) Kindb.
Drepanocladus sp(p).
Scorpidium scorpioides (Hedw.) Limpr.
Calliergon giganteum (Schimp.) Kindb.
C. cuspidatum (Hedw.) Kindb.
Isothecium myosuroides Brid.
Homalothecium sericeum/lutescens
cf. *Brachythecium* sp(p).
Pseudoscleropodium purum (Hedw.) Fleisch
Eurhynchium striatum (Hedw.) Schimp.
Hypnum cupressiforme Hedw.
cf. *Rhytidiadelphus triquetrus* (Hedw.) Warnst.
R. squarrosus (Hedw.) Warnst.
PTERIDOPHYTA
Filicales (fern)
Pteridium aquilinum (L.) Kuhn (bracken)
ANGIOSPERMAE
Salix sp(p). (willow)
Populus sp(p). (poplar/aspen)
Myrica gale L. (bog myrtle/sweet gale)
Betula sp(p). (birch)
B. cf. *pendula* Roth. (?silver birch)
Corylus avellana L. (hazel)
Quercus sp(p). (oak)
Ficus carica L. (fig)
Cannabis sativa L. (hemp)
Urtica dioica L. (stinging nettle)
U. urens L. (annual nettle)
Polygonum aviculare agg. (knotgrass)
P. hydropiper L. (water-pepper)
P. persicaria L. (persicaria/red shank)
P. lapathifolium L. (pale persicaria)
Bilderdykia convolvulus (L.) Dumort. (black bindweed)
Rumex acetosella agg. (sheep's sorrel)
Rumex sp(p). (docks)
Chenopodium Section *Pseudoblitum* (red goosefoot etc.)
C. polyspermum L. (all-seed)
C. album L. (fat hen)
Atriplex sp(p). (oraches)
Arenaria serpyllifolia L. (thyme-leaved sandwort)
Moehringia trinervia (L.) Clairv. (three-nerved sandwort)
Stellaria media (L.) Vill. (chickweed)
S. cf. *neglecta* Weihe in Bluff & Fingerh. (?greater chickweed)
S. graminea L. (lesser stitchwort)
Cerastium sp(p). (mouse-ear chickweeds)
Scleranthus annuus L. (annual knawel)
Spergula arvensis L. (corn spurrey)
Lychnis flos-cuculi L. (ragged robin)
Agrostemma githago L. (corncockle)
Silene vulgaris (Moench) Garcke (bladder campion)
S. vulgaris ssp. *maritima* (With.) A. & D. Löve (sea campion)
S. alba (Miller) Krause in Sturm (white campion)
Caltha palustris L. (marsh marigold)
Ranunculus Section *Ranunculus* (meadow/creeping/bulbous buttercup)
R. sardous Crantz (hairy buttercup)
R. sceleratus L. (celery-leaved crowfoot)
R. flammula L. (lesser spearwort)
R. cf. *lingua* L. (greater spearwort)
R. Subgenus *Batrachium* (water crowfoots)
Ranunculus sp(p). (buttercups, etc.)
Thalictrum flavum L. (common meadow rue)
Papaver somniferum L. (opium poppy)
P. dubium L. (long-headed poppy)
P. argemone (long prickly-headed poppy)
Papaver sp(p). (poppies)
Fumaria sp(p). (fumitories)
Isatis tinctoria L. (woad)
Rorippa islandica (Oeder) Borbás (northern marsh yellow-cress)
Brassica rapa L. (turnip)
B. cf. *nigra* (L.) Koch in Röhling (?black mustard)
Brassica sp./*Sinapis arvensis* (brassica/charlock)
Brassica sp(p) (cabbages, etc.)
cf. *Sinapis arvensis* L. (?charlock)
Raphanus raphanistrum L. (wild radish)
Reseda luteola L. (weld/dyer's rocket)
Filipendula ulmaria (L.) Maxim. (meadowsweet)
Rubus idaeus L. (raspberry)
R. fruticosus agg. (blackberry/bramble)
R. cf. *caesius* L. (?dewberry)
Rubus/Rosa sp(p). (blackberry, etc./rose)
Rosa sp(p). (roses)
Potentilla palustris (L.) Scop. (marsh cinquefoil)
P. anserina L. (silverweed)
P. cf. *erecta* (L.) Räuschel (?tormentil)
P. cf. *reptans* L. (?creeping cinquefoil)
Fragaria vesca L. (wild strawberry)
Malus sylvestris Miller (crab apple)
Crataegus monogyna Jacq. (hawthorn)
Prunus spinosa L. (sloe)
P. domestica ssp. *domestica* (plums, etc.)
P. Section *Cerasus* (cherries)
Prunus sp(p). (sloe/plum/cherry, etc.)
Leguminosae (pea family)
Genista tinctoria L. (dyer's greenweed)
Vicia hirsuta (L.) S.F. Gray (hairy tare)
V. faba L. (field bean)

Vicia sp(p). (vetches, etc.)
cf. *Pisum* sp(p). (?peas)
cf. *P. sativum* L. (?garden/field pea)
Medicago lupulina L. (black medick)
Linum usitatissimum L. (cultivated flax)
L. catharticum L. (purging flax)
Euphorbia helioscopia L. (sun spurge)
E. peplus L. (petty spurge)
Ilex aquifolium L. (holly)
Viola sp(p.) (violets/pansies, etc.)
Umbelliferae (carrot family)
Hydrocotyle vulgaris L. (marsh pennywort)
Anthriscus sylvestris (L.) Hoffm. (cow parsley)
A. caucalis Bieb. (bur chevil)
Scandix pecten-veneris L. (shepherd's needle)
Berula erecta (Hudson) Coville (narrow-leaved
    water-parsnip)
Oenanthe lachenalii C.G. Gmelin (parsley water-dropwort)
cf. *Oe. aquatica* (L.) Poiret in Lam. (?fine-leaved
    water-dropwort)
Oenanthe sp(p). (water-dropworts)
Aethusa cynapium L. (fool's parsley)
Conium maculatum L. (hemlock)
Apium graveolens L. (wilde celery)
A. nodiflorum (L.) Lag. (fool's watercress)
Peucedanum ostruthium (L.) Koch (master-wort)
cf. *Daucus carota* L. (?wild carrot)
Menyanthes trifoliata L. (bogbean)
Galium aparine L. (goosegrass, cleavers)
Galium sp(p). (bedstraws, etc.)
Rubia tinctorum L. (dyer's madder)
Buglossiodes arvensis (L.) I.M. Johnston (corn gromwell)
Marrubium vulgare L. (white horehound)
Galeopsis Subgenus *Ladanum* (hemp-nettle)
G. Subgenus *Galeopsis* (hemp-nettles)
Lamium Section *Lamiopsis* (annual dead-nettles)
Stachys cf. *sylvatica* L. (?hedge woundwort)
S. cf. *arvensis* L. (?field woundwort)
Stachys sp(p). (woundworts)
Nepeta cataria L. (cat-mint)
Prunella vulgaris L. (selfheal)
Lycopus europaeus L. (gipsywort)
Mentha (sp(p). (mints)
Hyoscyamus niger L. (henbane)
Solanum nigrum L. (black nightshade)
S. dulcamara L. (woody nightshade)
Pedicularis palustris L. (marsh lousewort)
Rhinanthus sp(p). (yellow rattles)
Sambucus cf. *ebulus* L. (?danewort)
S. nigra L. (elder)
Sambucus sp(p). (elder, etc.)
Valerianella dentata (L.) Pollich (narrow-fruited cornsalad)
Valerianella sp(p). (cornsalads)
Dipsacus sativus (L.) Honckeny (fuller's teasel)
Anthemis cotula L. (stinking mayweed)
Achillea millefolium L. (yarrow)
Chrysanthemum segetum L. (corn marigold)
Senecio sp(p). (groundsels/ragworts, etc.)
Arctium sp(p). (burdocks)
Carduus/Cirsium sp(p). (thistles)
Centaurea sp(p). (knapweeds, etc.)
Hypochoeris sp(p). (cat's ears)
Leontodon sp(p). (hawkbits)
cf. *Picris hieracioides* L. (?hawkweed ox-tongue)

Sonchus asper (L.) Hill (prickly sow-thistle)
S. oleraceus L. (sow-thistle)
S. arvensis L. (corn sow-thistle)
Taraxacum sp(p). (dandelions)
Lapsana communis L. (nipplewort)
Alisma sp(p). (water-plantains)
Triglochin maritima L. (sea arrowgrass)
Potamogeton sp(p). (pondweeds)
Juncus inflexus/effusus/conglomeratus (hard/soft/compact
    rush)
J. gerardi Loisel. (saltmarsh rush)
J. bufonius L. (mud rush)
J. cf. *acutiflorus* Ehrh. ex Hoffm. (?sharp-flowered rush)
J. cf. *articulatus* L. (?jointed rush)
Juncus sp(p). (rushes)
Luzula sp(p). (woodrushes)
Gramineae (grasses)
Gramineae/Cerealia (grasses/cereals)
Cerealia indet. (cereals)
cf. *Poa annua* L. (?annual meadow-grass)
Glyceria sp(p). (sweet-grasses)
Triticum aestivo-compactum (bread/club wheat)
Triticum sp(p). (wheats)
Triticum/Secale (wheat/rye)
Triticum/Hordeum sp(p). (wheat and/or barley)
cf. *Secale cereale* L. (?rye)
Hordeum sp(p). (barley)
Avena fatua L. (wild oat)
A. sativa L. (cultivated oat)
Avena sp(p). (oats)
cf. *Alopecurus* sp(p). (?foxtails)
Danthonia decumbens (L.) DC. in Lam. & DC. (heath grass)
Cyperaceae (sedge family)
Scirpus maritimus/lacustris (sea club-rush/bulrush)
Scirpus lacustris sl (bulrush)
Eleocharis palustris sl (common spike-rush)
Cladium mariscus (L.) Pohl (great sedge/saw-sedge)
Schoenus nigricans L. (bog-rush)
Carex sp(p). (sedges)
NEMATODA
Ascaris sp(p).
Trichuris trichiura (L.)
Trichuris sp(p). indet.
ANNELIDA
Oligochaeta sp. (egg capsule)
CRUSTACEA
CLADOCERA
Daphnia sp. (ephippium)
Ceriodaphnia sp. (ephippium)
Cladocera sp. indet.
OSTRACODA
Ostracoda sp.
INSECTA
DERMAPTERA
Dermaptera sp.
MALLOPHAGA
Trichodectidae sp.
SIPHUNCULATA
Siphunculata sp.
MALLOPHAGA OR SIPHUNCULATA
Louse (s.l.) sp.
THYSANOPTERA
Thysanoptera sp.
HEMIPTERA

Lygaeidae sp.
Anthocoris sp.
Lyctocoris campestris (Fabricius)
Miridae sp.
?Saldula sp.
Heteroptera sp.
Heteroptera sp. (nymph)
Auchenorhyncha spp.
Trioza urticae (Linnaeus)
Aphidoidea sp.
Coccoidea sp.
Hemiptera sp. (nymph)
TRICHOPTERA
Trichoptera sp.
COLEOPTERA
Loricera pilicornis (Fabricius)
Trechus obtusus Erichson or *quadristriatus* (Schrank)
Bembidion lampros (Herbst)
Bembidion spp.
Pterostichus sp.
Carabidae spp.
Hydroporinae sp.
Colymbetinae sp.
Anacaena sp.
Helophorus spp.
Sphaeridium bipustulatum Fabricius
Cercyon analis (Paykull)
C. atricapillus (Marsham)
C. haemorrhoidalis (Fabricius)
C. ?quisquilius (Linnaeus)
C. terminatus (Marsham)
C. ustulatus (Preyssler)
Cercyon sp. indet.
Cryptopleurum minutum (Fabricius)
Hydrobius fuscipes (Linnaeus)
Chaetarthria seminulum (Herbst)
Hydrophilinae sp.
Histerinae sp.
Histeridae sp. indet.
Ochthebius minimus (Fabricius)
Ochthebius sp. indet.
Ptenidium sp.
Acrotrichis spp.
Silpha atrata Linnaeus
Scydmaenus tarsatus Müller and Kunze
Micropeplus fulvus Erichson
Micropeplus sp. indet.
Olophrum sp.
Lesteva longoelytrata (Goeze)
Lesteva sp. indet.
Dropephylla sp.
Omalium excavatum Stephens
O. caesum Gravenhorst or *italicum* Bernhauer
O. ?rivulare (Paykull)
Omalium spp. indet.
Xylodromus concinnus (Marsham)
Xylodromus sp. indet.
Omaliinae sp.
Carpelimus bilineatus Stephens
C. ?corticinus (Gravenhorst)
C. elongatulus (Erichson)
C. fuliginosus (Gravenhorst)
C. pusillus (Gravenhorst)
Carpelimus sp. indet.

Aploderus caelatus (Gravenhorst)
Platystethus arenarius (Fourcroy)
P. degener Mulsant and Rey
P. nitens (Sahlberg)
Anotylus complanatus (Erichson)
A. nitidulus (Gravenhorst)
A. rugosus (Fabricius)
A. sculpturatus (Gravenhorst) groups
A. tetracarinatus (Block)
Anotylus sp. indet.
Oxytelus sculptus Gravenhorst
Stenus spp.
Lathrobium sp.
Paederinae sp.
Leptacinus sp.
Phacophallus parumpunctatus (Gyllenhal)
Gyrohypnus angustatus Stephens
G. fracticornis (Müller)
?Xantholinus sp.
Neobisnius sp.
Philonthus spp.
Philonthus or *Gabrius* sp.
Staphylininae spp. indet.
Tachyporus sp.
Tachinus laticollis Gravenhorst or *marginellus* (Fabricus)
Cilea silphoides (Linnaeus)
?Cordalia obscura (Gravenhorst)
Falagria caesa Erichson or *sulcatula* (Gravenhorst)
Falagria or *Cordalia* sp. indet.
Aleocharine spp.
Pselaphidae sp.
Aphodius spp.
Oxyomus sylvestris (Scopoli)
?Phyllopertha horticola (Linnaeus)
Clambus sp.
Cyphon sp.
Elateridae sp.
Anobium punctatum (Degeer)
Tipnus unicolor (Piller and Mitterpacher)
Ptinus fur (Linnaeus)
Ptinidae sp. indet.
Lyctus linearis (Goeze)
Brachypterus sp.
Monotoma longicollis (Gyllenhal)
M. picipes Herbst
Monotoma sp. indet.
Cryptophagus acutangulus (Gyllenhal)
C. scutellatus Newman
Cryptophagus spp.
Atomaria spp.
Ephistemus globus (Paykull)
Corylophus cassidoides (Marsham)
Orthoperus sp.
Mycetaea hirta (Marsham)
Lathridius minutus (Linnaeus) group
Enicmus sp.
Dienerella sp.
Corticaria ?punctulata Marsham
Corticaria spp.
Lathridiidae sp. indet.
Typhaea stercorea (Linnaeus)
Aglenus brunneus (Gyllenhal)
?Blaps sp.
Anthicus formicarius (Goeze)

A. formicarius or *floralis* (Linnaeus)
Gracilia minuta (Fabricius)
Cerambycidae sp.
Bruchus ?rufimanus Boheman
Donaciinae sp.
Phyllotreta nemorum (Linnaeus) group
Phyllotreta sp.
Halticinae spp.
Chrysomelidae sp.
Apion (Taenapion) urticarium (Herbst)
Apion spp.
Sitona lineatus (Linnaeus)
Sitophilus granarius (Linnaeus)
Bagous sp.
Notaris aethiops (Fabricius)
Ceutorhynchus contractus (Marsham)
Ceutorhynchus spp.
Rhinoncus sp.
Rhynchaenus foliorum (Müller)
Curculionidae sp. indet.
Coleoptera spp.
HYMENOPTERA
Proctotrupoidea sp.
Hymenoptera Parasitica sp.
DIPTERA
Bibionidae sp.
Syrphidae sp. (larval spiracular process)
Melophagus ovinus (Linnaeus)
Diptera spp. (adult)
Diptera spp. (puparium)
SIPHONAPTERA
Pulex irritans Linnaeus
Siphonaptera sp. indet.
Insecta sp. (larva)
ARACHNIDA
Aranae sp.
Acarina sp.
MOLLUSCA
Theodoxus fluviatilis (Linnaeus)

Valvata cristata Müller
V. piscinalis (Müller)
Bithynia tentaculata (Linnaeus)
B. leachii (Sheppard)
Aplexa hypnorum (Linnaeus)
Lymnaea truncatula (Müller)
L. palustris (Müller)
L. stagnalis (Linnaeus)
L. peregra (Müller)
Anisus leucostoma (Millet)
A. vortex (Linnaeus)
Bathyomphalus contortus (Linnaeus)
Planorbarius corneus (Linnaeus)
Oxyloma pfeifferi (Rossmässler)
Cochlicopa lubrica (Müller)
Vertigo sp.
V. antivertigo (Drap.)
V. pygmaea (Drap.)
Pupilla muscorum (Linnaeus)
Lauria cylindracea (da Costa)
Vallonia costata (Müller)
V. pulchella (Müller)
V. excentrica Sterki
Discus rotundatus (Müller)
Vitrea crystallina (Müller)
Nesovitrea hammonis Ström
Aegopinella nitidula (Drap.)
Oxychilus cellarius (Müller)
O. alliarius (Miller)
Zonitoides nitidus (Müller)
Limax sp(p).
Deroceras sp(p).
Cecilioides acicula (Müller)
Trichia cf. *plebeia* (Drap.)
T. cf. *hispida* (Linnaeus)
Cepea/Arianta sp(p).
Helix aspersa Müller
Pisidium personatum Malm
Ostrea edulis Linnaeus

4.3 The animal bones

by Roberta Gilchrist

with a contribution by Terry O'Connor

Summary

The report considers sieved and hand-collected bone from the 1986–7 excavations at the Priory. Issues pertinent to assemblages of bone from urban monastic sites are considered, in particular the sources of food supply and methods of waste disposal. The identified fragments were dominated by domestic species: cattle, sheep, pig and domestic fowl. Few species or fragments of wild bird or game were present. Eighteen species of fish were identified: these were mainly marine, with the cod fishes, herring and eel most numerous. The waste from the primary butchery of cattle was absent from the assemblage, suggesting that animals arrived as partially dressed carcasses. Concentrations of fish body waste and the small bones of domestic fowl and sheep were noted in certain areas of the site. It is suggested that this 'table waste' was allowed to accumulate close to living/eating areas. Similarities to secular sites in Beverley include the lists of species identified, their biometric details and methods of butchery, perhaps indicating that by the later medieval period some of Beverley's secular and monastic sites were sharing common urban market sources.

Introduction

Recent excavations at the Priory have yielded 5351 fragments of hand-collected bone, and 7670 recovered from bulk-sieving of selected soil samples. This report considers the identification and interpretation of the animal remains.

Certain objectives may be recognised as appropriate to the study of material derived from an urban monastic settlement. In particular, the social composition of the house and its specific religious aims may have determined the diet observed on the site. Members of mendicant communities were restricted in their consumption of meat, although these prohibitions were less strictly observed from the 14th century onwards. Consequently, a high proportion and range of bird and fish species might be expected to occur on the site. Houses of friars, however, were vowed to complete poverty, so that diversity of food sources or inclusion of unusual types may have been avoided deliberately. The recognition of religious observances in the animal bone assemblage is complicated by the unknown social composition of the house. Many friaries had a subsidiary, or little cloister constructed beyond the main cloister. Its function varied, but may have included industrial use as kitchens or workshops, or as accommodation for an infirmary, school, or guest house for secular visitors or paying lodgers. The observance of a specifically monastic diet, therefore, may have varied spatially across the site. In addition, adherence to a strict diet may have fluctuated over time. An attempt will be made to compare the composition of this particular assemblage with those from contemporary secular sites in the locality, and to determine the uniformity of the assemblage across spatial and temporal boundaries within the monastic precinct.

Very few excavated monastic sites have yielded large assemblages of animal bone. While the numbers of fragments considered here may seem insignificant in relation to many secular medieval urban sites, they are considerable in terms of urban monastic assemblages (O'Connor 1993). This rarity of recovery begs certain questions regarding the organisation of refuse disposal at monastic sites. The degree of order achieved in monastic routines, in addition to the constricted nature of friary sites, may have prompted a highly efficient programme of refuse collection and its disposal off-site. Sanitary provisions were made in the form of extensive systems of drainage. These were maintained in order to avoid the accumulation of refuse within the vicinity of the occupied area. Human waste, and the products of animal slaughter and butchery, and the remains of food preparation and table waste were disposed of systematically. This factor may affect the representativity of bone assemblages which have been excavated from within the area of the cloisters. Most bone-yielding contexts are dumps associated with construction and demolition activities. Few deposits represent actual monastic occupation layers. From this it may be deduced that waste was regularly collected and deposited away from the cloisters, perhaps even beyond the precinct walls.

Houses of the mendicant orders were prohibited from owning private property or estate property in the way that other monastic communities did. In contrast to the self-sufficient aims of rural monasteries, friars were obliged to subsist on the gifts and alms of benefactors. A house might cultivate a garden and keep an orchard, but they did not own lands away from the precinct until the latest phases of their occupation. The area within the precinct walls was generally only 2–2.5 hectares; at Beverley it was 1.8 hectares. It is not known to what extent friaries produced their own food or participated in raising, slaughtering and butchering animals. From the animal bone evidence it may be possible at least to determine whether animal food sources entered the precinct whole or partially processed, and to what extent the friary shared the food sources of the town.

A sample of floor silt material was examined after the production of the main body of the report. The numerous animal bones from this sample — drawn from Phase 5B — have not been included in the quantification of material from the excavation, though a note by Dr. Terry O'Connor considers the character and interpretation of this group.

The Excavations

Excavations at the Priory have shown that the final plan of the site consisted of buildings grouped around a main cloister to the north of the church, beyond which was a partial subsidiary cloister. The latter was a triangular area north of the main cloister. It was formed by two cloister walks initially separated from a triangular garth by an arcade. It is in this area to the north of the main cloister that recent excavations have concentrated. Contexts which yielded animal bone are associated with the north range of the main cloister and the secondary cloister to the north.

The earliest monastic occupation is associated with a mid.-to-late 13th-century timber building (Phase 3A), constructed in the area of the later subsidiary cloister. This structure may have provided temporary accommodation during the construction of the church and main cloister during the first half of the 13th century. The timber building was replaced by another (possibly aisled) structure in Phase 3B, perhaps with a stone-built cross-wing. Very late 13th/early 14th-century occupation of this structure (Phase 3C) was followed by its disuse, and possibly by horticultural use of the area (Phase 3D). In the early 14th century the area was redeveloped with the construction of a subsidiary cloister (Phase 5A). This consisted of a narrow west range and a larger, two-chambered north range, of which the west end may have incorporated an upper storey. The chambers of the north range may have functioned differently: the western chamber had an ornamental fireplace; the eastern chamber brick benches facing a central hearth. The range provided abundant deposits of small bones, and may have functioned as a Prior's lodge, infirmary *misericord*, or corrodian accommodation. It has been

suggested that a service area or ancillary accommodation at the west end of the north range was integral to its layout.

Access to the main cloister was by an alley running south. Modifications to the little cloister (Phases 5B/C) may have accompanied the construction of a substantial refectory (or *frater*) on the north side of the main cloister (Phase 6A). Support for this attribution of function may come from the integral footing protruding from its north wall, possibly supporting a wall-pulpit. The refectory may have been located on the ground floor, with storage facilities or a kitchen area at one end of the range. Following the construction work of the later 14th century (Phases 5C/6A), activity in the east chamber of the subsidiary cloister's north range became less intense. A water tank, perhaps pre-dating the refectory, lay beyond its north-west corner.

Hand-collected animal bone has been studied from a pre-Priory deposit of dark earth (plough soil or infill for construction), and layers derived from the construction, occupation and demolition of the little cloister and north range, in addition to post-medieval features. Of particular interest are those contexts which represent sequences of occupation. These include the 13th-century timber hall, 14th-century occupation of the little cloister, and the occupation of the north range of the main cloister.

The animal bone is generally well-preserved. Some material from Groups B, C and D (see Table 23 for an explanation of groups), associated with the timber building, were slightly more abraded in appearance. Only three contexts yielded burnt fragments of bone; these were all associated with the 13th-century occupation of the timber building. (A further small quantity of material identified as either clinker or burnt bone was also recovered from the west chamber of the little cloister north range, Phase 5B, group G). Two contexts attributed to 14th-century occupation of the little cloister contained bones stained green, which had presumably been in contact with objects of copper alloy.

Few contexts produced large assemblages of bone. The exceptions are dump deposits associated with the stripping of fixtures and the demolition of the little cloister (quantification group H). The identifiability of the hand-collected material varied, ranging from 52% to 94.2% of the total fragments considered in the quantification groups. Many of the unidentifiable fragments represent fragments of long bones of the major domesticates.

Method (Table 23)

For the purposes of quantification the animal bone assemblage has been considered in groups which respect the stratigraphic phase groups. Larger animal bone quantification groups (ABQ) have been formed which divide material according to spatial zones and their chronological phases, and activity sequences such as construction, occupation and demolition. Groups A–K refer to the little cloister area; L–P represent the main cloister; Q and R represent the occupation of the west end of the north range of the little cloister, the putative 'service area' (see Table 23 for summary of quantification groups). The animal bone quantification groups were formed with reference to the matrix groups of the Level III archaeology report. They respect, but do not always directly correspond with the division of the material by the final phase groups. For example, it was necessary to split Phase 6A into groups L and M, representing the construction of the north range of the great cloister, and its occupation, respectively. Similarly, the post-monastic activities, grouped as Phase 8, were split into robbing of buildings (I), post-medieval pits (J), and 19th and 20th century activity (K).

Quantification of the animal bone has been by a simple fragment count of hand-collected and sieved material. The small numbers of bones in any single context would make any calculation of minimum numbers of individuals fruitless. While this method of quantification is biased toward the bones of mature larger animals (particularly cattle), these biases may be recognised through reference to assemblages recovered by sieving.

Attempts to distinguish goat from sheep bones included the examination of post-cranial elements. In general, however, 'sheep' may include a small number of goat bones not easily recognisable as such.

Ageing of the material was approached through the recording of dental attrition of mandibles (after Grant 1982). Fusion of the epiphyses of long bones was also used to identify individuals, with fused elements from early, intermediate and late-fusing bones (after O'Connor 1984). These two methods of ageing have been used together to suggest approximate ages at death for the main domestic species.

Biometric data were collected wherever possible, and in accordance with von den Driesch (1976). From these data, it is sometimes possible to reconstruct ratios of the sex of the individuals represented in the assemblage.

Hand-collected bones

Species present and their occurrence (Tables 24–6)

The animal bone from all contexts was dominated by the bones of the major domesticates: cattle (*Bos* f. domestic), sheep (*Ovis* f. domestic) and pig (*Sus* f. domestic). Small numbers of fragments of horse (*Equus* f. domestic), deer (fallow, *Dama dama* and roe, *Capreolus capreolus*), dog (*Canis* f. domestic), cat (*Felis* f. domestic), hare (*Lepus europaeus*), rabbit (*Oryctolagus cuniculus)* and goat (*Capra* f. domestic) were also present (see Table 24).

Fragments of the bones of cattle were predominant in most of the groups examined for quantification. In certain notable exceptions, however, the bones of sheep were more numerous. These include the contexts considered as quantification groups F, G, M and Q. The proportion of fragments of sheep in these groups may be significant, since the groups constitute a large number of fragments (particularly F and G), and because the method of quantification may discriminate against the less robust sheep skeleton. Groups F, G, M and Q represent occupation layers of 14th and 15th century phase groups. Groups F and G derive from the east chamber of the north range of the little cloister; Q is composed of material from the west chamber of the same range; M is occupation of the north range of the great cloister. Fragments of cattle were more numerous in the groups that represent pre-Priory activity, Priory construction and demolition sequences and the 13th-century occupation of the timber hall. Pig was relatively well represented (*c*.10%) in groups reflecting pre-Priory activity and

Table 23　Animal bone quantification (ABQ) groups

	ABQ Groups	Activity Phase
A	Pre-Priory activity	1–2
B	Construction of timber hall	3A
C	13th/early 14th-century occupation of timber hall	3A,3B,3C
D	Very late 13th/early 14th-century occupation, post-dating hall	3D
E	Construction of little cloister	5A
F	Early to mid. 14th-century occupation of little cloister	5A
G	Occupation of little cloister, later 14th-century onwards	5B,5C
H	Stripping of little cloister	7
I	Robbing of north range building	8
J	Post-medieval pits	8
K	19th/20th-century activity	8
L	Construction of north range, great cloister	6A
M	Occupation of north range	6A
N	North range and cistern	4,6A
O	Latrine and fills	4–7
P	Demolition and robbing of north range	7–8
Q	Construction and occupation (west end of north range, little cloister)	5A,5B,5C
R	Post-Priory activity	8

	Cattle	Sheep	Pig	Horse	Deer	Dog	Cat	Hare	Rabbit	Goat	Bird	Fish	UFR	Total
A	38	11	23	1	1						2		30	106
B	22	14	7								5		5	53
C	34	17	6								4		33	94
D	32	23	24			1					8	6	41	135
E	239	116	80					1		1	41	3	302	783
F	55	79	64						3		136	71	242	650
G	86	138	80			1		3	1		152	38	331	830
H	444	276	172	5				1		2	76	16	680	1667
I	88	72	41			2					18	2	131	354
J	56	47	31								6	4	9	153
K	20	14	5			1					1	2	36	79
L	7	3	1								2		12	25
M	22	30	17								7	6	20	102
N	10	8	8	2			1						16	44
O	15	4	4							1			2	26
P	60	48	19			1			1	1	6	6	85	227
Q	6	7	1								15		14	43
R	19	19	13								5	1	15	72

5351

Table 24   Quantification of hand-collected bone fragments occurring in animal bone quantification groups

the construction and occupation of the little cloister.

Fragments of bird skeleton were present in all but two groups considered for quantification (N and O, both located to the north-west of the main cloister). They were particularly numerous in F, G and Q, representing 20.9%, 18.3% and 34.9% of the total number of hand-collected fragments. These groups, it may be recalled, contain mainly 14th and some 15th-century occupation of the little cloister north range east and west chambers. The highest percentage of bird fragments (34.9%) came from the west chamber.

Of the species of bird present on the site, domestic fowl (*Gallus* f. domestic) is predominant (see Table 25). In groups F and G, the largest assemblages considered, domestic fowl makes up 66.2% and 71.7% of the total number of fragments of bird. Other species exploited as food sources include (in decreasing order of occurrence) domestic goose (*Anser anser*), duck (*Anas platyrhynchos*), pigeon (*Columba livia*), jay (*Garrulus glandarius*) and pheasant (*Phasianus colchicus*). Non-food species

	Fowl	Goose	Duck	Pigeon	Jay	Pheasant	Rook	Raven	Blackbird	Marsh Harrier	UFR	Total
A	2											2
B	1										4	5
C	2	2										4
D	6	2										8
E	12	4	1	6	1	1					16	41
F	90	5	1								40	136
G	109	4	9			1					29	152
H	44	18	8	1			2	1	1	1	4	80
I	12	1				1						14
J	5	1										6
K											1	1
L	1	1										2
M	4		1								2	7
N	1										4	5
O												-
P	1	1	1								2	5
Q	11	1	1								1	15
R	4	1										5

488

Table 25   Quantification of hand-collected bird bone occurring in animal bone quantification groups

	saithe	cod	ling	haddock	plaice	UFR	total
D		4	1			1	6
E		1				2	3
F	1	9	1	3	2	55	71
G		10	2	1		25	38
H	1	6	1	2		6	16
I			1		1		2
J		3				1	4
K		2					2
M		4				2	6
P		2		2		2	6
R							
Total	2	41	6	8	3	95	155

Table 26   Quantification of hand-collected fish bone occurring in animal bone quantification groups (by fragment)

present include rook (*Corvus frugilegus*), raven (*Corvus corax*), blackbird (*Turdus merula*) and marsh harrier (*Circus aeruginosus*). The greatest range of species occurs in Group H, which is derived from demolition activity. In the occupation phases, a limited range of species (domestic fowl, goose and duck) occur in groups from the timber hall (13th century), little cloister and north range (14th and 15th century). Occurrences of fragments of duck bone are highest for groups M and Q, representing occupation of the north range of the great cloister, and the west chamber of the north range, little cloister, respectively.

Small numbers of fish bones were recovered by hand-collection (see Table 26). Relatively large numbers of fish bones came from Groups F and G (14th/15th-century occupation of the little cloister). The species present include saithe (*Pollachius virens*), cod (*Gadus morhua*), haddock (*Melanogramus aeglefinus*), ling (*Molva molva*), and plaice (*Pleuronectes platessa*). Cod bones were predominant in all groups containing fish remains.

Small quantities of oyster shell (*Ostrea edulis*) were recovered from contexts representing Phases 3–8. Larger numbers (over 30) were recorded from reworked fills associated with construction (E) and robbing activities (I, P), and from dumping linked to the final phases of monastic use (H). Considerable quantities were recovered from two phases of occupation: a 14th-century floor in the east chamber of the north range, little cloister (F), and later 14th-century occupation levels of the same area (G).

One non-edible mollusc was present in the hand-collected material: from Group F (14th-century occupation of the little cloister) came a shell of *Oxychilus cellarius*, a synanthropic, facultative carnivore which can be found near human habitation, particularly in damp, shady environments.

Two fragments of fossil belemnite (Upper Cretaceous) were incorporated into a large context which constituted the make-up and construction of the little cloister (Group E).

Ageing of individuals (Table 27)

Ageing according to stages of tooth wear provides more precise chronological ranges for attributing an age at slaughter than ageing according to fusion of epiphyses, which yields categories of juvenile, sub-adult, and adult (Table 27). The number of mandibles available for recording tooth attrition, however, was limited to nine cattle, ten sheep and seven pig, for the whole assemblage. Wherever possible, therefore, the two methods have been used together.

A single cattle mandible representing pre-Priory activity (Group A) may be aged at 5–6 years. From the construction layers of the timber hall (Group B) came a specimen aged 6–7 years; the fusion data confirm that a fully adult individual was present. From the very late 13th or early 14th century deposits post-dating the hall (Group D), a cattle mandible was aged 4–5 years at death; fusion data confirm that sub-adult specimens were present in the group. From Group E, the construction of the little cloister, came one individual aged 3–4 years, and two aged 4–5 years at death; fusion data suggest that some juveniles were present, but that mainly sub-adult beasts were represented. Groups I, J and Q each produced single cattle mandibles aged 4–5 years; fusion data for I and J suggest that mainly adult animals were present, with some sub-adult individuals. Fusion data from additional groups representing occupation (C, F, G) confirm only that sub-adult specimens were present. Data from Group M (occupation of the north range of the main cloister) indicate that the individuals present were juvenile when slaughtered.

Fusion data for sheep bones in Group A suggest that the individuals were at a sub-adult stage of development when they were killed. Data for Group C (occupation of the timber hall) indicate that a fully

	cattle			sheep				pig		
	early	intm.	late	early	intm.A	intm.B	late	early	intm. A/B	late
A	1/1			3/3		0/1	0/1			1/1
B			1/1	2/2						
C		1/1		2/2		2/2	1/1	2/2	1/1	
D		0/1	1/2	1/1						
E	0/3	5/6	0/5	8/8	2/2	2/3	0/1	4/4	0/1	1/4
F		1/1		1/1	2/2	1/5		0/1	0/4	1/3
G	1/1			1/1	1/2	9/10	1/1			3/3
H	6/6	3/4	5/17	33/35	5/10	12/21	16/16	2/2		6/8
I	2/2	1/1	2/3	3/3	5/5	2/2		1/3	0/1	4/5
J	3/3	2/2	7/11	1/1	5/5	4/4				2/3
K	3/3	1/3	1/2		1/1	1/1		0/1		
L										
M	1/1	0/1	0/1	2/2			0/2			
N		1/2	1/1			1/1				
O			0/1						1/1	
P	1/1	1/1	2/4	4/5	1/1	4/4	1/2			0/5
Q										
R		2/2	0/3		1/1	1/1	1/1			

* (after O'Connor 1984, 18)

Table 27   Proportions of fused epiphyses in the animal bone quantification groups (fused/total) *

adult individual was present. From Group E (construction of little cloister) come two mandibles, respectively aged at 2–2.5 years and 3 years at death; fusion data suggest animals were killed as sub-adults. Fusion data for Group F (earlier occupation of little cloister) show that the sheep were sub-adult at death. A mandible from Group G (later occupation) was aged 2–2.5 years; fusion data suggest that mature adults were present. Mandibles representing Group H (demolition) were aged 2–2.5 years (N=1) and 2.5–3 years (N=2); the considerable amount of fusion data indicates that both sub-adult and adult individuals were present. Groups I, N, Q, and R each yielded a single mandible aged 2.5–3 years; fusion data merely confirm that adults were included in the group. Fusion data for occupation sequences represented by Group M (north range of main cloister) suggest that animals were killed as sub-adults.

Pig mandibles from Groups A (N=2), E (N=2), and H (N=1) were aged at 3–4 years at death. Two additional mandibles from H were aged at 2–3 years. Evidence from the fusion of epiphyses indicates that some adults and juveniles were present, but that the majority of individuals represented were at a sub-adult stage in their development.

Results of the ageing indicate that the remains of cattle incorporated in construction material, and individuals consumed in the initial stages of monastic occupation, were fully adult. In later phases of use, juvenile, sub-adult and adult beasts were present. The majority of sheep and pig consumed were sub-adult,

prime meat specimens, although adult individuals were present.

Sexing of individuals

Biometric data for certain skeletal elements may sometimes be harnessed to provide profiles for the sex of domestic animals. Such a profile is useful in evaluating the importance of dairying as a criterion for keeping cattle, sheep and goats on a site, and for determining the composition of the breeding stock for herds kept by a community. The measurements of horn cores and long bones are particularly useful in this respect.

It is preferable to examine a large, well-defined assemblage (chronologically and stratigraphically). Only context 15 (quantification group H) yielded a large number of measurable bones. This context represents a dump deposited in the little cloister garth during demolition activities. Its origins and date are, therefore, not certain. From context 15, only the sample of sheep radii was considered complete enough for the possible detection of sexual differences. Plotting a measurement of the greatest length of sheep radii against minimum breadth of shaft (N=9) produced a fairly dense cluster, in which ewes, rams and wethers cannot be distinguished. Sexual differentiation within the breed may not have been particularly pronounced; alternatively, a single sexual group may be represented in the scattergram.

ABQ Group	species	no.	element	description
C,D	pig	1	vertebra	halved through axis
	sheep	1	atlas	halved through axis
E,F,G	sheep	1	humerus	trochlea chopped across the axis
	cattle	1	radius	chopped longitudinally from proximal
	pig	1	vertebra	chopped through long axis
	cattle	3	scapulae	chopped from base through axis of bone
	sheep	6	vertebrae	chopped through axis
	cattle	1	vertebra	chopped through axis
	pig	1	vertebra	chopped through axis
H	cattle	1	atlas	split longitudinally
	sheep	4	atlas	split longitudinally
	cattle	3	calcanea	chop-marks across shaft above distal
	cattle	6	astragali	chopped oblique to long axis
	sheep	1	pelvis	chopped through acetabulum
	cattle	1	femur	chopped across proximal
	sheep	5	vertebrae	chopped through long axis
	cattle	1	tibia	chopped longitudinally from proximal
	sheep	1	metapodial	chopped through axis from proximal
I,J,K	cattle	1	radius	'chattering' at mid-shaft where chopped with cleaver
	sheep	1	astragalus	chopped oblique to long axis
	cattle	1	astragalus	chopped through axis
M	sheep	2	vertebrae	halved through axis
P	cattle	1	astragalus	chopped oblique to long axis

Table 28   Evidence for butchery

Patterns of butchery (Table 28)

Table 28 lists the evidence recorded for butchery. Occupation layers of the 13th-century timber hall and the later little cloister produced evidence mainly for the simple halving of vertebrae of cattle, sheep and pig through the long axis of the bone. A sheep humerus was chopped across the axis of the trochlea. A cattle radius was chopped longitudinally from the proximal end. Three cattle scapulae showed evidence of having been chopped from the base through the axis of the bone.

More systematic butchery was detected for Group H (demolition of little cloister), primarily from the large garth dump context 15. Sheep and cattle vertebrae were halved through their long axis. Three cattle calcanea displayed chop-marks across the shaft above the distal end; six cattle astragali were chopped obliquely to their long axis. These two patterns may have been produced through one action — the severing of metapodials as waste from the bovine carcass. A cattle femur was chopped across the proximal articulation and a tibia was chopped longitudinally from the proximal end. A sheep pelvis was chopped through the acetabulum and a metapodial was chopped from the proximal end through the axis of the bone.

Groups representing post-Priory activity in the region of the little cloister (I, J, K) contained a sheep astragalus chopped obliquely to the long axis, and a cattle astragalus chopped through the axis. A cattle radius showed evidence of 'chattering' at the mid-shaft, where it had been chopped through by a cleaver.

From the occupation of the north range of the main cloister, were recovered two sheep vertebrae which were halved through the axis of the bone. Demolition deposits in this area yielded a cattle astragalus which was chopped obliquely to the long axis.

Anatomical analysis (Table 29)

Some hand-collected groups were examined for the occurrence of skeletal elements of the major species (Table 29). This exercise may shed light on the nature of animal food sources entering the site, whether as dressed carcasses or 'on the hoof', and also on the extent of animal-based activities which were conducted within the precinct. The groups chosen for anatomical analysis included those representing supposed sequences of occupation (C, D, F, G, M, Q) and the large sample provided by the dump context 15.

The results of the analysis for cattle, sheep and pig were fairly uniform in their representations of meat-yielding parts of the carcass (ribs, vertebrae,

	C	D	F	G	M	Q	15
Cattle:							
Horncores	-	-	-	-	-	-	-
Mandible, maxilla, atlas	1	2	-	1	-	1	5
Vertebrae	-	3	16	5	4	2	27
Scapula, pelvis	5	5	3	9	4	-	50
Humerus, radius, ulna	1	1	2	3	3	-	34
Femur, tibia, calcaneum, astragalus	1	7	3	1	2	1	35
Metapodials	1	1	-	-	-	-	11
Phalanges	1	1	3	7	2	-	20
Ribs	16	9	22	49	3	3	161
Sheep:							
Horncores							
Mandible, maxilla	-	2	-	1	1	1	6
Vertebrae	1	5	7	34	6	-	13
Scapula, pelvis	3	3	8	14	6	1	36
Humerus, radius, ulna	6	2	4	3	5	-	87
Femur, tibia, calcaneum, astragalus	4	2	8	16	1	-	31
Metapodials	3	3	5	8	1	-	9
Phalanges	-	2	14	16	3	-	4
Ribs	2	3	34	38	4	3	19
Pig:							
Mandible, maxilla	2	1	-	-	-	-	1
Vertebrae/ribs	4	9	38	45	6	1	87
Scapula, pelvis	-	1	1	-	-	1	8
Humerus, radius, ulna	1	1	4	4	1	-	13
Femur, tibia, fibula, calcaneum, astragalus	1	-	2	3	2	-	6
Metapodials	-	-	4	1	-	-	7

Table 29   Anatomical analysis of some hand-collected groups (by hypothetical butchery zones)

scapulae, pelves, long bones) and the waste products of slaughter and butchery (skulls, mandibles, teeth, phalanges) which occurred in small numbers. In contrast to their representation for sheep and pig, cattle metapodials were conspicuously absent from the occupation groups and dump contexts. Within the species analysis, there was no apparent chronological or spatial difference in the distribution of skeletal components.

These results bring the status of the occupation groups into question. Within these groups are the waste products of activities which would not normally be associated with monastic quarters of accommodation. In addition to the remains of meals (ribs, vertebrae, long bones), the bones within these groups reflect the slaughter and initial butchery of animals (skulls, mandibles, phalanges), the dressing of the carcass (metapodials, calcanea, astragali) and the preparation of food for table (scapulae, pelves). It is likely that these groups (C, D, F, G, M, Q) are composed both of accumulation of occupation deposits and extraneous dumped material. While the contents of the dumps may indeed represent monastic activities, they cannot be related closely to a particular zone or phase of use.

While it has been established that a small quantity of waste from slaughter is present in the groups, there is some evidence to suggest that the Priory was importing partially prepared carcasses from market. Results of the anatomical analysis indicate an absence of cattle metapodials. This negative occurrence seems to apply to all periods and areas of occupation, although only Groups F and G and context 15 may be considered large enough samples of bone in which this pattern might be detected adequately (little cloister area, late 13th-century to its demolition). The absence of bovine metapodials and the low occurrence of cranial fragments suggest that much of the beef entered the site as dressed carcasses.

Certain patterns of butchery which were noted on the cattle bones, in particular the obliquely chopped astragalii and chop-marked calcanea, confirm that feet were systematically removed from the carcass. The metapodials of sheep and pig, however, did occur in substantial numbers. Neither sheep nor cattle horn cores were observed in any groups contemporary with monastic occupation. This may, to some extent, support the notion that prepared carcasses were imported to the site. It may be possible, however, that cattle horn was collected for working, and that hornless sheep dominated the assemblage of sheep bones; however, no hornless sheep skulls were noted.

The proposed sites of the priory refectory and kitchen were severely constricted by the western precinct boundary. It is unlikely that space was available for the keeping of large animals, or for the initial preparation of their carcasses. The restricted nature of the area available for food preparation, in addition to the results of the anatomical analysis, suggest that dressed cattle carcasses were obtained at market. Sheep and pig were probably prepared, if not slaughtered, on site. The presence of a single goat horn core from Group E (construction of the little cloister) may indicate that these animals, at least, were kept in the precinct.

Results of the analysis may clarify the status of context 15. This deposit of garth soil from the little cloister has been defined as a dump associated with demolition activities. Its authenticity as a monastic assemblage may, therefore, be questioned. According to its profile of skeletal elements, however, context 15 does not differ from the so-called occupation groups. Although it may be a dump deposit, the material incorporated within it is consistent with other assemblages which were more securely linked to the occupation of the Priory. Context 15 seems to have derived from monastic use. If it is assumed to be of

monastic character, the systematic butchering observed within the group (Table 28, H) supports the hypothesis that dressed cattle carcasses were imported onto the site.

Bone from bulk-sieved soil samples (Table 30)

Bone from sieved samples of selected contexts was dry-sorted and identified, in order to redress the bias inherent in hand-collection toward the bones of larger species. Twenty-three samples were chosen in an attempt to represent a wide range of feature types and dates (see Table 30). The deposits from which the samples were derived include sequences of pre-Priory dark earth (958, 1186, 1188); 13th-century occupation (807) of the timber building; one of a series of possible soakaway pits dug at the south-western edge of the site in the later 13th century (1048); occupation of the eastern chamber of the north range of the little cloister (dated to the 14th century: 110, 2009, 2053, 2054); occupation contemporary with 2009, 2053 and 2054 in the western chamber (see below, appended summary of context 772) and later 14th-century occupation of the western end of the corresponding western chamber (3006, 3051, 3092); and the area (3020, 3064) at the west end of the same range. These

	Description	Date*	Phase
958	pre-priory dark earth	C.11/12	2
1188	pre-priory dark earth	C.12 +	2
1186	clay fill	?	1
807	timber building occupation	C.13	3C
1048	?cess pit, SW edge of site	C.13	3A
110	E chamber, little cl. N range, silt	C.14	5A
2009	E chamber, little cl. N range, floor silt	C.14	5B
2053	E chamber, little cl. N range, burnt clay/hearth	C.14	5B
2054	E chamber, little cl. N range, ash/burnt silt	C.14	5B
772	W chamber, little cl. N range, floor silt	C.15	5B
3006	W chamber, little cl. N range, floor silt	C.14/15	5C
3020	W chamber, little cl. N range, floor silt	C.14/15	5C
3064	W chamber, little cl. N range, floor silt	C.14/15	5C
3092	W chamber, little cl. N range, floor silt (w/lead melt)	C.14/15	5C
3051	W chamber, little cl. N range, floor silt (w/lead melt)	C.14/15	5C
3110	Little cl. area, floor silt	?post-priory	8
944	occup/flooring of N range	C.14/15+	6A
1109	'primary' fill, water tank	?mid. C.15	4
1106	fill, water tank	?C.15	4
1107	fill, water tank	?C.15	4
1094	fill of garderobe/culvert	C.16	7
1095	fill of garderobe/culvert	C.16 Priory	7

* dates given are based on pottery spot dates and/or stratigraphic relationships. Discrepancies in date or nature of deposit are discussed in the text.

Table 30   Description of sieved samples

	110	944	1094	1095	1107	1109	1188	2009 (52)	2009 (579)	2009 (589)	2009 (5100)	2009 (5101)	2054	3006	3020	3051	3069	3092
Rajidae (ray)		1	1					1					1					
Raja claraton (thornback ray)									2	3		4						3
Clupea harengus (herring)	126	24	8	1		18	4	35	286	288	39	227	2	7	69	13	45	35
Salmonidae sp.	2	3																
Esox lucius (pike)										11								
Cyprinidea sp.	1								2									
Leuciscus leuciscus (dace)								1	1		1							
Anguilla anguilla (eel)	102	10						47	533	437	52	396		26	13	4	11	26
Conger conger	3					1											1	
Abrauis brama (bream)										1								
Gadidae sp.		2			1	6			18	16	2							
Merlangius merlangus (whiting)	15	9				1		13	69	51	1	51	2		1	2	1	15
Pollachius pollachius (pollack)						7												
Gadus morhua (cod)	5					21			7	2	17	14			1	4		7
Melanogramus aeglefinus (haddock)	1	3				11		1	7	8		12				2	1	6
Molva molva (ling)				1	3		4		2							3		1
Labridae sp. (wrasse)									1									
Scomber scomber (mackerel)		5							5	2								2
Gutrigla gurnardus (grey gurnard)		1							1	1								
Lottus gobia (bullhead)	1																	
Scopthalmus chombra (brill)	9	7																
Limanda limanda (dab)	5																	
Pleurorectes platessa (plaice)	12	9	1	1		5		3	27	15		13		8	3	2	2	4
Sub-total	282	74	10	4	4	75	8	101	960	837	112	717	5	42	88	30	61	99
UFR	180	150	17			120	16	47	410	480	65	380	4		75	57	34	80
Total	**462**	**224**	**27**	**4**	**4**	**195**	**24**	**148**	**1370**	**1317**	**177**	**1097**	**9**	**42**	**162**	**87**	**95**	**179**

Table 32 Quantitification of fish bone from sieved samples

	Sample Numbers:	110	944	2009 (S79)	2009 (S89)	2009 (S101)	3020	3064	1109
Region	*Element**								
(olfactory)	prevomer			2					
(orbital)	lacrimal	1			1				
(otic)	otolith	3	5	1	2	1		1	2
	otic bullae	2							
(oromandibular)	articular		1		1	2			1
	dentary					1			
	maxilla				4	4			1
	premaxilla	2	1	12	6	6			5
	quadrate	1	1	3	4	1	1	1	
	dermal denticle		1	2		1			
	teeth		4	2	3	3			
(hyoid)	ceratohyal						1		1
	hyomandibular								1
(branchial)	pharyngo - br.	1			1				
(pectoral)	supra-cleithrum								1
(girdle)	cleithrum					1			
	post-cleithrum						1		
(vertebral column)	precaudal	125	50	827	792	688	81	58	42
(caudal skeleton)	caudal	45	11	110	24	9	3	1	21
Total		180	74	960	837	717	87	61	75

*terminology follows Harder 1964

Table 33   Anatomical analysis of fish bone from selected samples

late floor surfaces contained lead melt and came. While the pottery dates attributed these latter silts to the late 14th or early 15th centuries, they may have included material which represented robbing following the Priory's suppression in 1539. A further floor silt in this area (3110) belonged to a post-monastic period of use. From the north range of the great cloister (refectory) a sample was examined which may represent an episode of occupation (944). 'Primary' (1109) and secondary (1106, 1107) fills of the water tank, perhaps dated to the 15th century, and post-Priory fills of the culvert (1094, 1095) were also analysed.

Species present and their occurrence (Table 31)

Table 31 (Mf.3 D14) indicates that all of the 23 sieved samples yielded unidentifiable fragments of large mammal, and a small number of fragments of cattle, sheep and pig. These samples also contained small quantities of egg shell and shell fish (oyster and mussel; *Mytilus edulis*). Mandibles of very young dog were recovered from the pit (1048) and culvert (1095). Rabbit was present in the early floor silt of the east chamber (110), and hare was recorded from the north range (944) and culvert fills (1094, 1095). Substantial numbers of fragments of small mammal were present in samples from the east and west chambers of the north range of the little cloister (except in Phase 5B in the west chamber, see below). House mouse (*Mus* sp.) was present in pre-Priory dark earth, in addition to the two chambers. Common shrew (*Sorex araneus*) was present in the early floor silt of the east chamber. Vole (*Microtus agrestis*) was identified from both chambers. Ship rat (*Rattus rattus*) and common shrew were detected in samples from the western end of the west chamber. All of these species thrive in a wide variety of urban habitats.

In addition to unidentifiable fragments of bird bone, fragments of domestic fowl were recovered from both chambers of the little cloister's north range, the north range of the great cloister and the fills of the water tank. Goose was identified from pre-Priory dark earth. Non-domestic species present included fragments of house sparrow (*Passer domesticus*) from the west chamber and single fragments of Laridae sp. (gulls and terns) and Fringillidae sp. (finches) from the east chamber. The non-domestic species are all gregarious birds associated with human settlement. House sparrows nest in buildings and hedges, finches in trees. The single fragment of gull/tern appears to have been a chance occurrence.

Small numbers of fragments of frog (*Rana temporaria*) were recovered from both the east and west chambers of the north range of the little cloister, the north range of the great cloister, and fills of the

Sample Numbers		110	944	2009 S79	2009 S89	2009 S101	3020	3064	1109
head									
	no.	15	13	23	21	19	2	2	11
	%	8.3	17.6	2.4	2.5	2.6	2.3	3.3	14.6
body									
	no.	165	61	937	816	698	85	59	64
	%	91.7	82.4	97.6	97.5	97.4	97.7	96.7	85.3
total		180	74	960	837	717	87	61	75

Table 34   Proportions of fish head to body waste from selected samples

culvert and water tank.

Fish (Table 32)

Eighteen of the 23 samples contained fish bone, totalling 5618 fragments (Table 32). It was possible to identify 18 species of fish, in addition to bones identifiable only to family (Rajidae sp., Salmonidae sp., Cyprinidae sp., Gadidae sp. and Labridae sp.). Marine species dominated the assemblage, with a small number of freshwater species present, in addition to those species which spend their life cycles in both marine and freshwater environments.

The marine fishes identified include the deep-dwelling cod fishes (whiting, cod, haddock and ling), surface-dwelling fish (mackerel), fish associated with shallow, muddy bottoms (thornback ray, grey gurnard, plaice, brill and dab), the inshore species found near rocks (wrasse and pollack), and fish which inhabit a variety of inshore and offshore environments (herring and conger eel). The wide range of species present would have been fished using a combination of nets and lines.

The freshwater species identified are all associated with lowland rivers and lakes: pike, dace, bream and bullhead. Two taxa present, eel and Salmonidae sp., spend portions of their lives in marine and freshwater habitats.

The densest occurrences of fish bones were recovered from the east chamber of the little cloister north range, from Phase 5B floor silts thought to represent mid.-to-later 14th-century occupation (2009). They were also numerous in silts from the broadly contemporary occupation of the west chamber (see below). Considerable numbers of bones were also recovered from the 14th-century occupation of this area (110), from the Phase 6 floor silt of the great cloister refectory (944), and from the supposed primary fill of the water tank (1109). Phase 5C occupation layers from the west chamber of the north range of the little cloister produced much smaller quantities of bone, between 42 and 179 fragments. Very little fish bone was recovered from the fills of the culvert (1094, 1095), the upper fill of the water tank (1107) and the pre-Priory dark earth (1188).

The proportional representation of species from the larger assemblages indicates that the occupation debris was dominated by the bones of herring and eel, with small but consistent occurrences of thornback ray, whiting, cod and plaice. There are, however, slight variations in the relative proportions of these species in samples recovered from different areas of the site. The largest samples, associated with the 14th/15th-century occupation of the east chamber of the little cloister's north range, are dominated numerically by the bones of eel (52.5–55.5% of identified fragments) with considerable numbers of herring (29.8–34.4%). This pattern is reversed for the 14th-century occupation of this same area, the later occupation of the west chamber, and the occupation of the refectory. In these areas, herring bones greatly outnumber those of eel. In the presumed primary fill of the water tank, the bones of cod fishes predominate over herring and eel. The respective characters of these contexts may be more fully elaborated with reference to an anatomical analysis of the identified fish bone.

Anatomical analysis of fish remains (Tables 33–4)

The identifiable fish bone from the occupation of the east and west chambers of the north range of the little cloister, the north range of the great cloister and the primary fill of the water tank were quantified according to regions within the body of the fish (Table 33). These regions were then classified as waste deriving from the fish head (olfactory, orbital, otic, oromandibular, hyoid, branchial), or body (pectoral girdle, vertebral column, caudal skeleton). This division between head and body waste represents the products of two separate phases of food preparation and consumption. At the stage of food preparation, where food sources are processed and cooked, fish heads would generally be removed and discarded. After consumption of the prepared meal, the resulting table waste, composed mainly of vertebrae, would be disposed of separately.

Results of the anatomical analysis (Table 34) elucidate both the activity represented by the bone assemblage and the manner in which it was deposited.

In fish-yielding contexts thought to represent sequences of occupation, a high body-to-head ratio would be expected. Table 34 indicates that body waste predominates in all of the samples selected for anatomical analysis. In the floor silts associated with the east and west chambers (little cloister, north range) the percentage of head fragments ranges from 2.3 to 8.3%, and where not quantified (Phase 5B, west chamber) appears broadly consistent with this. The proportion of head waste from the refectory silt (944), however, is considerably higher at 17.6%. Fragments identified from the primary fill of the water tank were 14.6% head waste. The latter two deposits (944, 1109), with their higher values for fish head waste, may be distinct from the occupational sequences in the activities and processes of deposition which they represent. These samples are relatively small, 74 and 75 fragments, but exhibit higher head waste values than other samples of similar size (3020 and 3064).

Context 944 is associated with the north-west corner of the north range of the great cloister. It was identified tentatively as an episode of occupation and flooring, post-dating the construction of the range in the later 14th century and sealed by demolition layers. Context 1109 refers to the 'primary' fill of a water tank which was constructed beyond the northwest corner of the refectory range, at an unknown date, to supply water to the west range of the great cloister. This fill has yielded pottery with a latest date of (mid.) 15th century. The high proportion of fish head waste (17.6 and 14.6%, respectively) suggests that these two deposits contain an unusually high level of kitchen waste produced by food preparation. It may be suggested that 944 represents the accommodation of kitchen waste, rather than a sequence of occupation. Similarly, the fill of the water tank may have been kitchen waste dumped or allowed to accumulate after this part of the Priory's system of water management had fallen into disuse. The upper fills of this feature (1106, 1107) contained large quantities of oyster shells which may have been deposited in a similar manner.

Animal bone from the west chamber, little cloister north range

by Terry O'Connor

Following recording and analysis of bone fragments from the 1986 excavations at the Priory, examination of one further assemblage was undertaken. This came from context 772, a Phase 5B ashy silt occupation deposit in the western chamber of the north range of the little cloister.

A sample comprising 70.5kg (six buckets) of sediment was wet-sieved on 1mm mesh, retaining a 0.5mm washover. The 1mm residue was dried, re-sieved on a 2mm mesh, and the 2mm+ residue was sorted for bone and shell fragments. The residue consisted of about 2kg of mortar and building stone 'gravel', and yielded several thousand fragments of bone. Because of time constraints, and because a large proportion of the bone recovered was clearly unidentifiable small fragments, a detailed quantification has not been attempted.

The bulk of the assemblage consisted of highly fragmented bird bones, the great majority of which were unidentifiable. Most of the latter were of domestic fowl, including much of the skeleton of one immature individual. Other bird bones were attributable to a thrush species (*Turdus* sp.), an unidentified small passerine, and a species of owl. This last specimen was part of the shaft of a humerus, and was consistent in size with barn owl (*Tyto alba*), though that should not be regarded as a secure identification.

The mammal bones in this sample included fragments of sheep or goat vertebrae and sternum, and most of one foot of a sub-adult pig. One of the sheep/goat sternum fragments bore tooth-marks clearly attributable to a cat.

Numerous fish bones were recovered. As is usual in medieval assemblages, the majority were of herring (*Clupea harengus*) and eel (*Anguilla anguilla*). The other taxa identified were haddock (*Melanogrammus aeglefinus*), plaice (*Pleuronectes platessa*), whiting (*Merlangius merlangus*), and another gadid. These fish species are quite consistent with later medieval assemblages from secular occupation elsewhere in Beverley and York.

Overall, the content of the assemblage indicates that this is waste from consumption of food, rather than its preparation. The deposit appears to have been fairly rapidly emplaced and sealed, as there were no bones of mice, rats or frogs. Shell fragments from the same sample included only four specimens of the eurytopic snail *Trichia* cf. *plebeia*, and a few fragments of oyster shell. The single fragment of owl is intriguing, and probably fortuitous. There is no other evidence to support the use of the (presumably abandoned) structure as a roost — the absence of small mammal bones directly gainsays this — and the bone must be a chance incorporation in what is otherwise residue from human activity.

I am grateful to John Carrott for undertaking the lengthy and onerous task of sorting this sample.

Discussion

The identified fragments were dominated by the three major domesticates: cattle, sheep and pig. Deer, hare and rabbit were present, but their small numbers indicate that hunted foodstuffs did not make up a significant proportion of the usual diet. Small numbers of fragments from dog, cat and horse were recorded.

A certain degree of variation in the relative importance of species was observed between spatial and chronological bone groups. Cattle bones were predominant in assemblages representing pre-Priory activity, Priory construction and demolition sequences, in addition to the deposits making up the 13th to early 14th-century occupation of the timber building. Sheep were more numerous in all 14th and 15th-century occupation groups of the little cloister and main cloister (north range). Fragments of pig occurred fairly consistently in medieval groups at *c*.10%, rising slightly in post-medieval assemblages. The limited data available for ageing indicate that during monastic use of the site, sheep and pigs were slaughtered as sub-adult/adult prime meat specimens. Bird bones made up a significant proportion of identified fragments from occupation of the little cloister, from 18–34.9%. The bird species represented were largely domestic (fowl, goose and duck). A greater range of species of bird was observed only in groups E and H, representing construction and demolition activity.

The results of the bone analysis may be compared with those of the animal bones from two other medieval sites in Beverley; Eastgate may be described as secular and low status in character; Lurk Lane may have been of higher status, associated with the Minster complex. The biometric data from Eastgate (Scott 1992) indicate that individual sheep and cattle were of a similar size to those at the Dominican Priory. In relative proportions of species, Lurk Lane (Scott 1991) is comparable to the Priory: sheep increase in fragment numbers over time, cattle decrease, and pig remains fairly constant throughout. Sieved samples revealed large quantities of herring and eel at Lurk Lane — a pattern noted at the Priory. Eastgate produced a range of fish bone identifiable to 15 species or families, and Lurk Lane yielded 23, in comparison to 24 from the Dominican Priory. The fish bone assemblages from all three sites were dominated by marine taxa. In contrast to the Priory, both Eastgate and Lurk Lane had a varied range of wild birds (24 and 28 species, respectively). Lurk Lane differed from both Eastgate and the Dominican Priory in the relative importance of hunted species (deer, hare, and wild boar). Although Eastgate and Lurk Lane yielded a greater range of species of small mammal/rodent than the Priory, none of the sites produced large quantities of fragments from occupation layers or floors.

Patterns of butchery noted on cattle bones from Lurk Lane were similar to those for the Dominican Priory. These included the slicing of vertebrae to split the carcass into two more easily handled units, the longitudinal chopping of scapulae, perhaps for glue or stock making, and the oblique cleaving of astragali for the removal of feet. The similarities in patterns of butchery between the Priory and Lurk Lane, and in the stature of animals between the Priory and Eastgate, may indicate that by the later medieval period Beverley's secular sites, Minster complex and Dominican Priory were sharing common urban market sources. A similar pattern has been noted for York, where by the 15th/16th centuries the Gilbertine Priory, Bedern and city shared the same sources of food supply (O'Connor 1993).

Results of the analysis may be compared to those from other medieval English urban monasteries. Few sites of this nature have provided large bone assemblages, with the exceptions of St. Andrew's Gilbertine Priory, York (O'Connor 1993), the Dominican Priory at Oxford (Lambrick 1985), the Austin Friars' Leicester (Thawley 1981), and the nunnery of Polsloe, near Exeter (Levitan 1989). Additional sites have yielded assemblages of a few hundred fragments. These include Guildford Dominican Priory (Done 1984), Kirkstall Abbey and Pontefract Priory (Ryder 1961). All of these sites provided a range of species similar to those identified at the Beverley Dominican Priory. Some sites differed, however, in the proportions of species present and the treatment of carcasses on site.

Beverley may be distinct in the high number of fragments of sheep in occupation layers of the 14th/15th centuries. Only the small assemblage from Pontefract Priory (about 300 fragments) indicated a similar predominance, although the importance of sheep relative to cattle at the York Gilbertine house increased over time. In contrast, the assemblages from the Dominican Priory, Oxford, and the Austin Friary, Leicester, indicate a bias toward cattle which was higher even than at contemporary secular sites within their regions (Lambrick 1985, 205). The high incidence of cattle from Kirkstall Abbey may be the result of the specialised nature of the deposit, which was recovered from an area described as the 'meat kitchen'. The varying emphasis on mutton in the monastic diet may in fact be a product of trends on a regional scale. Monastic houses at Beverley, York and Pontefract fit a general pattern of an increasing reliance on sheep for the meat supply of later medieval towns in the north-east and east of England.

From the small sample of mandibles from Beverley, it seems that the majority of animals were killed as young adults. The animals consumed at other monastic sites were predominantly adult, although the small sample from Pontefract suggested that animals were killed before 2 years.

The relative importance of domestic fowl increases in the later occupation of Dominican Beverley, Gilbertine York and Dominican Oxford. In comparison with York and Austin Leicester, the ratio of domestic fowl to goose is particularly high at

Beverley. This pattern may reflect the character of refuse from a relatively small area of the site (i.e. the north range of the little cloister). Fragments of the bones of deer were noted in greater relative proportions at Pontefract and Kirkstall than at Beverley. In contrast to Beverley, fragments of fallow deer, which may be considered a semi-domestic species, and horse, occurred in considerable quantities at Austin Leicester. From the 15th century onwards, the Gilbertine Priory at York enjoyed an increased diversity of wild bird species. At Beverley and Leicester, however, the emphasis remained on domestic bird species throughout the monastic occupation.

The range of fish species represented at monastic sites varies according to their geographical region. At all sites the bones of marine fishes were more numerous than those of freshwater species, whether the assemblage was hand-collected (Guildford, Leicester) or sieved (York, Oxford, Beverley). The bones of herring, eel and the cod fishes predominate. The reliance on marine fishes may have been due to their greater availability and lower cost within the urban market. Urban monasteries seldom had their own fishponds, and may not have had fishing rights to their adjacent rivers. Although a reference exists to ponds, fishponds and fisheries within the enclosure of the Dominican Priory (PRO C66/740), these sources did not enable the house to achieve self-sufficiency. The anatomical analysis of the Beverley fish remains suggests that whole fishes were imported to the site, fresh, in brine, or dried. The presence of skin bones at Leicester (Thawley 1981, 174) indicates that the skin was removed on site. It is commonly believed that fish made up the majority of the monastic diet. While sieved samples from monasteries have indeed yielded an impressive list of species, comparisons with contemporary secular sites in Beverley suggest a similar diversity of fish taxa. It is possible, however, that the proportions of fish fragments to the bones of mammals and birds may be higher at monastic sites. At Dominican Oxford it was noted that the concentration of fish from a drain was 'probably several hundred times greater than in most medieval channel deposits in Oxford' (Lambrick 1985, 198).

Anatomical analysis of the bones of the major domesticates has provided comparative evidence for the importing of animals to urban monasteries. It may be recalled that waste of the primary butchery of cattle was absent from Beverley. In contrast, all elements of the skeleton were well represented at Dominican Oxford and Austin Leicester, where meat apparently arrived as whole carcasses or 'on the hoof'. At Polsloe Nunnery, Exeter, it seems that whole animals and/or halved carcasses were brought onto site. Secondary butchering, in which carcasses were cut into joints and boned out, was conducted within the priory precinct

(Levitan 1989, 171). At York, the low incidence of sheep feet may indicate that sheep were imported as dressed carcasses, or that their feet remained attached to skins deposited elsewhere (O'Connor 1993). The patterns observed for the York and Beverley material may relate to the differential deposition of bone.

The precinct of an urban monastery was defined according to discrete activity areas. The nature of the waste which accumulated in these areas may be representative of a specialised task or of the type of occupants in the area, and not of monastic habitation across the whole site. At Polsloe the bone assemblage was studied with special reference to lateral variation. It was concluded that the larger bones, representing kitchen waste, were disposed of in the immediate vicinity of the kitchens. Small bones, representing the remains of meals, were subject to a more haphazard and variable disposal. They were deposited closer to the eating and living areas (refectory, dormitory). At Dominican Beverley there was no apparent spatial variation in the distribution of skeletal components of cattle, sheep and pig. 'Large' and 'small' bones were not specifically recorded, but concentrations of small fragments of the bones of sheep and bird (mainly domestic fowl) were apparent in certain quantification groups. In groups F, G and Q, sheep made up 12.2, 16.6 and 16.3% of the identified fragments. Fragments of bird bone accounted for 20.9, 18.3 and 34.9%, respectively. These groups are the accumulations from occupation in the east and west chambers of the north range of the little cloister (late 13th to 15th century). The extremely high concentrations of domestic fowl probably represent the remains of meals. The food waste in this area was not disposed of systematically, in the way that kitchen waste may have been. Instead it was allowed to build up within the structures. A process similar to that described for Polsloe may be suggested, in which table waste was allowed to accumulate close to a living/eating area.

Disposal of refuse on monastic sites may be understood through the nature of the bone assemblages and the feature types from which they were excavated. Bone evidence for some sites is largely negative, with the majority of fragments coming from pre- and post-monastic sequences. The largest groups of fragments from Beverley were associated with construction and demolition activities, although it was possible to link bone from floor surfaces with phases of occupation. The largest groups of fragments from most urban monastic sites are dump deposits, which may be difficult to define spatially or temporarily in relation to monastic occupation. The paucity of bone from monastic sites indicates that it was systematically collected and disposed of. The general absence of gnawed fragments from Beverley may confirm that bone was not left exposed for any great period of time. Leicester and Beverley produced very little burnt material, suggesting that it may not have been normal practice to incinerate bone waste. It is most likely that kitchen waste was collected and dumped outside the precinct. At Beverley the less offensive table waste was allowed to accumulate within an accommodation area. Kitchen waste from the final period of monastic use was dumped in the cloister garth, the north-west corner of the cloister, and the (presumably) disused water tank.

In conclusion, it has been possible to confirm that the little cloister was used for an eating/living area, but the lack of comparable bone assemblages from the great cloister makes it impossible to establish its lay or monastic character. The occupational sequences of this area may lend credence to the notion that the monastic diet held a high proportion of fish, and more especially, bird. The range of bird species represented was certainly less diverse than at contemporary secular sites, while the variety of fish taxa was comparable. Evidence for the stature, butchery and relative proportions of species at the Priory and contemporary Beverley sites suggests that the Priory shared the food sources of the town. The monastic institution was essentially 'urban' in its acquisition of food stuffs. A specifically 'monastic' character is more easily recognised in the well-ordered systems of sanitation and waste disposal which operated there.

5. Analytical Reports

5.1 Archaeomagnetic dating

by A.J. Clark

Summary

Six samples were taken for archaeomagnetic assay from hearths of Phases 3B, 5A, 5B, 5C and 7. Some of the determinations were clearly anomalous, and none is crucial to the dating of the site.

(The full report can be found on Mf.3, frame E5.)

5.2 The slags and residues

by J.G. McDonnell

Summary

A total of 1.2kg of slag and other residues was recovered from the site; these were present in pre-Priory levels, contexts relating to the monastic occupation, and also in a small number of post-Dissolution contexts.

Evidence for industrial metalworking activity is negative, except for the reclamation of the lead at the Dissolution. There was no evidence for ironworking in the areas excavated, at any period of the site's use (despite the fact that some constructional ironworking activity might have been expected.) This evidence can be contrasted with that from two other Beverley sites - Lurk Lane (McDonnell 1991) and Eastgate (McDonnell 1992) -both of which indicated nearby iron smithing activity.

(The full report can be found on Mf.3, frames E6–8.)

5.3 Chemical analysis of glass

by Julian Henderson

Full details of the chemical analyses of glass fragments catalogued in sections 3.8 and 3.13 are listed in Table 36. This is reproduced on Mf.3, frame E9.

5.4 Sources of coal

by P.D. Spriggs

Summary

Some Phase 5B contexts contained coal derived from seam(s) of Middle Coal Measure age, and the reflectance value of the coal was 1.03%. Some Phase 5C/6A contexts also yielded coal from the Middle Coal Measures, and the reflectance value was 0.99%. The age of the coal present in these two phases was the same, and the rank of the coal was similar, thus, indicating that the coals could have been derived from the same source.

Coal ranks maps compiled by the Coal Survey (1960) show outcrops of coal of the same age and similar rank to that of the coal under investigation in the coalfields of Northumberland, Durham, Yorkshire and Lancashire, but it is, however, most widespread in Durham.

(The full report can be found on Mf.3, frames E10–11.)

5.5 Dendrochronological dating

by Jennifer Hillam

Six out of eleven tree-ring samples proved suitable for measurement, and of these three were dated by comparing their ring patterns against those of dated reference chronologies. Using a sapwood estimate of 10-55 rings (95% confidence limits), it was calculated that timber 15 was felled during the period AD1098-1143.   Timbers 4A and 4B, from a contractor's sewer trench on the Eastgate street front, were felled some time after AD1048 and AD1042 respectively. The ring widths from the three timbers were averaged to produce a new tree-ring chronology spanning the period AD967-1092.

(Further details can be found in Tables 37-8 and Fig. 91 on Mf. 3, frames E12-13.)

6. Discussion

by Martin Foreman

The discussion is divided into three parts. The first (6.1) loosely follows the order of the excavation report, amplifying the topographical evidence with material drawn from artefact and environmental studies, and with comparative data from other sites. Where appropriate, the use or identification of structures is considered. The second (6.2) briefly considers the metrology employed at the Priory. The third (6.3) summarises the evidence for the Priory as a mendicant site, and its contribution to the understanding of the local urban economy.

6.1 The development of the site

Phases 1 and 2 — early topography

The south side of Beverley was the subject of near-continuous archaeological research between 1979 and 1987. The collation of the results of this work has gone far towards indicating the general character of the landscape, while indicating significant variations within a relatively small area. The local landscape was undoubtedly influential upon the progress of early settlement, and on the development of those areas peripheral to the early focus or foci of occupation. The beginnings of this process at the Priory site are undated, but it apparently continued into the 12th century.

The subsoil in the southern part of Beverley is a stiff boulder clay laid down in the last period of glaciation over the weathered surface of underlying chalk. Gravels outcrop in the north and north-east parts of the medieval town (British Geological Survey, Sheet 72, Drift), and there is evidence here for Romano-British occupation (Miller *et al.* 1982, 3: Frere 1986). The earliest occupation in the southern part of the town was of later Bronze Age or early Iron Age date, represented at Lurk Lane by indeterminate features and a buried soil horizon. This activity took place on a natural hummock of boulder clay at a level of *c*.6.50m OD. Although only a little higher than the surrounding land, this area was to attract Middle Saxon occupation (Armstrong *et al.* 1991, 8–11).

Recent work at Park Grange Farm, Woodmansey by Peter Didsbury has demonstrated that localised post-Roman peat formation took place in some areas, perhaps due to a rise in groundwater levels. The coincidence of cropmarks with slightly elevated ground may betray the colonisation of islands in the flood plain of the River Hull. Excavations at Minster Moorgate (Watkins and Williams 1983, 73–4), at

Butcher Row (Sanders and Armstrong 1983, fig. 4), and at Dyer Lane, Beverley have identified early peat horizons. The absence of peat from the northern part of the Dominican Priory may imply that, like the Lurk Lane site, it was a slightly drier area more suitable for habitation than the surrounding wetlands.

To the north-east of the Minster the subsoil fell to a level of *c*.5.40m OD at the Eastgate streetfront. This area was not inhabited until after the Norman Conquest; prior to this, various attempts had been made to drain and infill a natural pond (Evans and Tomlinson 1992, 7–10 and 271). The identification of early water-filled features immediately west of the later Dominican precinct may argue that at least the first stages in this reclamation work were extended to include what would later form the full depth of the Eastgate tenements. The boulder clay subsoil here achieved a maximum level of *c*.5.75m OD. The ground may then have risen gently; in the north-east part of Trench 3 deposits taken to be a natural subsoil lay at 6.30m OD.

Evidence for early activity here was restricted to the view afforded by trial trenches. These established the presence of a series of pits (Phase 1) — some with threshing debris and carbonised grain in their fills, others containing occupation debris, and one containing charcoal and burnt daub. The fill of this last pit also included slag-like products considered to have been formed as residues from the burning of wood. This evidence may be regarded as indicating an area peripheral to agrarian settlement (see above, section 4.2). It was certainly used for rubbish disposal, but this activity is undated. Comparable evidence was uncovered at Highgate, north of the Minster, where occupation or industrial debris lay at a level of *c*.6.50m OD, and was sealed by 'brushwood' deposits considered to be of artificial origin which yielded a radiocarbon determination of 920 ± 70 B.P. (HAR–2736: Watkins and Williams 1983, 73–4).

The early pits were truncated by the excavation of a wide shallow depression (Phase 2). This may have been related to the winning of clay for structural activity elsewhere; from the 10th century onwards large quantities of clay were used, for example, in works south of the Minster, and this may have been common elsewhere in the early medieval town (Armstrong *et al.* 1991, 17; Sanders and Armstrong 1983, fig. 4).

The infilling of the depression is dated to the later 11th or 12th century; it is uncertain whether this was a sudden or a gradual accumulation. The presence of marsh plants is attested by the plant macrofossils, though these were accompanied by other occupation debris. One pit is suggested to have been used for the disposal of peaty debris — the use of peat for fuel has been recorded at Eastgate (Evans and Tomlinson 1992, 230 and 278). The interpretation of evidence for a marshland habitat should be qualified by the possibility that these soils were imported — either from nearby areas of occupation, being dumped in an area it was desired to reclaim, or as scourings from nearby ditches or watercourses. The Phase 2 soils lay between c.5.40m and c.6.30m OD. At Eastgate, the early medieval layers at an equivalent level retained their richly organic character (Evans and Tomlinson 1992), but at the Priory site they had decomposed to a dark grey loam. Iron-staining which was noted between contexts 957 and 958 has been taken to indicate a fairly high level for percolating ground water. This is perhaps confirmed by the strenuous efforts to seal floors and footings made by the friars when they came to develop the site. The balance of evidence therefore appears to indicate that the Phase 2 soils were laid down after their clearance from another area, and after the elapse of enough time for the greater part of their organic content to rot away.

Dr. R. McPhail of the London Institute or Archaeology has kindly commented that the soils of Phase 2 may have been cultivated to acquire their relatively homogeneous character. Some attempt to cultivate the site has also been suggested to explain the apparent ridging of the surface of context 958, but this was followed by the deposition of further soils. The extent of reclamation may not have been adequate to permit intensive agricultural use. The area was to be sealed by a clay raft held to be associated with the Dominican occupation of the site, established by 1240. The landfill operations represented by Phase 2 may also be reflected in some of the undated activity immediately west of the precinct boundary (see below).

Trench 2 — the precinct boundary

Introduction

The identification of a relict fragment of the western precinct wall of the Beverley Priory and the interpretation of this discovery in the light of documentary evidence have been presented by Armstrong and Tomlinson (1987, 49–51, fig. 27). They considered that the four and a half acres of the Priory precinct surveyed at the Dissolution probably represented little gain on the original size of the site, though Dr. R. Horrox suggests (pers. comm.) that piecemeal acquisition of land had taken place in the 13th century. The Dissolution survey allowed the divisions within the north part of the precinct, an area of gardens and closes, to be charted. They lay to the

north of an internal wall dividing the precinct, recorded at its junction with the precinct wall. The routing of a Phase 5C drain northwards may tend to confirm this interpretation, as *Pondegarth* (Armstrong and Tomlinson 1987, fig. 27) is held to have lain just north of the buildings of the house, fixing the rest of this interdependent survey.

The findings of the recent excavation have illuminated the original character of the land granted to the Dominicans. As indicated above, it was a damp and low-lying area, the reclamation of which had perhaps failed to enhance its agricultural value. This presented a contrast with the intensive and recurrent activity recorded to the west of the later precinct boundary. The latter may therefore have served to restate a pre-existing limit confining activity of an urban character, and thus arguing that the Priory was a suburban foundation at its inception.

The precinct boundary

The section views at the east end of Trench 2 indicate that pits or gullies were superseded by an embanked watercourse. The fill of the earliest features included plant and invertebrate macrofossils which suggested nearby occupation, and activity of a possibly industrial character. This is likely to have been associated with the development of the Eastgate tenements from the early 12th century onwards (Evans and Tomlinson 1992).

The use of flat roof tile in the bed of the watercourse provides a *terminus post quem* of the mid. 12th century for its construction, as this material has not certainly been recorded in use in Beverley before this date. This watercourse was perhaps an improvement upon earlier schemes designed to canalise or control the flow of water through or around the town. Given the 12th or early 13th-century establishment of the cloth industry on the banks of the Walker Beck, in the north part of the town (Dyer Lane, in prep.: Allison 1989, 41), it is unlikely that the watercourse in the Priory precinct could have been expected to supply unpolluted water. It may indeed be identified with the '*commune fossatum*' recorded in the 15th century, whose putative outfall on Hellgarth Lane received the evocative name of 'Shittendyke' in the post-medieval period (Armstrong and Tomlinson 1987, 50–2; Witty 1929, 4).

It is considered that the southward extent of the Priory watercourse should be identified with that flushing the *reredorter* or latrine of the Blackfriars (Armstrong and Tomlinson 1987, fig. 12), though the identification of a northern terminal to this ditch should now be regarded with circumspection (*ibid.*). The eccentric position of the Priory latrine block implies that this watercourse route was established before the formal claustral plan. The discovery of a large ditch south of the extant 'Old Friary', with fills dated to the 11th or 12th century (Armstrong and Tomlinson 1987, 24–5), hints at the earlier presence of substantial drainage or boundary features. Evidence of an early ditch of comparable size was not, however, forthcoming from the investigation of deposits west of the precinct wall.

Watching-brief work on the east side of the precinct, near Chantry Lane, has established the presence of numerous ditches, two of which appear to have corresponded closely to the presumed course of the precinct boundary. One contained pottery of 14th or 15th-century date. The foundations of a substantial wall were perched precariously on the edge of one of these ditches; a juxtaposition formerly considered unlikely for the precinct wall (Sanders and Armstrong 1983, 57–8), though one which reflects the more closely examined alignments of sewer and wall to the west. The latter wall had a drain emptying through it, suggesting that its position could indeed have related to that of a conduit.

The use of ditches to mark property boundaries is a feature of Beverley, dictated by its low-lying position. The town defences were marked by earthworks or by the maintenance of natural watercourses (Miller *et al.* 1982, 39–45; Youngs *et al.* 1986, 154). At the south end of the town the 12th-century hospital of St. Nicholas was surrounded by an irregular moat; the Preceptory of the Knights Hospitaller and the Archbishop of York's manor house of Hall Garth were also moated enclosures (Miller *et al.* 1982). The privacy afforded by such a boundary could be economically enhanced with the planting of hedges; this is recorded in the 13th century at the Dominican houses of Wilton and Salisbury (Hinnebusch 1951, 206–7). Material from the early features close to the precinct boundary included flora perhaps to be associated with hedged boundaries. The precincts of mendicant Priories in the larger towns were walled before the end of the 13th century, as at Norwich Blackfriars or the York Greyfriars (Hinnebusch *op. cit.*; Goldthorp 1934, 271).

The materials chosen to build precinct walls varied with local resources. At Canterbury Blackfriars they were of brick (Martin 1929, 173); at Ipswich Blackfriars of mudstone blocks (Loader 1986); and at York Greyfriars and Hulne Whitefriars of stone (Goldthorp 1934, 271; Hope 1890, 107). At Beverley the choice of brick was presumably prompted by its local availability, and perhaps by its donation (see above 3.3). The precinct wall was often a substantial structure; at Ipswich it survives over 2m high in places (Loader 1986), and at Guildford the churchyard wall was partially demolished in 1606 leaving an elevation of *c.*2.40m remaining (Poulton and Woods 1984, 7). At Beverley the relocated gates from the Priory wall stand over 2m high. Even with donated materials, the erection of the precinct wall would have represented a

considerable investment of labour. No further evidence has been recovered to date the Beverley precinct wall, save the confirmation that the surviving structure includes bricks of Type 1, whose use in the little cloister is known from the early 14th century onwards.

The site of the Priory

As noted above, excavation has so far failed to indicate a substantial ancient boundary along the east side of Beverley. No advance has been achieved on the formerly stated view of the suburban position of the Dominican Priory relative to the early eastern boundary of the town, which is held to have been ill-defined in the early 13th century (Armstrong and Tomlinson 1987, 50).

The excavation of Trench 2 did, however, indicate the contrasting character of early medieval land use on either side of the precinct alignment. There is little evidence for early (i.e. pre-Conquest) reclamation in the excavated areas of the Priory. Neither have industrial features been identified within the Priory precinct — though they have been recorded elsewhere in Beverley in contexts spanning at least the 11th to the mid. 14th centuries.

The position of the Priory downwind (south-east) of the noisome dyeing trade practised on the adjacent Eastgate properties (Evans and Tomlinson 1992) may suggest that the site had certain insalubrious aspects. The complaints and sufferings of the mendicants from the location of their sites are widely recorded. At Ludgate Blackfriars, London, for example, petitions against the stench of the neighbourhood were lodged in 1290 and 1368 (Hinnebusch 1951, 33–4); while at the Exeter Greyfriars the setting of the first site was so unpleasant as to prove fatal to nine brethren in the space of two years (Little 1917, 12–13). At Beverley it is possible that a changing character of occupation along Eastgate may have ameliorated the lot of the friars by the later 14th century (Evans and Tomlinson 1992).

Eastgate in the early 13th century was an area in which a burgage layout had already been achieved. The tenements saw intense use, though it is not certain that a settled population occupied residential accommodation amongst a plethora of sheds, workshops and industrial processes until the later 14th century (*ibid.*, 270). The focus of economic life in Beverley developed around the market area in the northern part of the town in the 12th and 13th centuries (Miller *et al.* 1982, 17, fig. 5: Allison 1989, 34). The establishment of the Dominican Priory, and indeed of other foundations endowed with land, was in areas lying away from this presumed axis of established or intensifying urban activity, in the south part of the town (Miller *et al.* 1982, 51–2). An attempt to expand the precinct westwards was quashed in

1309 (see above, Chapter 1).

A comparable zoning of religious houses is detectable elsewhere; the mendicants were particularly prone to such constraints, being comparatively late arrivals on the urban scene. At Northampton, the Franciscan and Carmelite precincts were adjacent to each other (Williams 1978, fig. 1), while at Leicester, the Dominican and Austin friars were both given sites on the damp western side of the town (Mellor and Pearce 1981, fig. 1). At Chester, religious foundations were fitted into the corners of a seigniorial town, the mendicant houses being closely grouped around the pre-existing Benedictine nunnery (Ward 1990, fig. 1); at Newcastle-upon-Tyne, all four mendicant Orders were granted peripheral sites (Butler 1987, fig. 78). At Nottingham and Hereford, peripheral and marshy areas were given over to mendicant use (Butler 1984, 123). In the case of Hereford the juxtaposition of the Dominican precinct with lands owned by the Knights Hospitaller (Hinnebusch 1951, 113) recalls the situation at Beverley.

The essentially marginal position of the Blackfriars house at Beverley may have been compensated by its proximity to the Minster. The provision of guest accommodation, tentatively identified beneath the extant 'Old Friary' (Armstrong and Tomlinson 1987, 55), and of a second cloister (see below: 'the little cloister'), could both relate to a pilgrim traffic which the Dominicans would have been ideally placed to exploit. Though the royal patronage of Hull from 1293 was to contribute to the eventual eclipse of Beverley, the Beverley Blackfriars at its foundation before 1240 was well-situated in relation to the town's port. The precinct was so formed as to permit access from the south and west, both entrances being marked in the later medieval period by formal pedestrian gateways (Miller *et al*. 1982, fig. 11).

Phase 3 — timber buildings (13th century)

Introduction

The formation of a clay platform appears to have been the first step taken by the Dominicans to facilitate settlement on previously marginal land. The platform achieved its greatest recorded depth over the position of an underlying hollow, indicating the deliberate choice of the building's position despite the somewhat unpropitious ground conditions. This could indicate either pressure on the available space for building — perhaps unlikely in a precinct of *c*.4½ acres — or an intention to establish a structure with a definite relationship to the church and great cloister laid out to the south. The alignment of the first structure set upon the platform was to match that of the Priory church.

The low-lying topography of the south side of Beverley has meant that landfill operations were a common and necessary precursor to settlement. At

Lurk Lane clays had been used to plug the redundant boundary ditches of the Anglian monastery in the 10th century, and occupation in the 11th century was preceded by further movement of soils (Armstrong *et al*. 1991, 15, 24–6). Along Highgate, north of the Minster, brushwood deposits may have helped to reclaim that area (Watkins and Williams 1983, 73–4); while on Eastgate, the medieval occupation was preceded by the gradual infilling of a large natural pond with organic detritus (Evans and Tomlinson 1992, 7–10 and 271).

The frequent location of mendicant houses in peripheral or unoccupied areas of towns made such works a normal first stage of their occupation. They have been reported from most such sites where archaeological investigations have taken place. At Bristol Greyfriars, rock and clay raised the ground level over much of that site by about a metre (Ponsford 1975). At Hartlepool, it is possible that ploughsoil was removed from the Greyfriars site before building began (Daniels 1986, 265). At the Austin Friars, Leicester, clay make-up for a building was probably derived from the digging of foundation trenches (Mellor and Pearce 1981, 17); the similar use of upcast is suspected at the Oxford Blackfriars (Lambrick and Woods 1976, 175). It is possible that the digging of footings for the church and claustral ranges at Beverley may have supplied boulder clay subsoil for rafting. Later documentary reference to *Pondegarth* lying north of the buildings might also suggest that other excavations had taken place close at hand within the Priory precinct.

Phase 3A — Sill beam structure (First half of 13th century)

The principal evidence for the first timber building to be set over the clay platform consisted of a linear band of chalk and cobble, forming its northern limit. The southern equivalent of this cobble footing is assumed to have been obliterated by the Phase 6A footings in the later 14th century. The north–south extent of the platform would therefore have been between *c*.7.5 and *c*.9.6m — an appropriate span for a timber building.

The usual interpretation of such an insubstantial footing would be as a feature of a timber-framed building — either supporting walls without a load-bearing function, or as the bedding for a timber sill. In the absence of other credible structural members, the latter explanation is preferred. The adoption of sill beam construction may indicate the building's temporary nature or low status. A combination of post and sill construction has been noted in early structures close to the west end of the Priory church, considered to have perhaps represented the first generation of Priory buildings in that area (Armstrong and Tomlinson 1987, 55, Pl. 4c).

The affinities of ground sill construction are with buildings of lower status. In the East Midlands the erection of buildings with major structural elements resting on the ground has been seen in a peasant context as a modest development upon the earth-fast post technique (Dyer 1986, 39). In Norwich, sill beam construction has been suggested for a later 13th-century brewhouse (Atkin *et al.* 1985, 149), and the use of ground sills edge-pegged into place has also been noted in an ancillary structure behind a town house in Hull, dated to the late 13th or early 14th century (Armstrong and Ayers 1987, 26). At Eastgate, a timber building was found with its sills still pegged together in an early 14th-century context (Phase 10, building B3), while interrupted sill construction was noted in a mid. or late 14th-century building (Evans and Tomlinson 1992, 57 and 287–90).

A re-evaluation of structural evidence from Wharram Percy has suggested the wide currency on the Yorkshire Wolds of cruck construction (Wrathmell 1989). Crucks have been recorded in the region as surviving in buildings of lower status; in South Yorkshire their use continued at least into the 17th century (Ryder 1987, 74, 77). The tentative suggestion of a base cruck construction for the Phase 3A hall is one which could account for the absence of load-bearing verticals along the course of the footing. The lower cost of timber for crucks is suggested by a letter dated 1355–6, addressed to John Thoresby, then Archbishop of York, asking him to 'Order the delivery of suitable timber, which consists more of bent trees than of those of greater price and value which grow straight up' (Salzman 1952, 239).

There is no evidence for the nature of walling materials used in the construction of the Phase 3A hall. This could be explained by a ground sill or cruck construction, in which the walls would serve only as weather screens. A ground sill could accommodate walls of planking or wattle. 'Hombre Borde' was used in quantity at Ely in the early 14th century, and may have been a common local building material (Salzman 1952, 244). The use of plank walling set in sills was observed in one of the excavated outbuildings at Eastgate (Evans and Tomlinson 1992, 57). A similar lack of visible side walls was noted in timber buildings at the Austin Friars, Leicester, where a storage function was suggested (Mellor and Pearce 1981, 14, fig. 3). The nature of the roof covering is also unknown. The absence of tile from the footings is probably significant, but a little Type 6 flat tile and fragments of roof furniture in later contexts could have derived from the demolition of this hall. Clay ridge or ventilator tiles would not have been out of place on a roof of shingle, or even of thatch.

Internal fittings

The hearth position set more or less centrally to the Phase 3A structure indicates that it fulfilled a domestic function, and that it was a single storey building open to the roof. This simple hall was equipped with an area of distinct use at one end, marked by heavily stained soils and irregular pits or hollows. The iron-staining in the pits indicates that water passed through them. Charcoal and a fragment of a curfew from their fill show that sweepings from an area with a fireplace also found their way to this area, though perhaps only with the disuse of the pits.

Whilst these pits could conceivably have served as urinals, this use is not supported by the environmental examination of their fills (see above 4.2). An alternative explanation for the use of this area could be in association with a kitchen area. Kitchens could frequently include cisterns, and would often be equipped with drains and soakaways leading out of the building. In urban contexts, waste-disposal pits, both lined and unlined, have been considered as possible kitchen features (cf. examples cited in Ayers 1987, 161); while in a rural setting, a round pit at Wharram Percy may have been used for water storage (Wrathmell 1989, 39). There is, however, little evidence for the disposal of food waste or kitchen vessels in the pits. The institutional kitchen was, moreover, usually a separate structure in the 13th century (Wood 1965, 247–55).

Another interpretation, arguing a specifically monastic character for the activity in this area, would be that the pits served as soakaways for a laver or *piscina* used for ritual washing before conventual meals. This was a facility more usually sited at the corner of the cloister nearest the entrance to the dining area, a location identified archaeologically at Guildford Blackfriars (Poulton and Woods 1984, 38, fig. 21). The provision of a laver in a regular site would, however, be contingent upon an established water supply and, indeed, an established claustral plan; neither can be assumed at the outset of the mendicant occupation. The position of a water pipe within an early refectory has been recorded at Kirkstall Abbey (Moorhouse and Wrathmell 1987, 19). The attenuated construction process recorded in the north range of the great cloister at Beverley (Phases 4A–B) may have dictated the retention of a temporary building until the completion of the stone range.

The use of the pits at the western end of the Phase 3A and 3B halls at the Beverley Priory is unclear; though the fact that they occupied similar positions in both buildings argues for those buildings being used for similar functions. An external pit at the east end of a 12th-century hall at Lurk Lane may originally have been dug as a water cistern, as there was no environmental evidence for faecal material in its primary fill (Armstrong *et al.* 1991, 33). At Waltham Abbey, Essex, a 'Viking-Age Hall' was equipped with soakaway pits of irregular form, also just beyond the east end of the building (Huggins 1976, fig. 31); however, as at Beverley, the archaeological evidence does not permit a firm identification of their function.

Phase 3B — The aisled hall (Later 13th century)

The principal characteristic of the Phase 3A building was its relatively ephemeral construction; nevertheless, by the later 13th century it merited reconstruction. This took a more elaborate form, though the spatial division into functional areas was to be restated within a new aisled hall.

This does not rule out a continuing interpretation of this area as providing temporary accommodation. Building projects on mendicant houses, dependent as they were upon the bounty of patrons, could extend over generations. At the Canterbury Blackfriars, payments towards building are recorded for the period 1237–59 (Martin 1929, 155). At Gloucester Blackfriars, a foundation of *c*.1239, the completion of structural work was achieved *c*.1270 (Rackham *et al.* 1978, 105). The first Dominican house in London was under construction between 1235 and 1273 (Hinnebusch 1951, 28). At York Blackfriars, grants of timber for building works span the period 1235–52 (Goldthorp 1935, 366). Although the Dominicans were established in Beverley by 1240, when a Provincial Chapter was held there, the grant of fifteen oaks by the King in 1263 shows that some building work continued to this date. The style of painted window glass later reused in the secondary cloister dates to the mid. 13th century: if this had originated in the Priory, it may hint at the glazing and completion of the church about this time. Later 13th-century works would presumably have been on the fabric of other ranges.

Against an identification as makeshift accommodation must be set both the persisting divisions (and consequently similar usage which they suggest for the Phase 3A and 3B halls) and the improved quality of the new building. The latter is most apparent in its aisled form, and is also suggested by evidence for the use of roof tile and decorative roof furniture, and the more marked delineation of internal spaces and features. The division of the new structure into bays is apparent, and the archaeological evidence may again suggest a formal arrangement modelled on the secular hall. A detachment from the great cloister is, however, suggested by the realignment of the new structure. This may have been enforced by constraints of land usage within the west part of the precinct, and, as with the later little cloister, was perhaps dictated by the course of the western precinct boundary.

Structure

The major structural elements of the new hall were vertical posts, which varied widely in their recorded scantling (see above, Chapter 2). This may indicate the reuse of donated materials of variable quality and size. On the south side of the hall, it appears that at least one post was to be replaced or supplemented by an adjacent member. Repair by the insertion of a new post would tend to suggest an original process of reversed assembly construction, in which the equidistant spacing of posts was not essential to maintain the structural integrity of the timber frame (Smith 1974, 239).

In the urban environment the earth-fast post style of construction, with a set module distance between the principal uprights, has been seen as a feature of buildings of early 12th to early 13th-century date at York (Addyman 1979, 72). There it was a method replaced by the use of padstones and sill walls by the mid. 13th century (*ibid.*). In King's Lynn most buildings erected before *c*.1250 were raised on earth-fast posts, a method abandoned between *c*.1250 and *c*.1300 in favour of sill wall construction (Clarke and Carter 1977, 439). Excavations in Norwich have indicated a customary reliance on earth-fast post construction before the 14th century, with the occasional use of the method for light or ephemeral structures thereafter (Atkin *et al.* 1985, 245). In situations where improvement of building stock was slow to come about, as in Lincolnshire, earth-fast post and stud-and-mud construction could persist into the post-medieval period (Dyer 1986, 39). There are methodological similarities in the setting of the earth-fast posts at 13th-century Eastgate and the Priory, especially with the use of planks in the bases of the post-pits. The adoption of this structural method may betray the cheap construction of the Phase 3B timber hall.

No evidence for the nature of the north wall of the new building was recorded; the putative north aisle was defined only by a single post, layers of soil, and by insubstantial timber verticals. The west end, however, was represented by a substantial footing which could have supported a stone superstructure — either a full height gable-end wall, or a low stone sill. This could alternatively represent a building of stone attached to the west end of the aisled hall, to serve as a cross-wing, kitchen or service block, perhaps suggested by the position of screens within the hall (though see below).

The evidence for the roofing of the hall consisted mainly of small fragments of roof furniture incorporated in external spreads to the north, and residual roof tile incorporated into later make-up deposits. Plain roof tile of Type 6 was incorporated into a variety of construction or occupation deposits of

Phase 3B. The roof furniture included functional ventilator or louvre fragments, and 'spinning-top' finials, of a purely decorative form (see above, 3.5). A linear spread of silt lying *c*.1.50m beyond the putative north wall could have marked a path, or possibly a shallow eaves-drip, indicating a roof extended well beyond the wall-plate. This would have protected the walls from weathering, but would also have shut off light from the north side of the building. External surfaces spread into the north aisle at its west end. This is taken to indicate an entrance. Here, it may be pertinent to anticipate the form of the Phase 5A buildings later to be erected in this area, which also had a north entrance.

Internal features

Spreads of chalk and crushed stone or mortar within the building could be interpreted either as construction horizons or as floors. At Hartlepool Greyfriars, a clay platform within a timber hall was surfaced with at least four layers of plaster (Daniels 1986, 265). In claustral ranges at Oxford Blackfriars, interleaved mortar floors were identified (Lambrick and Woods 1976, 183); at the Austin Friars, Leicester, some floors consisted only of patches of mortar (Mellor and Pearce 1981, 21). The floor of the east range at the Carmelite house, Newcastle-on-Tyne, was formed by mortared chippings (Harbottle 1968, 184); at Denny Abbey there were plaster and mortar floors in the refectory (Christie and Coad 1980, 179–82). These spreads were laid down at the outset of the occupation. They did not recur in the eastern part of the hall — an apparent change in flooring which could have related to internal divisions within the building.

A footing which extended between the timber principals divided the second and third bays of the hall, and may mark the position of a dias. The failure of the mortary floor surfaces to appear at the east end of the hall could have arisen from a boarded floor for the dias end of a hall: the division between the lower end of the hall — the 'swamp' or 'marsh' (Braun 1968, 161) — and the 'high table' need have been no more substantial than a joist to support floor boards. Such an interpretation would, however, suggest the limitation of the hall structure to only three bays. The division of high and low areas of the hall implies a formal purpose, which in a conventual setting could indicate a function as a refectory. A raised dias has been identified within the refectory of the Carmelite House at Linlithgow (Lindsay 1989, 86).

The continuing function of the building as an open hall was indicated by the reinstatement of a central fireplace. This was constructed with tiles of Type 6, the first plain roof tile to be used at the Priory. The occasional patching of the fireplace indicated the continuing residential status of the building through Phases 3B and 3C. The pits or soakaway in the Phase

3A hall were also renewed with the cutting of a rectangular pit at the west end of the south aisle. The pit was recut at least once, an operation which almost obliterated its first phase, indicating the restriction to this location of the activity it represented. Elements of timber hinted at either the lining of the pit or a superstructure over it.

The pit was apparently screened by a partition extending from the south side of the south aisle to a point half way across the hall. The alignment did not carry all the way across the building, arguing against an interpretation as a full screens passage. The space between the partition and the west wall conformed fairly closely to the *c*.2m width of the aisles. It is possible that this marked a route from the south, over the (necessarily covered) soakaway, and functioned as a draught-excluding screen. The partition ran from a principal timber vertical, which could have accommodated a truss housing the upper ends of the 'speres' of the screen (cf. Braun 1968, 166), and ended on a substantial hollow.

The grouping of stakeholes set centrally against the west wall of the hall appeared too close to it to define a passage. This could represent a bench or furniture position — as identified in a medieval building in Norwich (Ayers 1987, 49). A further east–west alignment of hollows was apparently related to the fireplace. Moveable firescreens were used within medieval buildings: in 1386 'a screen (was) made for the King to have between him and the fire' and in 1390 'a wooden skrene for a fireplace' was ordered for royal apartments at Dover (Salzman 1952, 260). The pairing of sockets suggests a robust structure, conceivably linked to the western partition, or even scaffolding used during the construction or repair of the building. All these fixtures had been removed by the time of the Phase 3C occupation, if not before.

The use of the aisled hall

In the West Midlands documentary research has indicated that the most common form of rural vernacular building between *c*.1350 and *c*.1500 was a structure of three bays; these findings are broadly corroborated by the lower level of research carried out in the East Midlands and elsewhere, and by excavated evidence for buildings of 13th-century date (Dyer 1986). The aisled hall was a common form in the Middle Ages, and where extensive building survey has been carried out, numerous examples have been identified in varying states of preservation (e.g. Hewett 1976, Ryder 1987). This form of building is found in both royal and baronial contexts, carrying on a tradition already established in Saxon times. Ecclesiastical magnates also constructed aisled halls, usually with services accommodated at the 'low' end of the building. This arrangement has been noted in episcopal halls at Lincoln, *c*.1224; Wells, *c*.1275–92;

and Norwich, *c*.1318–25 (Smith 1955, 30).

Institutional timber-framed halls have also been identified. Great Bricett Hall, Essex, was a four bay hall erected *c*.1250 as guest accommodation for an Augustinian Priory. A hall at Kersey Priory, Essex, is of similar form, and is perhaps related to an early 13th-century hospital (Hewett 1976, 46–8). At Thornholme Priory, South Humberside, aisled halls have been dated to the mid. 13th century (Coppack 1989). The aisled hall could achieve monumental proportions: at the 'Bedern' site in York, a later 13th-century aisled hall was at least 40m long with bays *c*.2.50m apart (M. Stockwell, pers. comm.). The aisled hall was also favoured for infirmary buildings where the structural divisions demarcated areas to be occupied by beds, usually in the aisles, and by the chapel, set at one end (Knowles 1963, 186–96). Where they occurred at the great rural monastic houses such as Fountains or Kirkstall, these were probably influential in establishing the wide use of this style (Moorhouse and Wrathmell 1987, 51–3), which was to recur in the quasi-monastic urban hospitals.

At Boston and Guildford Blackfriars, timber structures of uncertain form have been attributed either to occupation pre-dating the priories or to early mendicant activity on these sites (Moorhouse 1972, 22–3; Poulton and Woods 1984, 17–22). At the Austin Friars, Leicester, six pairs of posts set 5m apart defined a building *c*.20m long, comparable in its span to the Phase 3B hall at Beverley. It was likewise swept away by the extension of the house beyond the original cloister (Mellor and Pearce 1981, 9, 14–15, fig. 3). At Pontefract Blackfriars, the Priory ranges were of timber from 1245 to the mid. 14th century (Butler 1984, 133). At Ipswich Blackfriars, a timber building, probably aisled, is considered to have served as the refectory from the time that the church and other ranges were under construction, until its replacement with a stone building on the conclusion of these works (Loader 1986). An early building at Hartlepool Greyfriars provides various points of similarity with the Beverley hall. There, a clay platform served as the bed for a plaster and mortar floor within a post-built aisled structure. Stakeholes indicated internal partitions or fittings at the east end and at the midpoint of one aisle of the hall. The use of this building was considered to have been contemporary with that of the church (Daniels 1986, 265–6). This was probably the case at Beverley, given the dating of *c*.1275 for the occupation of the hall.

A particular feature of the Phase 3 buildings is their detachment from the great cloister. During Phase 3A the building nevertheless followed the (ritual) east–west alignment of the church. It was, however, so positioned as to leave ample room for the development of claustral ranges. The shift in alignment, much closer to compass east–west, which occurred in Phase 3B may betoken a functional separation from the cloister to the south. This eccentric position was to recur in the arrangement of the Phase 5 little cloister.

The alley which later served the little cloister was to be aligned so as to intersect, if projected, the north-west corner of the great cloister. An earlier path, alley or slype, on the same alignment would have given access to the south-west corner of the Phase 3B hall. A detached structure set away from the public access to the complex, but nevertheless linked to the great cloister, is often interpreted as an infirmary in a monastic plan. In the early stages of mendicant occupation this could be a quite lowly building: at Oxford Greyfriars the first infirmary stood to 'barely a man's height' (Little 1917, 62).

Later occupation of the aisled hall (Later 13th century)

The Phase 3C occupation of the aisled hall post-dated the removal of the internal features at the west end and around the fireplace. The silting over the floor, like the chalk and mortar spreads below it, did not extend eastward to the putative dias position: changes in the nature of the occupation cannot, therefore, be substantiated by evidence from the eastern end of the building. The repair of the fireplace and the deposit of ashy silts indicate its continuing residential function.

The animal bone found in floor deposits was significantly different from that recovered from other occupation deposits within the Priory ranges. The 14th-century assemblages were marked by a high proportion of fish and poultry. Occupation deposits from the aisled hall, however, showed a predominance of cattle and other meat bones which might more usually be associated with a secular occupation (see above, 4.3). This was the last recorded use of the hall before its demolition. It may represent a *misericord* regime in which flesh-meat was permitted. An alternative interpretation may also be considered: food-waste at Mount Grace Priory, North Yorkshire, sealed below the Prior's cell, has been identified as secondary rubbish introduced onto the site with construction materials because of the abundance of meat bones, absent from the monastic occupation of that site (Dr. G. Coppack, pers. comm.). The animal bone from the Phase 3C and 3D deposits in the area of the aisled hall included waste products which reflect the slaughter and initial butchery of animals, the dressing of carcasses and the preparation of food for table. It is likely that these groups include both occupation deposits and extraneous dumped material: the latter suggests that a now disused building was being used as a convenient site for the disposal of rubbish.

Phase 3D post-dated the occupation of the timber hall, though activity could have taken place within the derelict shell of the building. There is a dearth of finds to indicate a clear destruction horizon for the Phase 3B hall. The slow deterioration of the Phase 3B structure is suggested by the survival in an advanced state of decay of the post-stubs: these were evidently cut off at ground level rather than being withdrawn for reuse.

Phases 4 and 6 — The great cloister (13th century onwards)

Introduction

The cloister forms the distinctive residential focus of a conventual house, and its relationship to the church as the ritual centre of the community is consistent across the range of medieval monastic houses (Knowles 1963, 181–5). Within this broad formula, however, the mendicant orders exercised a flexibility which was notable even at the time of their flourishing: 'We have nearly as many different plans and arrangements of our buildings and churches as there are priories' wrote a Dominican in the mid. 13th century (Hinnebusch 1951, 132). This flexibility applied especially to the English houses, typically snuggled into an urban or suburban locale where pre-existing topography would impose the adaptation of plan forms to take advantage of the sounder ground, established drainage, or access to the site. Thus, at Beverley, the situation of the great cloister north of the church may have been imposed by the presence of established thoroughfares to the south and west of the precinct. This would have rendered the friars' devotions accessible, and their accommodation secluded. The situation of the latrines over a conduit on the western periphery of the cloister may suggest that the dormitory or *dorter* would have been set in the west or north range. Whilst admitting this flexibility, it should be recalled that certain ritual aspects of the monastic life did not lend themselves to modification. Thus, the division of a mendicant church into public and private areas, and the setting of the chapter house to the east of the cloister, were standard practices as soon as anything approaching a claustral layout was achieved.

The following discussion of the great cloister at Beverley proposes an outline scheme of development. The church is dealt with first, followed by the east, west and north ranges. The consideration of evidence for the west and north ranges draws together evidence assigned to Phases 4 and 6 in the excavation report (see above, Chapter 2).

The church — choir and sacristy

The choir, the east end of the church set aside for the singing of the divine offices and for private devotions, was the focal point for communal worship in all monastic houses. The Dominican order was unusual in the precedence which it afforded to study, but the efficacy of the public duties of preaching and taking confessions sprang also from the application which the friars brought to prayer. The importance of communal prayer was stated and restated both by Chapters Provincial and General, and by the anecdotal tradition of the order (Hinnebusch 1951, 216–31).

The excavations carried out between 1963 and 1989 have indicated the overall dimensions of the church. The original preaching nave was *c*.6.60m wide internally (Armstrong and Tomlinson 1987, 52), and *c*.25m long. Such dimensions support the view that the church was of average size for a mendicant community (*ibid*.). The choir, however, has been shown to have been *c*.21m long (foundations recorded during watching brief work in 1980 have been considered as marking the end of the church, reported by Sanders and Armstrong, 1983) and *c*.7m wide internally: the discrepancy in the width of nave and choir merits discussion.

The excavations have shown that the alignment of the south wall of the choir conformed with the south wall of the nave. This would suggest that the original building matched the standard pattern of the early mendicant church, as seen at Carmelite Hulne, Northumberland. This was a long single-cell building, internally divided (Hope 1890, plan). The north wall of the choir at Beverley, however, fails to align with that of the nave: it lies *c*.1m to the north. This slight deviation may bear some significance for the development of the church and the complex. The medieval builder could use '*rayngyng line*' for setting out buildings (Salzman 1952, 340). A straight line would not, perhaps, have been so easily achieved, if the buildings of the east claustral range had already been under construction. The deviation in alignment may, therefore, represent no more than a surveying error, perhaps due to the early progress of work on the east range.

An alternative interpretation is that the footings, which were exposed, but not thoroughly examined, may represent either a rebuilding of the north wall of the choir, or the separate modelling of choir and nave; the latter is less likely, given a tradition of single-cell churches. The form of the footings may hint at two distinct structural episodes: chalk rubble extending south of wall C3 could perhaps have marked an earlier wall alignment, though one that was not recognised at the time of excavation. The overall dimensions of the choir show a ratio of internal length to width of 3 to 1. Such a ratio is not recorded in the plans of the earlier churches. It occurred at the second site of the London Blackfriars at Ludgate, established by 1286 (Hinnebusch 1951, 145), where recent excavation (1989) has confirmed that the 16th-century survey giving the dimensions of the choir relates to its internal measurements (B. Watson, pers. comm.). This ratio was also to be approached at Chichester Greyfriars, where the choir remains extant (Martin 1937, 23), and at Southampton Greyfriars, a church indicated by excavation to have been of near identical plan to Chichester (S. Hardy, pers. comm.) and dated to *c*.1287 (Little 1917, 74). The triune proportion of the choir was a feature of Walsingham Greyfriars, founded *c*.1347 (Martin 1935, 229), and of the second Carmelite church at Aylesford, of uncertain date, but probably later 14th-century (Rigold 1965, 9–15). Similar, though not identical, proportions occurred at Bristol Blackfriars (Leighton 1933, 162); at Bristol Greyfriars' new choir of *c*.1386 (Ponsford 1975), and at the Greyfriars at Lichfield and Great Yarmouth — both later churches with aisled naves (Martin 1937, 23, 151–3). At King's Lynn Greyfriars, it is considered likely that building work was carried out in the 14th century (Martin 1937, 23, 105); here too the length and breadth of the choir observed an approximate ratio of 3 to 1. At Beverley, there is ample evidence for the extension of the preaching nave by the addition of a south aisle in the 14th century. Both ends of the south aisle have been recorded by excavation, and defined an internal space of *c*.31.50m by *c*.5.10m. The ratio used here closely approaches 6 to 1, which may represent a doubling of the system perceived in the choir.

Given the non-intrusive investigation of the choir, the evidence for a rebuilding remains circumstantial. Two other pieces of evidence may relate to this question. The first is the identification of wall C30, the western limit of the choir, as being butted to the original south wall of the choir. The second is the north wall of a sacristy, C18 and C19. The character of these footings, and the floors they enclose, is markedly different, possibly suggesting two phases of construction.

The identification of light footings within the choir appears to indicate the extension of the stalls half way up the choir — a normal situation noted at Hulne Whitefriars (Hope 1890, 114) and London Greyfriars (Martin 1937, fig. 13). At Guildford and Oxford Blackfriars, low walls were considered to have served as a base for timber stalls (Poulton and Woods 1984, 34, fig. 17; Lambrick and Woods 1976, 175). Ephemeral internal footings set parallel with the south wall of the choir at Newcastle-upon-Tyne Blackfriars have been interpreted in the same way (B. Harbottle, pers. comm.). The stalls appear to have been a little over half as wide as those at Oxford Blackfriars (Lambrick and Woods 1976, 175), perhaps only accommodating a single rank of friars on either side.

Burials within the choir included a brick-lined tomb which may have been disturbed by robbing for the retrieval of a lead coffin, an activity commonly reported from Dissolution horizons (e.g. Lambrick

and Woods 1976, 190). The '*White Lady*' presently resting against the wall of the 'Old Friary' is a grave slab depicting a woman in 14th-century costume; a slab would likewise have capped the lined grave. The names of some of the noteworthy individuals buried in the church and cloisters of the Beverley Blackfriars are known (see Mf.1. A2–8). Previous limited investigations of the west end of the nave have shown burials in coffins within the church, and burials apparently without coffins in the cloister (Armstrong and Tomlinson 1987, 26–9). Burials were not observed beyond the east end of the choir stalls, save for a single tomb in an ancillary structure, perhaps a chantry chapel (see below). Where, as at Ipswich Blackfriars, large numbers of burials have been excavated, only a few were in lined graves (Loader 1986). No *in situ* flooring was seen, although a few fragments of green or yellow glazed floor tile may suggest the former paving of the choir. The paving of the interior of the Blackfriars church at Newcastle-upon-Tyne with yellow and green tiles, set diagonally, has been recorded at the main entrance from the cloister (B. Harbottle, pers. comm.)

A building identified as the sacristy or vestry lay on the north side of the choir. The location of the sacristy on the cloister side of the choir is usual; this appears to have been structurally independent of the east claustral range, perhaps to admit light from the south into the chapter house. There were two distinct structural forms identified which may relate to a similar sequence of construction activity to that indicated above. The flat-laid roof tile at the east end of the building may mark the position of an item of furniture. At Ludlow Whitefriars, 'inner' and 'outer' sacristies were described by the suppression inventory: the inner sacristy contained vestments, the outer sacristy was used to store furniture and an arras for use on festival days (Klein and Roe 1987, 23).

The south aisle and chantry chapel

The clearance of the junction of the south aisle with the choir allowed the definition of the full extent of the aisle. This extension of the church had been attended by the replacement of the south wall of the nave with an arcade of piers set on octagonal bases. These have been recorded as features of work on the churches of Hartlepool Greyfriars and Chester Blackfriars. The resultant twin-aisled form of the church has been compared to those at Guildford, Brecon and Chelmsford Blackfriars, and at Hartlepool and Gloucester Greyfriars (Armstrong and Tomlinson 1987, 53). As noted above, the internal dimensions of the south aisle, *c*.31.50m by *c*.5.10m, indicate that it was constructed with a length to width proportion of 6 to 1, rather than with reference to the breadth of the nave. The new aisle is considered to be of 14th-century date, probably before 1350, and was work of an inferior quality compared to the primary build of the nave (*ibid.*). It terminated on a line with the west end of the choir, as was the case at Cardiff Greyfriars, Brecon Blackfriars (where the west end of the aisle accommodated a chapel), Cardiff Blackfriars (Clapham 1927, figs. 4, 2, 3), and the Chester Blackfriars rebuilding (where it may be associated with a semi-transeptal form: Ward 1990, 62–9). The new work was buttressed, as were most of the more substantial buildings at the Priory, helping to match the new work to the old. It nearly doubled the public preaching area of the church, and provided a correspondingly increased area for the burial of patrons. Bequests to the friars, some specifically linked to burial within the church, are recorded from 1311 (Mf.1. A2–8), and reached a peak *c.*1391–1410. The inferior workmanship of secondary building work was a feature also noted at Guildford Blackfriars when the choir was extended in the 14th century (Poulton and Woods 1984, 34), and at the Blackfriars church at Oxford (Lambrick and Woods 1976, 189).

The identification of the structure added to the south side of the choir as a chantry chapel rests on the discovery of a large brick-lined tomb at its east end; this burial would have been beside the altar. The chapel post-dated the extension of the preaching nave. The method of construction, with a rubble core faced with brick, is analogous to that used for ashlar walling on the site. The slightly more robust construction at the east end, where the walling was *c.*0.10m thicker, may have been intended to allow for the setting of an east window. A double tomb, stone-lined, has been excavated at Northampton Greyfriars (Williams 1978, 106); while at Bristol Greyfriars, a group of eleven individuals including children was found in a vault within the church (Ponsford 1975). Palmer (1882, 42) commented that a quarter oxgang of land at *Coldon Magna*, listed among the holdings of the house in the Dissolution survey, was probably the endowment of a mortuary foundation. In 1421 John de Holme, son of Richard de Holme, desired to be buried within the Priory church at Beverley. In 1448 the church is recorded as containing the '*Holme Awtir*'. This structure cannot, however, be more specifically associated with these references.

At Guildford Blackfriars, a chantry chapel was attached to the church at an angle buttress position; as at Beverley, this relationship is held to indicate that it is of 14th-century date or later (Poulton and Woods 1984, 34). A chantry chapel was identified at Oxford Blackfriars (Lambrick and Woods 1976, 178). At the Dominican house in London, a Lady Chapel was built before 1437, and rebuilt *c.*1470 adjoining the choir (Clapham 1912, 64). At Beverley, however, the will of William Horn, proved 1476, requested his burial before the image of St. Mary in the middle of the nave. This may imply that there was not a separate Marian chapel attached to the church at this late date.

The chapter house

The buttressed corner of a building to the north of the choir may be identified as the chapter house, on the basis of its apparent projection east of the cloister. This forms the only evidence yet recovered for the eastern side of the great cloister. (Butler is mistaken in referring to the *east* range as adjacent to the *reredorter:* 1984, 132). The rest of the east claustral range remains inaccessible to investigation, beneath the Hull-Scarborough railway line. The position of this structure was predicted by making two assumptions. The first was a similarity in this aspect of layout — the eastward projection of a chapter house — with most other Dominican houses (Hinnebusch 1951, 186). The second assumption was that the proportion and size of the east range were similar to those of the Phase 6 north range (see below, for further discussion of that structure).

While the discovery of a building in the position it had been suggested to occupy was immediately satisfying, the problems which it raises are intractable without further excavation, and may be summarised as follows. First, the footings are undated. The use of clasping buttresses, if this is indeed what the footings represent, is not a diagnostic trait of any one period of building at the Beverley Priory. Secondly, the Phase 6 north range, upon the dimensions of which the calculation of the position of the chapter house was based, is considered to be work of the later 14th century, while the chapter house might be expected to be early work. Thirdly, the indications of rebuilding along the division between north range and cloister garth, and the apparent asymmetry of the great cloister, could hint at its reorganisation. Finally, the chapter house was almost certainly a narrower structure than the *ad hoc* estimation of its position has suggested, and its position relative to the final form of the great cloister may not have been central. To conclude, an identification of a chapter house projecting east of the cloister may be acceptable; however, this remains undated, and the possibility of rebuilding, or of an aberrant plan on the east side of the cloister, should not be ruled out. The brick-faced walling which runs across the buttress-footings could represent either a rebuilding of the buttress, or an altogether distinct building which is not otherwise recorded.

Phase 4 — Great cloister, west side

The west side of the great cloister has been recognised as a complex area since the excavations of 1963, which recorded the irregular plan of the west range. MacMahon identified two major periods of building, and considered them to have been of 13th and 15th-century date, recognising that the west range in its later form post-dated the *reredorter* (Armstrong and Tomlinson 1987, 55, fig. 12). The recent detailed re-examination of parts of MacMahon's trenches, and in particular the elevation view obtained of the east wall of the range (Figure 26), has confirmed the previous view of extensive rebuilding activity, and may tend to confirm the suggestion that the area had been subjected to a major episode of replanning (cf. Armstrong and Tomlinson 1987, 55). The evidence for an early plan of a different form from that finally achieved is considered below, and is advanced as a provisional interpretation, which is qualified throughout by the incomplete examination of these structures.

Phase 4A — Great cloister, north and west ranges (?13th century)

The 1986–7 excavations revealed that the earliest structures on the west side of the cloister were two apparently independent foundations; the northern one was associated with two pairs of buttresses marking the ends of a north–south wall *c*.8.32m long. No original superstructure of this wall survived, save these buttresses. Their position may indicate, by analogy with their use elsewhere at the Priory, that they were part of the west end of a building set parallel to the church. This structure would therefore have formed part of an early north range.

Other evidence may tend to corroborate this interpretation. A footing which ran across the cloister alley, and which has been identified as marking the position of responds on either side of a step (Armstrong and Tomlinson 1987, 54, fig. 12), formed the entrance to the putative north range. The south wall of the range may have been continued by a footing running eastwards from the arch. The north wall of the range was represented by an external ashlar plinth course lying *c*.14m to the east. The use of a chamfered plinth is characteristic of the early masonry on the site. The south wall footing has not been traced this far east, perhaps because excavation was only carried down to a level of *c*.6.70m OD. What would have served as a median internal footing within this range has, however, been located. The early north range was internally arched or vaulted, as indicated by the survival *in situ* of a demi-hexagonal respond. This would indicate a two-storied building, which was longitudinally divided.

The postulation of arches or vaults within the north range may permit a reconsideration of previously published evidence for the footings of the west range. As reported by Armstrong and Tomlinson (*op. cit.*), the alignment which was later to form the wall between the garth and the west cloister alley was intermittently buttressed externally. It also carried walling of a narrow gauge which was perhaps not part

of the original structure. The west side of this foundation featured footings protruding at a spacing of *c*.1.50m centre-to-centre, though not without interruption. These may bear interpretation as the bases for responds, and could therefore indicate an arched or vaulted form for an early west range.

According to this scheme the north range would have been *c*.6.50m wide, with a length of over 14m internally, whilst the west range would have been *c*.15m long, with an uncertain width. These dimensions may relate to those of the original nave of the church. One or both ranges could have been arched or vaulted at ground floor level, with first-floor apartments above. Overshot apartments are known to have existed at Dominican houses at Bristol, Hereford, and Norwich (and at Ribe, Denmark, on all three sides of the cloister — a continental parallel kindly suggested by Dr. L. Butler); at Greyfriars houses at Ware, Walsingham, Dunwich, and perhaps also London, Bedford and Yarmouth; and at Carmelite Aylesford (Martin 1937, 30). The presence of an overshot west range has previously been regarded as unlikely because of the disparate widths of the alley and range (Armstrong and Tomlinson 1987, 54). This disproportion is suggested to exist between elements of different periods of construction; the overshot alley is, however, often considered as a secondary feature of a mendicant plan (Dr. G. Coppack, pers. comm.). Vaulting in the cloister is rare in a mendicant context; it survives only at Coventry Whitefriars and Great Yarmouth Greyfriars, but may have been torn down or defaced at the Greyfriars houses at Southampton and London (Martin 1937, 31). Vaulting has also been inferred within the Dominican church at Great Yarmouth, from the survival of brick columns supporting a Caen-stone springer (Rye 1973, 501), in undercrofting at Lincoln Greyfriars (Martin 1937, pl. 11; Stocker 1984), and in the sacristy of the Newcastle Blackfriars.

The firm identification of the function of the Phase 4A ranges considered above is impossible given the fragmentary nature of the evidence. The proximity of the latrine or *reredorter* makes it likely that one of these ranges served as the dormitory or *dorter*. This would have been a location dictated by the western position of the drain (see above). A situation for the refectory or *frater* opposite the church would be usual in a regular monastic plan (Knowles 1963, 185–6). It is recorded at Dominican houses at London (Clapham 1912, 75), Newcastle-on-Tyne (Hinnebusch 1951, 163), and perhaps at Guildford (Poulton and Woods 1984, 38–9). The Phase 6 building erected in the later 14th century on the north side of the great cloister at Beverley has been identified as a refectory (see below).

The west range could also serve as the refectory: this has been suggested at Bristol (Leighton 1933,

172); Ipswich (Gildyard-Beer 1977, 16), Canterbury (Martin 1929, 162–3) and Gloucester (W.H. Knowles 1932, 181). At Beverley, a footing within the alley lies on the convergence of three conduit alignments, perhaps marking a laver position (Armstrong and Tomlinson 1987, fig. 12). A further strengthened footing on the west wall could bear interpretation as a wall pulpit-base — it has formerly been considered to mark a chimney (Armstrong and Tomlinson 1987, 55). It is, therefore, possible that a western refectory was resited on the north of the cloister in the later 14th century.

The interpretation offered above is necessarily tentative. The duration, or even completion, of an original arrangement is uncertain, though it was redundant by the later 14th century when the Phase 6 north range was built, and possibly even before that date. It does at least offer objectives for any future work in this area. An alternative interpretation of the early form of the north range is presented below, p.244.

Phase 4B — Great cloister, north range (?13th or 14th century)

The Phase 4B rebuilding appears to have been carried down to foundation level on the east, and offset over footings on the west side of the wall; the footings could be attributed to either Phase 4A or 4B. The only elements of the Phase 4A superstructure to survive were buttress bases, and these were masked by the new work.

The use of rough-tooled stone for the Phase 4B walling is a common feature of mendicant ranges (Martin 1937, 30). It represents lower quality work than was recorded on the church, and than was suspected on the Phase 4A north range. A distinction between better early work on the church and inferior later construction has been noted above. At Sandwich Whitefriars, 13th-century work set on an ashlar plinth contrasted with later coursed rubble walling (Rigold 1965, 13–14). At Newcastle-upon-Tyne, the Carmelite church was built on an ashlar plinth, whilst the 14th-century east range was of rough-dressed stone, with ashlar reserved for mouldings (Harbottle 1968, 179, 184). A lower quality of 14th-century work has also been recorded at the Austin Friars, Leicester (Mellor and Pearce 1981, 33) and elsewhere.

The new wall, 0.88–0.95m thick, would have been adequate to support a two-storey superstructure of stone. It extended along the west end of the putative Phase 4A north range, and returned eastwards, showing the reconstruction or completion of this building. The use of chalk on the west face of the wall may indicate that the area to the west was now enclosed, though a northern limit for the later western range has never been identified. The new work terminated short of the first putative respond position associated with the west range. It is therefore possible that the Phase 4B work was accomplished without the immediate disruption of pre-existing structures along the west cloister alley.

The west range of the Phase 4A layout did not, however, escape modification altogether. An east-west wall formed a subdivision of, or addition to, this building, to be rebuilt or completed in Phase 4C. It is not possible to state how far this work immediately altered the form of the west range. The lesser width of this new wall may relate it to Phase 4C, when further modification was accomplished.

Phase 4C — Great cloister, west range (?14th century)

The structural episodes recorded in Phases 4B and 4C may have been closely linked. The Phase 4B work has been discussed above as a rebuilding of the Phase 4A north range, demonstrated at its western end. Phase 4C was wholly concerned with the west range. The thick plaster render applied indiscriminately over both the Phase 4B and Phase 4C structures along the cloister alley, presumably as a cosmetic measure, may betray their close relationship. They should perhaps be viewed as discrete episodes in a general refurbishment of the great cloister.

The use of mixed media — brick, limestone and chalk — to construct a wall *c*.0.60m thick suggests a less substantial character for the new west range. It paid no detectable respect to the projecting footings along the easternmost wall, and may therefore indicate a total reconstruction. The walling which MacMahon's plan records as an intermittent survival above the eastern footing (Armstrong and Tomlinson 1987, fig. 12) may indicate a light structure dividing alley and garth, in keeping with the lighter Phase 4C walling, and supporting only a pent roof. A similar disparity between garth wall and footings was also noted along the north claustral alley, though in neither case was the depth of the footings established.

Aspects of the Phase 4C building reflect the structural detail of the little cloister ranges. Brick of Type 4 formed the east face of the wall; this was recorded in the little cloister, dated to the early 14th century. The thickness of the Phase 4C walling is also similar to that of the little cloister ranges, and may indicate a sill or ground floor wall supporting a timber frame. This contrasts markedly with the stone walling of the Phase 4B north range, and more markedly still with the vaulted or arched construction of Phase 4A. It may betoken a diminished status or altered function for the west range from this period, perhaps to be related to the updating of the Priory's building stock elsewhere. The tripartite subdivided form achieved by the later west range compares with that at

Newcastle-on-Tyne Blackfriars, which is considered as a guest hall accompanied by other chambers of uncertain purpose (B. Harbottle, pers. comm.).

The staining of the plastered wall face indicated that an alley surface lay at *c*.6.80m OD — close to the mid. 14th-century (Phase 5B) level of occupation at the south end of the little cloister alley, and about 0.20m below the level from which the Phase 6 north range was to be built. This may represent the achievement of a near-level surface across both cloister alleys, and may even hint at the contemporaneity of Phases 4C and 5B. The plaster rendering of the alley walls was carried across the position of the earlier arch or step, arguing for its redundancy by Phase 4C. It may follow that by the time that the Phase 4C works had been completed, the alley had been lengthened to achieve its final extent, which could imply a connection between these works and the construction of the Phase 6 north range in the later 14th century.

Phases 4A (alternative interpretation), 6A and 6B

Great cloister north range

The interpretation of buildings on the west side of the great cloister has included consideration of the early north range; an alternative interpretation of the Phase 4A building is presented below. Most of the evidence, however, relates to the later Phase 6 structure, whose construction post-dated Phase 4B. This new building incorporated major structural elements of an earlier north range, and fixed the final form of the great cloister. It is dated to the later 14th century, and is considered as broadly contemporary with Phase 5C in the little cloister.

Phase 4A (?13th century)

The identification of an external wall and a footing *c*.3.20m to the south of it was initially associated with the Phase 6A building. The wall was considered to mark the south side of this range, with the footing beyond supporting a lighter garth wall. This interpretation was reviewed. Not only did the position of an ashlar plinth-course on the north side of wall 566 argue against its construction as an internal face, but its construction also differed from the coursed rubble of the Phase 6 range. The faced wall to the south is accordingly regarded as part of a pre-existing range which was reused to form the south side of a new structure. An interpretation of this wall as part of the north range constructed during Phase 4A, and partially rebuilt in Phase 4B, has been offered above.

The most compelling argument against the identification of the walling on the north-west and north sides of the cloister as elements of a single structure is the failure to identify the continuation of a

south wall. Further to this, the full character and depth of footings in this area has not been established. MacMahon illustrated a footing which continued eastwards: it is not clear from his plan whether it terminated within or beyond his excavation (Armstrong and Tomlinson 1987, fig. 12). The garth wall footings shown on MacMahon's plan were shown by re-excavation in 1986–7 to survive up to a level of *c*.6.40m OD. The trench which identified walling to the east was not, however, carried below a level of *c*.6.70m OD. It is therefore possible that this overcautious investigation failed to reach earlier footings, which had been robbed to a similar depth as on the west side of the cloister.

If the excavated evidence *is* a full record of the form of the Phase 4A north range, it would represent an extremely narrow building with no more than an alley below and a gallery above. Such a range could not have fulfilled a communal role. It would, however, have had to fulfil some essential purpose to earn its place in the early plan. Amongst known 13th century works at British mendicant sites it would be unparalleled. A 15th-century range at the Austin Friars, Leicester, was 24m long by 4m wide, and is considered to have perhaps provided extra accommodation (Mellor and Pearce 1981, 35, 41–2). Narrow ranges at Ipswich Blackfriars, in the second cloister, have been considered as perhaps accommodating study cubicles, by analogy with continental houses (Gilyard-Beer 1977, 20–21). Study cells have been firmly identified at Gloucester Blackfriars, where the individual cells measured *c*.1.62m wide by *c*.2.50m long (Hinnebusch 1951, 171): about a dozen such cells could have been fitted into a narrow range set along the north side of the Beverley cloister. Small cells have also been identified at Cardiff Blackfriars, and have been reported to have measured *c*.2.30m by *c*.2m at Lancaster (Conway 1889, 104). Documentary evidence has also indicated that study cells existed at the Dominican houses at King's Langley (Salzman 1952, 292), Warwick (Hinnebusch 1951, 180), and York (Goldthorp 1935, 377), and at the Franciscan houses at London and Richmond, North Yorkshire (Martin 1937, 37). It is rare, however, for study cells to have occupied a narrow range; they more usually formed a subdivision of the dormitory (Hinnebusch 1951, 167). (Dr. L. Butler kindly comments that they also tend to be a late medieval development, citing their appearance at Richmond, Surrey, founded in *c*.1500.) This interpretation is thus regarded as less likely than the integration of the Phase 4A north range with the other early work, as discussed above. Quite apart from the unique character this plan would impose on the early cloister at Beverley, it would also carry with it a shortage of communal space unusual in mendicant houses which had actually achieved a claustral form.

Phase 6 (Later 14th century)

The substantial nature of the Phase 6 footings and walls indicates that they formed an important element of the Priory's building stock — almost certainly a stone building of two storeys. Although the masonry was of indifferent quality, it was in keeping both with the previous modifications, and with mendicant standards of domestic architecture.

The variable scale and character of the footings — the north wall footing was trench-built, while the west wall foundation was built as a free-standing structure — may relate both to the local topography and to the pre-existing layout into which the new range was to be fitted. The considerable width of the pitched footings was a characteristic of work on major buildings where ground was poor — the foundations of the choir of the Oxford Blackfriars were 2.50m wide (Lambrick and Woods 1976, 173–4). At Chelmsford Blackfriars, on the site of the latrine block, changes in the character of subsoil are suggested to have dictated a variable form of foundation (Drury 1974, 43). In the case of the Phase 6 building, spreads of loam and rubble were used to build up the ground level around the foundations. The incorporation of a conduit into the footing of the north wall may have related either to the local control of ground water, or to a more extensive system of water supply (see below, Phase 5).

The construction of the new range post-dated the Phase 4B works at the north-west corner of the great cloister, though there is no evidence to indicate the length of time which had elapsed. The continuing use of clasping buttresses at the north-west corner of the new building does, however, show that it was probably of a style which matched the old. The internal width of the new structure may also have been determined by reference to existing buildings (see below, Chapter 6.2).

The size of the new building — *c*.7.44m by over 19m — indicates that it was a major conventual building. The presence of an integral footing which projected from the north side of the range initially suggested its identification as a *frater* or refectory, equipped with an integral wall pulpit. In a mendicant setting, wall pulpits have been identified at Dominican Norwich (Sutermeister 1977, 28), Canterbury Blackfriars (Martin 1929, 164); at the Franciscan convent at Denny (Martin 1937, fig. 18) and perhaps at Winchelsea Greyfriars (Martin 1937, 33), at Sandwich Whitefriars (Rigold 1965, pl. 11) and at the Austin Friars Leicester (Mellor and Pearce 1981, 24). In such a setting the pulpit itself would be within the thickness of the wall, with a window lighting the reader's desk. This was not an invariable feature: free-standing pulpits have been recorded at Bridgnorth and Reading Greyfriars, Ludlow Austin Friars (Martin 1937, 33) and Ludlow Whitefriars (Klein and Roe 1987, 63). The thickening of walls in the west claustral range at Beverley has been tentatively ascribed to the provision of kitchen fireplaces (Armstrong and Tomlinson 1987, 55). The 'pulpit footing' may, therefore, be inadequate evidence on its own to permit the identification of the Phase 6A range as a refectory.

The two doorways at the west end of the building could give access, either from the ground floor or from both ground and first floors, to services lying west of the range. These included a cistern and the latrine — an early feature to judge from the quality of its stonework. Access to water supply would be important for the functioning of a kitchen. There is further circumstantial evidence for access through the range along a north–south axis. Without this the construction of the Phase 6A range would have severed communication between the little and great cloisters. This route, if maintained, could have imposed a division within the ground floor of the building.

The ground floor saw use intensive enough to require the replacement of its clay floors, identified at the north-west corner and along the north side of this building. No extensive occupation deposits were recorded in the central part of the range, which may argue that a tiled or suspended floor was fitted in the main ground floor chamber. The alignment of brick running parallel to the north wall could be interpreted as a sleeper wall for a wooden floor (cf. Martin 1973, 27), or as indicating the position of benches (see below, Phase 5). According to such an interpretation the clay floor along the north side of the building would have been a distinct surface, separated from the boarded or tiled part of the range. At Newcastle Blackfriars, the floor was tiled in the centre of the refectory, with clay platforms along the walls (B. Harbottle, pers. comm.).

The later occupation deposits in the north-west corner of the range contained an unusually high proportion of bone from fish-heads, which may indicate that food was prepared in this area. A similar concentration of food preparation waste was recovered from the bottom of the cistern immediately to the west of the range (see above, section 4.3). This may illustrate the use of the west end of the ground floor as an ancillary area to a refectory — food being prepared there before being taken to table. The refectory may therefore have occupied a chamber further to the east at ground-floor level. In this case, the route connecting the great and little cloisters would have functioned as a screens passage. At Dominican Ipswich, the ground-floor refectory was screened at one end from a chamber, tentatively identified as a parlour (Loader 1986). A first-floor position for the Beverley refectory cannot, however, be ruled out, given the substantial structure of the range. Walsingham Greyfriars, founded *c*.1347, had a refectory set at first-floor level in a range which was similarly located between the great and little cloisters (Martin 1935, plan). When the large area and two-storey form of the Beverley north range are taken into consideration, it is even possible that the twin constraints of water supply and drainage enforced the accommodation of both dormitory and refectory in a single large range, the former above the latter. This may be confirmed by the northwards extension of the *reredorter*, which was apparently intended to maintain a connection between the latrine and the first floor of the north range.

The construction of a narrow wall, which was buttressed in brick, and which formed the division between the north cloister alley and the garth, was secondary to the original north range. The disproportion between the footings and the wall has been interpreted above as marking the building of a garth wall on footings which were originally provided for a more substantial structure. According to this interpretation, an original internal division (Phase 4A) became the limit of a garth which had been extended northwards. The provision of a separate foundation for the Phase 6B buttress and wall, at a higher level than the original footings, may confirm this hypothesis. This wall may have supported the pent roof of a new alley.

The bench footings along both sides of the alley are similar to those set in the north range of the little cloister in Phase 5C (see below). Benching in the cloister alley is not common in mendicant houses, though a south-facing alley would be the sunniest position for such seats. They may also betray a temporary shortage of space for the pursuit of private study, which was more usually carried on in a library or in study carrels. In this context, the documentary evidence for a fire in the library and dormitory in *c*.1449 may be significant. The wear to which the alley surface had been subjected, thereby forming a silted hollow, shows that its more common use was for access between areas of the convent.

The latrine block and cistern (?13th or 14th century onwards)

The identification of the chutes and culverts of the latrine block or *reredorter* confirmed the nature of this eccentrically positioned building, which had been previously recorded by MacMahon, and was again glimpsed in 1983. Its position was dictated by a pre-existing watercourse whose form and development have been discussed above. It was originally an independent structure, as is considered to have been the case at the Canterbury (Martin 1929, 166, pl. 8) and Rhuddlan Blackfriars (Clapham 1927, 97, pl. 3). The extension of the west wall of the west claustral range, however, effected a later junction with the south-east corner of the building.

The lower part of the structure was distinguished by a chalk floor and a basal plinth course on the east side; the latter feature has been considered above to denote earlier work. The rebuilding of its superstructure is suggested by its junction with the later west range, the extension and subdivision of its north end, and by the attached elements of brick. These last may relate to the provision of first-floor access to the Phase 6 north range, carrying a timber walkway. This structure did not continue at ground-floor level, as this would have taken it across the position of the nearby cistern. Its apparent engagement with the later 14th-century north range may suggest this extension to be of similar date. The revetment of the west side of the culvert in brick is undated, though at Chelmsford Blackfriars a comparable conduit was of 14th-century date (Drury 1974, 49).

No deposits survived within the culvert to indicate the variety of waste deposited in it, though the latrine was so positioned as to be accessible from both the north and west ranges of the great cloister. Drains from the great cloister emptied into this culvert, and the presence of sluices in the west range may indicate the disposal of liquid waste (Armstrong and Tomlinson 1987, fig. 12, pls. 8A–B; see above, Chapter 2).

The cistern beyond the west end of the Phase 6 north range is the second such feature to be identified at the Beverley Priory. The first was a tank built of reused materials, and which was perhaps in use in the 15th century; it lay adjacent to a putative detached guesthouse on the site of the extant 'Old Friary' (Armstrong and Tomlinson 1987, 16–17). Many Dominican houses were provided in the course of the 13th century with conduits supplying sweet water; the chalk-lined cistern was perhaps integrated into such a system. Its close juxtaposition with the Phase 6 north range need not argue the contemporaneity of cistern and range: the cistern may have served an earlier building. A cistern fed by four conduits has been identified at Denny Abbey; it was no earlier than the mid. 14th century, and was related to the Franciscan occupation of that site (Christie and Coad 1980, 189, fig. 15).

The initial interpretation of the second cistern at the Priory was as a reservoir, from which water might be drawn for kitchen or ritual use. The apparent redundancy of this cistern in this role was marked by the deposition within it of food preparation and fuel waste, and is dated to the 14th century — perhaps a contemporary episode with the use of the Phase 6 range. This prompts a reconsideration of this interpretation. The Irish Franciscan house at Ross had a round stone fishpond in the kitchen, to keep live fish until they were required for the table (Mooney 1956, 132). Such fixtures are also known in English mendicant houses — e.g. at Guildford Blackfriars, there were '*ii framies of leade to water fische*' in the little kitchen (Poulton and Woods 1984, fig. 3). Wooden vats for the keeping of live fish have been excavated at Blaydes Staithe in Hull (D. Evans, pers. comm.); Beverley, too, was a port with access to both marine and freshwater fish. The presence of waste in the base of the cistern need not imply its complete disuse, as eel and carp can both tolerate turbid water for short periods (Dr. A. Jones, pers. comm.). The former are known to have formed an important component of the diet observed at the Priory in the 14th century. A period of changed use for the cistern may thus be considered: as either a freshwater reservoir, or as a fish tank it could indicate the proximity of an area used for the preparation of food.

Further evidence relating to water supply or drainage has been recorded, particularly with reference to a conduit along the west side of the little cloister (see below, Phase 5). This has been considered to have extended through the Phase 6A range, though its integration with other conduits in the great cloister is unknown. A further conduit route along the outside of the Phase 5C little cloister ranges is also suspected (see below, Phases 5 and 7). These features add to a general picture of water supply and drainage which was routed on a north–south alignment. The possibility that some of the conduit routes, which were formerly presented by Armstrong and Tomlinson, may relate to a laver mounted on the wall of the west range of the great cloister, has been alluded to above.

The apparent direction of some conduit routes towards the centre of the great cloister garth could suggest that a header tank or cistern was situated here, which would feed pipes that redistributed water about the complex. A cistern survives in the centre of the cloister garth of Chester Abbey, and a similar site for a cistern has been suggested by Dr. C.J. Bond to have been a feature of the 12th-century layout of St. Peter's Abbey, Gloucester (pers. comm.). A cistern stood in the garth of the London Charterhouse, feeding water to the ranges set about it (Hope 1902, map 4). The identification of hollow brick or stone features as drains may sometimes be a misinterpretation of a system of cased conduits which protected lead water pipes, as noted with pipes *in situ* at Wells (Dr. C.J. Bond, pers. comm.) and Kirkstall Abbey (Dr. S. Wrathmell, pers. comm.). The central area of the great cloister garth at Beverley has yet to be investigated.

Phase 5 — The little cloister (14th century onwards)

Introduction

The setting out of a secondary cloister at the Beverley

Blackfriars was an operation which post-dated the Phase 3 timber buildings lying to the north of the great cloister. The evidence of coins and pottery argues that this took place in the first half of the 14th century. This followed a period during which the recorded numbers of friars at Beverley reached a peak: between 1299 and 1310 they had increased from 33 to 42; by 1328 only 30 friars were present to receive royal alms. Although the mobility of the mendicants could lead to wide variation in the numbers present in any house at any one time (Little 1917, 70; Hinnebusch 1951, 273), the English Dominican Province is held to have reached maturity towards the end of the 13th century (Hinnebusch 1951, 271–8). This general trend appears to accord with that noted for the Franciscans (Martin 1937, 11).

A consideration of monastic planning practice in medieval England has indicated the relationship of the numbers accommodated in a house to the scale and extent of building projects subsequently undertaken (Gammill 1981, 133). The burden of Gammill's thesis is to indicate the application of principles of allocation of personal space to monastic architecture. Although she excludes the mendicant Orders from her study on the grounds of their 'ideological' divergence from the monastic mainstream, the widespread improvement of their building stock nevertheless follows the increase of their membership. At Beverley, the initial claustral plan of Phase 4A was subjected to modification and expansion through the episodes described above as Phases 4B to 6 — the latter, at least, post-dating the establishment of the secondary cloister.

Dominican houses are known to have had a secondary cloister at Oxford and Ludgate, London — the latter house perhaps modelled on the former (Lambrick and Woods 1976, 197–207) — at Bristol (Leighton 1933, 179–82), Cardiff (Clapham 1927, 95–6, fig. 3), and possibly at Gloucester (Rackham *et al*. 1978, 120). Either detached ranges, or a formally planned second cloister are suspected at Chelmsford (Harris forthcoming) and Newcastle-upon-Tyne (B. Harbottle. pers. comm.). A second cloister is also known at Ipswich (Gilyard-Beer 1977, 22). With the possible exceptions of Ipswich and Chelmsford, these houses and Beverley may all be regarded as foundations of the first generation of Dominican activity in important towns, many of them ports. The dating of second cloisters is generally presumptive. At Oxford the second cloister is no later than the early 14th century (Lambrick and Woods 1976, 207); at Ipswich it is considered to post-date the construction of a Decorated, probably 14th-century, great cloister (Loader 1986). At Brecon, outlying buildings, perhaps answering a similar purpose to a secondary cloister, are also of 14th-century date (Clapham 1927, 94). At Cardiff (*ibid.*, fig. 3), as at Beverley, the little cloister is of an irregular form and eccentric alignment, probably betokening its later addition to the complex.

The distribution and range of Franciscan houses known to have had second cloisters is more varied. At London (Martin 1937, 30) and Northampton (Williams 1978, 102), the host town was a long-established urban centre. At Richmond, North Yorkshire (Goldthorp 1934, 303–10), Carmarthen (Youngs *et al.* 1986, 196, fig. 13) and Walsingham (Martin 1935, 260–1) the settlements were of strategic, or in the case of Walsingham, religious importance, with space to spare in the unconfined precincts. Lichfield, and perhaps Chichester also, had the second cloister attached to the church, rather than appended to the great cloister. The houses considered above were founded between *c.*1224 and *c.*1346. Dating evidence for the Franciscan little cloisters is rare. At London, the second Greyfriars church was begun in 1306 (Little 1917, 75); the little cloister must be later than this. At Carmarthen, the second cloister has been archaeologically dated to the late 13th or early 14th century (Youngs *et al.* 1986, 196), while Walsingham's is of the later 14th or early 15th century (Martin 1935, 260–1). The others are known only from passing documentary references. Of the seven towns, London, Carmarthen and Chichester were ports, Walsingham and Lichfield were centres of pilgrimage, and Richmond was set on both the trans-Pennine and north-eastern land routes which persist today.

The Carmelites had a secondary cloister at their house at Sandwich on the south coast, and a south court at Aylesford (Rigold 1965, 11–12, 17, fig. 3), and at Denbigh (Clapham 1927, 103–4). Footings at Hulne — founded *c.*1265–88 — also suggest a little cloister which pre-dates the extant infirmary (Hope 1890, 105, plan). Aylesford was only completed to a claustral plan in the late 14th or early 15th century. Sandwich was established *c.*1272, but its little cloister is later (Rigold 1965, 1–4, 12–14, fig. 2). Either a second cloister or an outer court at Denbigh is known only from the Dissolution survey of the house (Clapham, *loc. cit.*). The Austin Friars at Leicester (Mellor and Pearce 1981, 29–32, fig. 7) and Clare (Butler 1984, 133) had secondary cloisters. At Leicester, this was built from the mid. 14th century, as part of a scheme of overall improvement which also saw the completion of the great cloister (Mellor and Pearce, *loc. cit.*).

The second cloister is usually identified as an infirmary in a regular monastic plan. The flexibility held to characterise mendicant architecture has encouraged its more varied interpretation. At Ipswich, for example, Gilyard-Beer (1977, 20–1) has considered the second cloister at the Blackfriars as perhaps reflecting the continental practice of providing study cells or school facilities there, while Butler (1984, 133) considers it to have formed secular

lodgings. There is no exclusive correlation between those houses recorded by documentary sources as having study cells, schoolrooms, infirmaries, guesthouses, or other facilities, and the existence of a second cloister. The second cloister is, however, a more common feature of houses in the south, south-west and midlands; of those known to date, only Richmond, Hulne and Beverley lie north of the Humber.

The twenty-one mendicant houses considered above include ten located in ports, at least two in towns which, although not ports, were considered to be of strategic or political importance at the time of the houses' foundation, and two known for their importance as destinations for medieval pilgrims. (Oxford, as a pre-eminent university town, and London as the capital, might both be regarded as exceptional cases within this total.) Beverley itself was both a port and a focus of pilgrimage to the shrine of St. John. The Dominican Priory at Beverley was physically dominated by the neighbouring Minster church, whose construction in its present form began a decade or so before the foundation of the Blackfriars' house. The addition of secondary cloisters to mendicant houses from the early 14th century onwards may have been related not only to the growth of the mendicant population, but also to a more general increase in popular mobility.

This need not imply that the usual purpose of a second cloister was as guest accommodation serving the full range of medieval travellers. Indeed, the typical setting of a second cloister was such that the privacy of the community would have been disrupted by the coming and going of lay people. This is usually held to be a reason for either a western or a detached setting for guesthouses, as at Franciscan Walsingham, Ware and Chichester (Martin 1937, 34, 63), and at Dominican Canterbury (Martin, 1929), Cardiff, Brecon, Gloucester, London, Newcastle-on-Tyne (Hinnebusch 1951, 193) and perhaps also at Beverley itself (Armstrong and Tomlinson 1987, 55–6). It is likely, however, that a general increase in mobility would have had a corollary in the traffic of religious who might require or prefer accommodation in a conventual setting. This might involve the retaining of apartments in urban houses for regular and important visitors; thus chambers were set aside for the Dominican Provincial at London and Winchester (Hinnebusch 1951, 197). The Bishops of Lincoln retained apartments at the Dominican House at York, and a Bishop's lodging at Lichfield Greyfriars may have dated from the foundation of that house (Martin 1937, 37–8). A detached suite of buildings could provide extra conventual accommodation, if necessary. A combination of the functions of infirmary and guesthouse has been suggested at Cardiff (Conway 1889), Brecon (Clapham 1927, 94) and elsewhere.

The Dominicans were noted for their relatively loose ties to their houses. Their services on diplomatic missions were highly regarded, not only because of their learning, but also 'because they were wanderers, and were acquainted with all countries' (Hinnebusch 1951, 421). Provision for the accommodation of members of the Order passing through the ports of the kingdom may have been seen as especially pertinent in mendicant houses. Dominican foundations up to 1300 indeed show a systematic bias towards not only the spacing of houses, but also towards the selection of sites well placed with regard to population, trade and communications (Reynolds 1977, map 3).

Two anecdotal examples drawn from the Dominican experience in the north-east of England may illustrate the range of occasional demands made upon conventual accommodation. The first concerns a shipwreck off Scarborough in 1327. Among the survivors were two Scottish Dominicans who made their way to the Dominican Priory in Scarborough and took refuge in the church. A state of war existed between England and the Scots at this time, so the king ordered the bailiffs of Scarborough to 'place the Scotch Friars under such diligent custody as they could, without injury of the liberty of the church, so that they might not escape from the realm' (Goldthorp 1935, 411). This reads very like a description of 'house arrest'. The second example concerns the Beverley Blackfriars. Friar Roger de Querndon, confessor to Edward III when the King was young, retired to Beverley, and 'when he was broken with old age' was granted a pension of £5 per annum in 1351-2 (Palmer 1882, 35). This suggests that infirmary or corrodian accommodation was available in Beverley, perhaps in the little cloister. Other grants of this sort specify the privacy, financial independence and even the servants to be retained by the fortunate corrodian (Little 1917, 76).

If the provision of extra space or the building of an infirmary which also functioned as a guesthouse were aspects of mendicant architecture in the 14th century, a subsequent trend towards the provision of more private accommodation characterised its later development. The provision of a separate lodging for the Provincial, recognised by the Dominican Constitutions in the 15th century, was to be extended by custom to the Prior (Hinnebusch 1951, 197), who might retain a detached lodging in retirement (Dr. L. Butler, pers. comm.). Priors' lodgings have been identified or recorded at the Dominican houses at London and Oxford, where they were separate ranges behind the chapter house (Lambrick and Woods 1976, 180), Bangor, Winchester (Hinnebusch 1951, 197), and perhaps also at Ipswich (Gilyard-Beer 1977, 22). At the latter house, they may have been adjacent to a hereditary lodging of the Lords Wentworth (Martin

1937, 38). The relationship of patron and house, or of the Prior as host to his important guests, may have tended to blur the distinction between residents and guests. The 15th-century north range of the great cloister at the Norwich Blackfriars is thought to have served as a guesthouse for important visitors, attached to the Prior's lodgings (Sutermeister 1977, 29). The widow Eleanor Wandesford made her will in the 'low chamber next to the parlour in the friary called Prior Chanmer' at York Blackfriars in 1472 (Goldthorp 1935, 382). The individual circumstances of a house may have been influential upon the use of its buildings. The Courtenay family maintained lodgings at Exeter Blackfriars from before 1305 (Hinnebusch 1951, 196). The provision of a decorative fireplace in the principal little cloister range at Beverley may betray the high status of its first resident.

The situation in Franciscan houses was similar and may serve to illustrate the variety of residents who could gravitate to a house. The Greyfriars provided royal lodgings at York in the 14th century; by the 16th century, there were also royal chambers recorded at Dorchester and Carmarthen (Martin 1937, 38). The old Templar church at Denny Abbey was converted at first to provide chambers for the founder of the Franciscan convent, and later may have accommodated the Abbess (Christie and Coad 1980, 152). The death of Lady Maud de Scudamore was recorded in 1478, while she was staying at Salisbury Greyfriars (Harvey 1969, 51). By the Dissolution, private lodgings of the gentry were recorded at the Greyfriars houses of Colchester, Winchester and Coventry (Martin 1937, 38). At Canterbury, in the late 15th or early 16th century, several chambers, a kitchen and a study were given over to Bishop Martin and to his brother's family (Little 1941, 160). At Reading, the suppression survey related that 'in the house are three pretty lodgings, the warden keeps one, Mr. Ogle the King's servant, another and an old lady called My Lady Seynt John the third' (Martin 1937, 110). Christopher Stapleton, an invalid for sixteen years, was staying at Beverley Greyfriars in October, 1536, apparently a regular holiday taken 'for the change of air' (Goldthorp 1934, 296). The settlement of secular residents within priories was especially characteristic of the 15th and 16th centuries, and was facilitated by the existence of building stock beyond the falling requirements of the host communities. It must imply the changing use of buildings within the precincts. An area laid out with the intention of providing infirmary or conventual guest accommodation in the 14th century could be put to various other uses, as the demands and size of the community changed. In the particular case of the Beverley Blackfriars, however, their property was recorded as being in the immediate occupation of the friars at the suppression, so a secular presence cannot here be attested.

Phase 5A — The plan of the little cloister (Early 14th century)

The laying out of the little cloister at Beverley followed an eccentric plan compared to that of the great cloister. The alignment of the north range restated that of the timber hall of Phase 3B, and may have been dictated by similar constraints or by a similar function. The most obvious feature which may have conferred such a form upon the new part of the complex was the precinct boundary, to which the west wall of the west range ran parallel at a distance of *c.*12.40m. The use of the space between the 14th-century precinct wall and the little cloister is unknown, though light structures extended into it from the little cloister in the course of Phase 5. The only other constraints for which evidence has been recorded were the probably noisome proximity of the *Commune Fossatum* channelled to flush the latrine, and the equally malodorous activity carried out in some of the tenements beyond it. It may further have been considered desirable to maintain the external access to the north part of the precinct which is indicated by a gateway adjacent to the precinct wall. An eccentric plan for the little cloister is likewise a feature of the Cardiff Blackfriars plan (Clapham 1927, fig. 3).

The little cloister at Beverley was an incomplete enclosure, which was open on the east side. The digging of a trench aligned roughly north–south may indicate an intention to add an east range or covered passage, which would have met the great cloister at right-angles. The rapid abandonment of this scheme, which was probably undertaken along with the excavation of other foundation trenches as a first stage of works in the area, was dated to *c.*1320–30 by a coin (no. 1020) and by pottery. Similar evidence has been reported at Denny Abbey, where the footing trenches for an extension to the church were dug, and then immediately backfilled (Christie and Coad 1980, 157); and at Newcastle Blackfriars (B. Harbottle, pers. comm.). The final form of the little cloister was accordingly an L-shaped pair of ranges, with access by an alley from the south. The alignment of the alley may suggest that it communicated with the north-west corner of the great cloister. The north range of the little cloister was the more substantial, and was divided into two major ground-floor chambers, perhaps with a light lean-to at the west end. The west range was narrower; an approximate parity between the width of range and alley could argue that it was intended to overshoot the alley at first-floor level.

A distinction between principal and subsidiary ranges was common, and may show a common intention in their initial provision. At Bristol

Blackfriars the range later known as the 'Bakers Hall' was subdivided at ground level, with a large room above; the ground-floor arrangement is comparable to that at Beverley. The adjacent range was probably narrower (Leighton 1933, figs. 19 and 20). At Cardiff Blackfriars, the three little cloister ranges have been identified as an infirmary, a large guest house, and a kitchen which was located between the guesthouse and the main *frater*, and is considered to have served both (Conway 1889, plan). The elaboration of this view illustrated the subdivision of both 'guesthouse' and 'infirmary' (Clapham 1927, fig. 3). At Walsingham Greyfriars, the surviving kitchen was similarly placed, though the identity of the other little cloister ranges is uncertain (Martin 1935, plan). At Carmarthen Greyfriars, the south range of the little cloister appears to have been the most important; as at Beverley, one end was furnished with benches. A central chamber is identified as a kitchen (Youngs *et al.* 1986, fig. 13). Sandwich Whitefriars also shows a marked similarity in its little cloister south range to the Beverley north range. A two-chambered ground floor was furnished with a back porch entry to one room, while the other had a wall fireplace. The extent of the west range is unknown (Rigold 1965, fig. 3). At the Austin Friars, Leicester, the west range was the earlier, and was to be completely rebuilt; the narrow north range was of uncertain purpose (Mellor and Pearce 1981, 35). Leicester is an exception to a fairly standard form of little cloister to which Beverley conforms, in which the most important range shared the general alignment of the church.

The south side of the little cloister may have remained open until Phase 5C/6A, when a new north range of the great cloister closed this aspect. An unenclosed form may not have been uncommon. At Cardiff Blackfriars (Clapham 1927, fig. 3), the east range failed to complete the enclosure of the little cloister. At Sandwich Whitefriars, its eastern side is entirely conjectural (Rigold 1965, fig. 3). At Bristol Blackfriars, the lesser cloister appears to have been incompletely enclosed on the south side, while to the west its medieval form is unknown (Leighton 1933, fig. 21). At both the Austin Friars, Leicester (Mellor and Pearce 1981, 35) and at Walsingham Greyfriars (Martin 1935, plan), the second cloister is assumed to have eventually formed a regular enclosure, but in both cases is conjectural on one side.

If the trench on the east side of the garth betrays a failure to complete an original design, so too does the north range. A decision to abbreviate the original scheme had been arrived at by the time the lighter west end footings were constructed, and was confirmed by the positioning of doorways with reference to the superstructure of the range, rather than to the foundation plan, and also by the absence of buttresses at its west end. There was also a break in the footings of the north wall of the east chamber. This break may relate to some interruption of work, to the control of ground water, or to the construction of the northern porch tower. The complex history of the porch tower, where footings were apparently laid down, partially removed and later reinstated, and the associated introduction of a stair-base after the construction of the main footings, may add to a picture of a somewhat attenuated programme of works. So too does evidence for fires lighted within the east chamber of the building before its completion. Though the west range may have been intended to overshoot the cloister alley, the early provision of supports for a pent roof may indicate that this scheme too was subject to modification, and may have been implemented only in the later 14th century.

Certain aspects of the work show that due consideration was given to local ground conditions. There was a marked disparity between the depths of foundations used for the north and south walls, which arose from a high subsoil level below the former and the presence of early pits below the latter. The south wall footings were packed externally with clay. A similar technique was applied to the west range. This may show an intention to counteract the tendency of rubble footings, in an area of clay subsoil, to act as land drains. Comparable precautions were taken by the builders at Oxford, where foundations were packed with clay when carried below the contemporary water table (Lambrick and Woods 1976, 173–4, 206). The footings of the *frater* at Ludlow Whitefriars were likewise packed with clay (Klein and Roe 1987, 59). The raising of the ground surface both along the alleys and within the buildings at Beverley may also indicate a preoccupation with damp. It is likely that debris from earlier buildings was gathered together to accomplish this, especially along the west alley of the little cloister. Similar groundworks were carried out when structures to the south-west of the great cloister were built (Armstrong and Tomlinson 1987, 56).

The little cloister ranges

The early 14th century was a period of architectural transition, not only in the decorative forms adopted for stone buildings, but also in the nature of the construction of their walls. In the 13th century the construction of stone walls with ashlar skins and rubble cores required a substantial overall thickness. This is visible in the construction of the Priory church at Beverley, and in the later work erected in the same style. In London, the minimum thickness of stone walls was fixed at three feet by municipal regulation in the 13th century (Schofield 1984, 75). In the 14th century a greater facility in the use of stone, and especially of larger blocks, could result in the thinner construction of walls, with the ashlar sometimes

making up the full thickness of a wall (RCHM 1972, xlvi). The use of heavier masonry is well illustrated by the externally visible fabric of Beverley Minster, where the Decorated nave is predominantly a 14th-century rebuilding, sympathetically appended to the 13th-century choir and transepts (Miller *et al.* 1982, 7–8). At the Dominican Priory, however, the mendicant status of the site, the expense of good stone, and the lack of a local source for it, must have combined to enforce a more economical approach to building. The older style of construction permitted the internal use of chalk and the external setting of smaller ashlar. Of the building stone recorded from the site, only the mouldings are cut in fine material, and much of the rest is either reused, or of mediocre or low quality (see above, section 3.2).

The north and south walls of the north range of the little cloister departed from the more substantial scantling employed for Phases 4A and 4B in the great cloister. They were built to a consistent thickness of c.0.55m, comparable only to the Phase 4C and 6B works in the great cloister. Despite this diminished scale, the conventions of a limestone outer face, a rubble core, and an inner skin of chalk were followed. Although the thickness of north and south walls was identical, faced ashlar was used for the south elevation (which was visible from within the Priory), but coursed rubble for the north wall (which faced out onto the precinct gardens). This contrast, though demonstrated only by the east chamber, appears to indicate an intention to dignify the south aspect of the building. The superstructure of the west range was apparently of coursed rubble.

The light scantling of the walls, when compared to other stone buildings on the site, may suggest that they were not intended to be carried up to the full height of the building. Sill wall construction is common in the area at this date, and has been noted on other buildings in Beverley (e.g. Armstrong *et al.* 1991, 33–50) and Hull (Armstrong 1980, 16, 18, figs. 6 and 7; Armstrong and Ayers 1987, 23–4). The use of jointed ashlar for a sill-wall, would however, be unusual. These considerations may suggest that low stone sills supported a superstructure which was at least partly timber-framed, but which may have incorporated either brick or stone elements on the ground floor. The buttressing of the east chamber of the north range hints at a stone construction, but buttress positions were not identified to the west; this again suggests that an original design for a stone building was modified in the course of building work which proceeded from east to west.

A half-timbered form of construction is characteristic of both vernacular and institutional survivals in Yorkshire, though it should be recognised that both the survival and the published record of vernacular buildings is woefully inadequate for the eastern part of the historic county. The Royal Commission surveys of York have identified this form as previously extant in 13th and 14th-century houses (RCHM 1972, lxi; RCHM 1981, 129, pl. 3, 181). In an ecclesiastical setting, the King's Manor was perhaps originally a ground-floor stone structure with a timber-framed storey above, built as a house for the Abbot of St. Mary's, *c.*1270 (RCHM 1975, 30); the Abbey *hospitium* or guest house was of similar form: the ground floor is 14th-century with an upper timber storey of 15th-century date (*ibid.*, 13, pl. 15). The Merchant Adventurer's Hall was built in timber over a stone ground floor which was to serve as a hospital, *c.*1357–61 (RCHM 1981, 82). St. Anthony's Hall, dated *c.*1450–1453, had a ground floor which was stone-walled on two sides; later brickwork may have replaced the timber framing of the upper floor and perhaps of the other walls of the building (*ibid.*, 91). St. William's College was built from *c.*1465 around a courtyard: here the ground-floor walls were of stone, save for the west end of the north range and the adjoining part of the west wall, which were originally fully timber-framed (*ibid.*, 62–8). This partial building of the ground floor in timber may be paralleled by the west end of the Beverley north range. The 'Bedern' excavation at York is considered especially important to the study of this form of construction (Addyman 1979, 73–4). The established forms of institutional architecture at York may have been influential upon those adopted at Beverley. The Archbishop of York was the Lord of the town. The Beverley Dominican Priory fell within the administrative 'Visitation' based on York; and Provincial Chapters held at Beverley enjoyed the support of the Archbishop. In the 13th century at least, craftsmen from York may have worked on the glazing of the Beverley Priory church (cf. section 3.8), and perhaps on other parts of the fabric.

The attribution of half-timbered construction to mendicant, or even monastic, buildings is relatively rare where archaeological evidence or Dissolution surveys are lacking. At Denny Abbey, the *dorter* was described as 'half-timbered' in the 18th century (Christie and Coad 1980, 187). An ancillary timbered building has been identified at Salisbury Greyfriars (Martin 1937, 31). The domestic ranges at Thelsford Trinitarian Priory were half-timbered for three centuries (Butler 1984, 133). At Nostell Priory, West Yorkshire, the buildings of the outer court, of 15th or early 16th-century date, survive (Ryder 1982, 54), and the earlier half-timbered form of claustral ranges is also suspected (D. Michelmore, pers. comm.). The stable block in the Guest House complex at Kirkstall Abbey is considered to have been a 15th-century conversion of an earlier hall, which was possibly built in this style (Wrathmell 1987, 14–19). Half-timbering also survives in vernacular buildings of the later

medieval period; 'such a combination of stone walls and timber framing would appear to be of common occurrence in the region' (Ryder 1987, 57).

It is possible that the differential treatment of walls, presenting the better face to view, was also a more widespread medieval practice than may now be apparent. At Walmgate Bar, York, and perhaps at Ludgate, London, stone facing concealed a timber-framed structure (Schofield 1984, 100). The inner court at Mount Grace Priory was constructed in timber *c.*1420, but rebuilt in stone *c.*1470–80 (Dr. G. Coppack, pers. comm.) Denaby Old Hall, South Yorkshire, had ranges faced externally with stone, but with the timber-framed structure revealed from the internal courtyard; this was a 15th-century building whose form may in part have been dictated by reasons of defence (Ryder 1987, 72). Horbury Hall, West Yorkshire, *c.*1480, also presents a stone-faced ground floor to the outside world, while the end of the solar and the upper walls of the hall are timbered, to allow adequate fenestration. Elland Hall, West Yorkshire, had a similar treatment of its half-timbered solar (D. Michelmore, pers. comm.).

Many of the buildings discussed above were built as jettied structures. The footings between the little cloister alley and the garth could indicate a series of verticals which supported the projecting first floor of a range or ranges that overshot the alley. There is, however, scant evidence for any structure linking the vertical positions during Phase 5A. The replacement of the timber uprights along the alley with brick walling, which presumably supported a sill beam, in Phase 5C, was to entail the displacement of many tiles — perhaps from a pent roof over the alley. An interpretation of the eventual form of the west range as overshooting the alley could explain the comprehensive nature of renovations during Phase 5C. It would also have permitted access at first-floor level from the upper chambers in the little cloister, via the Phase 6 great cloister north range, to the *reredorter*. As the north range had major chambers at ground-floor level, it is considered likely that the north cloister alley was to be covered only by a pent roof. At Newcastle-upon-Tyne Whitefriars, cloister roofs are considered to have been pent structures because of the light character of the garth walls, and because of the inequality in width of alleys and ranges (Harbottle 1968, 194).

An alley was not always carried round a secondary cloister: it does not appear to have been a feature of Cardiff Blackfriars (Clapham 1927, fig. 3), or the Austin Friars, Leicester (Mellor and Pearce 1981, fig. 2). In such cases, access to the principal range would have been through the subsidiary one. At Beverley, as at Bristol (Leighton 1933, fig. 21), there is no evidence for an alley on the great cloister side of the secondary cloister; in both cases, it was probably reached through the ground floor of the range opposite the church. A similar arrangement for access existed at Sandwich Carmelite Priory (Rigold 1965, fig. 3); a 'dark entry' lay at the east end of the *frater* of Leeds Priory, Kent, giving access to the area beyond the great cloister (Tester 1979, 82).

The west range

This afforded very cramped ground floor space, perhaps no wider than *c*.2.50m. A doorway at the north end may be inferred from the variant construction of the lower wall and from the later route of a drain. The failure to identify early occupation surfaces within this range could be taken to indicate that a tiled, flagged or suspended floor was set within it; or that its completion was delayed. It is possible that, although the range was intended to incorporate the west alley when the footings were set out, it was to be completed to this form only in Phase 5C. A few fragments of floor slabs (nos B27–8) and floor tiles (nos B232–4), were recovered during the excavation of reused materials or redeposited soils, some of which lay in this area. These, and the lesser breadth and heterogeneous walling of the range, may both suggest that its ground floor performed a service function, that was perhaps ancillary to the occupation of the north range. It is possible that a pipe may have brought water to, or through, the west range. The northern course of a conduit was robbed in Phase 5C (see below), while a further extent was identified running east–west — perhaps leading out from this range and feeding into a conduit routed alongside the alley. The east–west conduit route was filled in Phase 5B, while the alley conduit (which it may have joined) was robbed in Phase 5C.

The north range

The east chamber of the north range was furnished with doors at its south-west and north-east corners. A jamb surviving *in situ* on the east side of the south doorway, no. B12, showed these to have been of a simple form. Both the angled chamfer on the jamb and a filled slot across the doorway indicated that a matching threshold had originally been installed. The north-east door was bodily removed in Phase 5B. A rectangular stair base at the north-west corner of the chamber led into the north porch tower. A newel would often be accommodated in a tower in the 13th century, assuring the privacy of the chamber above (Braun 1968, 167, 176).

The dominant feature of the chamber was its large central fireplace, which was surrounded on three sides by benches. Such an arrangement is suitable to a warming house or parlour, or to a refectory. Though a parlour might have been appropriate in guest chambers or private lodgings, it would not normally have figured among the conventual buildings of a Dominican house. Not only was there no time allotted in the Dominican regime to post-prandial relaxation, but St. Dominic's disapproval of the parlour as 'the place for laughter, and folly, and idle talk', was set down in the didactic *Lives of the Brethren* (Hinnebusch 1951, 188); however, such behaviour might be countenanced in an infirmary (Gwynn 1940, 6).

In a refectory, the diners would have sat round the fireplace, probably with their backs to the wall (Gilyard-Beer 1977, 18). Features probably to be identified as bench footings have been recorded at Ipswich Blackfriars (Blatchly and Wade 1977, 25), in the principal range of the little cloister at Carmarthen Greyfriars (Youngs *et al.* 1986, 196, fig. 13), and in the guest hall and refectory of the Blackfriars at Newcastle-upon-Tyne (B. Harbottle, pers. comm.). An open off-centre hearth was a feature of the refectory at Ludlow Whitefriars (Klein and Roe 1987, 59) where, as at Beverley, it is taken to indicate a chamber open to the roof. The west claustral range at Bristol Blackfriars is thought to have been composed of a single-storey refectory and a two-storey building with a chimney, serving perhaps as the Prior's lodging (Leighton 1933, 172) — a division comparable to that of the Beverley north range. At Cardiff Blackfriars, the little cloister included a lesser refectory 'wherein the infirm would partake of flesh-meat by dispensation from the common rule of abstinence perpetually observed in the greater' (Conway 1889, 105).

Considerable quantities of fish and poultry bone were identified by sieving of floor silts (sections 4.2 and 4.3), together with lesser quantities of sheep, pig and cattle. Amongst the fish, herring were especially prominent. This material is considered to represent table waste, and may indicate a partially abstinent diet, perhaps followed on only some days of the week, and supports an interpretation of the chamber as a refectory. The snails in the silts may indicate that the clay floor was covered with hay and rushes, which is held to have been a usual provision. (Those snails indicating a wetland habitat might alternatively have arrived in peat cut for fuel, for which the large fireplace would be well suited).

The west chamber was entered from the north-west corner of the alley; it is possible that there was an opposed north door. A screen may have been set towards the west end of the room. As with the west range, negative evidence could point to the former presence of a tiled, flagged or suspended floor. The dominant feature of the chamber was a formal fireplace set against the east wall, where substantial footings supported a chimney.

The fireplace was flanked by a pair of shafts, which were set on semi-octagonal bases (nos B14–15), and possibly painted to resemble Purbeck marble. These were decorative features, perhaps supporting a lintel or a projecting hood. The form of the fireplace may be compared to one ordered for royal apartments at Clarendon, which was to be rebuilt with a marble column on each side supporting a mantelpiece (Salzman 1952, 101–2). The chimney flue may have been plastered; a practice recorded in building contracts of 14th-century date (*ibid.*, 99). At the end of Phase 5A, plaster fragments were incorporated into spreads of material which were used to level up the chamber for the laying of a new floor. The original hearth was a clay surface; this was replaced with a raised tile-on-edge structure which was retained into Phase 5B. Both the hearth and the chimney continued in use after the pillared fireplace surround was removed.

The lack of silting in the chamber makes comment on its use difficult. The hearth implies a residential function of some status for the chamber, though one which it may subsequently have lost — a transition suggested by the defacing of the fireplace. Later finds of coins, from Phases 5B and 5C (but some perhaps residual from the early occupation) may indicate the presence of visitors from outside the community. In this context, a group of Scottish coins (no. 1026) is especially interesting, recalling as it does the detention of the 'Scotch friars' at Scarborough. An interpretation of the range as accommodating a guesthouse and guest hall has been suggested by Dr. Glynn Coppack, comparing similar plans at Mount Grace, North Yorkshire, dated to *c.* 1420, and at the Almonry, Thornholme Priory, South Humberside (Coppack 1989).

The cloister garth

The accumulation of material within the little cloister garth, principally context 65, post-dated the demolition of the Phase 3 timber hall, but was impossible to relate by stratigraphical evidence to any particular sub-phase of the Phase 5 occupation. The consideration of the finds evidence has provided equivocal evidence for the nature of deposition in the garth.

The pottery from the garth is considered as a group to be most closely related to either the Phase 5C occupation, or to the heavily residual collection of material from construction horizons (see section 3.16). It does not, however, include any material which need be later than 1400. Part-glazed roof tile of Type 4 occurred in the ranges from Phase 5C; three fragments of this distinctive fabric were also found in context 65. The numerous nails and nail fragments may have been residual from the dismantling of the Phase 3 timber buildings; they do not occur elsewhere in such quantity. A similar residual component was also identified in both the pottery and the tile from context 65. The debris in the garth included categories of

material which were to recur in a later deposit at the close of occupation, context 15. Like 15, garth soil 65 is considered likely to represent dumps of material, laid down either at the outset of the little cloister occupation or at Phase 5C, but derived from within the precinct.

External aspects

The external appearance of the little cloister, as suggested by the structural evidence, may be summarised as follows. The north range was the larger of two ranges, set at right-angles to each other, and was entered by two doorways from the cloister alley. The ashlar facing of at least the ground-floor elevation facing onto the cloister distinguished the north range from its narrower neighbour. A chimney was set centrally, perhaps with a circular stack. This may have marked a change in the roof line, as the east chamber was probably only of a single storey. A tower projected from the back of the range, where the lower elevation was of coursed rubble rather than ashlar. The west end of the range, its western upper storey, and perhaps the back wall, could have been of timber-framed construction. A lean-to may have been set against the west end of the building.

The west range was a narrow building, though still perhaps of two storeys. The back wall at least may have been timber-framed. An alley, initially covered by a sloping pent roof supported on timber uprights, ran around the garth, perhaps extending southwards as a covered slype leading towards the great cloister. A slype between the great cloister and the infirmary at the Cluniac Priory, Pontefract, was defined by an insubstantial wall without foundations (Bellamy 1965, 68), and a comparable structure may be indicated by the footing glimpsed in the south-west corner of the Trench 3 excavations (Figure 40). It is possible that the first floor of the west range was originally intended to overshoot the alley, though structures permitting this may not have been constructed until Phase 5C.

The finds from the construction horizon of Phase 5A, from the Phase 5 garth deposits, and from later renovation or demolition horizons, elaborate this outline. The roofs of the ranges and alleys were covered by flat clay roof tiles (section 3.4), with the ridge sealed by glazed and unglazed ridge tiles, which were simply decorated with low crests. The ridges would have been punctuated by ventilator tiles, to allow the circulation of air in the roof spaces, and a louvre may have been set on the east chamber's roof to vent smoke from the open hearth (section 3.5). A few fragments of lead came and glass indicate that glazed windows were present, in the north range at least. To judge from its distribution in Phase 7, more decorated glass may have been used in the better-lit first-floor apartments. This glass was mostly painted with a simple, and by this period slightly old-fashioned, grisaille design, that was well suited to fill fairly narrow window spaces. It is possible that undecorated glass may have been set in the ground-floor west chamber of the north range (section 3.8). The north range therefore appears to have been a residential area, with a communal refectory at one end, and an apartment with a fireplace, and chamber above, at the other.

The garth in front of the buildings was probably a simple lawn. The rubbish which accumulated there included a light scatter of book or dress fittings (nos 872, 892, 894), and an eraser (no. 762), which could suggest a conventual presence. Needles (nos 913–18) may suggest that the clothing of the community was mended nearby: this was a particular task of the lay-brothers, who would be occupied with cleaning, mending, and watching the dormitories when on the premises, and with the gathering of provisions when at work outside. The lay-brothers are considered to have made up a small part — perhaps 15% overall — of Dominican communities (Hinnebusch 1951, 217, 242, 331). It is possible that at Beverley they may have been accommodated or employed in the rather cramped west range of the little cloister. The lack of spinning and cloth-working gear is striking, as such finds are almost ubiquitous on sites in Beverley. This may indicate that women and family groups had never become established as residents within the Priory precinct.

The examination of animal bone from the site has indicated the later accumulation of material in the little cloister garth. Phase 7, Context 15, was comparable with the groups drawn from the occupation of the ranges (see section 4.3). It follows that other finds from the garth may also relate to the later occupation of the ranges. They would thus form a group, like that from Mount Grace Priory (Roebuck and Coppack 1987), of materials cleared from the little cloister ranges, or from the north range of the great cloister.

The animal bone itself may show evidence for the slaughter and butchery of sheep and pigs. An area used for food preparation has been suggested to have occupied the west end of the ground floor of the Phase 6 north range, during its later occupation at least (see above). The garth soils also included fragments from several cooking or kitchen vessels — though not in such quantities as would indicate their frequent disposal there. Both sources of evidence may indicate the proximity of service areas.

Phase 5B (Mid. 14th century)

The structural modification of the north range formed a unified programme in the west chamber, and may betoken a change in status or function. The east chamber alterations may have been more piecemeal. The renovation extended to the west range (as indicated by scaffolding positions), and to the mid-point of the north range, a location later to see extensive works on both external and internal fabric. A little window glass was deposited in the alley, suggesting work on glazing.

The north range, west chamber

The demolition of the west wall of the range may have been facilitated by the timber-framed construction of its west end. It has been remarked that 'The nature of timber frame construction is such that a partial dismantling is entirely feasible and the removal of one or more cross frames to allow rebuilding can be undertaken without danger or disturbance to the remainder' (Armstrong and Ayers 1987, 23). The dismantling of the fireplace, the replacement of the floor with a clay platform, and the encroachment of screens into the chamber may all relate to changes in status. The defacing of the fireplace and the building of a new hearth may have been late episodes in this process, as the reuse of one of the bases flanking it occurred early in Phase 5C. The reuse of pier fragments from a formal setting to build a later hearth kerb has been recorded at Fountains Abbey (Coppack 1986, 62) in a building also undergoing a change in status.

The function of the new partition at the west end of the chamber is uncertain. This may indicate the conversion of the chamber to a more private area, perhaps served through a screens passage. In this context the evidence of animal bone from the floor silts in the chamber is illuminating. Though not subject to detailed quantification, these deposits indicated the prominence of domestic fowl and of fish, especially herring and eel. The absence of vermin suggests that these silts were sealed soon after their deposition, and perhaps that the occupation was short-lived. The finds included copper alloy objects which could reflect a conventual occupation (nos. 896, 898), but the presence of fused copper alloy in the silts may indicate that these objects were gathered together only to be melted down.

The nature of activity west of the encroaching partition appears, from limited evidence, to have been essentially unchanged. A new clay platform was laid down over an earlier floor of similar character. The modification of the west end of the range would, however, have allowed more space for this activity to continue. The western limit of the space, thus enlarged, is unknown, though it would presumably have been enclosed by a timber-framed structure.

North range, east chamber

The east chamber of the north range underwent structural modifications as did the west, but the effect of this more attenuated scheme was to facilitate and enhance its former role. Thus, the laying of a new floor in the part of the chamber furnished with benches, and the renovation of the hearth, indicate an intention to maintain its function. The removal of a screen from before the south door may have dictated the insertion of a wattle structure shielding the north entrance, perhaps to control an uncomfortably strong through-draught. The dismantling of the south screen may further betray an increased traffic between the cloister and the stair tower. The removal of a stone threshold and the trampled soils between stair and south door may also have related to an intensified use of this route.

The blocking of the north-east door followed a period during which the screening of the fireplace was found to be either inadequate or inconvenient. In addition to the imperfect control of draughts which the screen may have allowed, its position, and that of the doorway itself, left little room for tables or seating along the north end of the east wall. The extension of bench footings round the position of the blocked doorway indicates the continuing communal character of activity here. The reinstatement of a more sheltered northern entrance in the base of the tower argues for an intention to maintain access and facilities, whilst enhancing comfort.

The structural history of the tower/porch is problematical. The ascription of the doorstep into the porch, and into the chamber itself, to Phase 5B is wholly circumstantial — a north door at ground-floor level would have been superfluous, before the blocking of the north-east entrance had taken place. The partial removal and reinstatement of the footings of the tower, and their weakness on the east side in particular, have been considered above as perhaps marking equivocation over the method of construction to be used here. The original footings of the west wall, perhaps attached to an external buttress, could have supported a structure of stone. Those which were reinstated on the north side, in contrast, would only appear adequate as the footings for a lighter timber-framed structure. This may be explicable in terms of the 'mixed media' style of construction considered above as a feature of the little cloister ranges. Structures identified as either porches or towers have been occasionally identified in a monastic setting, as at Pontefract Cluniac Priory (Bellamy 1965, 18) and in the local urban vernacular, as in Hull (Armstrong and Ayers 1987, 21). The two-storey porch is held to have been a feature absorbed into domestic practice from ecclesiastical architecture to improve living conditions in buildings with an open fireplace (Braun 1968, 166). A close mendicant parallel to the Beverley plan, at Sandwich, is noted above.

Material collected from the floor indicated the continuing deposition of table waste. The diet observed in the chamber retained its character of partial abstinence with fish, particularly eel, and poultry prominent. A very small collection of pottery remained dominated by jug forms, while a fragment of vessel glass (no. 989) hinted at the occasional use of finer tableware. A few fragments of lead came (nos 541–4) and window glass (nos 10–15), together with lead melt (nos 712–13), may show that work had been carried out on windows — perhaps using the hearth to recast lead. This was the first evidence to suggest the glazing of windows in this chamber; they were probably of clear undecorated glass.

Phase 5C (Later 14th century onwards)

Phase 5C saw works in the little cloister which are considered to have been interdependent with the extension of the great cloister (Phase 6A). These involved rebuilding of the west range, and of the west and south sides of the north range, and a re-covering of the cloister alley. The works on the west range and west alley were closely associated, and could represent the inclusion of an overshot alley within the west range, thereby permitting its junction with the new great cloister north range. It is less certain that work extended to the eastern part of the north range, save in so far as it may have been affected by the changes in the character or use of other areas in the little cloister, or at first-floor level. The ground-floor chambers were to see a diminished use after the completion of these schemes; this is suggested by both environmental and ceramic evidence.

The cloister alley

The most significant activity recorded in the cloister alley entailed the replacement of the timber verticals, which had hitherto supported the alley roof, with a sill-wall of brick. This post-dated the laying of new floors in the west chamber of the north range — a sequence indicated by the stratigraphic relationship between the new garth wall, a contemporary drain taking water from the roof, and a floor in the north range through which the drain was cut. This had been preceded by the removal of a conduit which ran along the west side of the cloister. The near contemporaneity of works on the roof and the conduit is indicated by the backfilling of the latter with broken roof tile.

The existence of guttering feeding a lead downpipe was inferred from the juxtaposition of a Dissolution-phase robber pit with the elevated inlet of the drain. A lead filter, no. 768, may have been associated with this system and was found in demolition deposits in the garth. The widespread medieval use of gutters, either lined or sealed at the joints with lead, is well known. At mendicant houses, it has been recorded at Hulne and Ludlow Whitefriars

(Hope 1890, 107; Klein and Roe 1987, 25), and at Coventry, Gloucester and Bristol Greyfriars (Martin 1937, 70, 85; Ponsford 1975). The provision of downpipes which the arrangement at Beverley implies is relatively rare; it is held to have been an unusual fixture in London at the Tower (Schofield 1984, 96), and is elsewhere recorded at castles from the later 13th to the 15th century, and in high-status sites thereafter (Salzman 1952, 266–7). Archaeological evidence for downpipes has, however, been recorded at smaller sites, as at Mount Grace Priory, North Yorkshire, dated to the later 15th century (Dr. G. Coppack, pers. comm.). If the roofs of the little cloister buildings and the great cloister north range had indeed achieved a structural unity, the large area of the roof would have necessitated the use of drains to prevent the inundation of the little cloister garth in wet weather. It is possible that lead was used as flashing for timber guttering; fragments of offcut lead (nos. 663–4, 668, 672–4, 676, 680, 694), were relatively common in Phase 5C contexts. The Phase 7 robbing at the south end of the drain suggests that the downpipe, or a silt trap, was perhaps of lead.

Several factors argue that this was an important episode in the development of the little cloister. It saw the provision of 'Great Bricks' for the construction of the drain: extensive roofing work was indicated by the deposit of nearly 6m² of non-diagnostic tile fragments; and lead-working was clearly associated with these works. It was also followed by levelling-up along the alley. This may have been necessary not only to maintain access southwards through the Phase 6 north range of the great cloister, but also to establish a parity of level within the west range.

The north range, west chamber

The activity in the north range is inseparable from the use of the area west of the partition which limited the west chamber during Phase 5B. Deposits here were allotted to Phase 5C, on the grounds of their stratigraphic relationship with the new west wall of the range.

The removal of the Phase 5B screen was a preliminary to the redefinition of the west chamber of the north range. The incorporation of the fireplace pillar-base (B15) into the south wall demonstrates that its rebuilding also took place at this time. It is possible that this repair was dictated by structural failure. Weakness at this point could have been engendered by the weight of the chimney structure, or by the thrust exerted upon the north end of the spine wall by the buttress and porch tower — a thrust which was not balanced by a corresponding buttress to the south. A doorway through the spine wall could have exacerbated such structural problems. It will be recalled that work here had been a feature of Phase 5B.

The alignment of the new west wall was continued southwards by a sill for the back wall of the west range — the whole perhaps representing a single structural episode. This may have accompanied the reconstruction of the west range to overshoot the alley, and the construction of a hipped roof at the junction of the ranges. The nature of this alignment was unclear where it formed the wall of the north range, as this had been robbed; however, its southward continuation along the back of the west range was marked by a rubble sill. The position of a brick socket at the junction of the north and west range walls is particularly suggestive of a single timber frame in an interrupted sill construction.

The occupation activity immediately west of the rebuilt wall was intense. Its extent suggests that it may have taken place in a structure which abutted both the north and west ranges. This should be considered as a successor of the western end of the Phase 5A north range. The repeated accumulation of silts rich in fish bone was accompanied by the patchy reflooring of the area with clay, and the burning of both silts and clays. This burning was not associated with any formal hearth structure, though it was concentrated in the north-west corner (of the excavated area). The character of these food waste groups was similar to that identified elsewhere in the conventual buildings during Phase 5C.

The presence of a fire may indicate a residential function for this area, while the food waste indicates that it served as an eating place. The apparent failure to provide a fixed hearth position, and the accumulation of fish debris (which presumably was the result of the recurrent sealing of matter beneath patchy clay flooring), both indicate an unusually casual regulation of activity in this area, which perhaps saw meals taken in an informal setting. The archaeomagnetic dating of a burnt patch of floor (context 3010) to AD1330–90 (at the 68% confidence level) falls within what, from other dating evidence, is considered the earlier part of Phase 5C (though the erratic reliability of archaeomagnetic data from the site must impose caution in its use). The intensive activity here could be related to the extensive scope of building work going on elsewhere in the precinct — on the great cloister Phase 6 north range as well as in the little cloister. It may, therefore, be interpreted as a temporary occupation, whilst construction or repair projects elsewhere in the precinct had rendered other buildings uninhabitable. Evidence for temporary accommodation interrupting a period of monastic occupation is comparatively rare, though the laying of 'intermediate floors' for occupation during episodes of building activity has been recorded at Denny Abbey (Christie and Coad 1980, 184).

The occupation of the refurbished main chamber left silts which included fish bones (especially herring), and notable amounts of sheep bone. They may suggest a less regulated diet than that observed before. The failure of more substantial deposits to accumulate between the late 14th and the 16th centuries does, however, argue for a markedly diminished intensity of activity at ground-floor level.

North range, east chamber

The energetic activity in the western part of the little cloister was reflected only at a subdued level within the east chamber of the north range. Structural modifications carried out here appear to have been related in the main to the upper chamber.

The light setting of bricks in the north-west part of the chamber has been identified as the base for a screen which may have been related to the stair. This is suggested both by the later distribution of window-fragments in Phase 7 (when they were apparently confined by this feature), and the juxtaposition of the brick footing with the stair base of Phase 5A. A doorway was probably provided in the screen.

The screen post-dated the construction and use of a bench-footing of tile at the west end of the room. This was identified only as a robbed feature, but appears to have represented the maximum extent of benches in the east chamber. The ascription on firm stratigraphic evidence of a comparable feature in the west chamber to Phase 5C (see above, Chapter 2) has also prompted the attribution of this bench-footing to the early stages of this phase. The intense activity at the west end of the north range has been considered as perhaps arising from the disruption of occupation elsewhere in the complex, and a similar explanation of the increased use of space in the east chamber might also be sought. The construction of the screen for the stair and north entrance should indicate that this provision — at the draughtier end of the room furthest from the fire — was of short duration.

The central position of a large footing is the most convincing evidence for its association with the roof or superstructure of the north range. It was placed so as to act as the load-bearing foundation for a vertical member, which divided two approximately equal spaces, each $c.4.80$m long (east–west). This may have been dictated by the original bay-spacing of the roof, a feature which could explain the off-centre site of the hearth. It may alternatively have related to the provision of residential accommodation at first-floor level, perhaps supporting a fireplace.

The occupation silting which accumulated within the east chamber contained fish bone, but less than had been previously remarked. The overall picture obtained from the study of food debris from the Priory indicates that mutton was becoming a more important component of diet through the later Middle Ages, a regional tendency noted also in a smaller assemblage

from Pontefract Blackfriars (see above, section 4.3). The silting ascribed to Phase 5C was recorded only in the western part of the room; its relative distance from the fireplace and benches, and hence the areas where food might have been consumed, may in part be responsible for the lower recovery of food-waste.

Of the other finds, the pottery includes 15th-century wares, which are rare on this site. As with the other material from the east chamber in Phase 5C, they originated in the western part of the room, away from the hearth. They may have been deposited during the use of the west end of the chamber for access to the stairs or north door, or as intrusive material from Phase 7. The latter probably applies to much of the glass and lead scattered on the surface of the silts. A French jetton (no. 1027), issued in the first quarter of the 15th century and probably deposited no later than $c.1450$, was found in Phase 7 deposits in this area, where it was probably residual. This coin is of interest because it is of a type considered unlikely to have travelled far from its port of entry into England, and may therefore show the presence of a visitor from abroad during the 15th century. One possible date range for the last use of the Phase 5B hearth (2011) in the east chamber is $c.$AD1400–50 (archaeomagnetic assay, at the 68% confidence level). The failure to provide a new clay floor within the ground floor of the east chamber between Phase 5B and the close of occupation would appear to confirm a relatively low intensity of occupation through the later history of the building. It may suggest a lesser importance for the communal aspects of the occupation which were a feature of the 14th-century use of the building. The disuse or reversion of the east chamber to storage from $c.1450$ onwards would not run counter to this evidence.

Phase 7 — The stripping of the ranges (early 16th century)

The stripping of the Priory ranges is held to represent activity at the suppression of the house in 1539. Although documents of 1524–5 described the house as 'dilapidated' and 'non-functional' before that date, their author may have exaggerated its previous state out of gratitude to Lord Darcy. A limited quantity of pottery and jettons (nos. 1028–31), amongst a larger residual component of material, tends to confirm this hypothesis.

The information pertaining to the great cloister was limited by the nature of the investigation carried out there; however, the detailed recording of the north range of the little cloister provided valuable detail as to both the objectives and the methods adopted at the suppression. It is likely that the shells of buildings here may have enjoyed a partial survival into the 17th century or later.

Two abiding motives may be identified in the activities carried out at the Dissolution. The first might be loosely defined as 'religio-political'. Writing of Warwick Blackfriars, the Royal Commissioner Dr. London reported that 'I pulled down no house thoroughly at none of the Friars, but so defaced them as they should not lightly be made Friaries again' (Hinnebusch 1951, 19). Buildings were to be rendered either uninhabitable or unsuitable for conventual occupation, rather than to be erased altogether from the townscape. A second factor was the value of certain fittings, especially plate, lead and bell-metal. The stripping of building fixtures at Coventry Greyfriars and Norwich Blackfriars, for example, may have been undertaken in haste because of the danger of opportunistic vandalism and theft by local people (Martin 1937, 70; Sutermeister 1977, 8).

The church and great cloister

Scanty evidence was recorded for the stripping of the great cloister ranges, as they were examined only by non-intrusive trenching. This has revealed essentially negative evidence for a tiled or suspended floor in the main part of the Phase 6 north range. The depth of mortar and crushed stone within the great cloister garth may indicate the movement of building materials into this area: the south wall of the Phase 6A building was robbed down to the level of its ashlar plinth. Finds from demolition deposits over the western part of the great cloister ranges included a little plain and decorated window-glass, the latter of a mid. 13th-century type found in the little cloister. The only glass of a later date from the Priory consists of a very few fragments from the little cloister north range, and a single piece from within the 'Old Friary' (Armstrong and Tomlinson 1987, 45, fig. 24: no. 37). It is possible that the larger tombs in the church were disturbed by the robbing of lead coffins, as they were filled with loose mortary soils.

The *reredorter* was filled with water-washed sand and gravel — perhaps debris from the dismantling of buildings. Though these fills included a closely datable group of pottery, only a single urinal was identified. This suggests the clearance of rubbish, rather than material associated with the area where it was found.

The little cloister

The record of the stripping of the north range of the little cloister indicated that a high priority had been attached to the retrieval of lead, and perhaps glass. Evidence for the removal of other materials was less prominent, though internal structures may have been affected by demolition activity at this time. The stripping of timber fixtures to fuel fires used to melt down lead has been suggested. At Hartlepool Greyfriars, wood ash containing many nails was

suggested to be the residue of such activity (Daniels 1986, 272). It is likely that roof tile was removed; although nearly 20m² of non-diagnostic tile were recovered from Phase 7 deposits, it included very few complete tiles, and would not have sufficed to cover any of the major structures. Concentrations of tile fragments in the upper part of the demolition horizon in the garth may indicate that this activity took place at a late stage in Phase 7. It is unknown whether structural timber was taken, though the removal of the roof covering may suggest that it was. The rarity of glazed floor tile hints at the systematic removal from the site of this material also.

The stripping of window-lead, room by room, is suggested by the distribution of hearths, and of lead (nos. 553–75, 582–613, 621–4, 627–37, 667, 680–3, 685–7, 695–9, 719–20, 727–46) and glass fragments (nos. 36–476). It would appear that this activity was carried out as close as possible to the place whence the lead originated, rather than in a specially designated area. This may have helped to render the premises uninhabitable. The immediate availability of fuel for the fires may also have been a factor. At Norwich Blackfriars, parts of the rood loft fuelled the plumbers' fires in the nave of the church (Sutermeister 1977, 10). The presence of such wooden fittings appears, from the evidence of plugged hearths at Beverley, to have been recognised as a fire risk during the execution of this work. At Carmarthen Greyfriars, an equivalent building to the little cloister north range burnt down in the course of operations involving the use of bowl-hearths to melt down copper and lead (Youngs *et al.* 1986, 196).

In the east chamber of the north range, the former fireplace was neglected in favour of a new bowl-hearth, which was built with brick removed from internal fixtures. Its position may have been related to that of the stairwell down which, the concentration of lead and glass suggests, window panels were flung for dismantling. At Pontefract Cluniac Priory, the concentration of glass in a corner may similarly have illustrated the collection of material for stripping (Bellamy 1965, 14). From Northampton Greyfriars, there is both documentary and archaeological evidence for the use of hearths in the church (Williams 1978, 106). At the Whitefriars at Ludlow, shallow scrapes were formed in the refectory floor to facilitate the casting of lead ingots (Klein and Roe 1987, 26, 62). The purpose of the very small bowl-hearth cut into the fireplace of the west chamber is uncertain, though its fill included lead. The reuse of an earlier hearth position in this fashion has also been recorded at Cluniac Pontefract (Bellamy 1965, 19–20). These operations would not, of themselves, have critically damaged the structure of a building; thus at Tynemouth Priory, in the 'Priests House', the excavation of furnaces for lead-burning was followed by another century of occupation (Jobey 1967, 57). The position of a larger and more intensively used hearth in the south doorway of the west chamber, and the failure to plug this hearth on its disuse, have both been taken to indicate that its use was a later — perhaps final — episode in the despoliation of the range.

These activities were all related to the retrieval of lead. Although the fragments of glass associated with this phase were very numerous, their overall measured area was not large: the total recorded from demolition horizons would barely have filled a pair of small window openings. The glass in better condition may have been removed from the Priory. No figurative pieces were recorded, and only one or two fragments bearing designs of a later style than the mid. 13th-century grisaille were recovered. The apparent concentration of undecorated glass in the west chamber of the north range may betray the different character of its glazing.

If the window lead was a principal target for the suppressors, the greater quantities of the material employed in water management at the Priory would also have been sought after; the robbing of a downpipe attached to a guttering system is suspected at the north-west corner of the little cloister. A conduit running along the west side of the west range may also have been robbed, though at what date is uncertain. A considerable extent of piping was discovered *in situ* beneath the west alley of the great cloister (Armstrong and Tomlinson 1987, fig. 12); this may have been part of a water-supply system which was disused by the time of the Dissolution, and thus overlooked. It is possible that some of the brick features formerly identified as drains may actually have served to protect lead pipes. If this was indeed the case, then enough piping may have been extracted to have dissuaded the suppressors from a further search. It is likely that lead flashing was also recovered, though the few fragments recorded in Phase 7 do not suggest its extensive use.

Both the dating evidence for the robbing of walls, and the location of features in Phase 7, indicate the constraint of activity by, and therefore the partial survival of, the north range. This is a widely reported feature of urban monastic houses; at Newcastle-upon-Tyne Whitefriars, for example, parts of the east range and the south wall of the church survived through their incorporation in a 17th-century house despite extensive robbing of the site (Harbottle 1968, 175, 181). The Newcastle Blackfriars' ranges too were substantially preserved by a change of use (Harbottle and Fraser 1987). At Canterbury Blackfriars, the church was demolished probably after 1584 (Martin 1929, 169–74); at Ipswich, the Dominican *frater* and *dorter* survived into the 18th and 19th centuries respectively (Blatchly and Wade

1977, 25).

The evidence for the later history of the Priory remains centred on the 'Old Friary' building (Armstrong and Tomlinson 1987, 55–7); only slight evidence for structures which apparently overlapped the west end of the little cloister north range has been recorded by more recent excavation.

The later activity in the little cloister area comprised the robbing of both walls and footings. The limited dating evidence for this activity argues that it took place in the 17th, or perhaps even the early 18th century. By the mid. 18th century the cloisters of the Priory had entirely disappeared from the plan of the town (Miller *et al.* 1982, fig. 5), though the street plan is held to show the partial fossilisation of the precinct boundary.

The delay of the final demolition activity has been noted above. The very slight recovery of architectural fragments from the site as a whole argues for the efficiency with which this robbing was executed. The incorporation of masonry from a number of churches into the rubble dumped on the site of Hotham House, on Eastgate, in the early 18th century, shows the use to which a wide variety of stone could be put (Evans and Tomlinson 1992, 276–7). The reuse on-site of a small quantity of masonry has been identified to the north, and it remains a debatable point whether greater quantities were incorporated into the 'Old Friary' and the rebuilding of the precinct wall (Armstrong and Tomlinson 1987, 55–7). Post-medieval floors of clay and brick in the little cloister area failed to relate convincingly to the medieval little cloister range, save in so far as the presence of wet features to the north, and the immediate availability of building materials, may have dictated their position over part of the earlier range. The evidence recovered here was too fragmentary to indicate the nature or duration of this activity. Nor is it known how systematic the use of this area may have been before the introduction of a sealing blanket of topsoil over the whole site.

6.2 Medieval metrology

The author's attention has kindly been drawn to the subject of medieval land measurement by Andrew Harris, who has presented the results of excavations at the Dominican Priory, Chelmsford (Harris forthcoming). The present note accepts the definition of the post-Conquest perch as 16½ feet, as in the modern imperial system (*ibid.*, and sources cited therein). The metrological implications arising from the study of the Beverley Dominican Priory are presented here in only a summary form.

As at Chelmsford Blackfriars (Harris *op. cit.*), the half-perch module appears to have dictated the position of the centre line of footings when used to lay out the putative Phase 4A north range in the 13th

Date	Structure	Total width	Internal Width	Setting Out (Mid-point of footings)
C13th	Church nave	*10.20m*	6.60m	8 52m
?C13th	Phase 4B north range	8.36m	6.68m	*7.60m*
Early C14th	South aisle, church	*7.80m*	5.44m	6.60m
Early C14th	North range, little cloister (Phase 5A)	6.60m	*4.84m*	5.60m
C14th	West range, great cloister (Phase 4C)	6.36m	*4.86m*	5.60m
Late C14th	West range little cloister — includes alley (Phase 5C)	6.40m	*5.20m*	5.88m
Late C14th	North range, Phase 6A	9.48m	*7.40m*	8.40m
?Late C14th	Church choir,	*c.9.40m*	*7.60m*	*c.8.40m*

Italicised figures are those which mostly closely approach multiples of a half-perch (*c.2.52m*) module.

century. It may have determined the overall width of the church footing plan.

The coincidence of the 14th-century structural measurements with the half-perch module is slightly less exact than in the earlier work, especially in the little cloister. This may be due to more casual mensuration accompanying building work of an inferior standard. It may alternatively represent a process of cumulative error arising from attempts to derive the module or proportions of the new buildings by estimation from the standing fabric of the old. The module apparently served to delineate internal spaces in the 14th century. The exception to this was the church, though this last figure may be distorted by the inclusion of pre-existing foundations.

The close relationship between the internal width of the early church nave and the Phase 4A/B great cloister north range may argue for their contemporary planning. The disparity in the extent of their footings may be explained by the system of arching or vaulting held to have been employed in the north range, but not in the church. Local ground conditions may also have been influential in this respect.

The close similarity between the Phase 4C great cloister west range and the Phase 5C little cloister north range complements the structural similarities noted in their construction (see above). The internal width of the extant Old Friary, 4.56m, perhaps erected on pre-existing footings, is also comparable (Armstrong and Tomlinson 1987, fig. 11). There is, therefore, a body of circumstantial evidence which could support the attribution of an early 14th-century date to the development of a variety of ancillary buildings to the north and west of the ritually significant areas of the great cloister. The full implementation of this scheme may have been retarded. This is perhaps demonstrable in the case of the little cloister west range, Phase 5C (see above).

The later 14th-century north range of the great cloister (Phase 6A) may be similarly linked to the suspected reconstruction of the choir of the church.

The evidence for this is weak, though it may find some indirect support in the increase of donations to the Friary made between 1391 and 1410 (see Mf.1. A2–8).

The findings of this admittedly limited survey of the Beverley Dominican Priory suggest three conclusions. First, it appears likely that a module of half-perches was used to accomplish the initial laying-out of the complex. Secondly, this system was most effectively employed when used to divide a virgin site. It appears, however, to have remained influential upon the design of later buildings. It was applied more exactly to structures of definite status, such as the church and refectory, and more casually to ancillary structures standing at a remove from the great cloister. Thirdly, it may suggest that buildings in different areas of the precinct were planned in unified campaigns of renovation, although the resources available may frequently have delayed the implementation of such designs.

6.3 The Priory and the town

Introduction

This section of the report is intended to summarise the contribution made by the excavation of this Priory to the understanding of the character of urban monasticism. It is the most extensively sampled mendicant house in the historic county of Yorkshire, and the application of modern research methods to aspects of its occupation enhances its importance in this respect. The recent archaeological investigations in the south part of Beverley have also offered the opportunity to compare the Priory with its lower-status neighbours on the Eastgate street front, and the nearby collegiate complex at Lurk Lane. These other excavations have provided a range of material culture against which the occupation evidence from the Priory may be measured. As with these sites, the Priory offers much detail covering the

13th and 14th centuries, but less about the later medieval period.

Excavation has shed light upon the siting of the Priory and the nature of its boundary: the 'temporary' buildings associated with it; the development of the church and both great and little cloisters; the occupation of some of their ranges; and the process by which this occupation was ended. These topics have been illuminated to varying degrees: the most detail has been recorded of the 13th-century timber buildings and the 14th-century little cloister, and of the Dissolution-period activity in the latter. The occupation deposits have yielded important environmental evidence for diet. In contrast, only structural evidence illustrates the development of the church and the great cloister. The shortcomings of this coverage are significant, and arise from the variable character and quality of the excavations between 1960 and 1989, the scanty examination of the eastern precinct, and the failure to achieve a complete understanding of any single area of the complex. No detailed structural survey of the 'Old Friary' — the only major extant remnant of the house — has been carried out. Many of these problems are common to urban monastic houses, and some are inevitable given the post-medieval expansion of the towns which initially attracted them.

The site of the Priory

The Priory lay to the east of a (probably) pre-existing channel which perhaps represented the restatement of earlier and more poorly defined boundaries (see above, sections 4.2 and 6.1). The relationship of the Priory to the town has been clarified by recent research into the establishment and use of tenements along Eastgate (Evans and Tomlinson 1992). This has indicated that intense use of some tenements — further illustrated by work immediately west of the Priory precinct (see sections 4.2 and 6.1) — is unlikely to have entailed residential occupation until over a century after the foundation of the Dominican House. As the northern and south-western boundaries of the Priory were defined by the precincts of pre-existing institutions, it is unlikely that the Priory was located in order to evangelise its urban neighbours. The land granted to the friars was probably peripheral to the town, had seen little or no recent occupation, and was damp. The area had been neglected by earlier drainage schemes, and had seen dumping of soils, perhaps in the 12th or early 13th century, which had permitted at best only slight agricultural activity (see sections 4.1, 4.2, and 6.1). By the early decades of the 13th century the industrial activity along Eastgate is also likely to have made this an evil-smelling quarter of the town. It was, in short, an area unattractive to settlement. These considerations are likely to have been influential in the donation of this land to the friars.

The occupation of this site by the Dominicans necessitated extensive soil movement, and the design of buildings with deference to unfavourable local ground conditions. In both respects the Beverley Priory was a typical mendicant house (see section 6.1). It did, perhaps, enjoy somewhat atypical benefit from its proximity to the Minster, a regional focus of both building activity and pilgrimage (see Chapter 1). The position of a building, which is thought to have been the predecessor of the extant 'Old Friary', has been compared to that of the detached guesthouse at Canterbury Blackfriars (Armstrong and Tomlinson 1987, 55–6) and might be taken to mark the deliberate exploitation of pilgrim traffic.

The definition of the precinct was initially by ditches, and possibly hedges. The former included a watercourse which was to serve to carry away waste from the Priory. Though this feature may have been of late 12th or early 13th-century date, it is uncertain whether its excavation was directly associated with the friars' arrival. As a boundary it was superseded by a wall, probably in the 14th century (see section 6.1). This enhanced the privacy of the precinct, and was to effect a clear definition of its extent which persisted into the post-medieval period.

The development of the precinct

The church constructed on the south side of the Priory precinct was at once the ritual focus of the community's religious life, its fixed point of contact with the townspeople, and a point of origin from which the buildings of the convent were to extend. This development, insofar as it has been traced, followed a traditional claustral plan, which was modified by the exigencies of site drainage. This is tentatively suggested to have been represented by a confined suite of ranges, the later reconstruction of which leaves their respective original functions in doubt. In their dimensions and their quality, they may have been intended to form a harmonious architectural unity with the church. This intention may have led to a relatively early (13th century) use of overshot ranges, as a way of meeting the twin demands of maintaining external appearances and providing adequate internal space (see section 6.1, above). The comparable high quality of masonry work on the early church nave (Armstrong and Tomlinson 1987, 7–8) and on the *reredorter* may hint at the contemporary execution of these works, which would be among the first required for both religious and practical reasons. It is tempting to see both skilled workmen and fine materials being drawn from the adjacent Minster site, where large-scale works were in progress at the time, to assist the establishment of the Dominican House. Both institutions enjoyed the support of the Archbishop of York, and the structural and modular similarity between disparate elements of the Phase 4A plan could suggest the implementation of a coherent overall design. The diminishing quality of work between Phases 4A and 4B may indicate, however, that the initial high standard of work could not be sustained.

The Phase 3A timber hall appears from its position to have related to this early claustral plan. The possibly attenuated achievement of this layout, illustrated by Phases 4A and 4B of the north range, may have forced the retention of this lowly structure until the completion of these works. Its position alongside the north range may be contrasted with the situation at Sandwell Priory, West Midlands, where timber buildings of the mid. 12th century were replaced in *c*.1200 by stone ranges built in the same position (Hodder and Jones 1987–8); it can also be compared with mendicant halls at Ipswich, Hartlepool and elsewhere (see above, 6.1).

If the dating of the window glass (which is presumed to have come from the church) to *c*.1250–85 is accepted (see section 3.8), then this, coupled with documentary evidence for a gift of oaks to 1263 (Mf. 1. A2–8), and the suggested date for the removal of the Phase 3A hall before *c*.1275, argues for the completion of the church and the stone north range by the last quarter of the century. This completion of the ritually significant building stock of the Priory was to be followed by occasional demands, such as the Provincial Chapter of the English Dominicans at Beverley in 1286, and by the expansion of the (admittedly fluid) establishment from 33 friars in 1299 to 42 in 1310. The membership of both Franciscan and Dominican orders in England was reaching a peak at this time. By *c*.1275 a proportion of the Beverley community would already have been ageing, thus providing an additional impetus for an expansion of the residential facilities. These factors may have dictated the replacement of the timber hall with a similar structure of somewhat enhanced status in Phase 3B. The realignment of the hall may indicate a functional separation from the rigours of full monastic observance. Either a *misericord* regime, or a lay occupation, may be indicated by the unregulated diet which is suggested by the environmental evidence from its latest occupation in Phase 3C (see section 4.3).

The recent focusing of archaeological attention upon the area to the north of the great cloister has allowed these developments to be followed through the 14th century. The use of half-timbered construction argues for a residential rather than a ritual function for the little cloister. The stone frontage of its principal range and other internal details also suggest some social pretensions. It is uncertain

whether infringement of the Dominican constitutions may have brought about the deposing of the Prior of Beverley in 1314, but it is significant that the house was considered to offer congenial corrodian accommodation for a retired Royal Chaplain by 1352 (Mf.1. A2–8).

In the period *c*.1275–*c*.1300 the aisled hall had become both structurally and socially anachronistic in lay terms, though it was still appropriate to communal life. With the construction of the little cloister, an approximate parity was granted to the private and communal spaces at ground-floor level; the former were probably duplicated upstairs. From the mid. 14th century, the subdivision of the private apartment, and the works related to the first-floor occupation gathered pace, leaving only scanty evidence of diminished activity on the ground floor from the later 14th century onwards. Similarly, the subdivision of the great cloister west range and its apparent reconstruction in timber-framed form may relate to the same trend towards privacy and comfort. Such timber-framed buildings are poorly represented amongst extant conventual survivals, though both documentary sources and the later medieval architecture of York are informative in this respect (see section 6.1).

The reconstruction of a refectory (possibly with a dormitory and library above it) in the later 14th century was a restatement of the communal ethos at the Beverley Priory, with a masonry construction denoting the formal status of the new range. Though a kitchen has not been unequivocally identified, both water supply and food preparation areas may suggest it to have been close at hand, probably in the ground floor of the west range (Armstrong and Tomlinson 1987, 55). The role of institutional meals in maintaining the coherence of the community is suggested not only by this physical centralisation of food preparation, but also by the consistent range of food debris found in the various parts of the complex (see section 4.3). The same meals appeared to have been served, whether consumed in a private or a communal setting. The prominence of poultry bones in the 14th-century floor deposits is consistent with an abstinent diet, as chicken was not classed as flesh-meat. Although meat was more prominent among later food remains, it rarely included the hunted game available to the upper echelons of local society (cf. Scott 1991).

Those works on the fabric of the church whose execution is certain — the development of a twin-aisled form by the early 14th century, and the construction of a chantry chapel in the later 14th or early 15th century — related to the involvement of the laity in the convent's devotions and religious activity. Bequests to the Priory are recorded from 1311 — about one a decade up to 1390, eleven between 1391 and 1410, and between two and four every ten years thereafter until the Dissolution (Mf.1.A2–8). If such bequests were linked to interment within the precinct, as is occasionally specified, they would indicate the increasing economic dependence of the Priory upon mortuary or chantry services. This would follow from the expansion of space available for burials. The most significant increase in bequests falls close to the known date of the rebuilding of the refectory. This suggests the importance of such sources of income — the fragmentary record of donations listing only a proportion of those necessary for the upkeep and development of the house. Fund-raising for building projects could also be energetically pursued beyond the local area; Chaucer's Friar in the Summoner's Tale was associated with a community in Holderness:

'Lordinges, ther is in Yorkshire, as I gesse,
A mersshy contree called Holdernesse,
In which ther wente a limitour aboute,
To preche, and eek to begge, it is no doute.
And so bifel, that on a day this frere
Had preched at a chirche in his manere,
And specially, aboven every thing,
Excited he the peple in his preching
To trentals, and to yeve, for goddes sake,
Wher-with men mighten holy houses make ...'

(Skeat 1912, 588).

This community has speculatively been linked with the Beverley Dominicans (*Hull Daily Mail* 22/3/89).

The Priory buildings

The various structures identified at the Dominican Priory span a wide range of vernacular and formal architectural types. The site has added to our knowledge of local timber-framed construction, and remains the only place in Beverley where a variety of stone or partly stone-walled buildings has been subjected to archaeological investigation.

The Phase 3 timber halls (attributed to the 13th century) incorporated forms of sill-beam and earth-fast post construction considered to have been, in regional terms, somewhat anachronistic (see 6.1, above). This may indicate the vernacular persistence of outmoded structural forms for residential buildings, especially those of lower or temporary status; there may have been many more buildings of this sort in 13th-century Beverley. The correspondence between the construction techniques used at Eastgate and at the Priory in the 13th century may confirm that they illustrate the contemporary local vernacular (see 6.1, above). The excavated timber halls at Lurk Lane were more sophisticated in their construction, perhaps a function of the wealth and status of that site.

The stone buildings considered to be of 13th-century date are, in contrast, of a high quality, as illustrated by early work on the church and the latrine block. The later masonry achieved a less competent or less costly standard, though construction methods saw little change (see 6.1, above). The tentative ascription of narrower wall construction to a half-timbered form familiar from the later-medieval architecture of York, may be of wider application in Beverley. Falling as it does between the stone construction of churches and the timber vernacular, this may have been commonly employed in a town distinguished by numerous charitable institutions (see Chapters 1 and 6.1).

Three major episodes of building work have been identified at the Priory. The first would have extended from before 1240 up to *c*.1263–75, and would perhaps have embraced Phases 3A, 3B and 4A — the timber halls and the establishment of the great cloister (see 6.1, above). The second episode for which evidence has been presented was the Phase 5A construction of the little cloister, in the early part of the 14th century (*ibid*.). The third major programme of building work to be recorded was in the later 14th century, and entailed the renovation of the little cloister in Phase 5C, and the rebuilding of at least the north side of the great cloister in Phase 6A (*ibid*.). Episodes such as Phases 4B, 4C and 6B are not readily placed in a chronological sequence with the others, though Phase 4B was completed before the later 14th century Phase 6A, and the subsequent Phase 6B. Given the dependence of the Dominicans upon local patronage, this should imply a high level of local prosperity through the 13th and 14th centuries, enabling these vigorous and recurrent episodes of building activity. No building work in the excavated areas is securely attributable to the 15th century, this may imply the waning of local prosperity as well as the recorded decline in the number of friars. This view should be qualified however, by documentary evidence for rebuilding in *c*.1449 (Mf.1.A2–8), the construction of a chantry chapel, and the debatable status of the extant 'Old Friary' (Armstrong and Tomlinson 1987, 55–7).

The choice of building materials available to the friars may itself have been dictated by the bounty of patrons; documentary sources describe the royal grant of timber in 1263 (Mf.1. A2–8), while the variable quality of the timber available has been inferred from the structural characteristics of the later 13th-century Phase 3B aisled hall (Chapters 2 and 6.1). The reuse of building stone is a practice remarked on every site to be excavated in Beverley. A few fragments are — as usual — considered to have been derived from the Minster, though the relocation of stone within the Dominican precinct has been identified during Phase 5C (see section 6.1, above). The assessment of the quality of building stone used at the Priory has indicated the selection of good freestone for mouldings, but the use of inferior material for simpler work or walling (section 3.2). This may reflect the mendicant status of the site, but also shows a clear appreciation of the relative merits of building stones despite their local scarcity. Both the Minster church and St. Mary's are known to have attracted craftsmen from outside the immediate locality, and evidence for a facility in the use of building stone at the Priory further illustrates the activity of skilled masons in the town.

Local industry and trade

The most prominent evidence for local industry was afforded by the large quantities of brick and tile used at the Priory, some types of which are convincingly related to a production site in the suburb of *Groval*, now Grovehill (sections 3.3, 3.4). These materials first appeared on this site in 13th-century contexts, increasing in both volume and variety in the 14th century.

The use of decorative roof-furniture was identified in 12th-century contexts at Lurk Lane, Beverley; at the Priory, similar decorative features adorned buildings dated to the later 13th century. Tilers are recorded in Beverley from 1202 onwards, and throughout the later Middle Ages (Allison 1989, 42). At the Priory, flat roof tile of two varieties was in use from the later 13th century. At least four distinct types were in use in the 14th century, illustrating the flourishing of this local industry. Two types of brick were used in early 14th century works; by the end of the century five types were available, most of which might be adapted as 'specials' (see section 3.3). Of the various brick and tile types, most were made from alluvial clay which was available along the banks of the River Hull. The variant character of brick Type 6, considered to be made from the glacial till which underlies the Priory itself, may mark its on-site production (section 3.3). This was perhaps a development which, ostensibly for environmental reasons, was to be restricted by the 15th century, when borough regulations forbade the migration of brick manufacture into the town.

As with the masonry, much of the brick and tile excavated at the Priory has been considered to have been of low quality (sections 3.3, 3.4). This may suggest that the Priory absorbed surplus production of goods which would not otherwise have been readily saleable within the town. The brick and tile makers of Beverley were accustomed to pay their Borough rents by the rendering of goods in kind, and the extension of this practice to the support of a mendicant house could have been an important source of building materials for the friars.

It was hoped that the investigation of the Dominican Priory would illuminate the character of the later medieval pottery in use in Beverley; however, the low level of material attributable to 15th-century activity, and a rigorous control exercised over the

accumulation of waste within the precinct, have combined to frustrate this aim. In common with other sites in the south part of the town, very few imported wares were present to illustrate foreign trading contacts, despite the proximity of the Dominican Priory to the port area. This may in part be due to the role of Wyke, later Hull, as a major port at the mouth of the River Hull; it may also mark the lack of a retail mechanism to convey goods from Hull to Beverley (section 3.16). Other imported goods, such as fine glassware and Norwegian hone stones, occur as rarely but consistently at the Priory as elsewhere in Beverley (sections 3.13; 3.14). Glass for windows may have been supplied from York (section 3.8). Coal too was imported, perhaps from Durham, from the mid. 14th century onwards (Mf. 3. E10–11). It is also likely that travellers from the Continent and from Scotland visited the Priory in the 14th and 15th centuries (section 3.15).

The trade in wool and cloth which formed the backbone of economic life in Beverley is better illustrated elsewhere; the Dominican Priory is indeed notable amongst sites in the town for the rarity of evidence for textile production. Evidence for dyeing and clothworking is drawn almost exclusively from outside the precinct, and complements the understanding already gained of the neighbouring Eastgate tenements (section 4.2: Evans and Tomlinson 1992, 278–87).

Environmental evidence for the diet observed at the Priory is of considerable importance, as such detailed information has rarely been presented from monastic sites. When compared with other sites in Beverley, the wide variety of fish from freshwater, coastal and deep-sea fisheries is usual, though fish may have been proportionally more important at the Priory. The prominence of domestic poultry (and eggs) at the Priory particularly distinguished it from other Beverley sites, and may indicate both a formal abstinence from flesh-meat and the relative poverty of the friars' diet. In a later dependence on mutton, and in the supply of part-prepared carcasses, the Priory is considered to have been similar to other sites in Beverley, and may have been supplied from the same market sources (section 4.3). This confirms the findings of pottery research which indicates little variation in ceramic usage, despite wide variations in the status of sites (section 3.16).

The friars' contribution to town life

The archaeological evidence has, of necessity, given a one-sided and materialistic view of the relationship between the Priory and the town. The spiritual or educational contributions of the friars to the quality of urban life are of their very nature not susceptible to quantification. Evidence has been recorded to denote the literacy of at least some of the residents, though this evidence is not restricted to ecclesiastical sites in the town (sections 3.9, 3.11, 3.12). The support in-kind which the archaeological record implies is one indirect measure of their success; so too is the recurrent vigour of their building programmes, the flow of bequests in their favour, and the recorded number of local worthies who chose their last resting place within the Dominican church. Lesser townsfolk were apparently associated with the friars, in either professional guilds or devotional organisations. The Beverley Priory was the scene of the Provincial Chapter of the English Dominicans on at least four occasions between 1240 and 1342 (Mf.1. A2–8), and this may itself be a modest measure of the honour and distinction which the house conferred upon the town.

The retention of the property by the friars until 1539, and the absence of families established within it, may point to a relatively vigorous monastic life. The Dominicans enjoyed a more durable place in the memory of the town than their Franciscan brethren: the outline of their precinct was to be perpetuated in the street plan, and elements of their house survived into the post-medieval period.

It is certain that the amelioration of the rigorous monastic life was in progress in advance of the formal recognition of change in the 15th century (e.g. Hinnebusch 1951, 197). The criticism of mendicant laxity voiced by Langland, Chaucer and others in the late medieval period should, however, be seen against a resurgence of religious interest which made the later 14th century a *renaissance* period for spiritual activity in England. A relaxation of standards of austerity may indeed have been imposed by a successful engagement in urban life. Polemics directed at the friars reflect the wide dissemination of the Christian *mores* against which negligent friars were seen to offend, and which they themselves had promulgated so successfully.

Bibliography

Addyman, P.V. 1979 'Vernacular Buildings below the Ground', *Archaeol. J. 136* (1979), 69–75.

Addyman, P.V. and Black, V.E. (eds), 1984 *Archaeological Papers from York presented to M.W. Barley*, York Archaeological Trust.

Addyman, P.V. and Priestley, J. 'Baile Hill, York: A Report on the Institute's 1977 Excavations', *Archaeol. J. 134* (1977), 115–56.

Allin, C.E. 1981 'The Ridge Tiles', in Mellor and Pearce 1981, 52–70.

Allison, K.J. (ed.) 1969 *A History of the County of York, East Riding Vol. 1: The City of Kingston upon Hull*, Oxford University Press, London.

Allison, K.J. (ed), 1989 *A History of the County of York, East Riding. Vol. 6: The Borough and Liberties of Beverley*, London.

Andrews, D.D. 1979 'Miscellaneous Small Finds', in Andrews and Milne 1979, 124–32.

Andrews, D.D. and Milne, G (eds) 1979 *Wharram, A study of Settlement on the Yorkshire Wolds* I, Soc. Med. Arch. Mon. Ser. 8, London.

Archibald, M. 1991 'The Other Coins and Jettons', in Armstrong *et al.* 1991, 168–72.

Armstrong, P. 1977 'Excavations in Sewer Lane, Hull, 1974', *East Riding Archaeologist 3* (Hull Old Town Report Series No. 1).

Armstrong, P. 1991 'The Floor Tile', in Armstrong *et al.* 1991, 199.

Armstrong, P. & Armstrong, S.J. 'The Clay Roof Tile', in Armstrong S.J. and Ayers 1987, 234–40.

Armstrong, P. and Ayers, B. 1987 'Excavations in High Street and Blackfriargate', *East Riding Archaeologist 8* (Hull Old Town Report Series No. 5).

Armstrong, P. and Tomlinson, D.G. 1987 *Excavations at the Dominican Priory, Beverley*, Humberside Heritage Publication *13*.

Armstrong, P., Tomlinson, D.G. and Evans, D.H. 1991 *Excavations at Lurk Lane, Beverley 1979–82*, Sheffield Excavation Reports *1*.

Armstrong, S.J. 1987 'Miscellaneous Finds', in Armstrong and Tomlinson 1987, 44–5.

Armstrong, S.J. 1992 'Clay Roof Tile and Roof Furniture', in Evans and Tomlinson 1992, 219–26.

Armstrong, S.J. and Didsbury, P. 1992 'The Roman Finds', in Evans and Tomlinson 1992, 121.

Aston, M. 1988 *England's Iconoclasts: Laws Against Images*, Oxford.

Aston, Michael (ed.) 1988 *Medieval Fish, Fisheries and Fishponds in England*, B.A.R. Brit. Ser. *182*.

Atkin, M., Carter, A. and Evans, D.H. 1985 *Excavations in Norwich 1971–78, Pt. 2*, East Anglian Archaeology *26*.

Atkinson, D. and Foreman, M. 1992 'The leather', in Evans and Tomlinson 1992, 175–87.

Axworthy Rutter, J.A. 1990 'Window Glass', in Ward 1990, 115–18.

Ayers, B. 1979 'Excavations at Chapel Lane Staith 1978', *East Riding Archaeologist 5* (Hull Old Town Report Series No. 3).

Ayers, B. 1987 *Excavations at St. Martin-at-Palace-Plain, Norwich, 1981*, East Anglian Archaeology *37*.

Aylmer, G.E. and Cant, R. (eds) 1977 *A History of York Minster*, Oxford.

Baker, J. 1960 *English Stained Glass* London, Thames and Hudson.

Barnard, F.P. 1916 *The Casting Counter and the Counting Board*, Oxford.

Bartlett, J. 1971 'The Medieval Walls of Hull', *Kingston upon Hull Museums Bulletins 3 and 4*, 1–28.

Barton, K.J. and Holden, E.W. 1977 'Excavations at Bramber Castle, Sussex 1966–67', *Archaeol. J. 134* (1977), 11–79.

Beer, R.J.S. 1976 'The Relationship between *Trichuris Trichiura* (Linnaeus 1758) of Man and *Trichuris Suis* (Schrank 1788) of Pig', *Research in Veterinary Science 20* (1976), 47–54.

Bellamy, C.V. 1965 'Pontefract Cluniac Priory, Excavations 1957–1961', *Publ. Thoresby Society 49* (1965), Leeds.

Biddle, M. 1961–62 'The deserted Medieval Village of Seacourt, Berkshire', *Oxoniensia 26–7* (1961–62), 70–201.

Biddle, M. (ed.) 1990 *Object and Economy in Medieval Winchester*, Winchester Studies 7, Pt. 2 (1990).

Bilson, J. 1896 'The North Bar Beverley', *Trans. East Riding Antiq. Soc. 4* (1896), 37–49.

Blatchly, J. and Wade, K. 1977 'Excavations at Ipswich Blackfriars in 1898 and 1976', *Proc. Suffolk Instit. Archaeol. and Hist. 34* (1977), 25–34.

Brainerd, G.W. 1951 'The Place of Chronological Ordering in Archaeological Deposits', *American Antiquity 16/4* (1951), 301–13.

Braun, H. 1968 *An Introduction to English Medieval Architecture*, London.

Brooks, C.M. 1987 *Medieval and later Pottery from Aldwark and Other Sites*, The Archaeology of York *16/3*, York Archaeological Trust/C.B.A.

Brooks, F.W. 1939 'A Medieval Brickyard at Hull', *J. Brit. Archaeol. Assoc.* (3rd Series) *4* (1939), 151–74.

Brown, M.M. and Gallagher, D.B. 1984 'St. Cuthbert's Church, Ormesby, Cleveland. Excavation and Watching Brief 1975 and 1976', *Yorks. Archaeol. J. 56* (1984), 51–63.

Butler, L.A.S. 1960 'Excavations at Blackfriars, Hereford, 1958', *Trans. Woolhope Nat. Field Club 36/3* (1960), 334–42.

Butler, L.A.S. 1984 'The Houses of the Mendicant Orders in Britain: Recent Archaeological Work', in Addyman and Black 1984, 123–36.

Butler, L.A.S. 1987 'Medieval Urban Religious Houses', in Schofield and Leech 1987, 167–76.

Caviness, M.H. 1981 *The Windows of Christ Church Cathedral, Canterbury, Corpus Vitrearun Medii Aevi, Great Britain 2*, British Academy, London.

Charleston, R.J. 1975 'The Glass', in Platt and Coleman–Smith 1975, 204–26.

Cherry, J. 1975 'Bronze circular brooch', in Steane and Bryant 1975, 111–12.

Christie, P.M. and Coad, J.G. 1980 'Excavations at Denny Abbey', *Archaeol. J. 137* (1980), 138–279.

Christy, M. 1926 *The Bryant and May Museum of Fire-Making Appliances. Catalogue of the Exhibits*, London: Bow Publishing.

Clapham, A.W. 1912 'On the Topography of the Dominican Priory of London', *Archaeologia 63* (1912), 57–84.

Clapham, A.W. 1927 'The Architectural Remains of the Mendicant Orders in Wales', *Archaeol. J. 84* (1927), 88–104.

Clapham, A.W. and Godfrey, W.H. 1913 *Some Famous Buildings and their Story*, London.

Clarke, H. and Carter, A. 1977 *Excavations in Kings Lynn 1963–1970*, Soc. Med. Archaeol. Mon. Ser. 7.

Clark, R. and Maull, A. 1989 'Dunstable Friary Excavations 1988', *Manshead Magazine* (J. Arch. Soc. Dunstable) 29 (1989), 26–8.

Clay, P. 1981 'The Small Finds — Non-structural', in Mellor and Pearce, 1981, 130–45.

Clifton-Taylor, A. 1972 *The Pattern of English Building*, London.

Congreve, A.L. 1938 'A Roman and Saxon Site at Elmswell, East Yorkshire: Second Interim Report, 1937', *Hull Museum Publications No. 198*, reprinted from *Trans. East Riding Antiq. Soc. 28*, Pt 3, Hull.

Conway, J.P. 1889 'The Blackfriars of Cardiff', *Arch. Camb.* (5th Series) *6*, No. 22 (1889), 97–105.

Coppack, G. 1986 'The Excavation of an Outer Court Building, perhaps the Woolhouse, at Fountains Abbey, North Yorkshire', *Med. Archaeol. 30* (1986), 46–87.

Coppack, G. 1989 'Thornholme Priory: the development of a monastic outer court landscape', in Gilchrist and Mytum 1989, 185–222.

Courtney, P. 1989 'Excavations in the Outer Precinct of Tintern Abbey', *Med. Archaeol. 33* (1989), 99–143.

Cox, G.A. and Gillies, K.J.S. 1986 'The X-ray fluoresence analysis of medieval durable blue soda glass from York Minster', *Archaeometry 28/1* (1986), 57–68.

Croft, R.A. 1987 *Graffiti Gaming Boards*, Finds Research Group 700–1700, Datasheet 6.

Crossley, D.W. 1967 'Glassmaking in Bagot's Park, Staffordshire, in the 16th Century', *Post-med. Archaeol. 1* (1967), 44–83.

Crossley, D.W. (ed.) 1981 *Medieval Industry*, CBA Research Report *40*.

Daniels, R. 1986 'The Excavation of the Church of the Franciscans, Hartlepool, Cleveland', *Archaeol. J. 143* (1986), 260–304.

Daniels, R. and Gill, W. 1986 'Stonework', in Daniels 1986, 286–91.

Davey, P. and Hodges, R. (eds) 1983 *Ceramics and Trade*, Sheffield.

Dent, J. forthcoming *Wetwang Slack: a prehistoric and Roman site on the Yorkshire Wolds*, Sheffield Excavation Reports, forthcoming.

Didsbury, M.P.T. 1990 *Aspects of late Iron Age and Romano-British settlement in the Lower Hull Valley*, unpublished M. Phil. thesis, University of Durham.

Didsbury, M.P.T. and Watkins, G. 1992 'The Pottery', in Evans and Tomlinson 1992, 81–120.

Done, G. 1984 'The Animal Bone', in Poulton and Woods 1984, Microfiche pp.159–60.

Von den Driesch, A. 1976 *A Guide to the Measurement of Animal Bone from Archaeological Sites*, Peabody Museum Bulletin 1 (1976), Harvard.

Drury, P.J. 1974 'Chelmsford Dominican Priory: The Excavation of the Reredorter, 1973', *Essex Archaeol. and Hist. 6* (1974), 40–81.

Drury, P.J. 1977 'Brick and Tile', in Williams 1977, 32–6.

Drury, P.J. 1981 'The Production of Brick and Tile in Medieval England', in Crossley 1981, 126–42.

D.U.A. 1984a *Lead Weights from Five London Sites*, unpublished survey (1984), Dept. of Urban Archaeology, Museum of London.

D.U.A. 1984b *Identifying Shoes*, Dept. of Urban Archaeology Information Sheet, Museum of London.

Duncan, H.B. and Moorhouse, S.A. 1987 'The Small Finds', in Moorhouse and Wrathmell 1987, 120–48.

Dunham, A.C., Fraser, A.G., Wilkinson, F.C.F. and Middleton, R., 1987 'Petrological Examination of Hull Tile Types', in Armstrong and Ayers 1987, 241–3.

Dunning, G.C. 1977 'Mortars', in Clarke and Carter 1977, 320–47.

Durham, B. 1977 'Archaeological Investigations at St. Aldates, Oxford', *Oxoniensia 42* (1977), 83–202.

Dyer. C. 1986 'English Peasant Buildings in the later Middle Ages (1200–1500)', *Med. Archaeol. 30* (1986), 19–45.

Eames, E.S. 1961 'A Thirteenth-Century Tile Kiln Site at North Grange, Meaux, Beverley, Yorkshire', *Med. Archaeol. 5* (1961), 137–68.

Evans, D.H. and Heslop, D.H. 1985 'Two Medieval Sites in Yarm', *Yorks. Archaeol. J. 57* (1985), 43–78.

Evans, D.H. and Tomlinson, D.G. 1992 *Excavations at 33–35 Eastgate, Beverley 1983–86*, Sheffield Excavation Report 3.

Evans, J. 1970 *A History of Jewellery 1100–1870*, Boston.

Farmer, D.H. 1982 *The Oxford Dictionary of Saints*, paperback, 1st edition, Oxford.

Farmer, P.G. and Farmer, N.C. 1982 'The Dating of the Scarborough Ware Pottery Industry', *Med. Ceramics 6* (1982), 66–86.

Fisher, R.A., Corbet, A.S. and Williams, C.B. 1943 'The Relationship between the Number of Species and the Number of Individuals in a Random Sample of an Animal Population', *J. Animal Ecology 12* (1943), 42–58.

Foreman, M. 1991a 'Objects of Lead', in Armstrong *et al.* 1991, 155–63.

Foreman, M. 1991b 'Objects of Stone and Fired Clay', in Armstrong *et al.* 1991, 105–14.

Foreman, M. 1991c 'The Bone and Antler', in Armstrong *et al.* 1991, 183–96.

Foreman, M. 1992a 'Stone Objects', in Evans and Tomlinson 1992, 122–32.

Foreman, M. 1992b 'Objects of Bone, Antler and Shell', in Evans and Tomlinson 1992, 163–74.

Foreman, M. 1992c 'Objects of Lead', in Evans and Tomlinson 1992, 148–50.

French, T. and O'Connor, D.E. 1987 *York Minster: A Catalogue of Medieval Stained Glass; Fascicule 1 — The West Windows of the Nave, Corpus Vitrearum Medii Aevi: Great Britain 3*, British Academy, Oxford.

Frere, S.S. 1986 'Roman Britain in 1985: 1. Sites Explored', *Britannia 17* (1986), 385–6.

Gamlen, St. John O. 1973 'Medieval Window Glass from the Priory, King's Langley', in Neal 1973, 73–7.

Gammill, D.G. 1981 *Space Allocation as a Planning Principle in British Medieval Monastic Architecture*, unpublished M.A. Thesis, University of Wales.

Gardner, J.S. 1955 'Coggeshall Abbey and its early Brickwork', *J. Brit. Archaeol. Assoc.* (3rd Series) *18* (1955), 19–32.

Gilchrist, R. and Mytum, H. (eds) 1989 *The Archaeology of Rural Monasteries* B.A.R. Brit. Ser. *203*.

Gilyard-Beer, R. 1977 'Ipswich Blackfriars', *Proc. Suffolk Instit. Archaeol. and Hist. 34* (1977), 15–23.

Goldthorp, L.M. 1934 'The Franciscans and Dominicans in Yorkshire: Part I; The Greyfriars', *Yorks. Archaeol. J. 31* (1934), 264–320.

Goldthorp, L.M. 1935 'The Franciscans and Dominicans in Yorkshire: Part II; The Blackfriars', *Yorks. Archaeol. J. 32* (1935), 365–428.

Goodall, A.R. 1979 'Copper Alloy Objects', in Andrews and Milne 1979, 108–14.

Goodall, A.R. 1991 'Objects of Copper Alloy', in Armstrong *et al.* 1991, 148–54.

Goodall, A.R. 1992 'Objects of Copper Alloy', in Evans and Tomlinson 1992, 138–42.

Goodall, I.H. 1987 'Padlock', in Armstrong and Tomlinson 1987, 37–8.

Goodall, I.H. 1991 'Objects of Iron', in Armstrong *et al.* 1991, 131–47.

Goodall, I.H. 1992 'Objects of Iron', in Evans and Tomlinson 1992, 151–61.

Grant, A. 1982 'The use of tooth wear as a guide to the age of domestic ungulates', in Wilson, B., Grigson, C. and Payne, S. (eds), *Ageing and Sexing Animal Bones from Archaeological Sites*, B.A.R. Brit. Ser. *109*, 91–107.

Graves, C.P. (forthcoming) 'Window Glass', in Lewis, J.H. and Ewart, G.T., *Jedburgh Abbey: the archaeology and architecture of a Border Abbey*, Soc. Antiqs. Scot. Mon. Ser., forthcoming.

Graves, C.P. (in preparation) *The Painted Medieval Window Glass from the Gilbertine Priory of St. Andrew, Fishergate, York*, The Archaeology of York 17.

Grew, F. and De Neergaard, M. 1988 *Medieval Finds from Excavations in London: 2. Shoes and Pattens*, London, H.M.S.O.

Gwynn, A. 1940 *The English Austin Friars in the Time of Wyclif*, Oxford.

Hall, A.R. 1992 'The last teasel factory in Britain, and some observations on teasel (*Dipsacus fullonum* L. and *D. sativus* (L.) Honckeny) remains from archaeological deposits', *Circaea, The Journal of the Association for Environmental Archaeology 9*, 9–15.

Hall, A.R., Jones, A.G.K. and Kenward, H.K. 1983 'Cereal Bran and Human Faecal Remains - Some Preliminary Observations', in Proudfoot 1983, 85–104.

Hall, A.R. and Kenward, H.K. (1990) *Environmental Evidence from the Colonia: General Accident and Rougier Street*, Archaeology of York *14/6*. London: C.B.A., 289–434, Pls. II–IX and Fiche 2–11.

Hamlin, A. 1977 *The Modern Traveller to the early Irish Church*.

Hamlin, A. and Hughes, K. 1983 *Celtic Monasticism: The Modern Traveller to the early Irish Church*.

Harbottle, B. 1968 'Excavations at the Carmelite Friary, Newcastle upon Tyne, 1965 and 1967', *Archaeol. Ael.* (4th Series) *46* (1968), 163–223.

Harbottle, B. and Fraser, R. 1987 'Blackfriars, Newcastle upon Tyne, after the Dissolution of the Monasteries', *Archaeol. Ael.* (5th Series) *15* (1987), 23–149.

Harder, W. 1964 'Anatomie der Fische', in Demoll, R., Maier, H.N. and Wundsch, H.H. (eds) *Handbuch der Binnenfischerei Mitteleuropas*, B. Schweizerbart'sche Verlagsbuchandlung, Stuttgart.

Hare, J.N. 1985 *Battle Abbey; The Eastern Range and the Excavations of 1978–80*, English Heritage Archaeological Report 2.

Harley, L.S. 1974 'A Typology of Brick: with numerical coding of brick characteristics', *J. Brit. Archaeol. Assoc.* (3rd Series) *25* (1974), 63–87.

Harvey, J.H. (ed.) 1969 *William Worcestre: Itineraries*, Oxford.

Harris, A.P. (forthcoming) *Excavations at Chelmsford Dominican Priory*, Draft typescript, 1989.

Hayfield, C. 1985 *Humberside Medieval Pottery*, B.A.R. Brit. Ser. *140*, 2 Vols.

Heathcote, J. 1990 'Excavation Round-Up, 1989, Part 1: City of London', *London Archaeologist 6/6* (1990), 160–7.

Henderson, J. 1988 'Electron Probe Microanalysis of mixed-alkali Glasses', *Archaeometry 30/1* (1988), 77–91.

Henderson, J. 1991 'The Glass', in Armstrong *et al.* 1991, 124–30.

Hewett, C.A. 1976 'Aisled Timber Halls and Related Buildings, chiefly in Essex', *Trans. Ancient Monuments Soc.* (New Series) *21* (1976), 45–99.

Hillam J., Morgan, R.A. and Tyers, I. 1987 'Sapwood estimates and the dating of short ring sequences', in Ward, R.G.W. (ed.) *Application of tree-ring studies: current research in dendrochronology and related areas*, B.A.R. Internat. Series S133 (1987), 165–85.

Hinnebusch, W.A. 1951 *The Early English Friars Preachers*, Institutum Historicum FF. Praedicatorum Romae AD S. Sabinae, Dissertationes Historicae Fasciculus XIV Rome.

Hodder, M. and Jones, C. 1987–8 *An Interim Report on Excavations at Sandwell Priory and Sandwell Hall, 1982–88*, Sandwell Valley Archaeological Project Report No. 6. Sandwell Metropolitan Borough Council.

Hope, W.H. St John 1890 'On the Whitefriars or Carmelites of Hulne, Northumberland', *Archaeol. J. 47* (1890), 105–29.

Hope, W.H. St John 1902 'The London Charterhouse and its Old Water Supply', *Archaeologia 58*, Part 1 (1902), 293–312.

Hope-Taylor, B. 1979 *Yeavering: An Anglo-British Centre of Early Northumbria*, Dept. Env. Archaeol. Rep. *7* (1979), HMSO.

Huggins, P.J. 1976 'The excavation of an 11th-century Viking Hall and 14th-century rooms at Waltham Abbey, Essex, 1969–71', *Med. Archaeol. 20* (1976), 75–133.

Humberside County Council 1987 *The Archaeology of a Medieval Roof Tile Factory in Grovehill, Beverley*, Humberside County Council, Beverley.

Jackson, S.J. 1979 'Metal, Wood and Bone', in Ayers 1979, 47.

Jobey, G. 1967 'Tynemouth Priory, Northumberland', *Archaeol. Ael.* (4th Series) *45* (1967), 33–104.

Johnson, A. 1974 'Excavations at Christchurch, Newgate Street, 1973', *Trans. London and Middlesex Archaeol. Soc. 5/25* (1974), 220–34.

Jones, L.W. 1946 'Pricking Manuscripts: The Instruments and their Significance', *Speculum 21* (1946), 389–403.

Keegan, T. 1973 The Heavy Horse, its Harness and Harness Decoration.

Kemp, R. forthcoming *The Gilbertine Priory of St. Andrew, Fishergate, York*, The Archaeology of York *11/2*.

Kenward, H.K., Hall, A.R. and Jones, A.G.K. 1980 'A Tested Set of Techniques for the Extraction of Plant and Animal Macrofossils from Waterlogged Archaeological Deposits', *Science and Archaeology 22* (1980), 3–15.

Kenward, H.K., Hall, A.R. and Jones, A.G.K. 1986 *Environmental Evidence from a Roman Well and Anglian Pits in the Legionary Fortress*, Archaeology of York *14/6*, 241–88, London: C.B.A.

Kerney, M.P. 1976 *Atlas of the non-marine molluscs of the British Isles*, Cambridge.

Kerr, J. 1983 'Window Glass', in Streeten 1983, 56–70.

Kerr, J. 1985a 'The Window Glass', in Hare 1985, 127–38.

Kerr, J. 1985b 'The Painted Glass', in Lambrick 1985, 170–2.

King, A.A. 1955 *Liturgies of the Religious Orders*, London.

Klein, P. and Roe, A. 1987 *The Carmelite Friary, Corve Street, Ludlow: Its History and Interpretation*, Historic Ludlow Research Paper No. 6. Ludlow Historical Research Group and Birmingham University Field Archaeology Unit.

Kloet, G.F. and Hincks, W.D. 1964–1977 *A Checklist of British Insects*, 2nd edition, London

Knowles, D. 1948 *The Religious Orders in England*.

Knowles, D. (ed) 1963 *The Historian and Character*, Cambridge.

Knowles, D. and Hadcock, R.W. 1953 *Medieval Religious Houses*, Longman, Green and Co. London.

Knowles, J.A. 1936 *Essays in the History of the York School of Glass-Painting*, S.P.C.K., London.

Knowles, W.H. 1920 'Monastery of the Black Friars, Newcastle-upon-Tyne', *Archaeol. Ael.* (Series 3) *17* (1920), 315–36.

Knowles, W.H. 1932 'The Black Friars of Gloucester', *Trans. Bristol and Gloucs. Archaeol. Soc. 54* (1932), 167–201.

Lafaurie, J. 1951 *Les Monnaies des rois de France: 1*, Paris.

Lambrick, G. 1985 'Further Excavations on the second site of the Dominican Priory, Oxford', *Oxoniensia 50* (1985), 131–208.

Lambrick, G. and Woods, H. 1976 'Excavations on the Second Site of the Dominican Priory, Oxford', *Oxoniensia 41* (1976), 168–231.

Larking, L.B. 1857 *The Knights Hospitallers in England*, Camden Society 65.

Lawson, G. 1980 *Stringed Musical Instruments; Artefacts in the Archaeology of Western Europe*, Unpublished Ph.D. thesis, Cambridge University.

Lawson, G. 1985 'Musical Instrument Pegs', in Hare 1985, 151–4.

Lawson, G. 1990 'Pieces from Stringed Instruments', in Biddle 1990, 711–18.

Lawson, G. 1991 'The Tuning Peg', in Armstrong *et al.* 1991, 118–19.

Lawson, G. (forthcoming) *Pig Metapodial 'toggles' and buzz-discs: Traditional Musical Instruments,* Finds Research Group 700–1700, Datasheet.

Leighton, W. 1933 'The Black Friars, Bristol', *Trans. Bristol and Gloucs. Archaeol. Soc. 55* (1933), 151–90.

Levitan, B. 1989 'Bone Analysis and Urban Economy: Examples of Selectivity and a Case for Comparison', in Serjeantson and Waldron 1989, 161–88.

Lindsay, W.J. 1989 'Linlithgow: The Excavations', in Stones 1989, 57–93.

Little, A.G. 1917 *Studies in English Franciscan History,* Manchester.

Little, A.G. 1941 'Introduction of the Observant Friars into England: A Bull of Alexander VI', *Proc. Brit. Academy 27* (1941), 155–6.

Loader, T. 1986 *The Ipswich Blackfriars — an Interim Summary of the Excavation of the Friary Levels 1983–86,* unpublished typescript. Suffolk Archaeological Unit (1986).

London Museum 1954 *Medieval Catalogue,* 2nd edition, H.M.S.O., London.

MacGregor, A. 1982 *Anglo-Scandinavian Finds from Lloyds Bank, Pavement and other sites,* Archaeology of York *17/3.*

MacGregor, A. 1985 *Bone, Antler, Ivory and Horn.* London: Croom Helm.

MacGregor, M. 1976 *Early Celtic Art in North Britain,* Leicester University Press.

McDonnell, J.G. 1991 'The Slag', in Armstrong *et al.* 1991, 239.

McDonnell, J.G. 1992 'The Ironworking Residues', in Evans and Tomlinson 1992, 254–5.

McGrail, S. (ed.) 1982 *Woodworking Techniques before A.D. 1500,* B.A.R. Internat. Ser. *129.*

McKenna, W.J.B. 1992 'The Environmental Evidence', in Evans and Tomlinson 1992, 227–33.

Madgett, P.A. and Catt, J.A. 1978 'Petrology, stratigraphy and weathering of Late Pleistocene tills in East Yorkshire, Lincolnshire and north Norfolk', *Proc. Yorks. Geol. Soc. 42* (1978), 55–108.

Margeson, S. 1982 'Worked Bone', in Coad and Streeten 1982, 241–55.

Martin, A.R. 1929 'The Dominican Priory at Canterbury', *Archaeol. J. 86* (1929), 152–77.

Martin, A.R. 1935 'The Grey Friars of Walsingham', *Norfolk Archaeol. 25* (1935), 227–71.

Martin, A.R. 1937 *Franciscan Architecture in England,* Brit. Soc. Franciscan Studies *18* (for 1933–34), Manchester: University Press.

Martin, D. 1973 *Hastings Augustinian Priory,* Hastings Area Archaeological Papers.

Mayes, P. 1965 'A Medieval Tile Kiln at Boston, Lincolnshire', *J. Brit. Archaeol. Assoc.* (3rd series) *28* (1965), 86–106.

Meaney, A. 1981 *Anglo-Saxon Amulets and Curing Stones,* B.A.R., Brit. Ser. *96.*

Mellor, J.E. and Pearce, T. 1981 *The Austin Friars, Leicester,* C.B.A. Res. Rep. *35.*

Miller, K., Robinson, J. English, B, and Hall, I. 1982 *Beverley: An Archaeological and Architectural Study,* R.C.H.M.(E.) Supplementary Series *4,* London: H.M.S.O.

Milne, G. and Milne, C. 1974 'Excavations on the Thames Waterfront at Trig Lane, London 1974', *Med. Archaeol. 22* (1974), 84–104.

Ministry of Agriculture, Fisheries and Food 1977 *Manual of Veterinary Parasitological Laboratory Techniques,* Technical Bulletin 18, London: HMSO.

Mitchiner, M. 1988 *Jettons, Medalets and Tokens Vol.1. The Medieval Period and Nuremburg,* London.

Mooney, C. 1956 'Franciscan architecture in pre-Reformation Ireland. Part II', *J. Roy. Soc. Antiq. Ireland 86* (1956), 125–69.

Moorhouse, S. 1972 'Finds from Excavations in the Refectory of the Dominican Friary, Boston', *Lincs. Hist. and Archaeol. 1,* No 7 (1972), 21–53.

Moorhouse, S. 1983 'Pottery roofing materials', in Mayes, P. & Butler, L.A.S., *Sandal Castle Excavations 1964–1973,* Wakefield, 308–16.

Moorhouse, S. and Wrathmell, S. 1987 *Kirstall Abbey. Volume 1. The 1950–64 Excavations: A Reassessment,* West Yorkshire Archaeological Service, Wakefield.

Morgan, N.J. 1983 *The Medieval Painted Glass of Lincoln Cathedral,* Corpus Vitrearum Medii Aevi (Great Britain) Occasional Paper II, Oxford.

Morris, C. and Evans, D.H. 1992 'The Wood', in Evans and Tomlinson 1992, 189–209.

Morris, R.K. 1978 'The Development of Later Gothic Mouldings', *Architect. Hist. 21* (1978), 18–57.

Morris, R.K. 1987 'Parish Churches', in Schofield and Leech 1987, 177–91.

Murray, H.J.R. 1952 *A History of Board Games other than Chess,* Oxford.

Mynard, D.C. 1969 'Excavations at Somerby, Lincs.', *Lincs. Hist.and Archaeol. 1,* No. 4, (1969), 63–91.

Mynard, D.C. 1979 'Some weights from the Rivers Great Ouse, Ouzel, Nene and Tove', *Rec. Bucks. 21* (1979), 11–29.

Neal, D.S. 1973 'Excavations at the Palace and Priory at Kings Langley, 1970', *Herts. Archaeol. 3* (1973), 31–72.

Newton, R.G. 1978 'Colouring Agents used by Medieval Glassmakers', *Glass Technology 19* (1978), 59–60.

North, J.J. 1960 *English Hammered Coinage. Vol. 2,* London (1960).

O'Connor, D.E. 1989 'The Medieval Stained Glass of Beverley Minster', in Wilson 1989, 62–90.

O'Connor, D.E. and Haselock, J. 1977 'The Stained and Painted Glass', in Aylmer and Cant 1977, 313–93.

O'Connor, T.P. 1984 *Selected Groups of Animal Bone from Skeldergate and Walmgate*, Archaeology of York *15/1*.

O'Connor, T.P. 1991 *Bones from 46–54 Fishergate*, Archaeology of York *15/4*.

O'Connor, T.P. 1993 'Bone assemblages from Monastic Sites: many questions but few data', in Gilchrist, R. and Mytum, H. (eds) forthcoming, *Advances in Monastic Archaeology*, B.A.R. Brit. Ser. *227*, 107–11.

Olsen, O. and Crumlin-Pedersen, O. 1967 'The Skuldelev Ships', *Acta Archaeologica*, Copenhagen.

Palmer, C.F.R. 1882 'The Friars Preacher or Blackfriars of Beverley', *Yorks. Archaeol. J. 7* (1882), 32–43.

Palmer, C.F.R. 1887 'The Friars Preacher or Black Friars of Guildford', *The Reliquary* (New Series) *1* (1887), 7–20.

Palmer, C.F.R. 1891 'Burials of the Priories of the Blackfriars', *The Antiquary 24* (1891), 28–30, 76–9, 117–20, 265–9.

Parker, G. 1982 *Northants. Past and Present*, 247–52.

Parker, J.H. 1900 *ABC of Gothic Architecture*, 11th edition, London.

Pevsner, N. and Harris, J. 1989 *The Buildings of England: Lincolnshire*, 2nd edition, London.

Platt, C. and Coleman-Smith, R. 1975 *Excavations in Medieval Southampton 1953–1969. Volume 2: The Finds*, Leicester University Press.

Ponsford, M.W. 1975 *The Greyfriars in Bristol*, Bristol Museum.

Poulson, G. 1829 *Beverlac: or the Antiquities and History of the Town of Beverley ....*, London.

Poulton, R. and Woods, H. 1984 *Excavations on the Site of the Dominican Friary at Guildford in 1974 and 1978*, Res. Vol. Surrey Archaeol. Soc. No. 9, Guildford.

Pritchard, F.M. 1982 'Textiles from Recent Excavations in the City of London', in Bender Jørgensen, L. and Tidow, K. (eds), *Textilsymposium Neumünster: Archäologische Textilfunde*, Neumünster, 193–203.

Proudfoot, B. (ed.) 1983 *Site, environment and economy. Symposia of the Association for Environmental Archaeology 3*, B.A.R. Internat. Ser. *173*.

RCHM 1972 *City of York Volume III, south-west of the Ouse*, H.M.S.O.

RCHM 1975 *City of York Volume IV, outside the City Walls, east of the Ouse*, H.M.S.O.

RCHM 1981 *An Inventory of the Historical Monuments in the City of York, Volume V, The Central Area*, H.M.S.O.

Rackham, O., Blair, W.J., and Munby, J.T. 1978 'The 13th Century Roofs of the Blackfriars Priory at Gloucester', *Med. Archaeol. 22* (1978), 105–22.

Reynolds, S. 1977 *An Introduction to the History of English Medieval Towns*, Oxford.

Richardson, K.M. 1959 'Excavations in Hungate, York', *Archaeol. J. 116* (1959), 51–114.

Rigold, S.E. 1965 'Two Kentish Carmelite Houses — Aylesford and Sandwich', *Archaeol. Cant. 80* (1965), 1–28.

Robinson, W.S. 1951 'A Method for Chronologically Ordering Archaeological Deposits', *American Antiquity 16/4* (1951), 293–301.

Roebuck, J. and Coppack, G. 1987 'A closely dated group of late medieval pottery from Mount Grace Priory', *Med. Ceramics 11* (1987), 15–24.

Ryder, M.L. 1961 'Livestock Remains from Four Medieval Sites in Yorkshire', *Agric. Hist. Rev. 9* (1961), 105–10.

Ryder, P.F. 1982 *Medieval Buildings of Yorkshire*, Moorland Publishing.

Ryder, P.F. 1987 *Timber Framed Buildings in South Yorkshire*, South Yorkshire County Archaeology Monograph No. 1.

Rye, C.G. 1973 'Great Yarmouth: Blackfriars Church', *Norfolk Archaeol. 35* (1973), 498–502.

Salzman, L.F. 1923 *English Industries of the Middle Ages*, Oxford.

Salzman, L.F. 1952 *Building in England down to 1540*, Oxford.

Sanders, G.B. and Armstrong, P. 1983 'A Watching Brief on the Beverley High Level Drainage Scheme 1980/81', *East Riding Archaeologist 7* (1983), 52–70.

Schofield, J. 1984 *The Building of London from the Conquest to the Great Fire*, British Museum, London.

Schofield, J. and Leech, R. (eds) 1987 *Urban Archaeology in Britain*, C.B.A. Res. Rep. 61.

Scott, S. 1991 'The Animal Bones', in Armstrong et al. 1991, 216–33.

Scott, S. 1992 'The Animal Bones', in Evans and Tomlinson 1992, 236–51.

Serjeantson, D. and Waldron, T. (eds) 1989 *Diet and Crafts in Towns*, B.A.R. Brit. Ser. *199*.

Skeat, W.W. (ed.) 1912 *Chaucer: Complete Works*, London, Oxford University Press.

Smith, A.J.E. 1978 *The Moss Flora of Britain and Ireland*, Cambridge University Press.

Smith, G.H. 1980 'The Excavation of the Hospital of St. Mary of Ospringe commonly called Maison Dieu', *Archaeol. Cant. 95* (1980), 81–184.

Smith, J.T. 1955 'Medieval Aisled Halls and their Derivatives', *Archaeol. J. 112* (1955), 26–44.

Smith, J.T. 1974 'The Early Development of Timber Buildings: The Passing Brace and Reversed Assembly', *Archaeol. J. 131* (1974), 238–63.

Spencer, B.W. 1968 'Medieval Pilgrim Badges', in Renaud, J.G.N. (ed.) *Rotterdam Papers: a Contribution to medieval archaeology*, Rotterdam, 137–53.

Spencer, B.W. 1992 'Objects of Lead Alloy and Pewter', in Evans and Tomlinson (1992), 143–7.

Stead, I.M. 1980 *Rudston Roman Villa*, Yorks. Archaeol. Soc. Mon.

Steane, J.M. and Bryant, G.F. 1975 'Excavations at the Deserted Medieval Settlement at Lyveden: Fourth

Interim Report', *J. Northampton Museums and Art Gallery 12.*

Steane, J.M. and Foreman, M. 1988 'Medieval Fishing Tackle', in Michael Aston 1988, 137–86.

Stewart, I. 1967 *Scottish Coinage*, 2nd edn., London.

Stocker, D.A. 1984 'The Remains of the Franciscan Friary at Lincoln: a Reassessment', in Addyman and Black 1984, 137–44.

Stones, J.A. 1982 'The Small Finds', in Murray 1982, 177–223.

Stones, J.A. (ed.) 1989 *Three Scottish Carmelite Friaries: Aberdeen, Linlithgow and Perth*, Soc. Antiq. Scot. Mon. Ser. No 6, Edinburgh.

Streeten, A. (ed.) 1983 *Bayham Abbey*, Sussex Archaeol. Soc. Mon. 2.

Stubbings, F.H. 1969 'The Church of the Cambridge Dominicans', *Proc. Cambridge Antiq. Soc. 62* (1969), 95–104.

Sutermeister, H. 1977 *The Norwich Blackfriars. An historical guide to the Friary and its Buildings up to the present day*, Norwich.

Tester, P.J. 1979 'Excavations on the Site of Leeds Priory (Part 2 –The Claustral Buildings)', *Archaeol. Cant. 94* (1979), 75–99.

Thawley, C. 1981 'The Mammal, Bird and Fish Bones', in Mellor and Pearce 1981, 173–5.

Thornton, J.H. 1973 'The examination of early shoes to 1600', *Trans. Museum Assistants Group* No. 12 (1973), 2–13.

Thorpe, C. and Sykes, R.F.R. 1967 'Analysis of Glass', in Crossley 1967, 72.

Tutin, T.G. *et al.* 1964–1980 *Flora Europaea 1–5*, Cambridge University Press.

Walton, P. 1989 *Textiles, Cordage and Raw Fibre from 16–22 Coppergate*, The Archaeology of York 17/5.

Ward, S.W. (ed.) 1990 *Excavations at Chester: The Lesser Medieval Religious Houses. Sites Investigated 1964–1983*, Grosvenor Museum Archaeological Excavation and Survey Reports 6, Chester.

Watkin, J. 1987 'Objects of Lead and Lead Alloy', in Armstrong and Ayers 1987, 200–8.

Watkins, J.G. 1983 'North European Pottery Imported into Hull', in Davey and Hodges 1983, 244–53.

Watkins, J.G. 1987a 'The Pottery', in Armstrong and Ayers 1987, 53–181.

Watkins, J.G. 1987b 'The Pottery', in Armstrong and Tomlinson 1987, 30–6.

Watkins, J.G. 1991 'The Pottery', in Armstrong *et al.* 1991, 61–103.

Watkins, J.G. 1993 'The Pottery', in Evans, D.H. (ed.), 'Excavations in Hull 1975–76', (Hull Old Town Report No. 2), *East Riding Archaeologist 4*, 75–144.

Watkins, J.G. and Williams, R.A.H. 1983 'An Excavation at Highgate, Beverley, 1977', *East Riding Archaeologist 7* (1983), 71–84.

Westlake 1881–94 *A History of Design in Painted Glass*, 4 Vols., London.

Williams, F. 1977 *Excavations at Pleshey Castle*, C.B.A. Res. Rep. *42*.

Williams, J.H. 1978 'Excavations at Greyfriars, Northampton 1972', *Northamptonshire Archaeol. 13* (1978), 96–160.

Williams, J.H. 1979 *St. Peter's Street. Northampton: Excavations 1973–6*, Northampton Dev. Corp. Archaeol. Mon. *2*.

Willis, R. 1868 'The Architectural History of the Conventual Buildings of the Monastery of Christchurch in Canterbury', *Archaeol. Cant. 7* (1868), 1–206.

Wilson, C. 1978 'The Architectural Fragments', in Williams 1978, 118–21.

Wilson, C. 1989 (ed) *Medieval Art and Architecture in the East Riding of Yorkshire*, Brit. Archaeol. Assoc. Conference Transactions for the Year 1983, Leeds.

Wilson, D.M. and Hurst, D.G. (eds) 1967 'Medieval Britain in 1966', *Med. Archaeol. 11* (1967), 262–319.

Wilson, D.M. and Hurst, D.G. (eds), 1970 'Medieval Britain in 1969', *Med. Archaeol. 14* (1970), 155–209.

Winston, C. 1867 *Memoirs Illustrative of the Art of Glass Painting with Hints on Glass Painting*, 2nd edition, London.

Witty, J.R. 1929 'Friars Lane', in *Beverley Guardian* November 30th (1929), 4.

Wood, M. 1965 *The English Medieval House*, London.

Woodland, R.R. 1981 'The Pottery', in Mellor and Pearce 1981, 81–129.

Wrathmell, S. 1987 *Kirkstall Abbey — The Guest House: A Guide to the Medieval Buildings*, West Yorkshire Archaeology Service, Wakefield, second edition.

Wrathmell, S. 1989 *Wharram. A Study of Settlement on the Yorkshire Wolds, VI. Domestic Settlement 2: Medieval Peasant Farmsteads*, York University Archaeol. Publ. *8*.

Young, G.A.B. 1983 'Archaeology in Hartlepool', in Vyner, B.E. (ed.) *Recent Excavations in Cleveland*, Middlesborough: Cleveland County Council, 44–54.

Youngs, S.M. and Clark, J. (eds) 1981 'Medieval Britain in 1980', *Med. Archaeol. 25* (1981), 166–228.

Youngs, S.M., Clark, J. and Barry, T.B. (eds) 1986 'Medieval Britain and Ireland in 1985', *Med. Archaeol. 30* (1986), 114–198.

Youngs, S.M., Clark, J. and Barry, T.B. (eds) 1987 'Medieval Britain and Ireland in 1986', *Med. Archaeol. 31* (1987), 110–91.

Abbreviated Index to the Microfiche

Fiche 1

Fiche 2

Fiche 3

Abbreviated index to the archive

1.	Beverley Eastgate watching brief: borehole survey.
2.	Public Record Office document copies.
3.1.	Context record sheets (eight volumes).
3.2.	Monthly summaries of work, July 1986–April 1987.
3.3.	Recorded finds sheets (four volumes).
4.1.	Section sheets (three volumes).
4.2.	Plan sheets (three volumes).
5.1.	Matrix, west end little cloister (roll).
5.2.	Matrices and phase groups (four volumes).
5.3.	Context synopsis sheets (four volumes).
6.1.	Plans and phase plans (three volumes; two rolls).
6.2.	Annotated publication plans (two volumes).
7.1.	Site photographs: seven volumes of black and white prints.
7.2.	Site photographs: 1506 colour slides.
7.3.	Catalogue and index of photographs.
8.1.	Pottery vessel record (two volumes).
8.3–8.12.	Pottery draft report and lists.
8.13.	Pottery illustrations.
9.1.	Finds register (seven volumes).
9.2.	Context/Finds sheets.
9.3.	Finds location plots.
9.4.	Finds illustrations (five volumes; one card index box).
10.1.	Masonry record (two volumes).
10.2.	Brick and tile record (three volumes).
10.3.	Building materials illustrations.
11.1.	Phasing supplied to E.A.U. for the environmental reports.
14.1.	X-rays (twenty-two strip packs).
17.1.	Research design.
17.2.	Administration records.
18.	Lectures and popular summaries.
21.	Draft report (three volumes).
22.	Archive of 1987 excavations: site code 1224/1987/BLY.

Plate 2. South cloister alley wall, Phase 6B, over earlier footing.

Plate 1. South wall of the north range, Phase 4.

277

Plate 3.   East wall of the west range, Phase 4 — plastered.

Plate 4.   East wall of the west range, Phase 4 — plaster removed.

Plate 5.   Conduit for latrine, west side.

Plate 6.   Chutes and conduit — floor of latrine, east side.

Plate 7. Cistern at north-west corner of great cloister.

Plate 11. Inlet to drain 426 and wall 21; north-west corner of little cloister.

Plate 9. The drain 426 — capping.

Plate 8. The internal wall 516 and bench 38, little cloister, north range.

Plate 12. Robbed bench position 482.

Plate 10. The drain 426 — brick conduit.

Plate 13.   Bowl-hearth 109, little cloister, north range.

Plate 14.   Bowl-hearth 753, inserted into hearth 347, little cloister.

Plate 15. Bowl hearth 579, inserted into a doorway in the little cloister.

Plate 16. RF 440, glass and came concentration in the little cloister, north range.

Plate 17.   Strap-end or book plate No. 880.

Index

(N.B. the names of pre-1974 historic shire counties have been used in this index to denote the location of places mentioned in the text)

washer 158
wire 61, 78, 89, 158–60
coprolites 205
corn 3, 205
cornfields 196, 201
corrodian accomodation 214, 249, 263
costume 240
court 248
inner court 252
Courtenay family 249
courtyard 252
Coventry (Warks.) 158
craft gear 150
craft practices 192
craftsmen 252, 265
creelers 3
crockets 135
cross-wing 236
cruck construction 235
crucks 235
cultivation 168, 232
culvert 41, 43, 91, 189, 221, 223, 224, 246

dairying 218
daub 9, 12, 22, 125, 197, 201, 207, 231
Decorated (style of architecture) 99, 247, 251
deer 215, 216, 225–27
demolition 7, 37, 38, 46, 49, 78, 86, 88, 89, 91, 97, 99, 101,
107, 115, 119, 122, 123, 126, 132, 136, 137, 145,
148, 155, 158, 159, 167, 168, 171, 175, 184, 186,
213–15, 218–21, 225, 226, 235, 238, 239, 254–56,
259, 260
Denaby Old hall (Yorks., W.R.) 252
dendrochronological dating 230
Denny Abbey(Benedictine; Knights Templar; Franciscan
nuns: Cambs.) 237, 246, 249, 250, 252, 257
desk 245
dias 237, 238
diet 195, 213, 227, 228, 247, 253, 256, 258, 262, 263, 265
dining area
see refectory
dismantling 91, 97, 254–56, 259
disposal of refuse
see waste disposal
Dissolution 86, 92, 96, 107, 129, 137, 147, 164, 184, 186,
229, 232, 240, 241, 248, 249, 252, 256, 259, 260,
262, 264
ditches 15, 17, 19, 20, 41, 86, 189, 197, 199, 203, 207, 208,
232–34, 262
documents 275, 276
dog 215, 216, 226
domestic fowl 213, 216, 217, 225–27, 255
duck 216, 217, 226
fowl 216, 223
goose 216, 217, 226
domestic
refuse 204
species 215
waste 197, 207
domesticates 214, 215, 227
Dominican houses
Bamburgh (Northumb.)
Bangor (Canarv.) 38, 249
Boston (Lincs.) 2, 176, 238

Brecon (Becon.) 240, 241, 248
Bristol Priory (Glos.) 137, 240, 242, 247, 250, 252, 253
Cambridge (Camb.) 97, 99
Canterbury (Kent) 38, 132, 233, 236, 243, 245, 246,
248, 260, 262
Cardiff (Glam.) 38, 241, 244, 247, 248, 250, 252, 253
Carlisle (Cumb.) 2
Chelmsford (Essex) 132, 147, 148, 240, 245–47, 260
Chester (Ches.) 99, 132, 240, 241
Dunstable (Beds.) 132
Exeter (Devon) 249
Gloucester (Glos.) 38, 99, 236, 240, 243, 244, 247, 248
Guildford (Surrey) 123, 132, 147, 155, 164, 168, 226,
227, 233, 235, 238, 240–42, 247
Hereford (Hereford.) 242
Ipswich (Suffolk) 38, 123, 233, 238, 240, 243–45,
247–49, 253, 263
Kings Langley (Hertfordshire) 97, 135, 137, 244
Lancaster (Lancs.) 2, 244
Lincoln 2
Ludgate (London) 132, 233, 236, 239, 241, 242,
247–49, 252
Newcastle-upon-Tyne (Northumb.) 2, 123, 132, 240,
242, 244, 245, 248, 250, 253, 260
Norwich (Norfolk) 38, 233, 242, 245, 249, 259
Oxford (Oxon.) 38, 147, 226, 227, 234, 237, 240, 241,
245, 247, 249
Pontefract (Yorks., W.R.) 2, 164, 226, 227, 238, 254,
256, 258, 259
Rhuddlan (Flint) 38, 132, 246
Ribe (Denmark) 242
Salisbury (Wilts.) 233
Scarborough (Yorks., N.R.) 2, 249, 254
Warwick (Warks.) 244, 259
Wilton (Wilts.) 233
Winchester (Hants.) 249
Yarm (Yorks., N.R.) 2
York 236, 244, 249
Dominicans 1–4, 6, 9, 15, 36, 38, 86, 91, 106, 107, 126,
132, 135, 145, 150, 164, 168, 176, 194, 195, 199,
207, 208, 226, 227, 231–34, 236, 239, 241, 242,
244–50, 253, 255, 260, 262–66, 276
donations
also grants 261, 262, 264
doors 68, 96, 97, 99, 102, 256
doorstep 52, 68, 115, 253
doorway 41, 46, 55, 57, 59, 61, 65, 68, 75, 83, 88, 107,
250, 253, 254, 256–58, 260, 284
dormitory 135, 239, 242, 244, 246, 255, 263
dorter 239, 242, 252, 260
Dover (Kent) 237
downpipe 72, 256, 257, 260
drain cover 148
drainage 46, 77, 80, 91, 92, 213, 233, 239, 246, 247, 262
drains 20, 22, 33, 46, 51, 59, 70, 72, 76, 78, 79, 96, 97,
101, 103, 107, 145, 148, 183, 204, 227, 232, 233,
235, 242, 246, 247, 251, 253, 256, 257, 260, 280–82
dung 201, 202
Durham 265
dyeing 265
dyeing trade 233
dyeplants 199, 200, 208
dyer 201
dyes 200